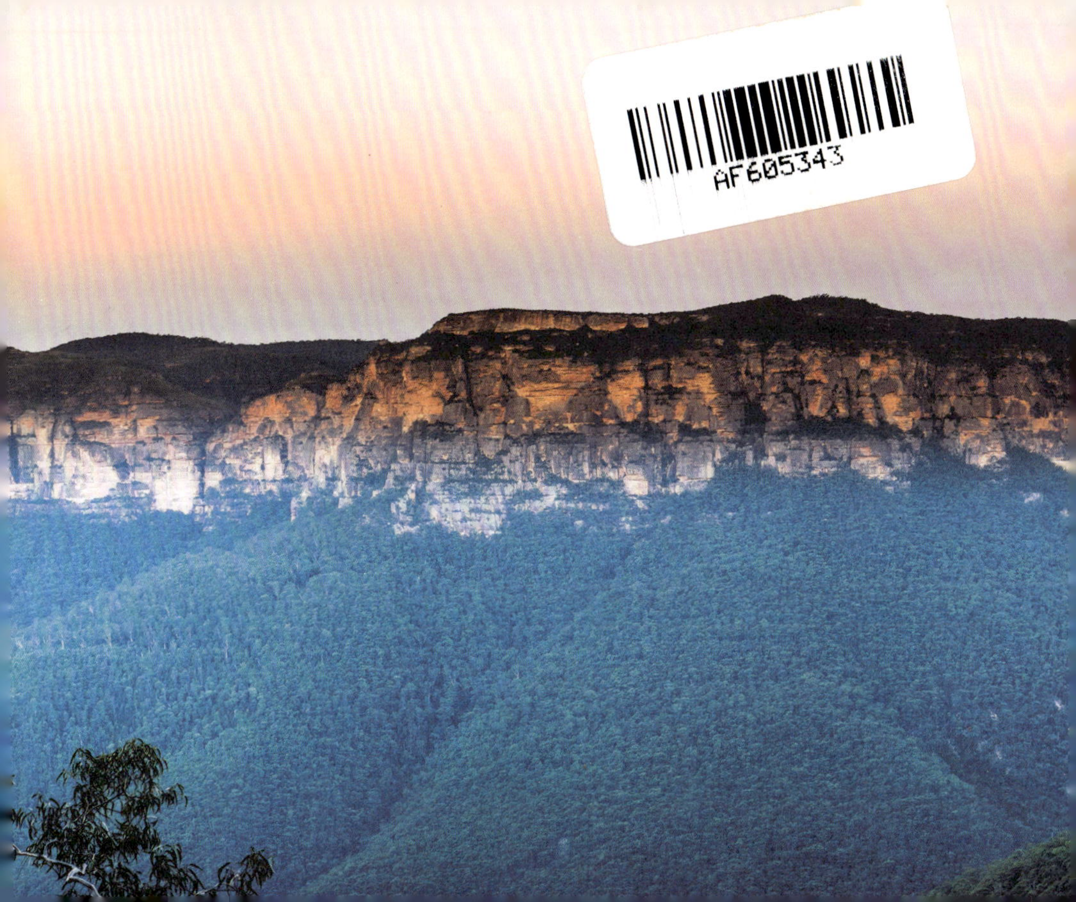

AF605343

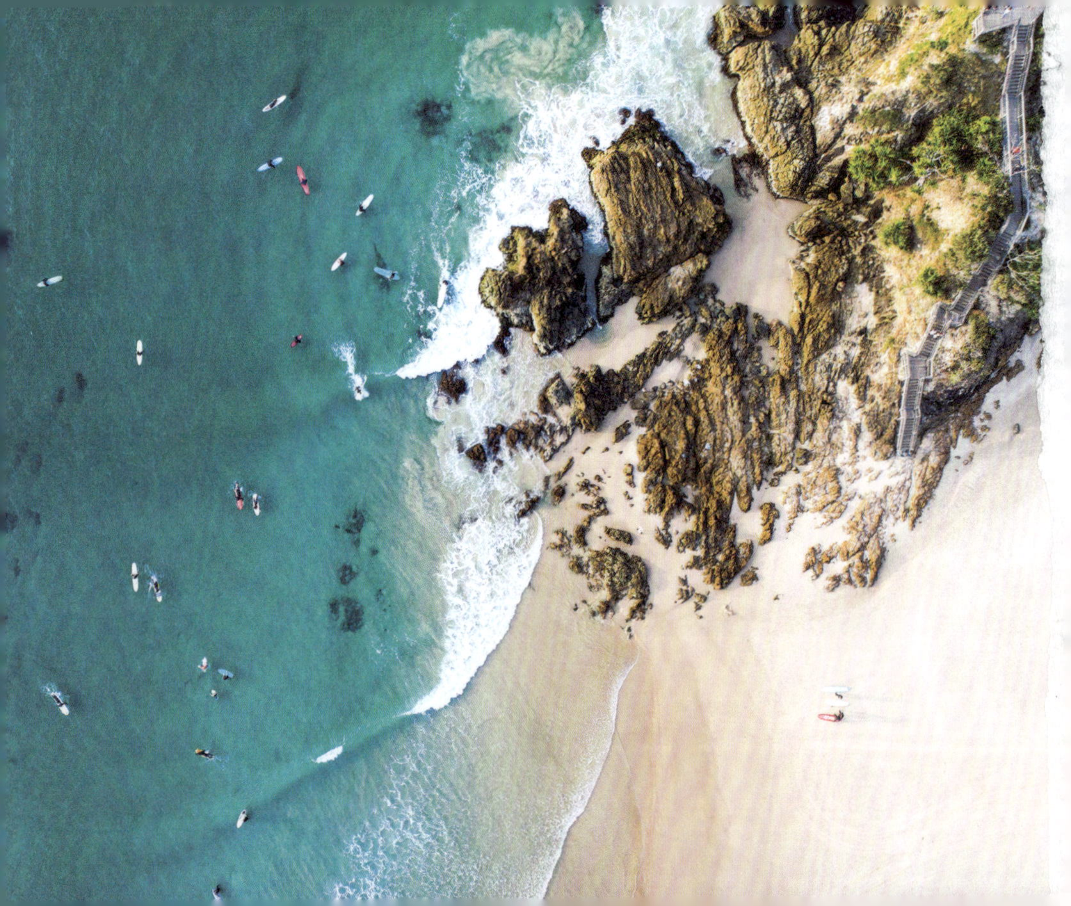

AUSTRALIA

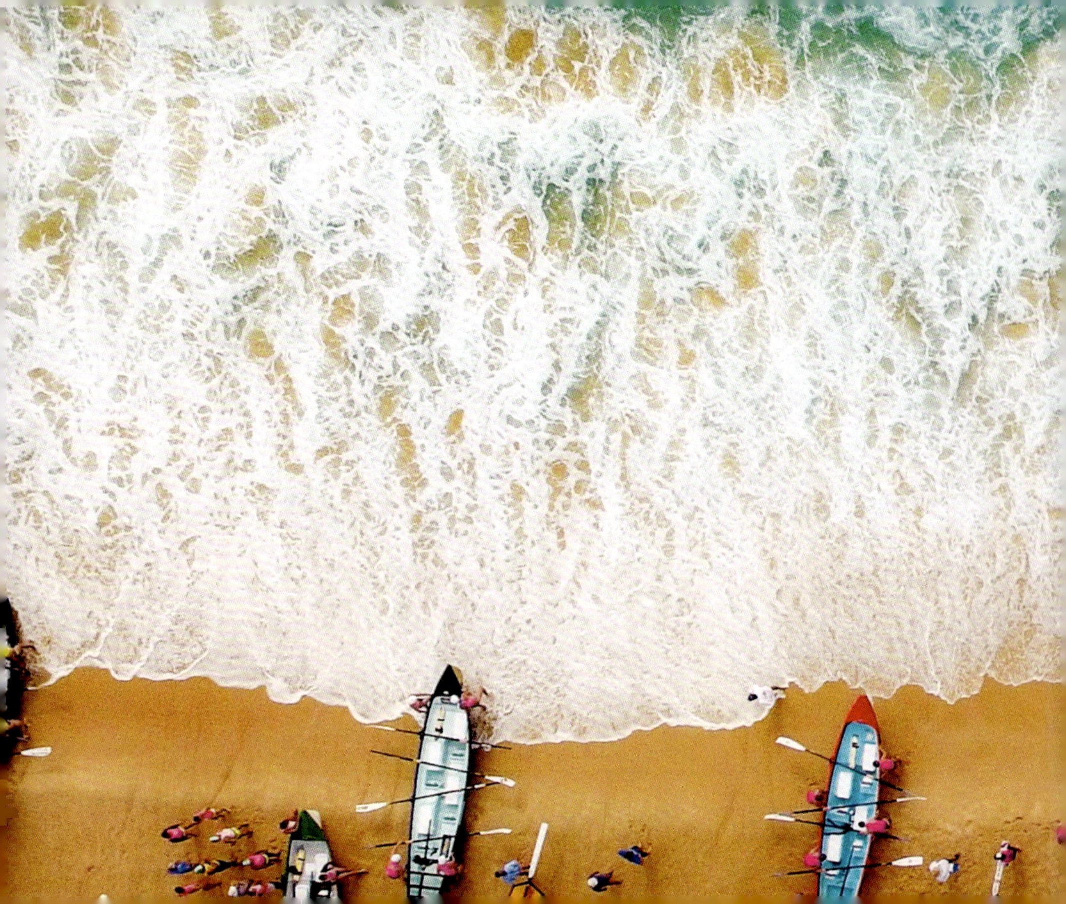

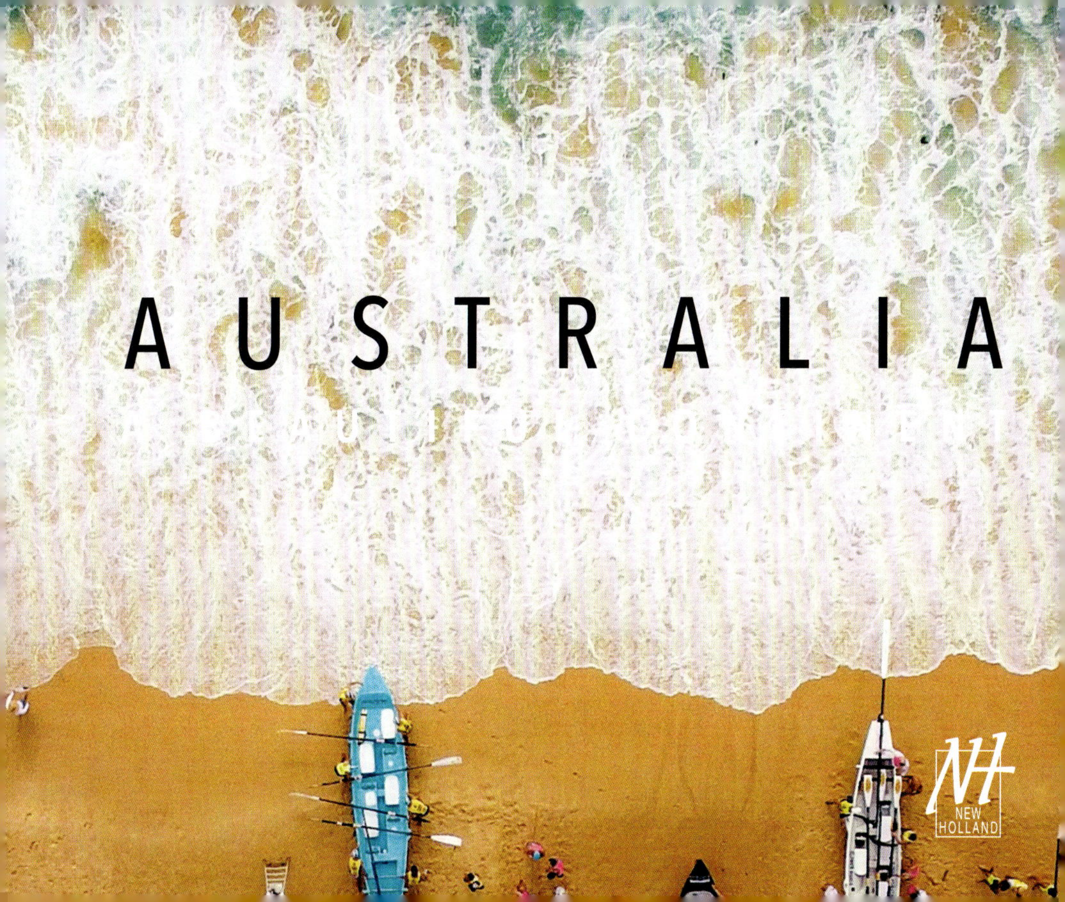
AUSTRALIA
NH
NEW HOLLAND

INTRODUCTION

Australia, often referred to as the 'Land Down Under', is a country that has amazing landscapes, unique wildlife, vibrant cities, and an indigenous history. Situated in the southern hemisphere, this vast small continent-large country is renowned for its stunning natural wonders, multicultural society, and laid-back lifestyle.

From iconic red deserts of the Outback to rainforests of Queensland and breathtaking coastal cliffs along the Great Ocean Road, the country offers an unparalleled array of natural beauty. The Great Barrier Reef, the world's largest coral reef system, stretches along the northeastern coast, offering an underwater wonderland of marine life and vibrant corals.

Australia is home to some of the world's most distinctive wildlife species. The kangaroo, with its powerful hind legs and pouch for carrying its young, is an iconic symbol of the country. The koala, known for its cuddly appearance and love for eucalyptus leaves, is another beloved marsupial. However, many are dangerous, including spiders, snakes, and the notorious Saltwater Crocodile.

Australia's history stretches back over 65,000 years, as it is home to the world's oldest continuous culture: the Indigenous Aboriginal and Torres Strait Islander peoples.

Their connection to the land, spiritual beliefs, and intricate art forms are an integral part of Australia's cultural fabric. Dreamtime stories, rock art, and traditional ceremonies are passed down through generations, offering insights into the connection between the land and its people.

Australia's major cities, Sydney, Melbourne and Brisbane, are dynamic centres of culture, innovation, and commerce. Sydney, with its iconic Sydney Opera House and Sydney Harbour Bridge, is a global landmark. Melbourne is known for its vibrant arts scene and diverse neighbourhoods, while Brisbane offers a subtropical atmosphere and a laid-back lifestyle. These cities reflect Australia's multicultural makeup, with a blend of cultures and cuisines from around the world.

While Australia's natural beauty is a source of pride, it also faces environmental challenges. The country is prone to bushfires, which can devastate large areas and impact wildlife. Climate change has intensified these challenges, leading to discussions about sustainable practices and conservation efforts.

Visitors to Australia often scratch their heads during an encounter with an Australian. Aussies are generally informal in both their behaviour and conversation, and the liberal use of slang is a feature of this informality.

Over half of the population live by the coastline of Australia which is why Australians love the ocean; and the waterways, canals, bays and rivers are hot spots for outdoor lifestyle in Australia.

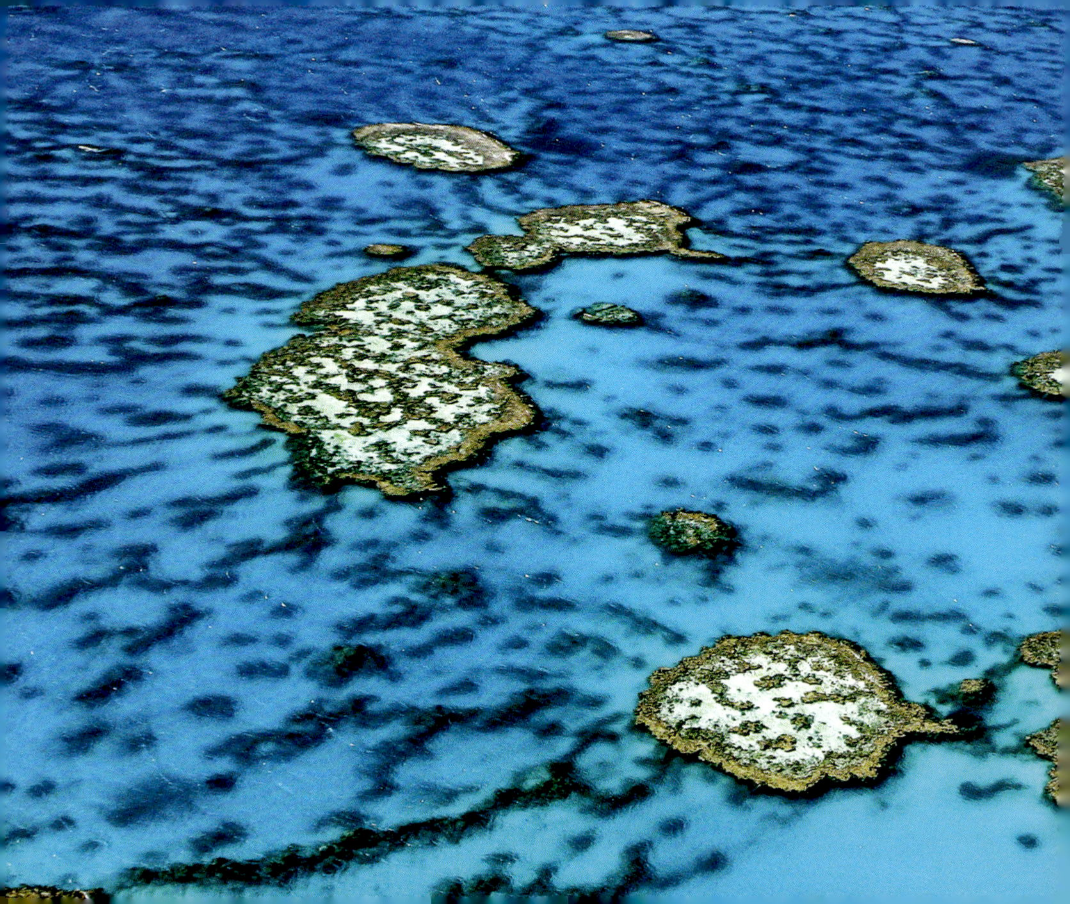

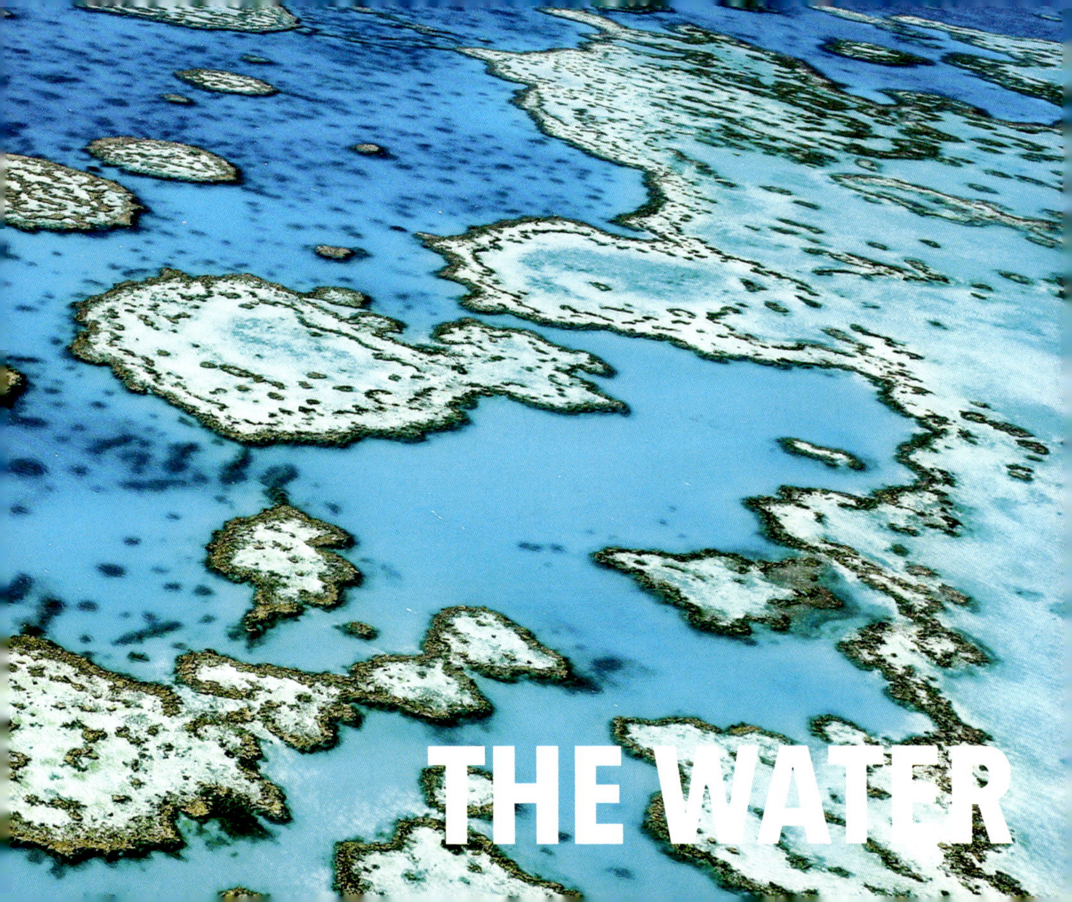
THE WATER

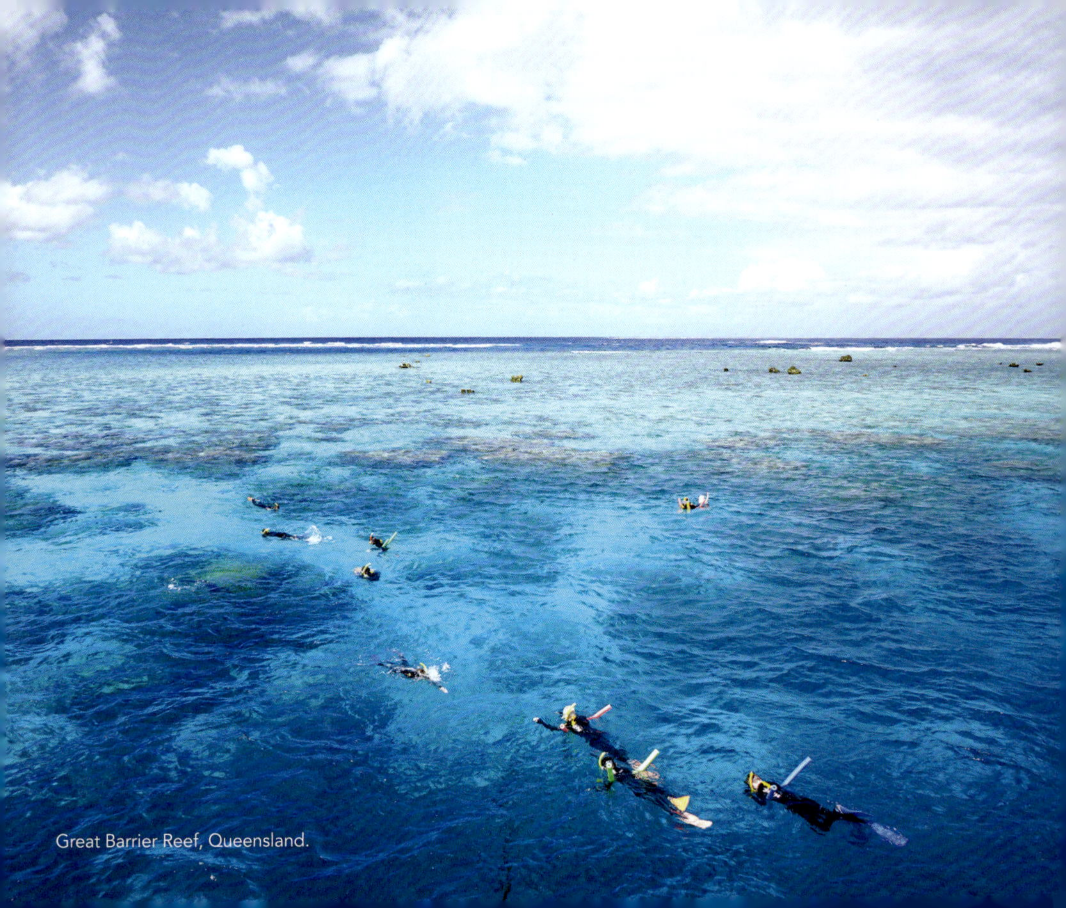

Great Barrier Reef, Queensland.

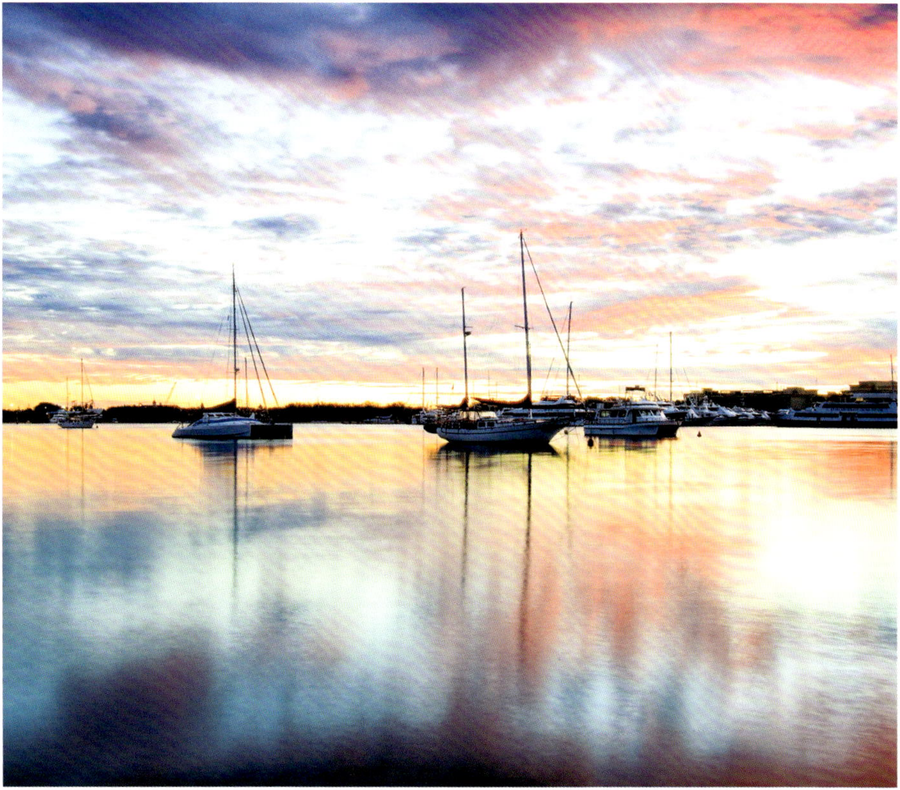

Broadwater, Queensland.

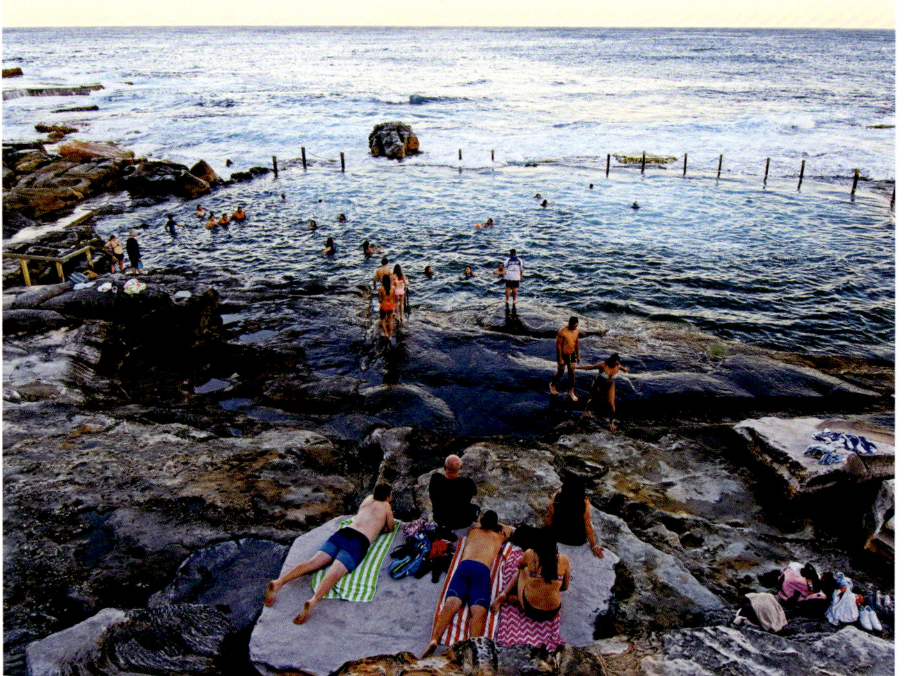

Maroubra Beach, Sydney.

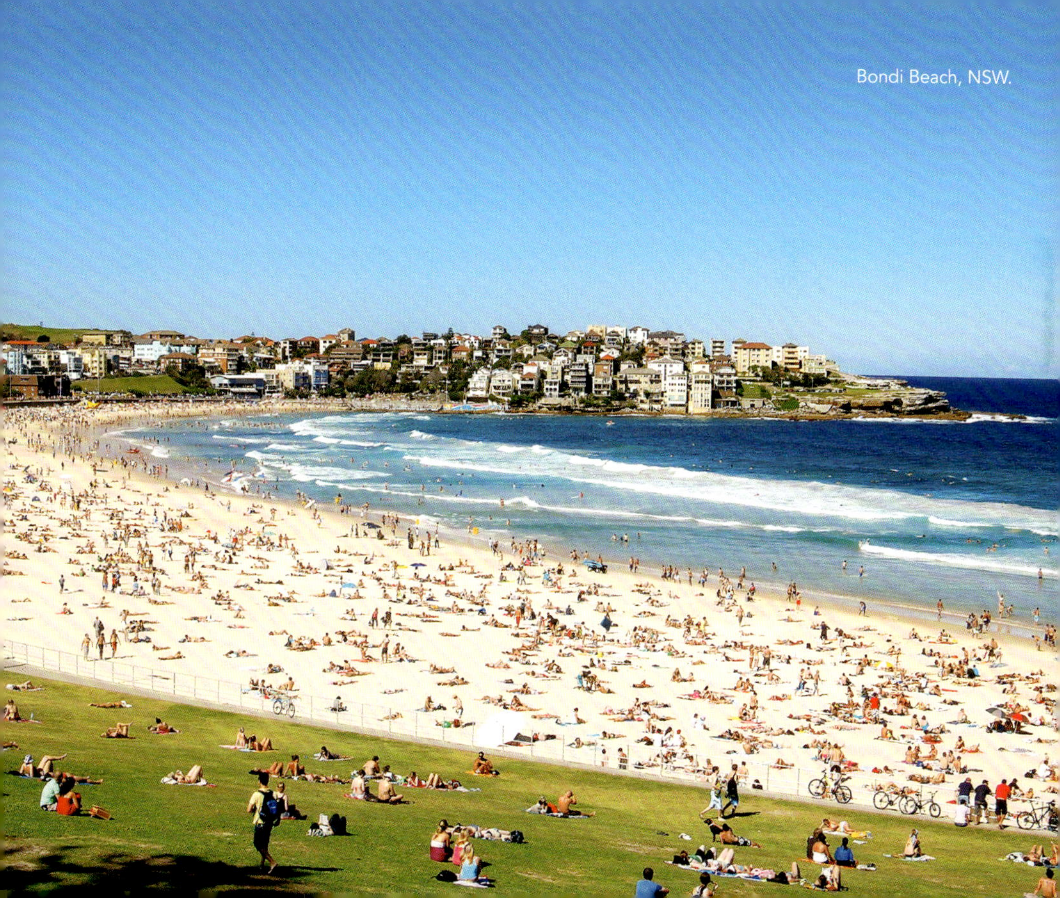
Bondi Beach, NSW.

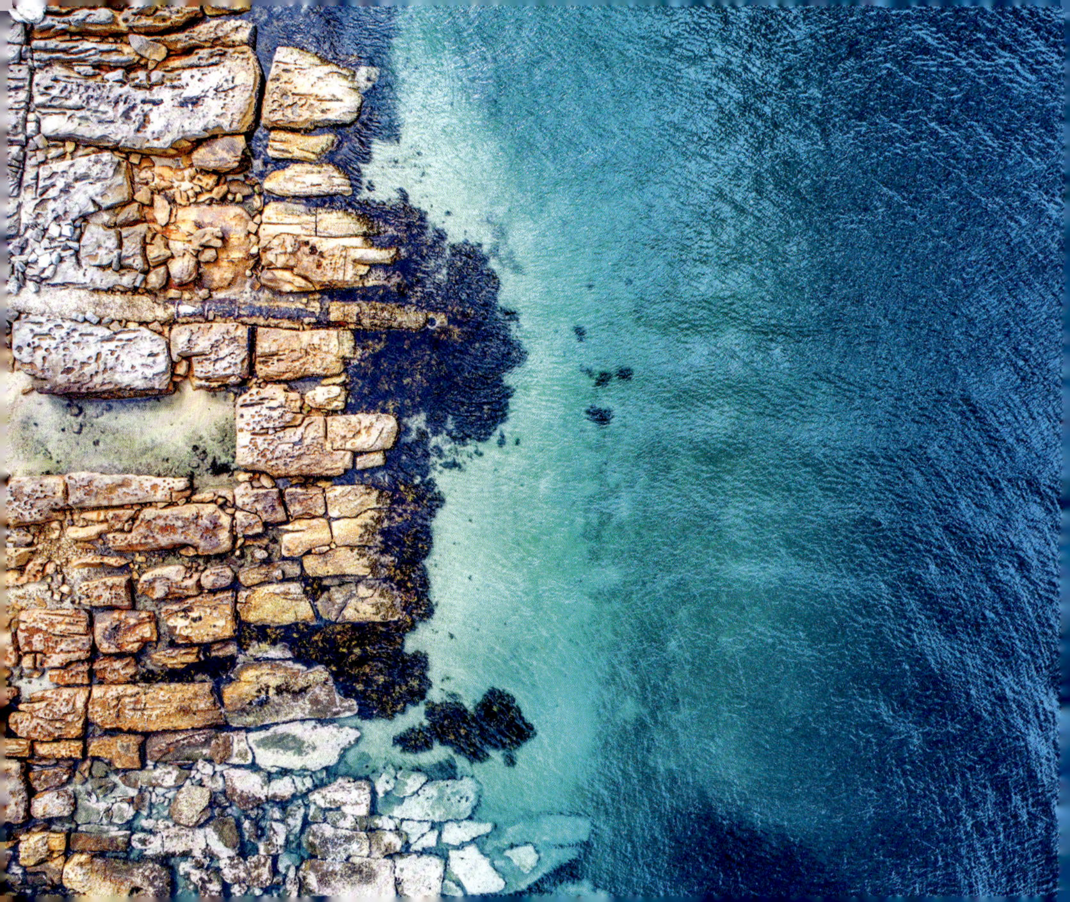

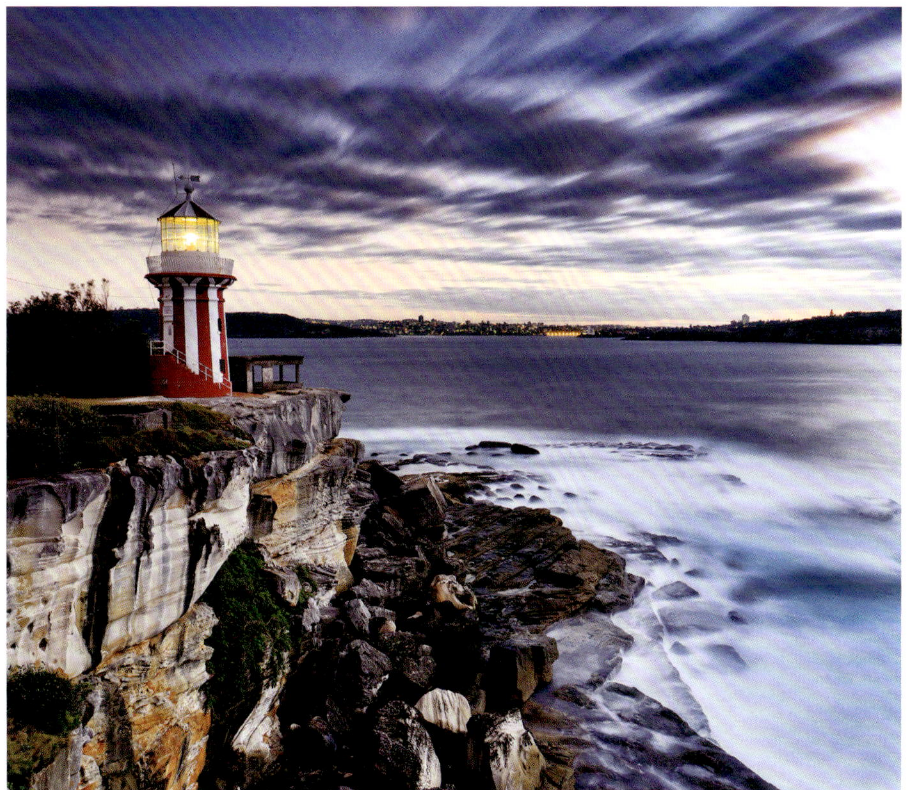

Hornby lighthouse, southern entrance to Port Jackson, Sydney.

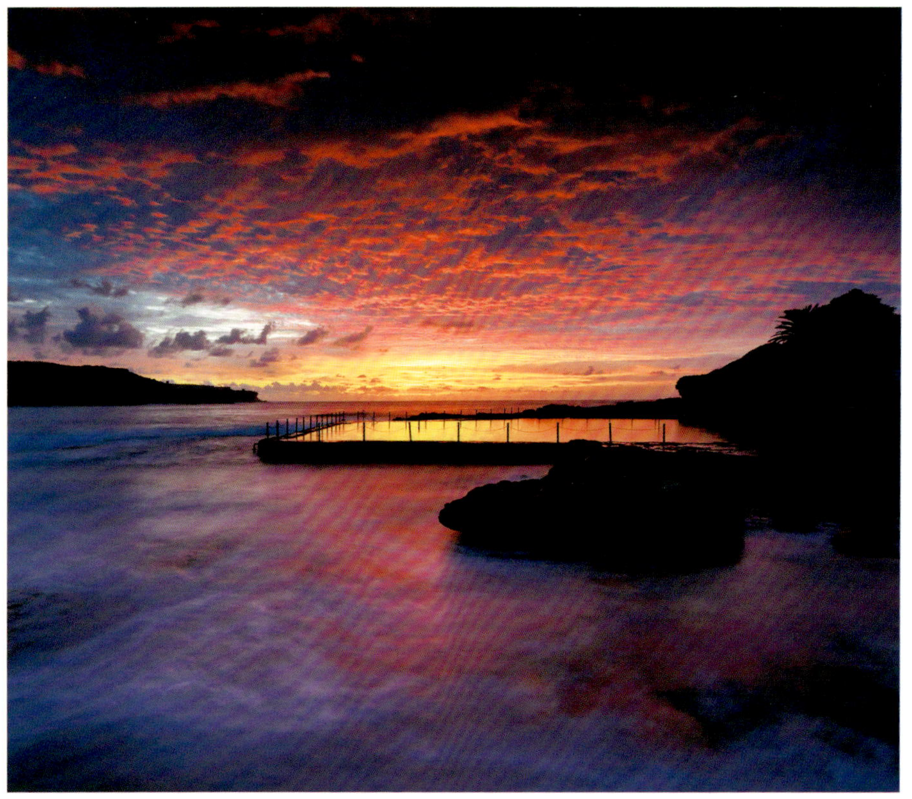

Malabar ocean rock pool.

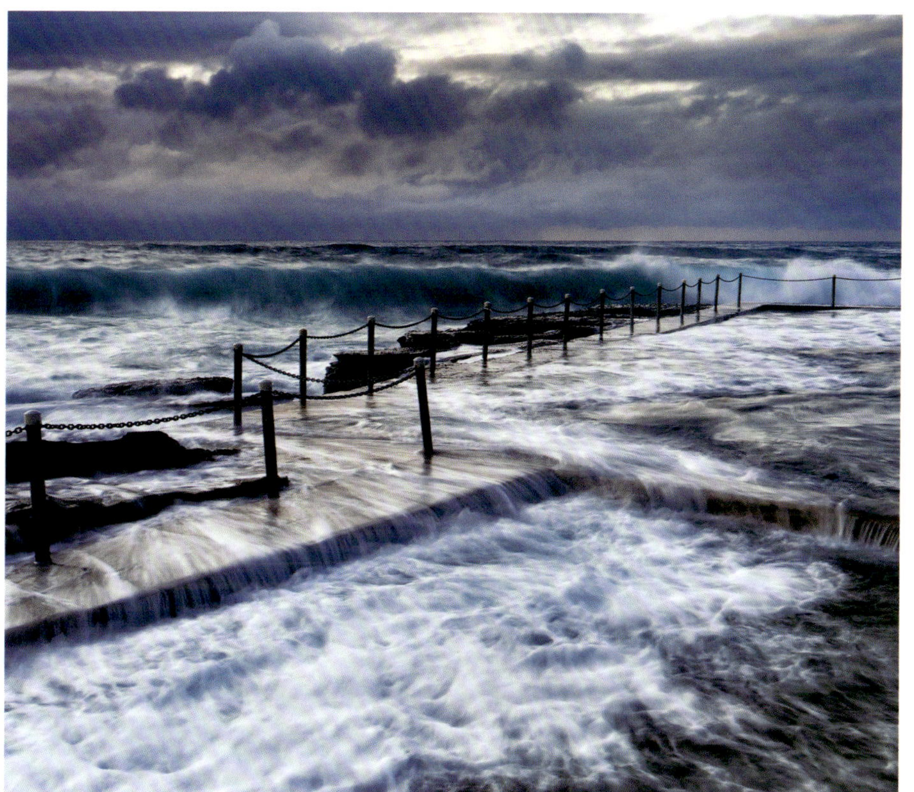

Avalon, Sydney.

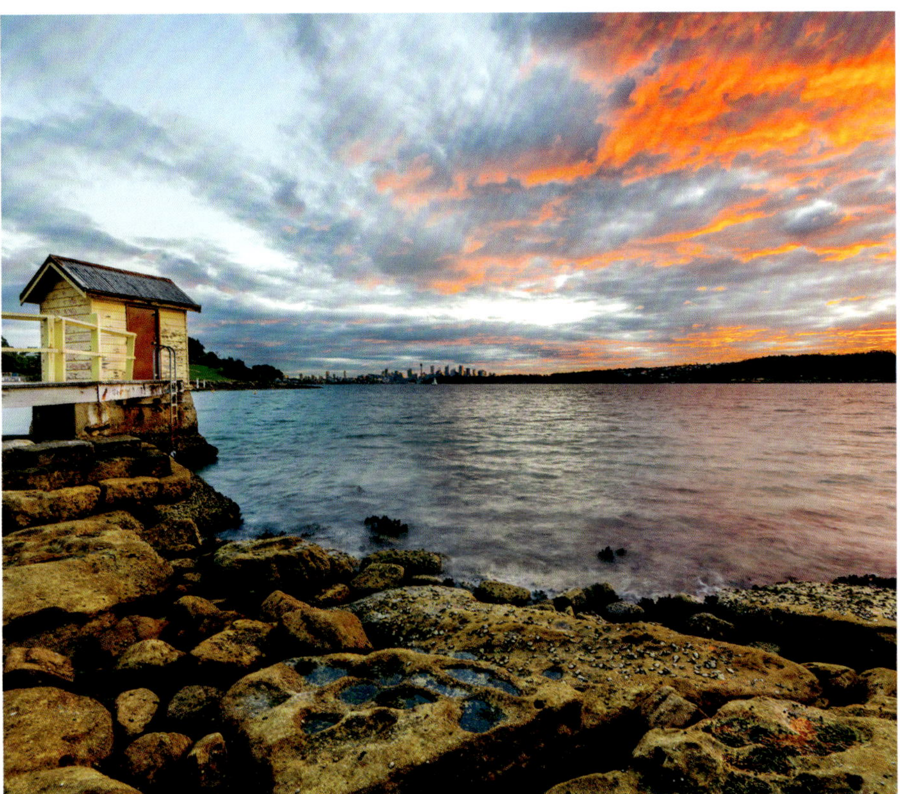

Watsons Bay, Sydney.

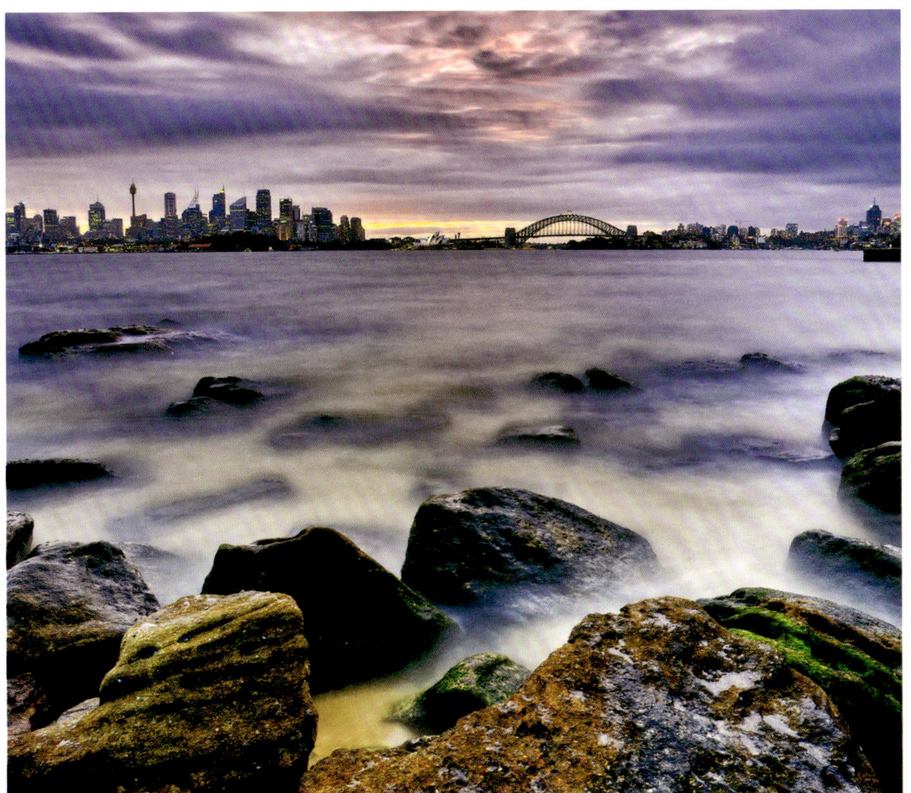

Sydney skyline.

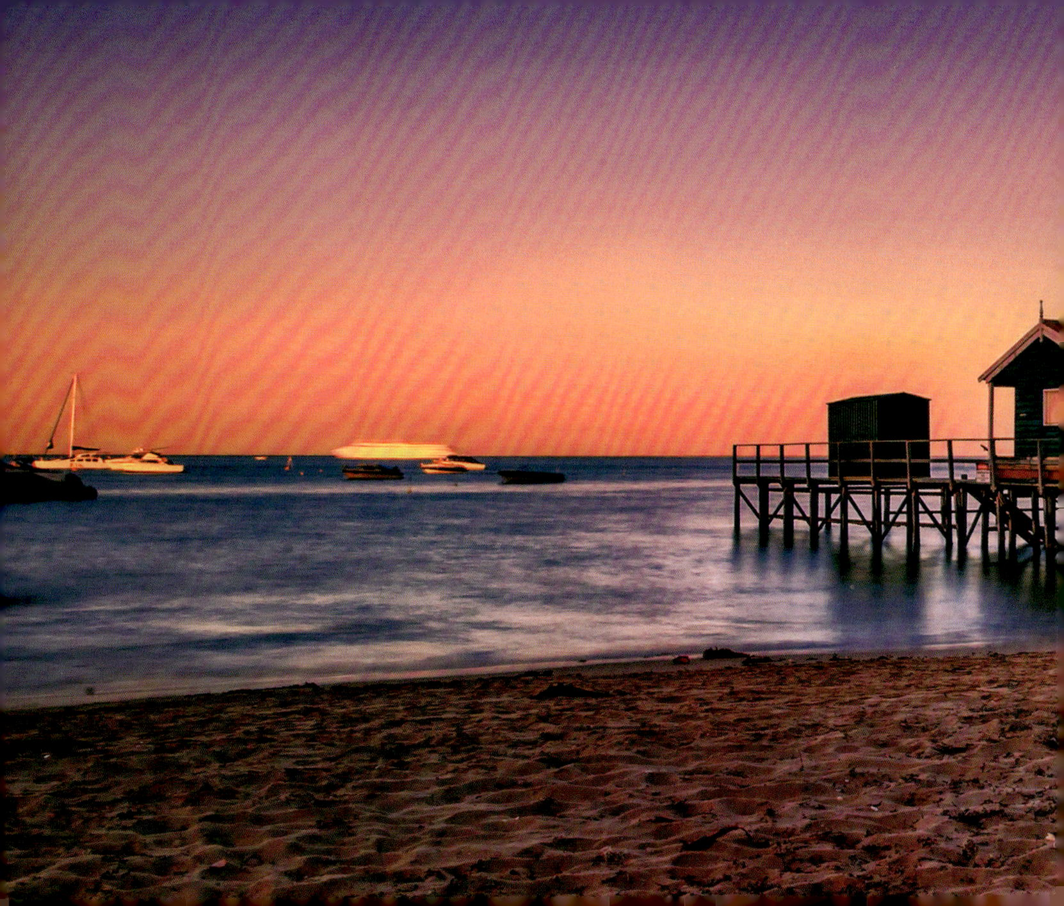

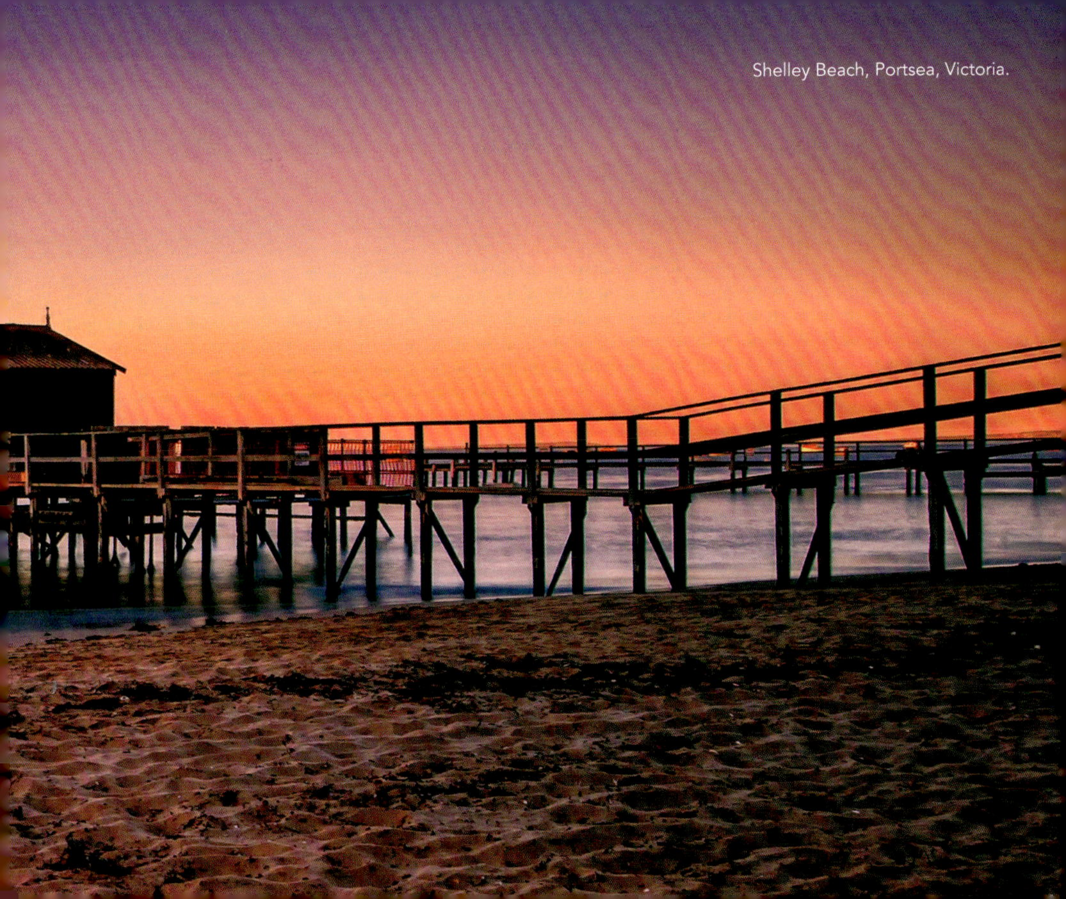

Shelley Beach, Portsea, Victoria.

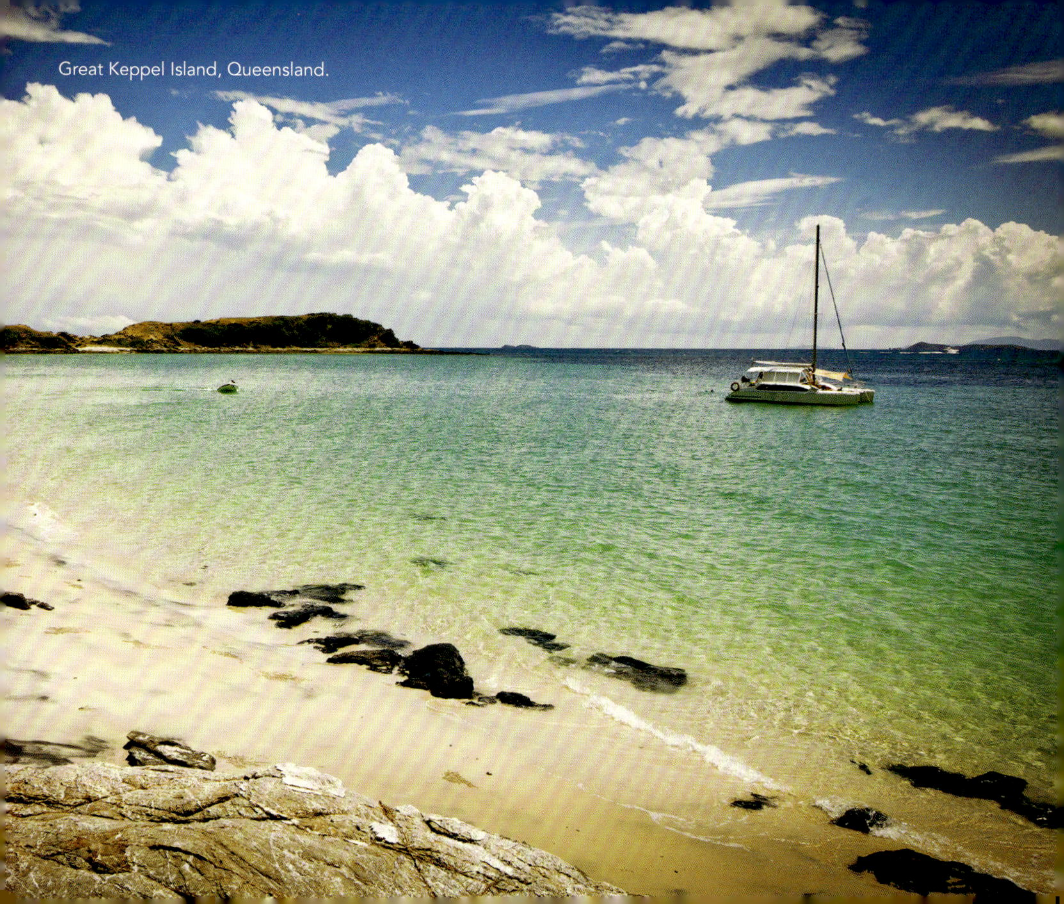
Great Keppel Island, Queensland.

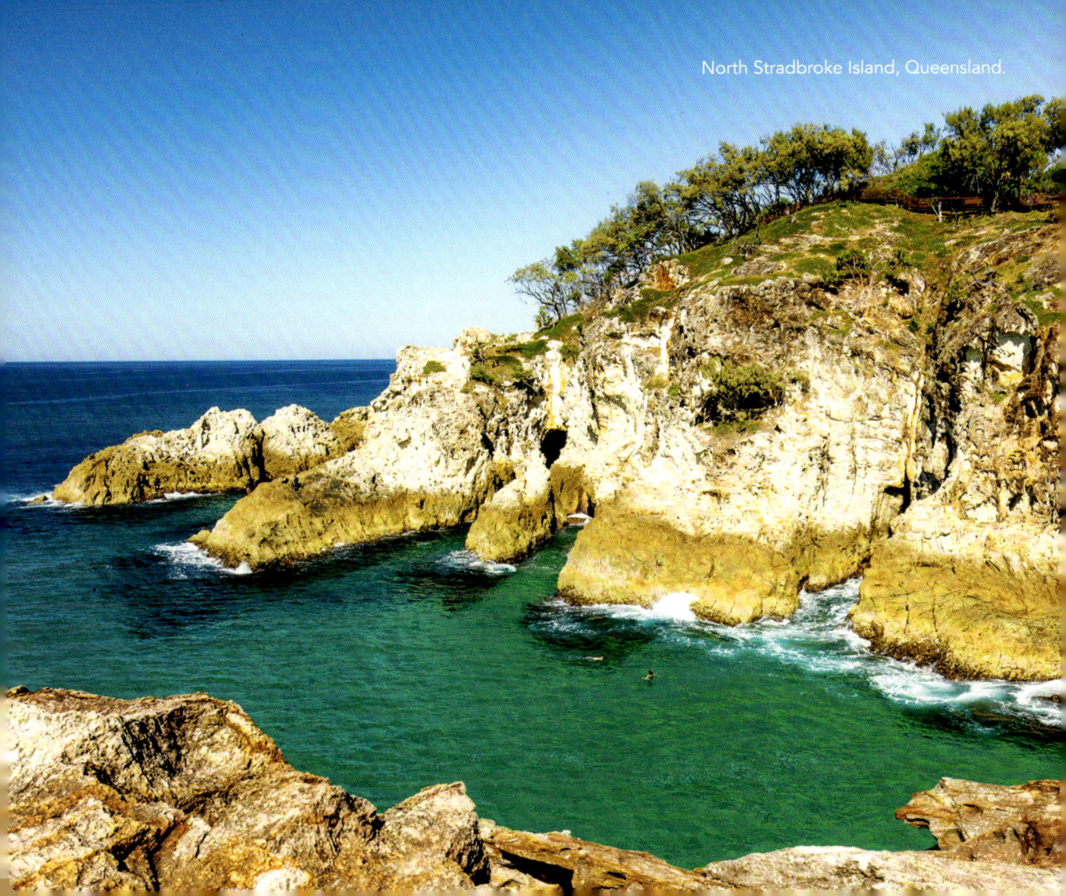
North Stradbroke Island, Queensland.

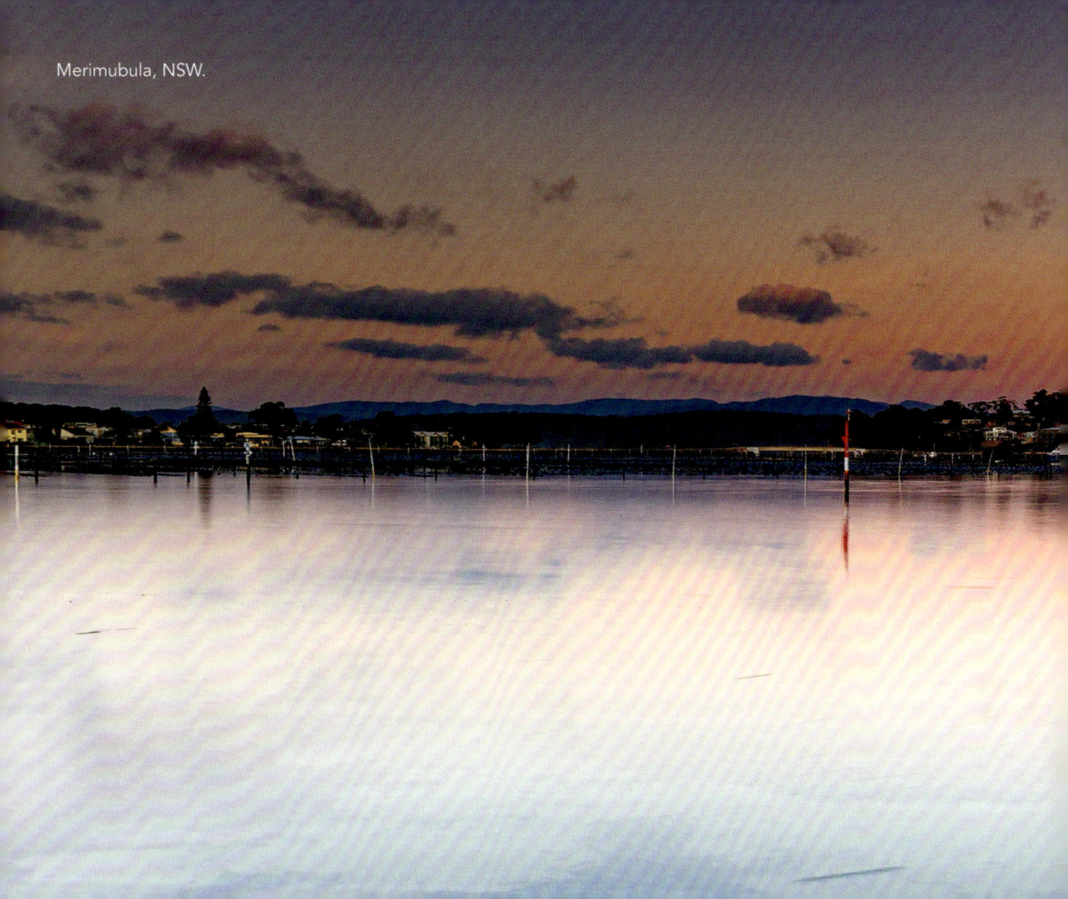

Merimubula, NSW.

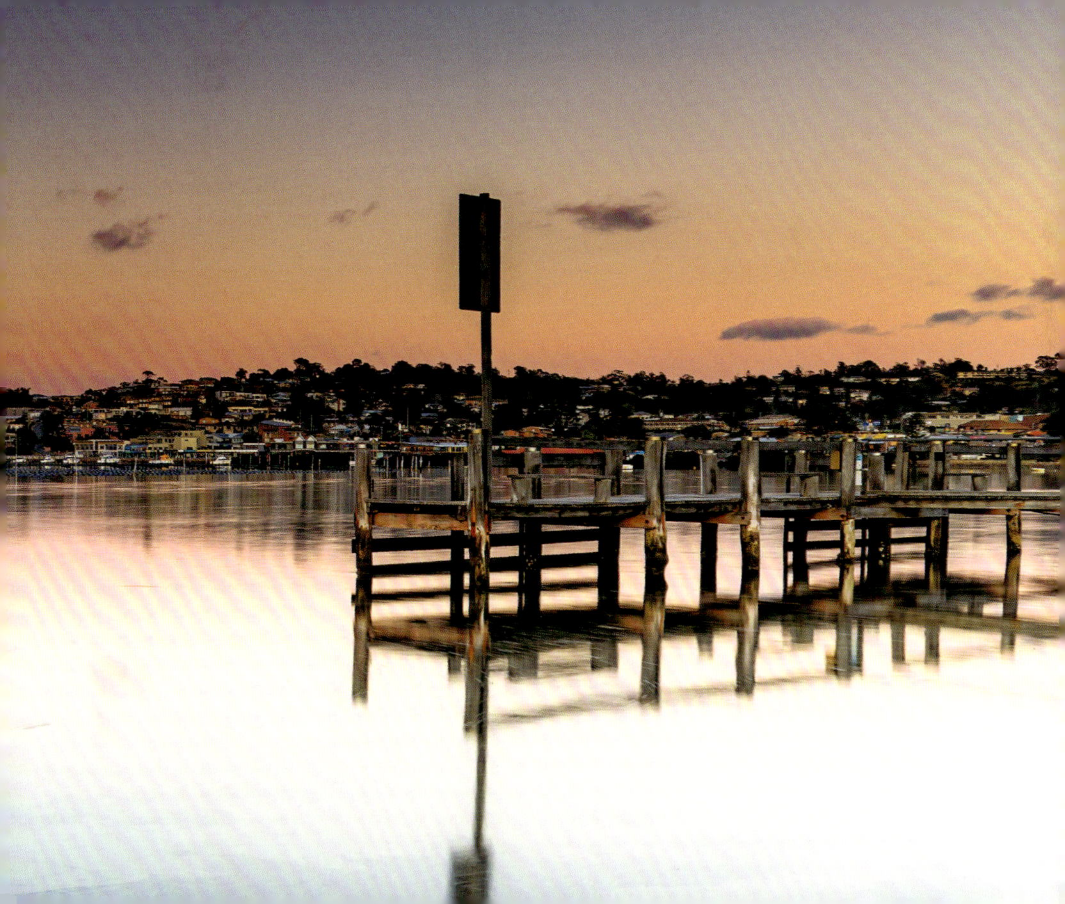

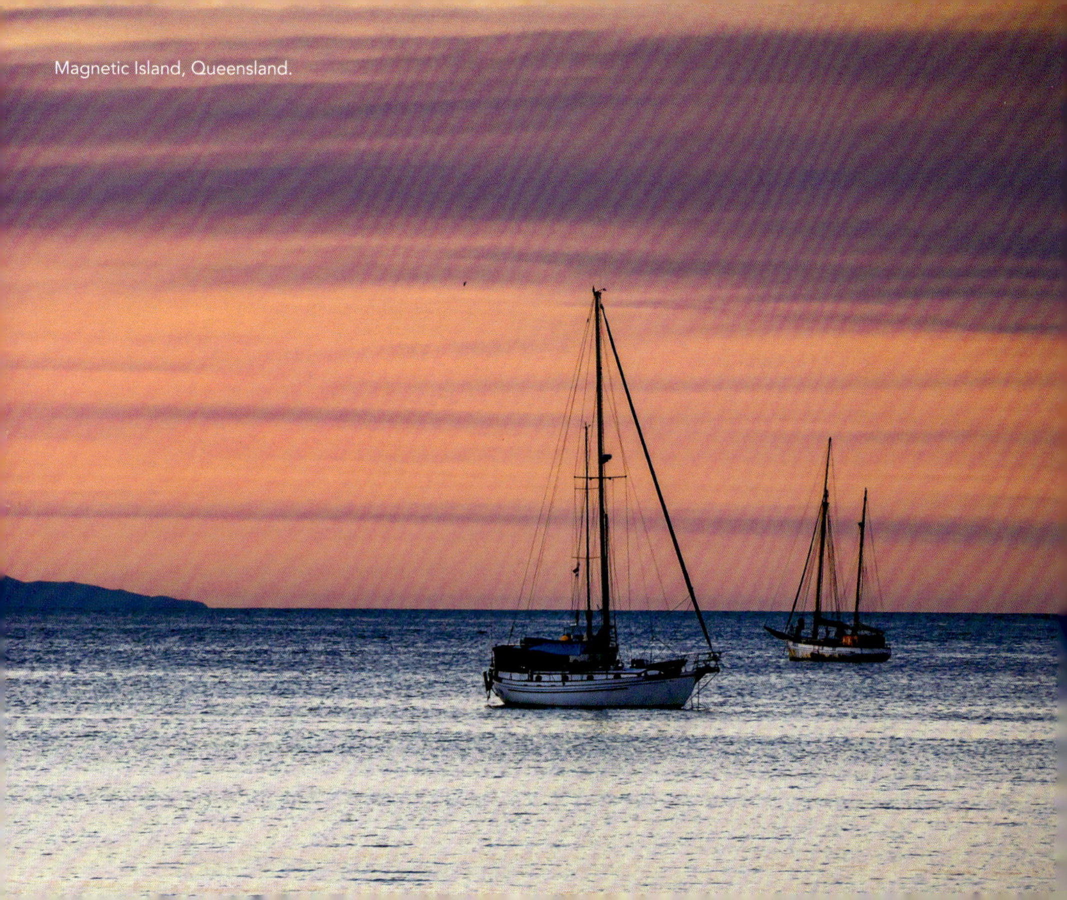
Magnetic Island, Queensland.

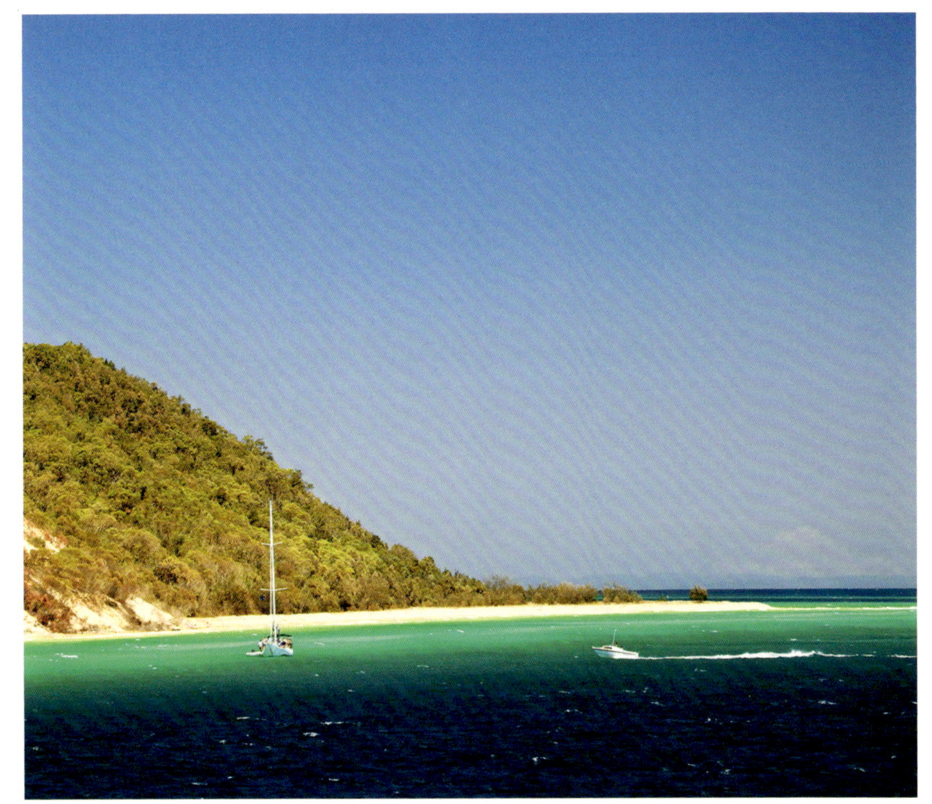

Moreton Island, Queensland.

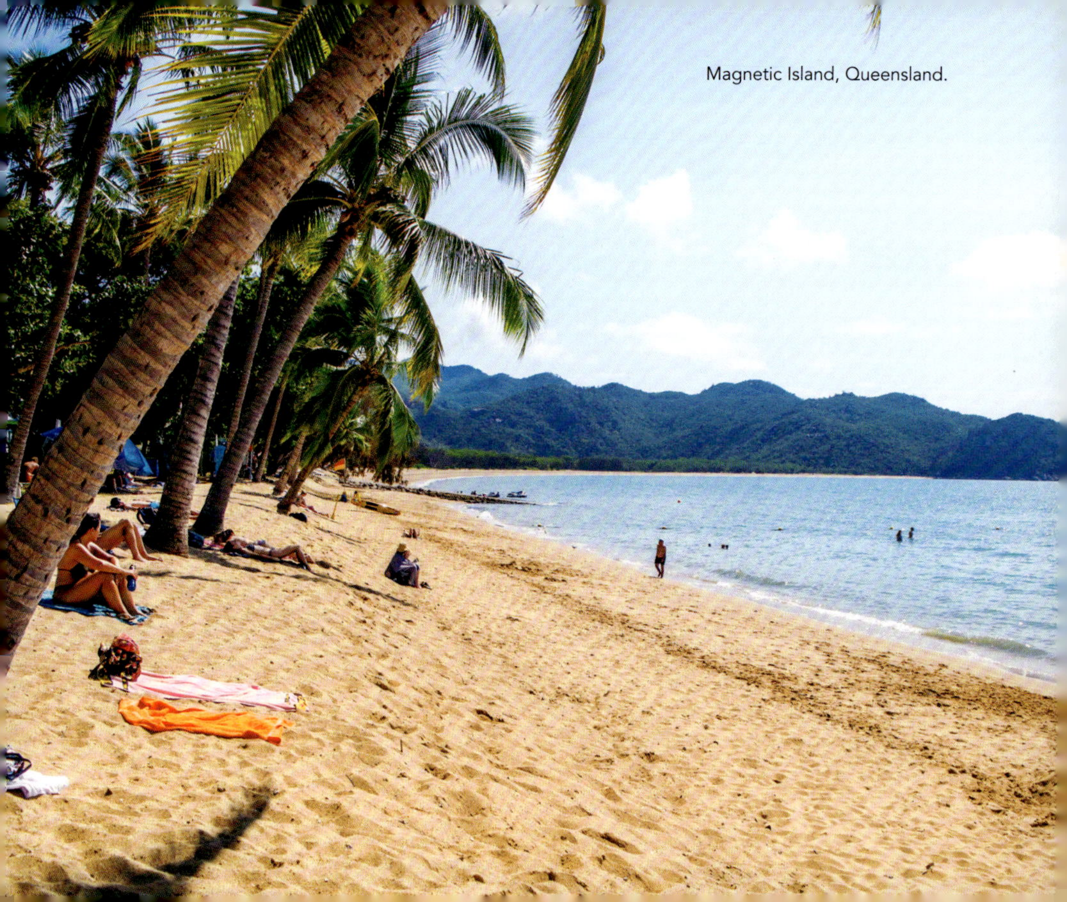

Magnetic Island, Queensland.

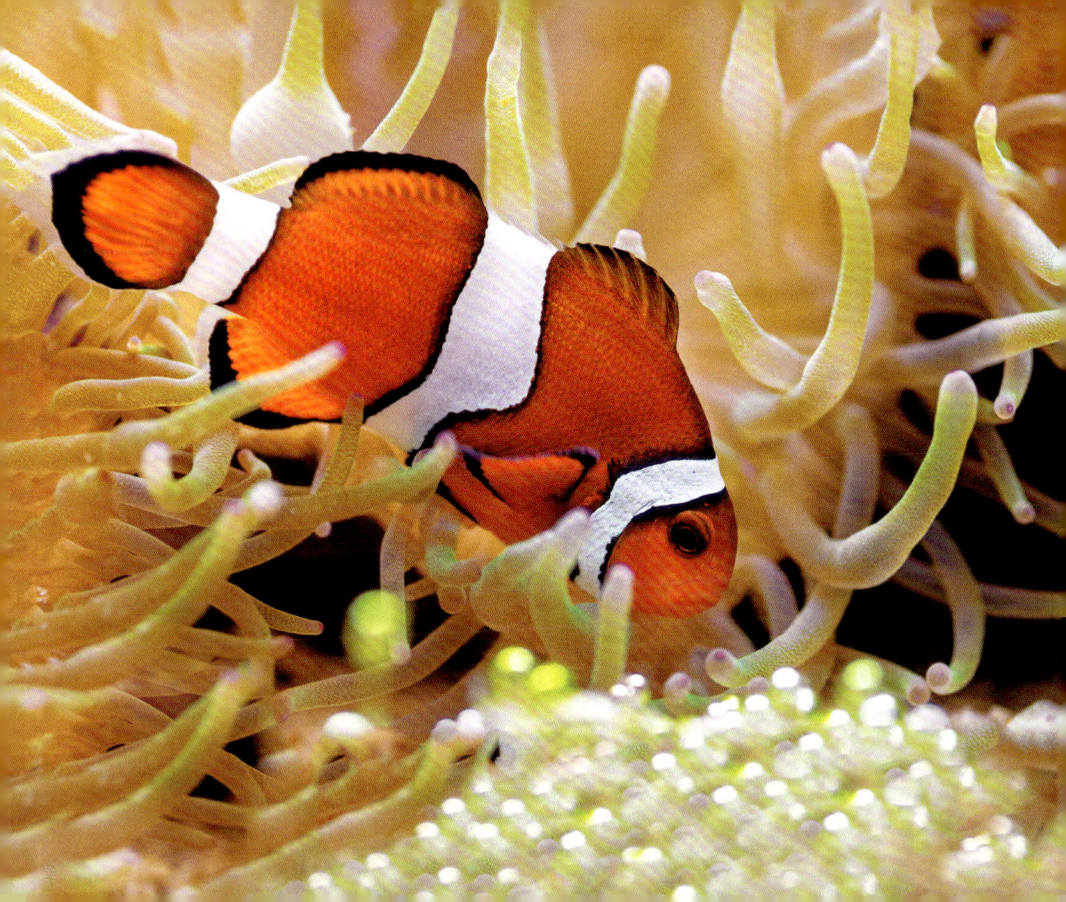

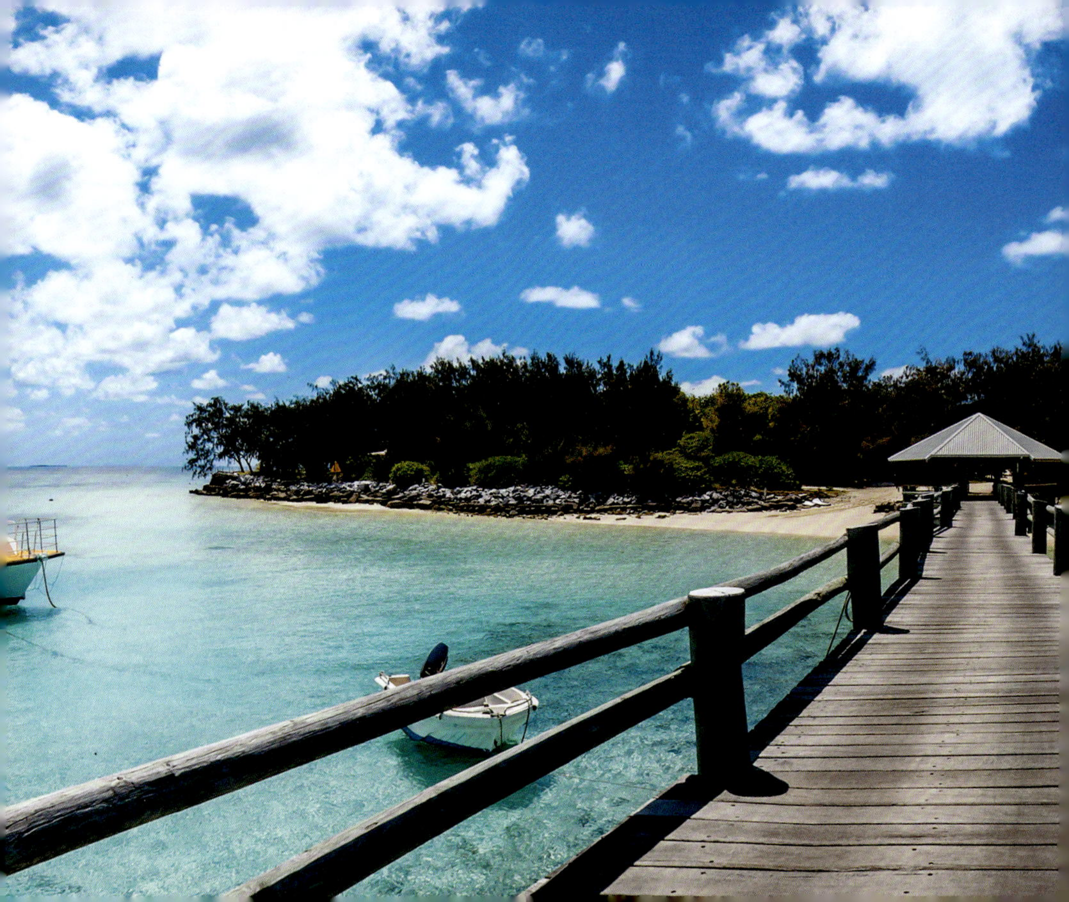

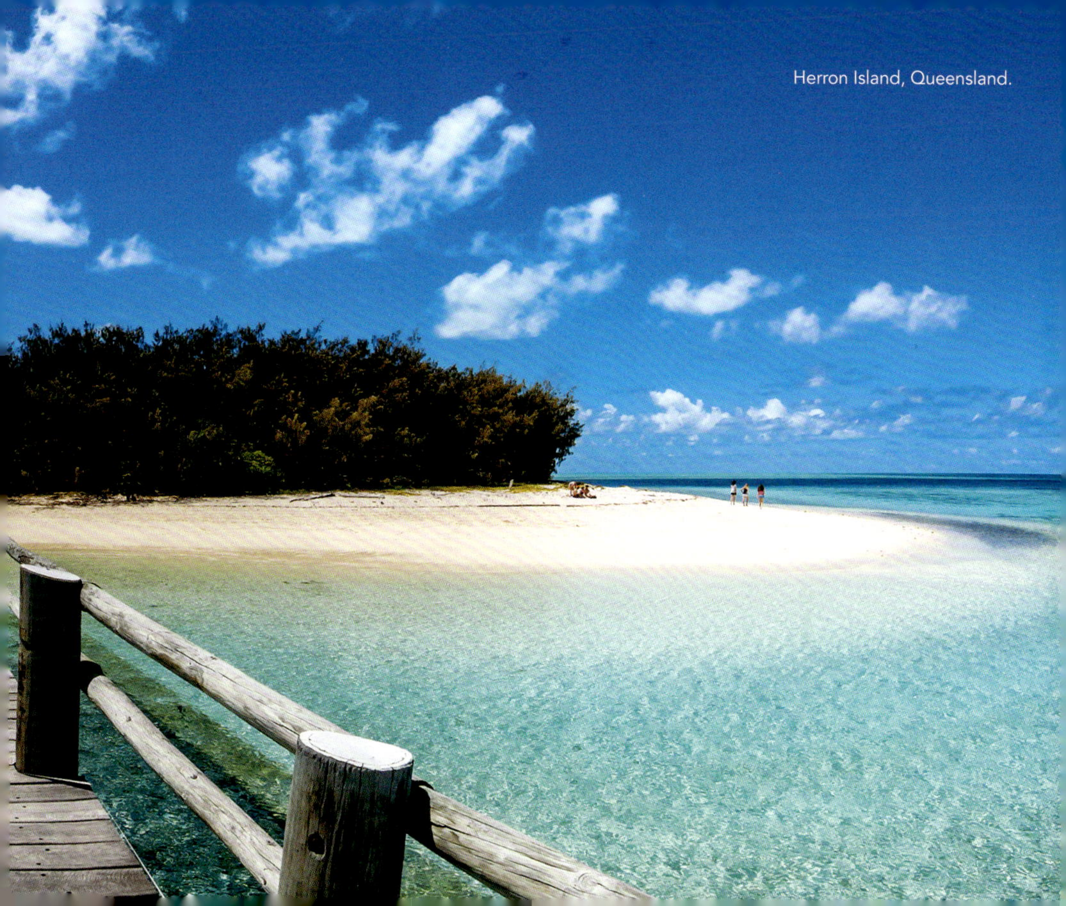

Herron Island, Queensland.

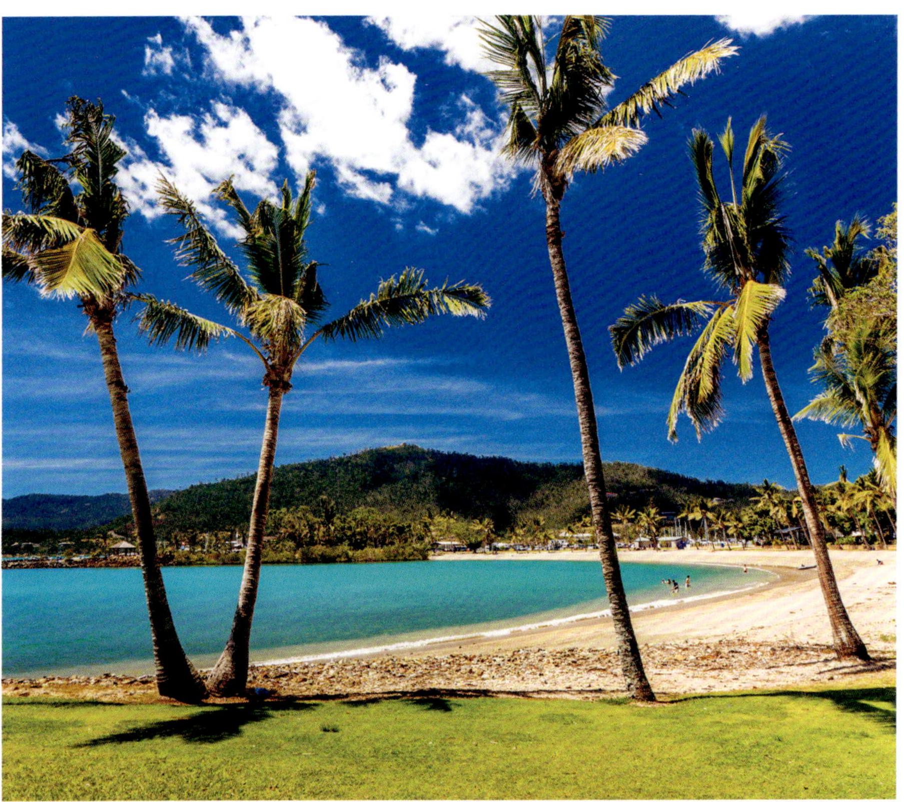

Airlie Beach, Queensland.

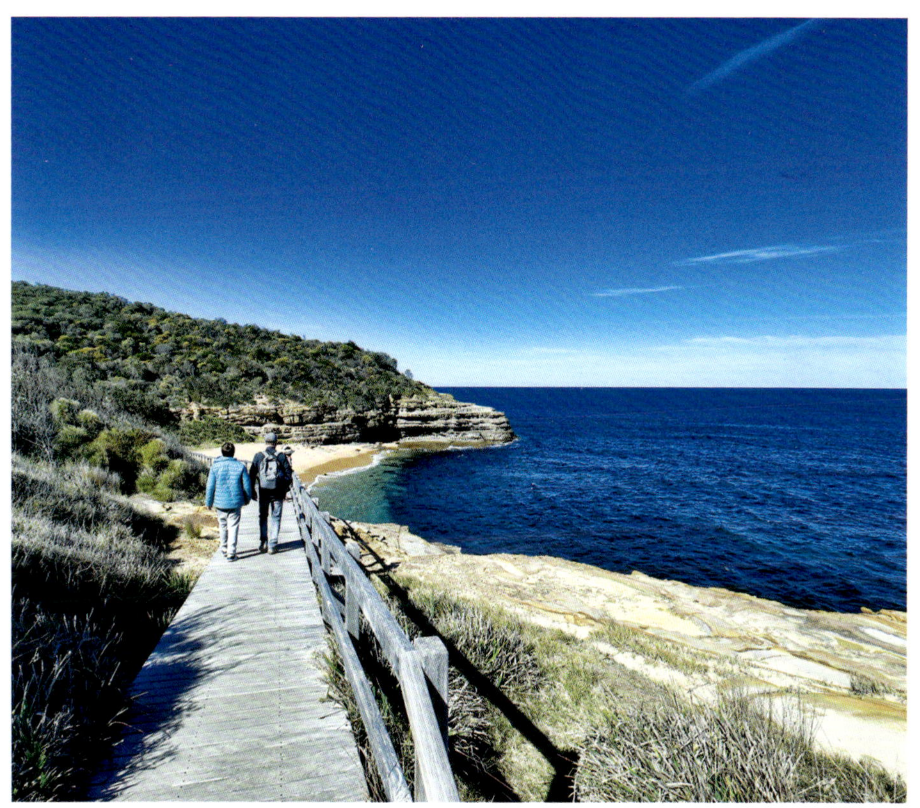

Bouddi National Park, NSW.

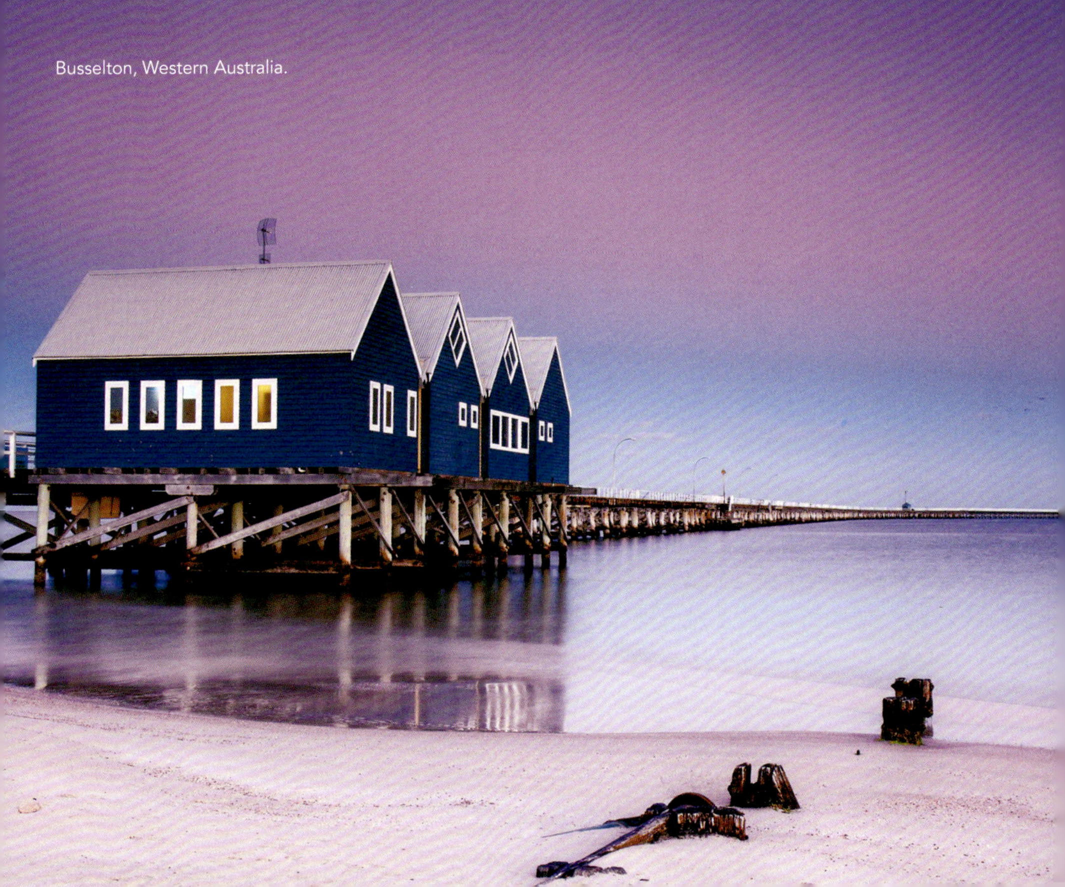
Busselton, Western Australia.

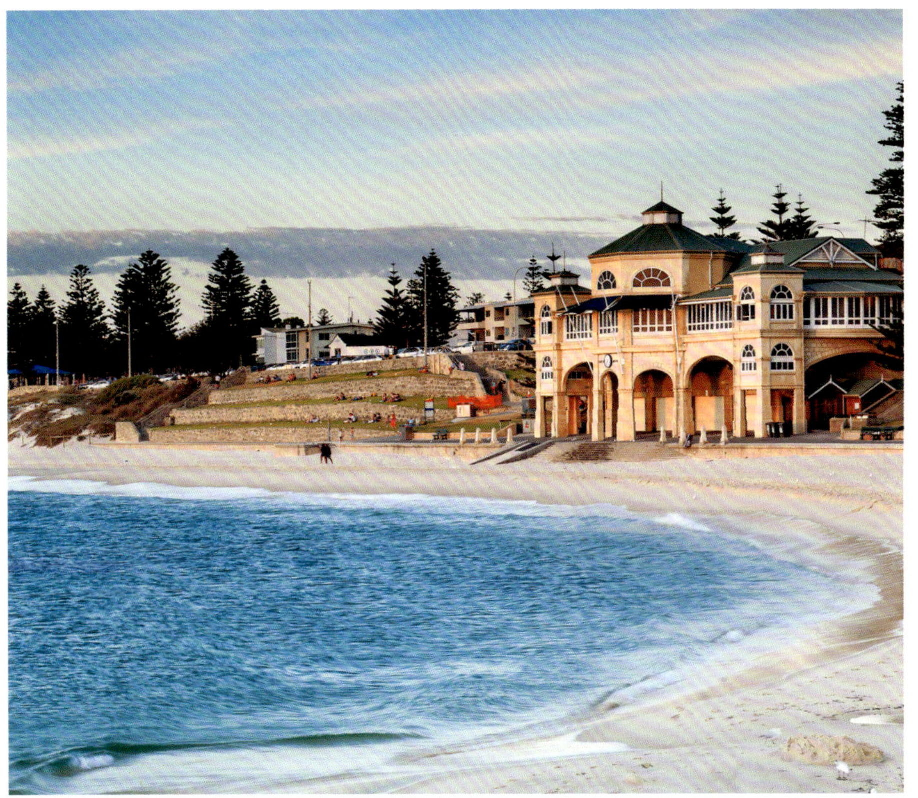

Cottesloe Beach. Perth.

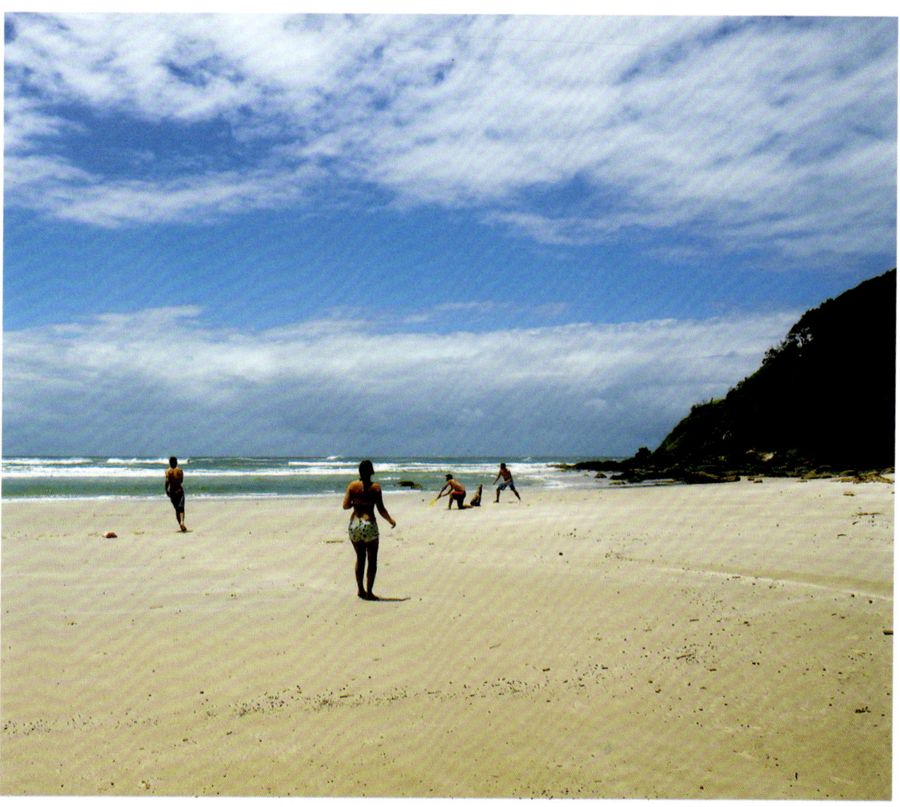

Byron Bay, NSW.

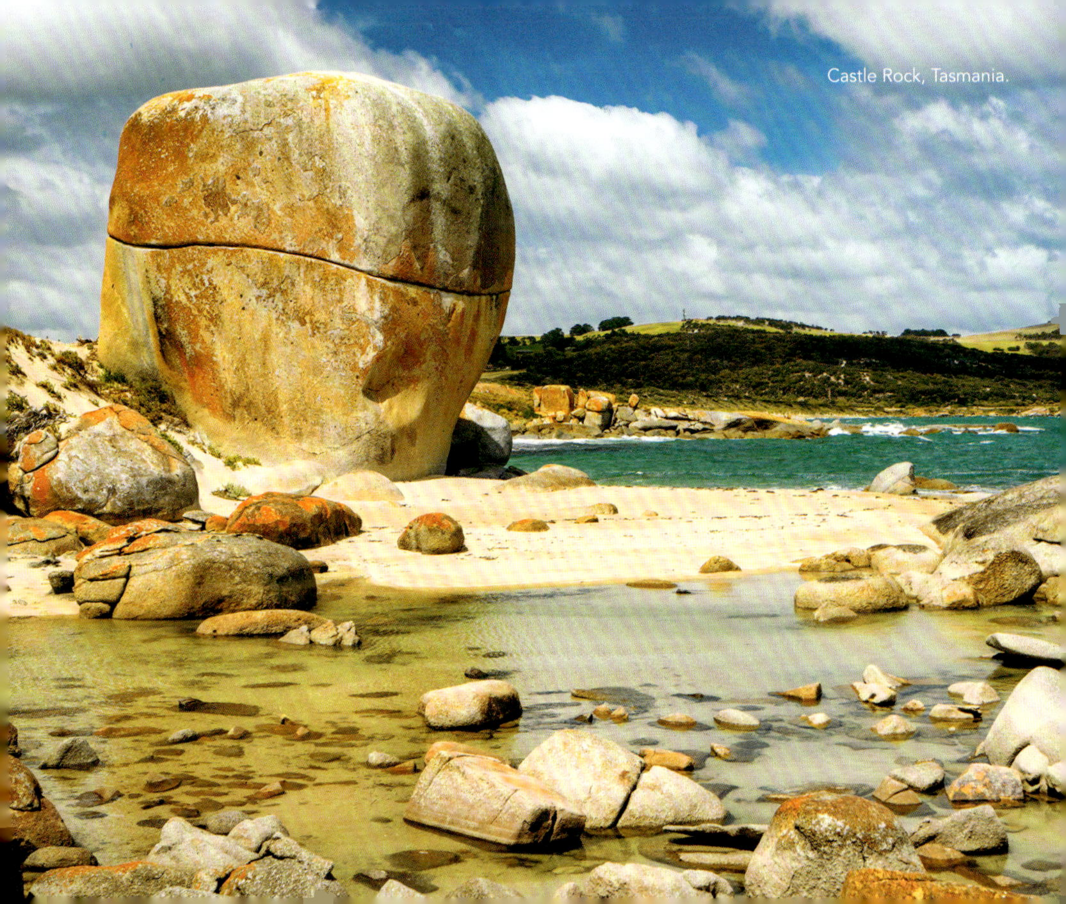

Castle Rock, Tasmania.

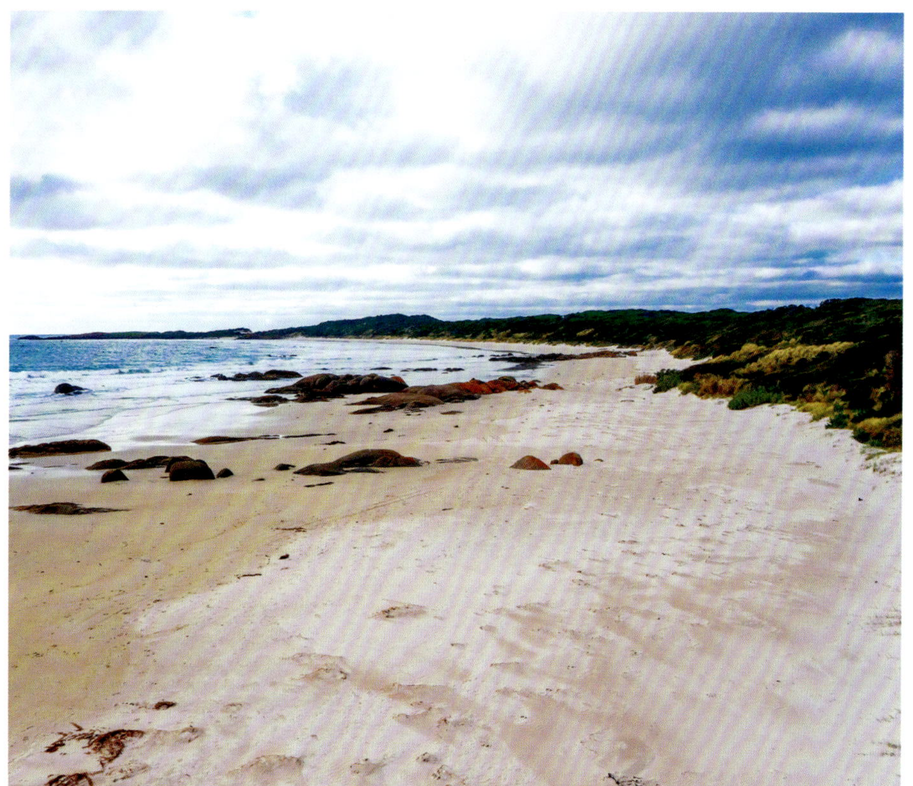

King Island, Tasmania.

Gippsland, Victoria.

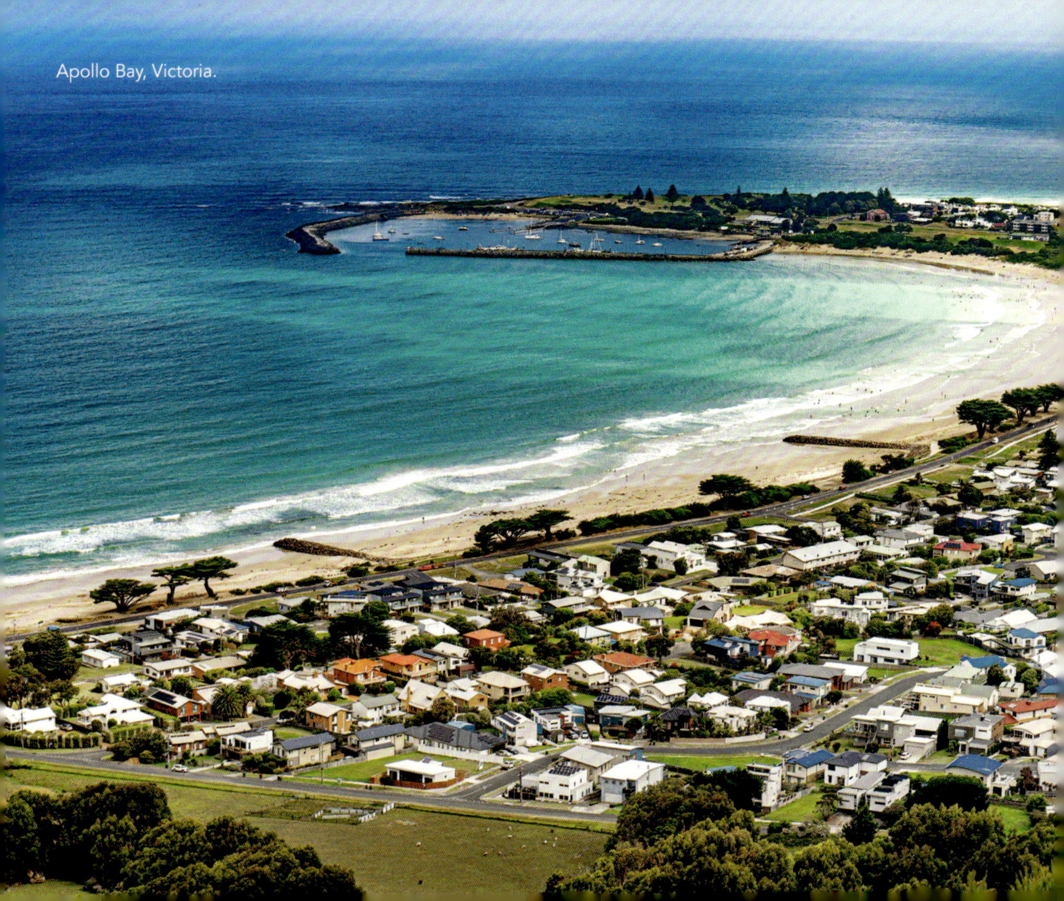
Apollo Bay, Victoria.

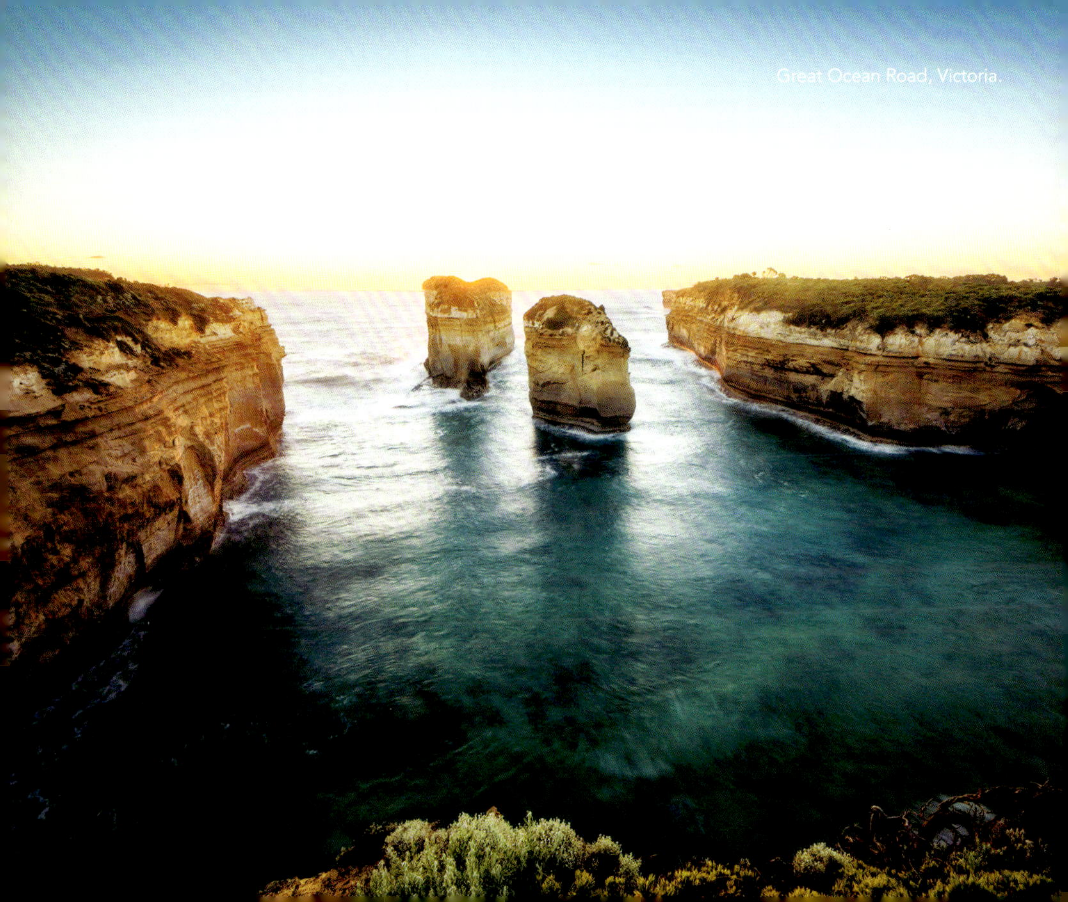

Great Ocean Road, Victoria.

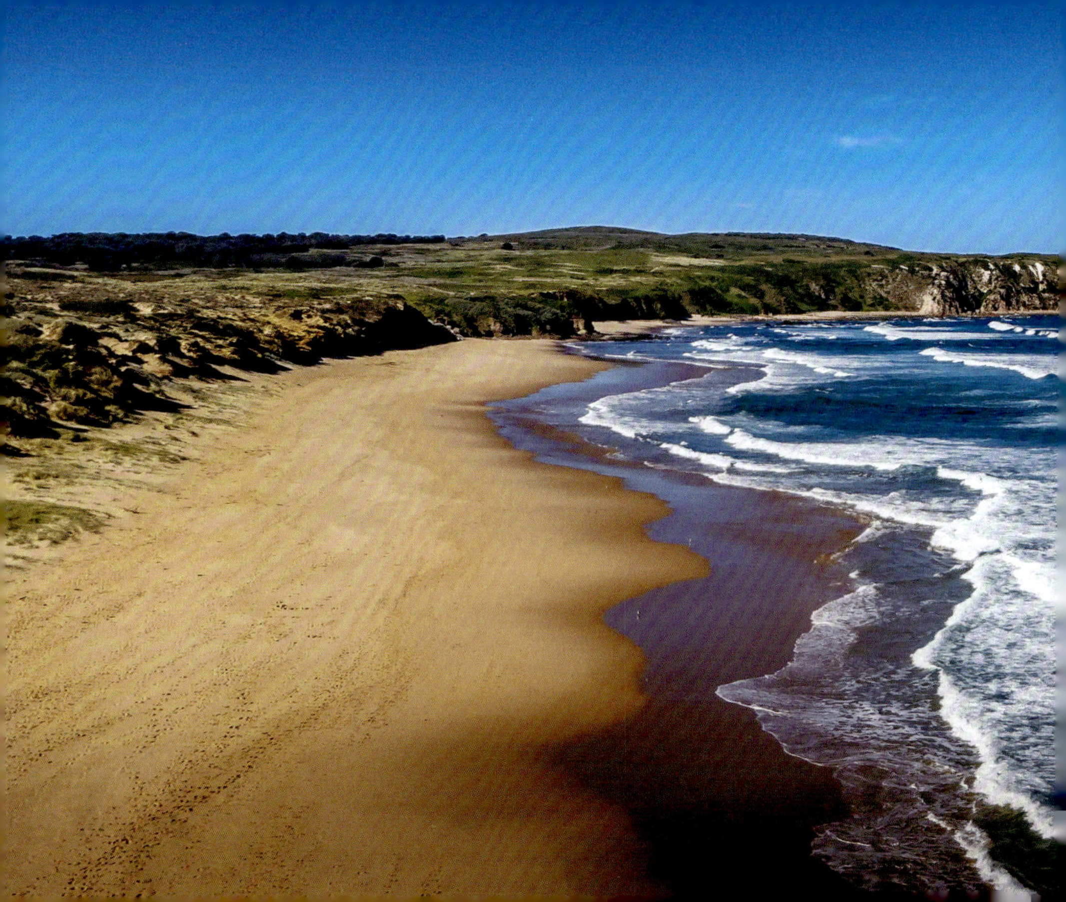

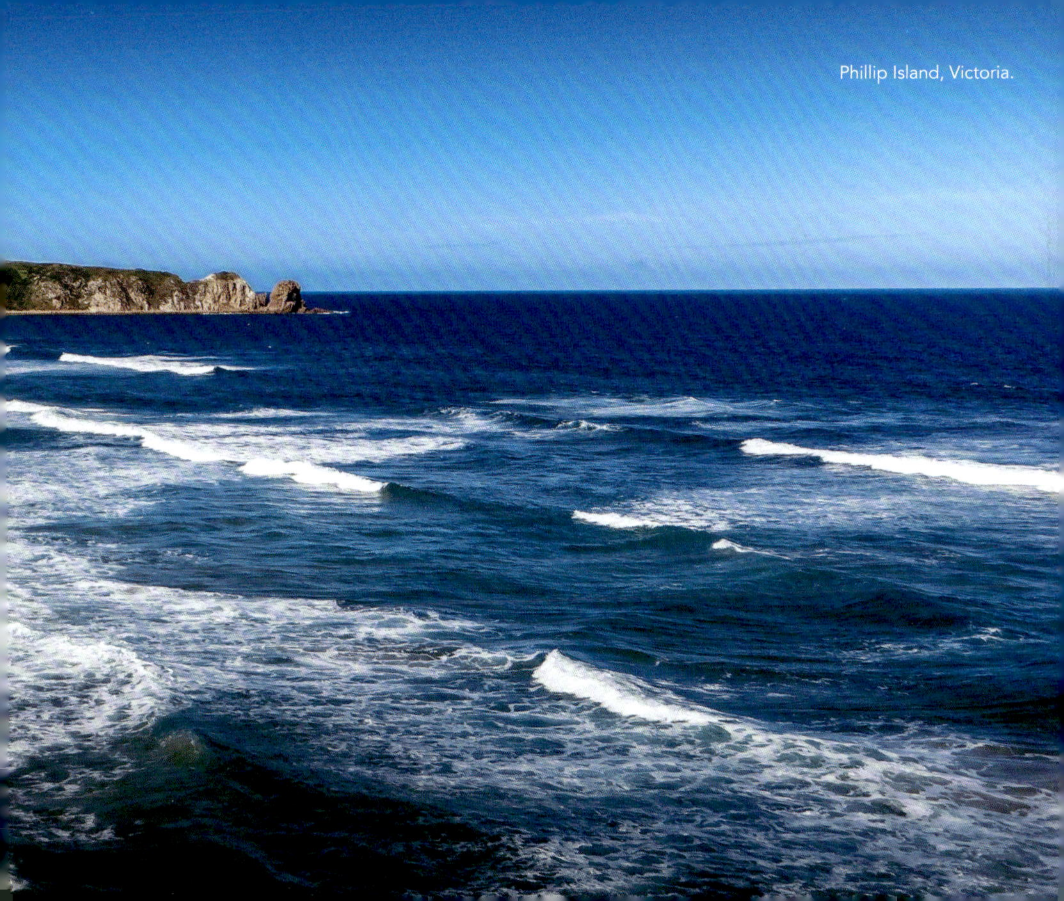
Phillip Island, Victoria.

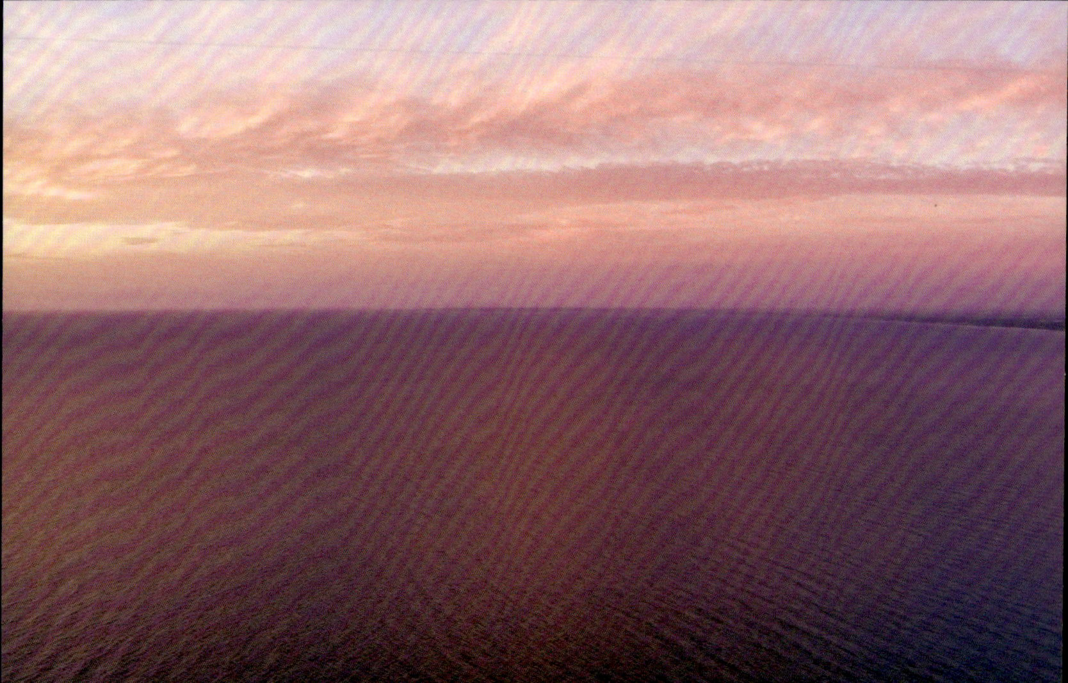

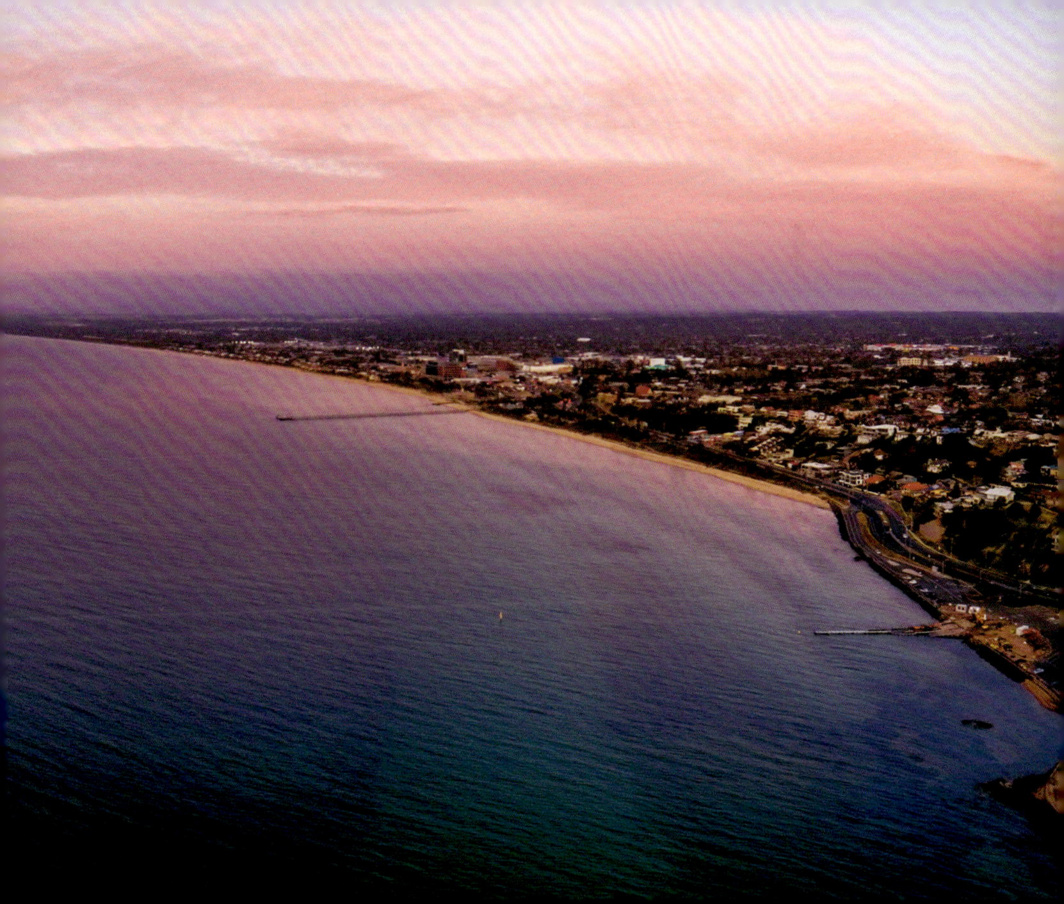

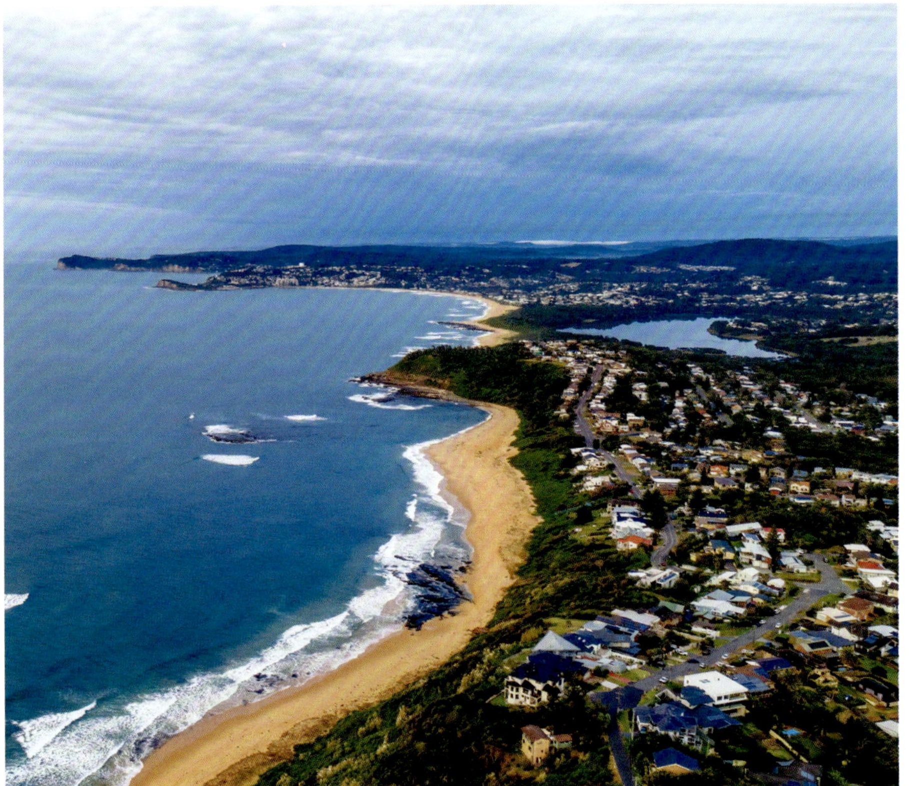

Forester Beach, NSW.

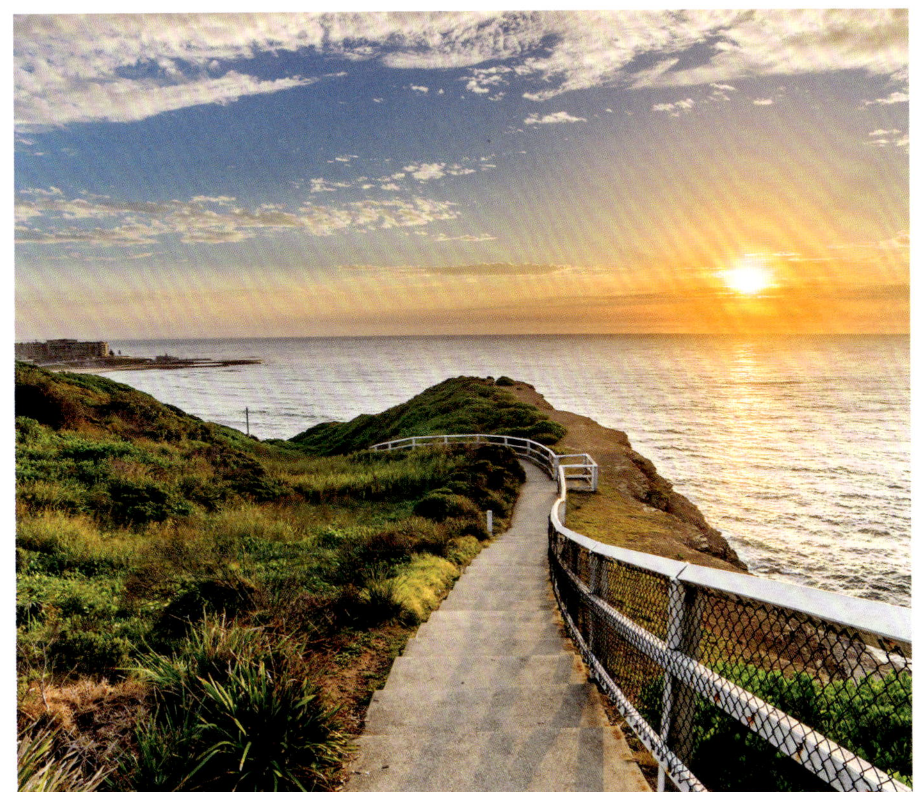

Bogie Hole, Newcastle, NSW.

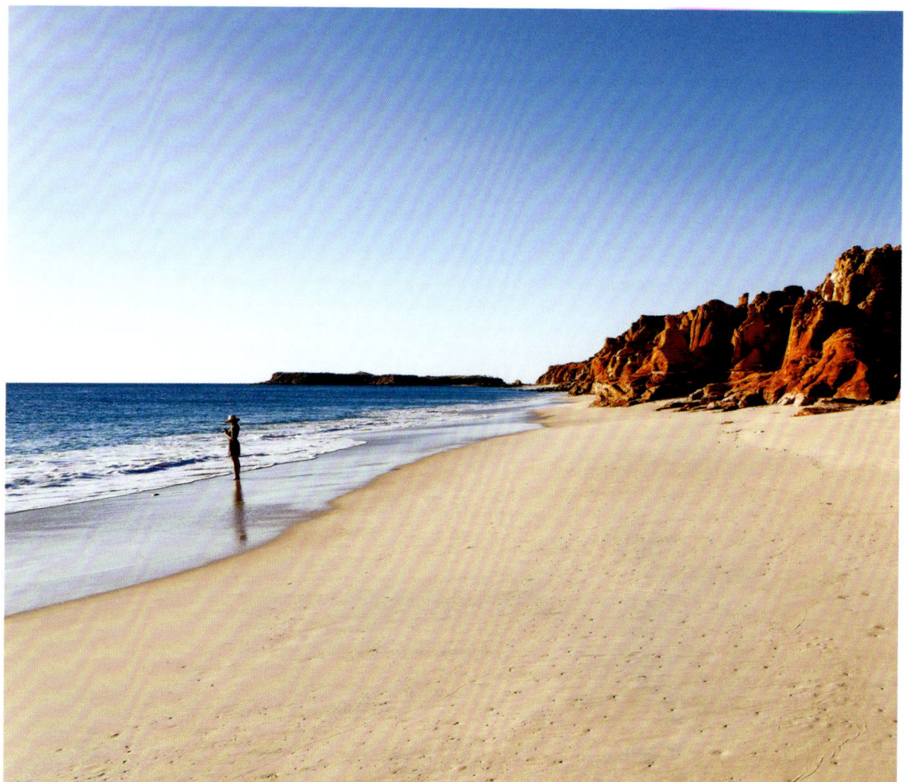

Dampier Peninsula in the Kimberley region of Western Australia.

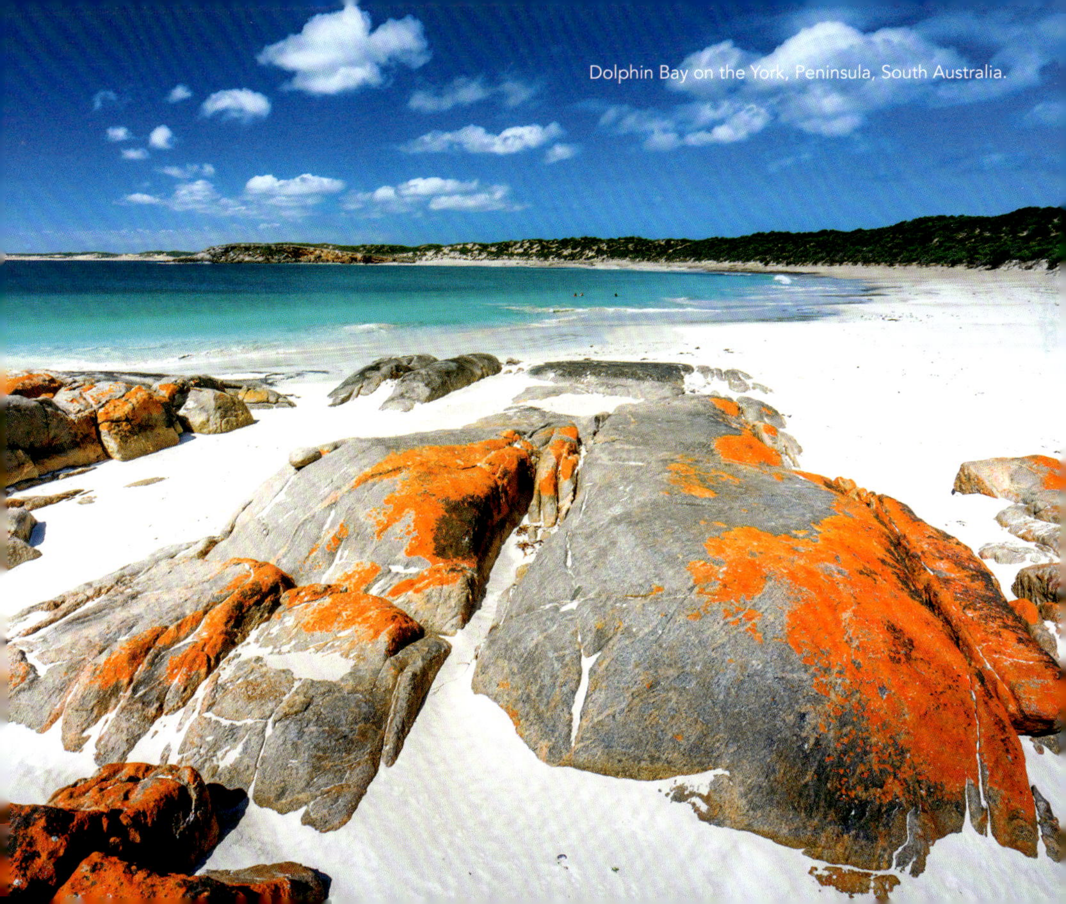

Dolphin Bay on the York, Peninsula, South Australia.

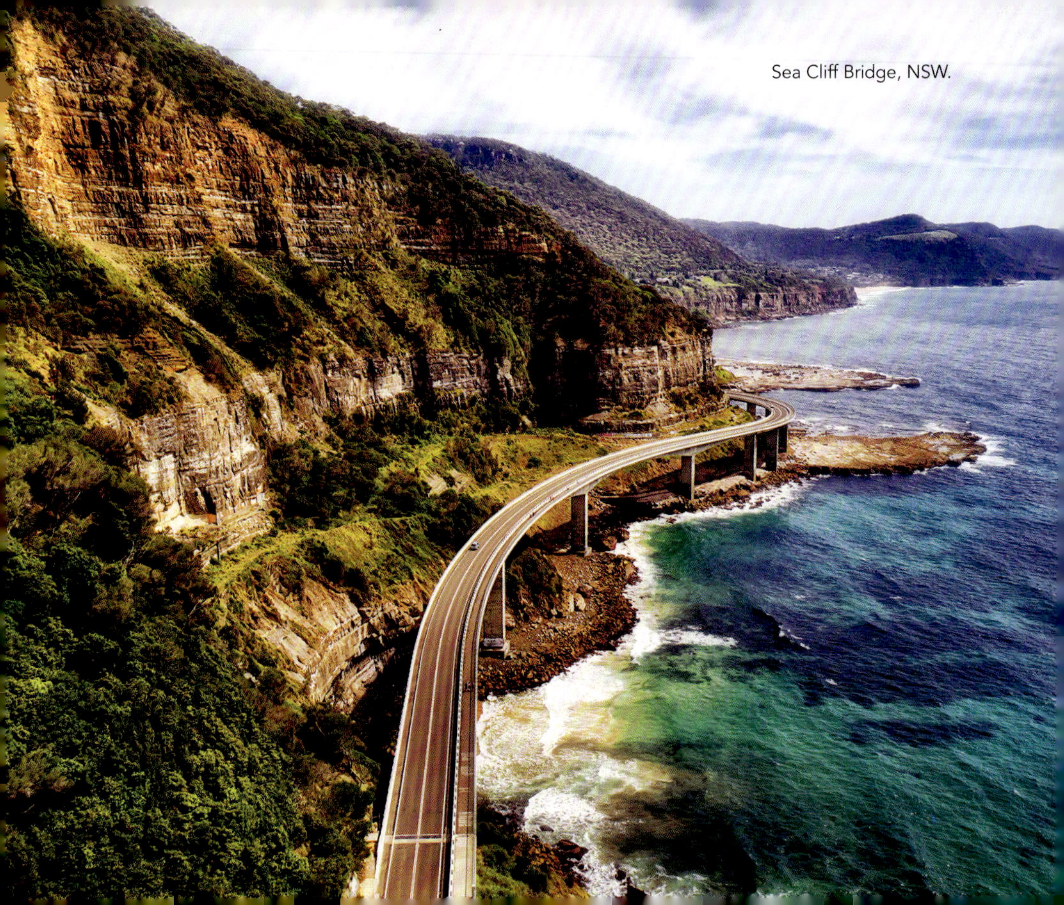
Sea Cliff Bridge, NSW.

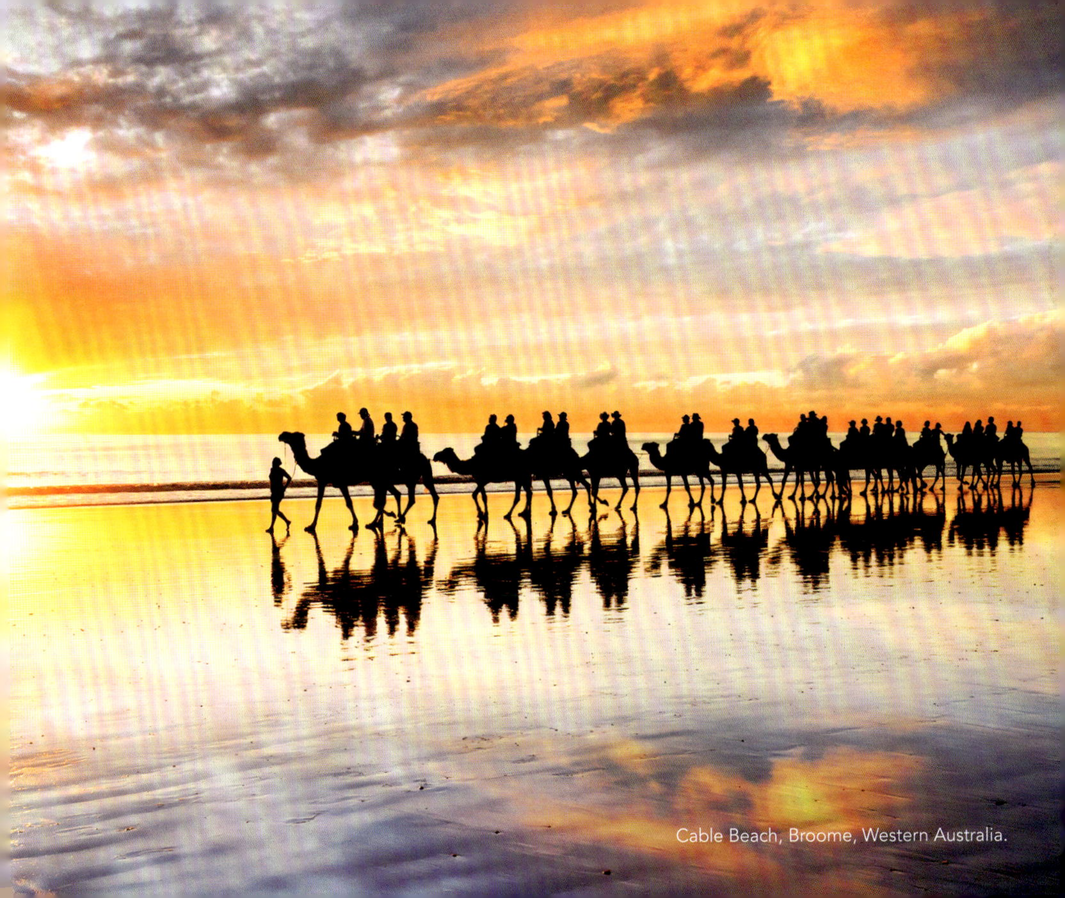

Cable Beach, Broome, Western Australia.

Kangaroo Island, South Australia.

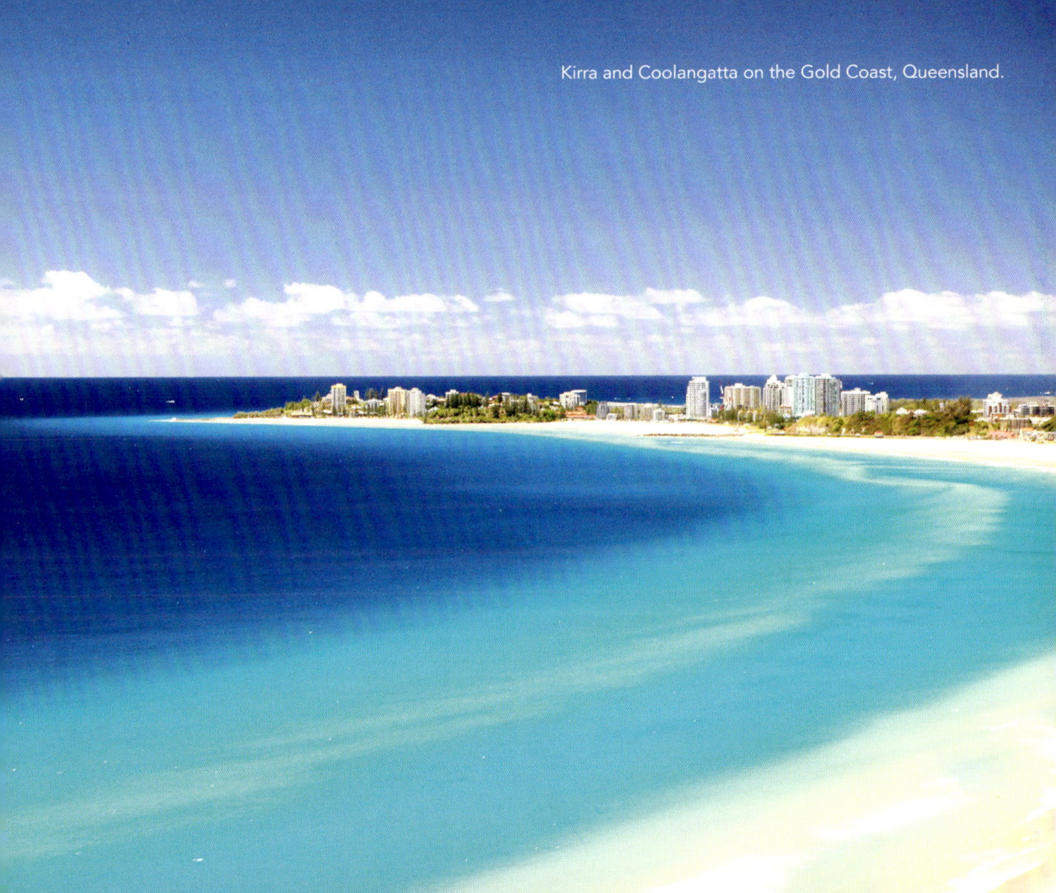

Kirra and Coolangatta on the Gold Coast, Queensland.

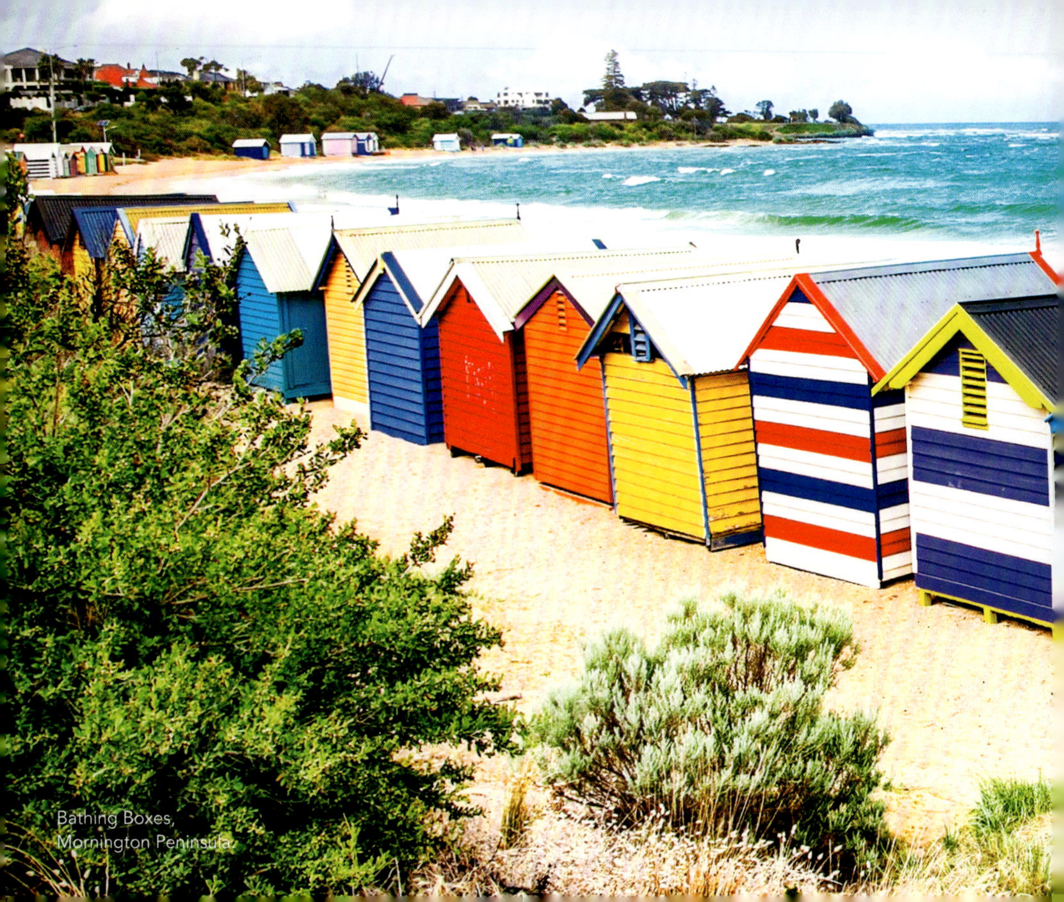

Bathing Boxes,
Mornington Peninsula

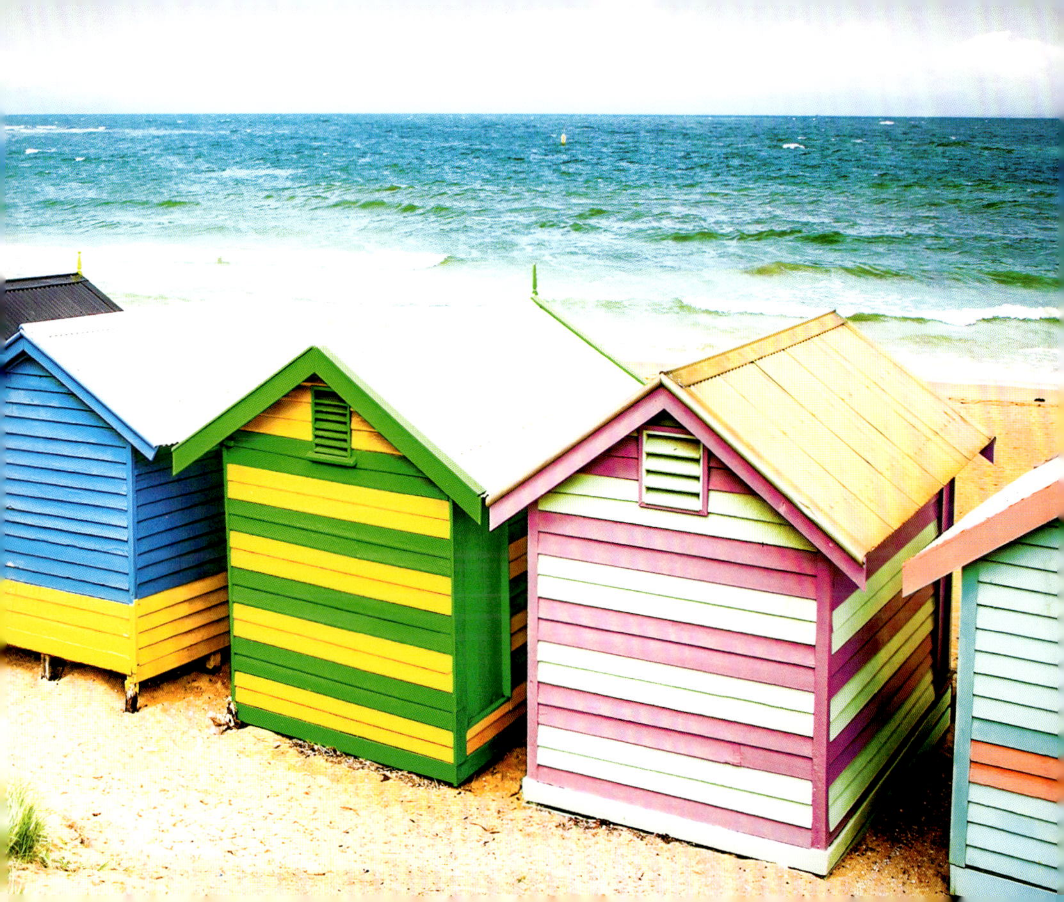

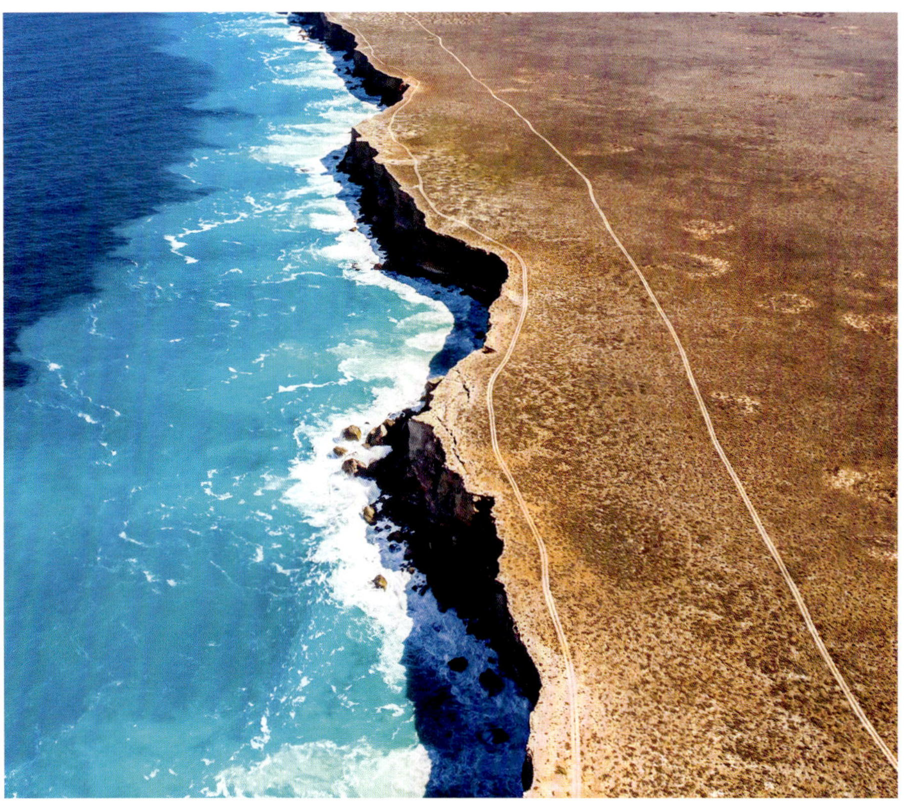

The coast near Nullarbor plain.

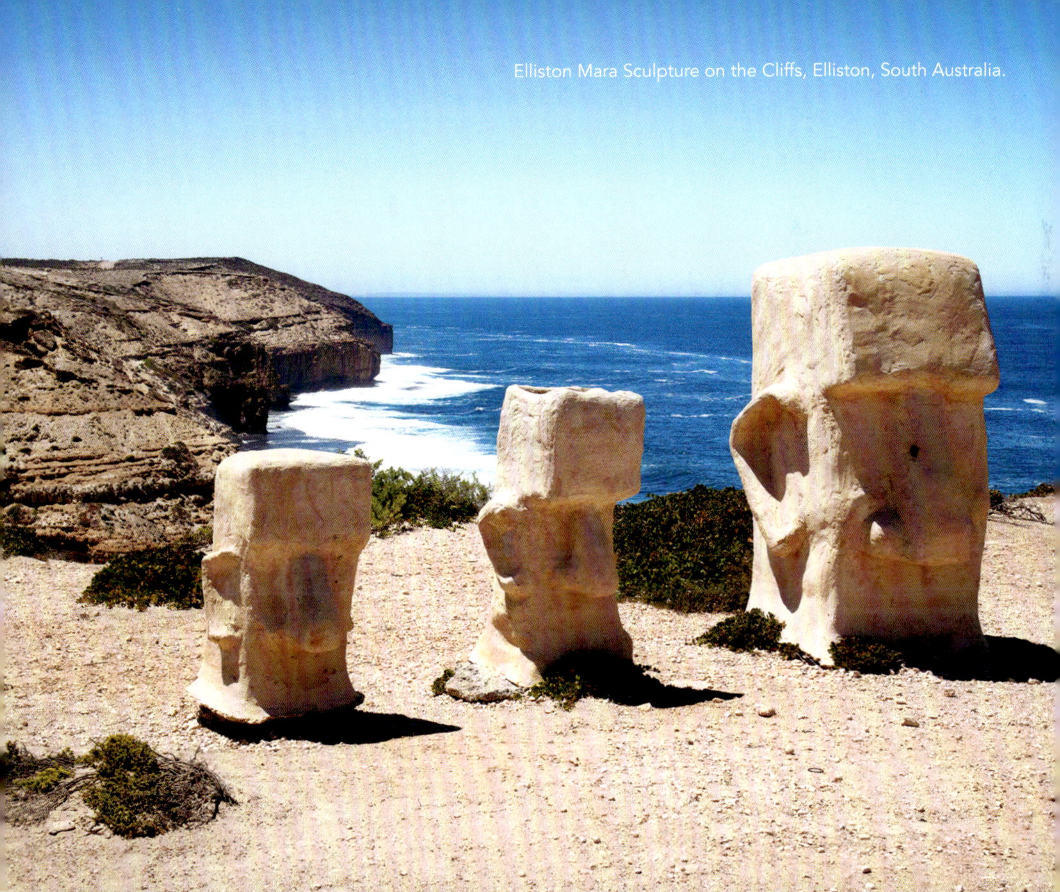
Elliston Mara Sculpture on the Cliffs, Elliston, South Australia.

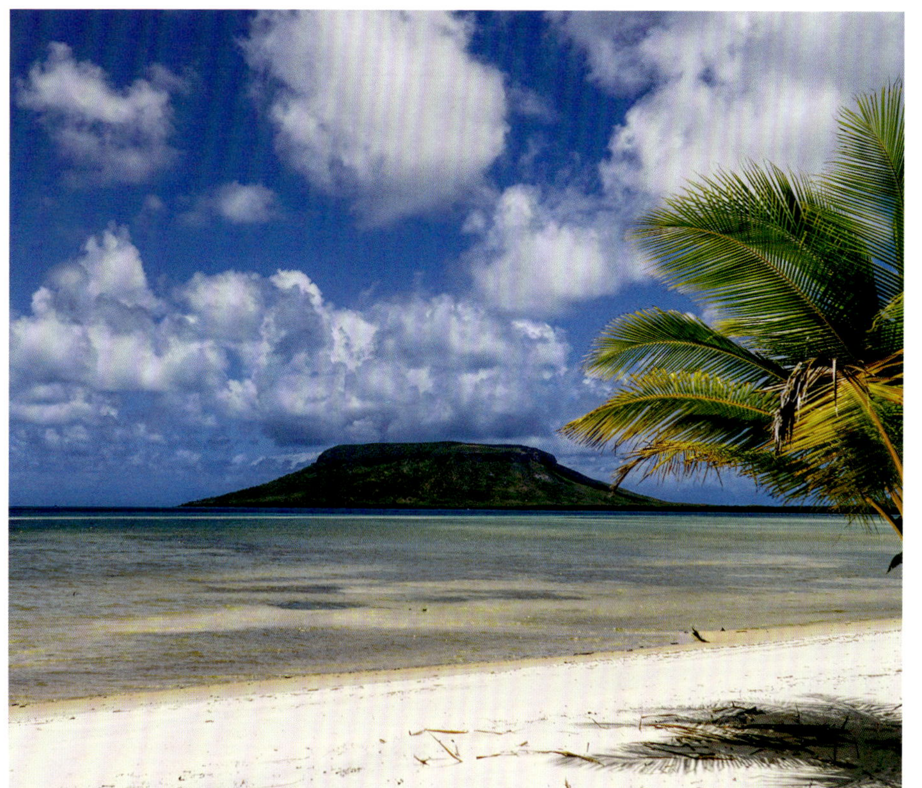

Elim Beach with Cape Bedford.

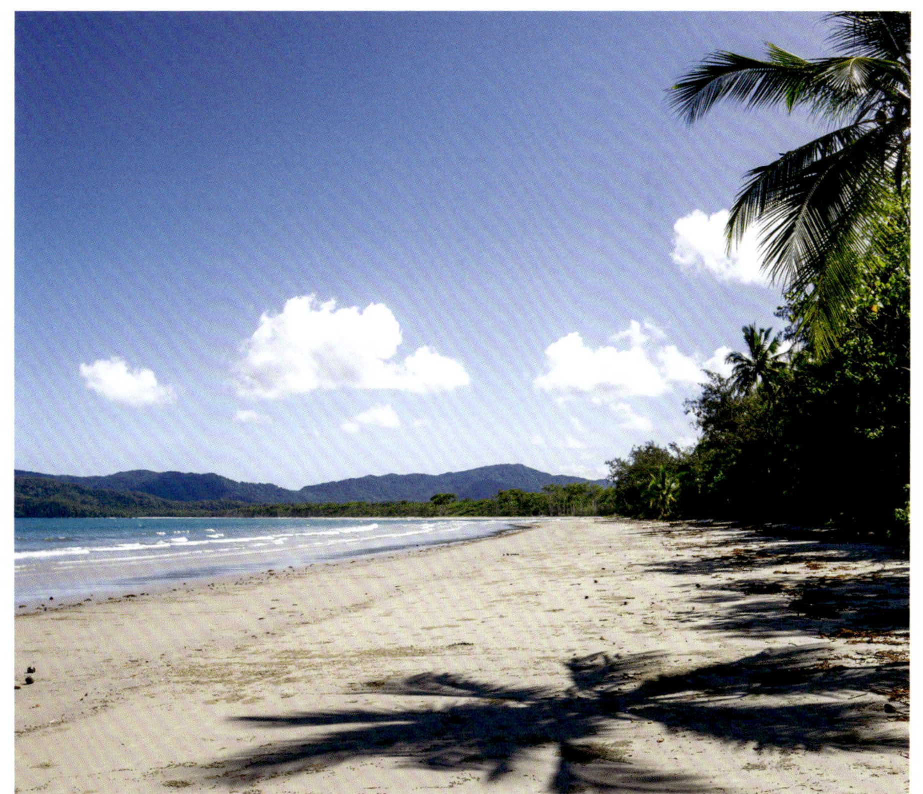

Daintree Rainforest, Queensland.

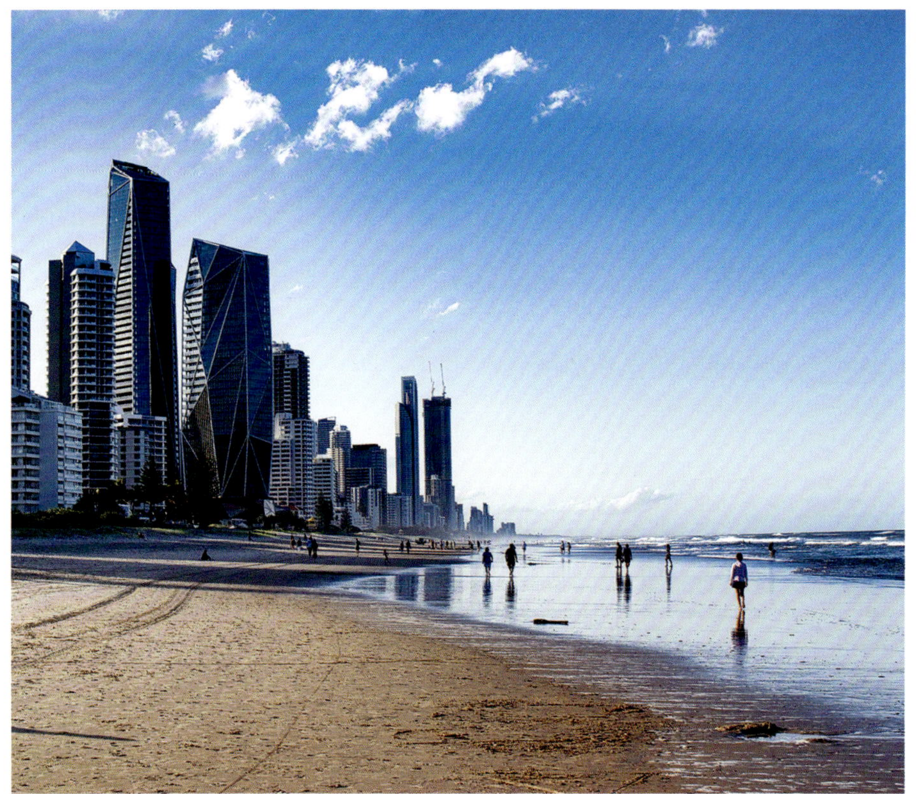

Sufers Paradise, Queensland.

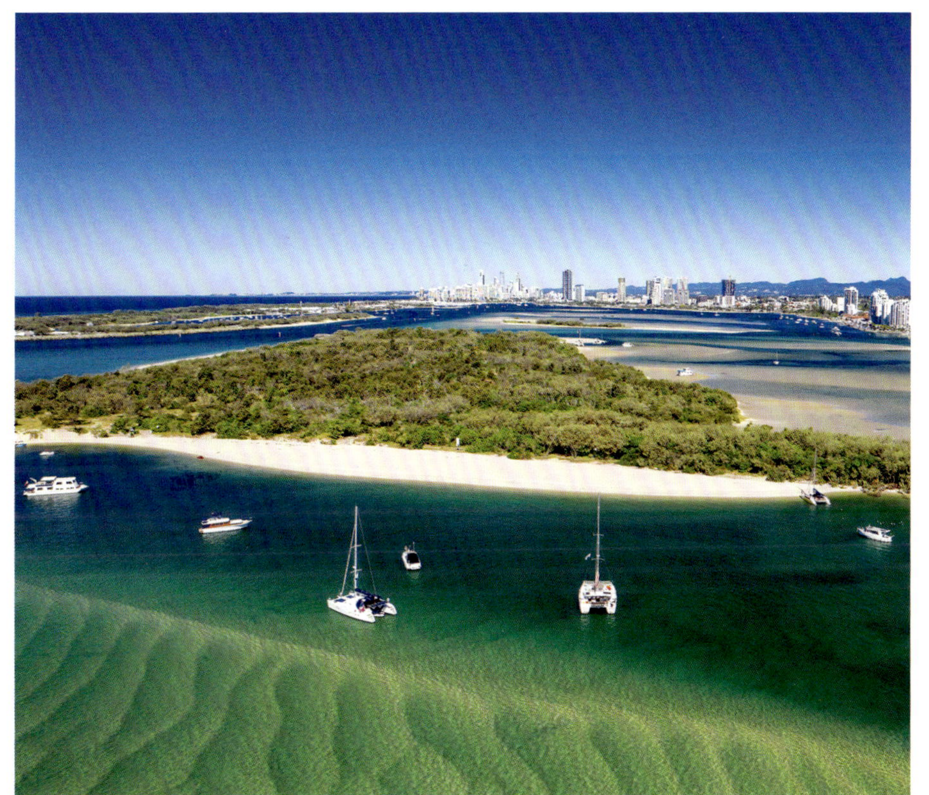

Gold Coast, Queensland.

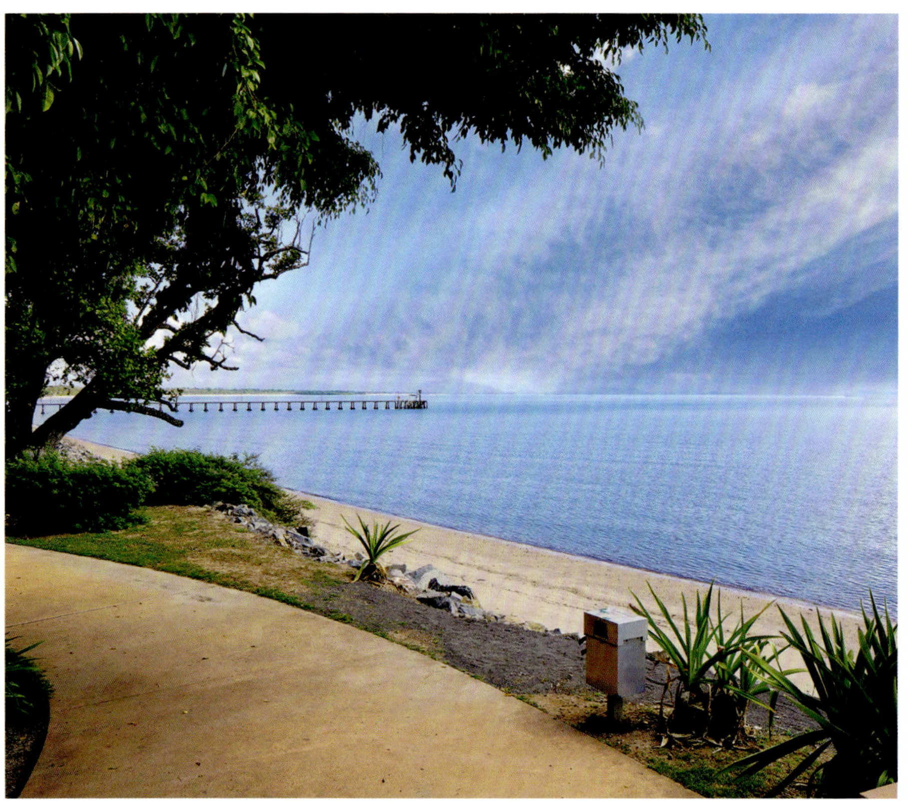

Cardwell Beach.

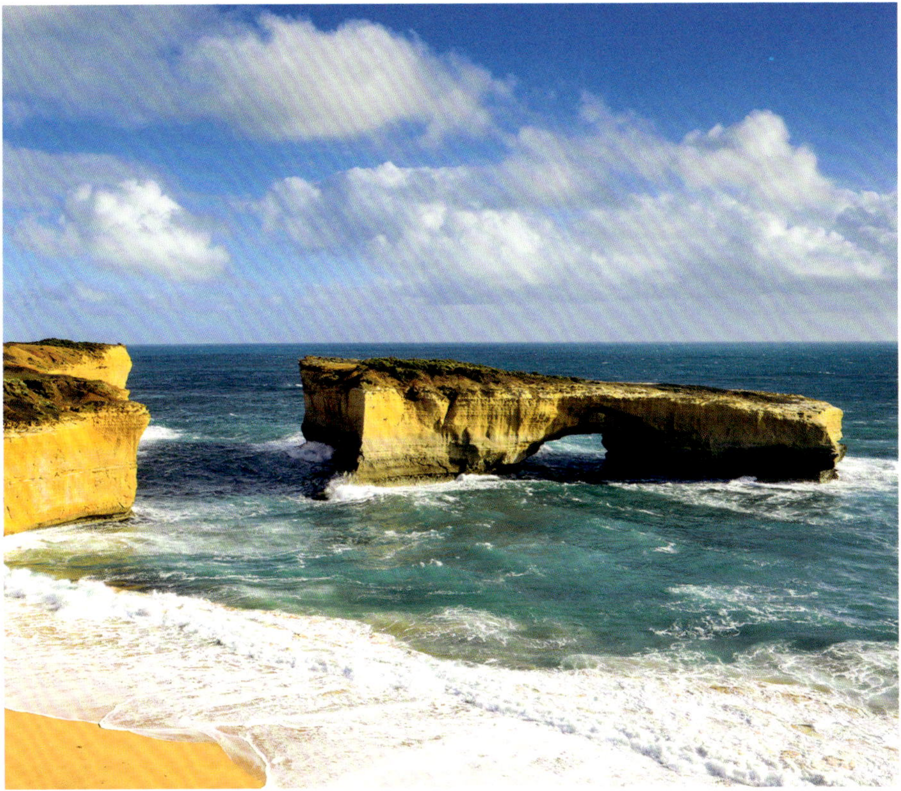

London Bridge, Port Campbell National Park at the Great Ocean Road, Apollo Bay.

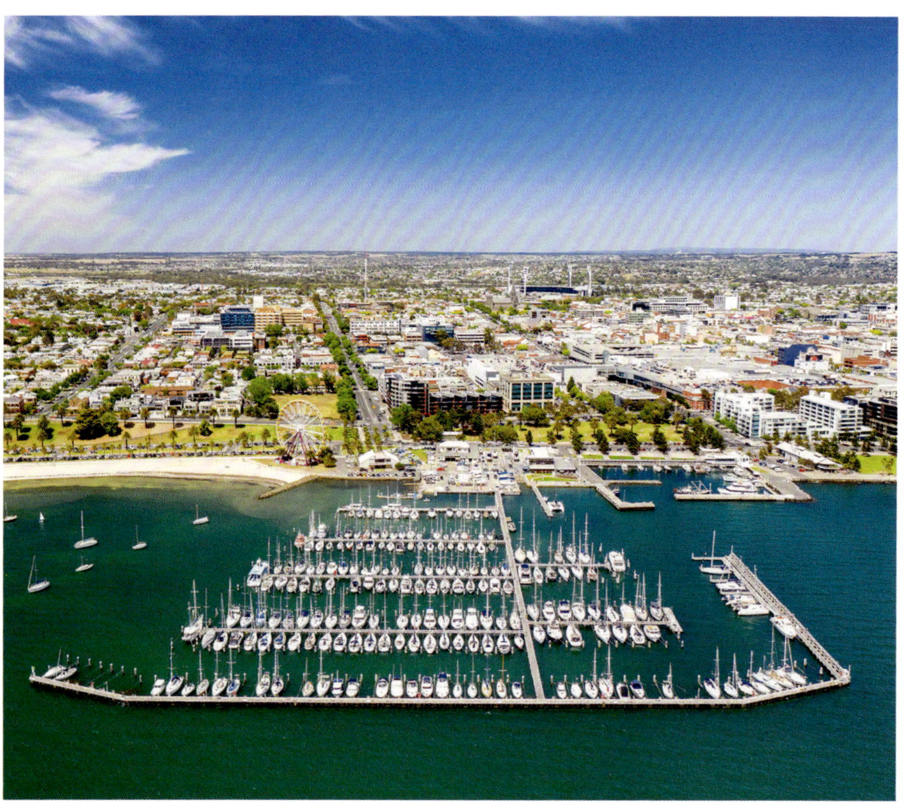

Geelong, Victoria.

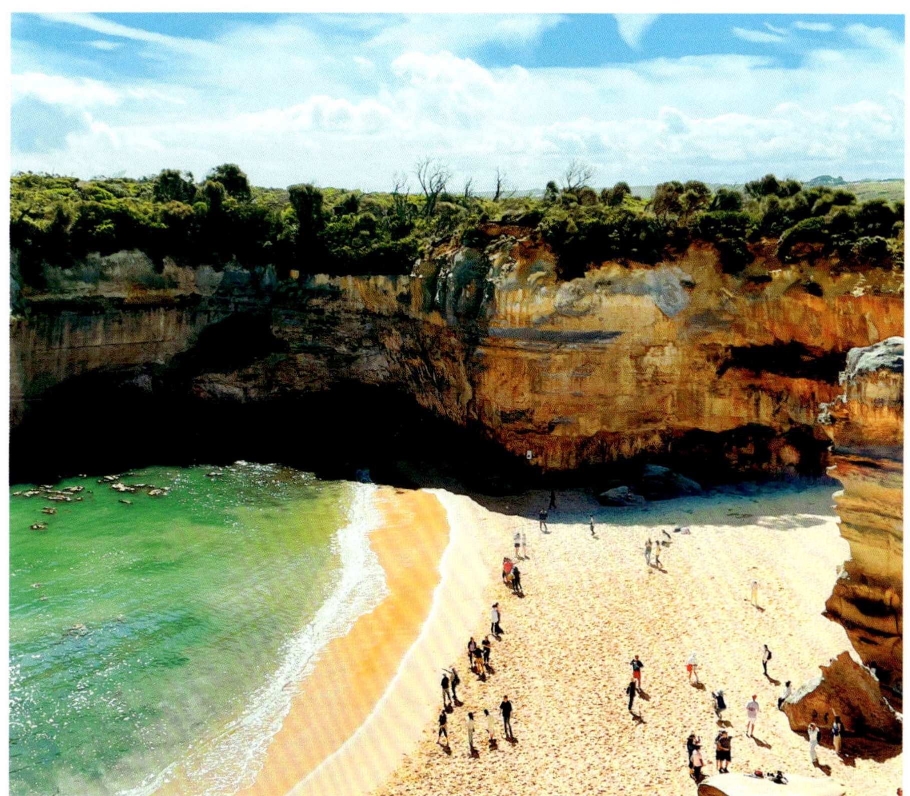

Loch and Gorge, Port Campbell National Park, Victoria.

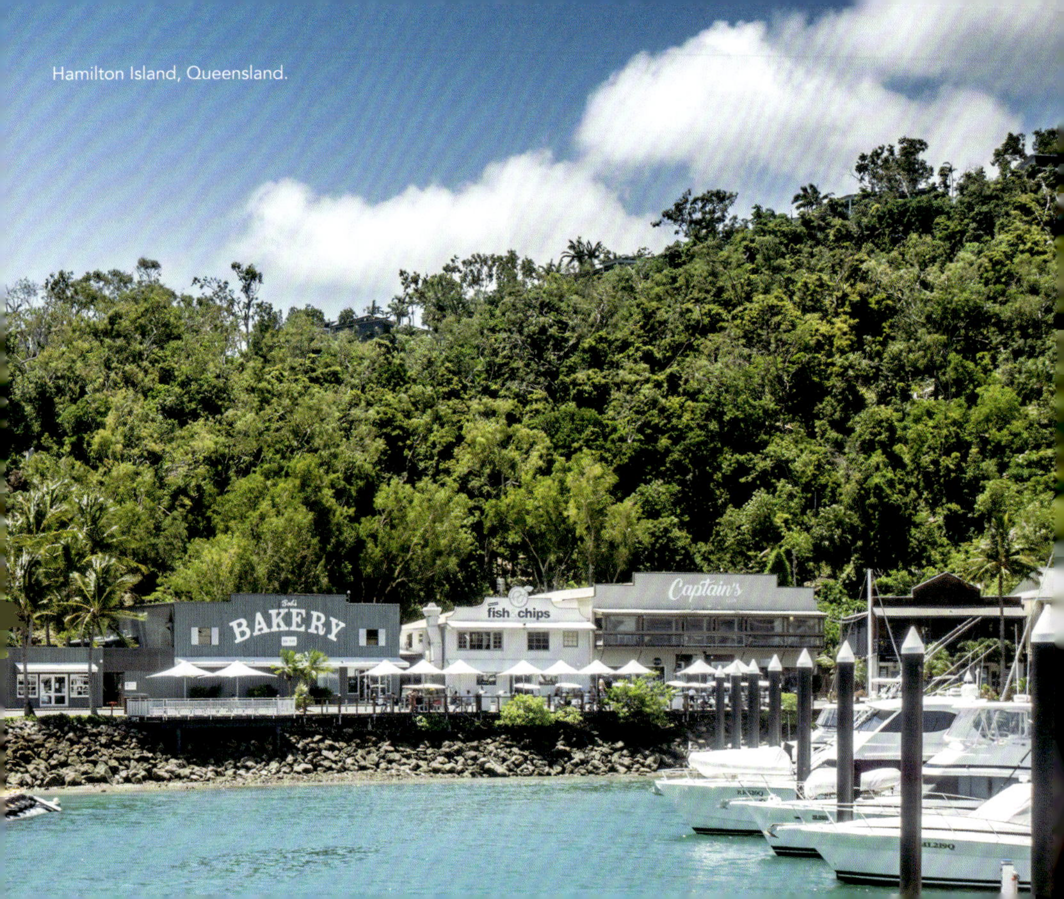

Hamilton Island, Queensland.

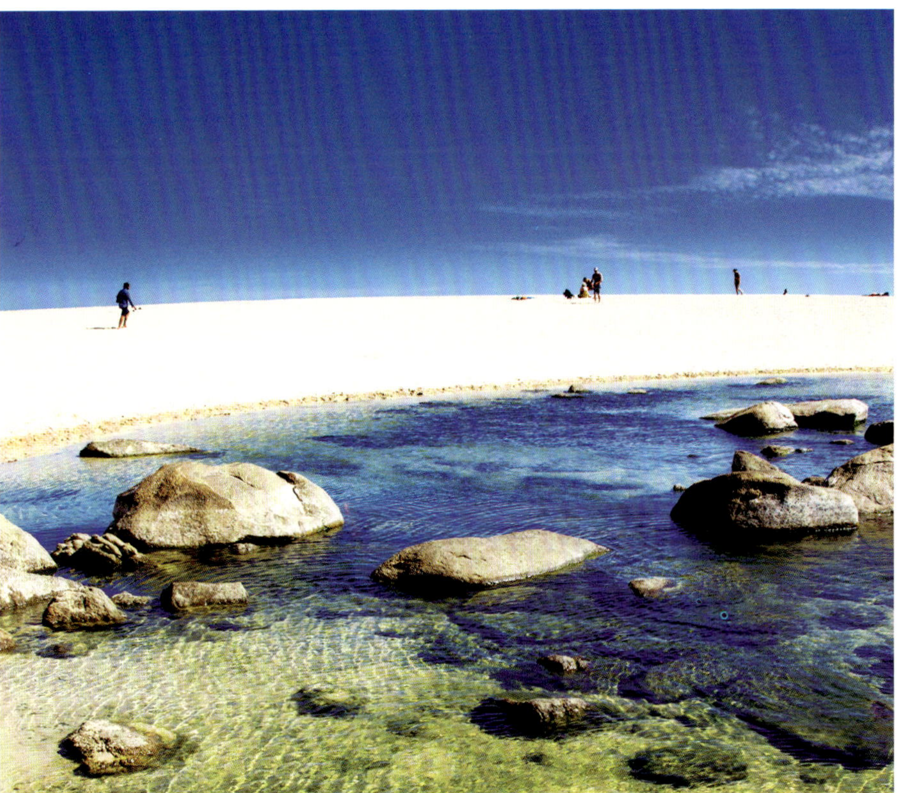

Margaret River, Western Australia.

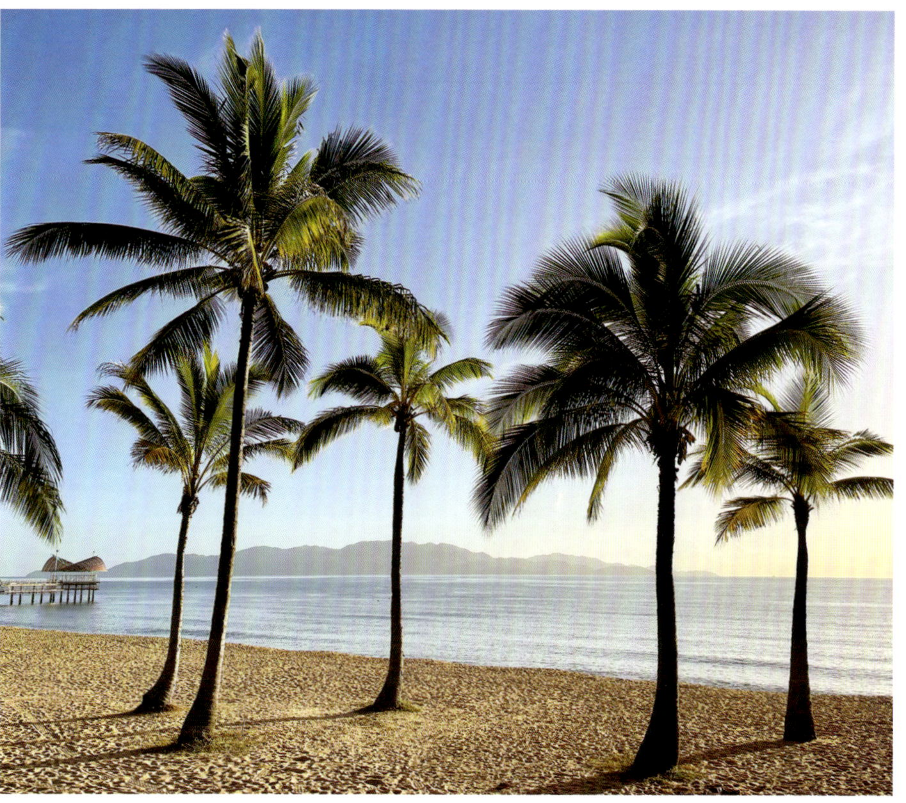

Townsville, Queensland.

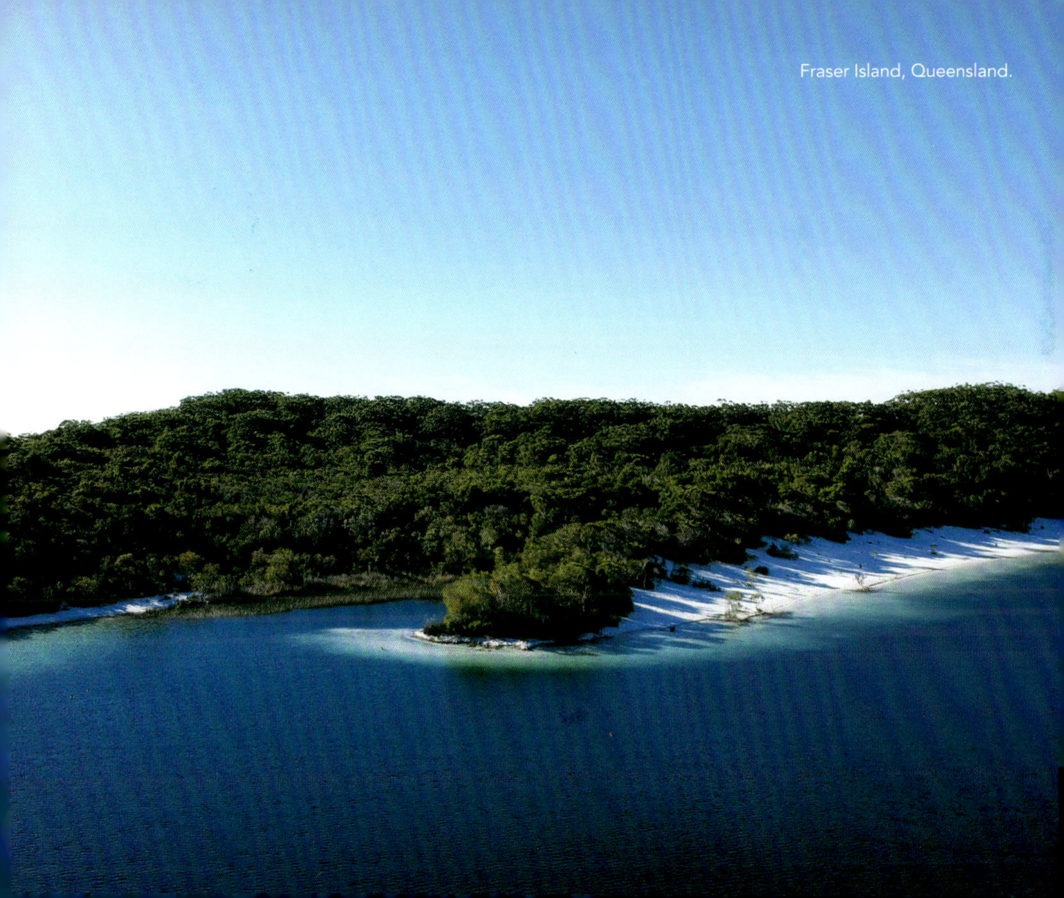
Fraser Island, Queensland.

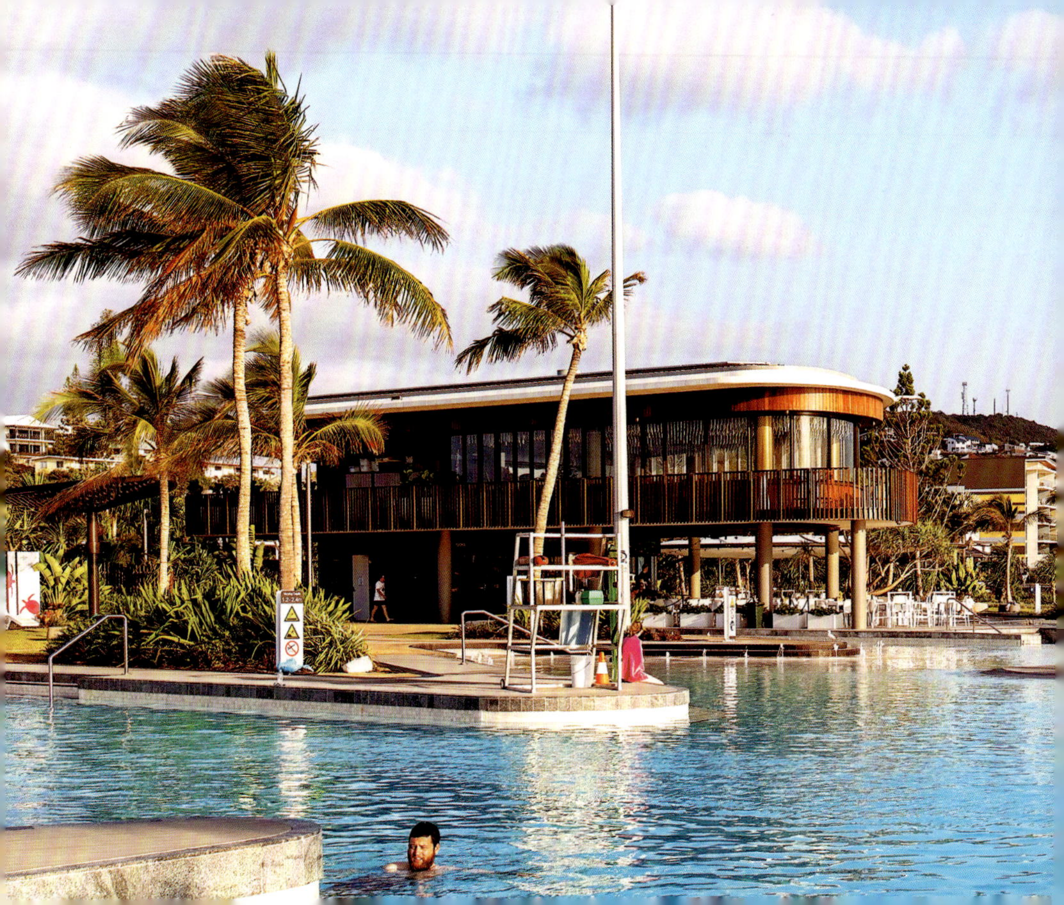

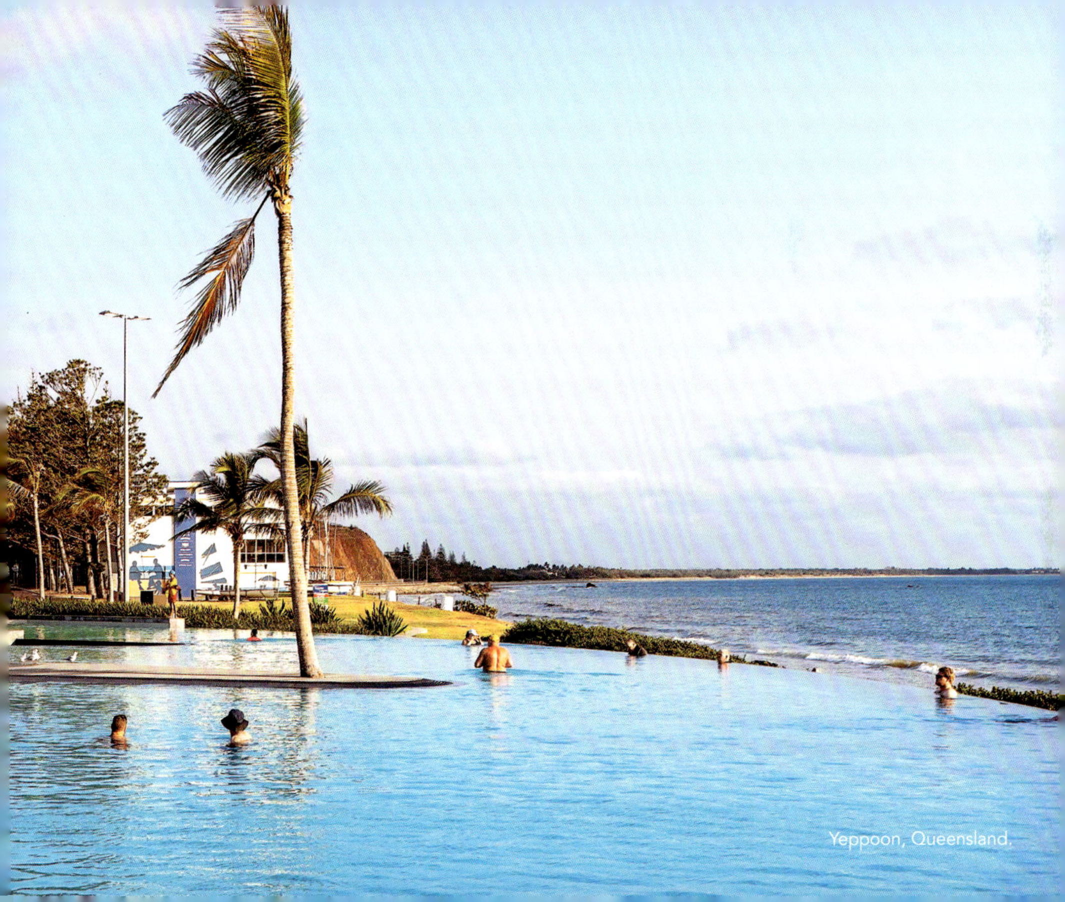

Yeppoon, Queensland.

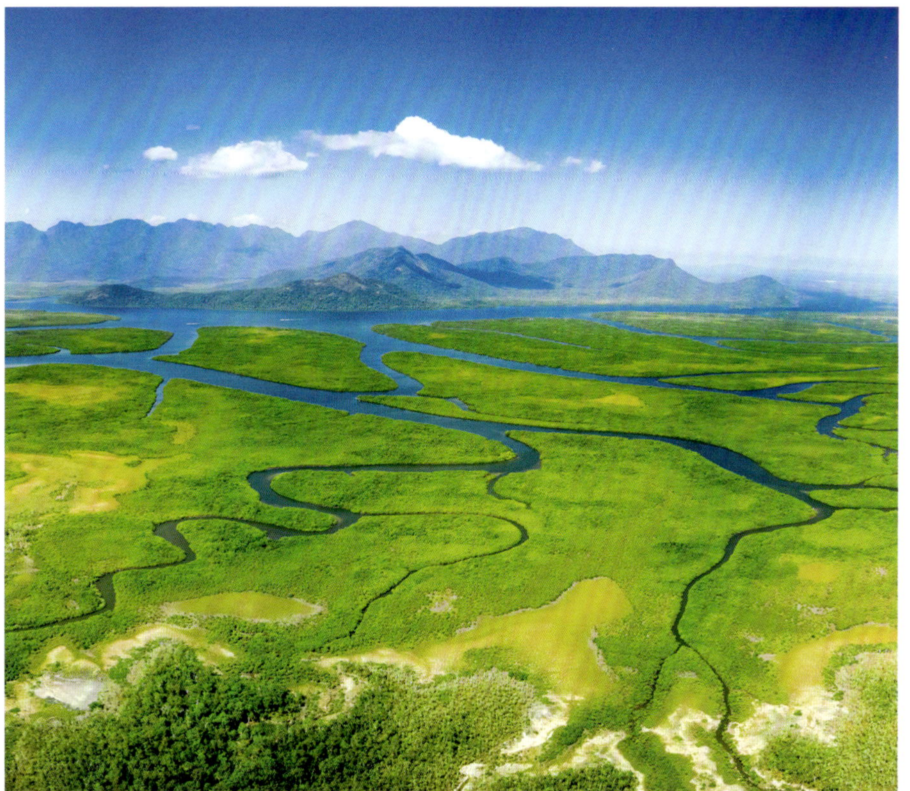

Hinchinbrook Island, Queensland.

Mornington Peninsula towards Point Nepean and Port Phillip Bay, Victoria.

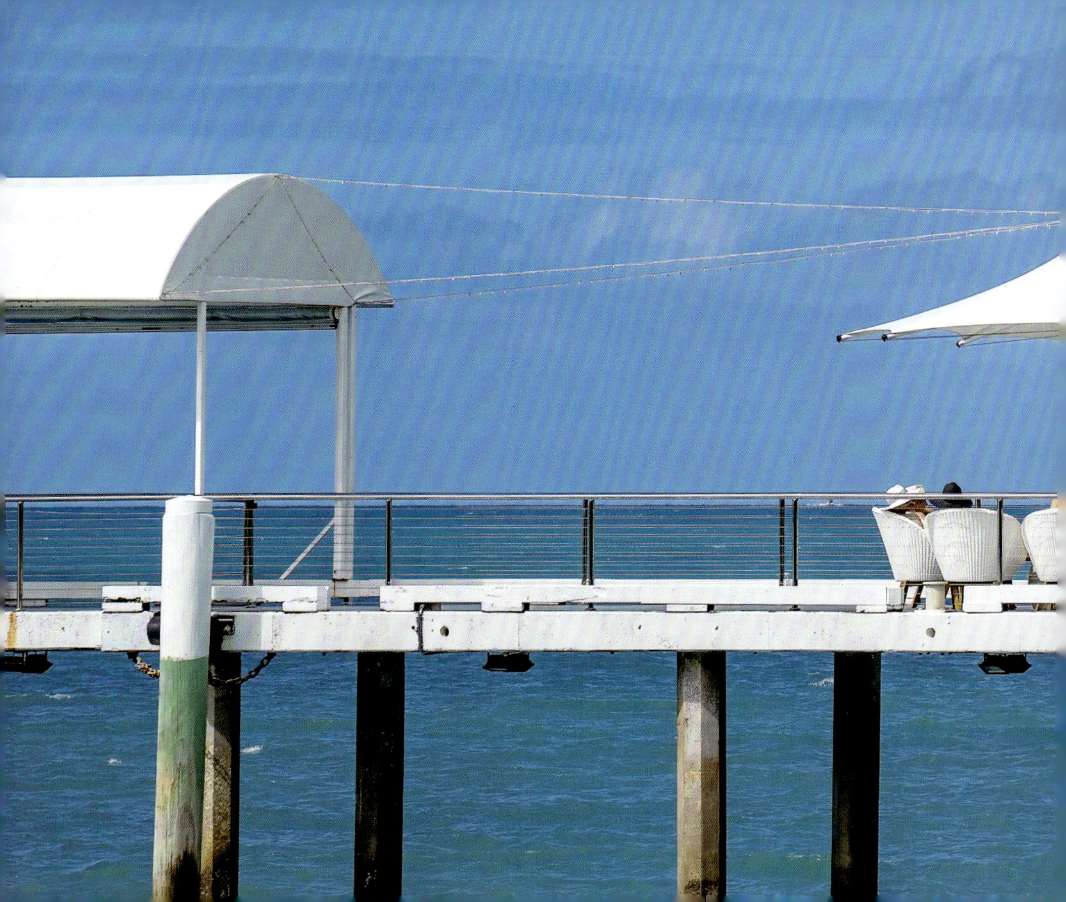

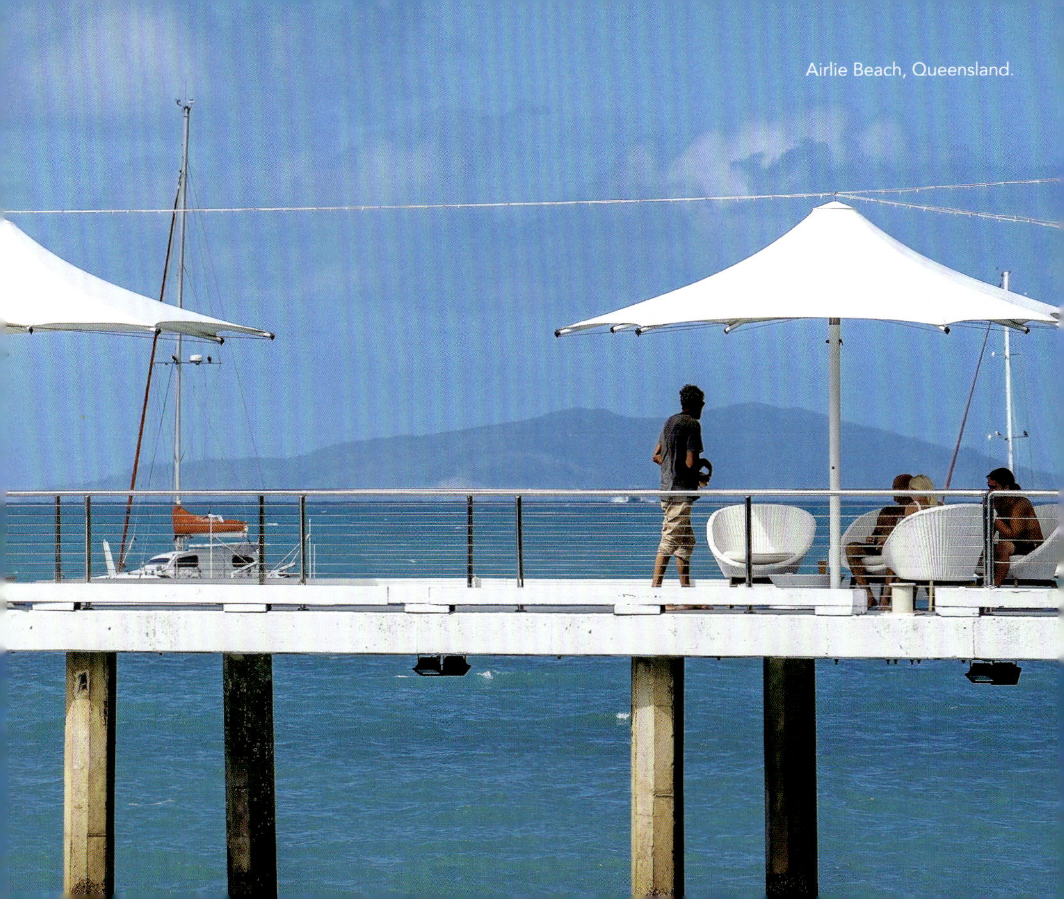
Airlie Beach, Queensland.

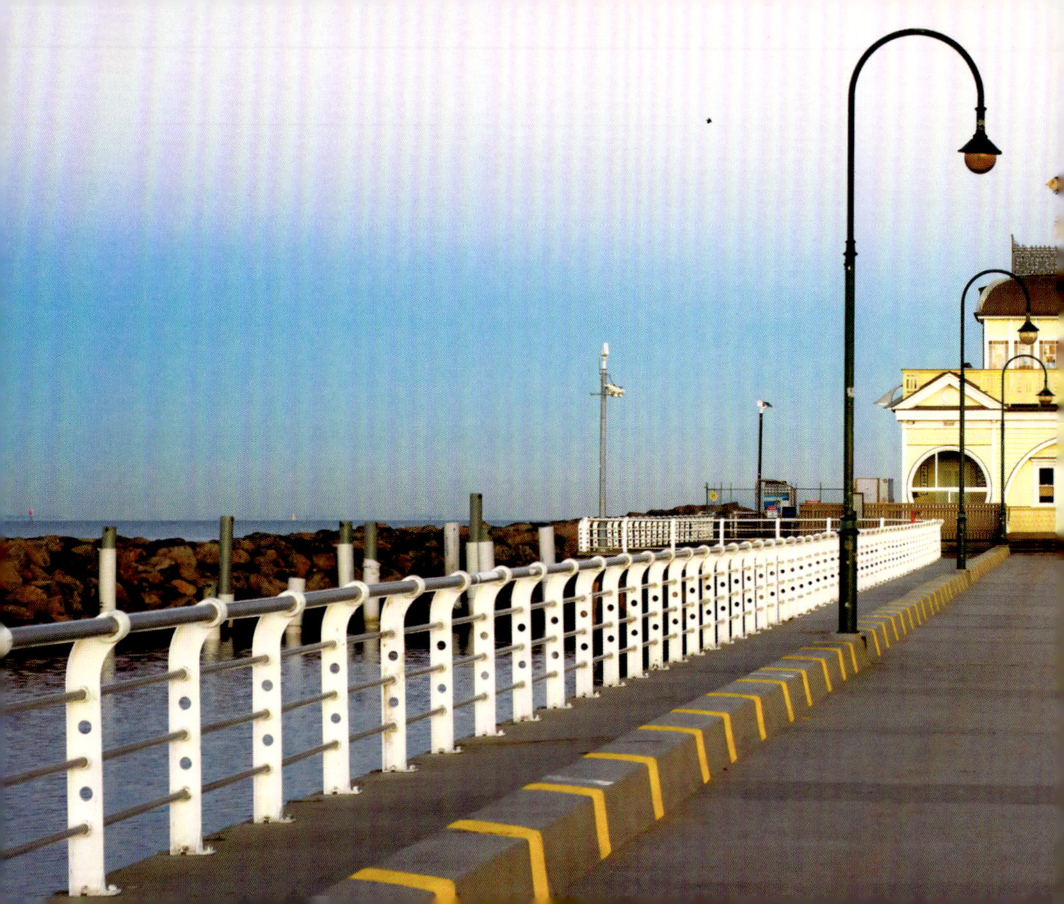

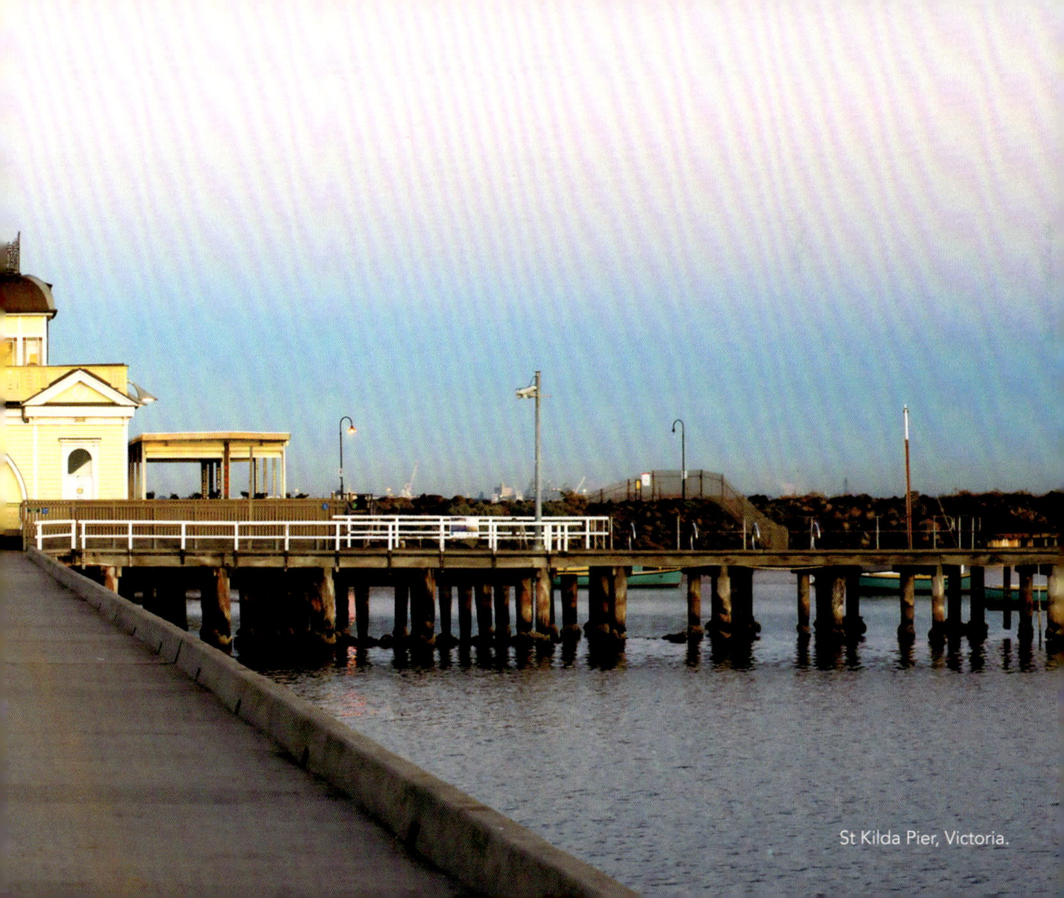

St Kilda Pier, Victoria.

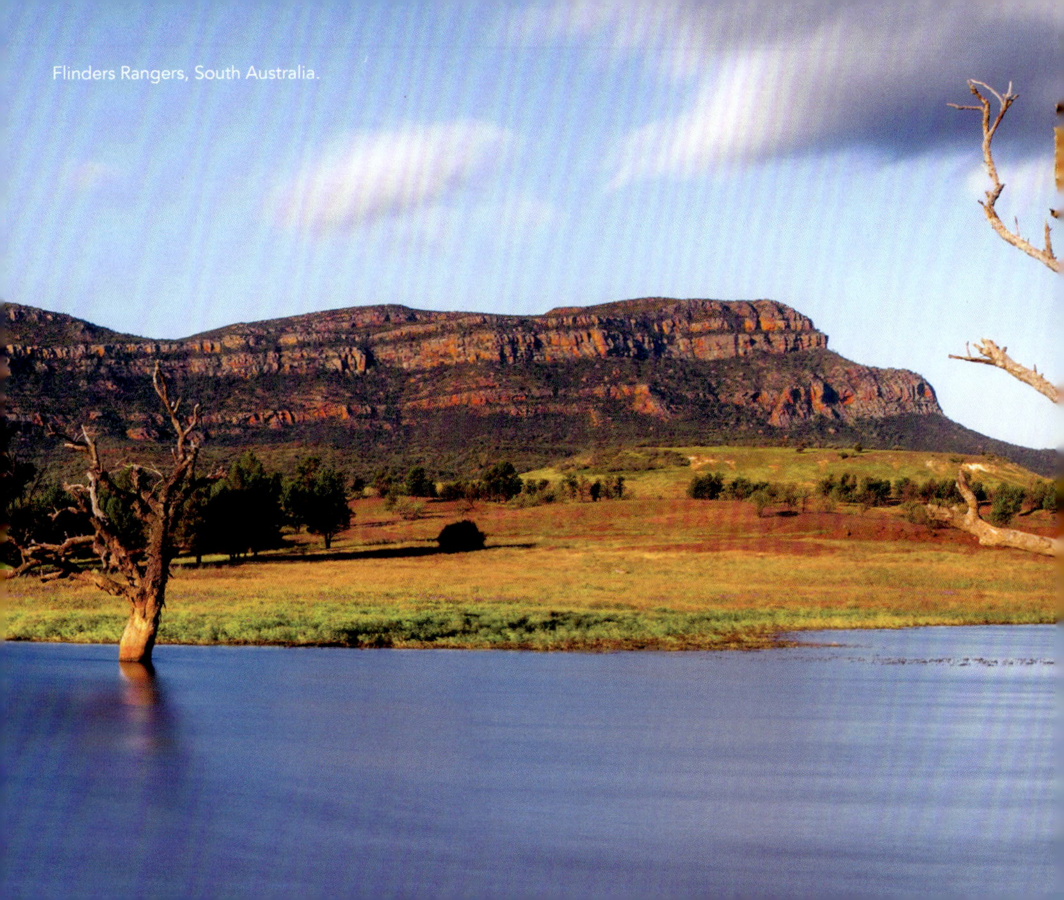

Flinders Rangers, South Australia.

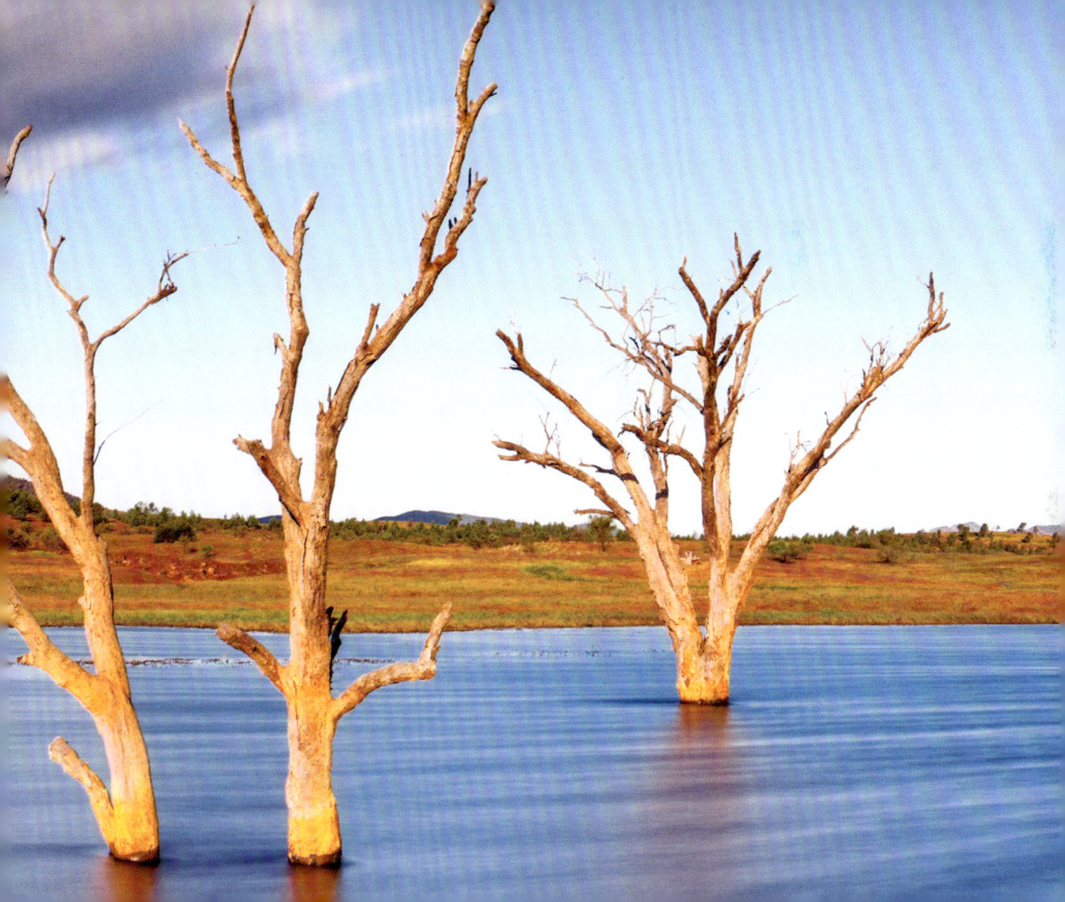

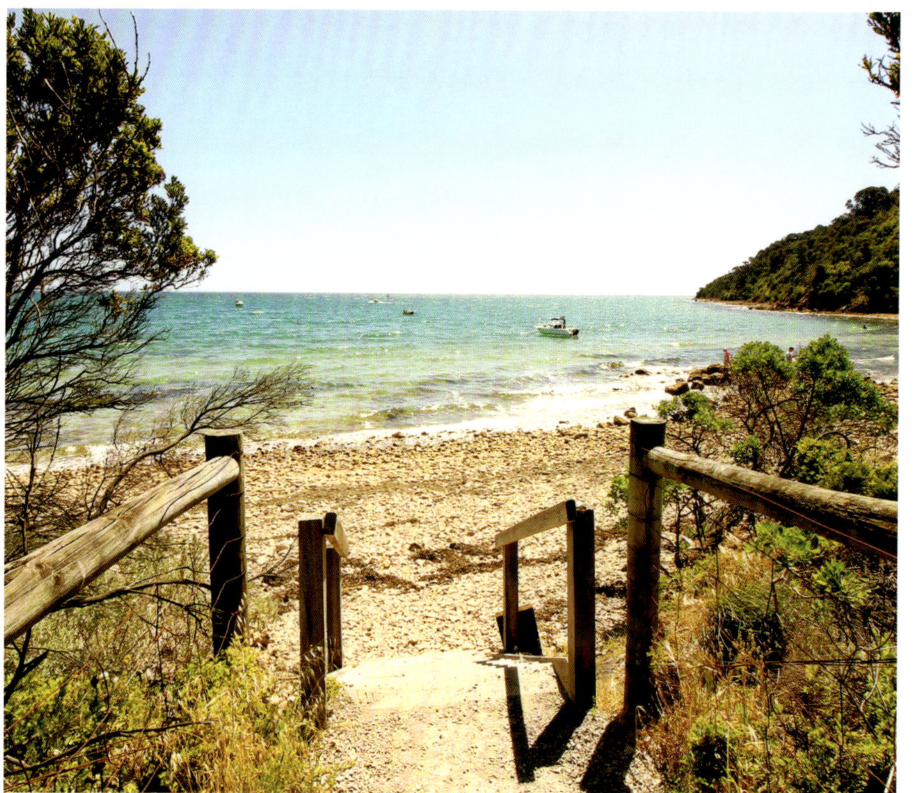

Safety beach, Mornington Peninsula, Victoria.

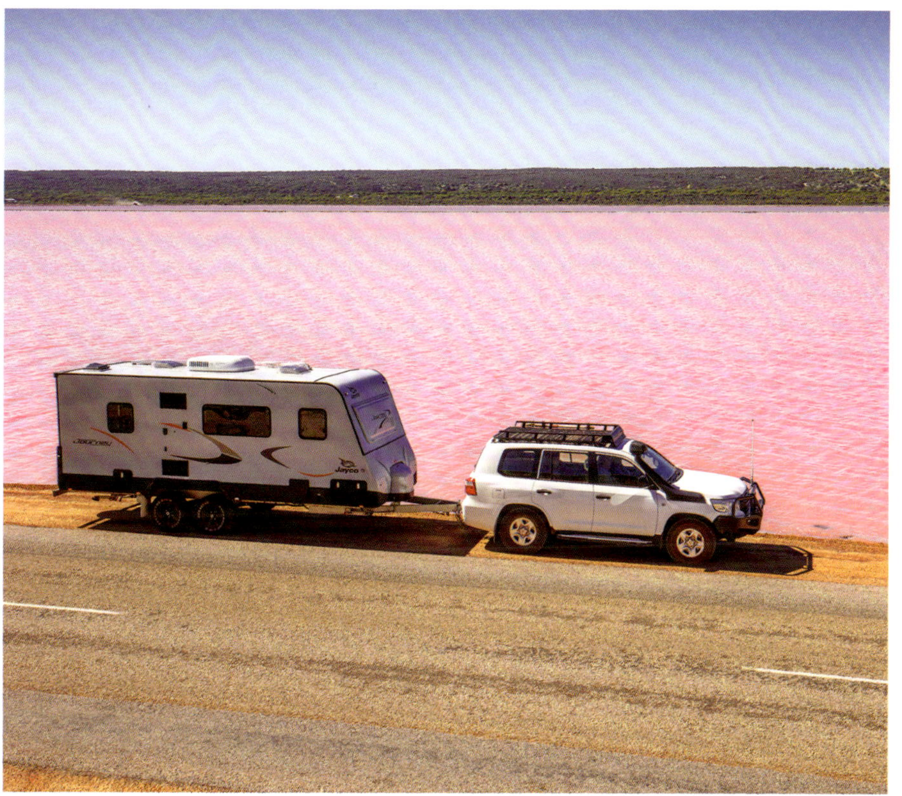

Port Gregory, Western Australia.

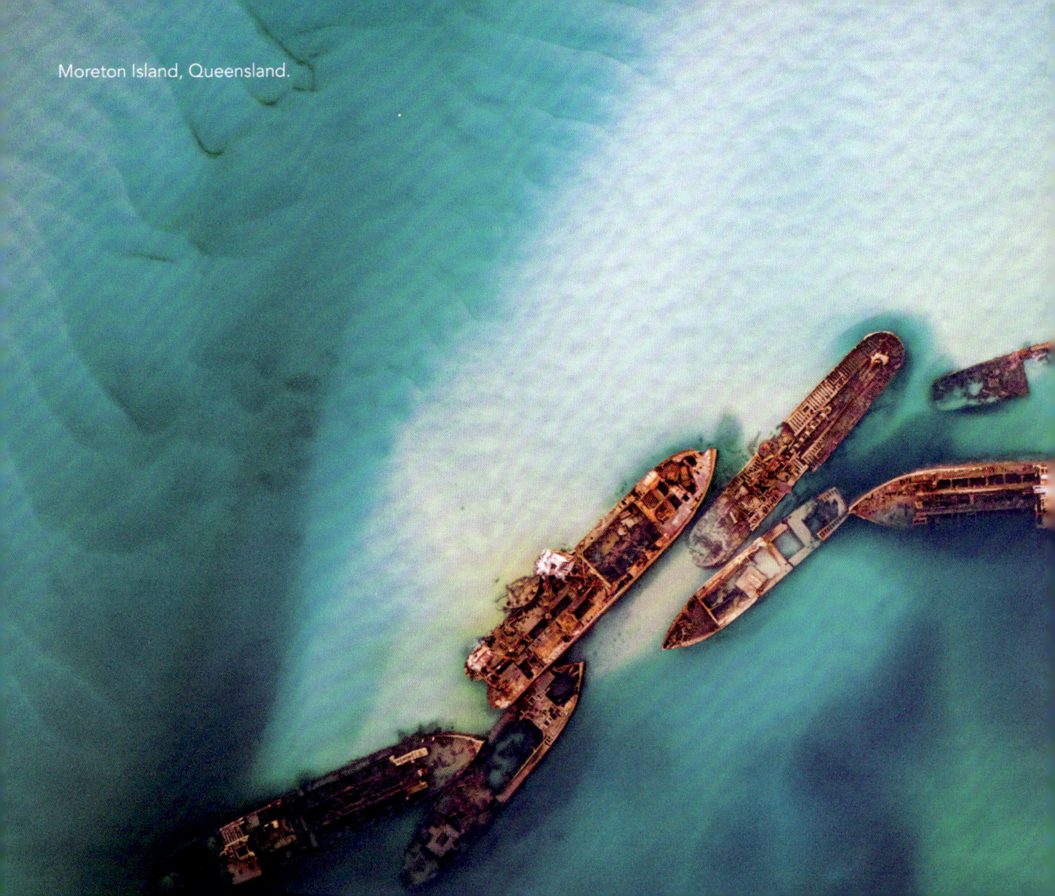

Moreton Island, Queensland.

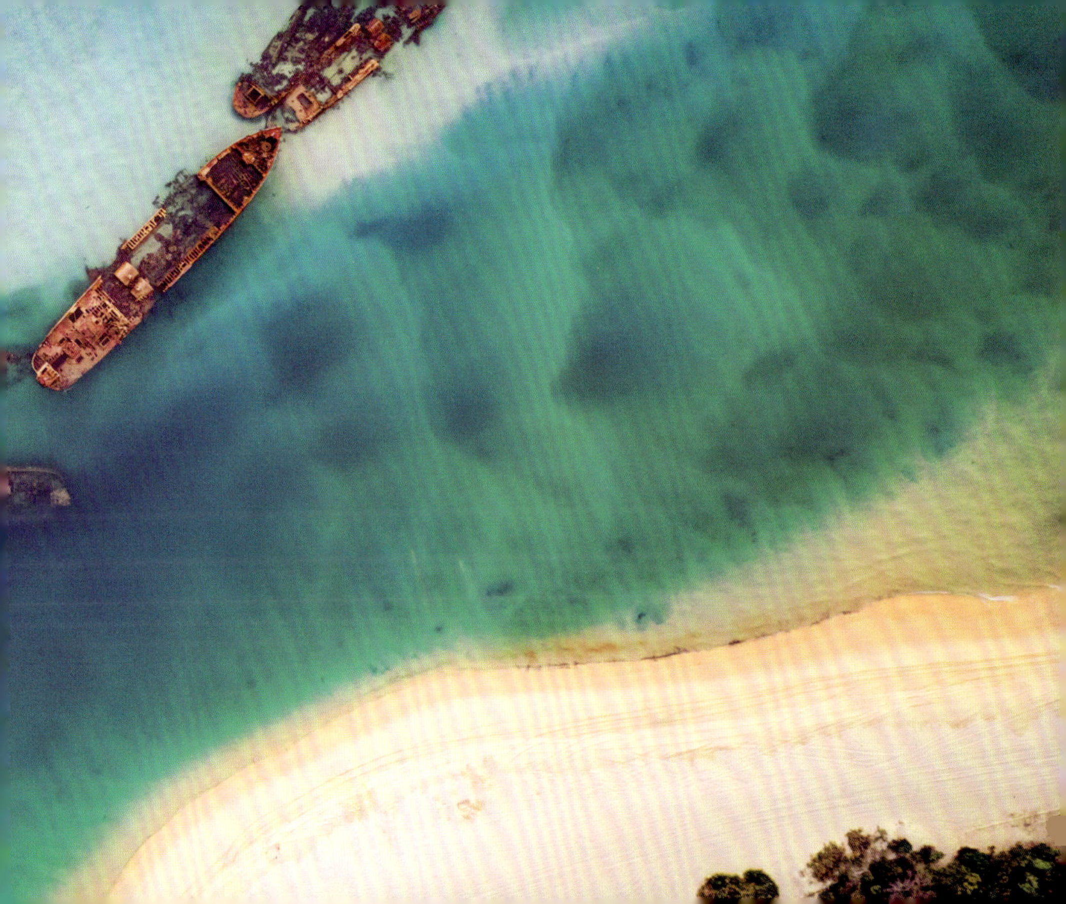

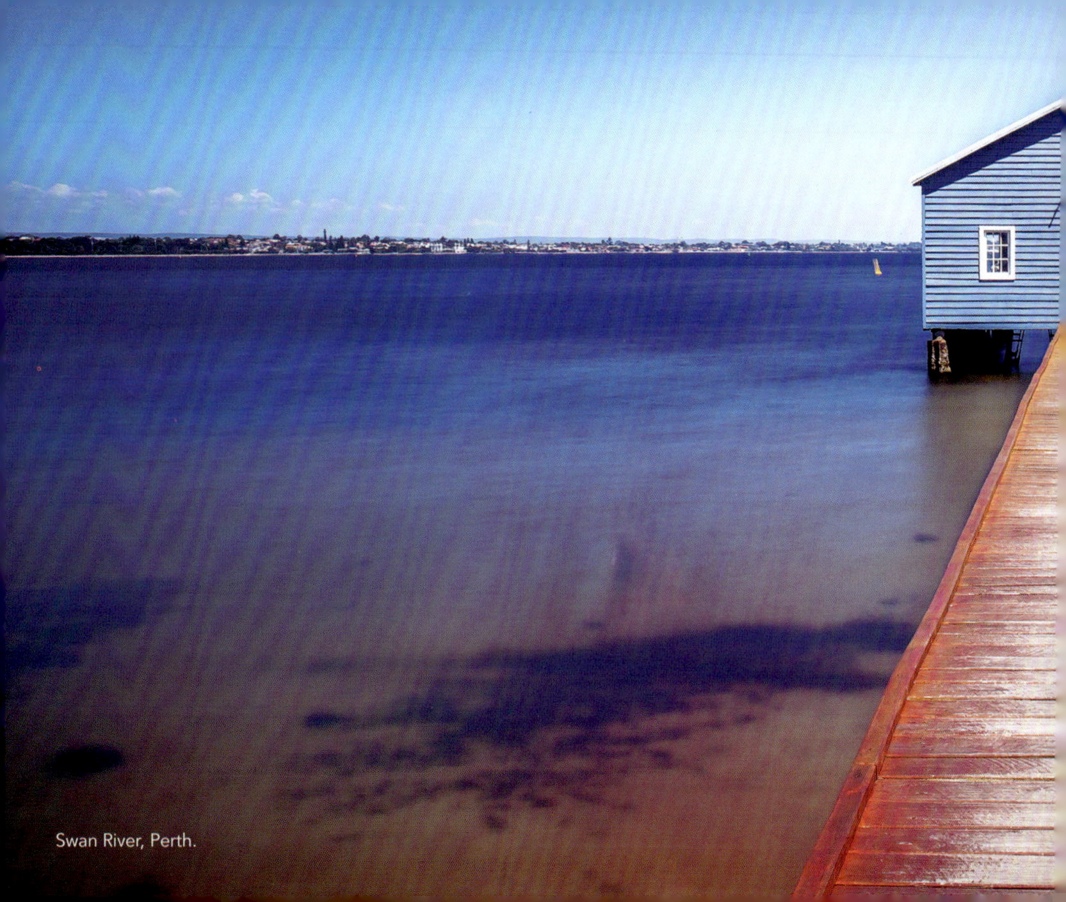

Swan River, Perth.

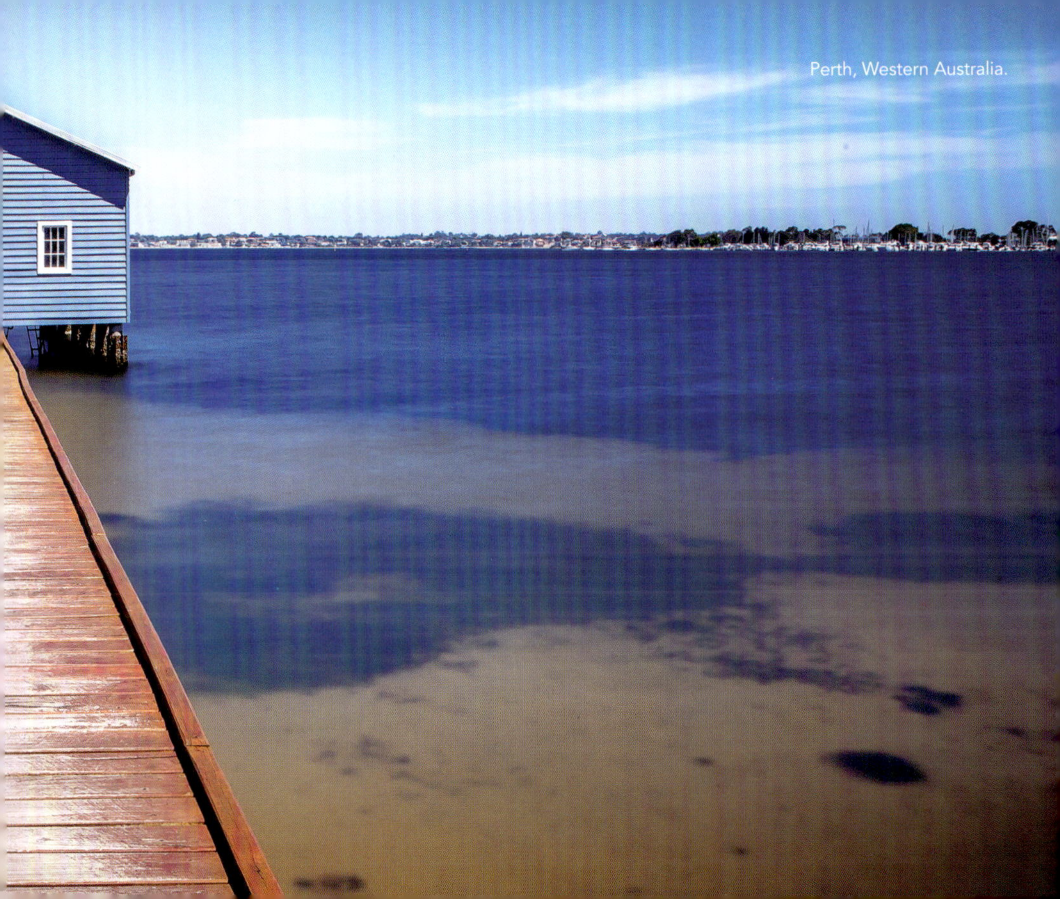
Perth, Western Australia.

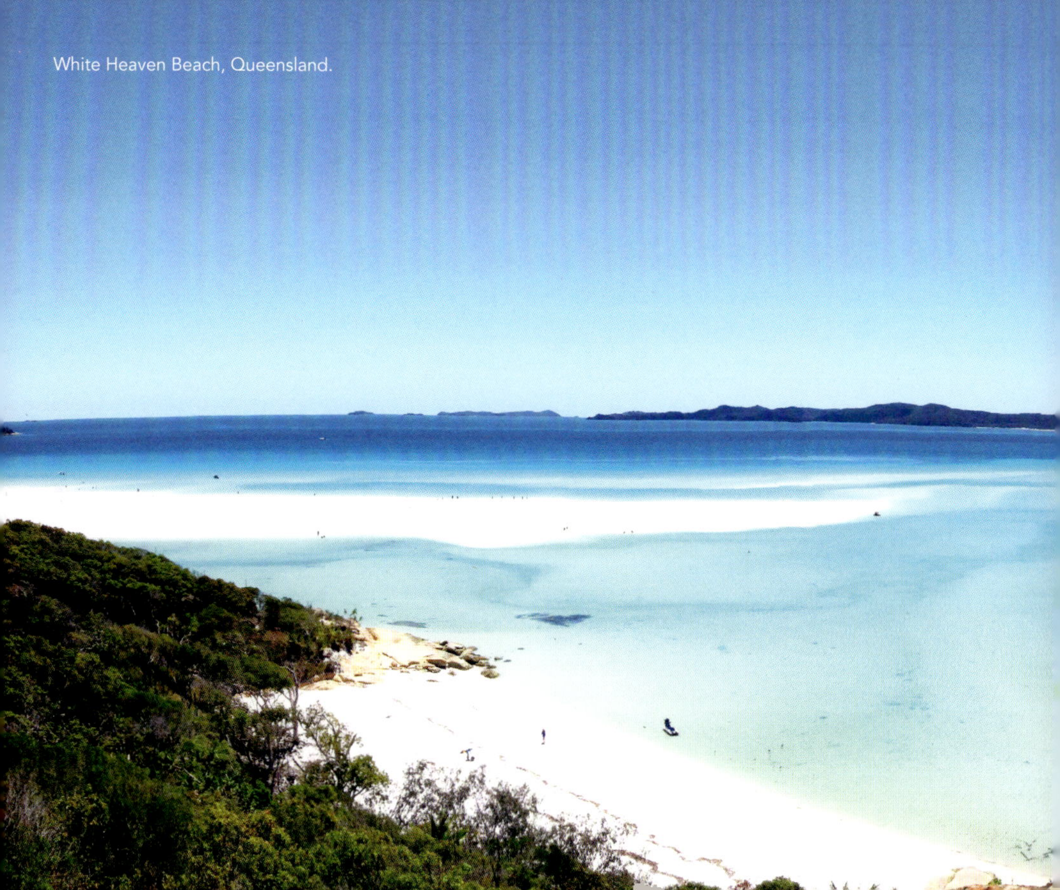

White Heaven Beach, Queensland.

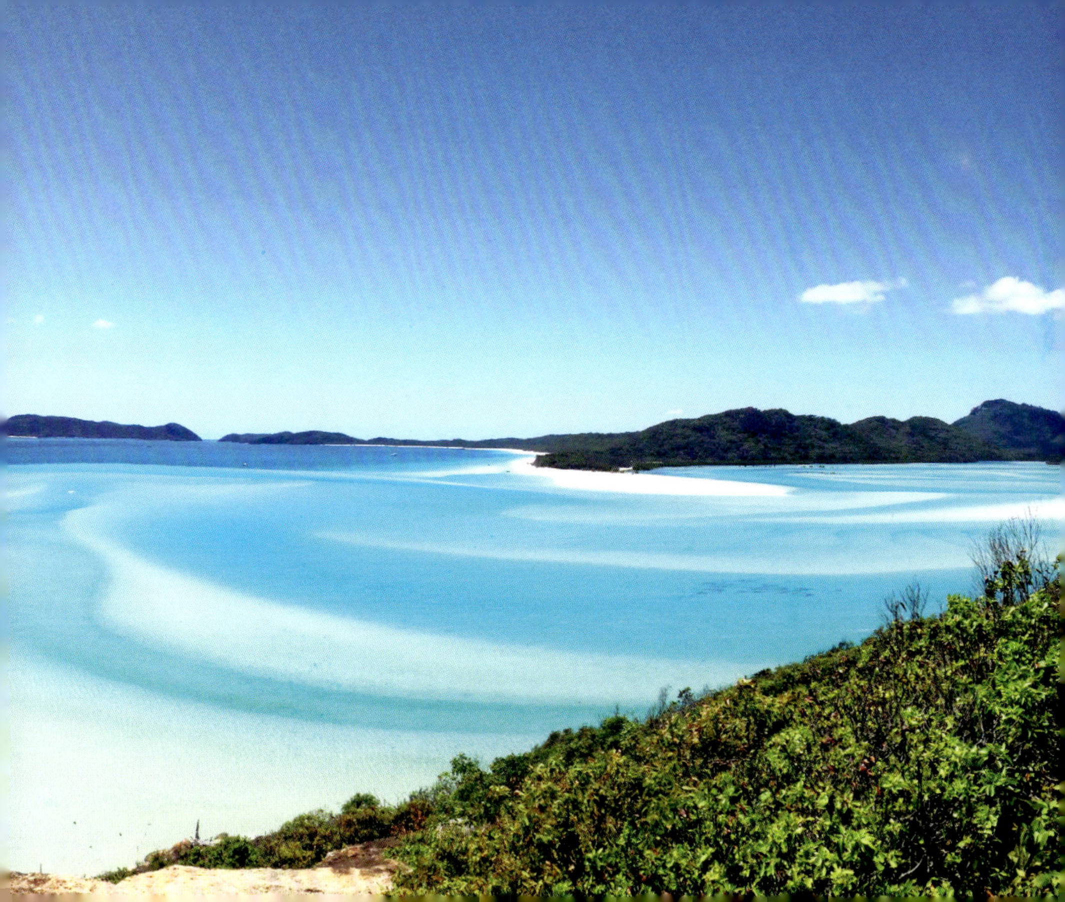

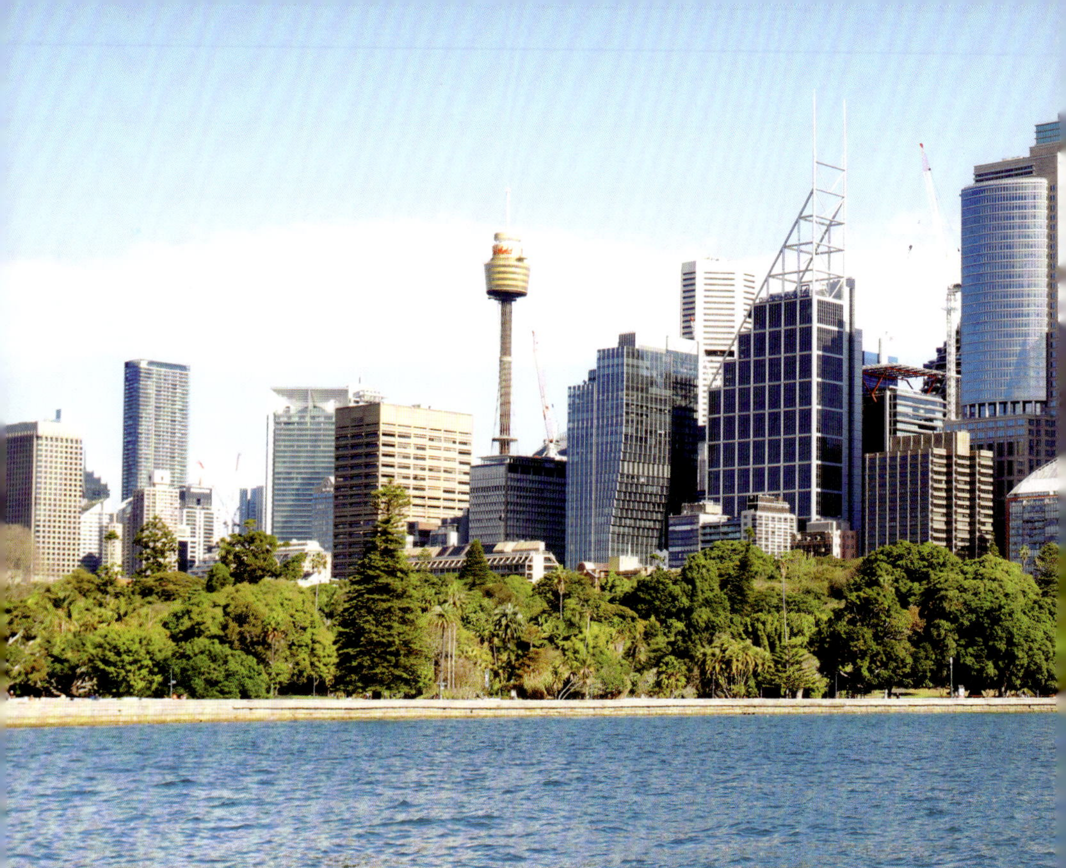

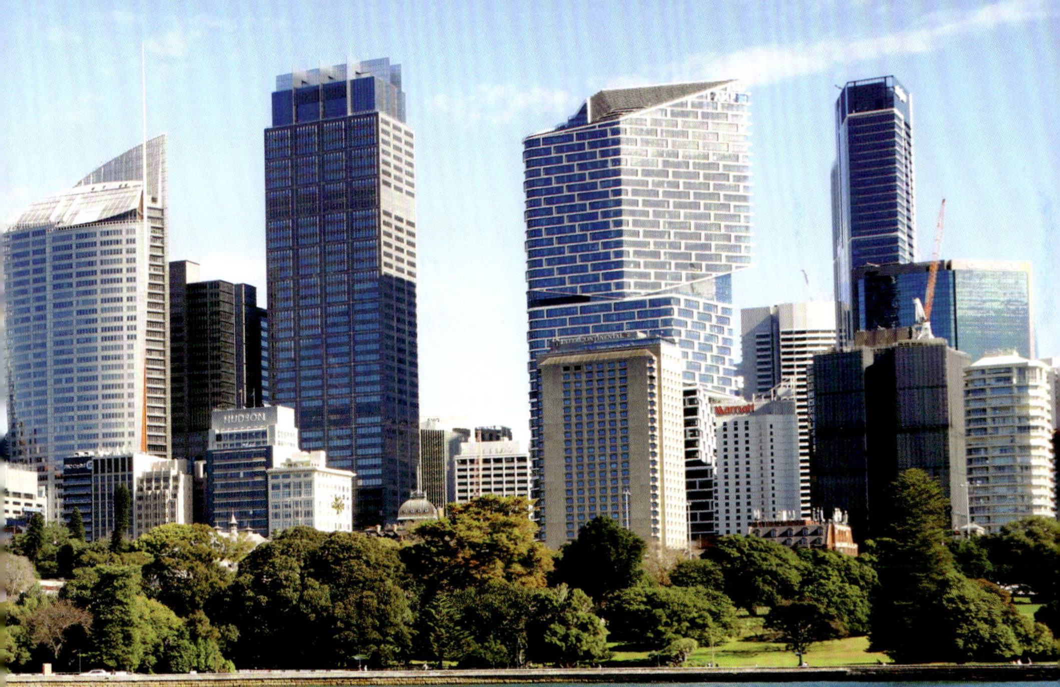

THE CITIES

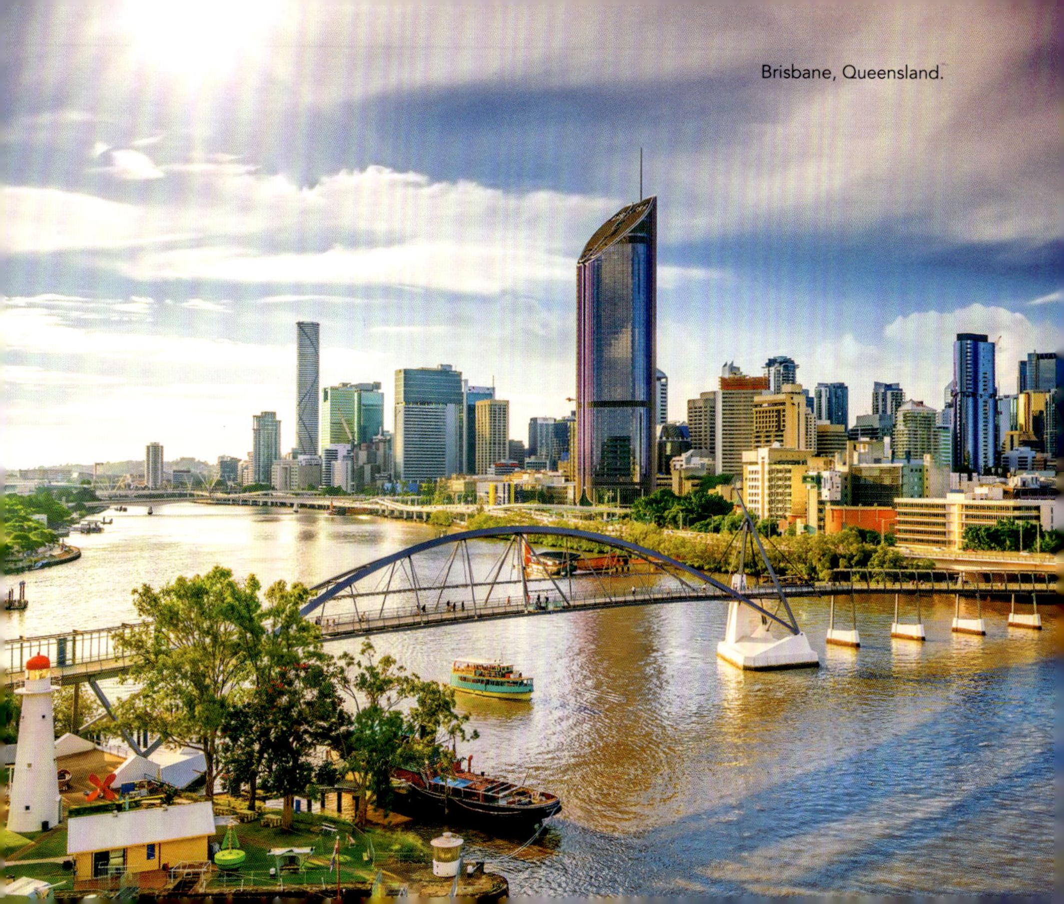

Brisbane, Queensland.

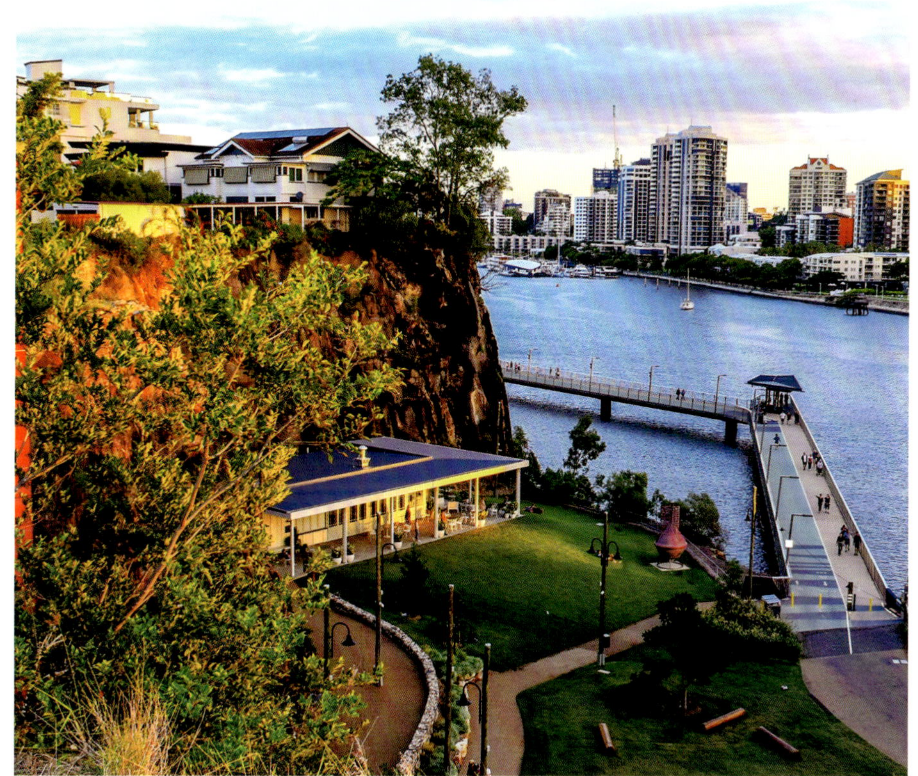

Brisbane, Queensland.

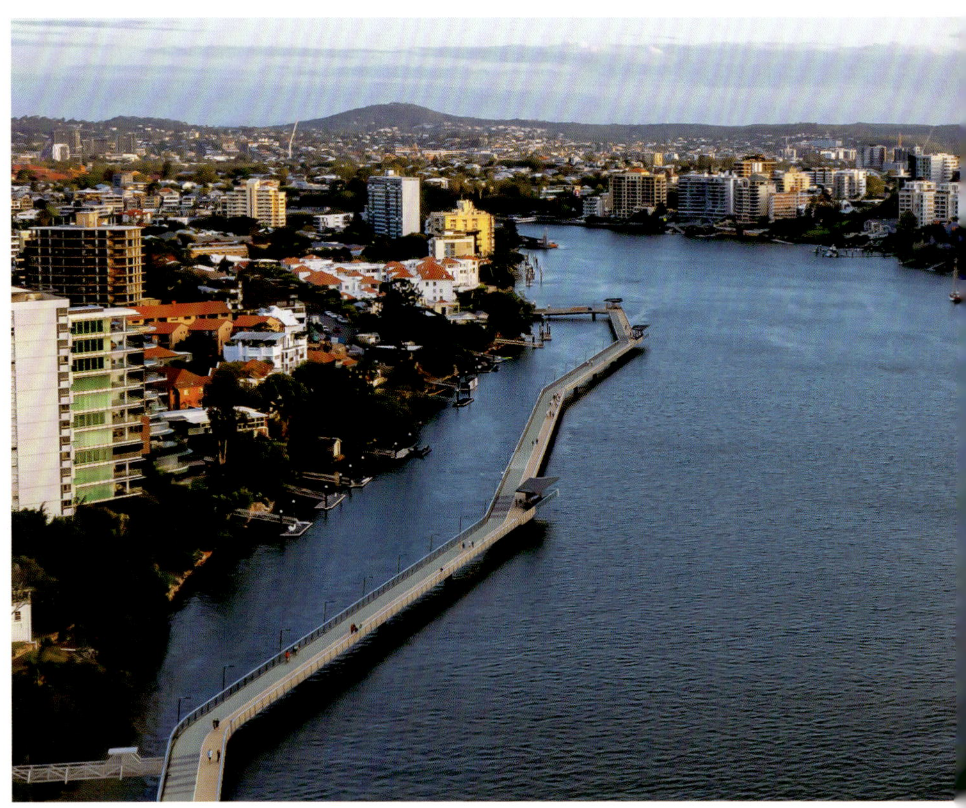

Brisbane River.

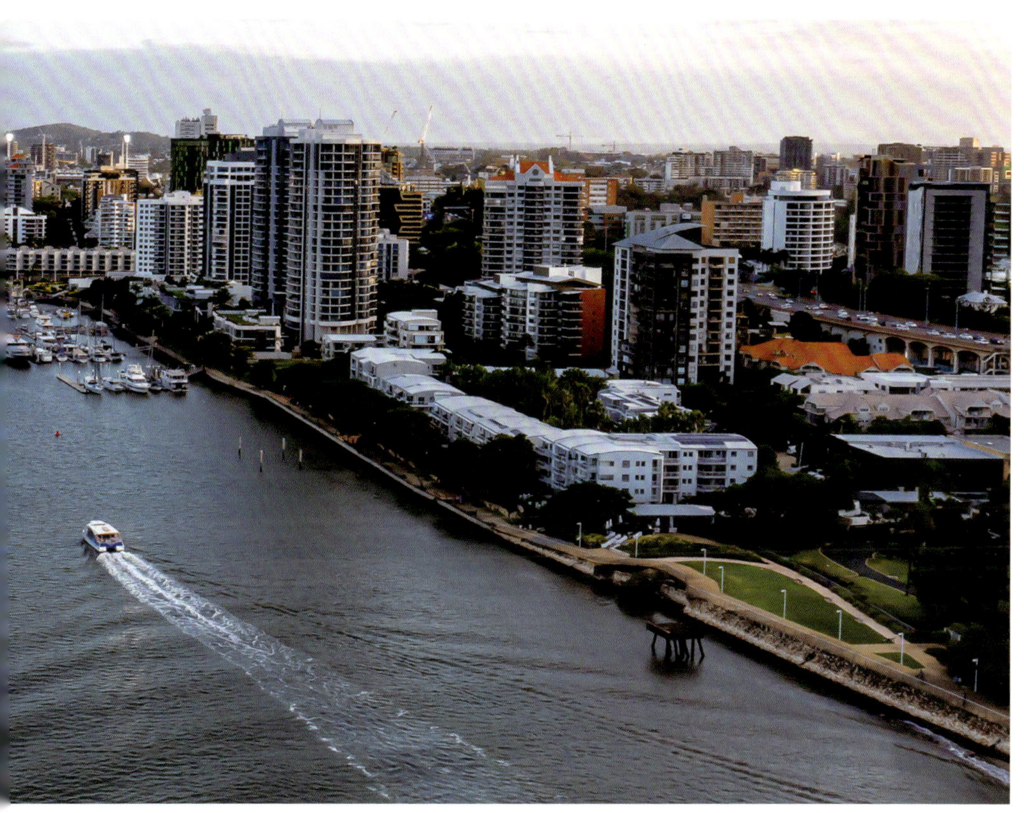

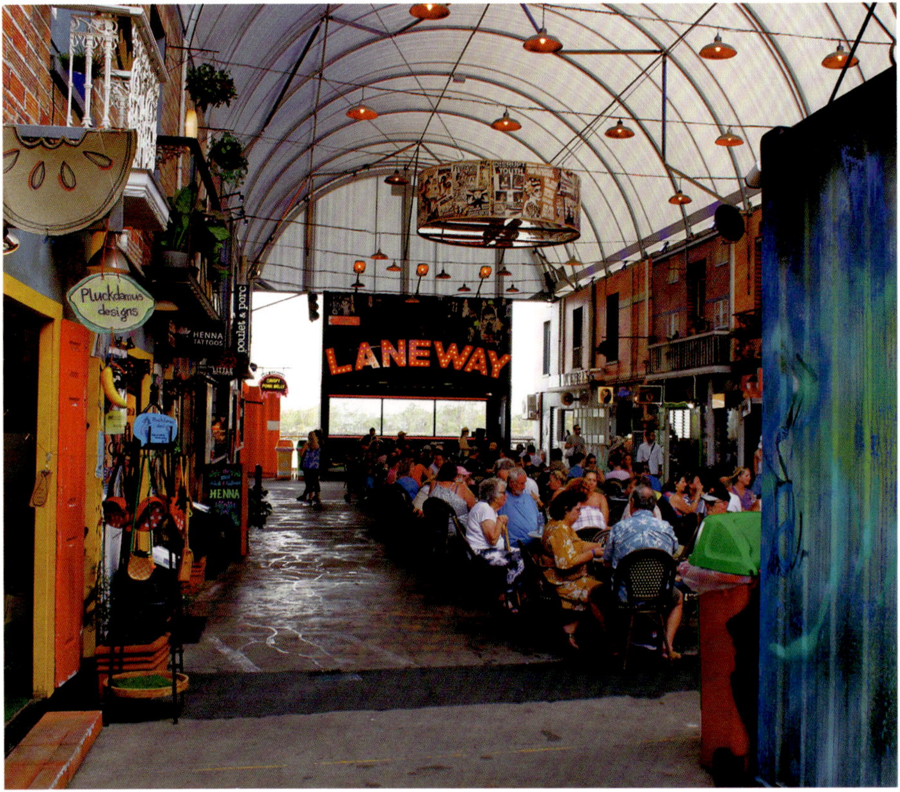

Eat Street Northshore, Brisbane River.

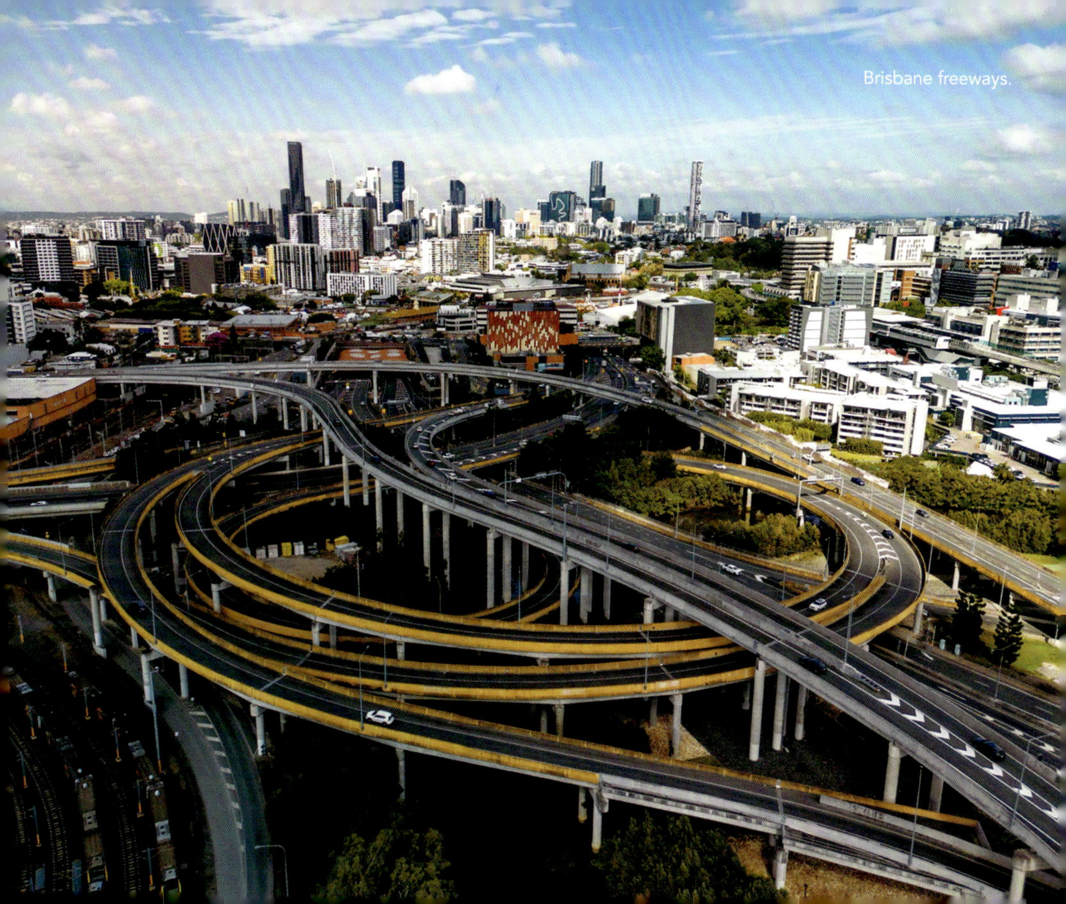
Brisbane freeways.

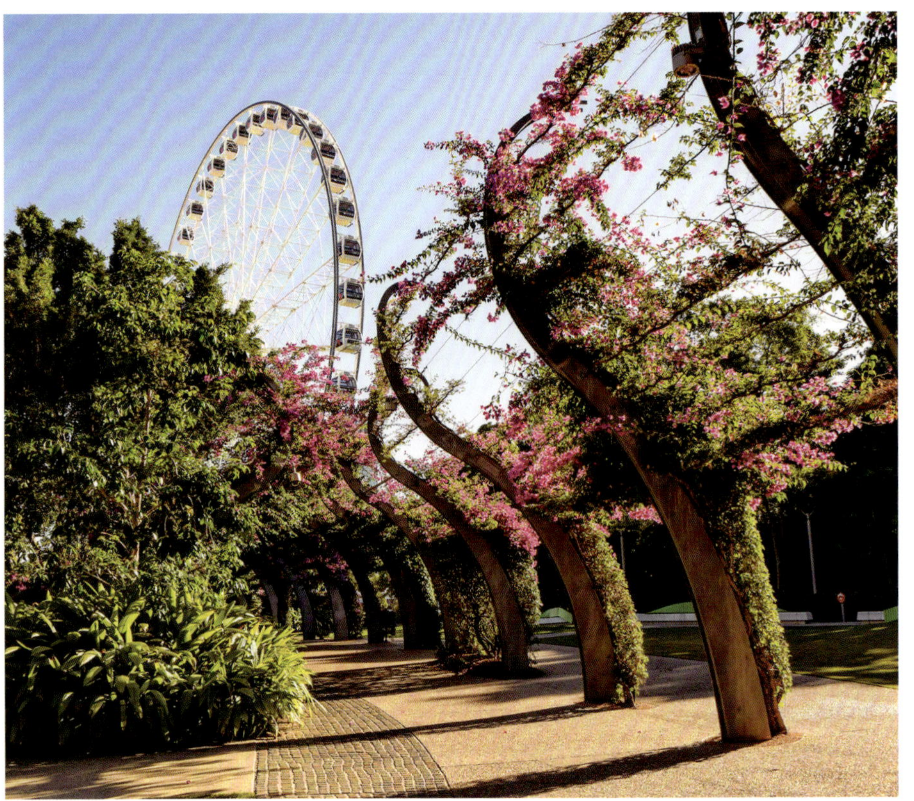

Ferris Wheel at South Bank, Brisbane, Queensland.

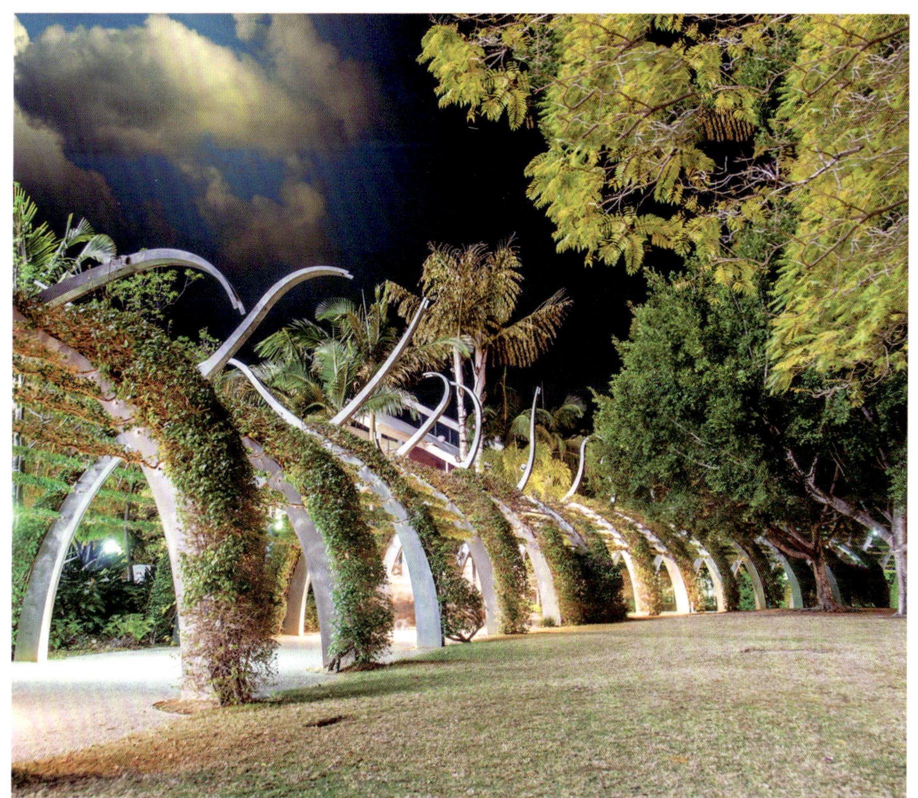

Brisbane, Queensland.

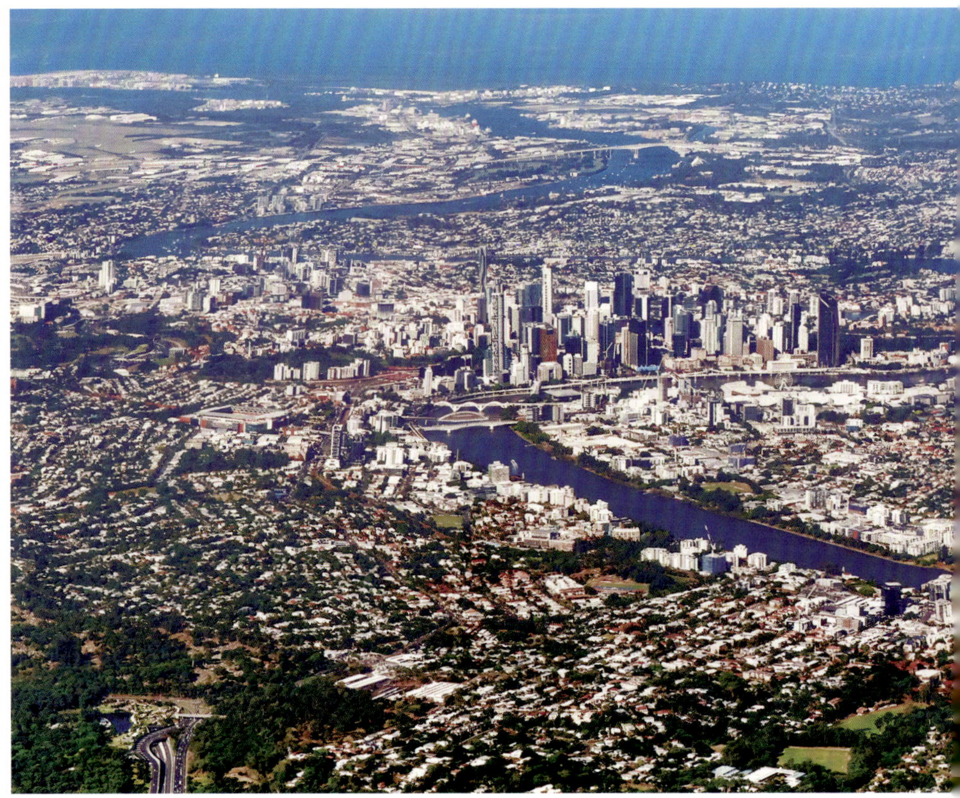

Brisbane, Queensland.

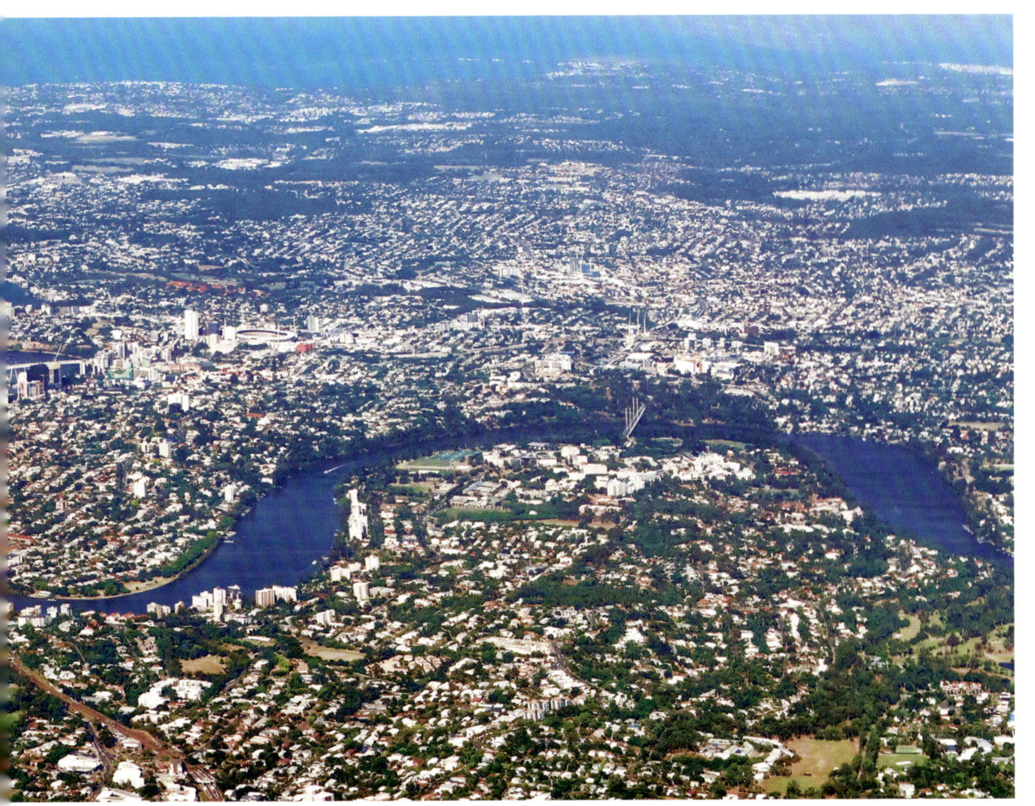

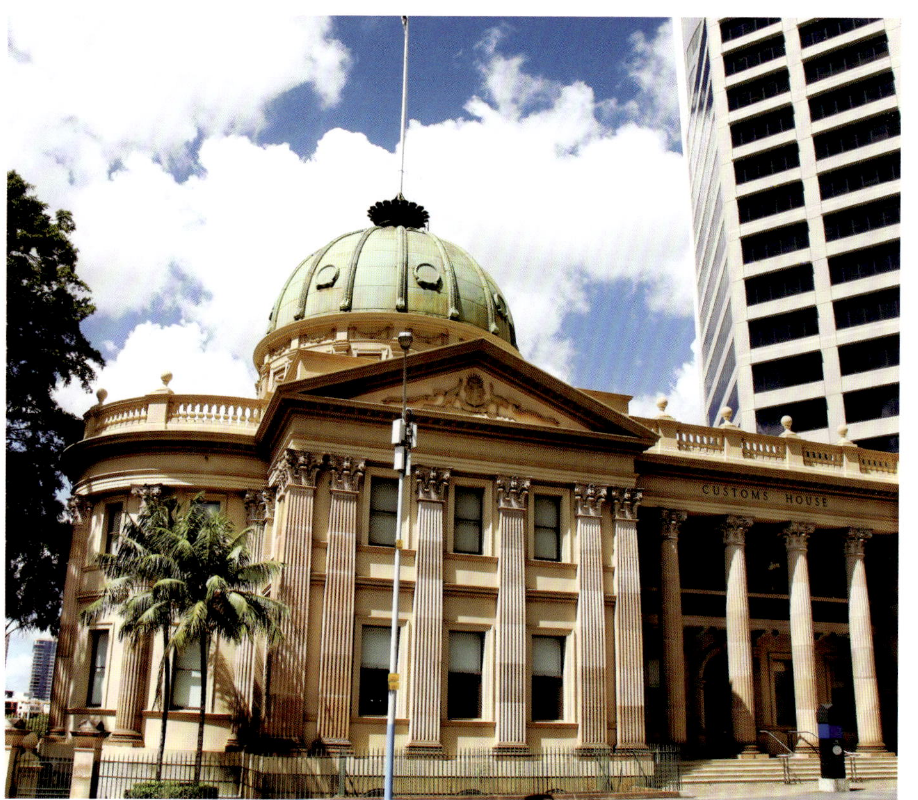

Customs House, Brisbane.

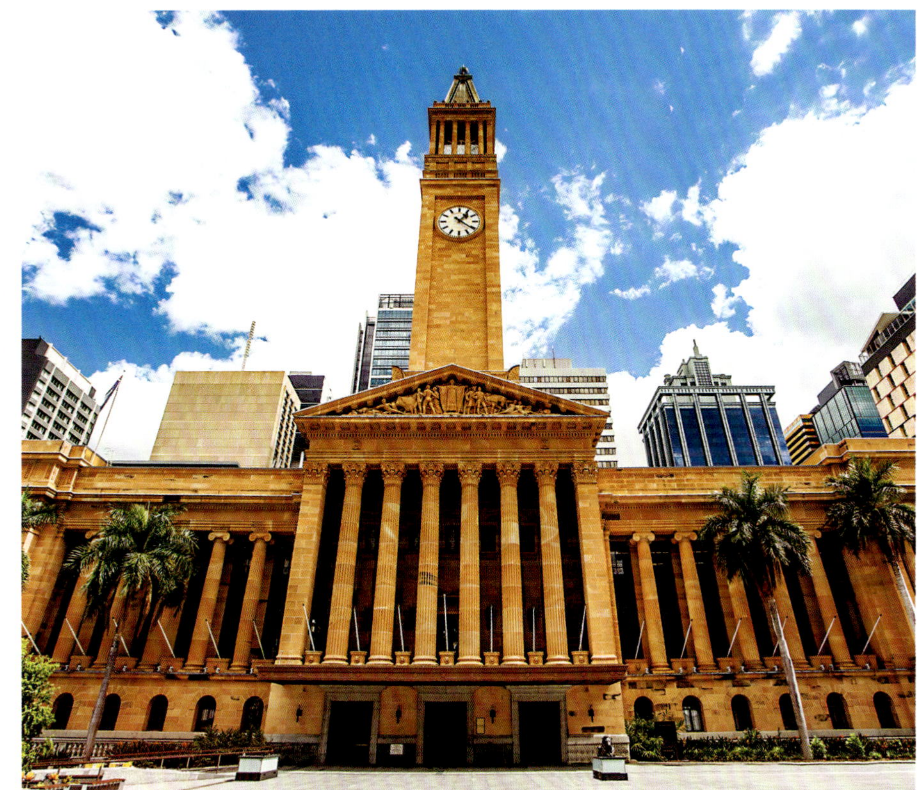

Brisbane City Hall in from King George Square.

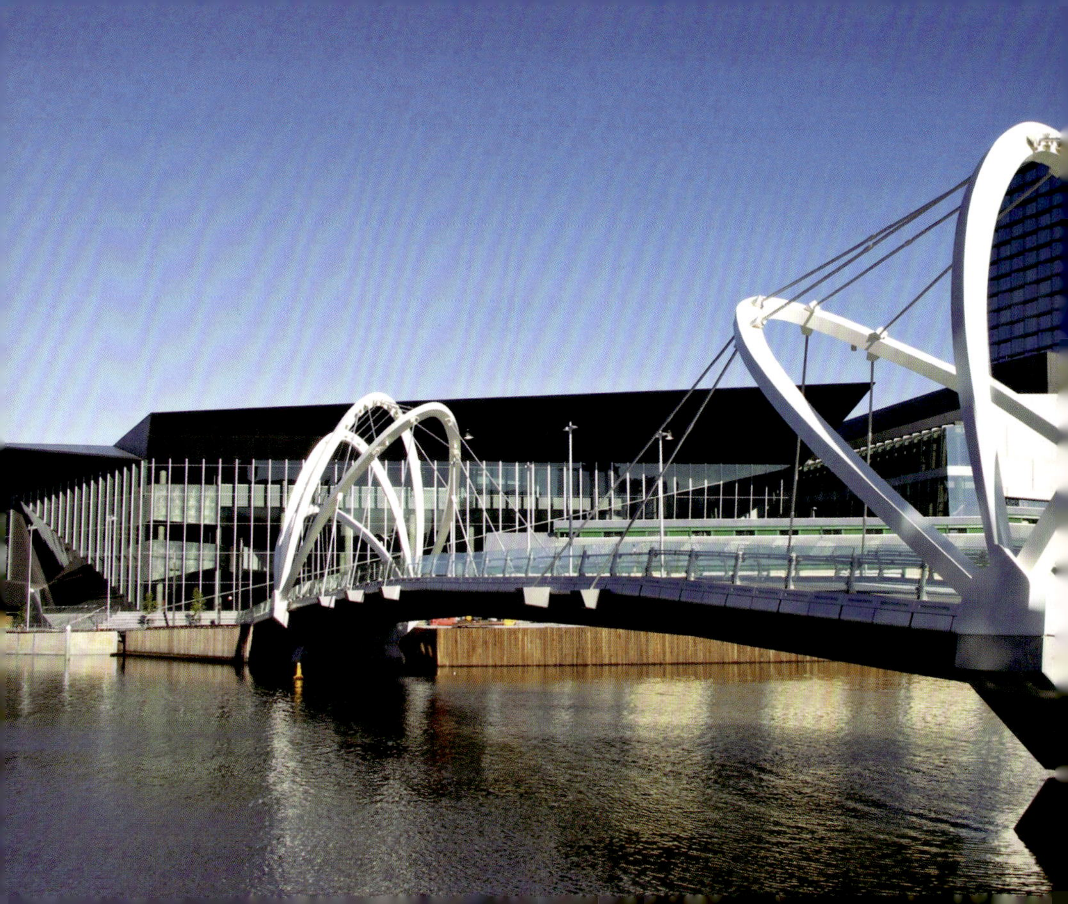

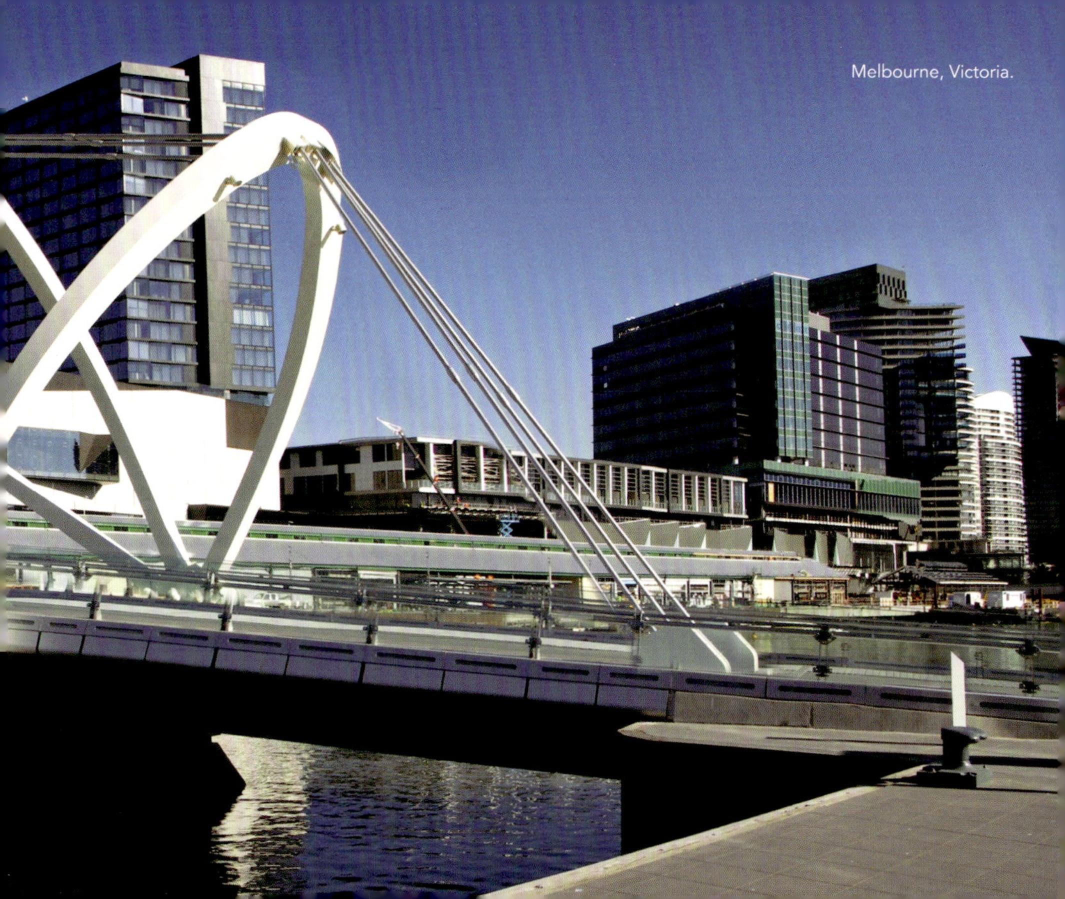

Melbourne, Victoria.

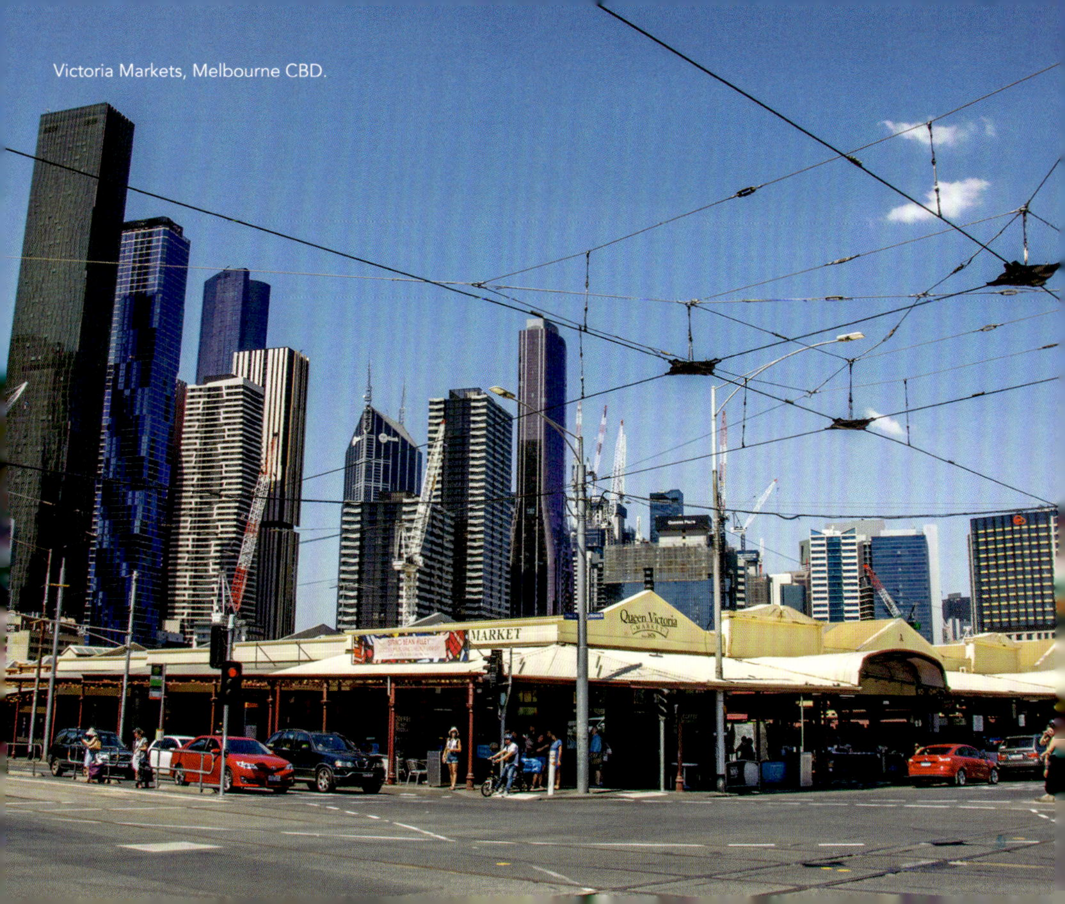

Victoria Markets, Melbourne CBD.

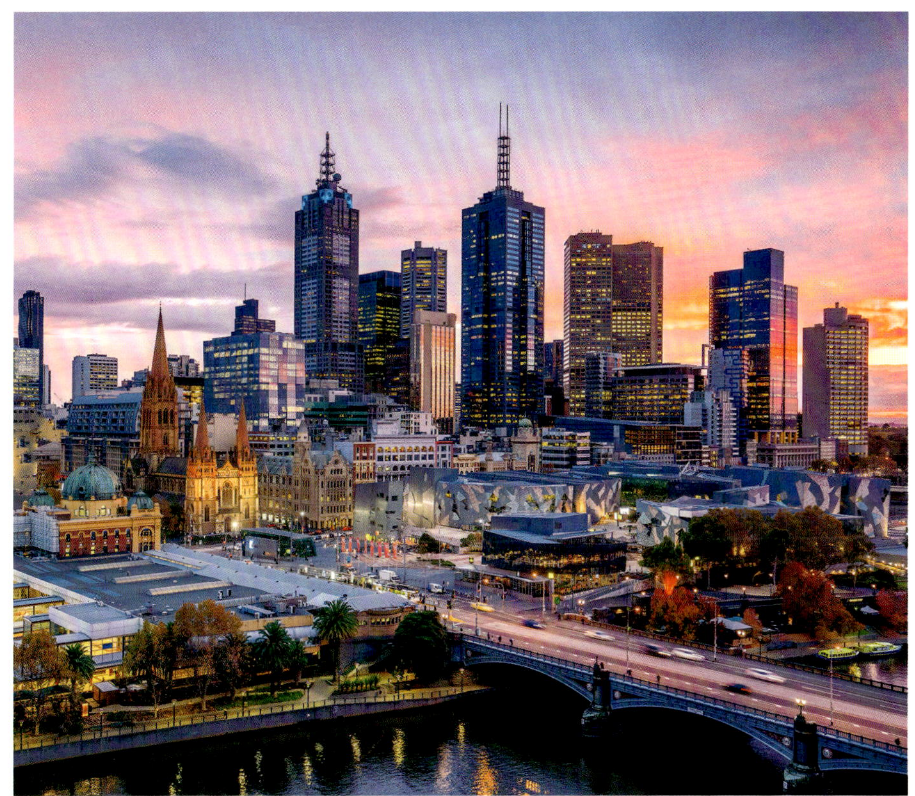

Melbourne, Victoria.

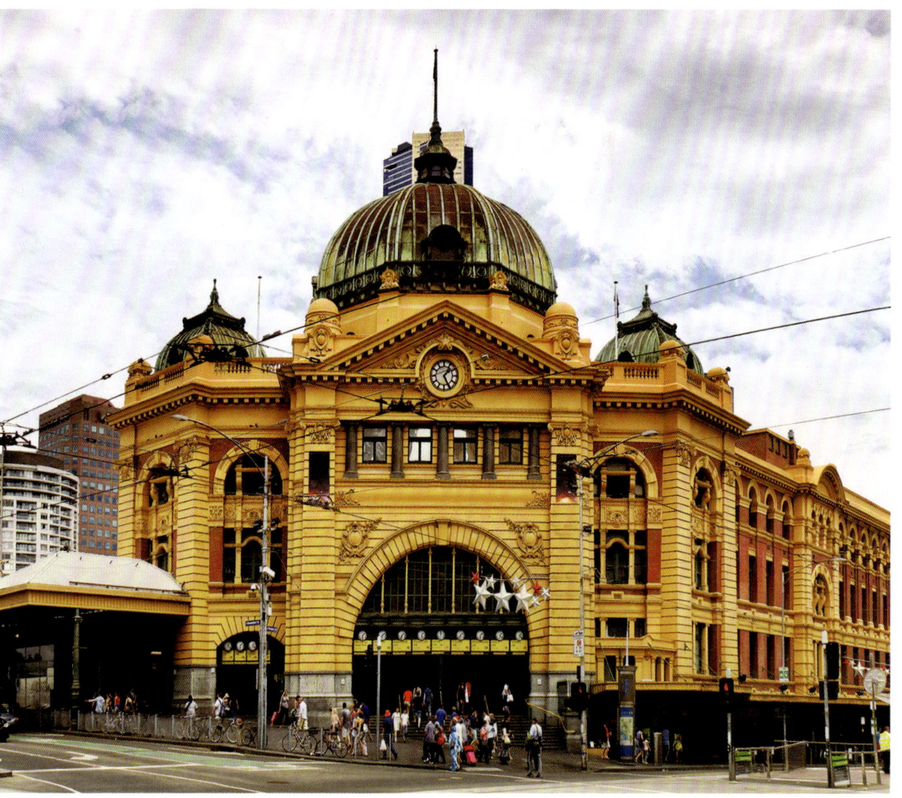

Flinders Station, Melbourne, Victoria.

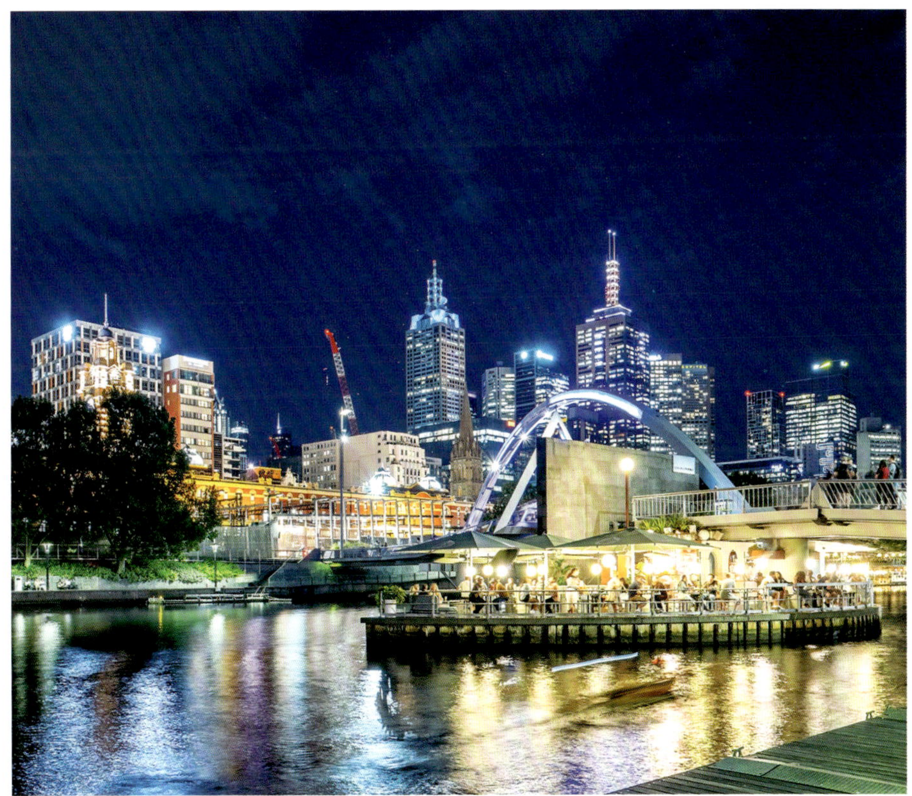

Melbourne, Victoria.

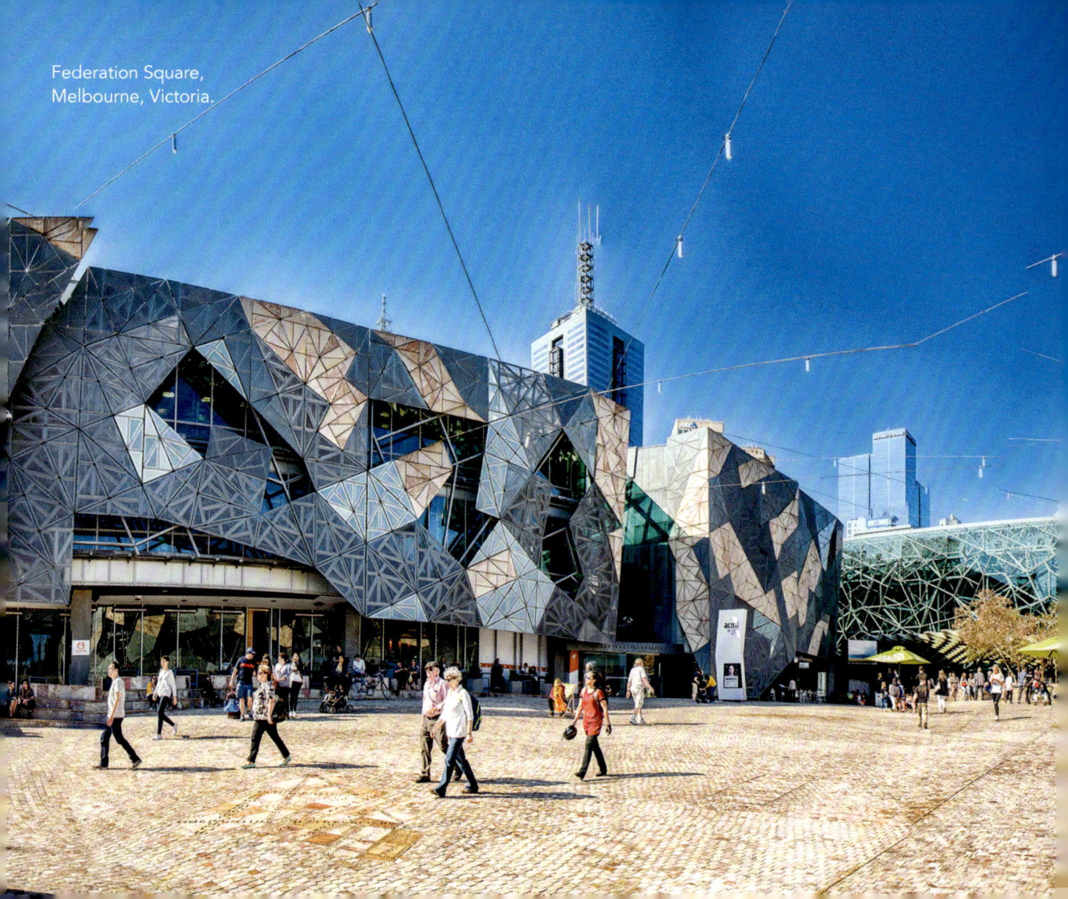

Federation Square,
Melbourne, Victoria.

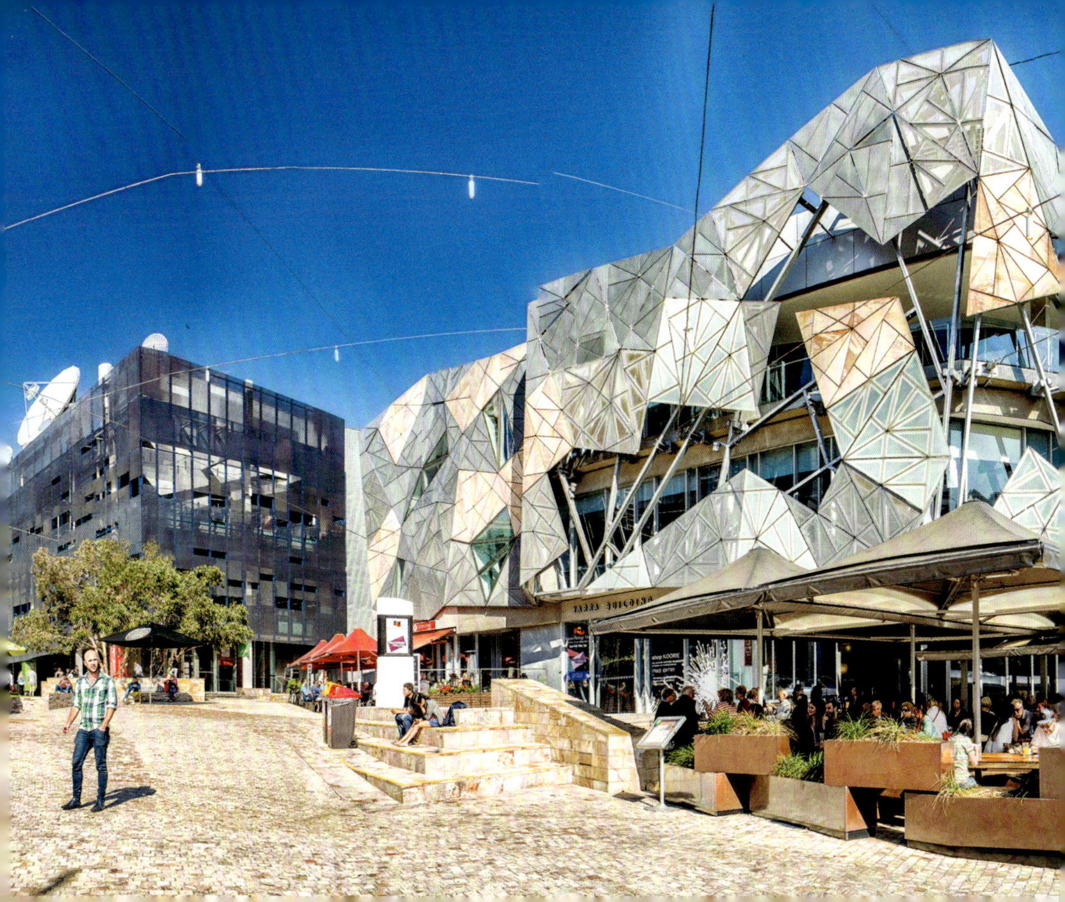
YARRA BUILDING
shop KOORIE
FREE ENTRY

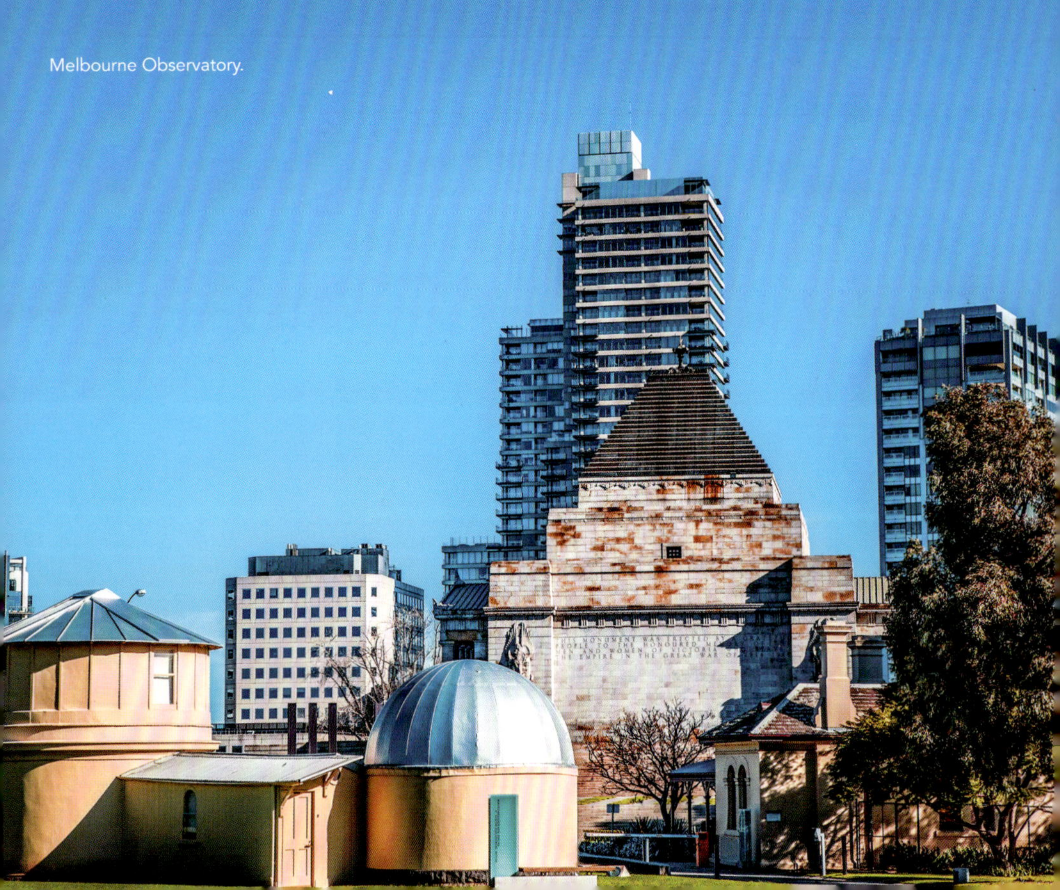

Melbourne Observatory.

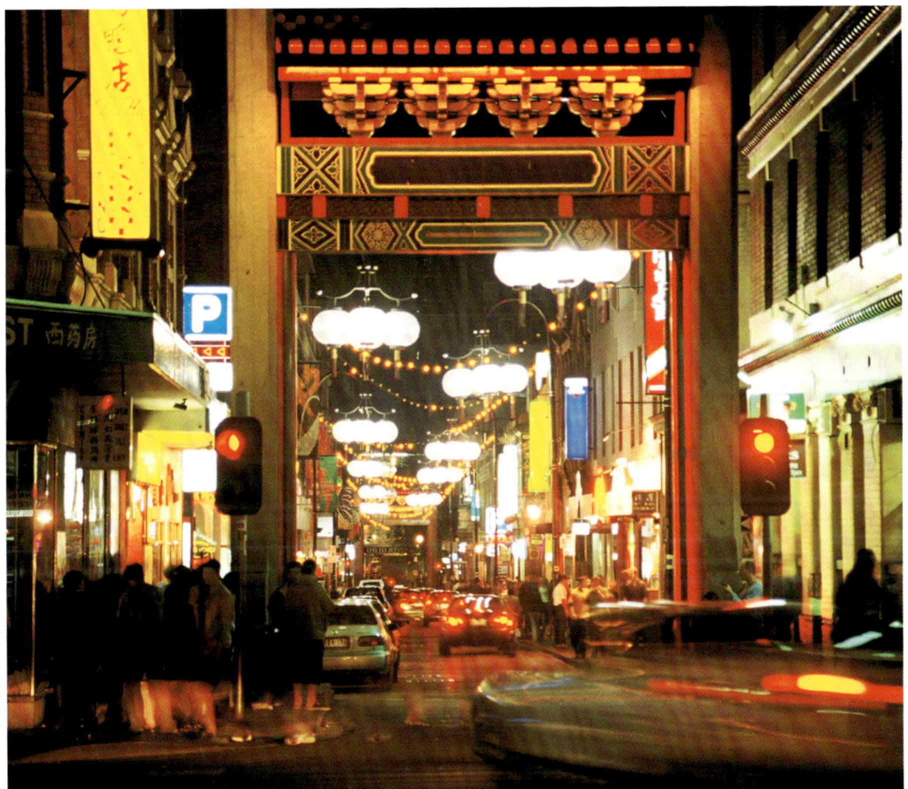

Chinatown, Melbourne.

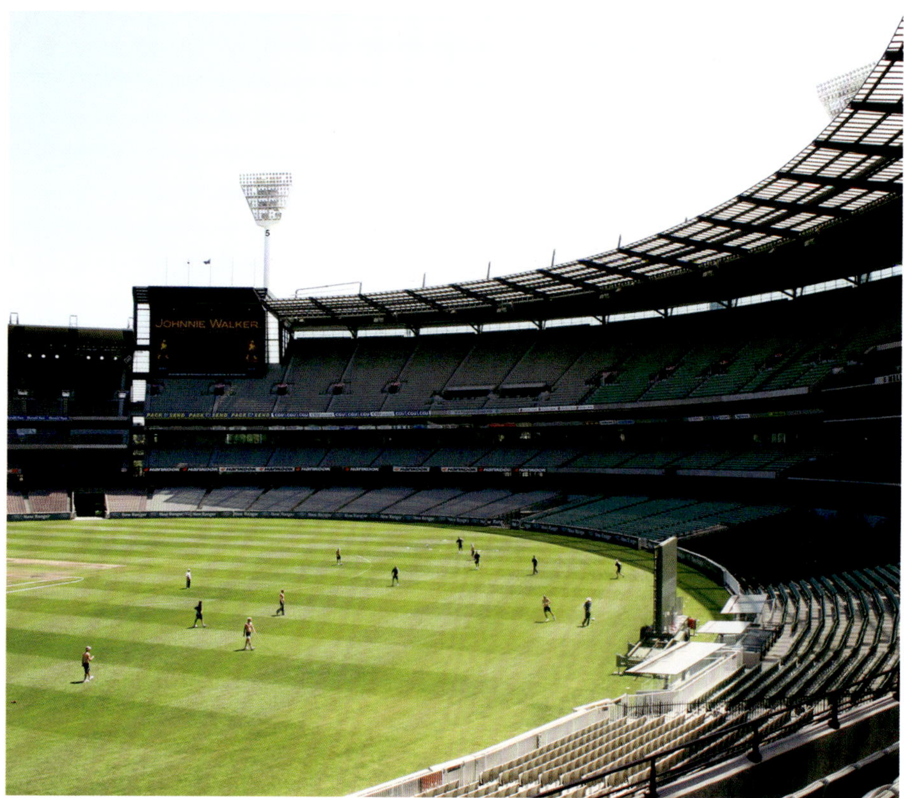

Melbourne Cricket Ground (MCG), Melbourne.

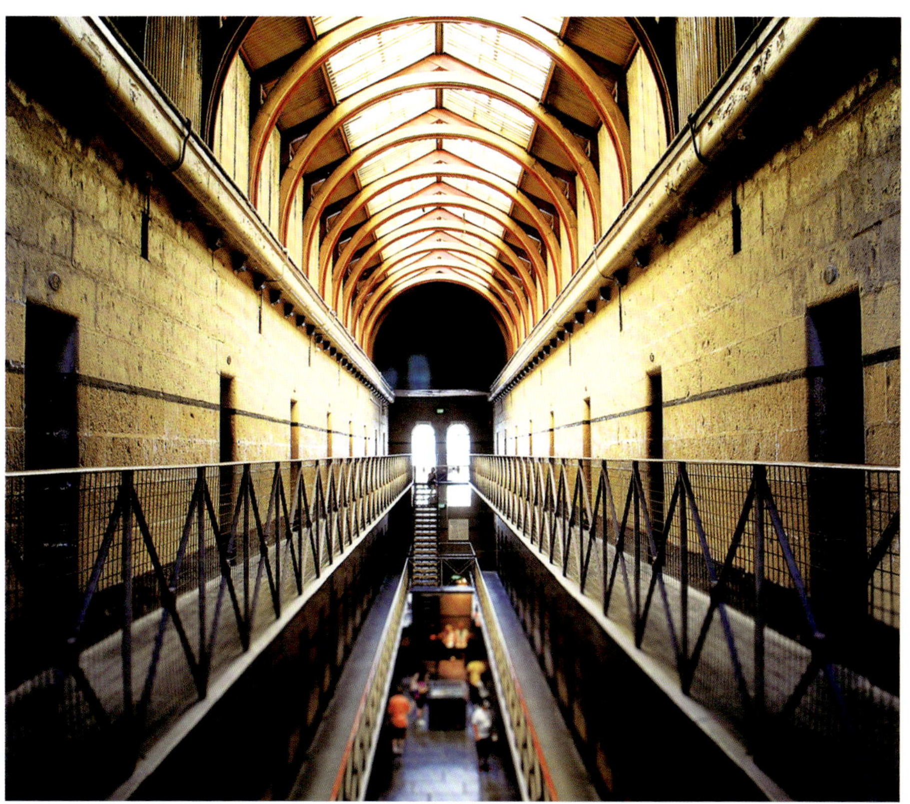

Old Melbourne Goal.

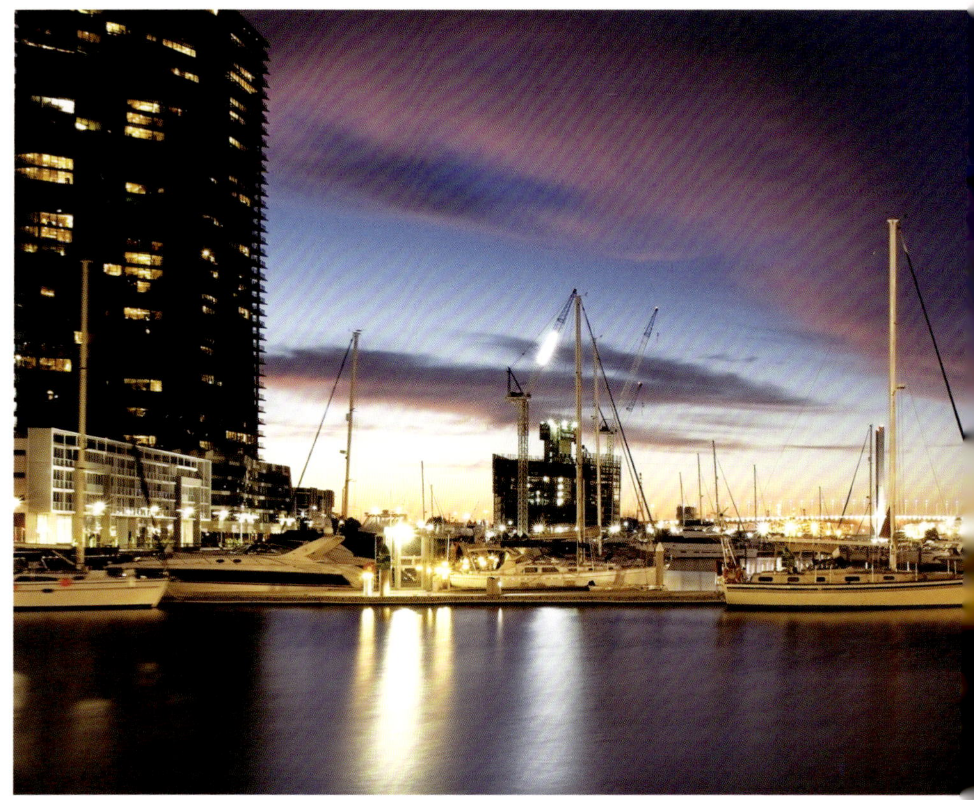

Docklands, Melbourne.

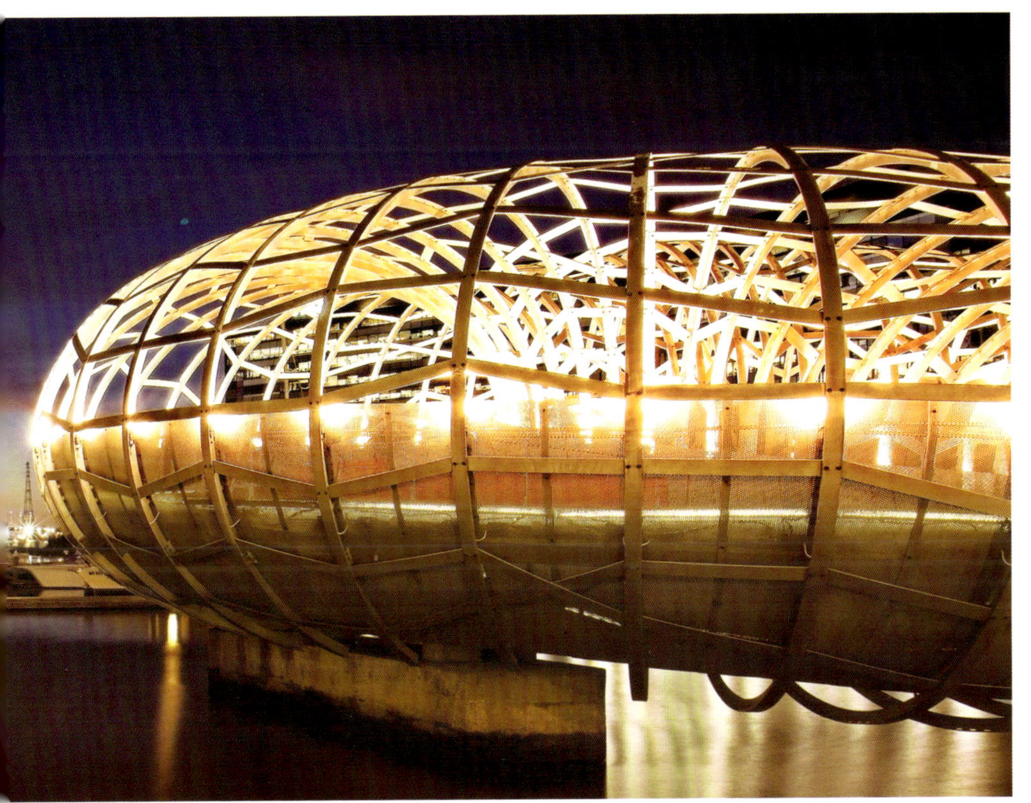

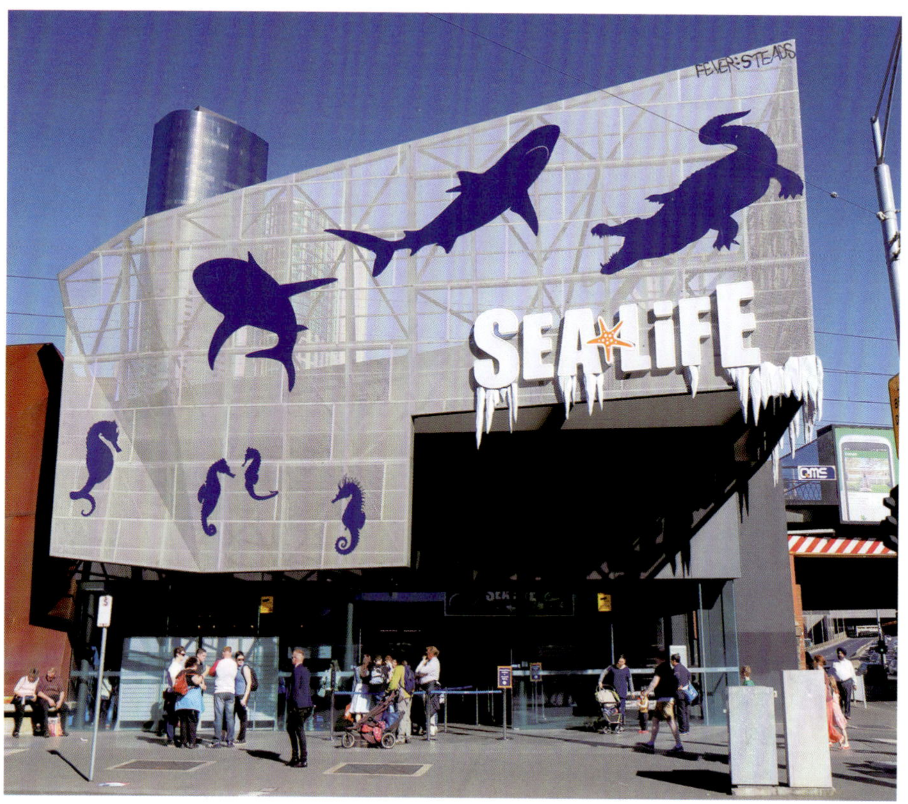

Sealife, Melbourne.

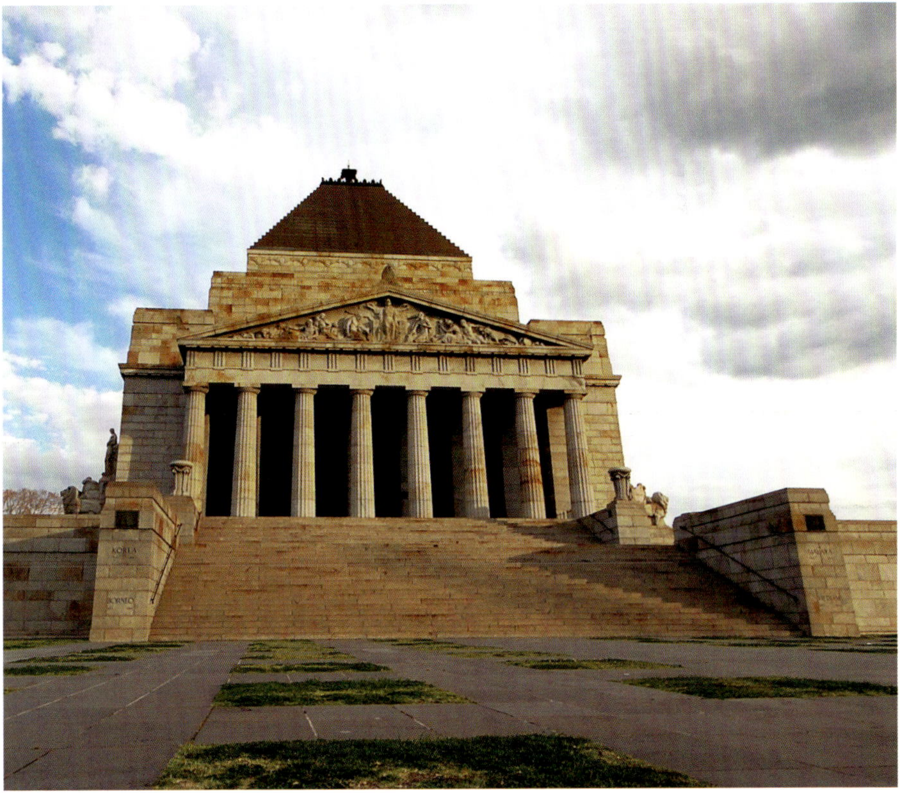

The Shrine of Remembrance, Melbourne.

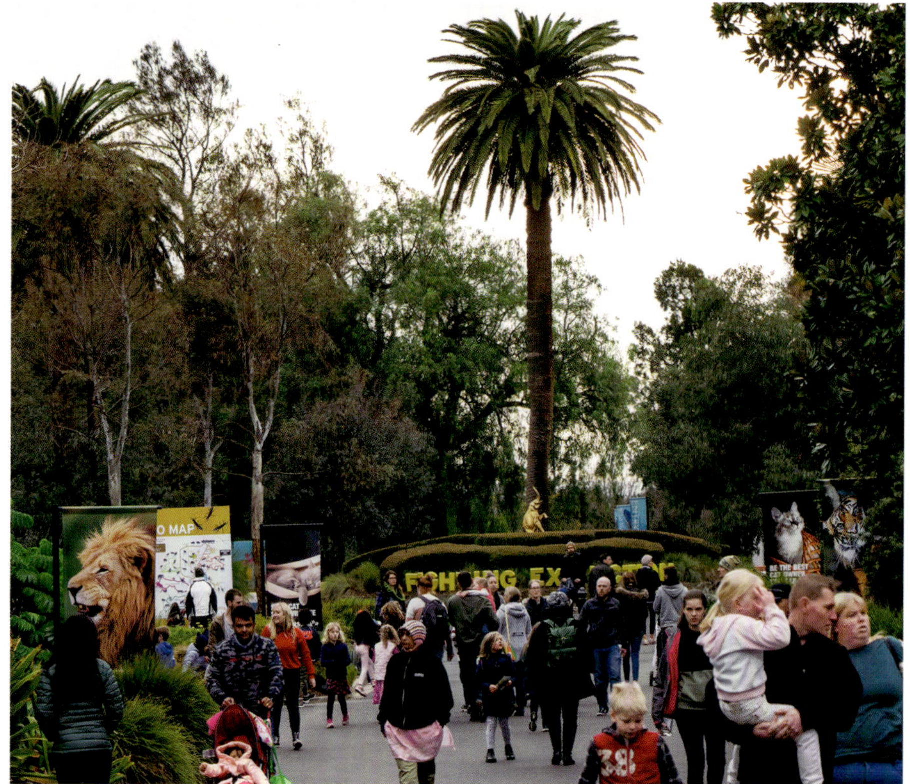

Melbourne Zoo.

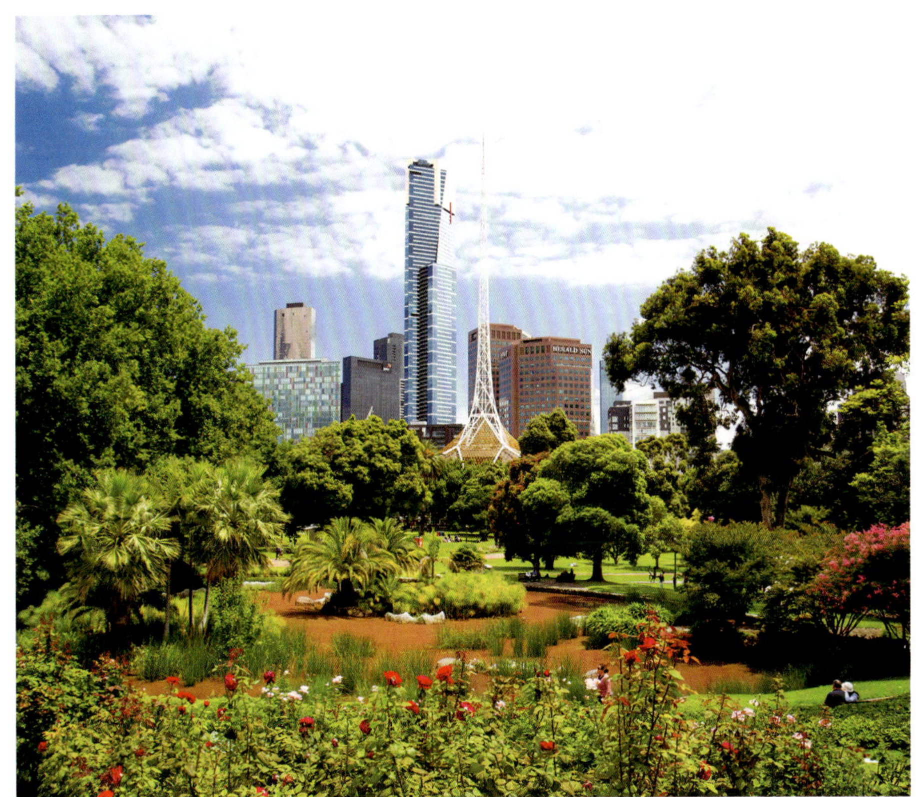

Southbank, Melbourne.

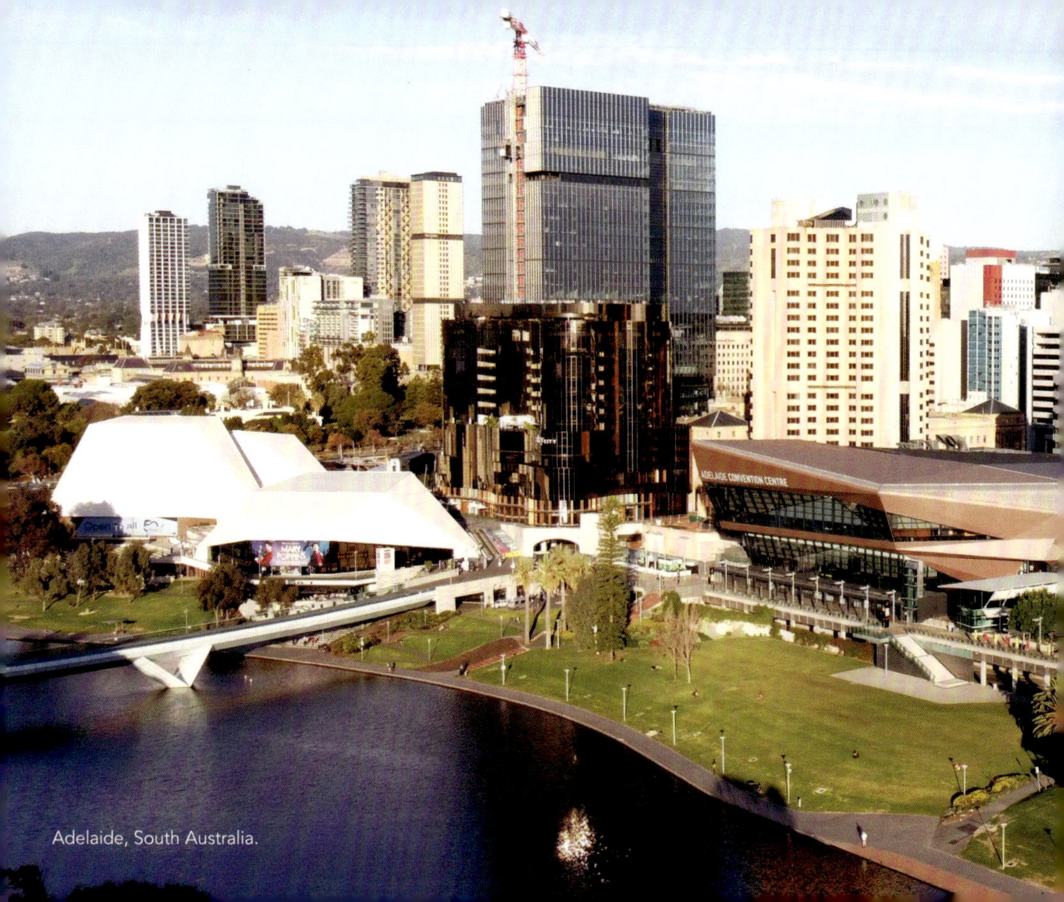

Adelaide, South Australia.

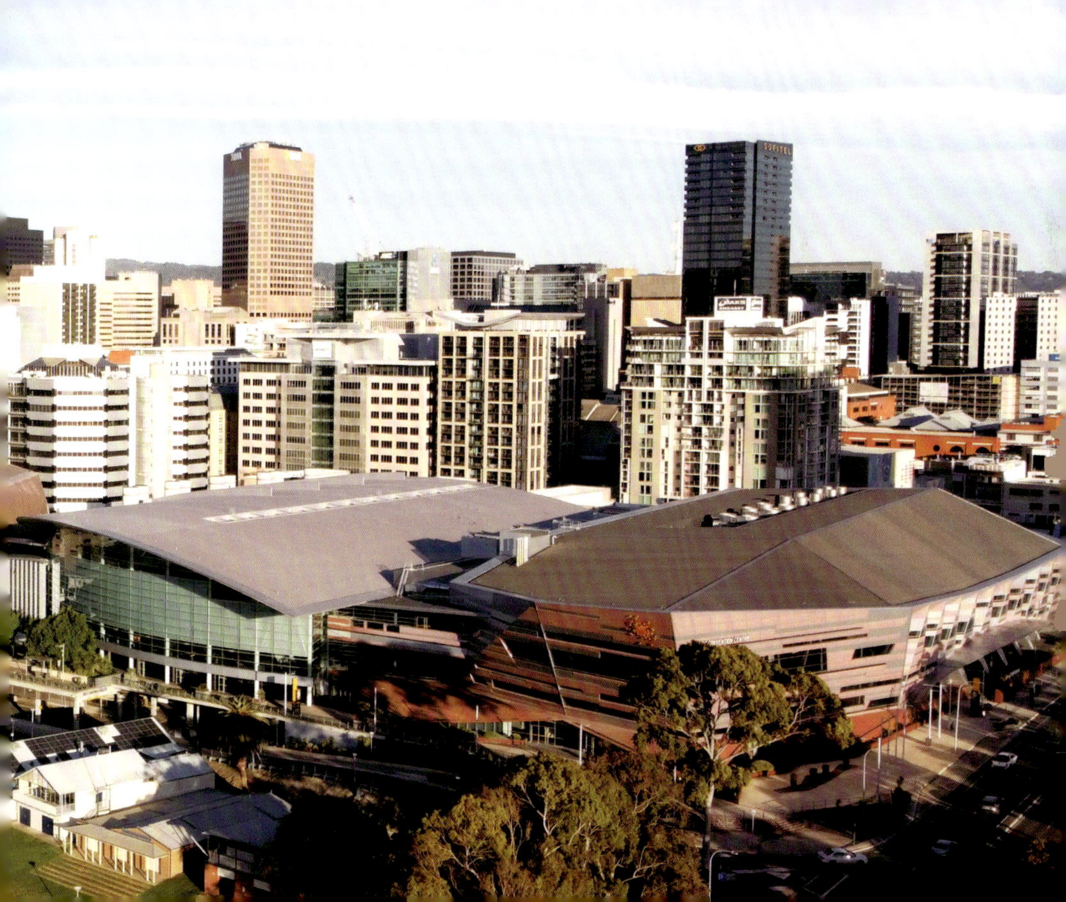
SOFITEL

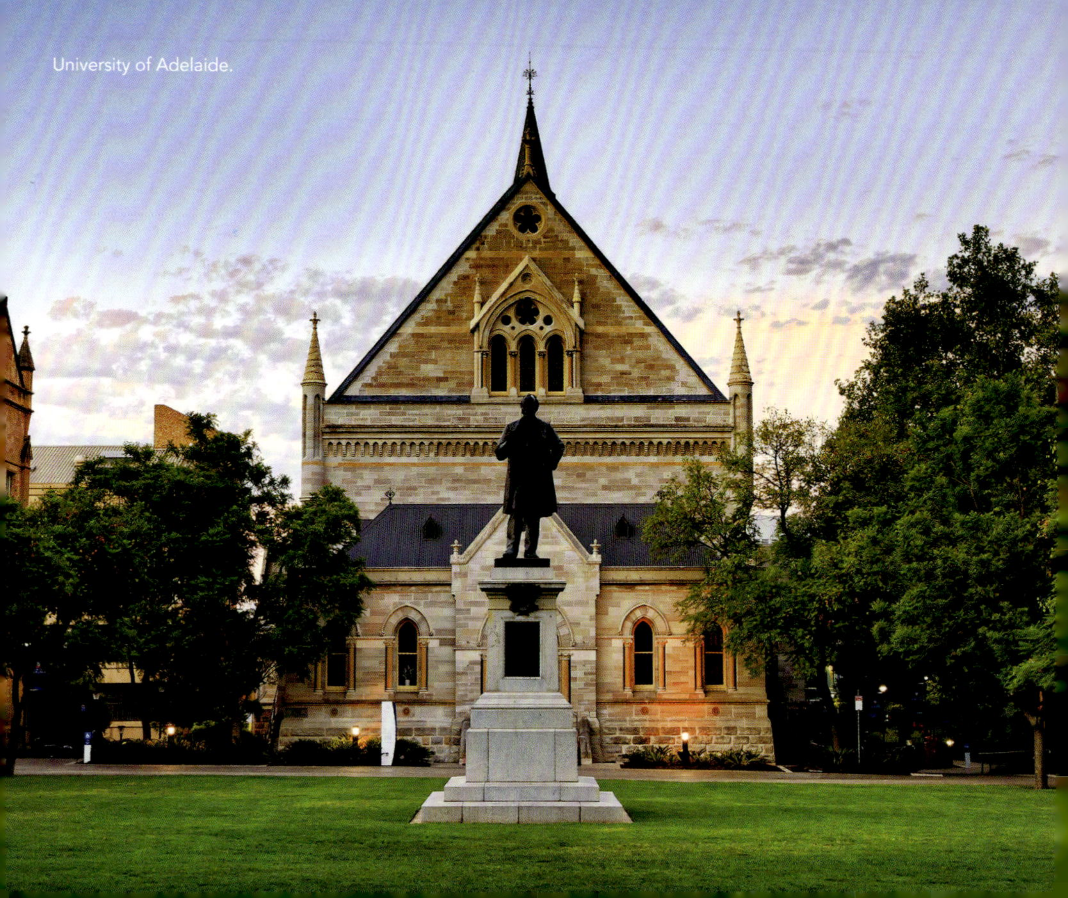

University of Adelaide.

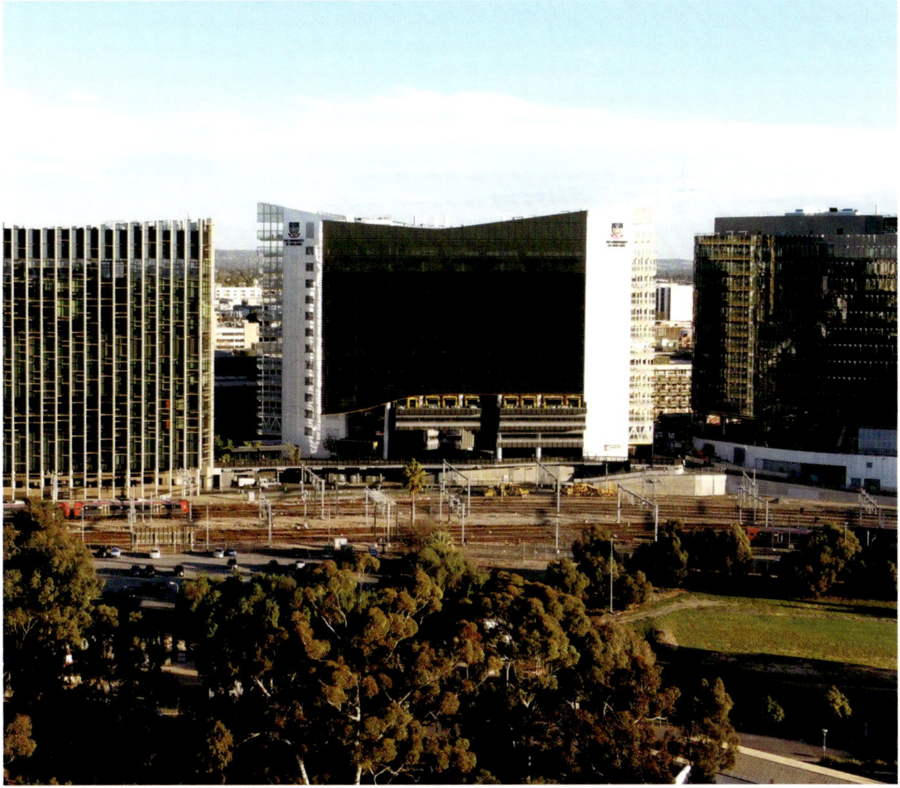

Adelaide Health and Medical Sciences building, The University of Adelaide.

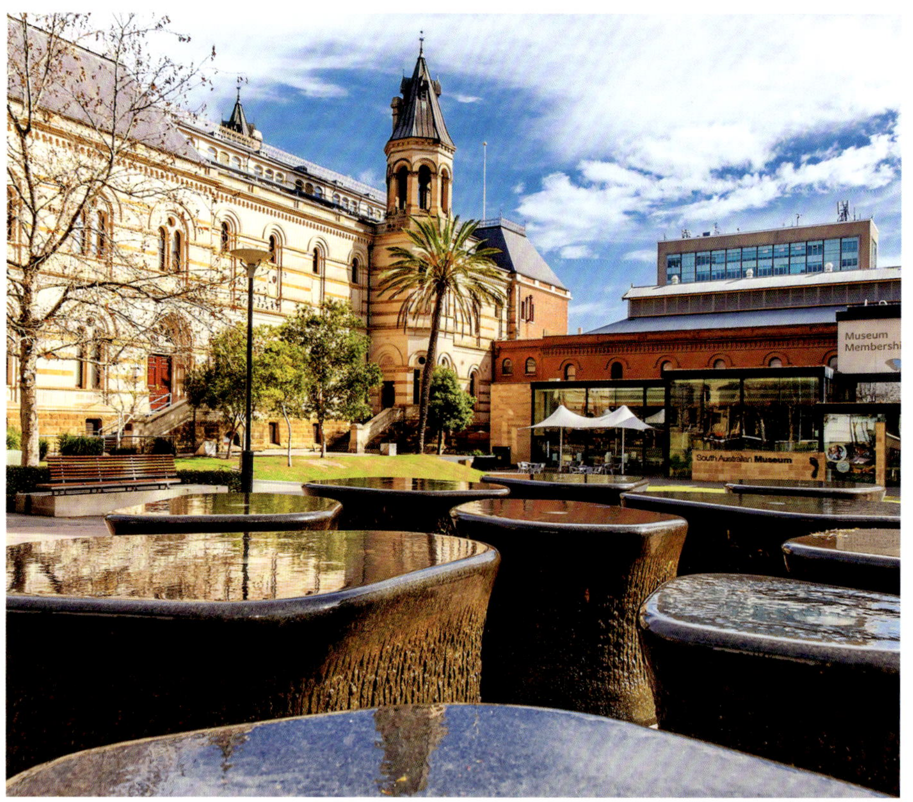

Adelaide Museum.

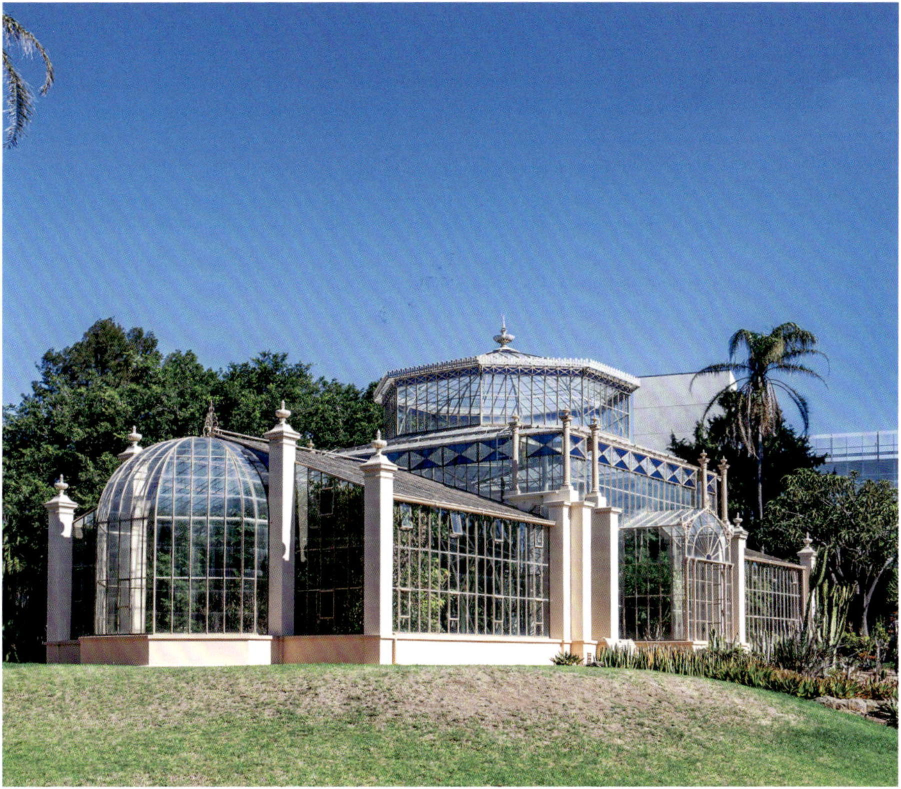

The 1877-built Palm House, Royal Botanic Garden, Adelaide.

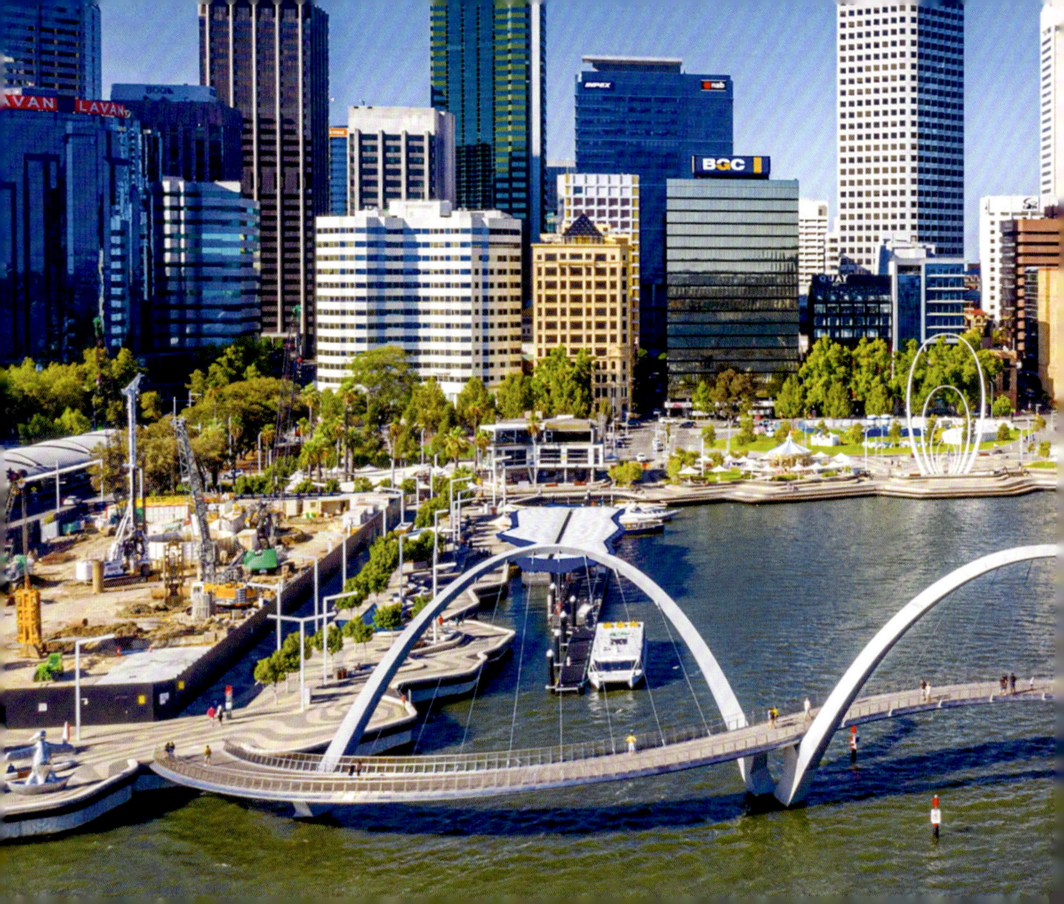
LAVAN
BGC
nab
QUAY

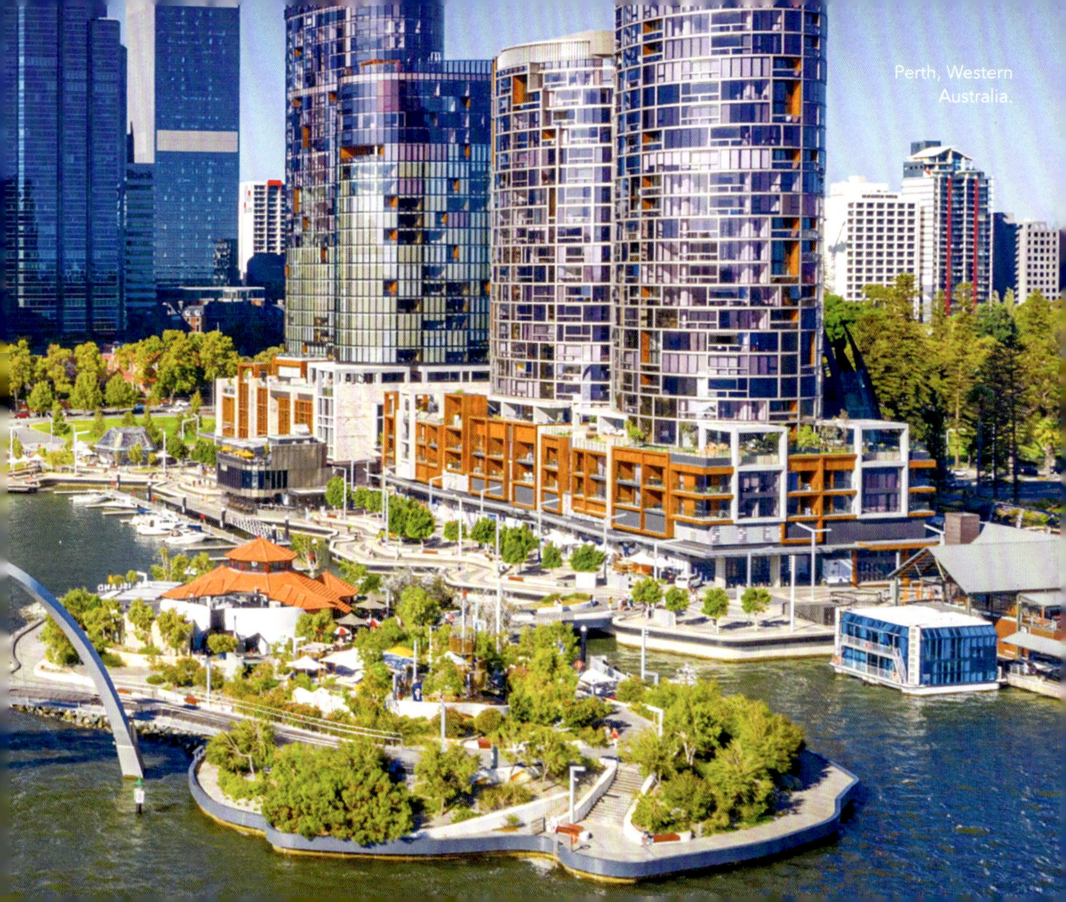

Perth, Western Australia.

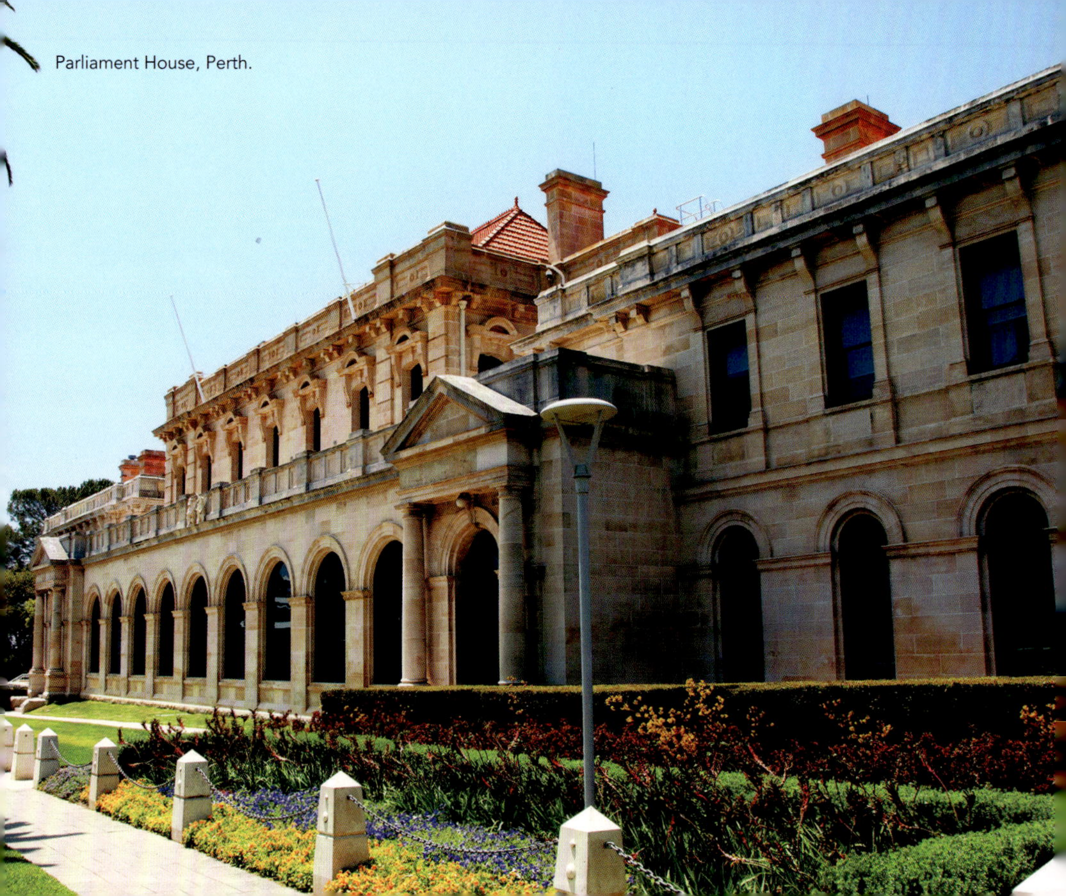

Parliament House, Perth.

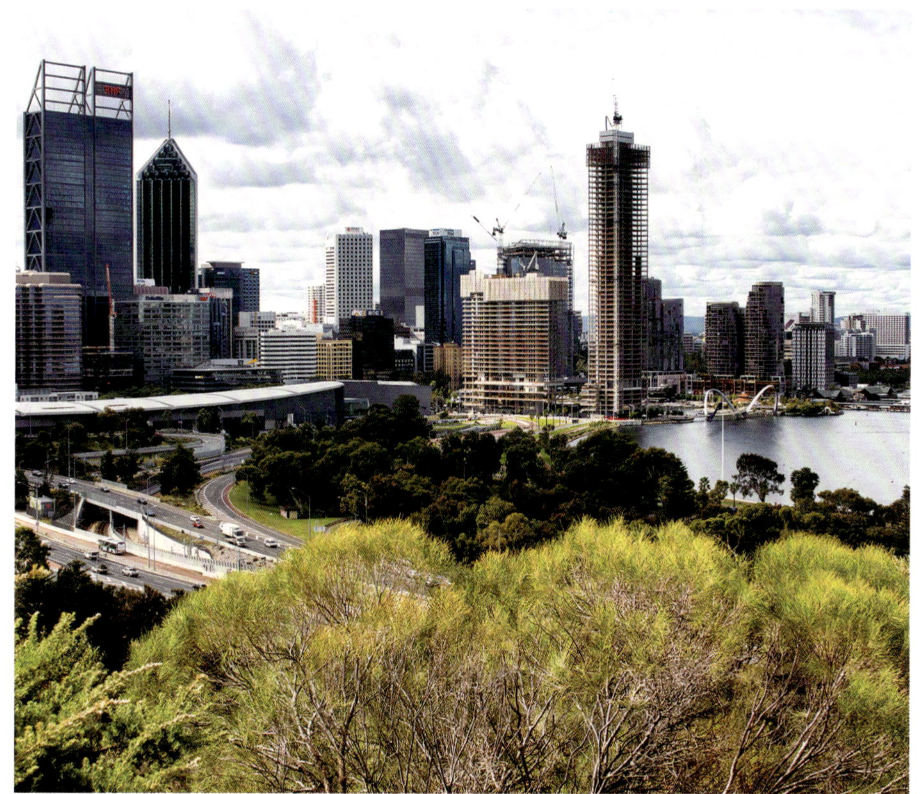

Perth, Western Australia.

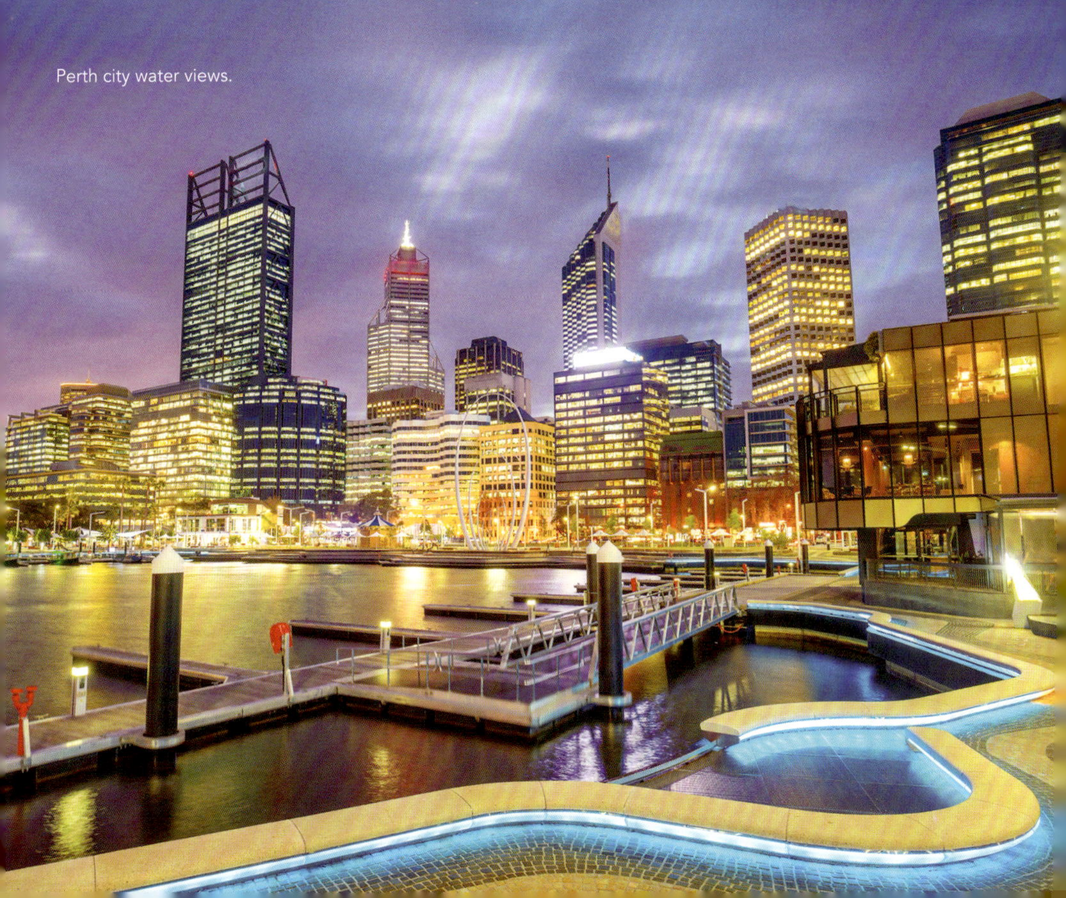
Perth city water views.

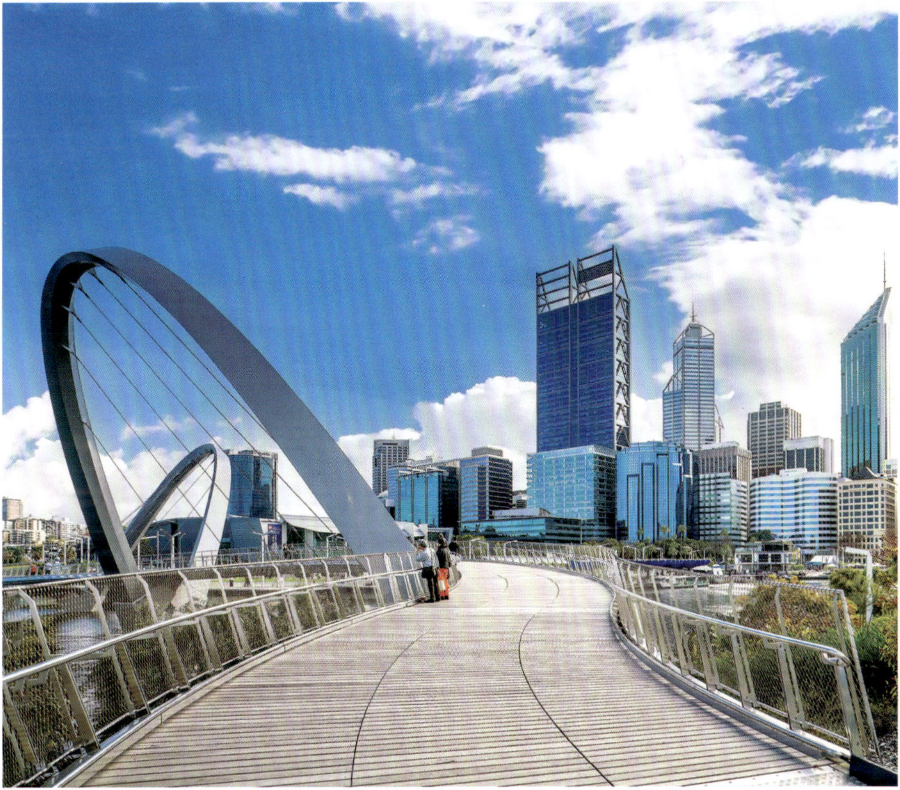

Downtown Perth city skyline.

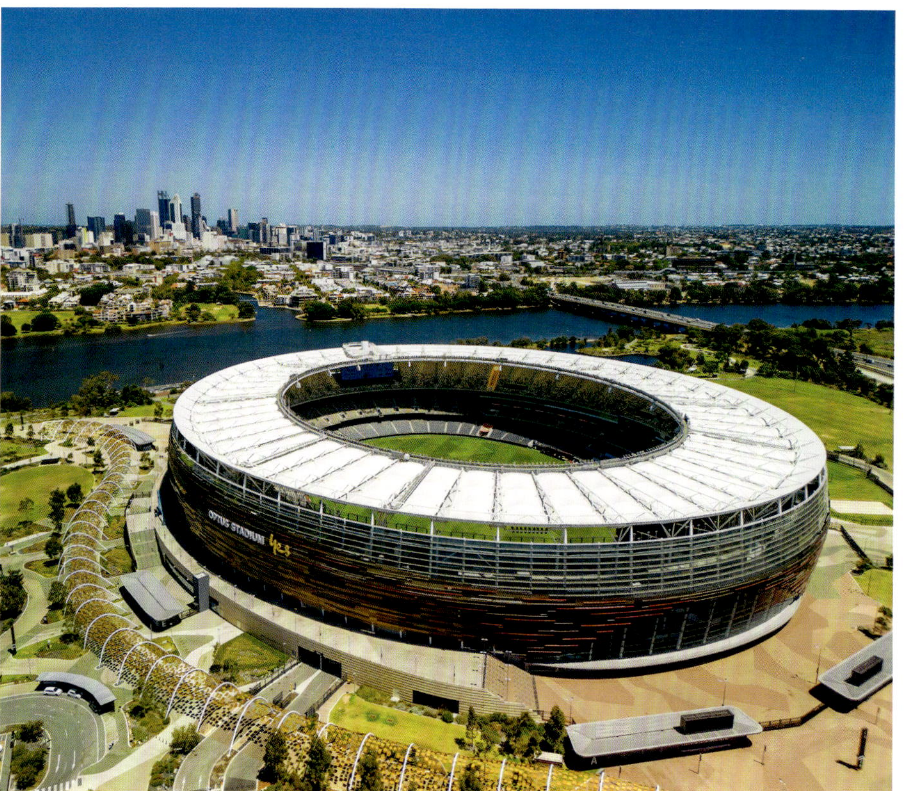

Perth Stadium and city skyline.

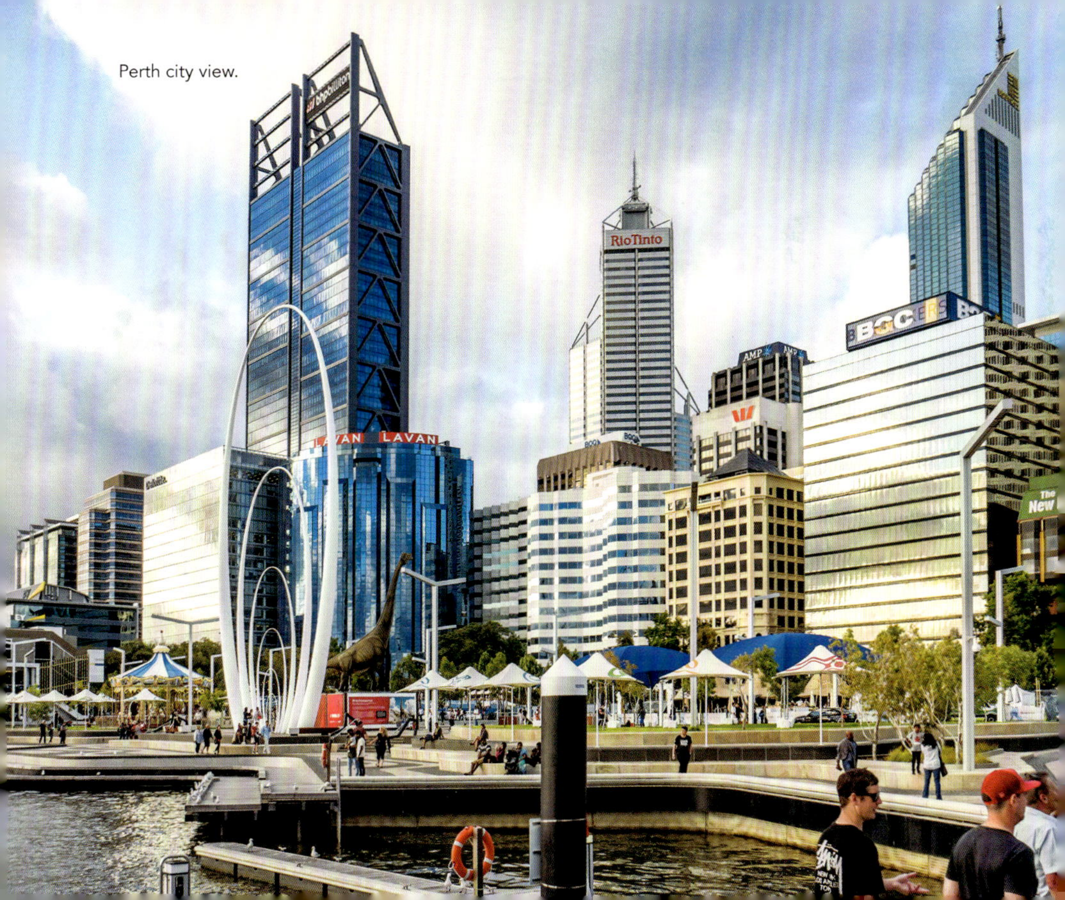

Perth city view.

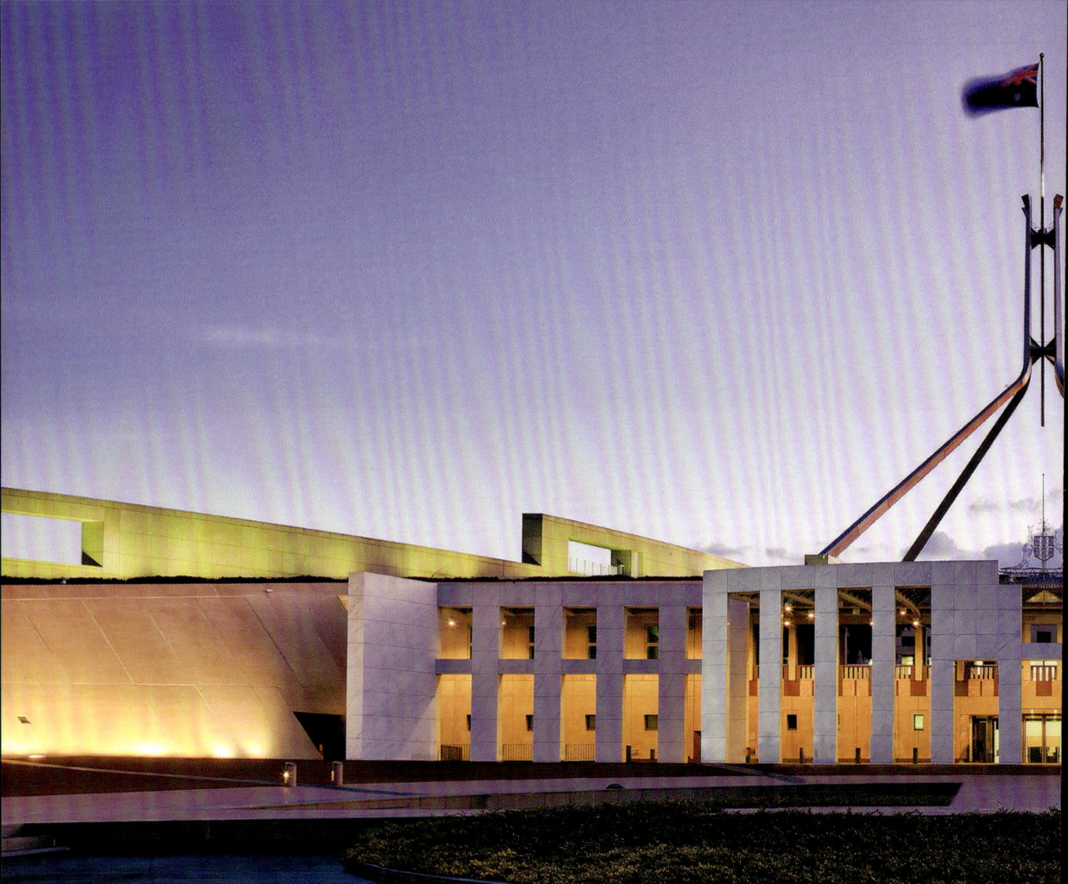

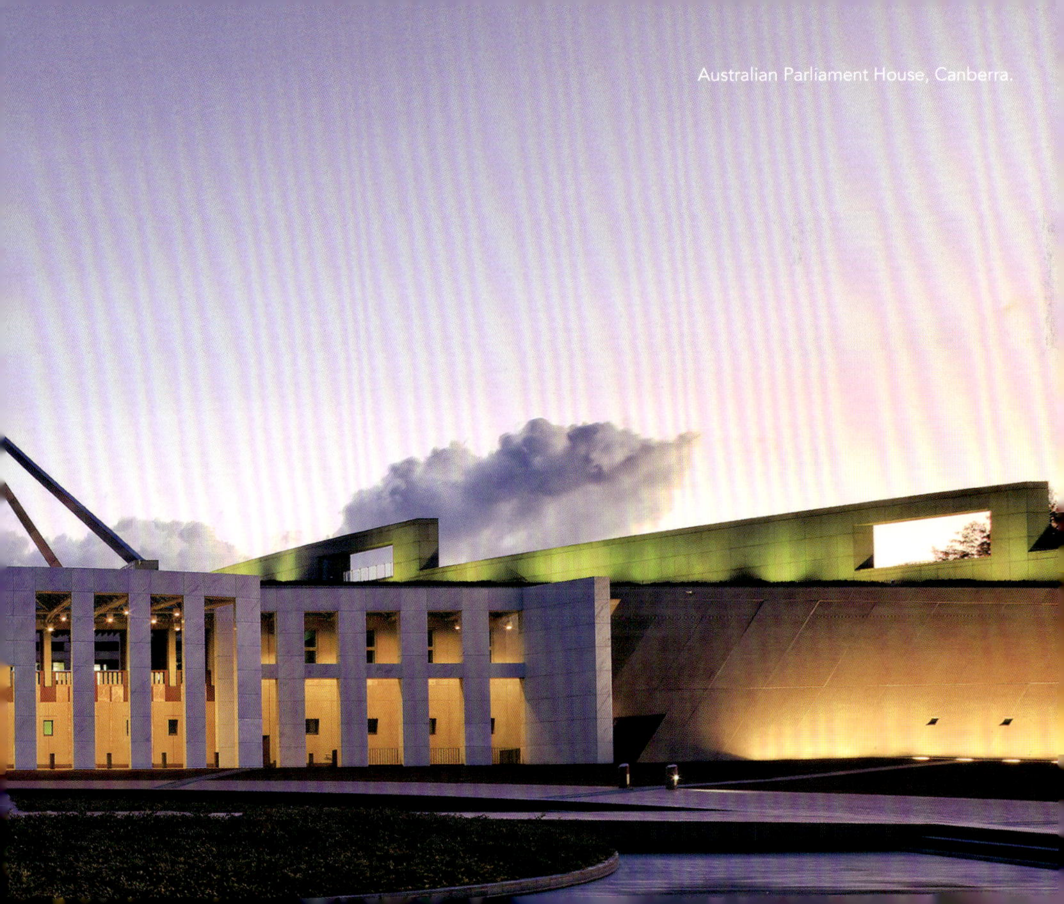
Australian Parliament House, Canberra.

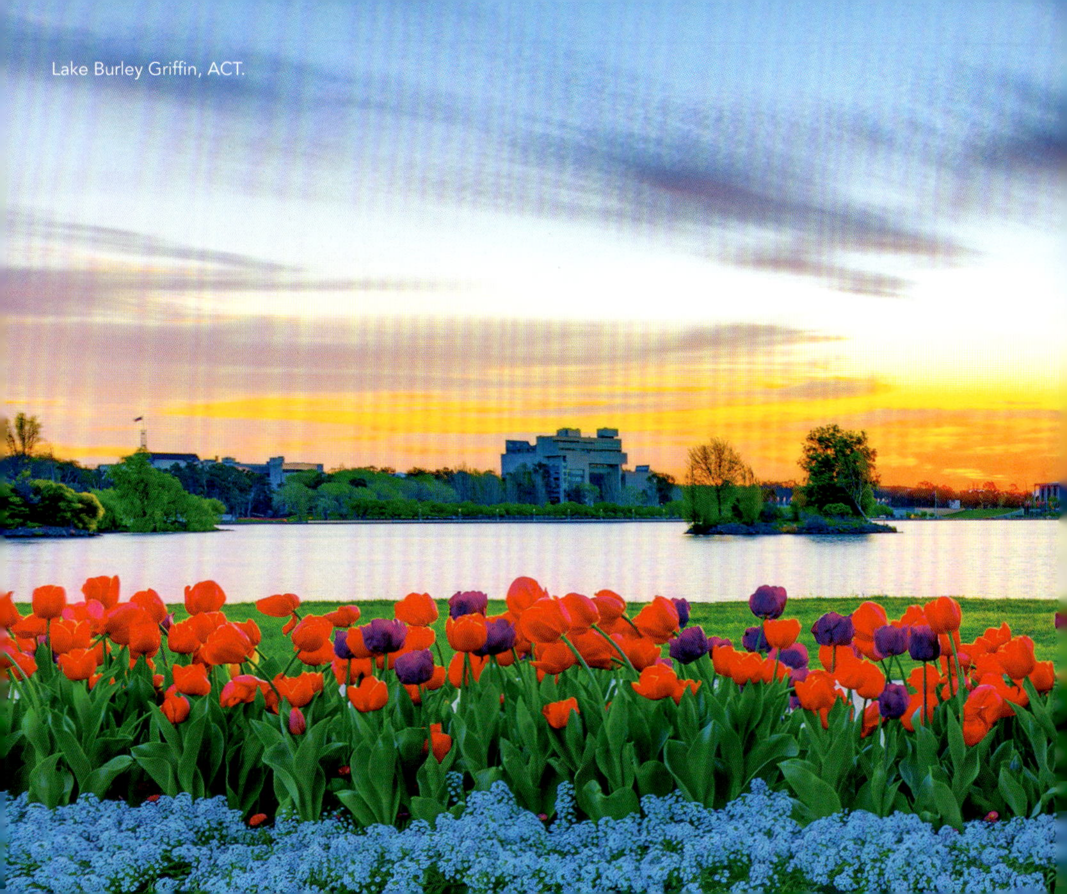

Lake Burley Griffin, ACT.

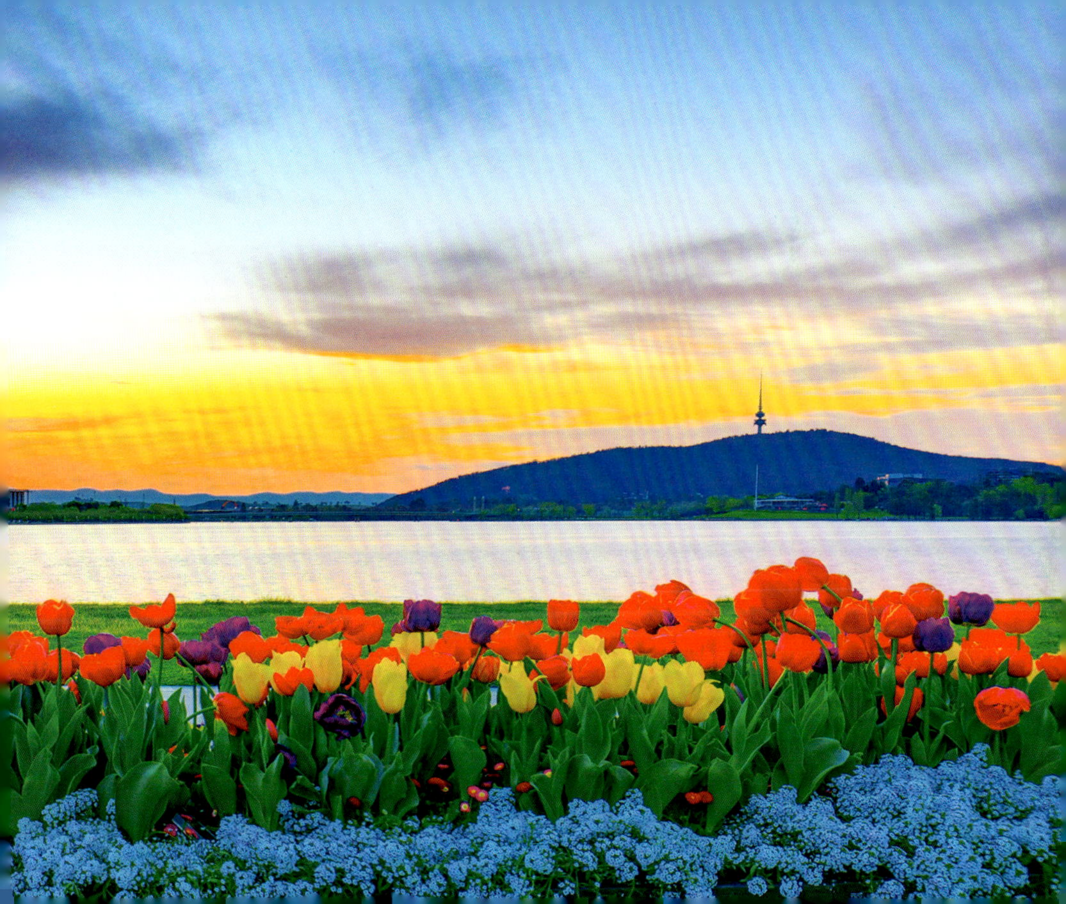

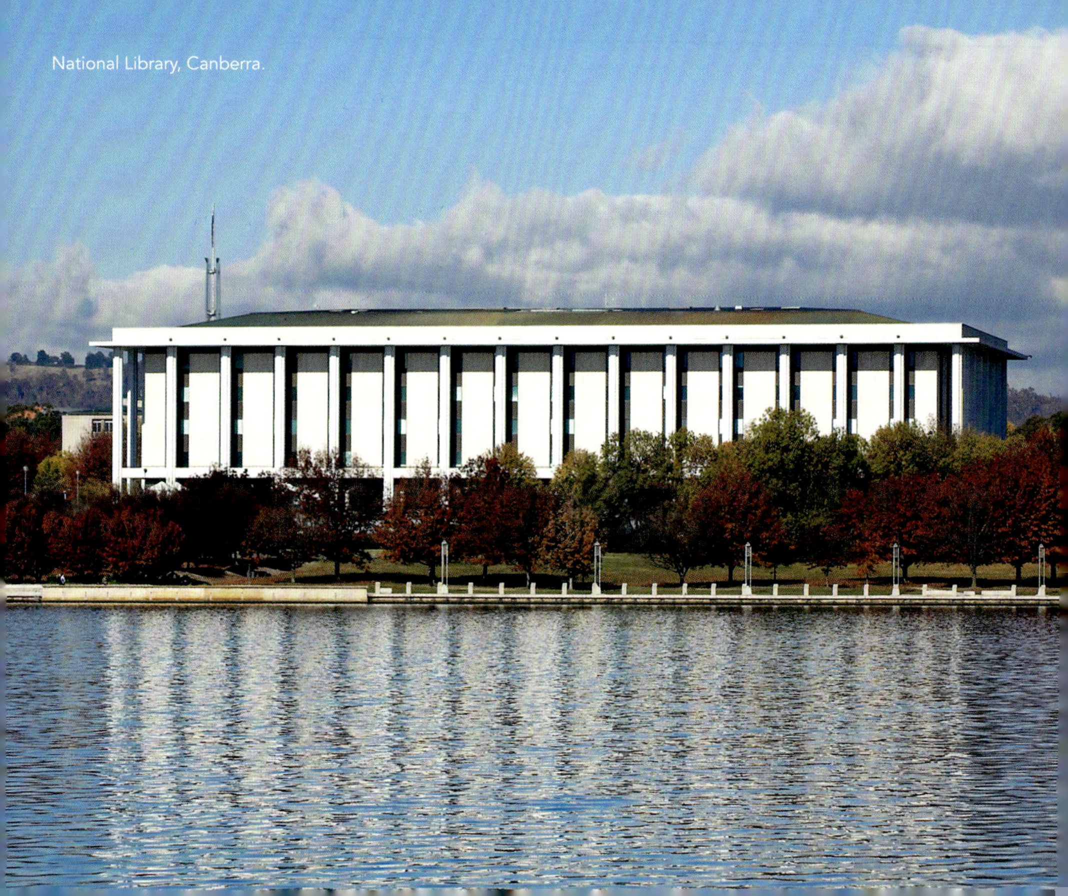

National Library, Canberra.

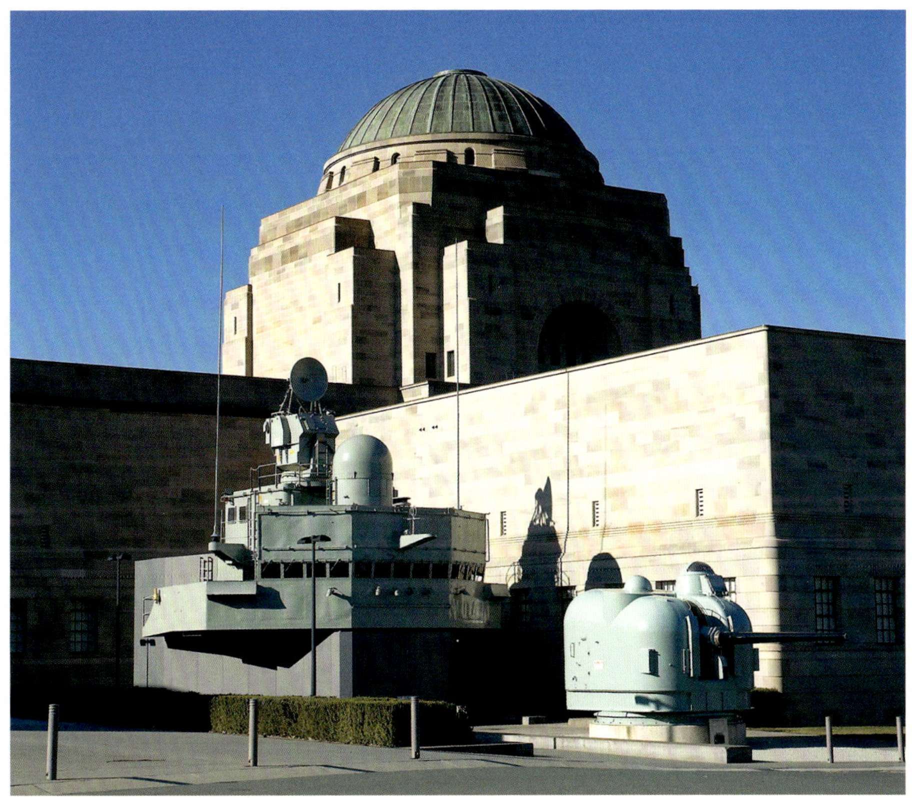

Australian War Memorial, Canberra.

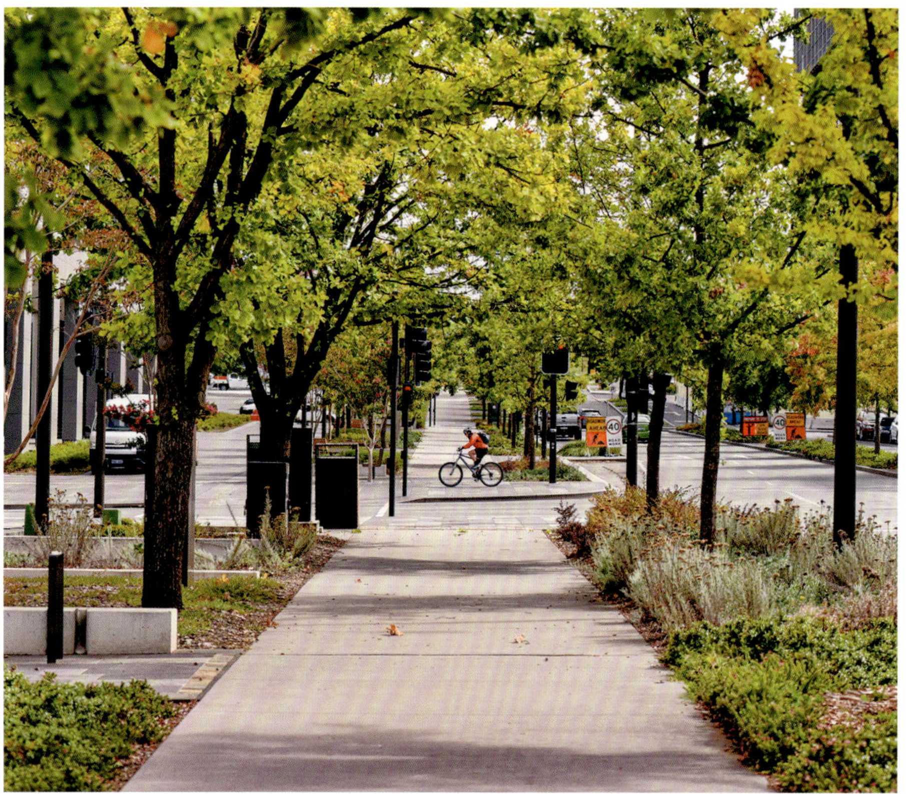

Streetscape, ACT.

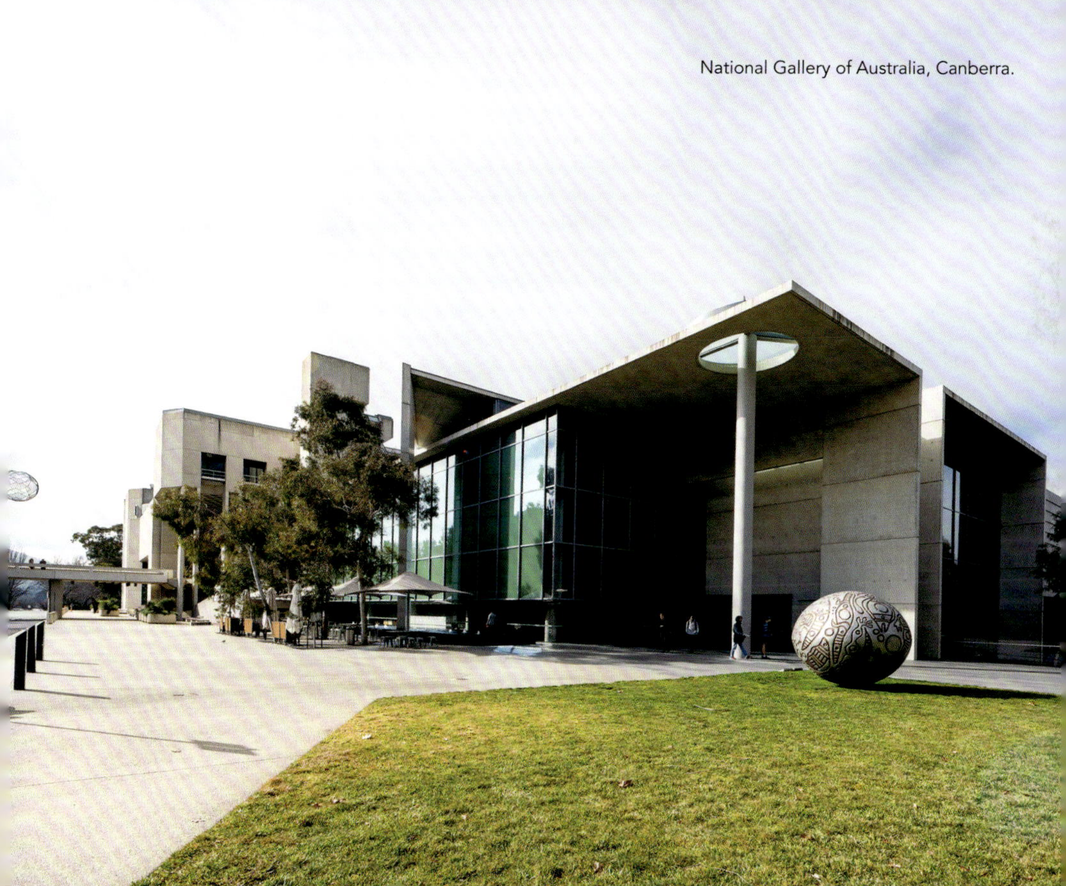
National Gallery of Australia, Canberra.

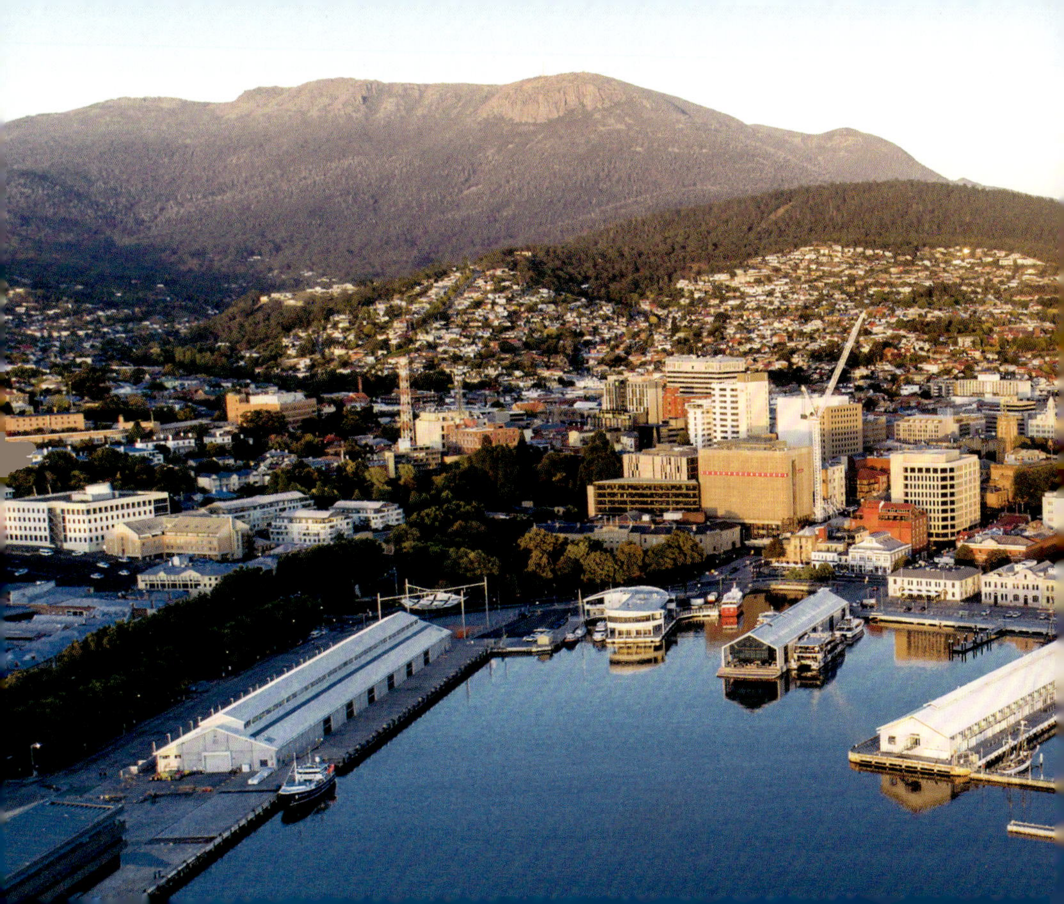

Hobart Harbour, Tasmania.

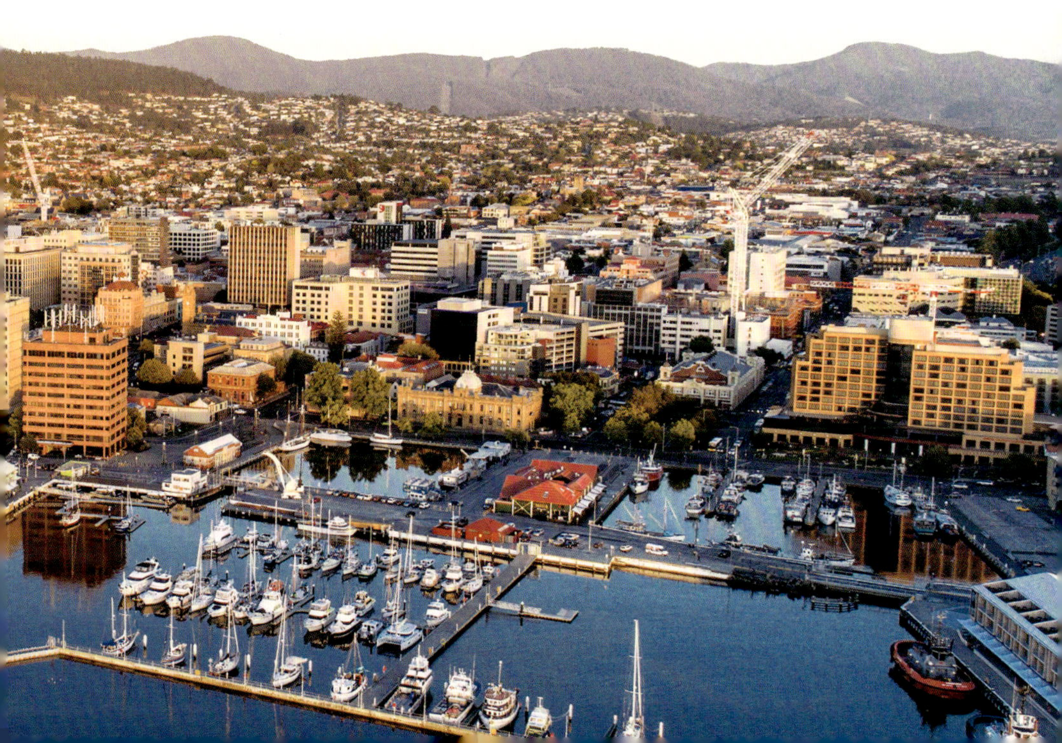

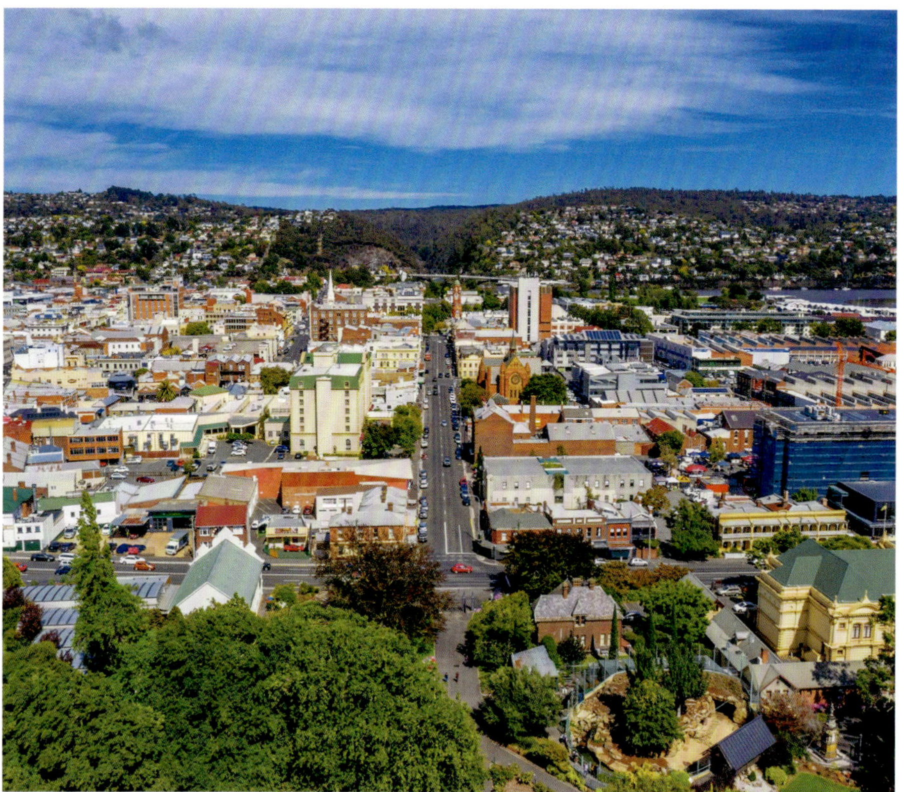

Launceston, Tasmania.

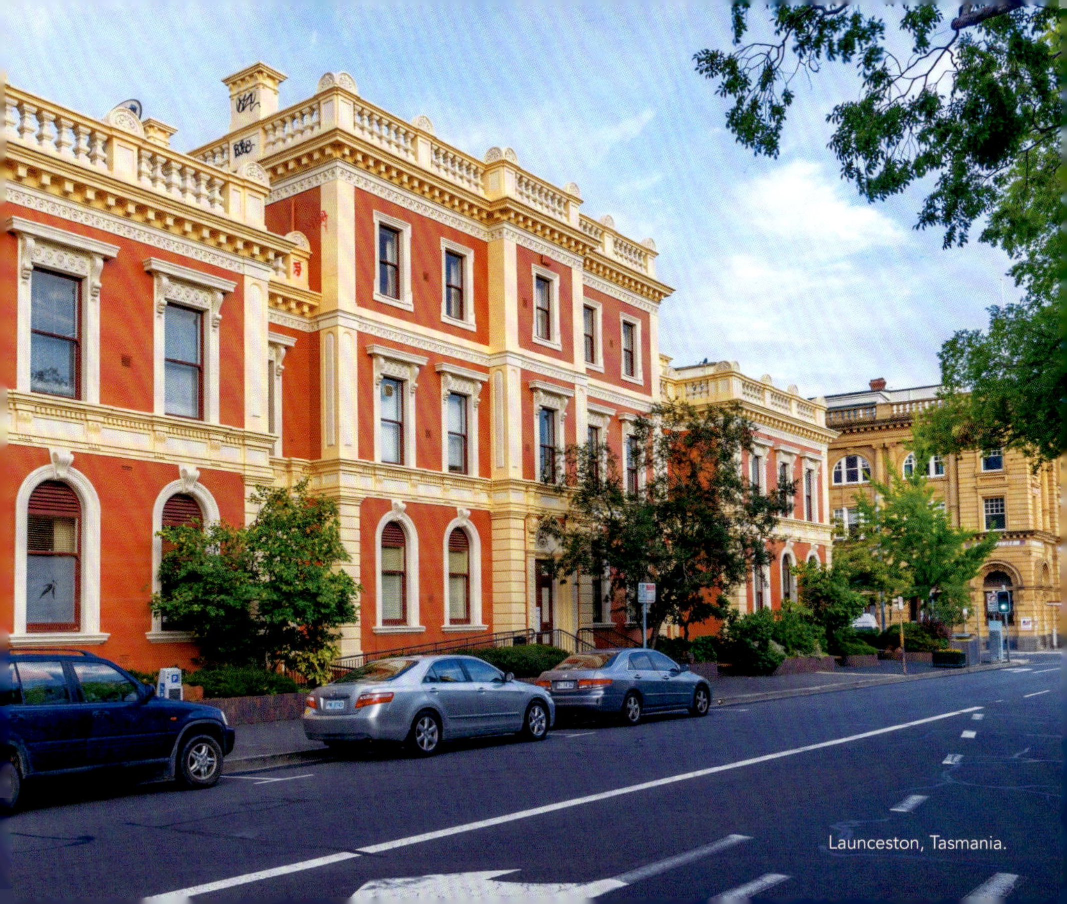
Launceston, Tasmania.

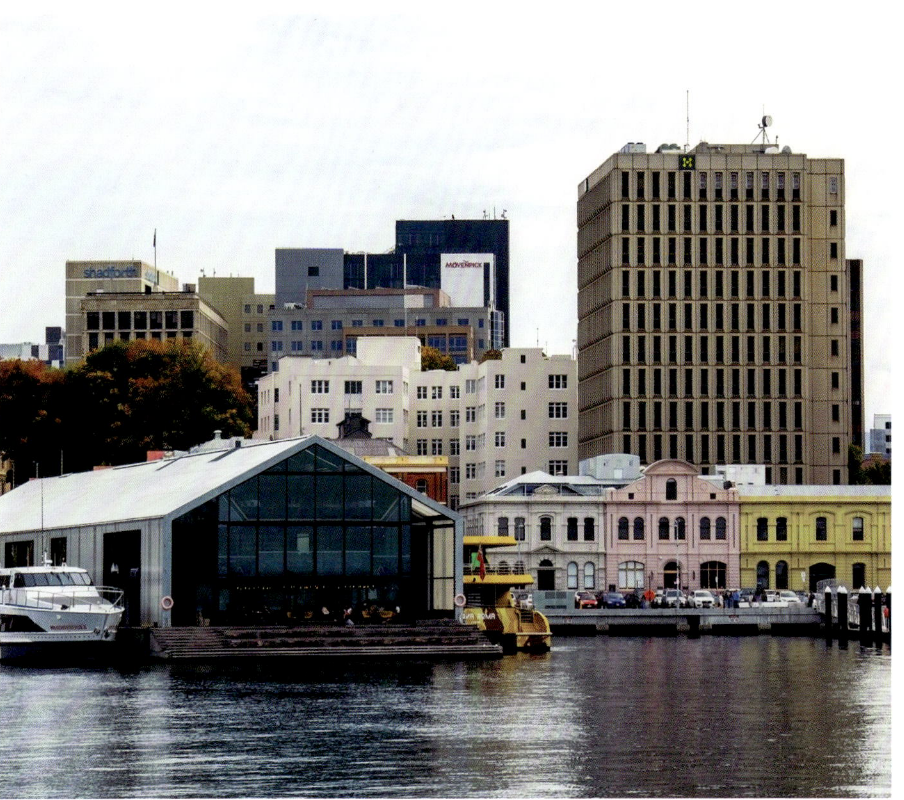

Hobart, Tasmania.

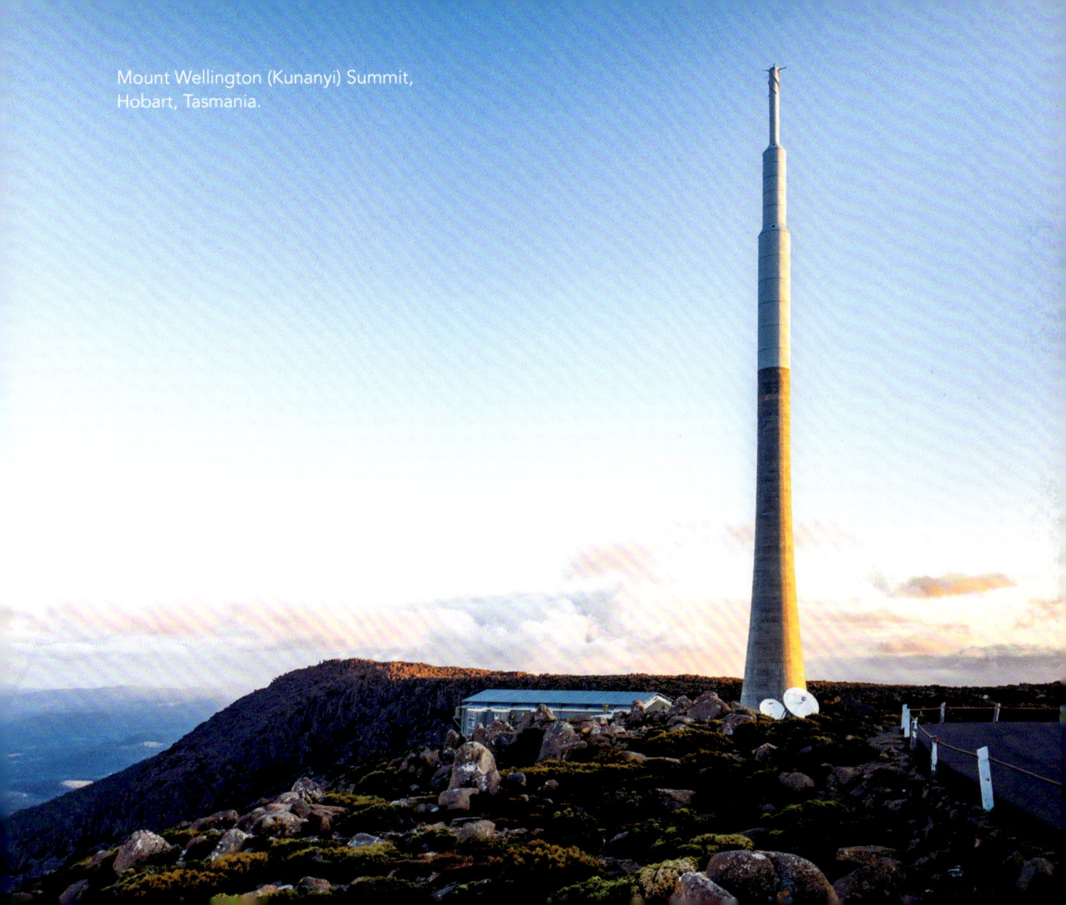
Mount Wellington (Kunanyi) Summit,
Hobart, Tasmania.

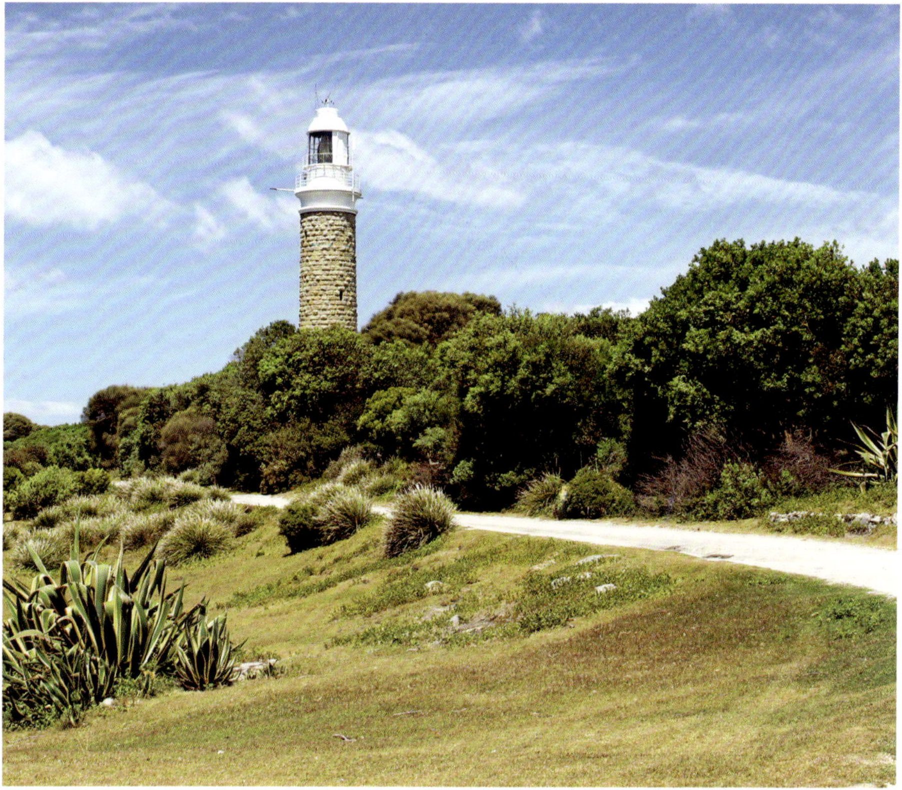

Eddystone Point Lighthouse, Tasmania.

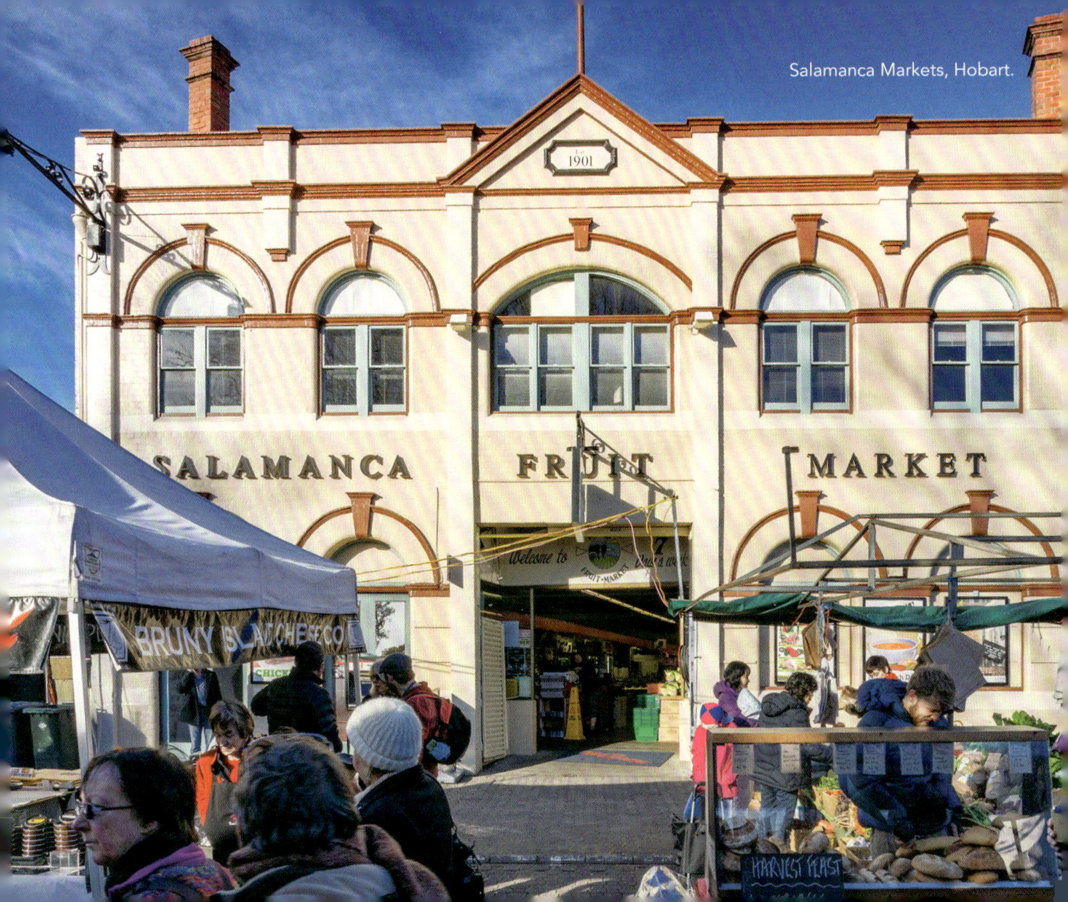

Salamanca Markets, Hobart.

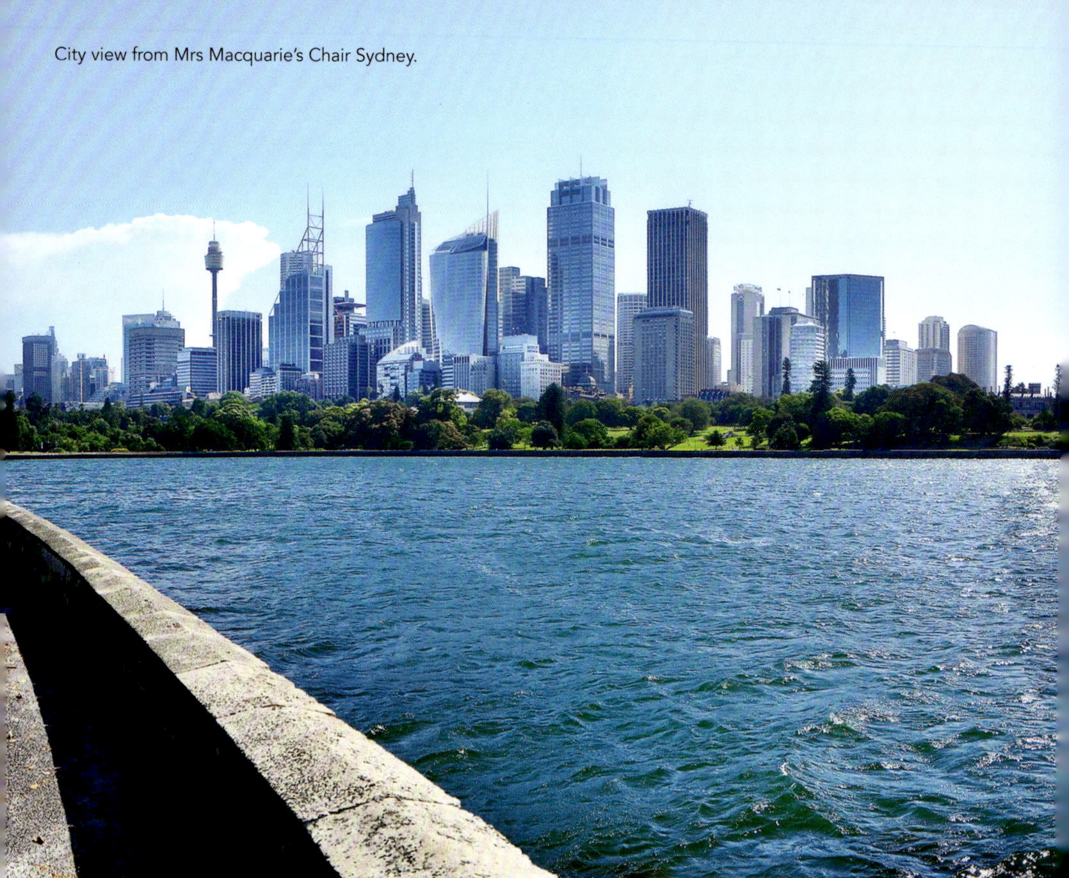

City view from Mrs Macquarie's Chair Sydney.

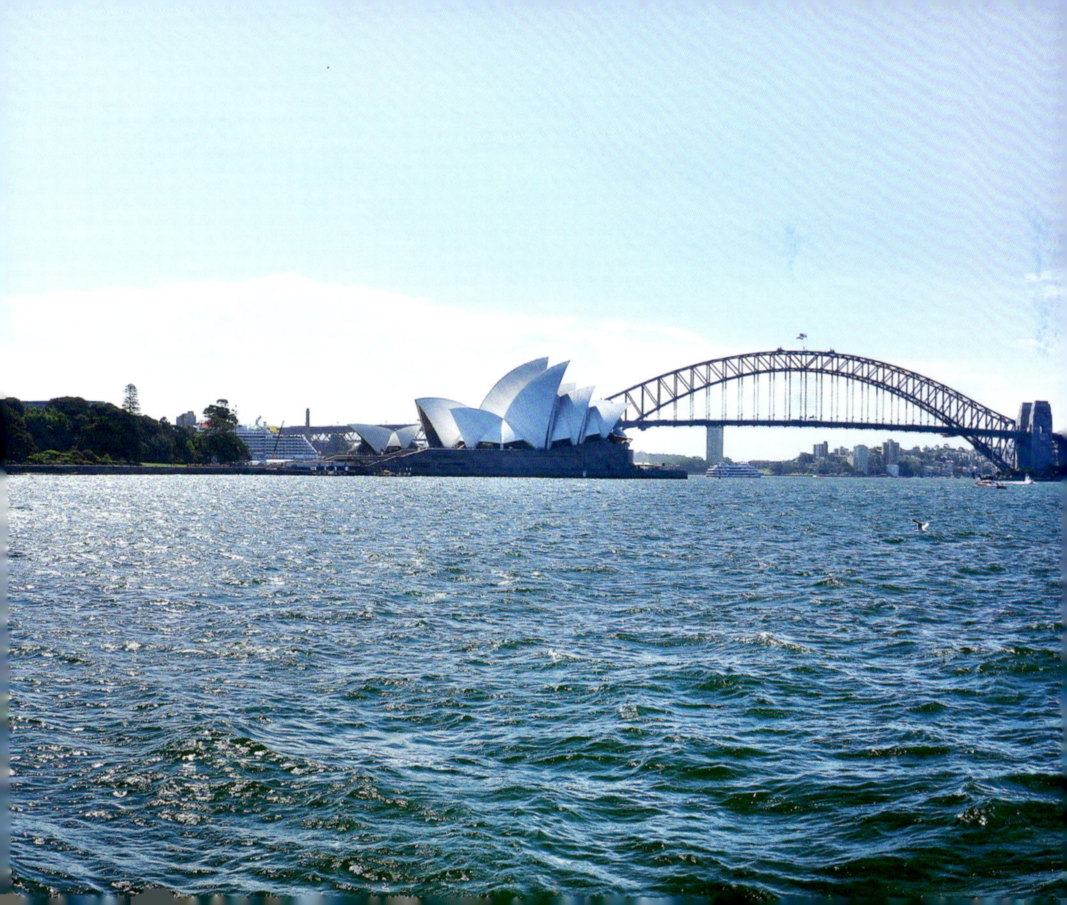

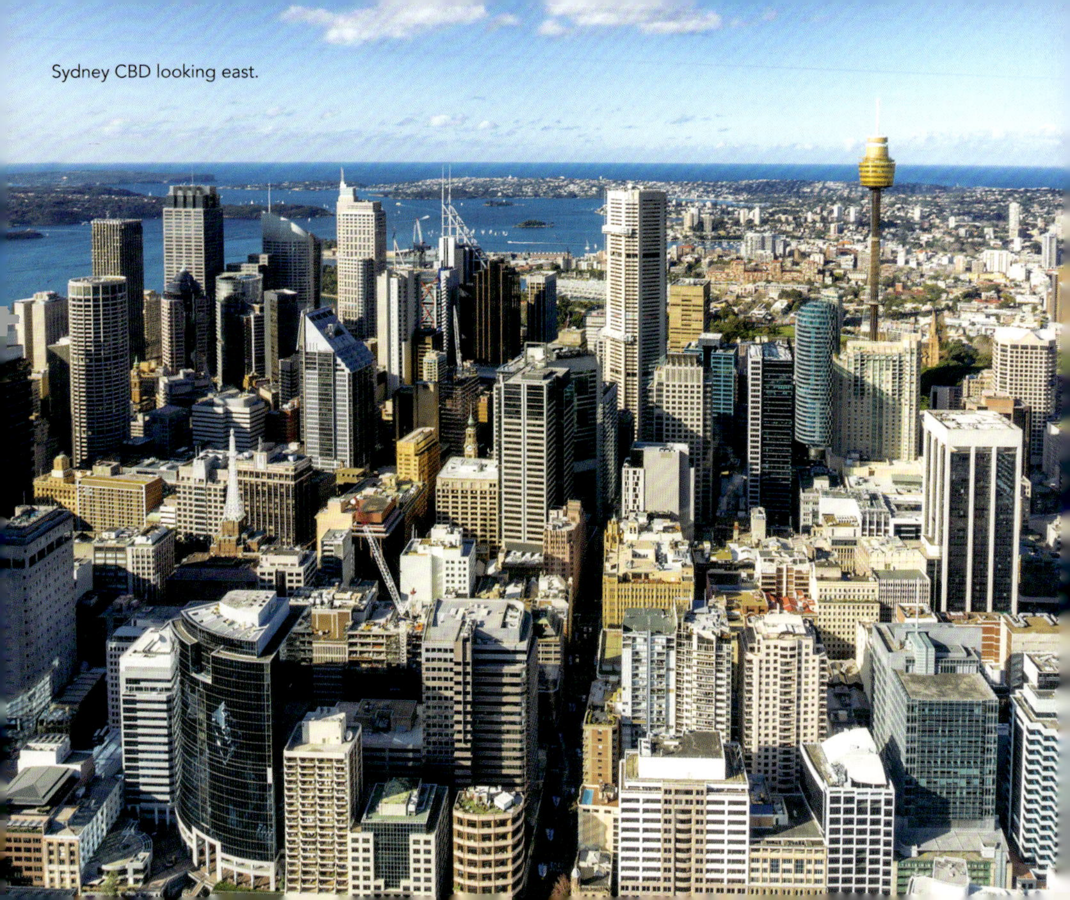

Sydney CBD looking east.

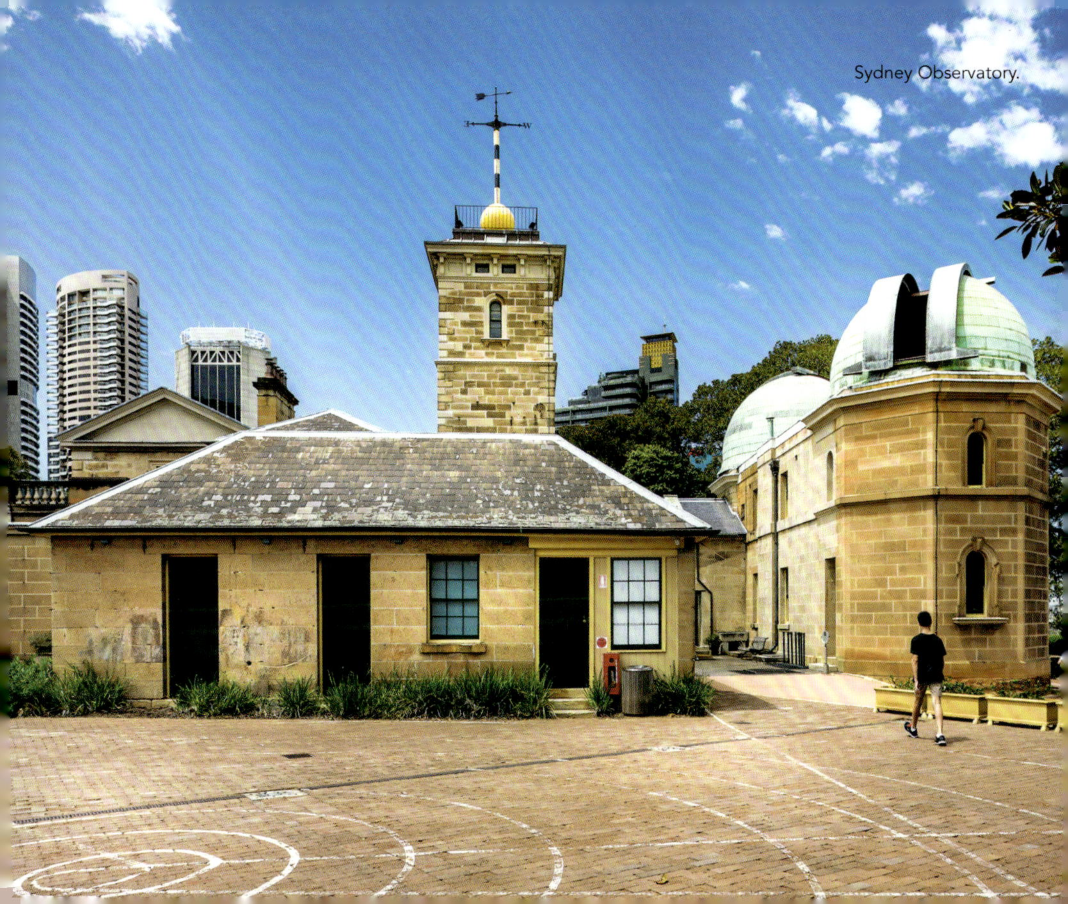

Sydney Observatory.

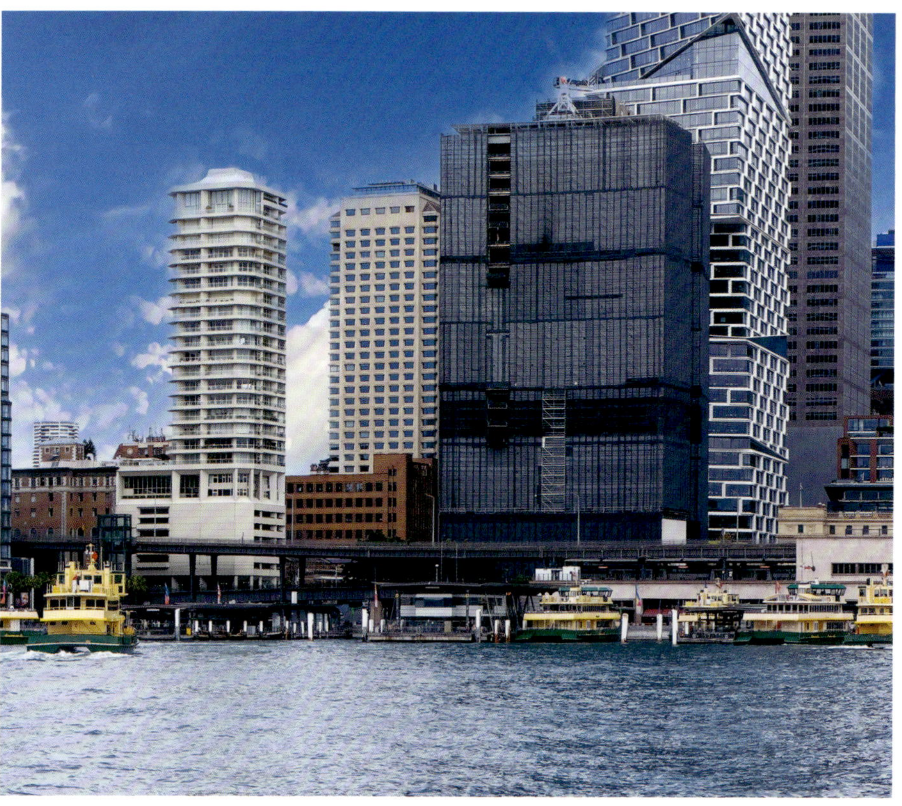

Circular Quay, Sydney.

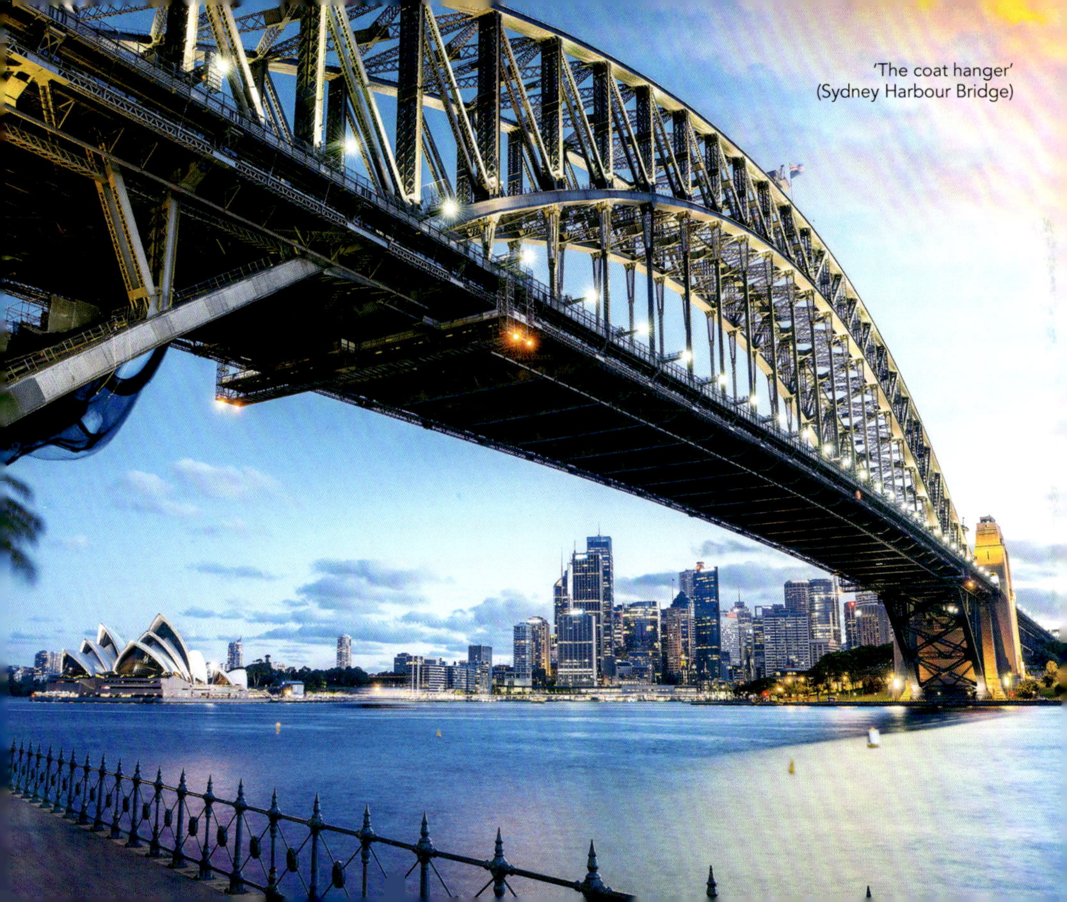

'The coat hanger'
(Sydney Harbour Bridge)

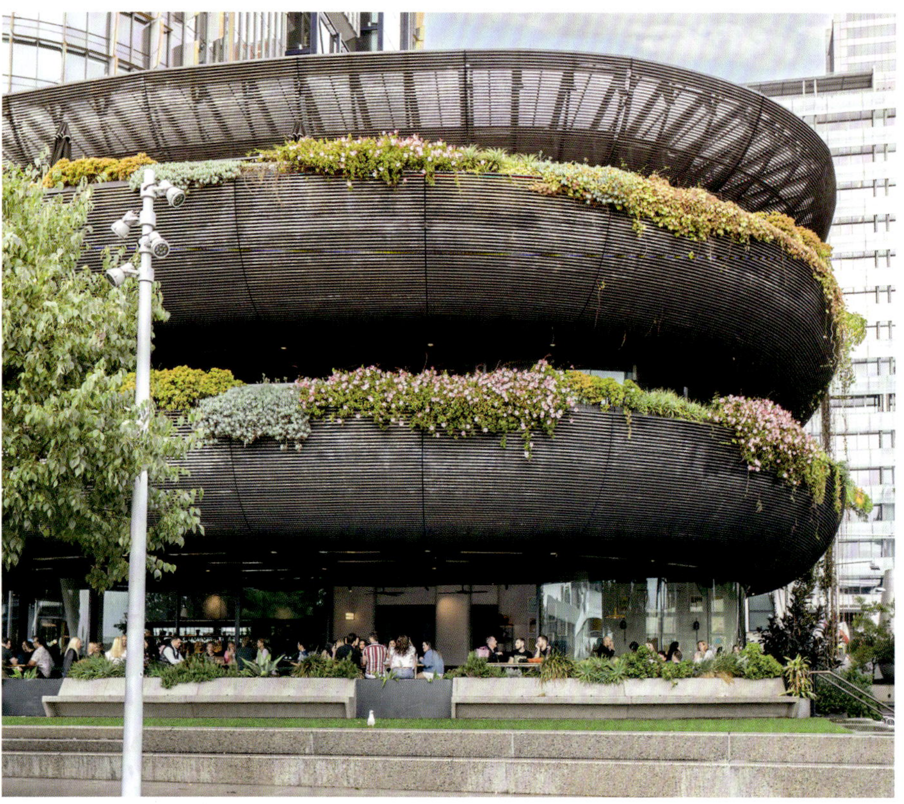

Barangaroo, Sydney.

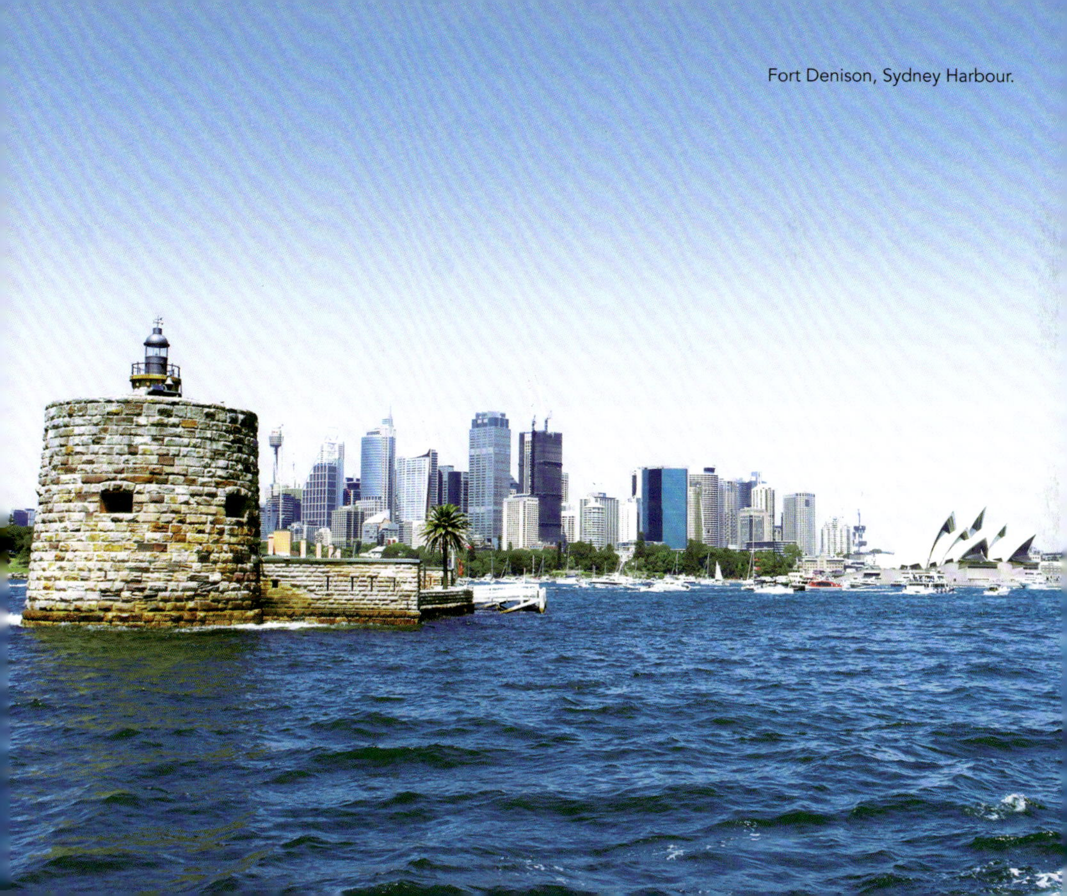

Fort Denison, Sydney Harbour.

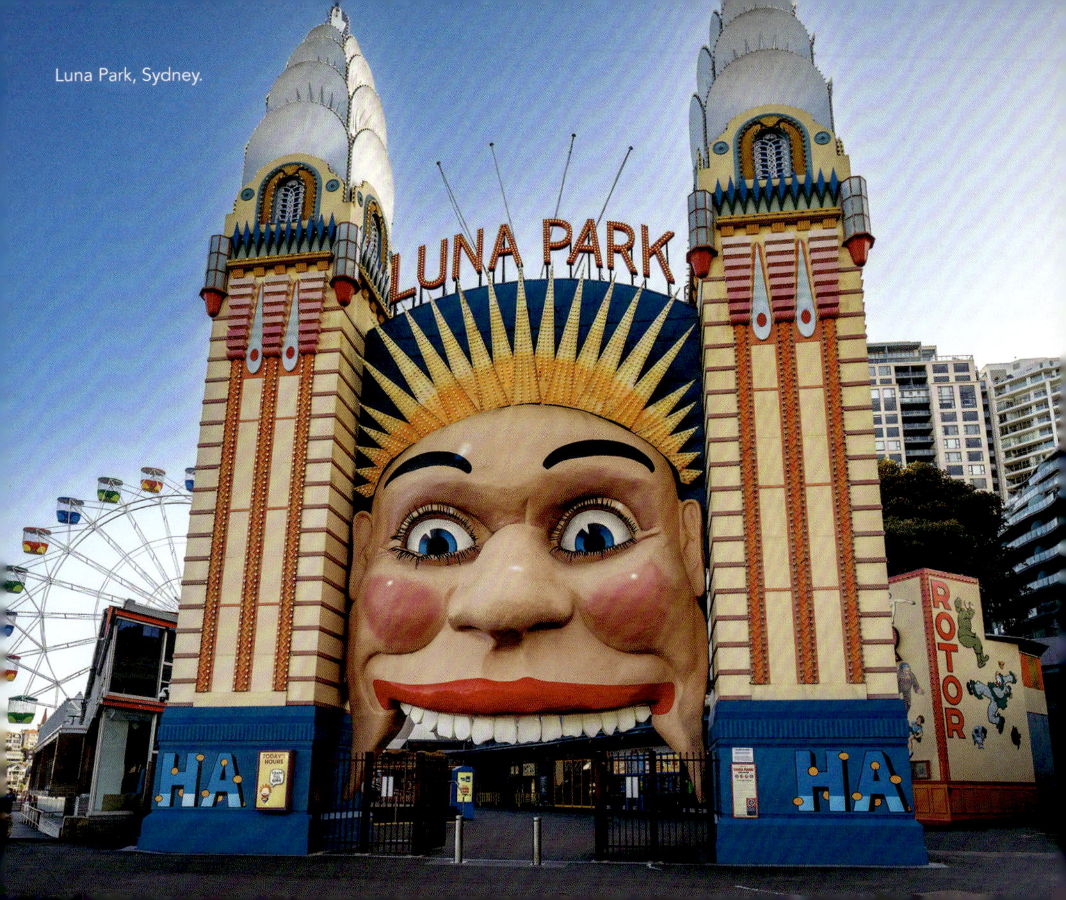

Luna Park, Sydney.

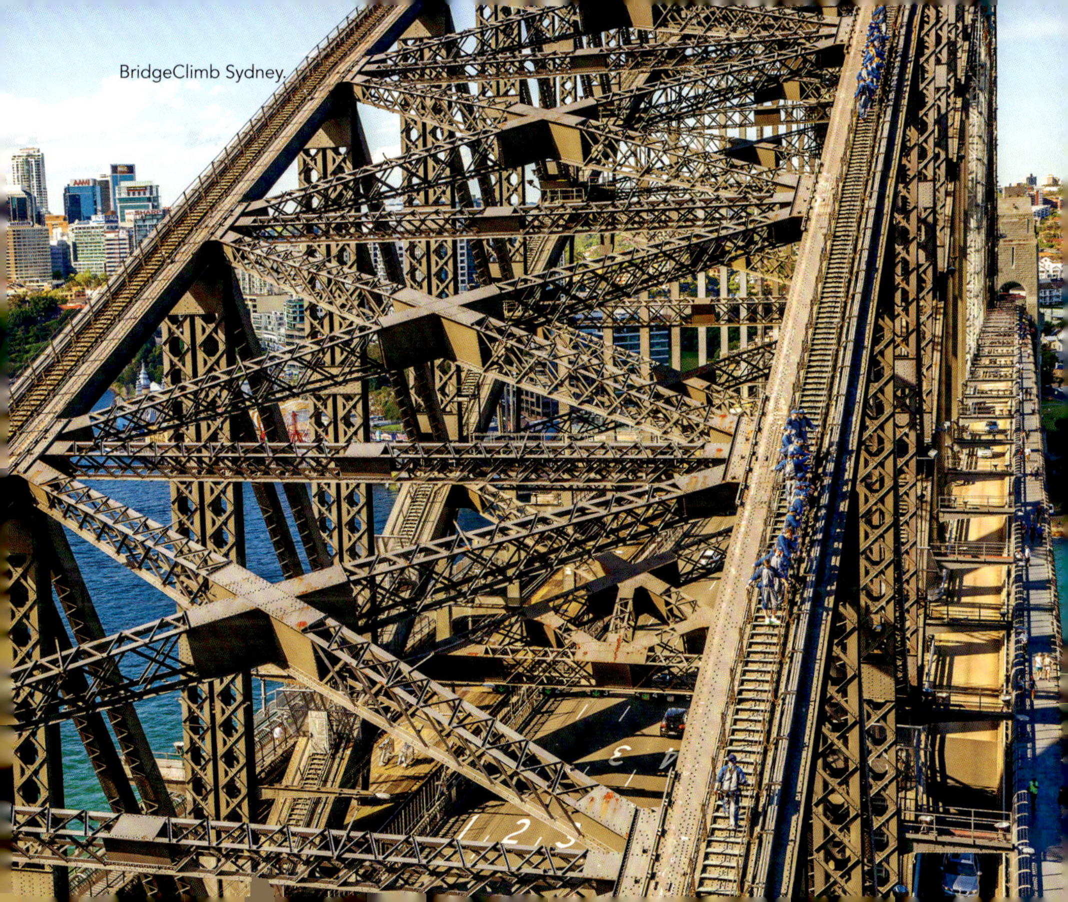

BridgeClimb Sydney.

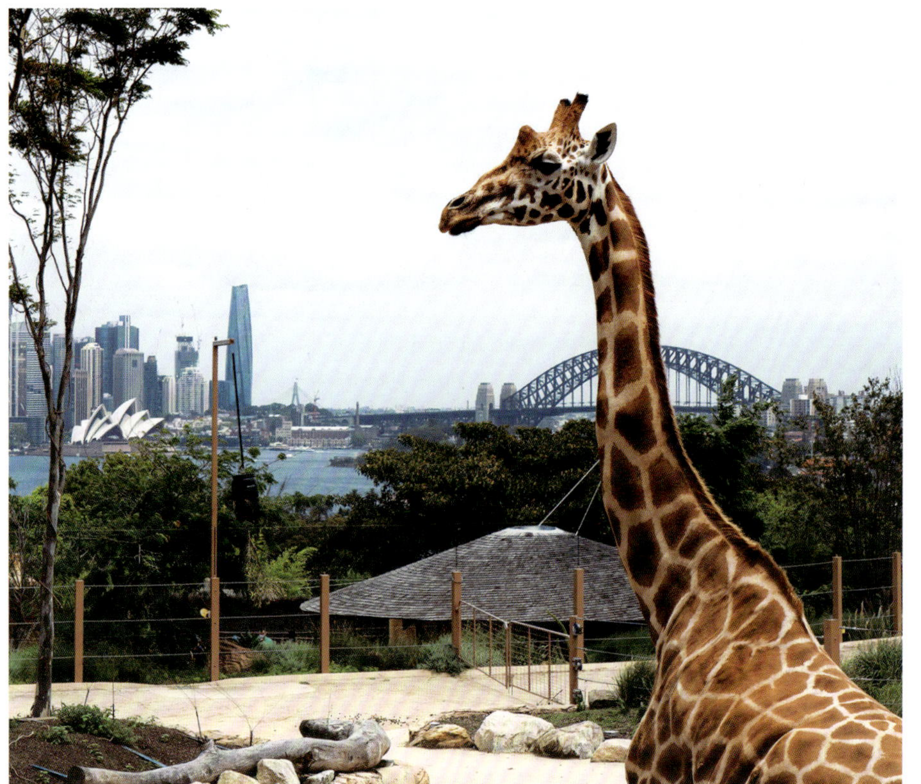

Taronga Zoo, Sydney.

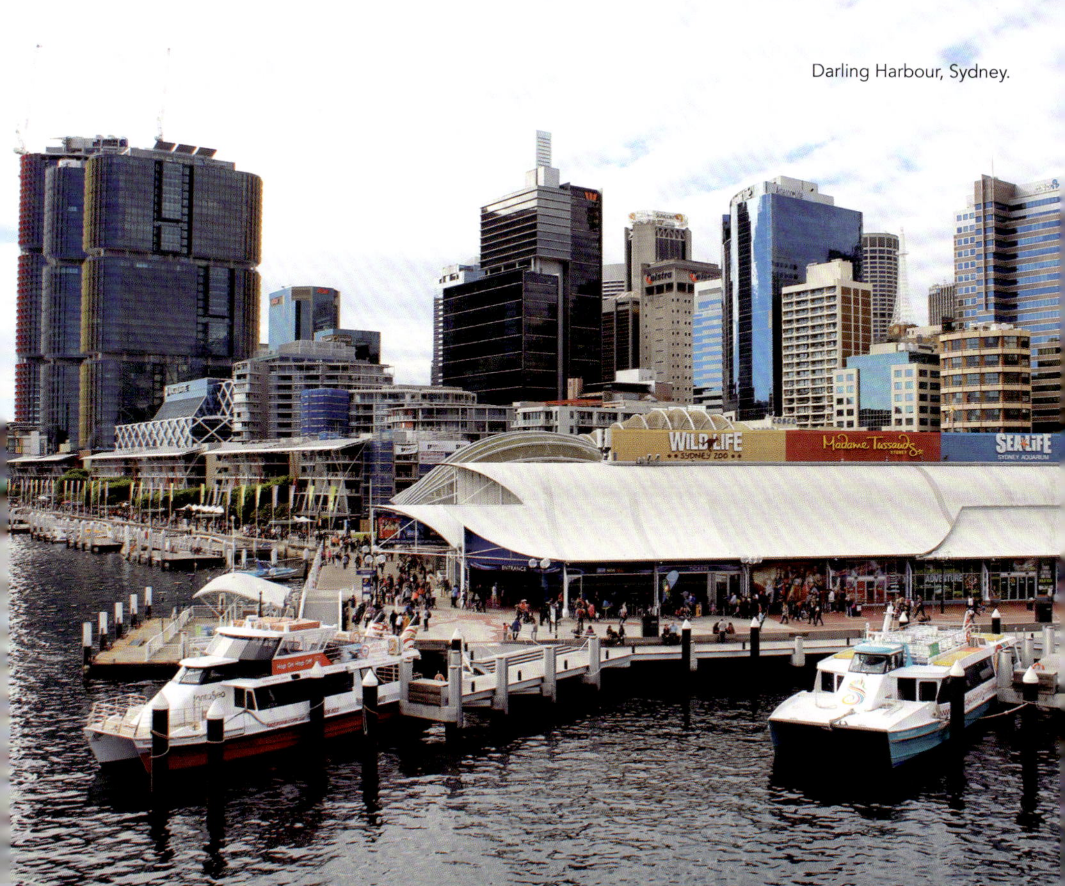

Darling Harbour, Sydney.

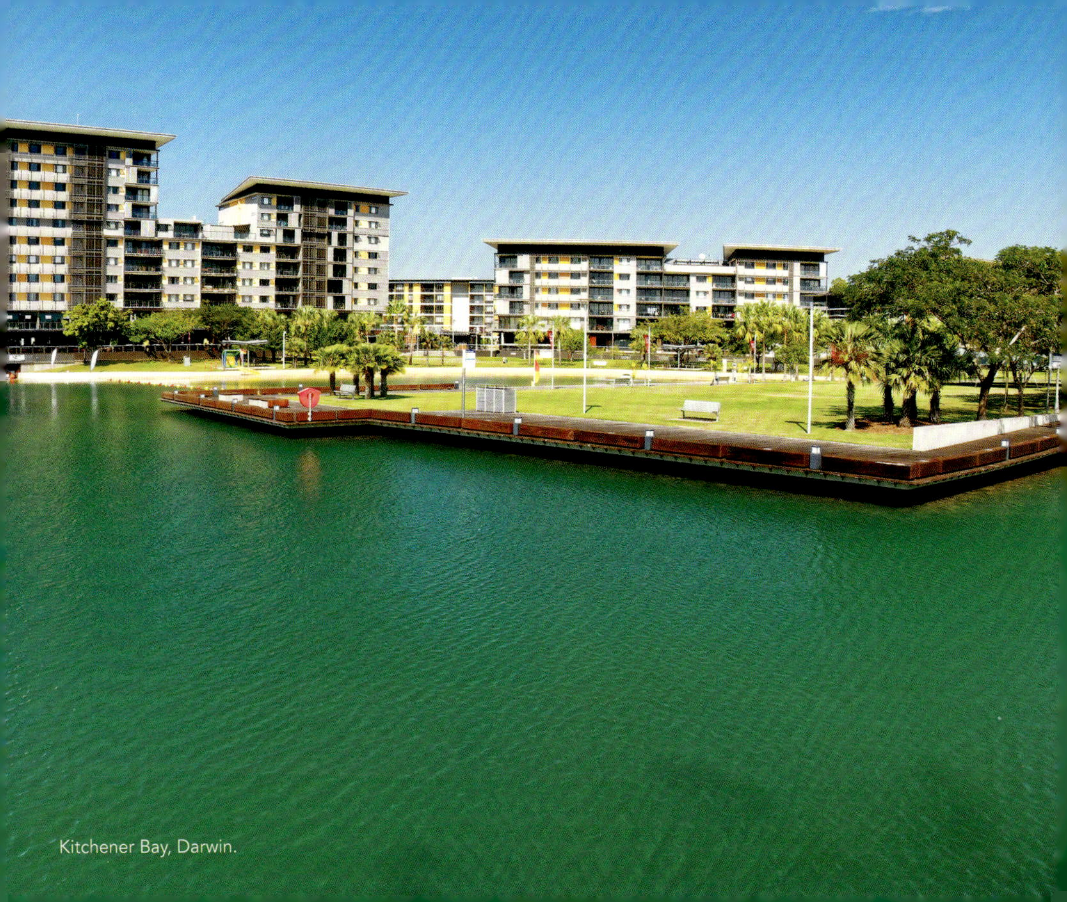

Kitchener Bay, Darwin.

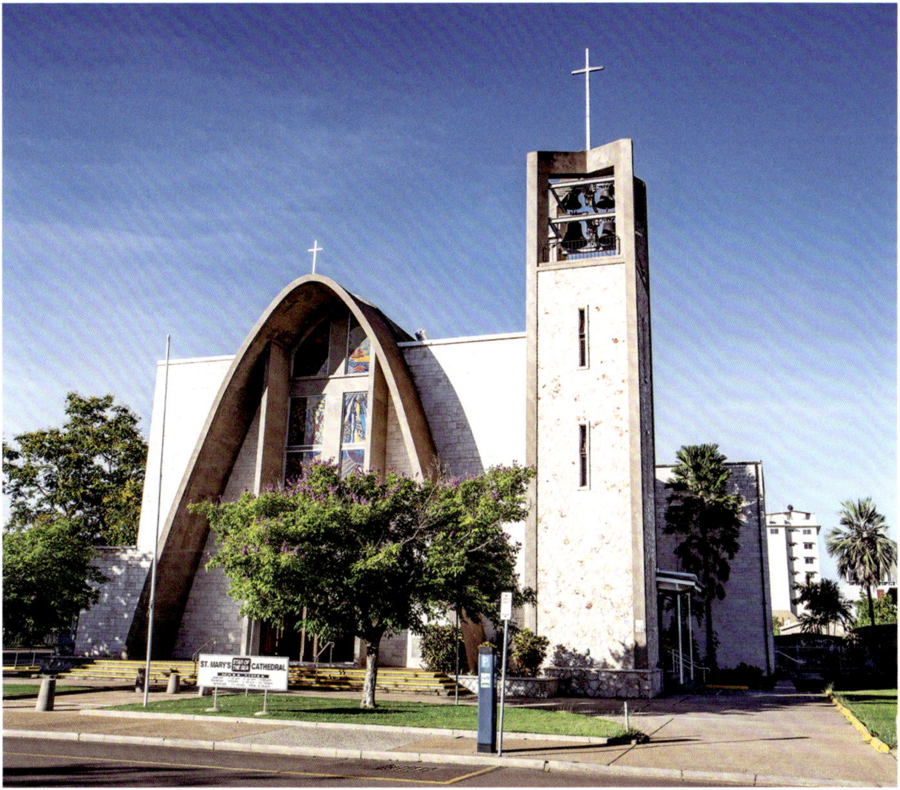

St Mary's Star of the Sea Cathedral, Darwin.

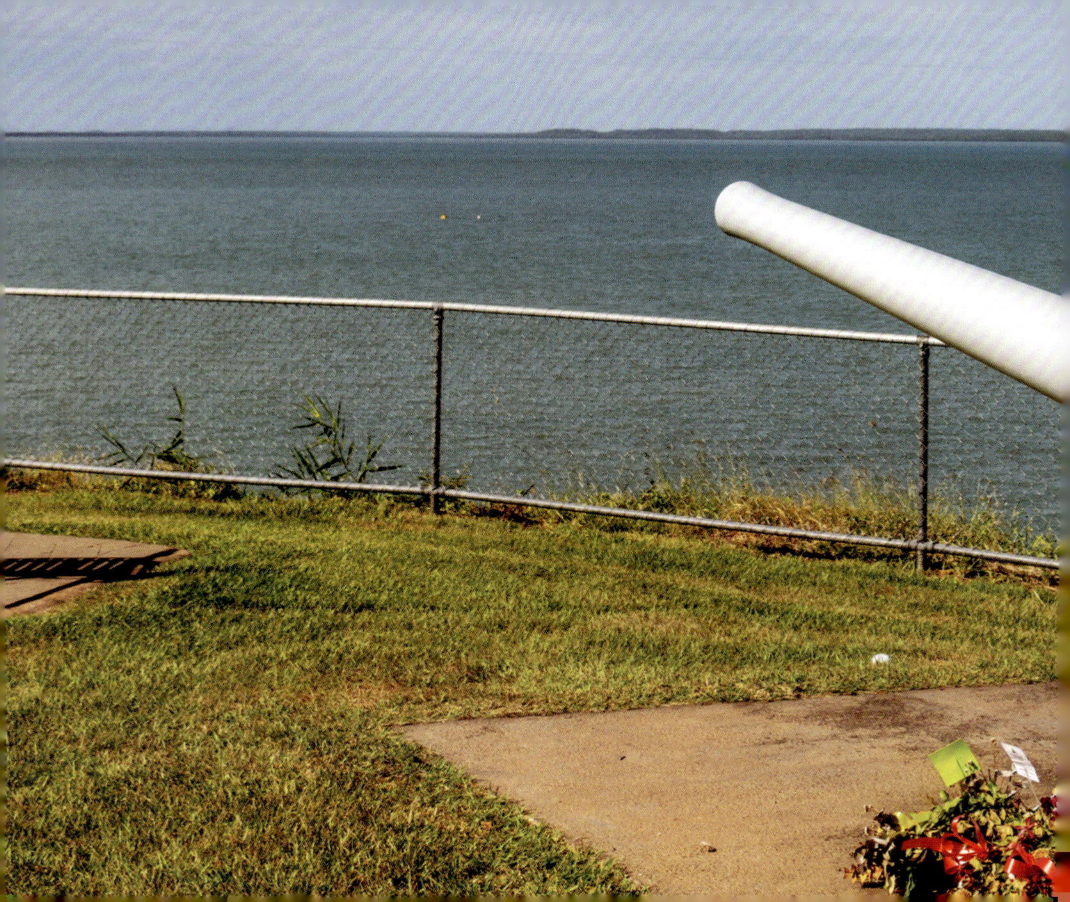

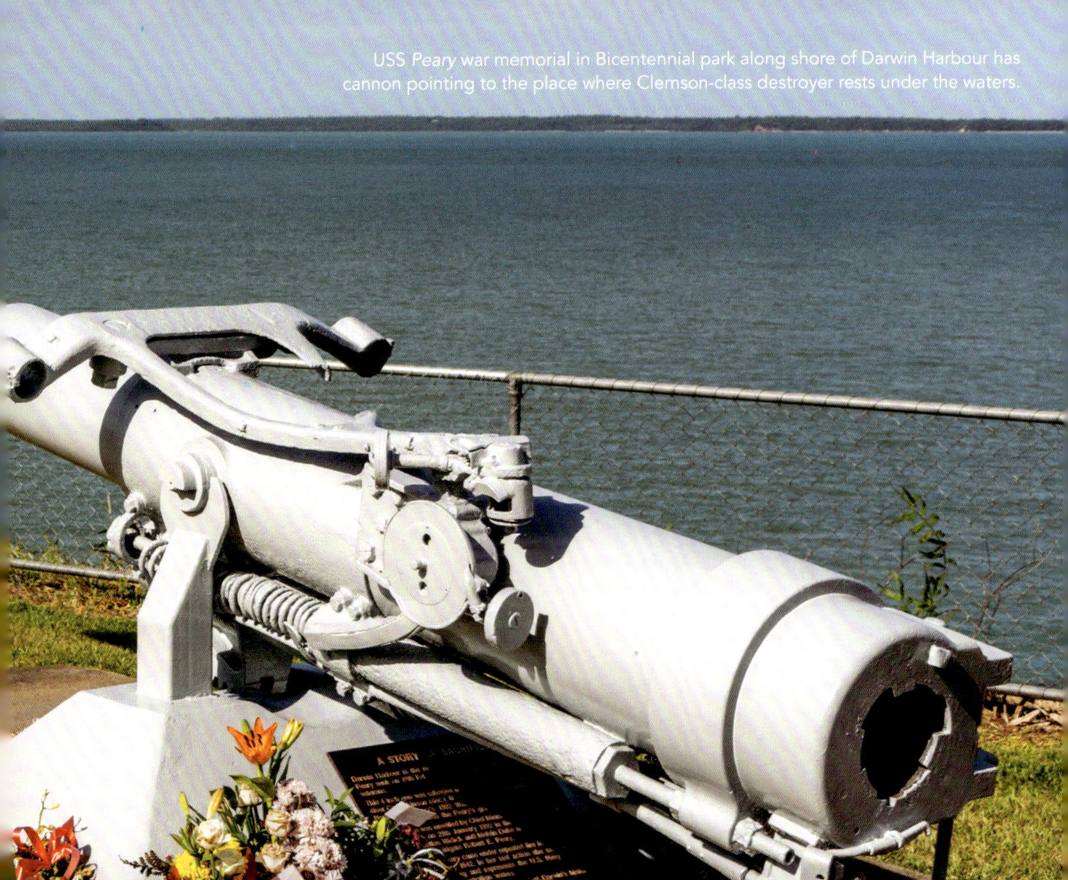

USS *Peary* war memorial in Bicentennial park along shore of Darwin Harbour has cannon pointing to the place where Clemson-class destroyer rests under the waters.

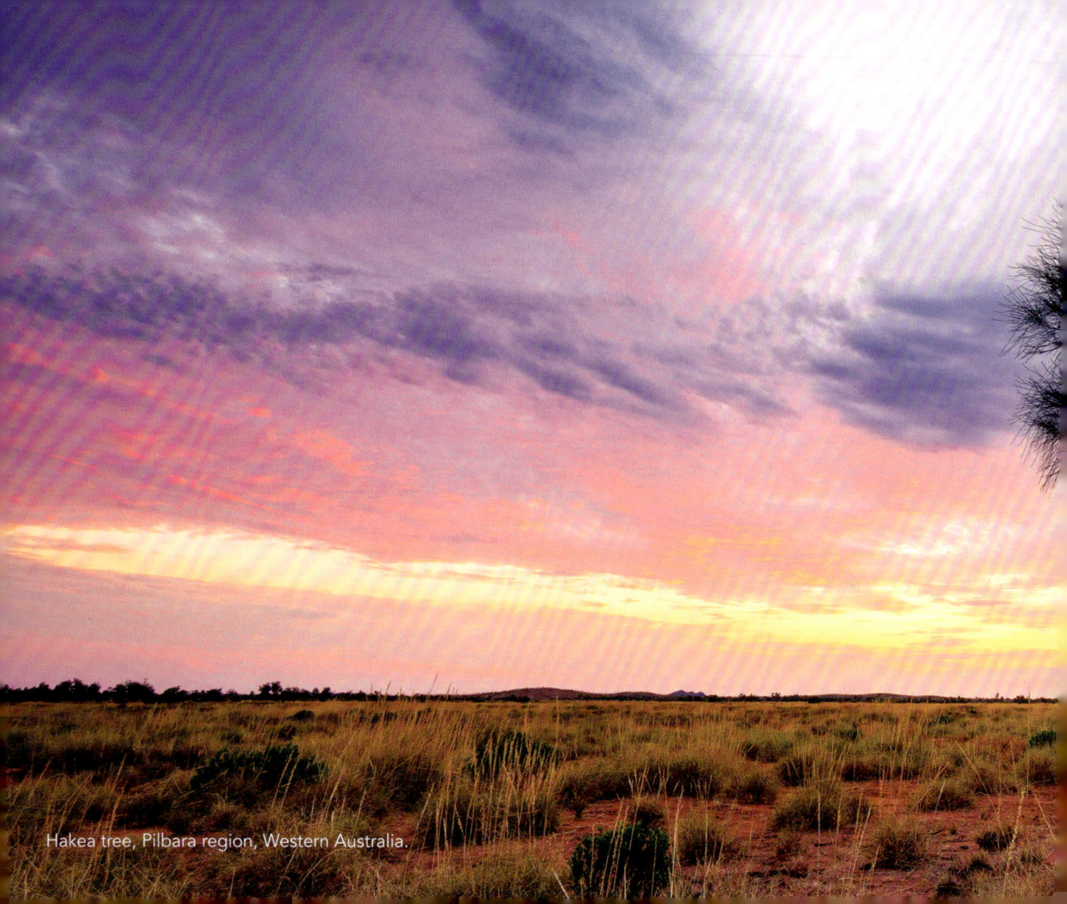

Hakea tree, Pilbara region, Western Australia.

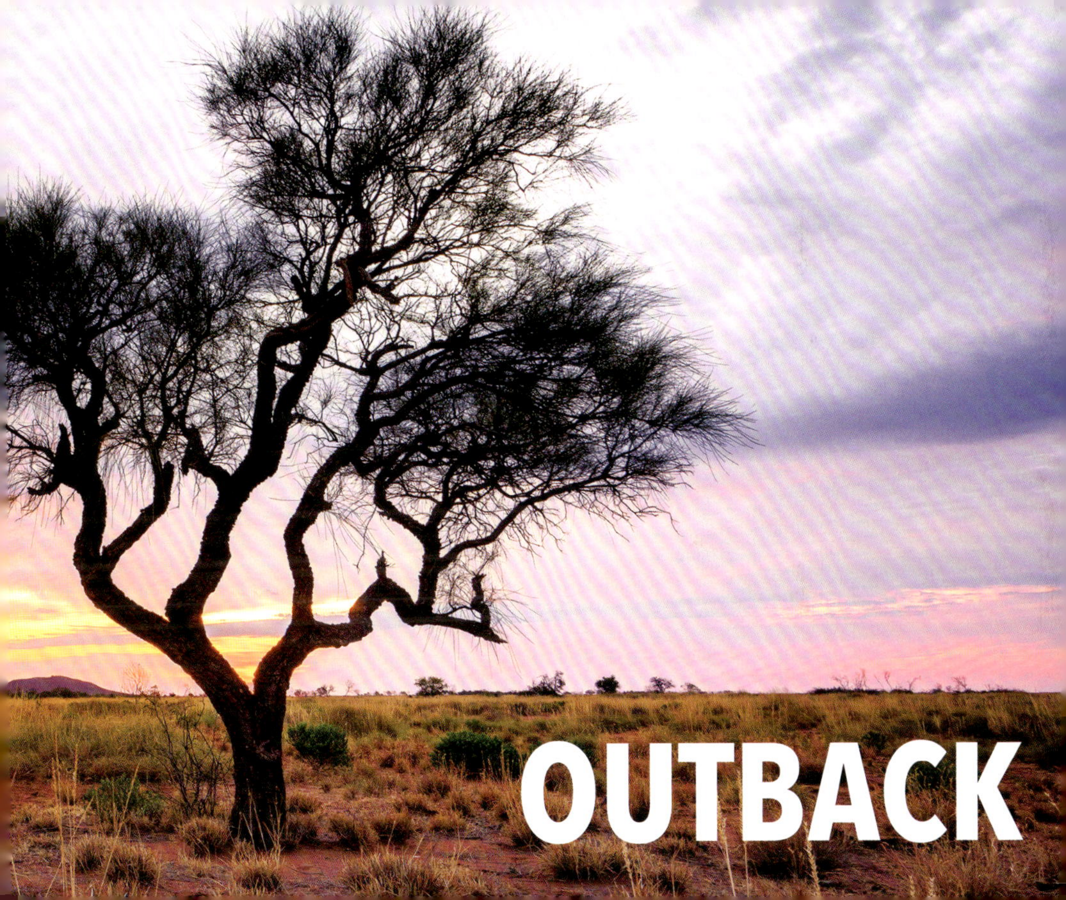
OUTBACK

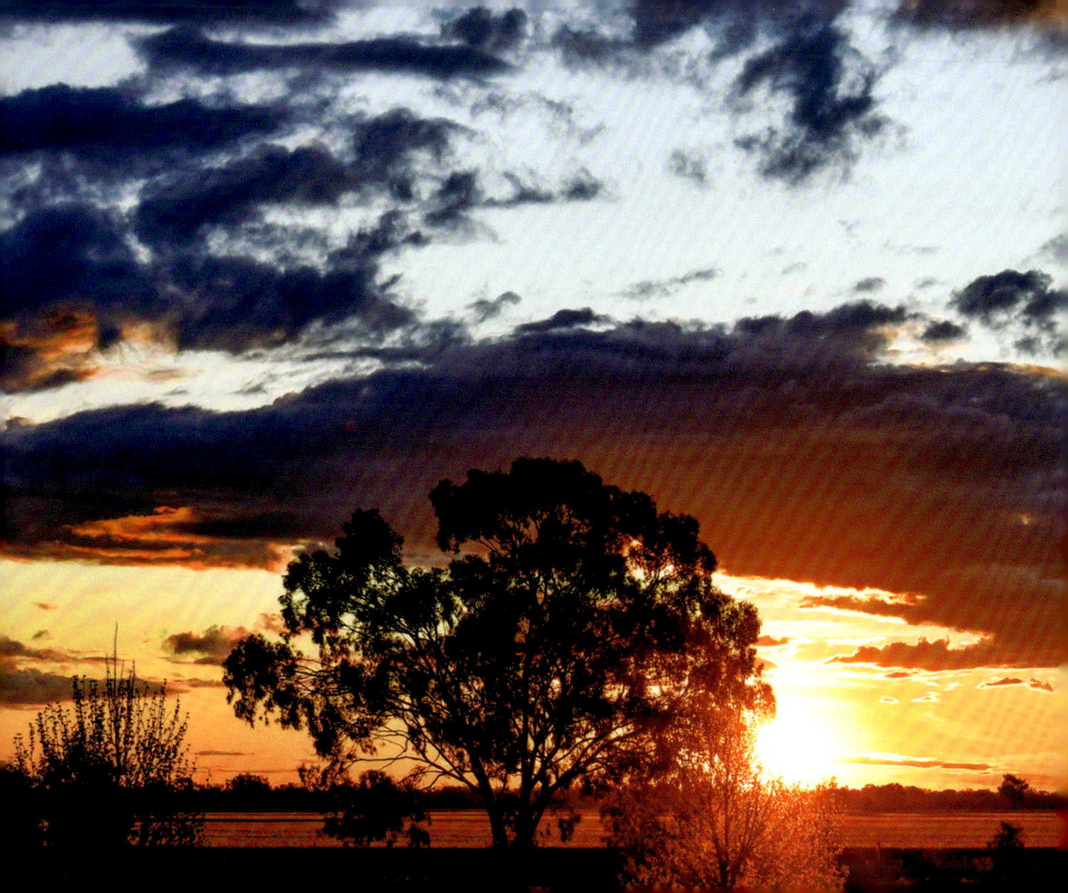

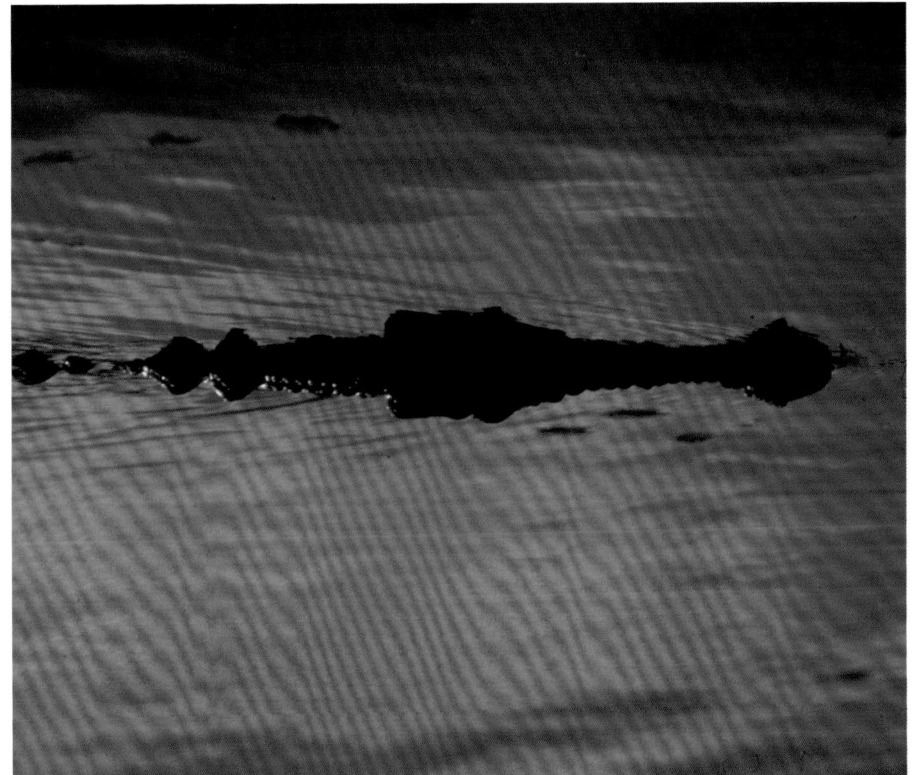

Crocodile.

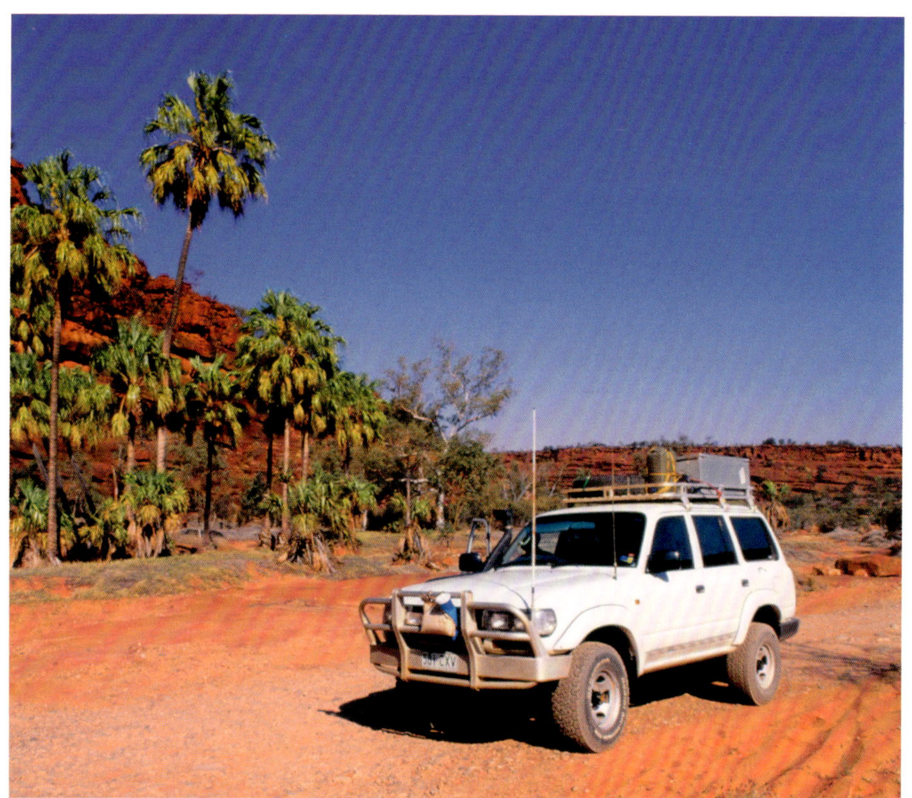

Finke Gorge National Park, Northern Territory.

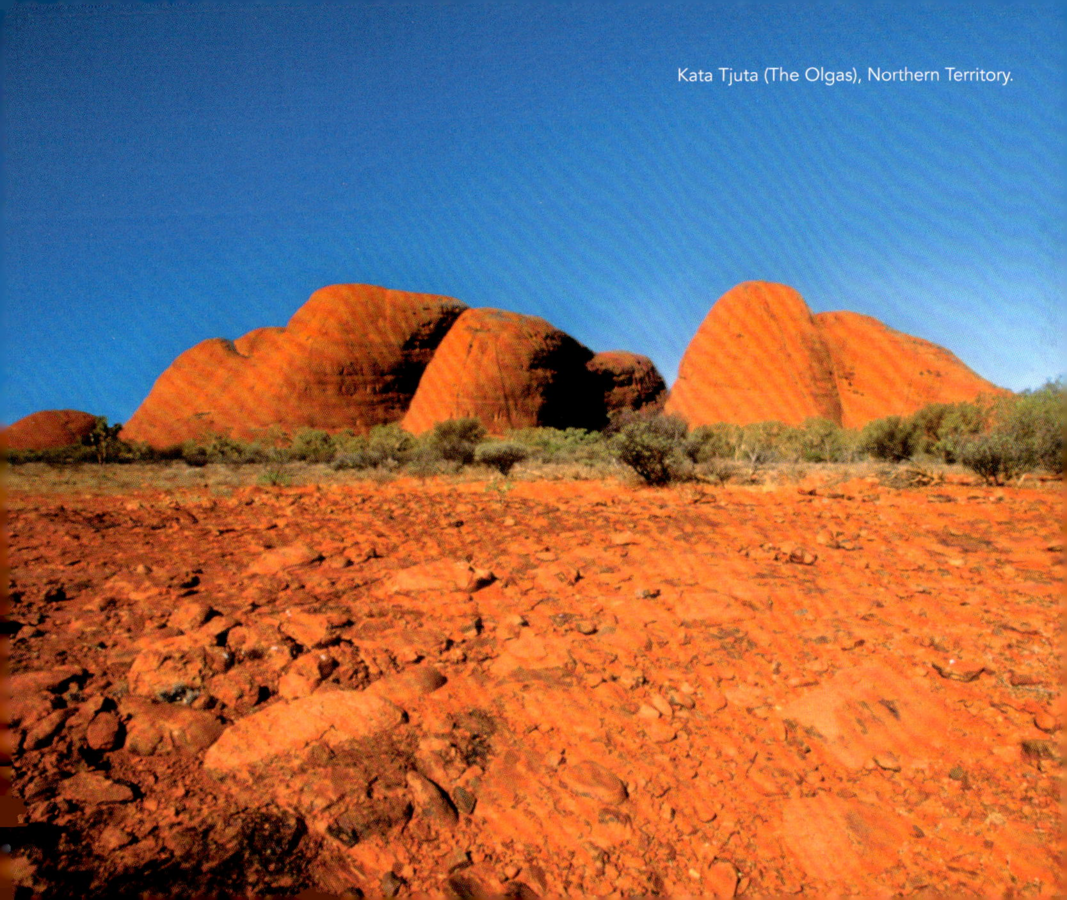

Kata Tjuta (The Olgas), Northern Territory.

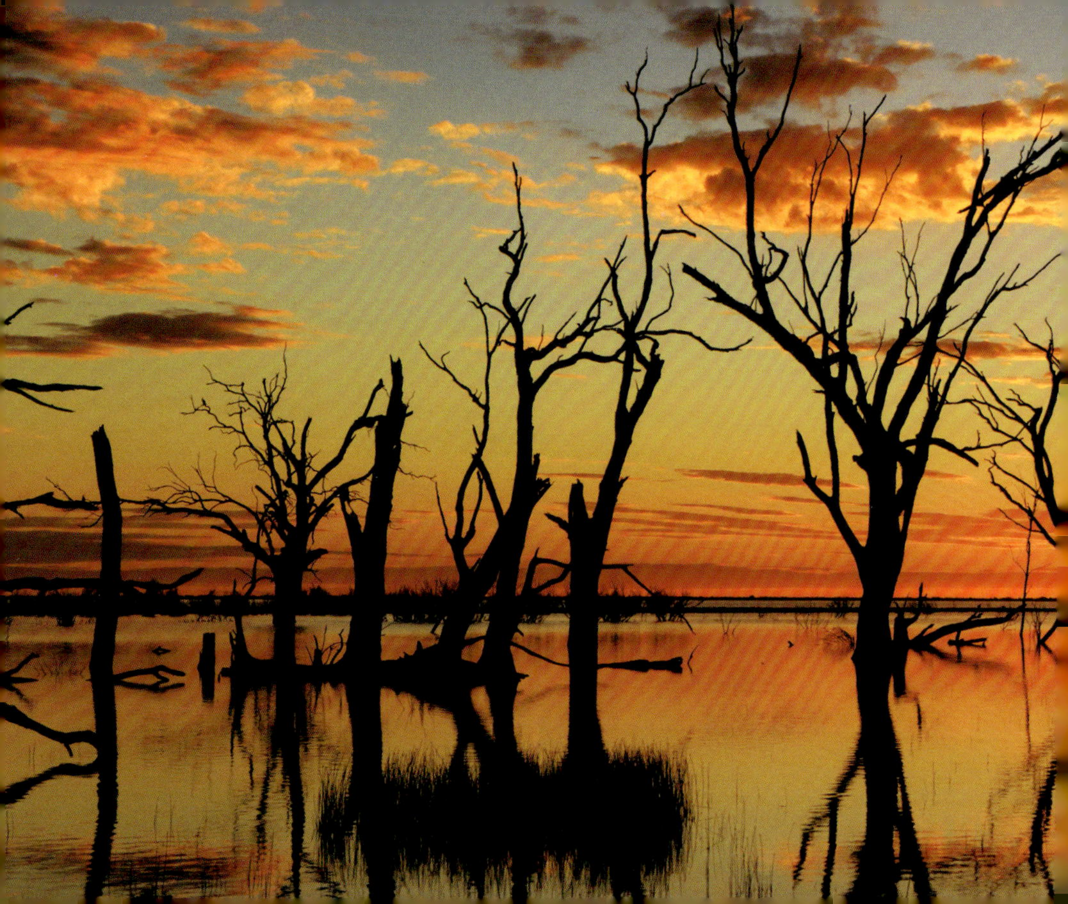

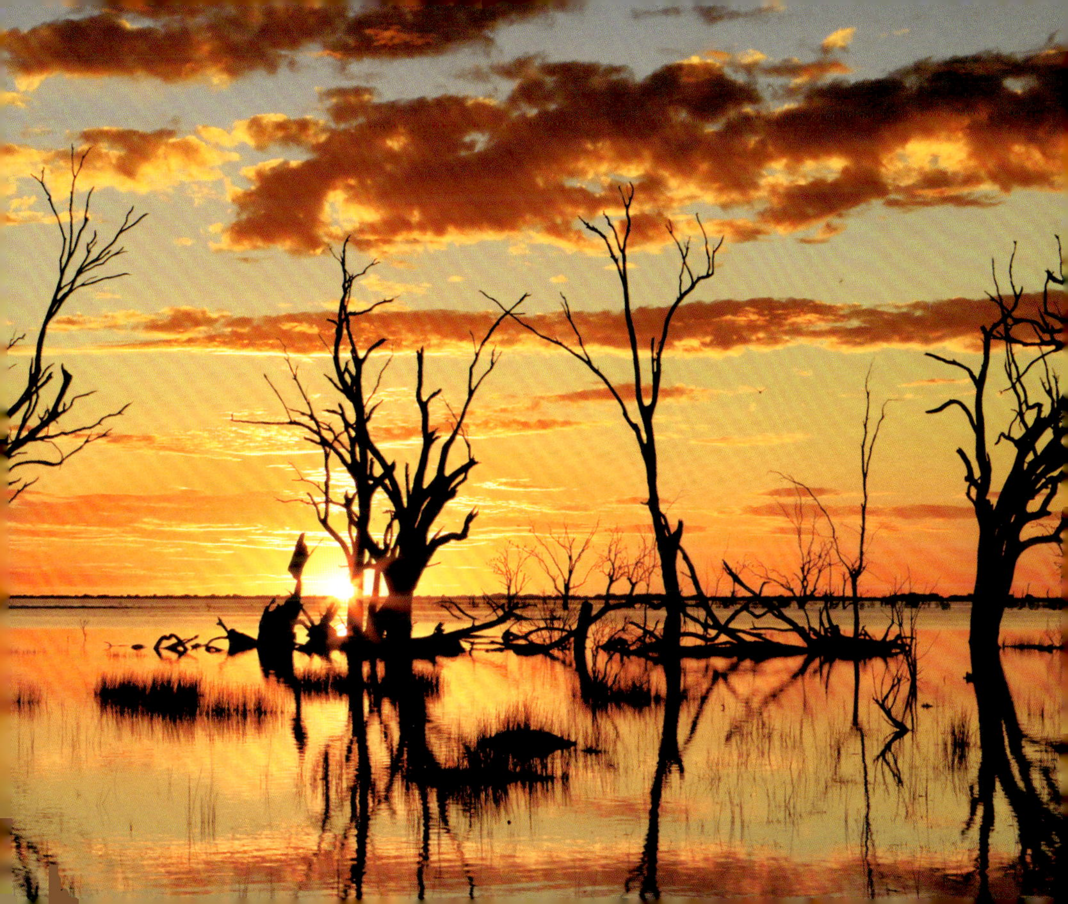

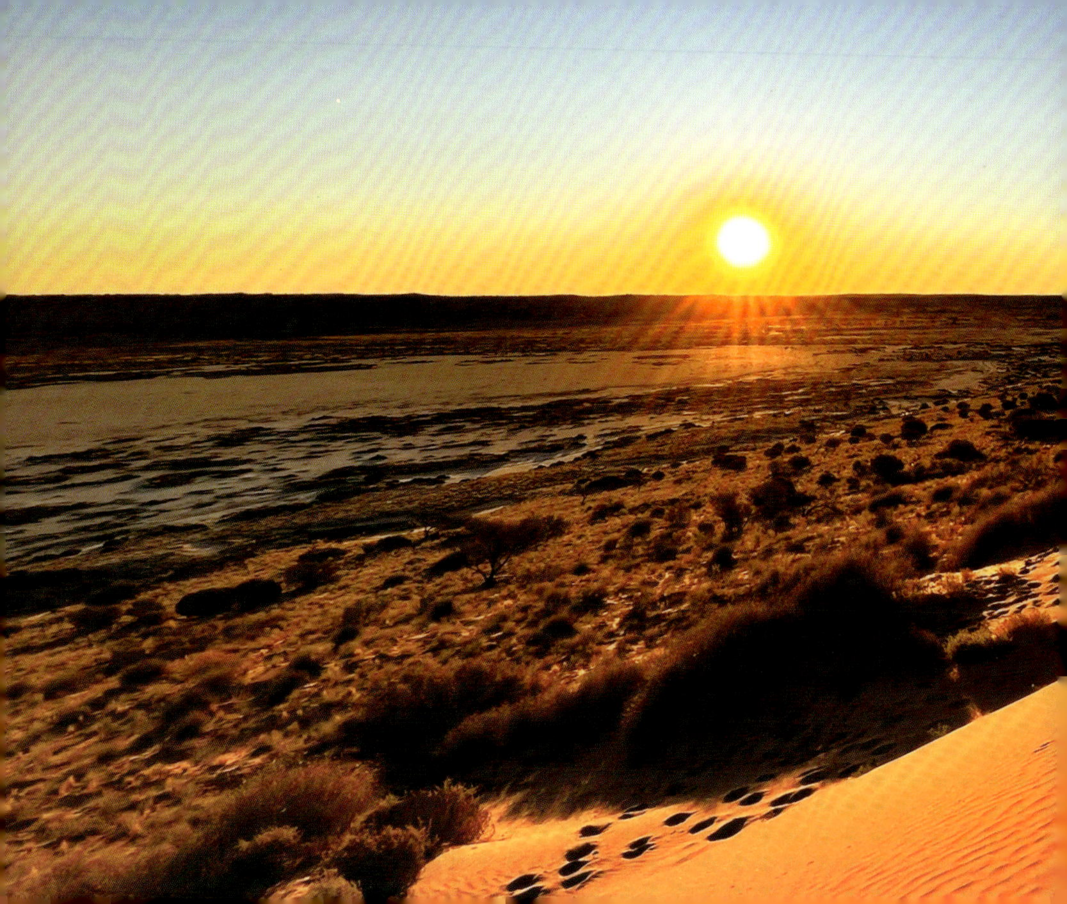

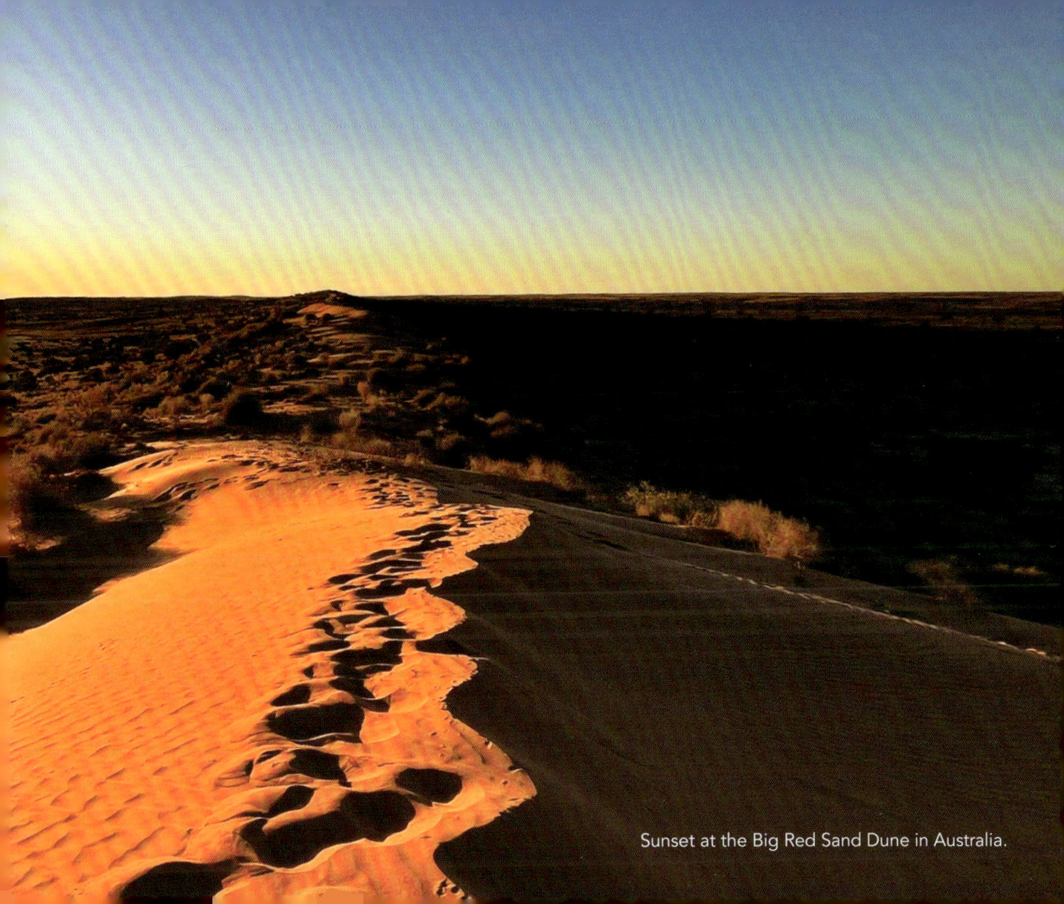

Sunset at the Big Red Sand Dune in Australia.

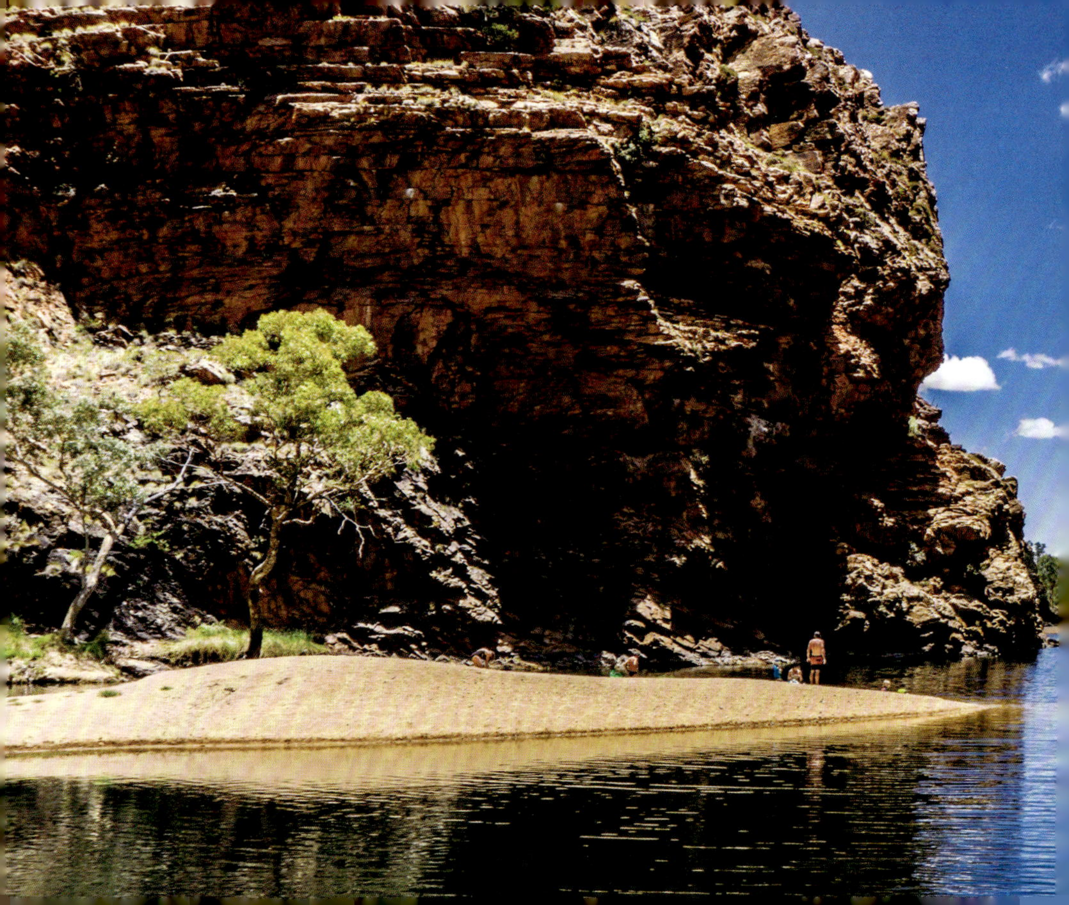

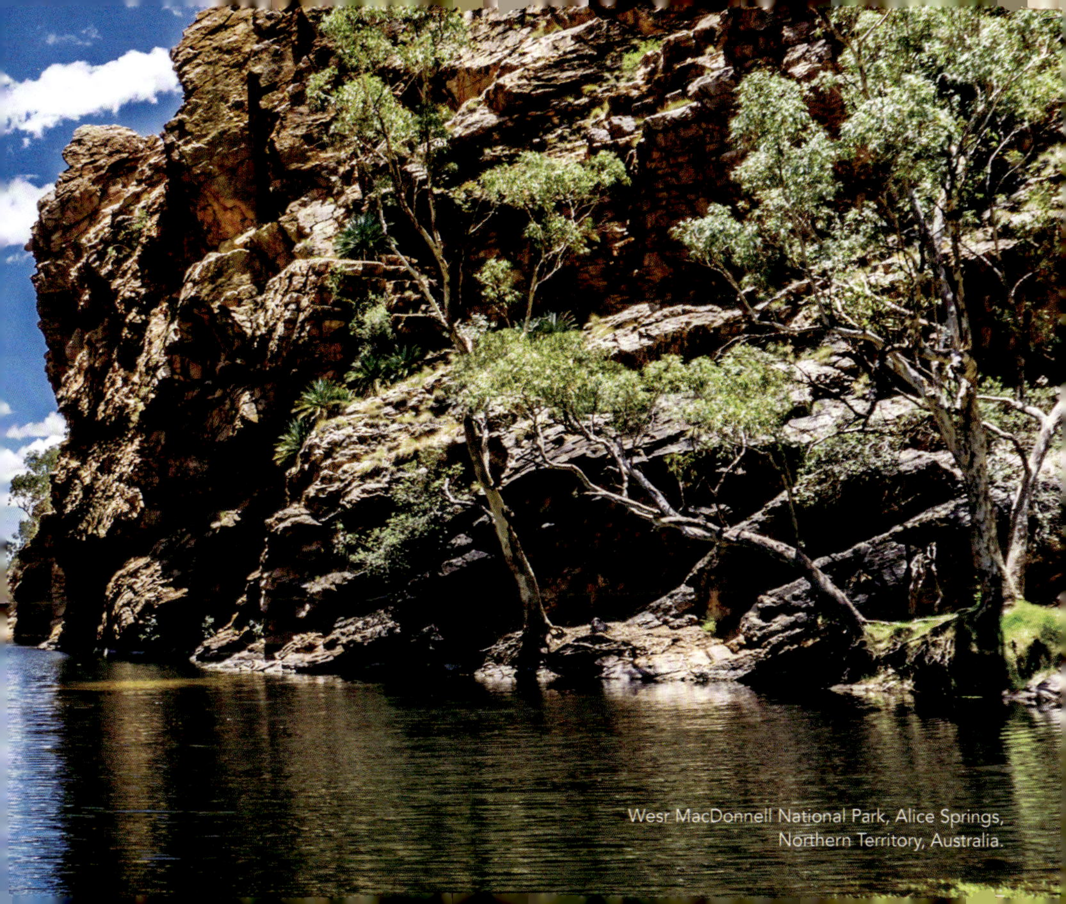

Wesr MacDonnell National Park, Alice Springs,
Northern Territory, Australia.

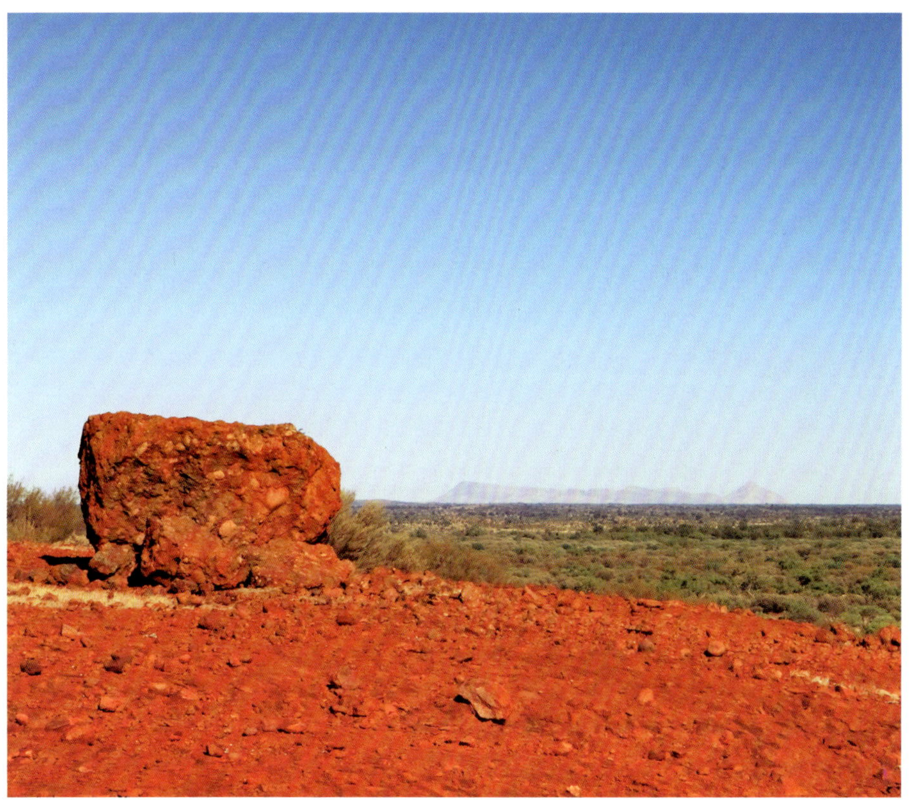

Glen Maggie Homestead, Northern Territory.

Yardie Creek Gorge, Exmouth.

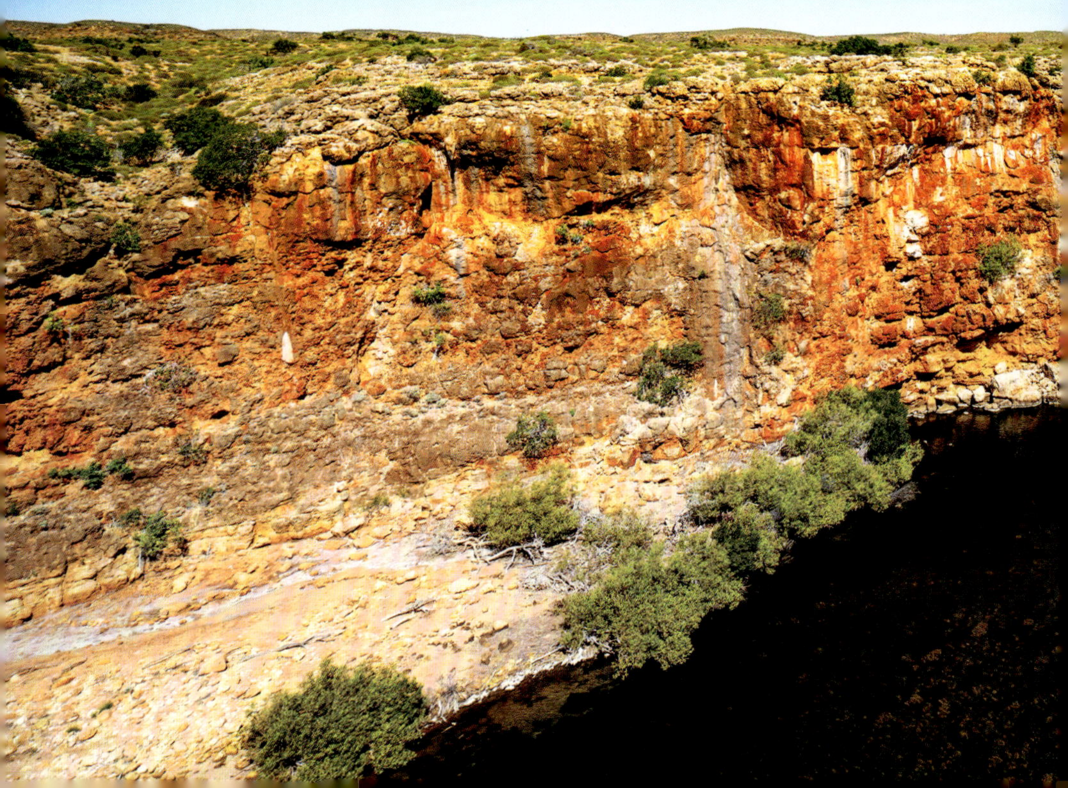

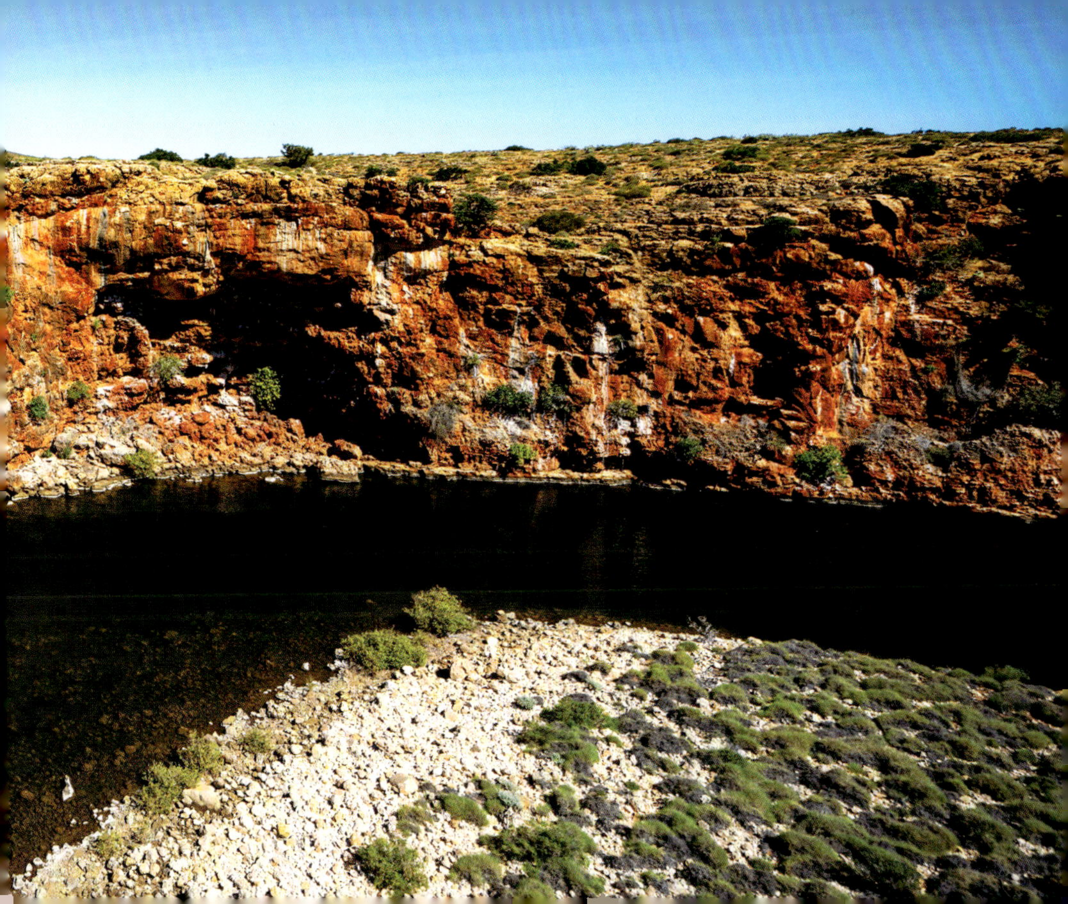

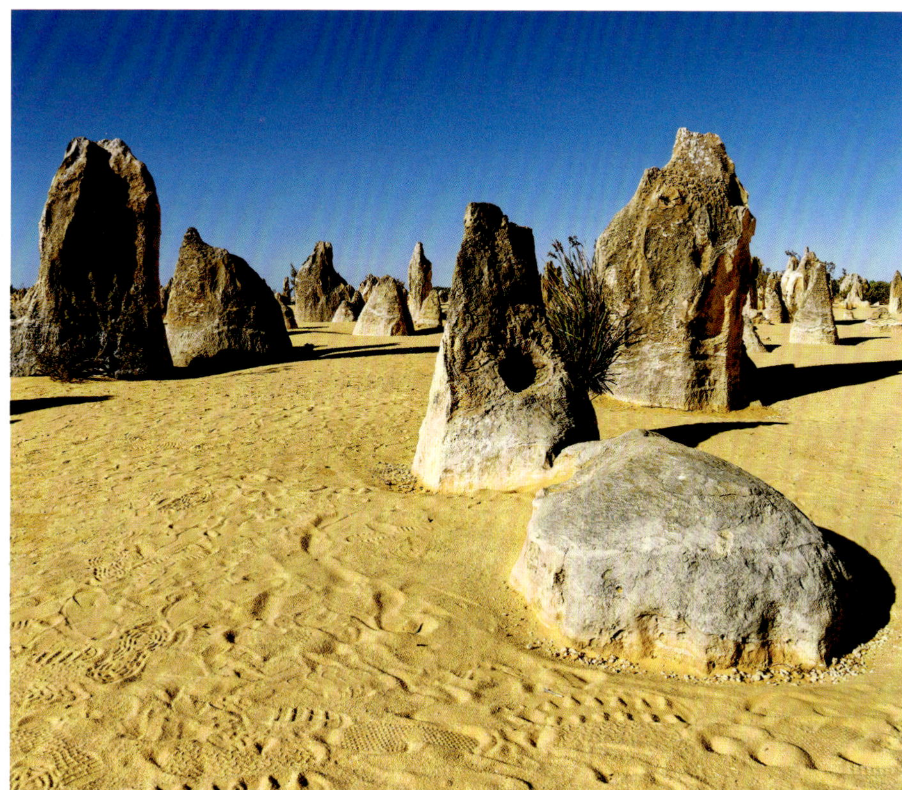

Pinnacles Desert in Nambung National Park.

Wave Rock in Hyden, Western Australia.

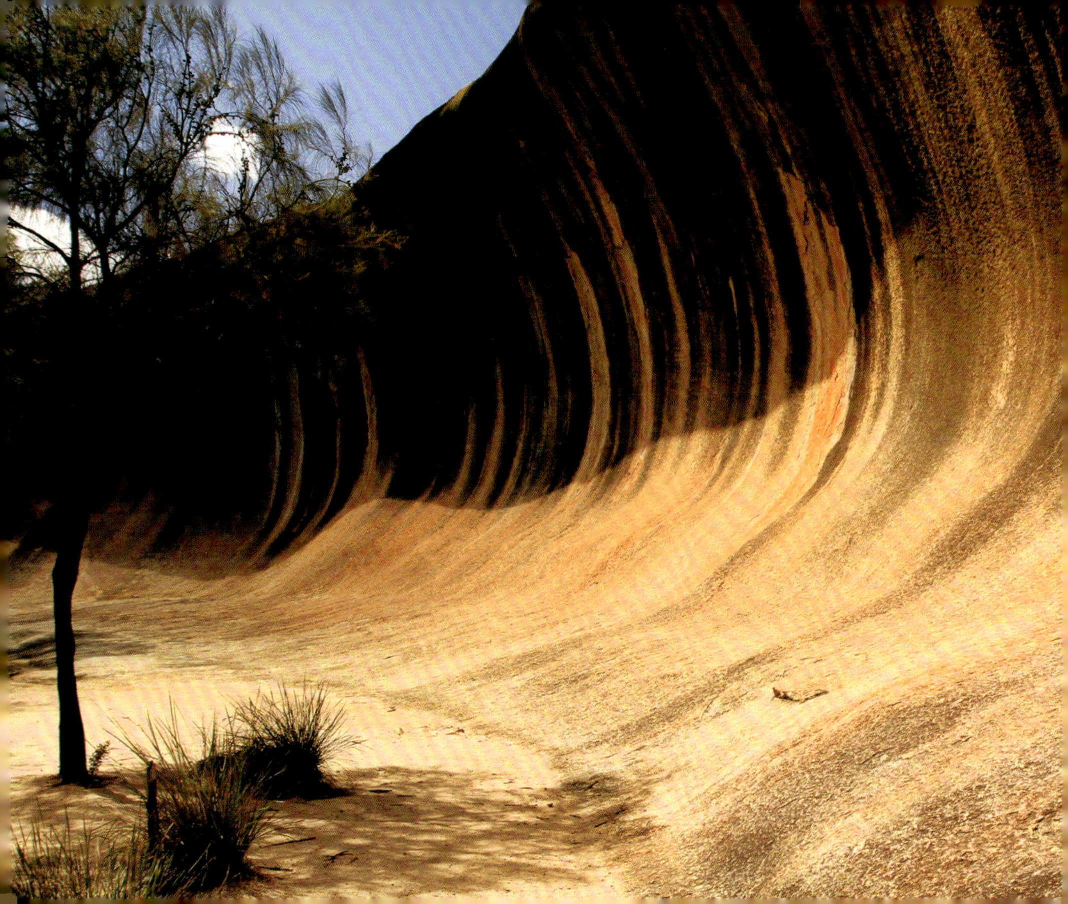

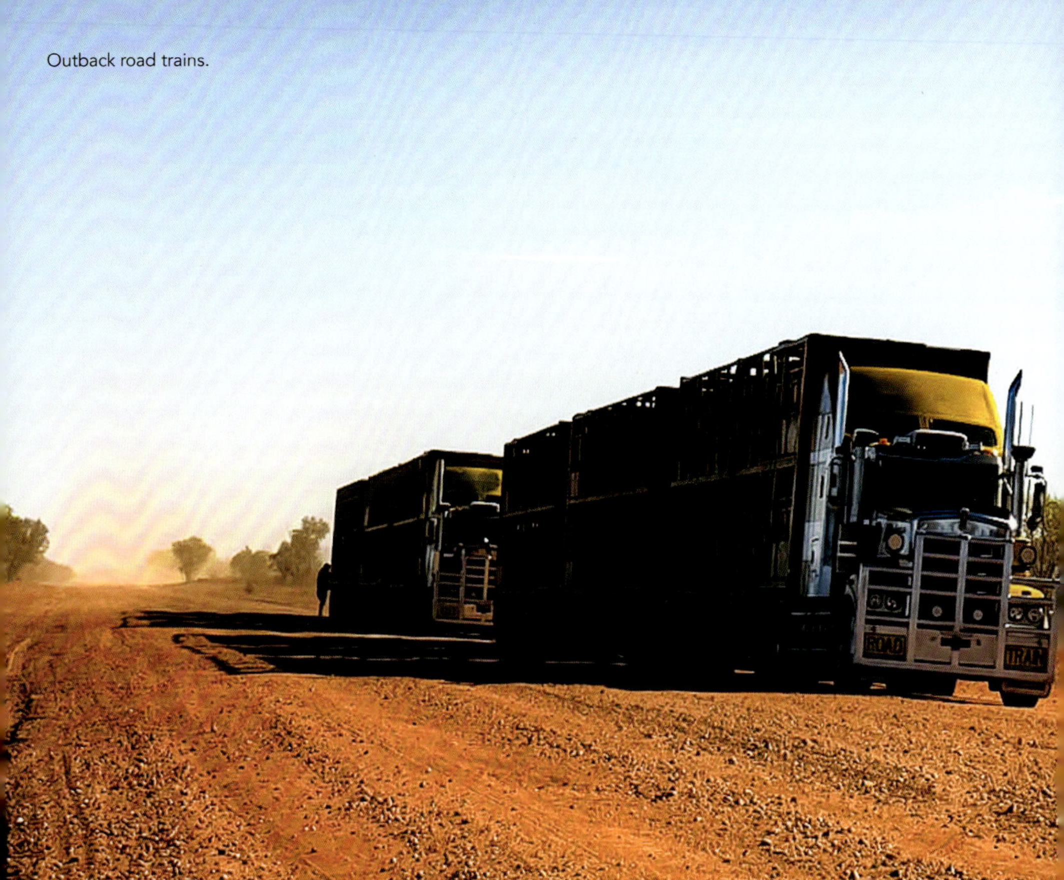

Outback road trains.

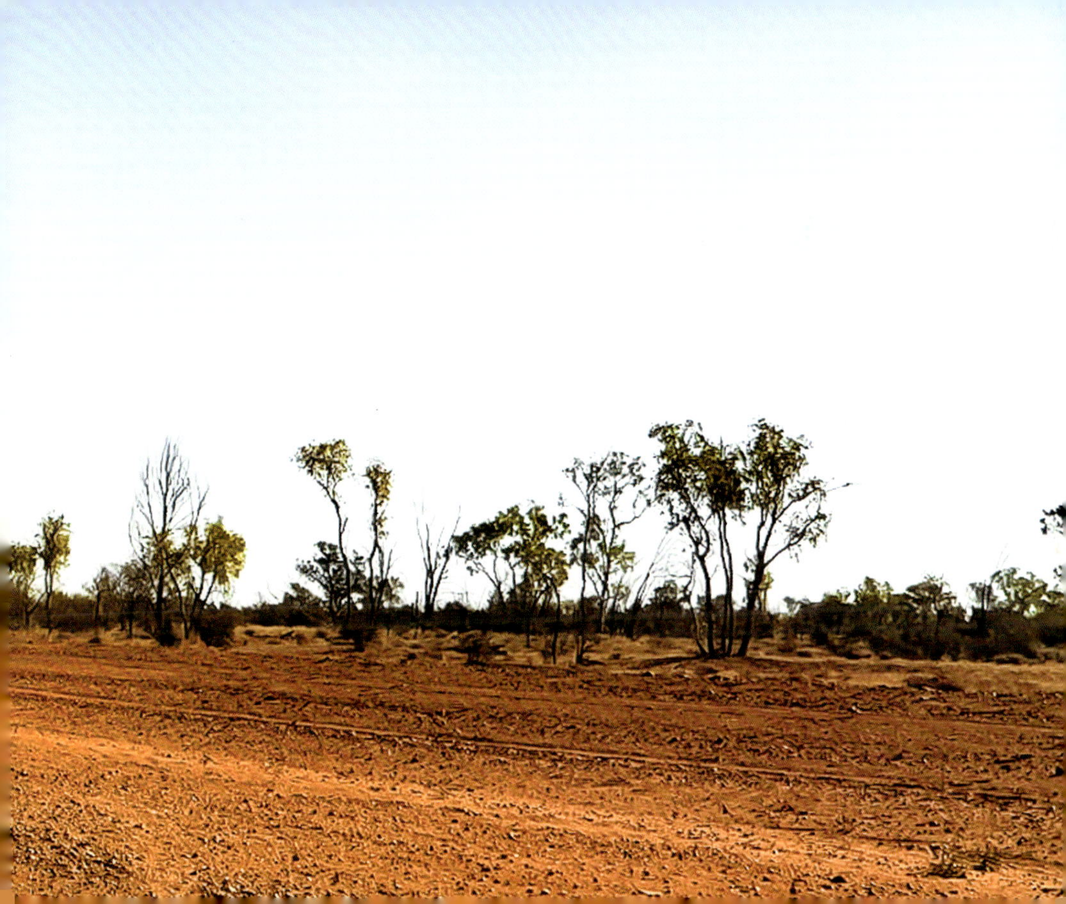

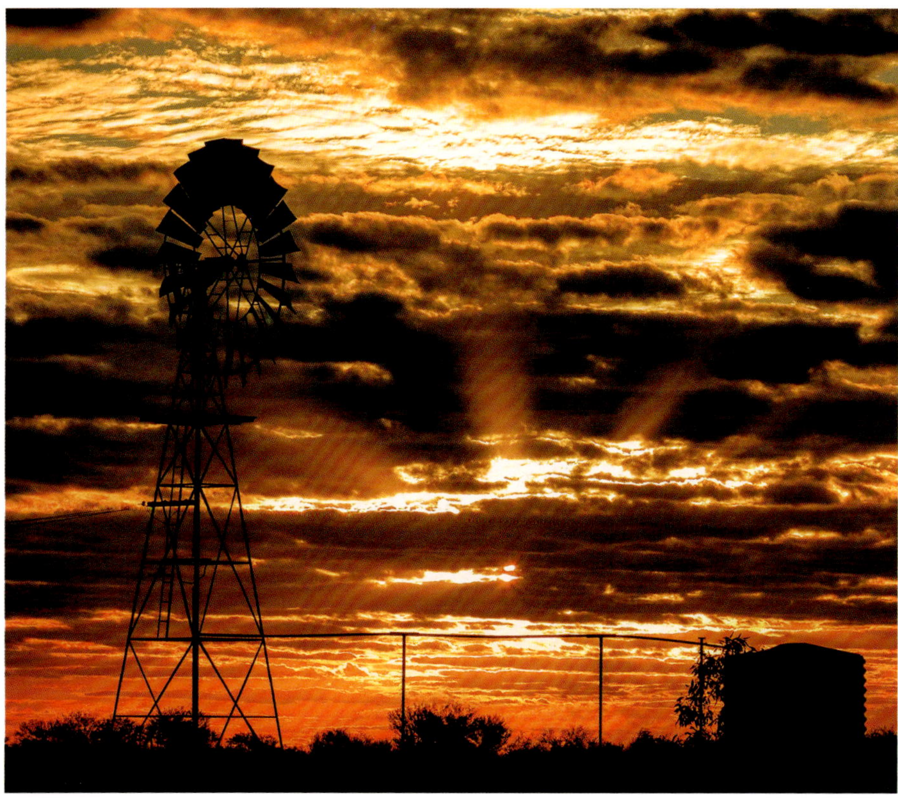

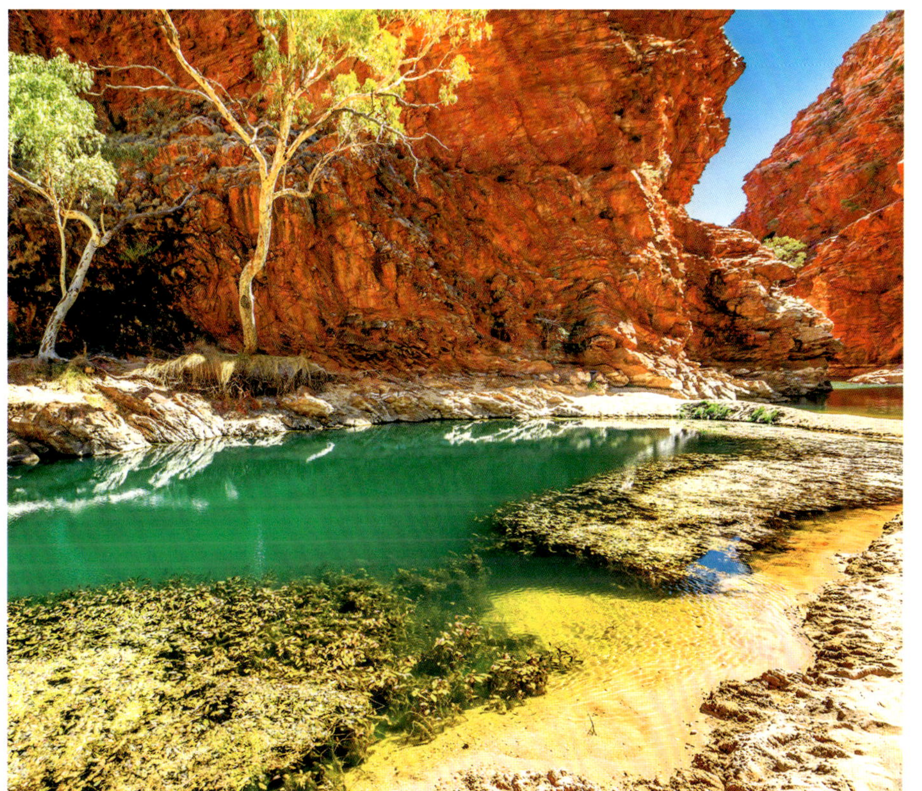

Ellery Creek Big Hole, West MacDonnell National Park, Northern Territory.

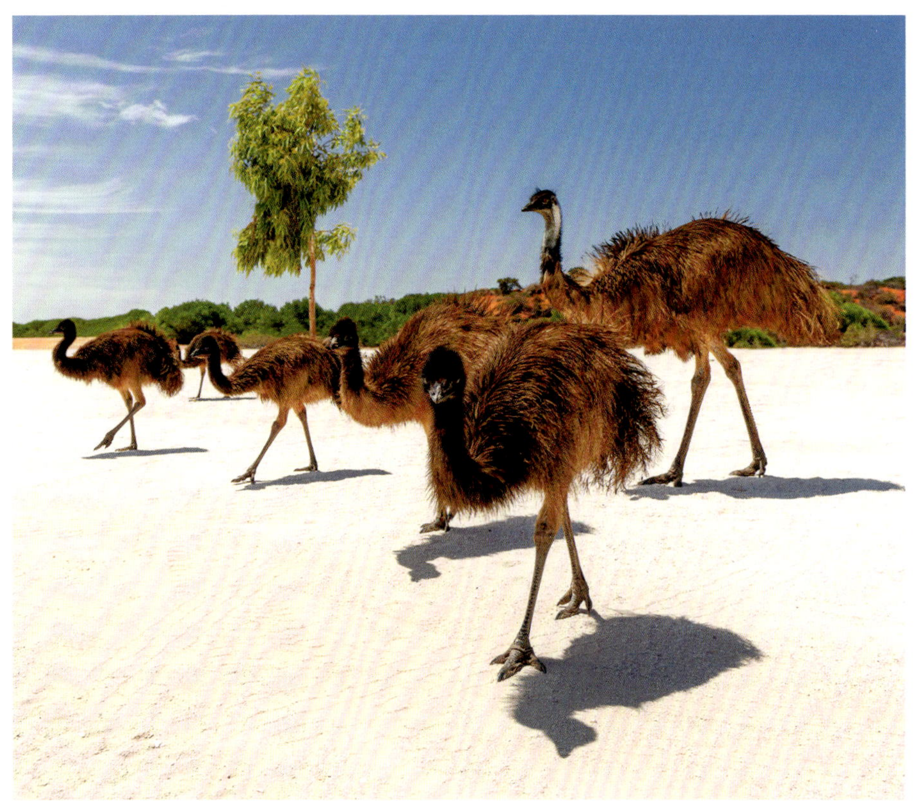

Emu.

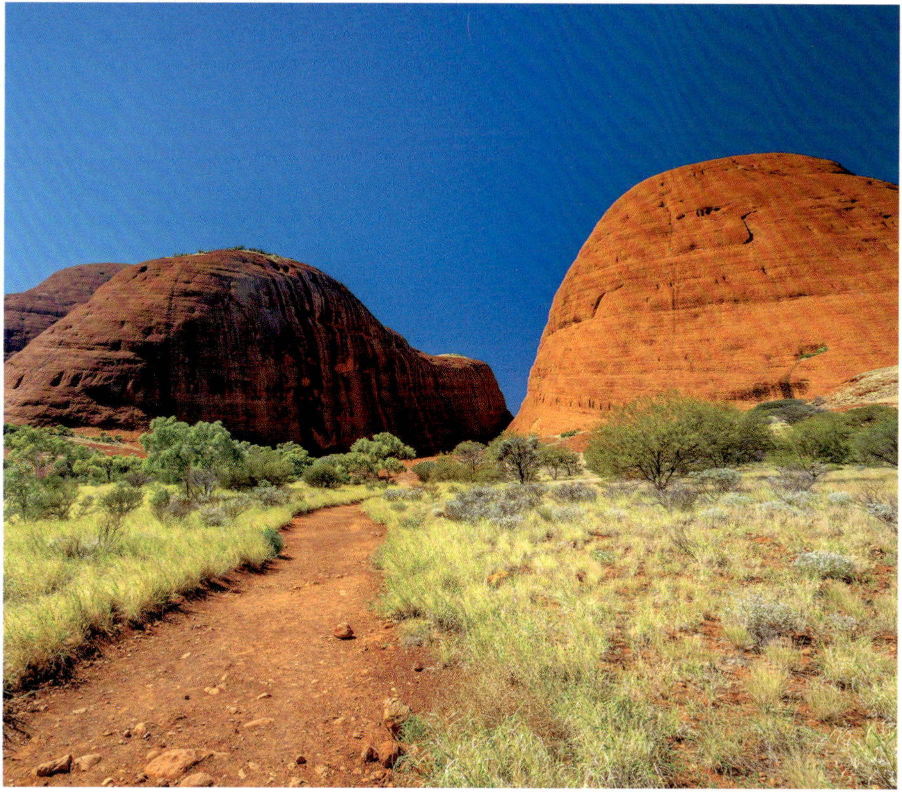

Kata Tjuta, Northern Territory.

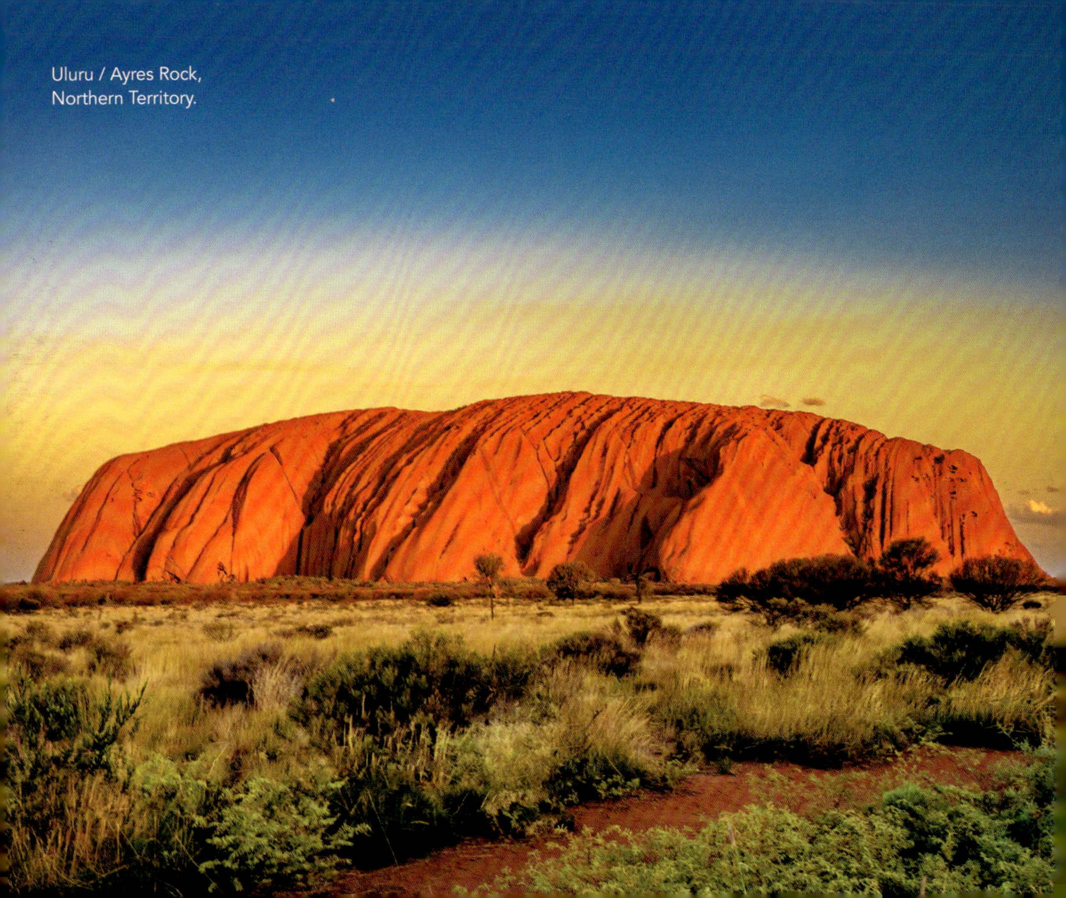

Uluru / Ayres Rock,
Northern Territory.

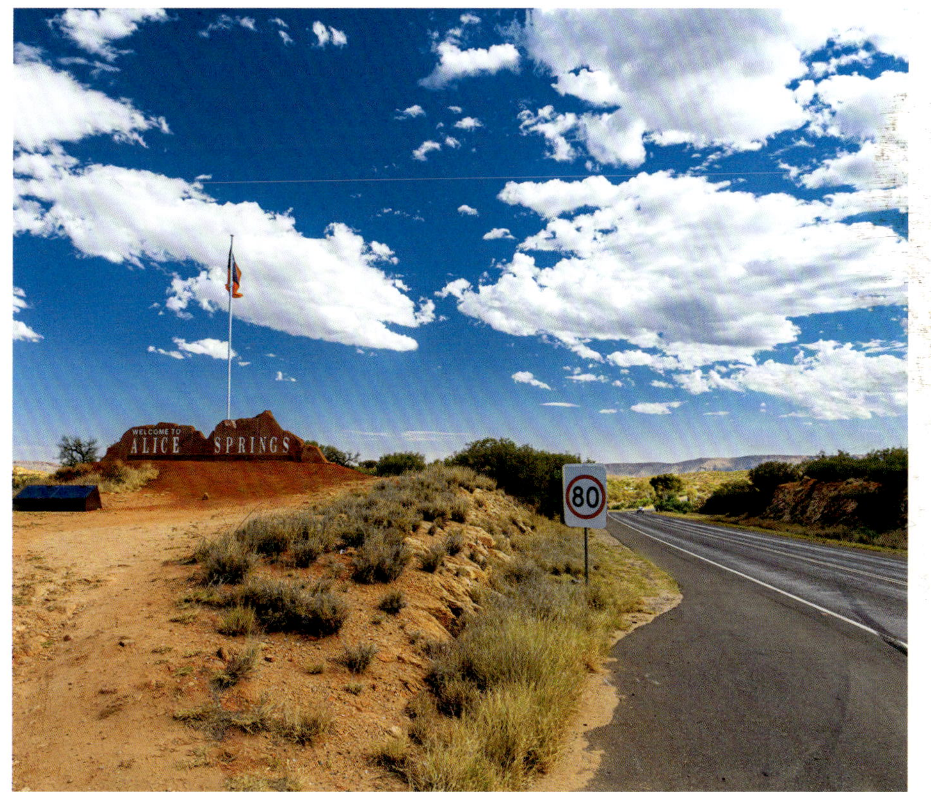
WELCOME TO
ALICE SPRINGS
80

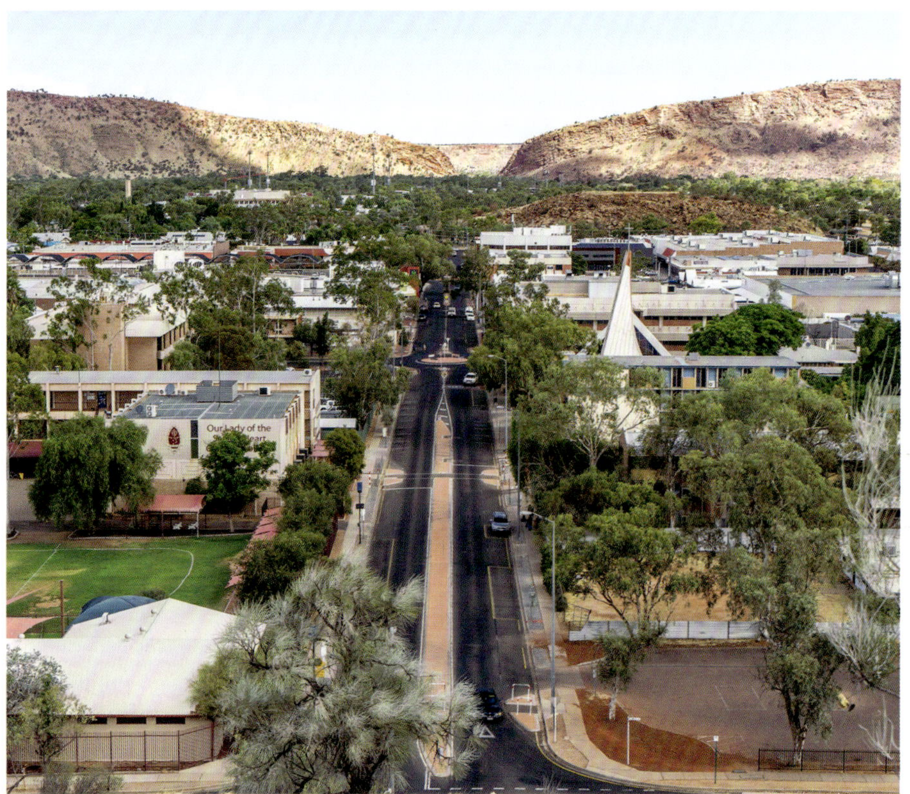

Alice Springs, Northern Territory.

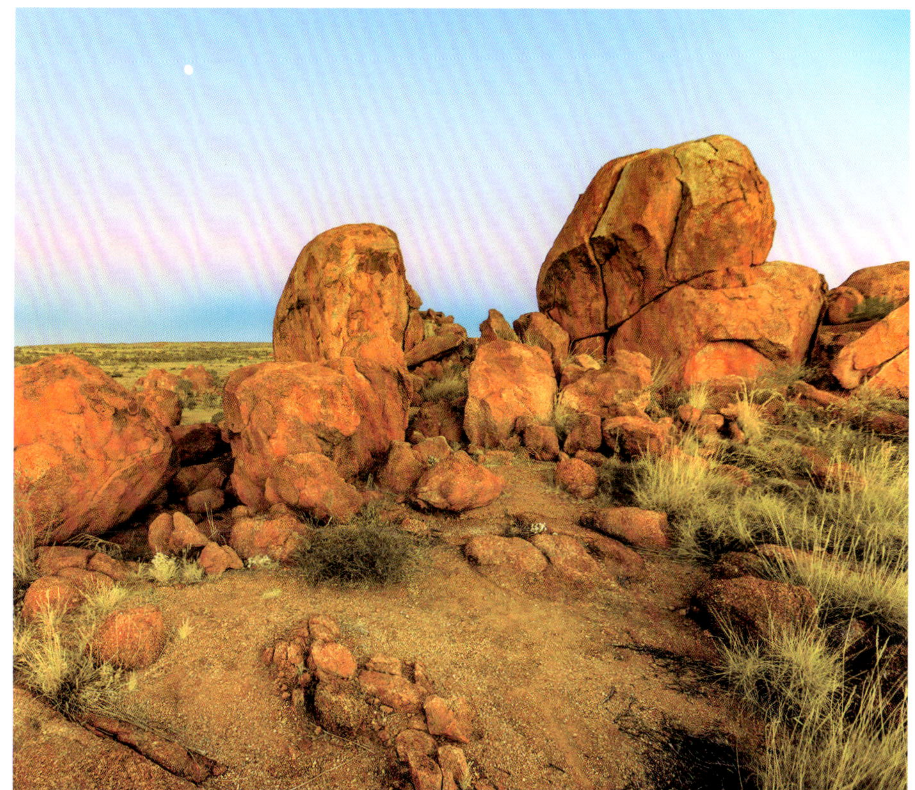

Karlu Karlu / Devils Marbles Conservation Reserve, Northern Territory.

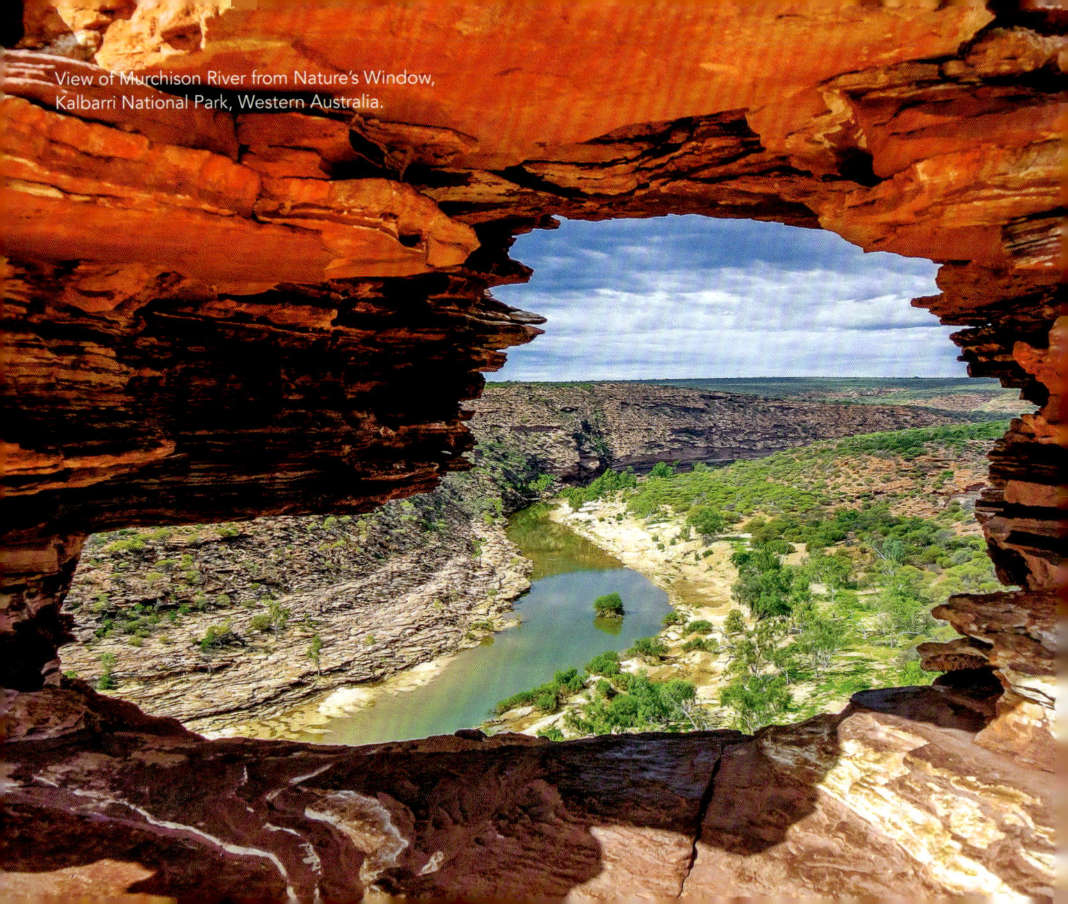

View of Murchison River from Nature's Window, Kalbarri National Park, Western Australia.

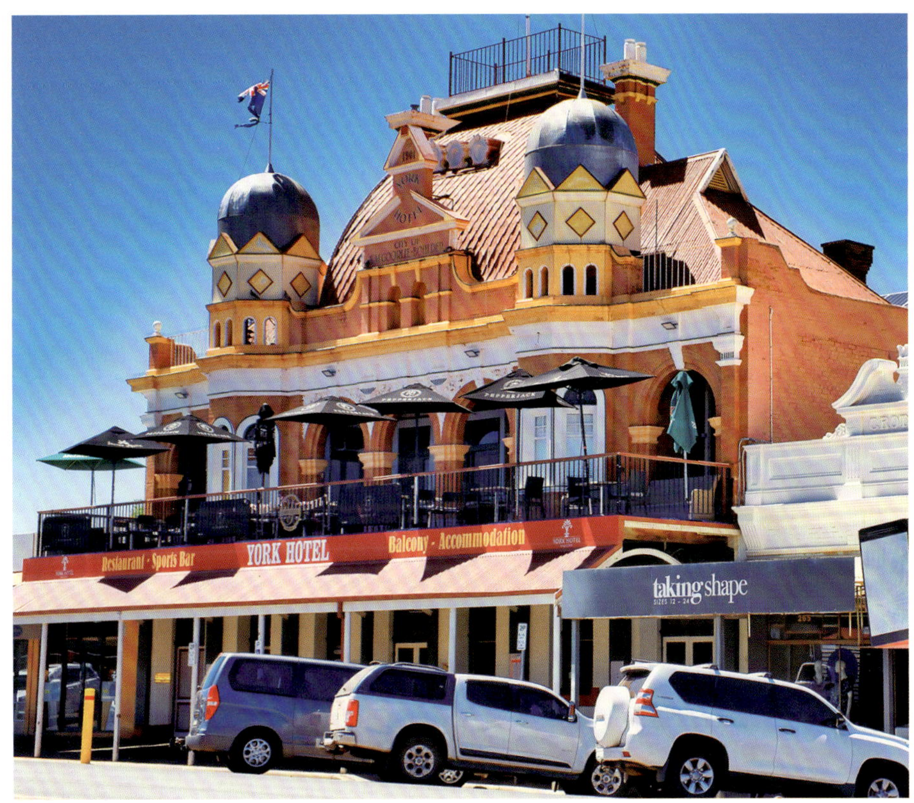

Kalgoorlie, Western Australia.

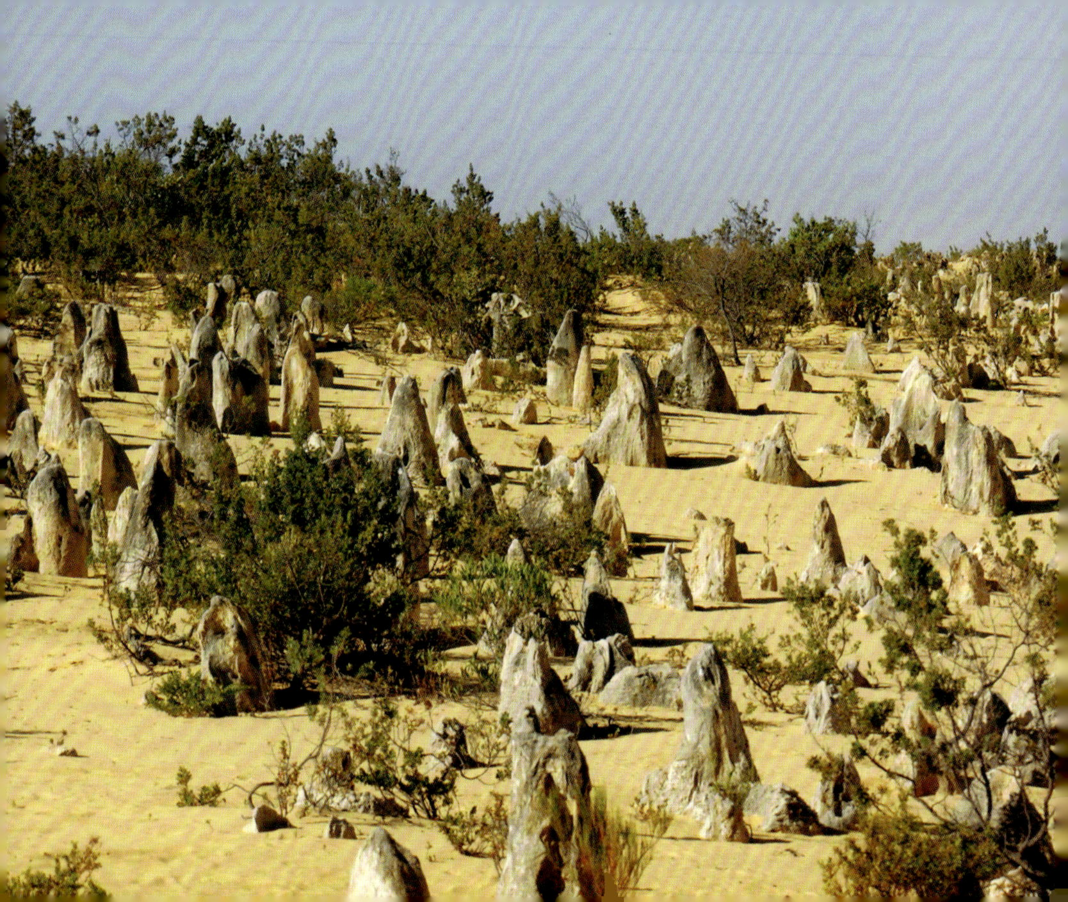

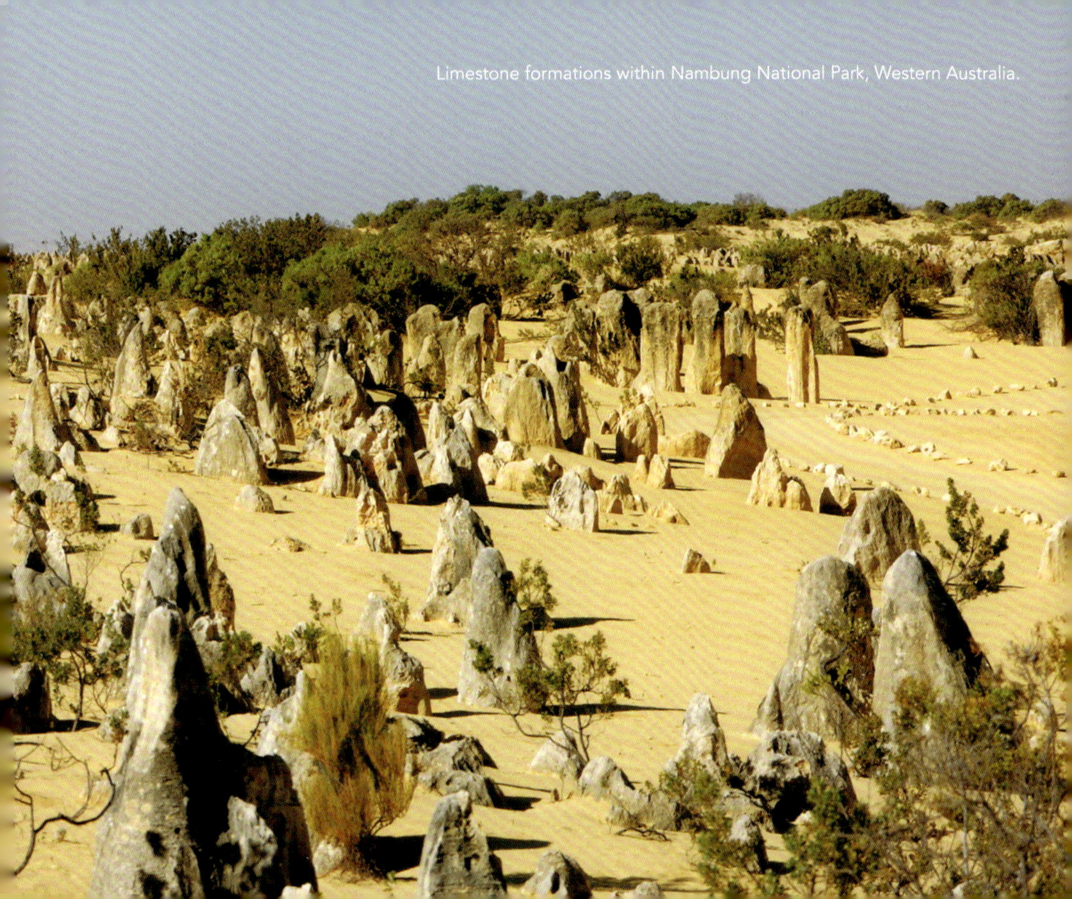

Limestone formations within Nambung National Park, Western Australia.

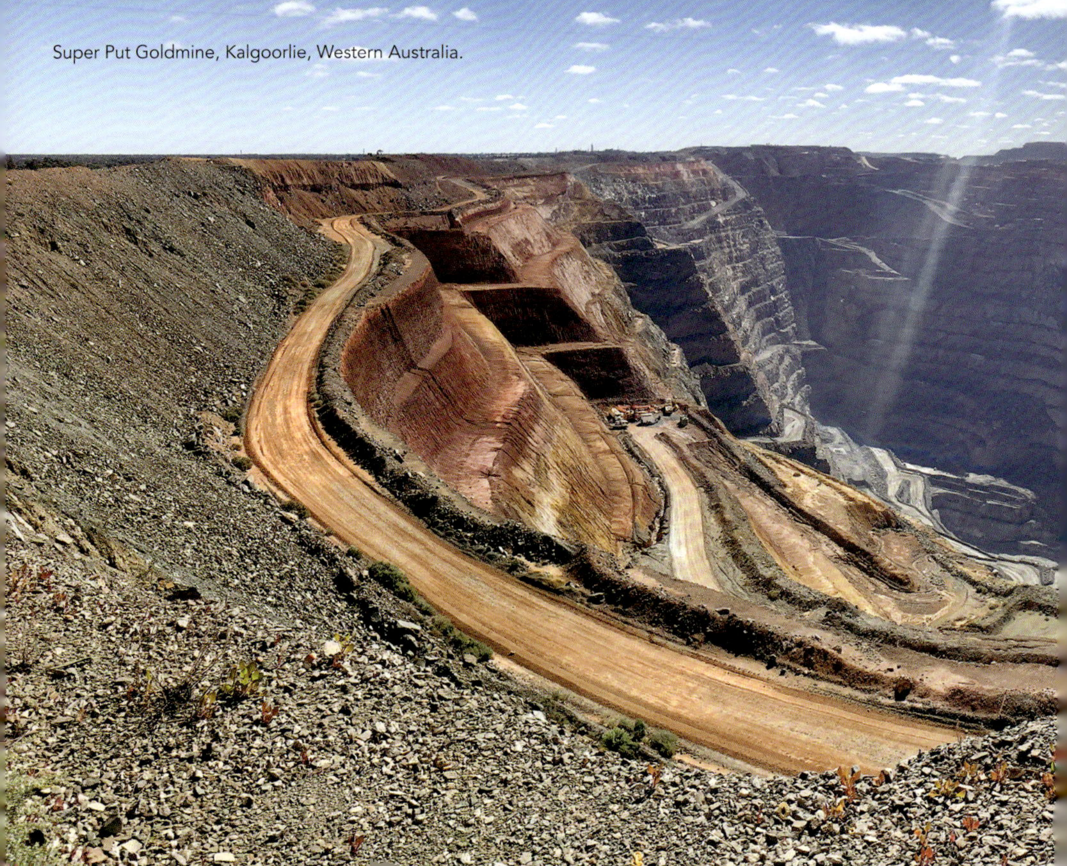
Super Put Goldmine, Kalgoorlie, Western Australia.

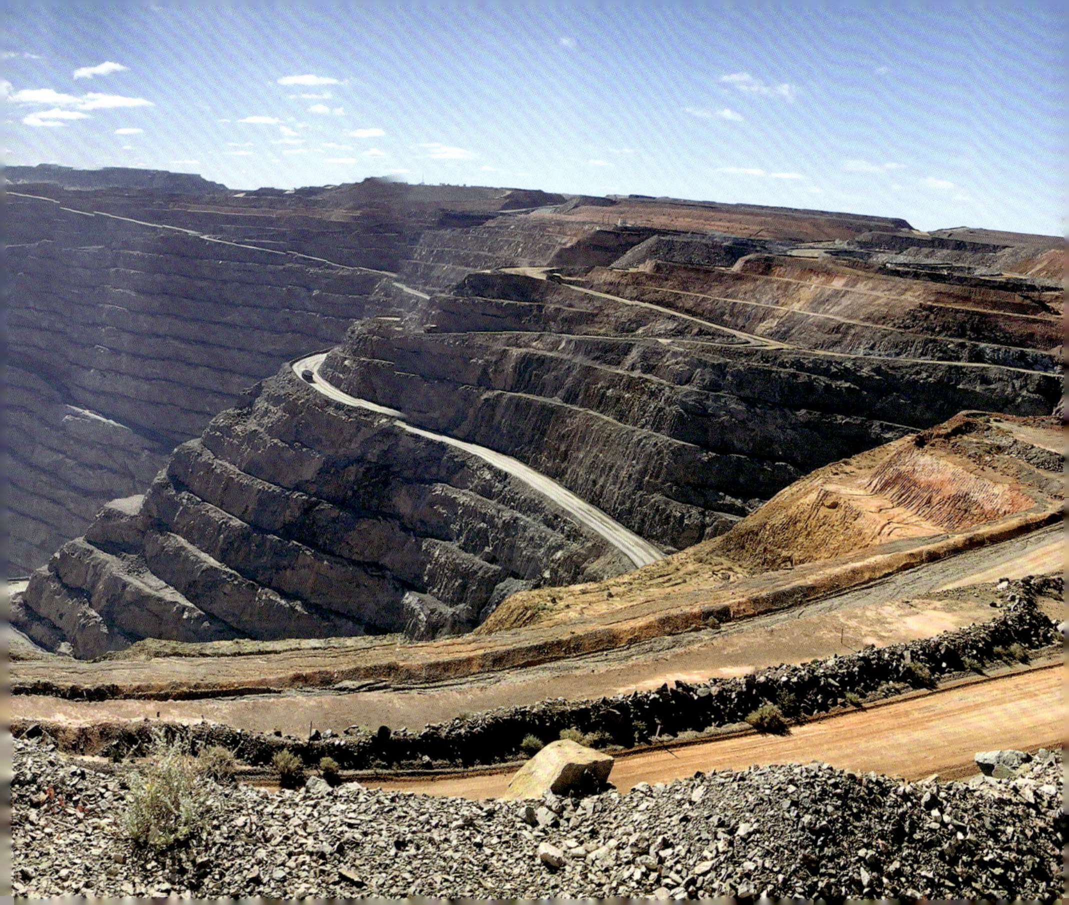

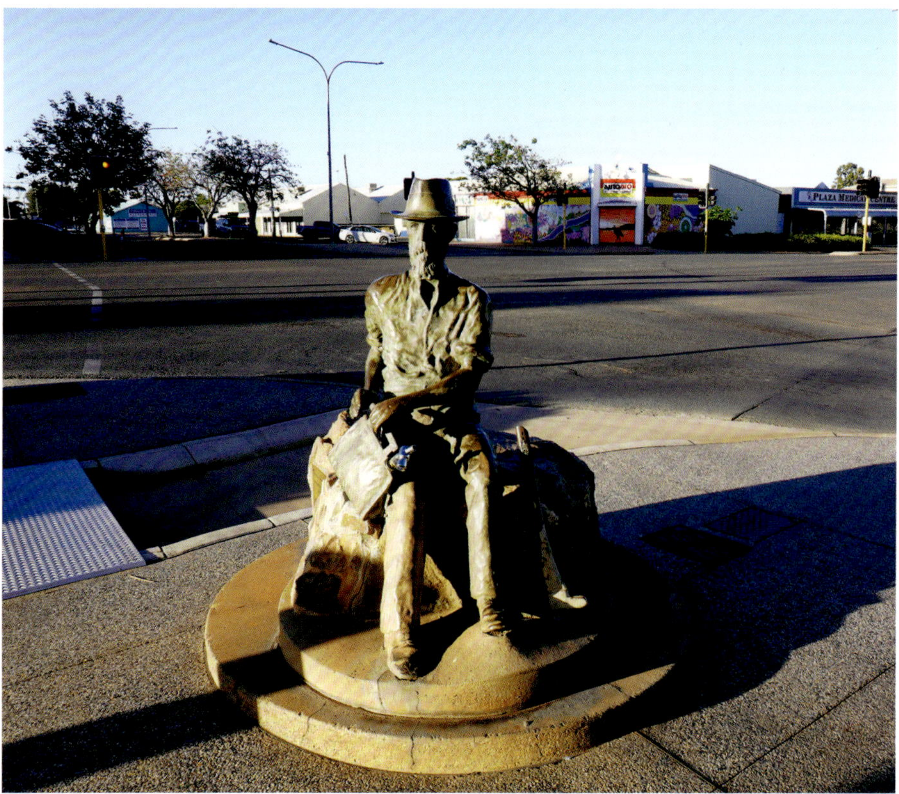

Kalgoorlie, Western Australia.

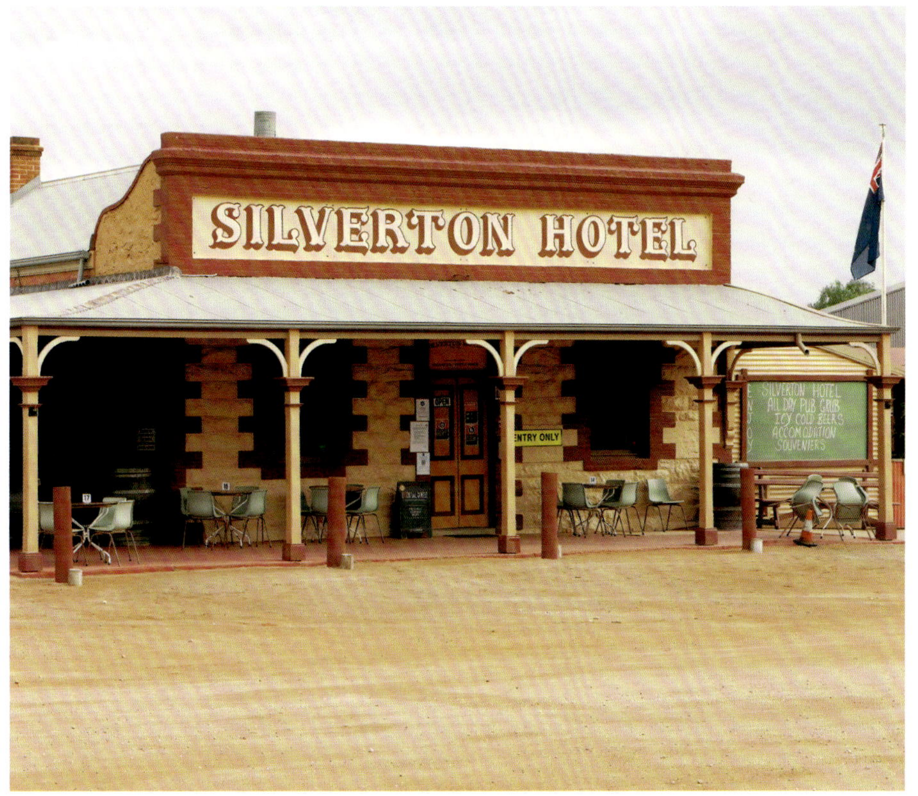

Silverton, NSW.

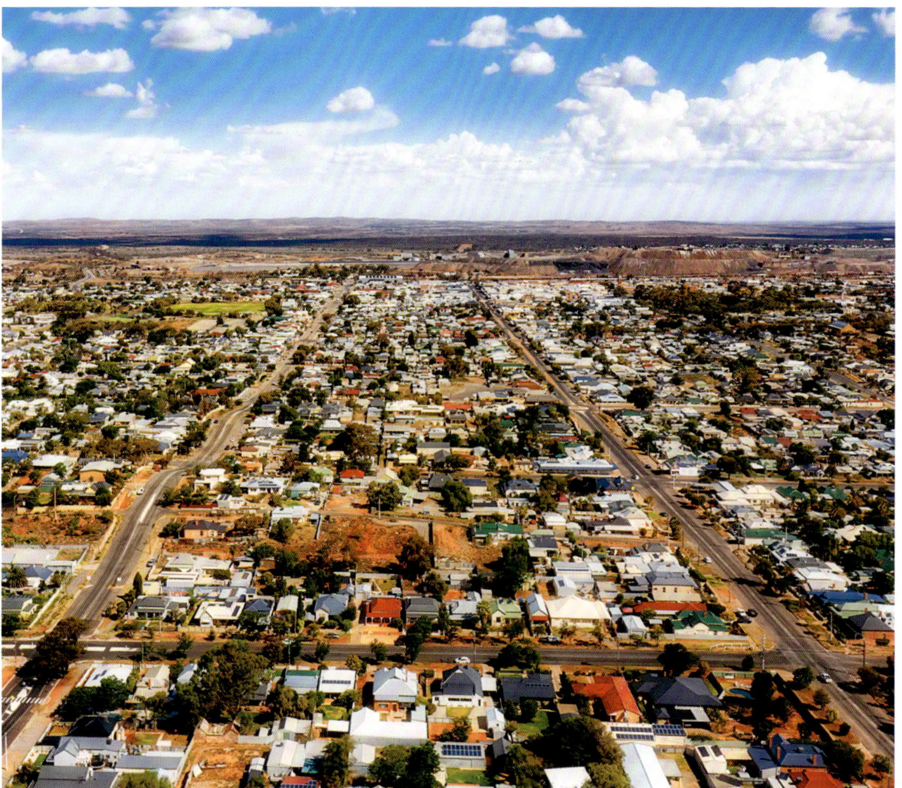

Broken Hill, NSW.

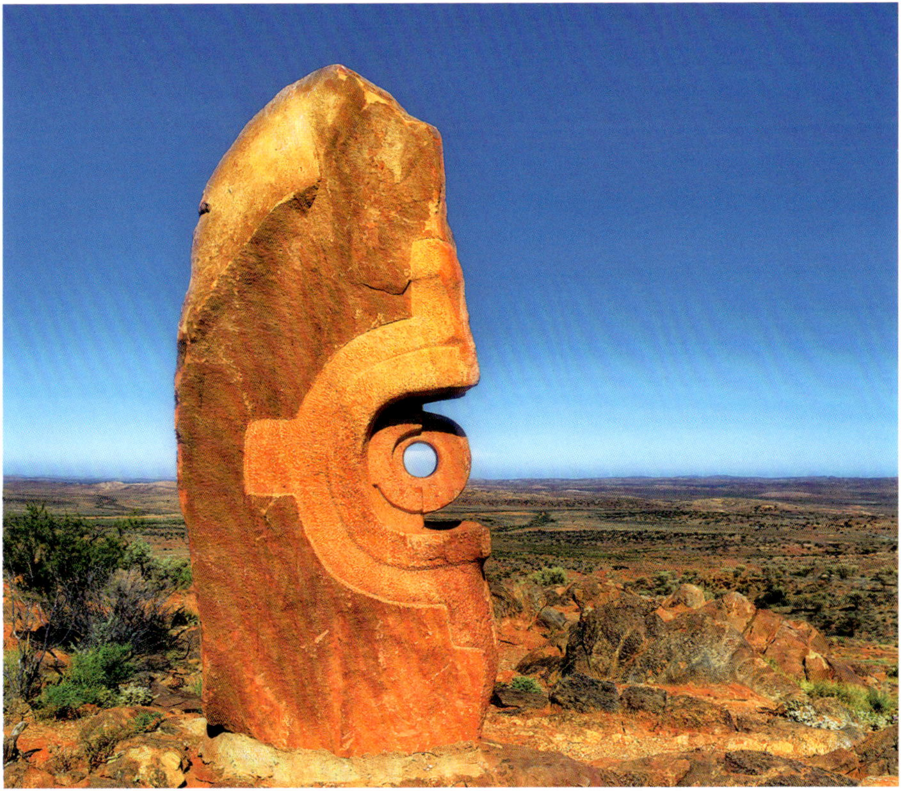

Stone sculpture in public sculpture garden near Broken Hill, NSW.

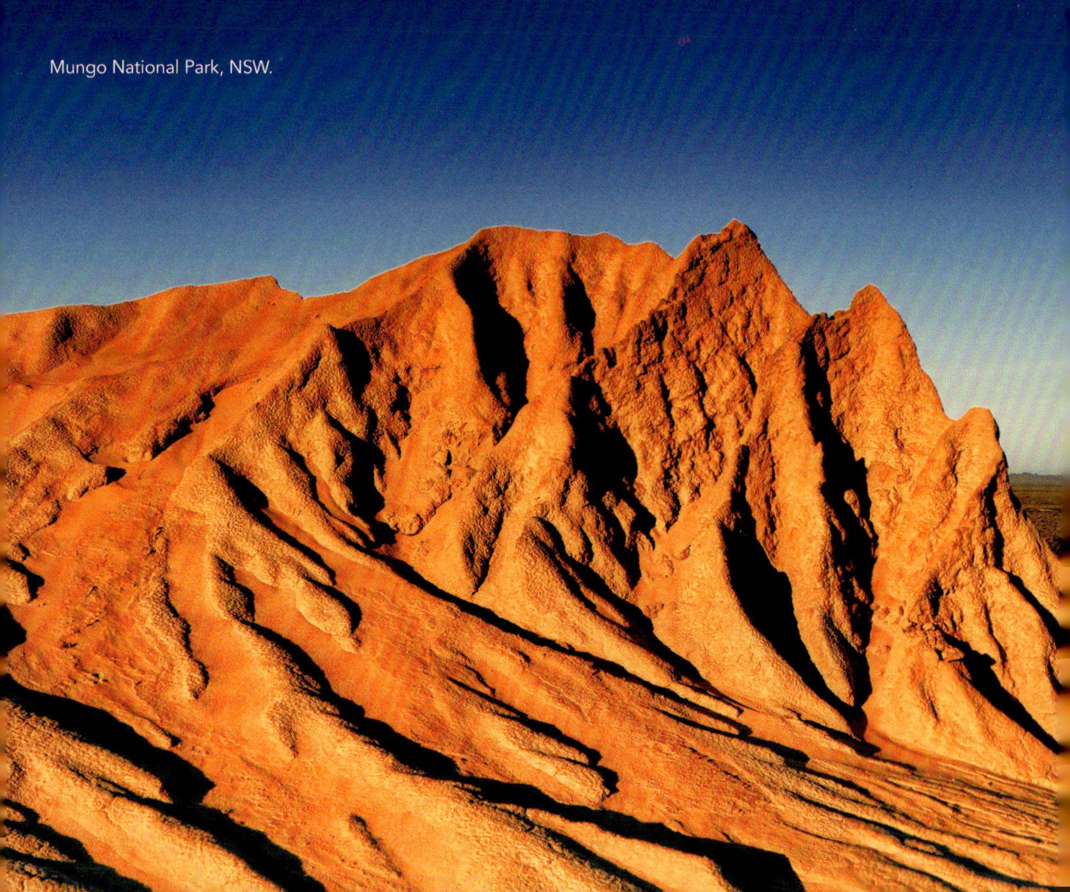

Mungo National Park, NSW.

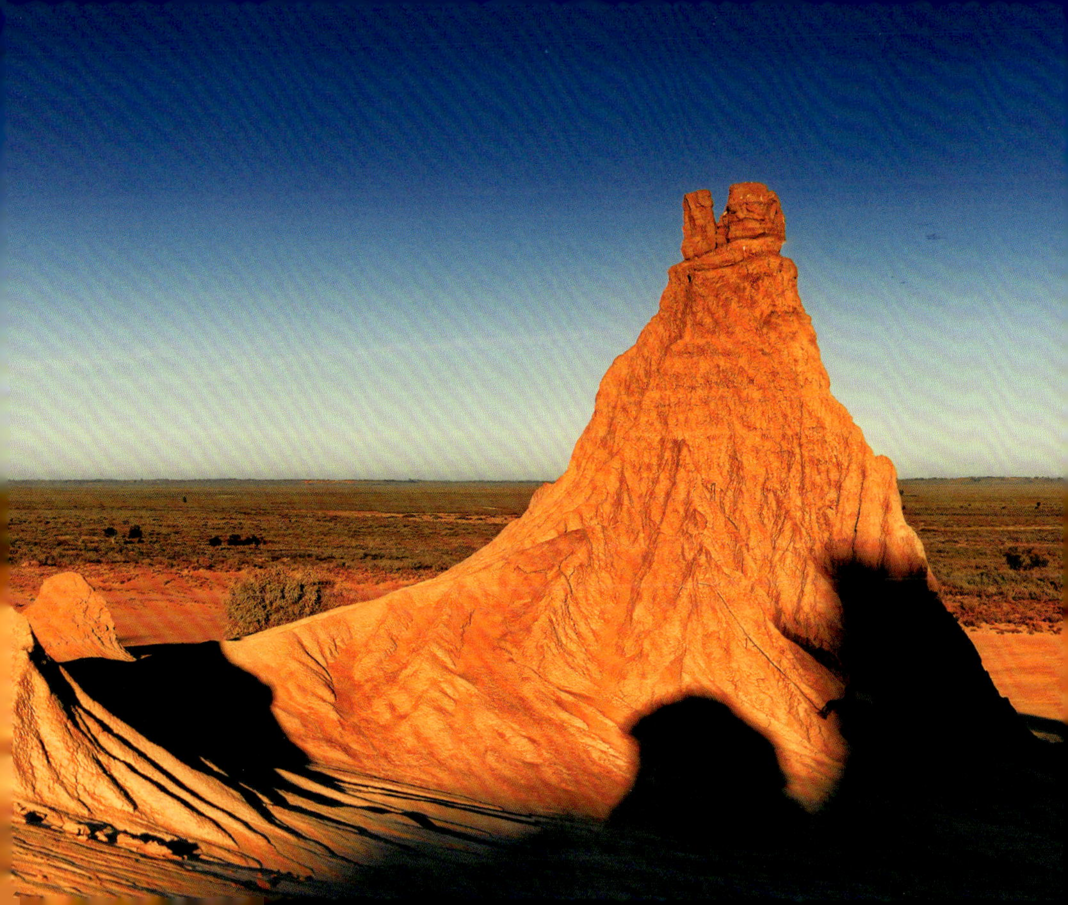

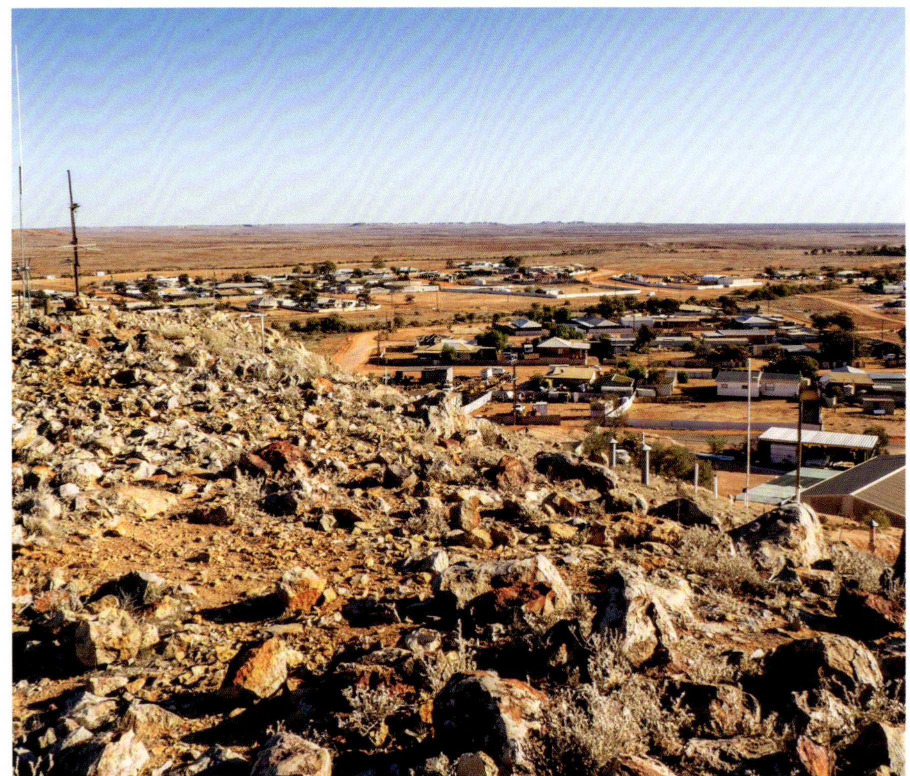

Town of Coober Pedy the underground city, South Australia.

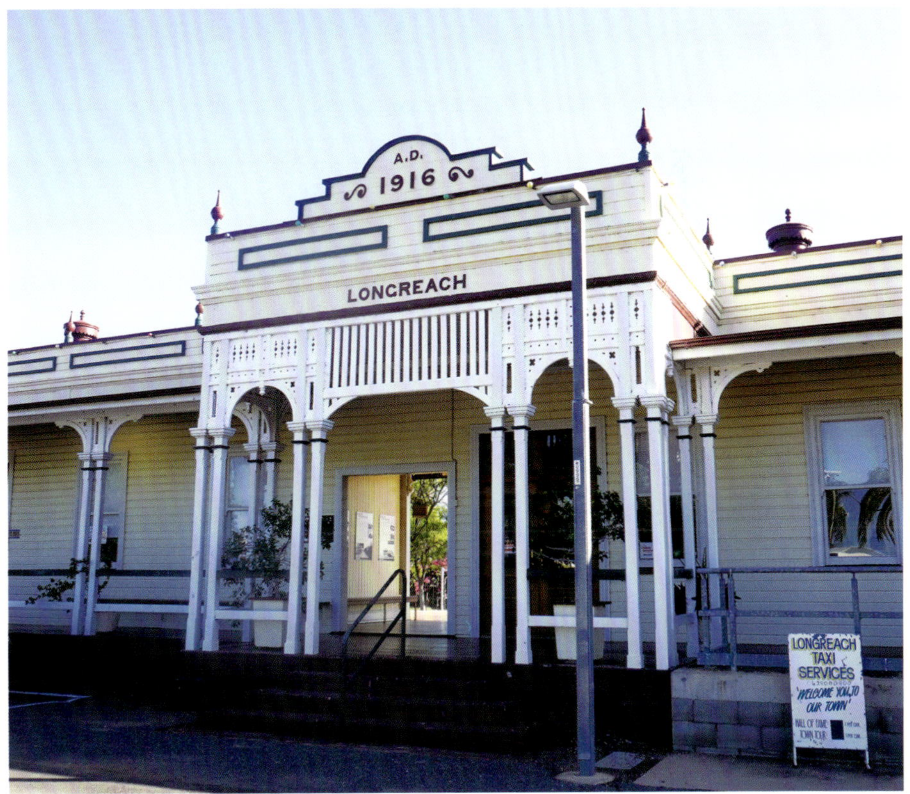

Historic Longreach Railway Station, Queensland.

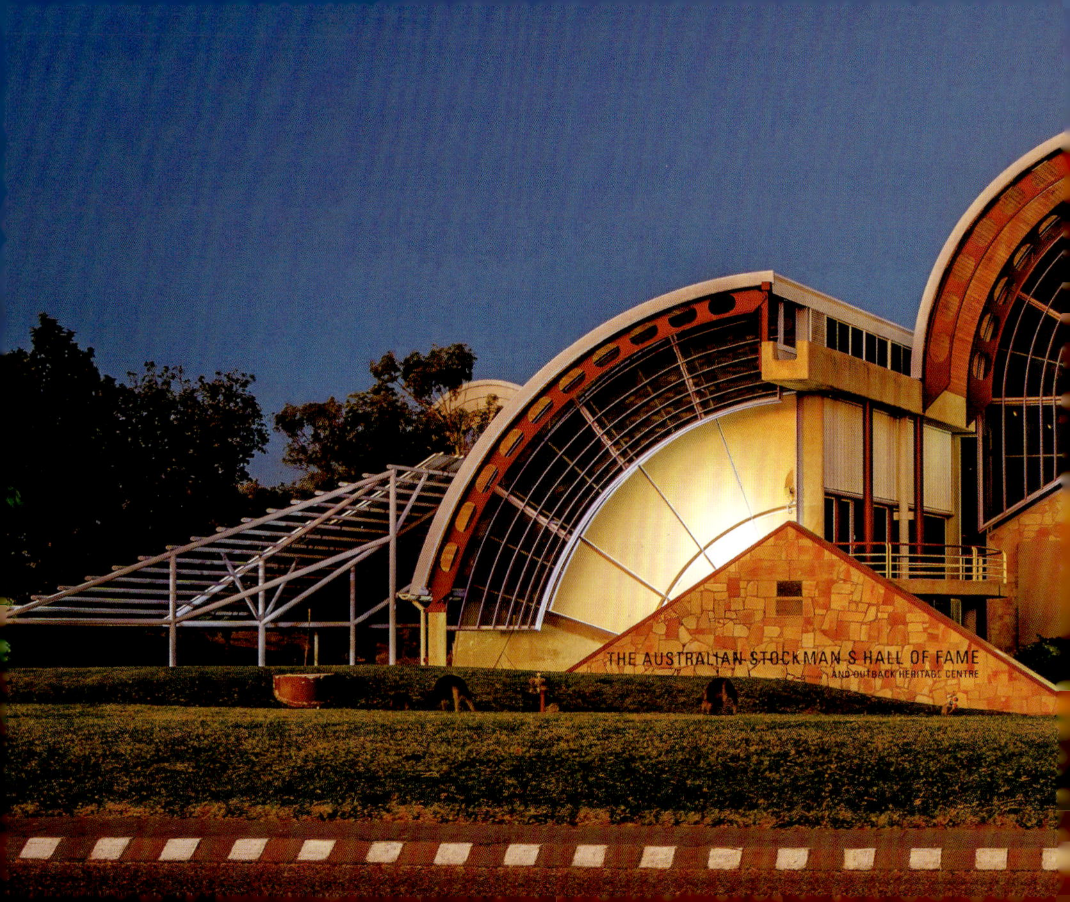
THE AUSTRALIAN STOCKMAN S HALL OF FAME
AND OUTBACK HERITAGE CENTRE

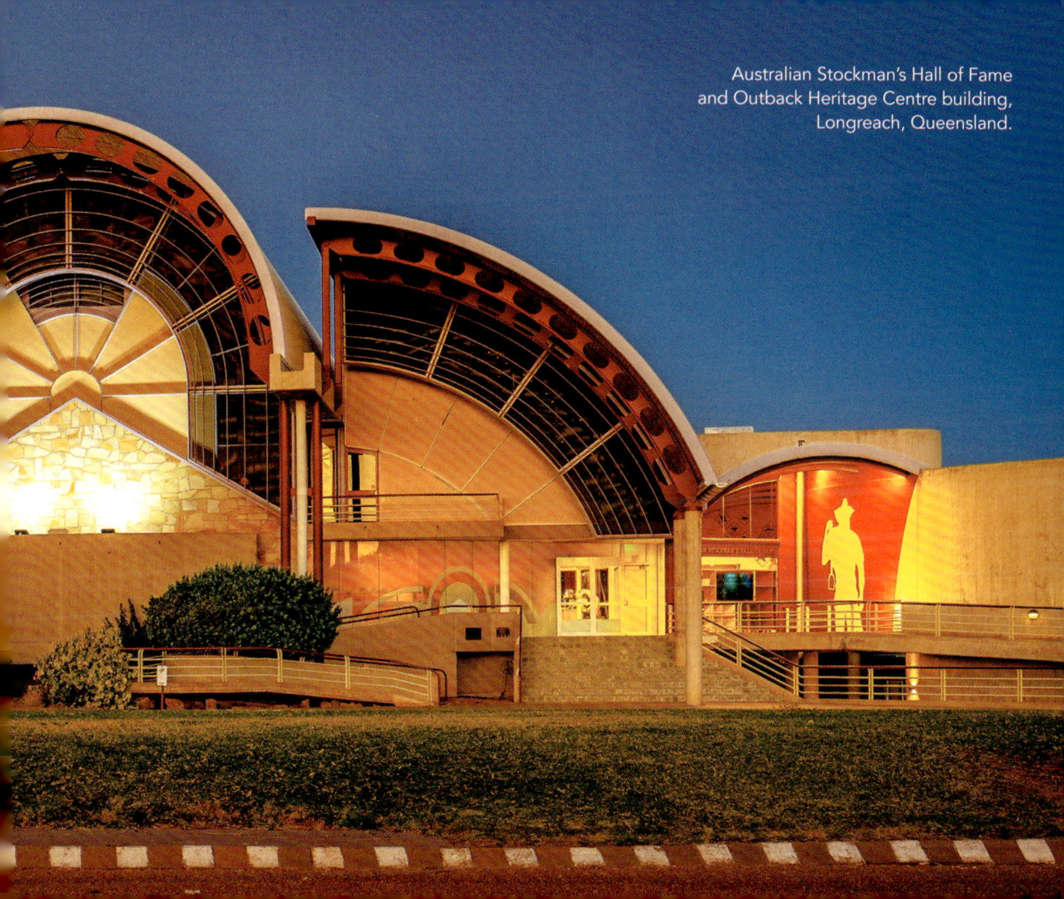

Australian Stockman's Hall of Fame and Outback Heritage Centre building, Longreach, Queensland.

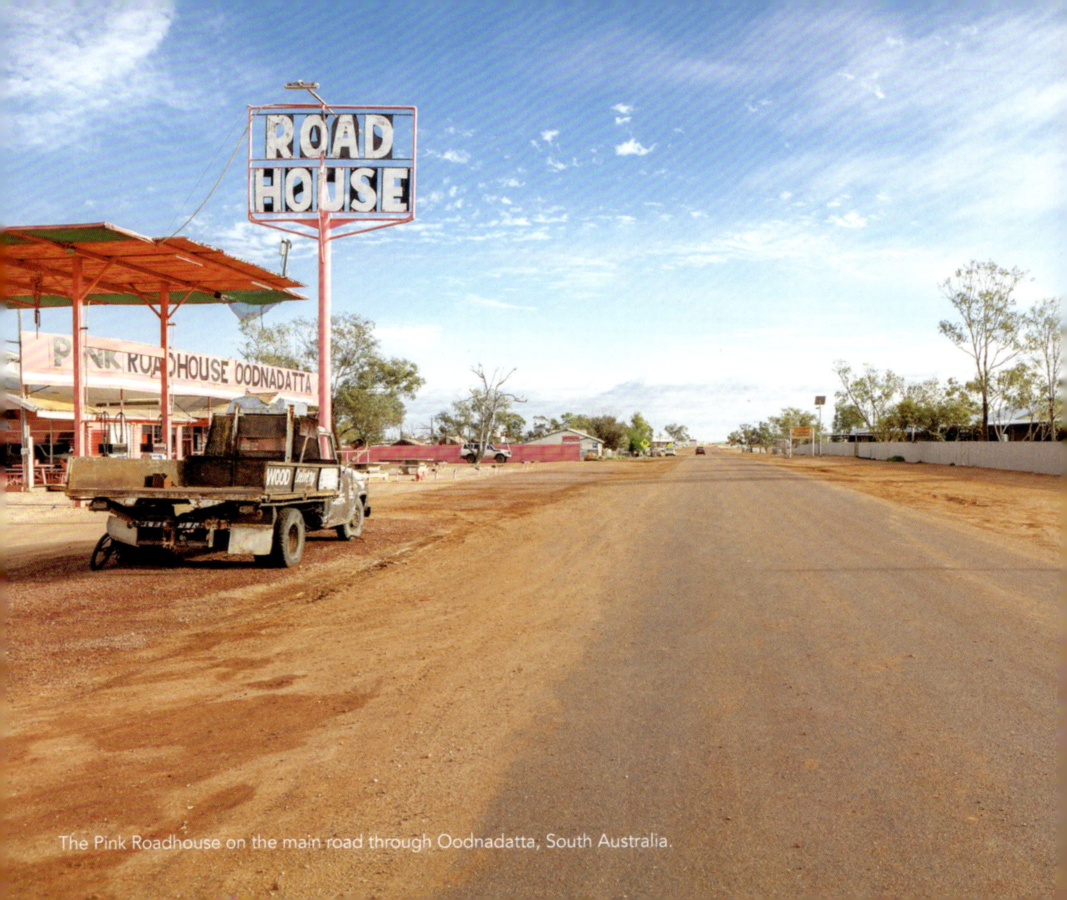

The Pink Roadhouse on the main road through Oodnadatta, South Australia.

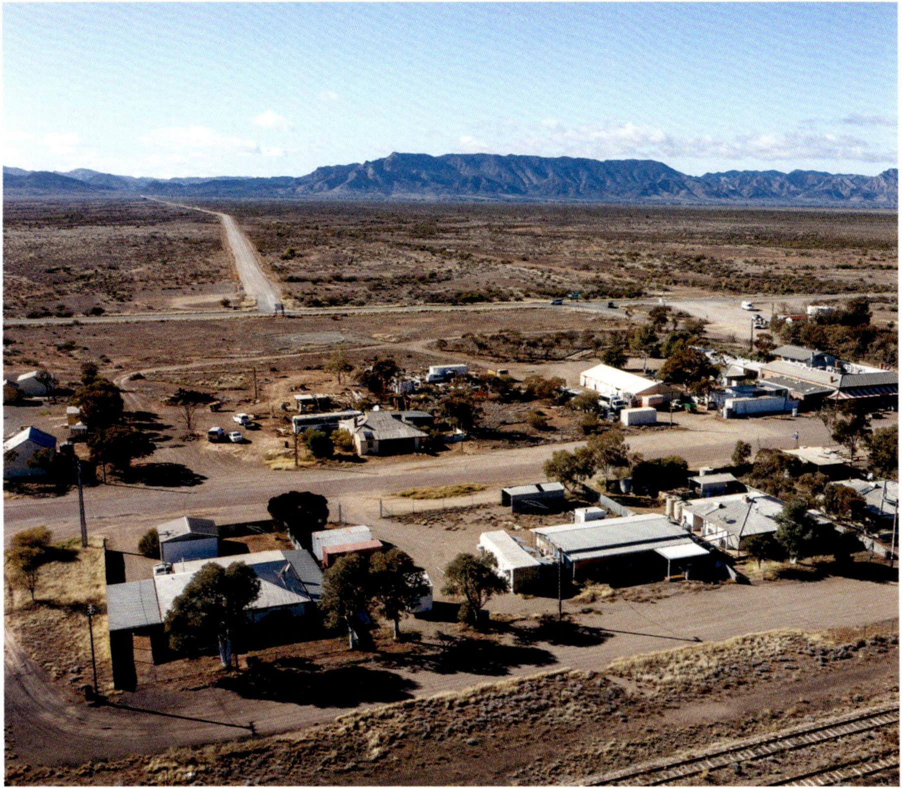

Parachilna near the Flinders Ranges, South Australia.

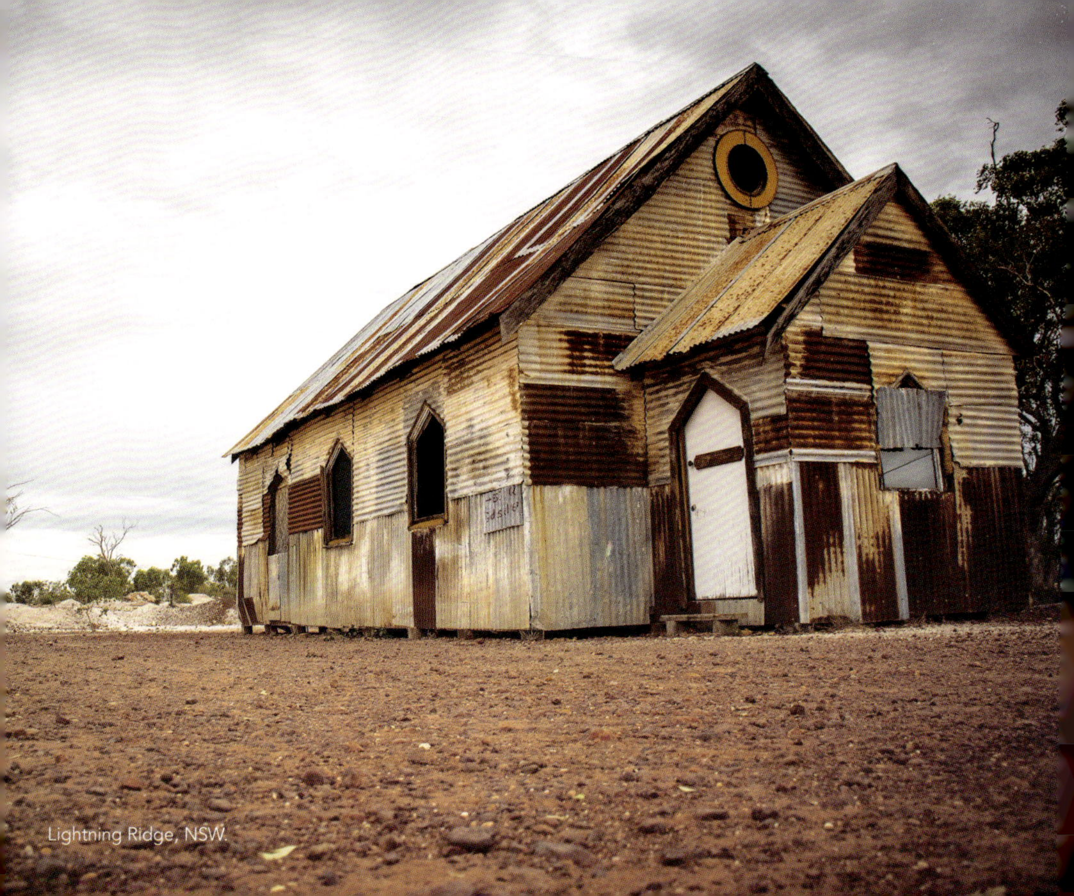

Lightning Ridge, NSW.

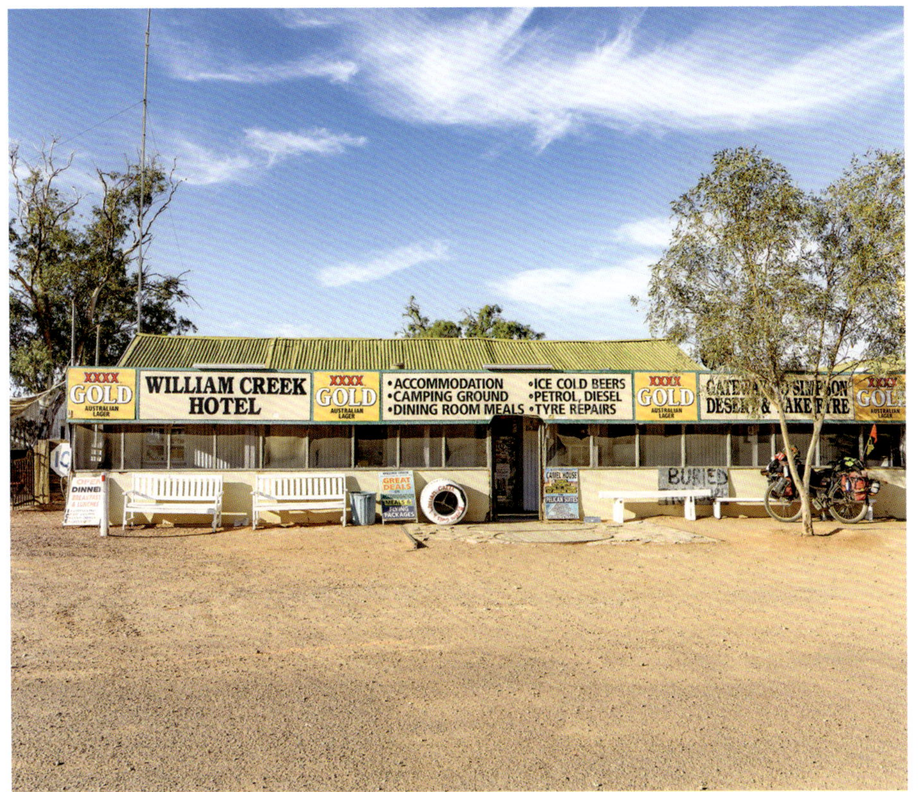

The William Creek Hotel on the Oodnadatta Track in South Australia.

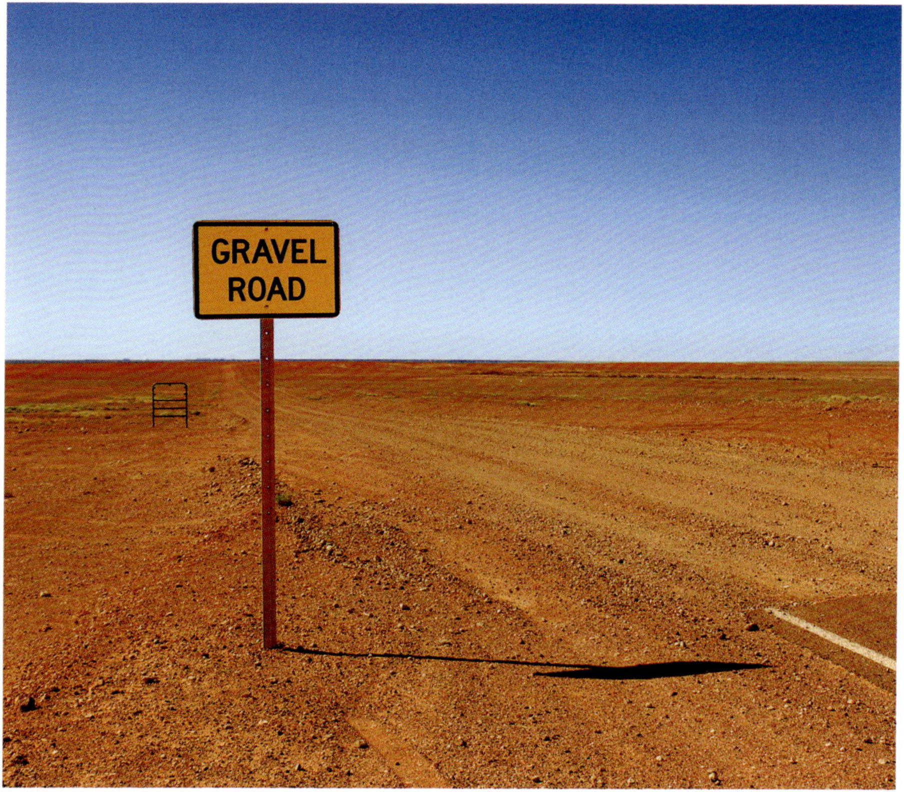

Road sign at the Oodnadatta Track, South Australia.

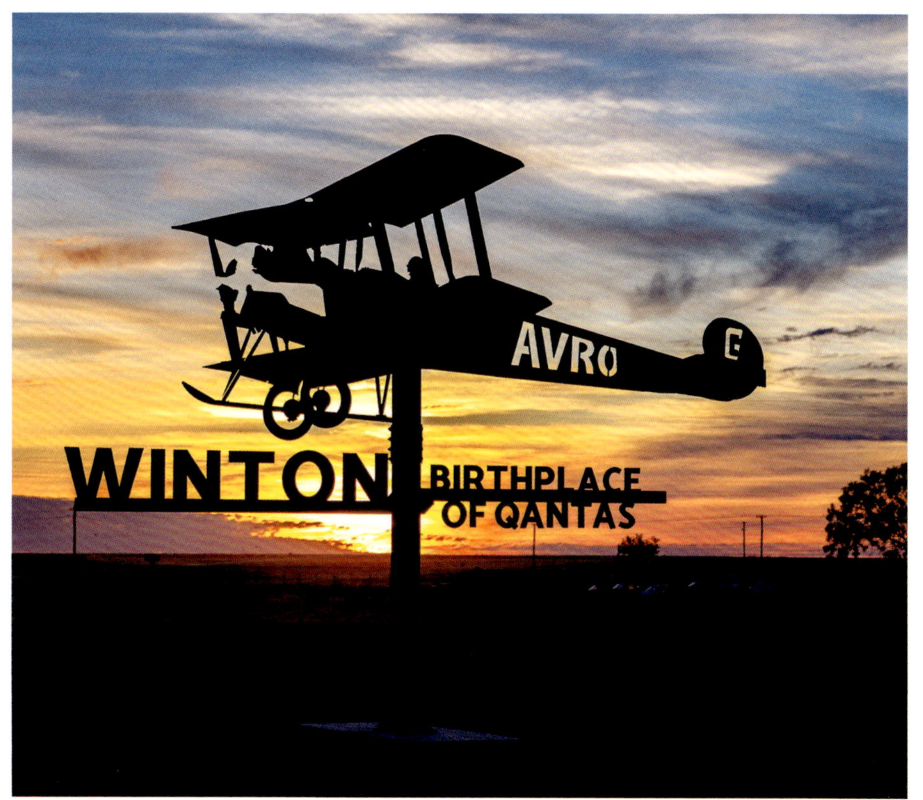

Winton, Queensland.

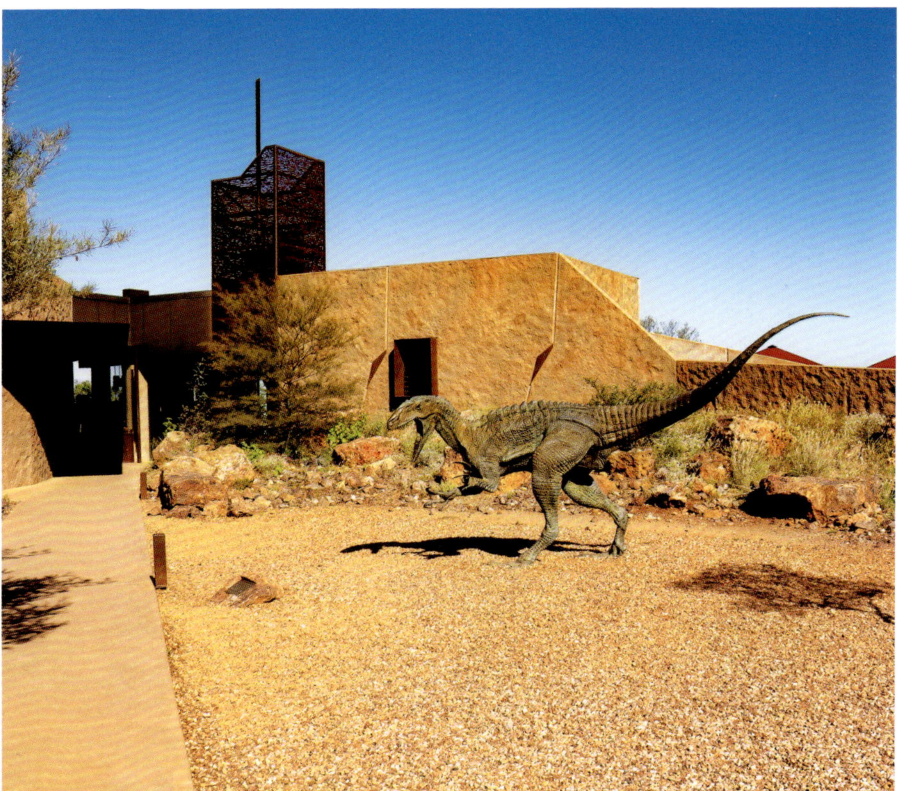

Australian Age of Dinosaurs Museum, Winton.

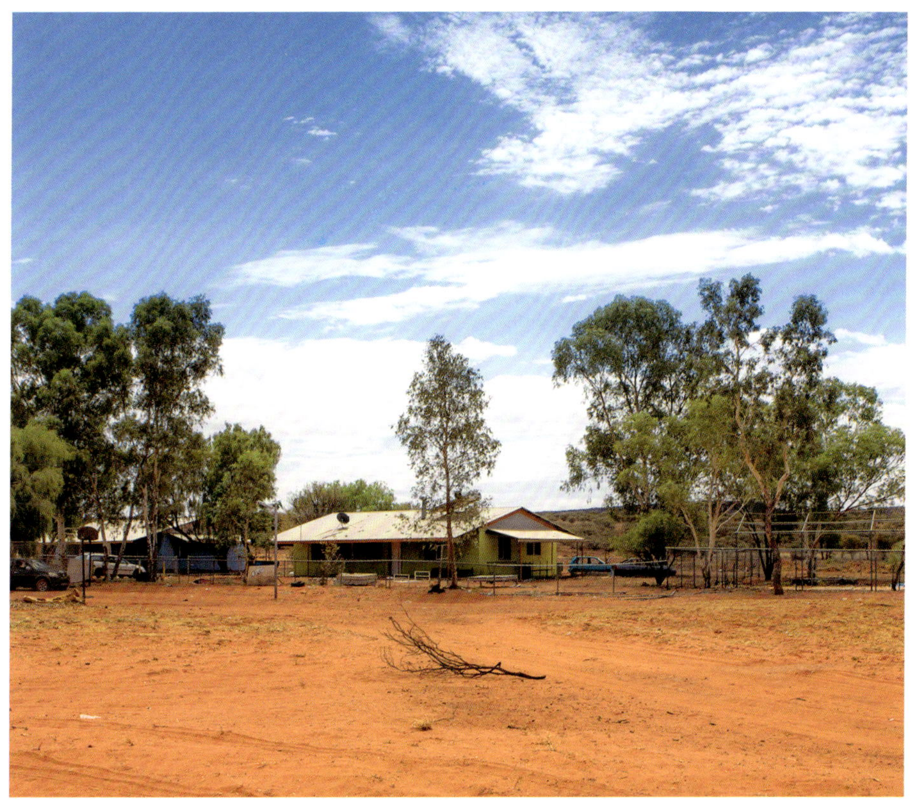

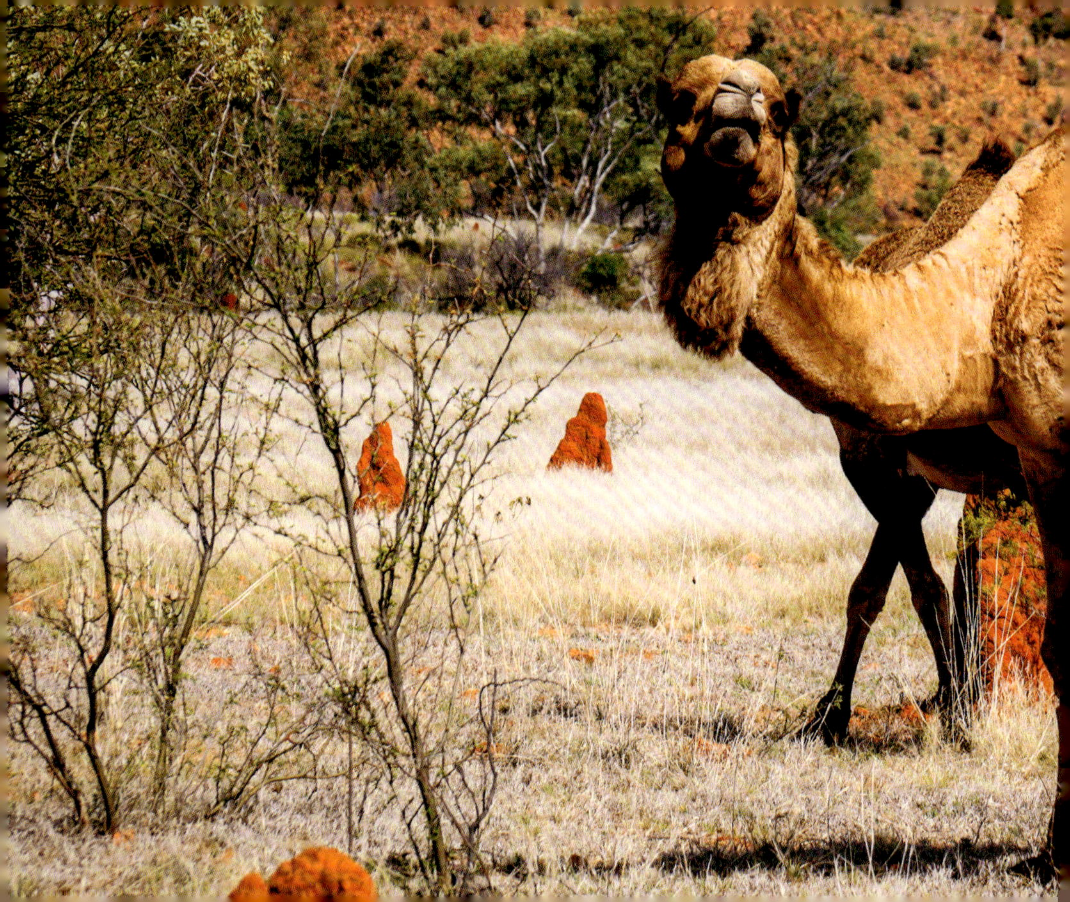

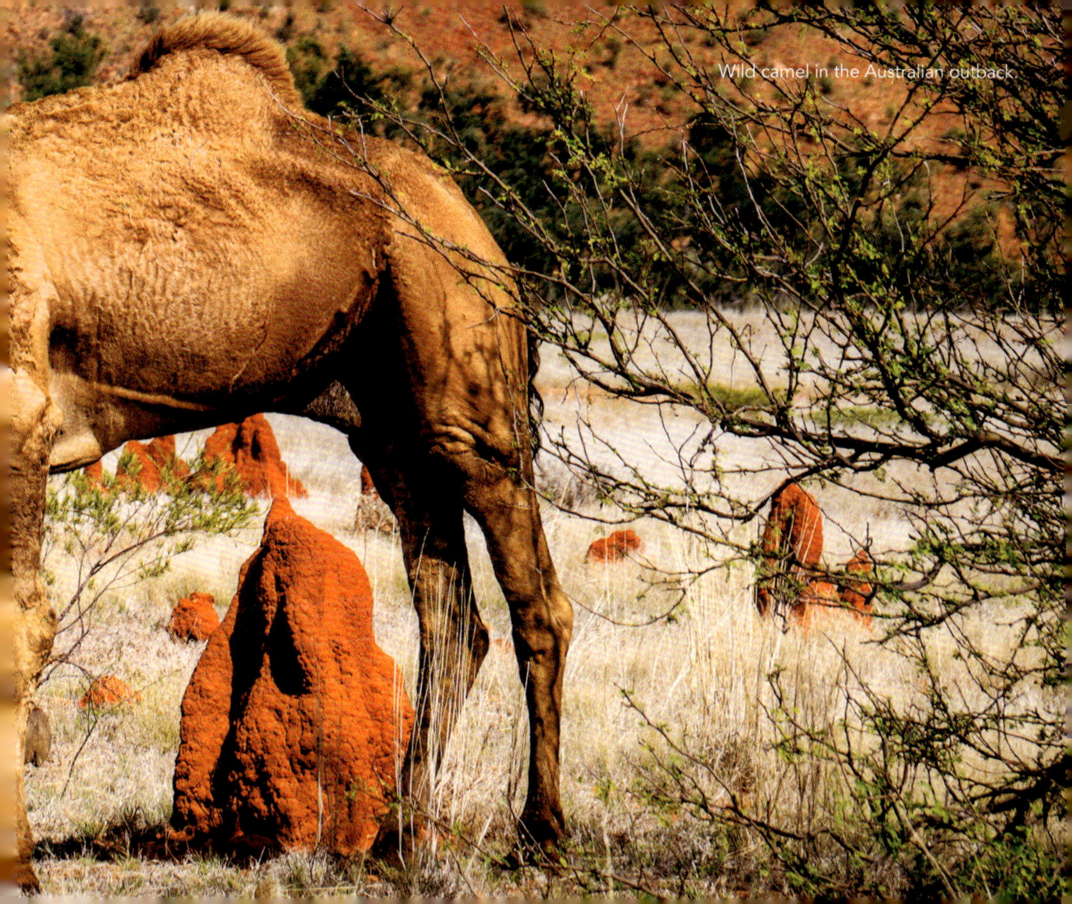
Wild camel in the Australian outback.

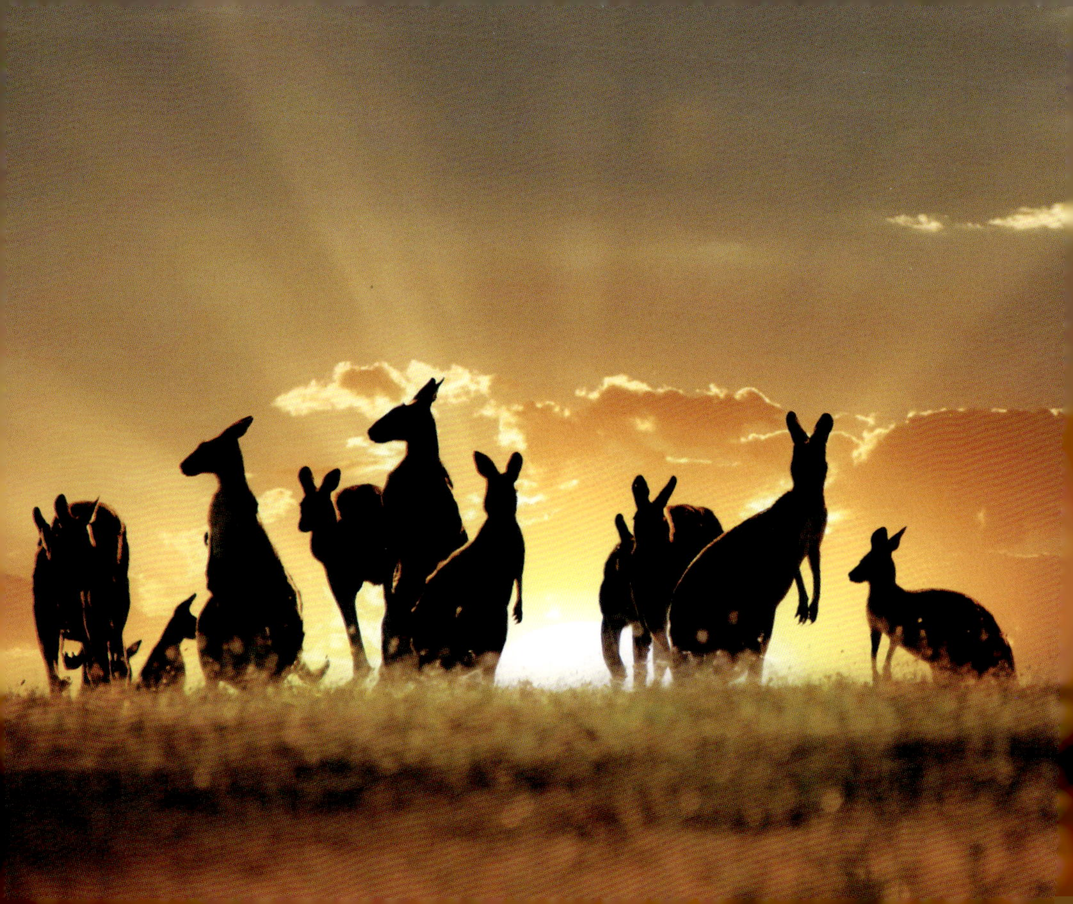

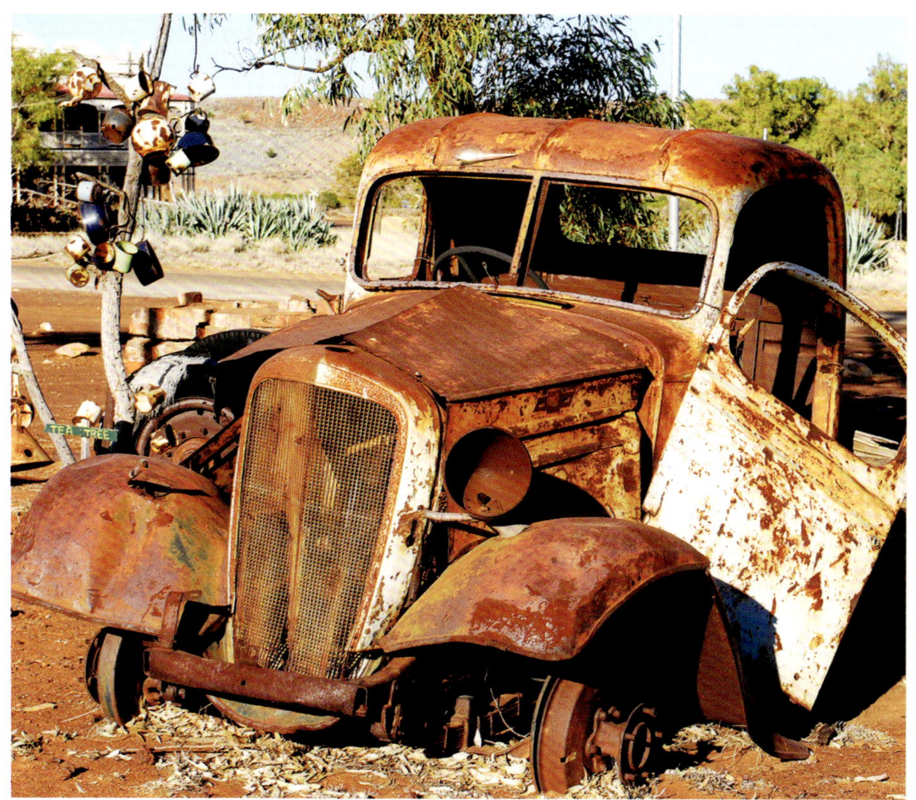

Western Australian desert.

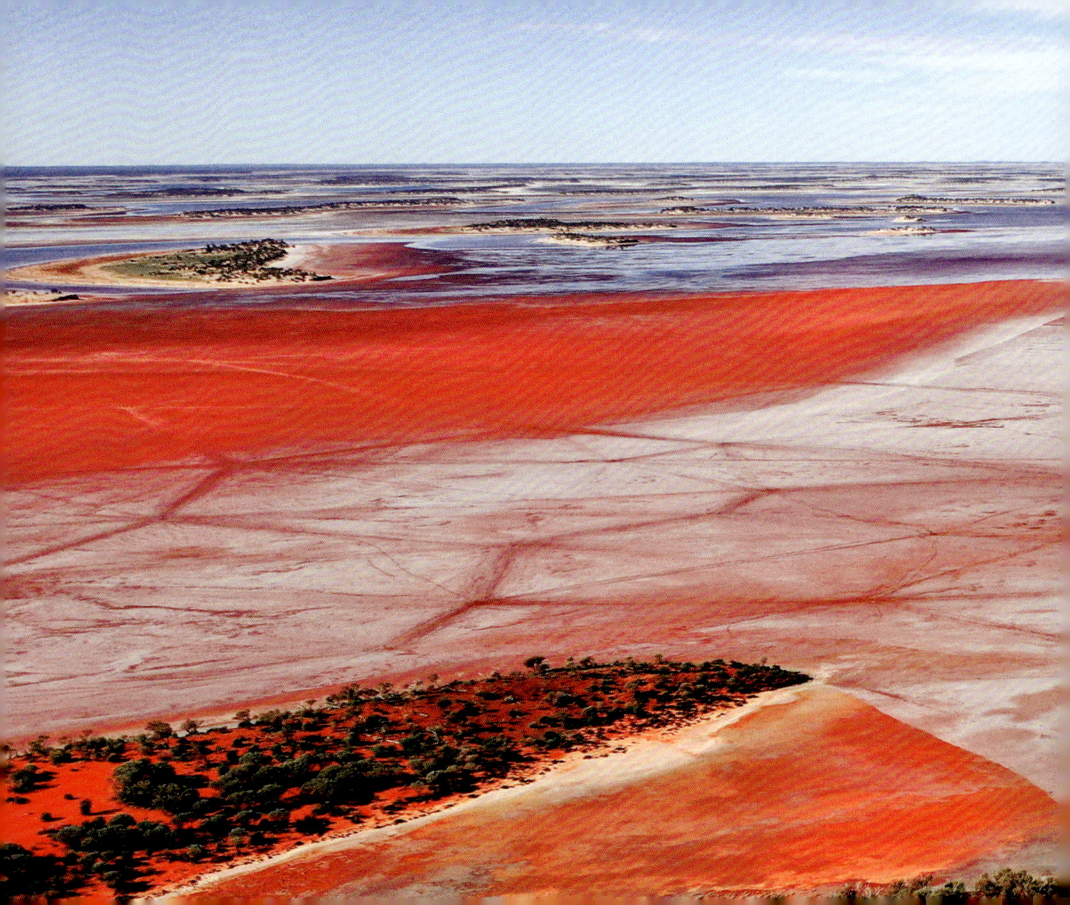

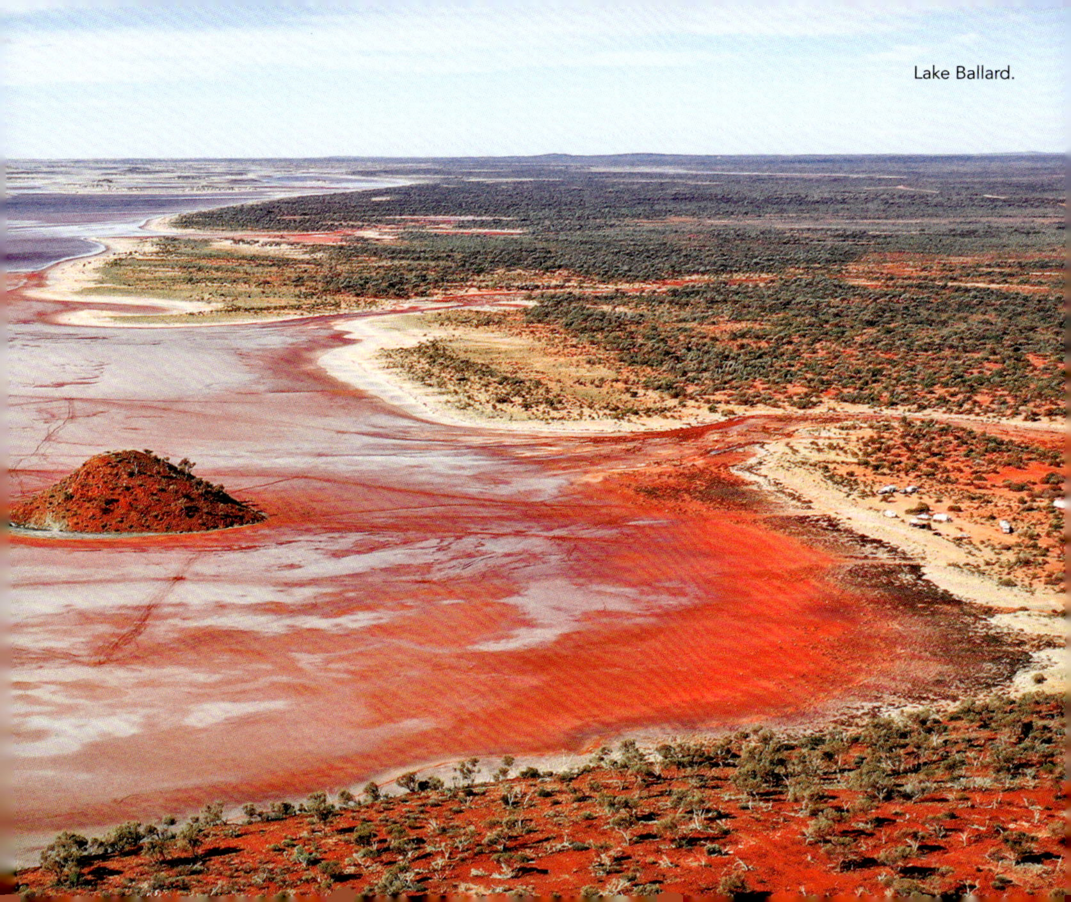

Lake Ballard.

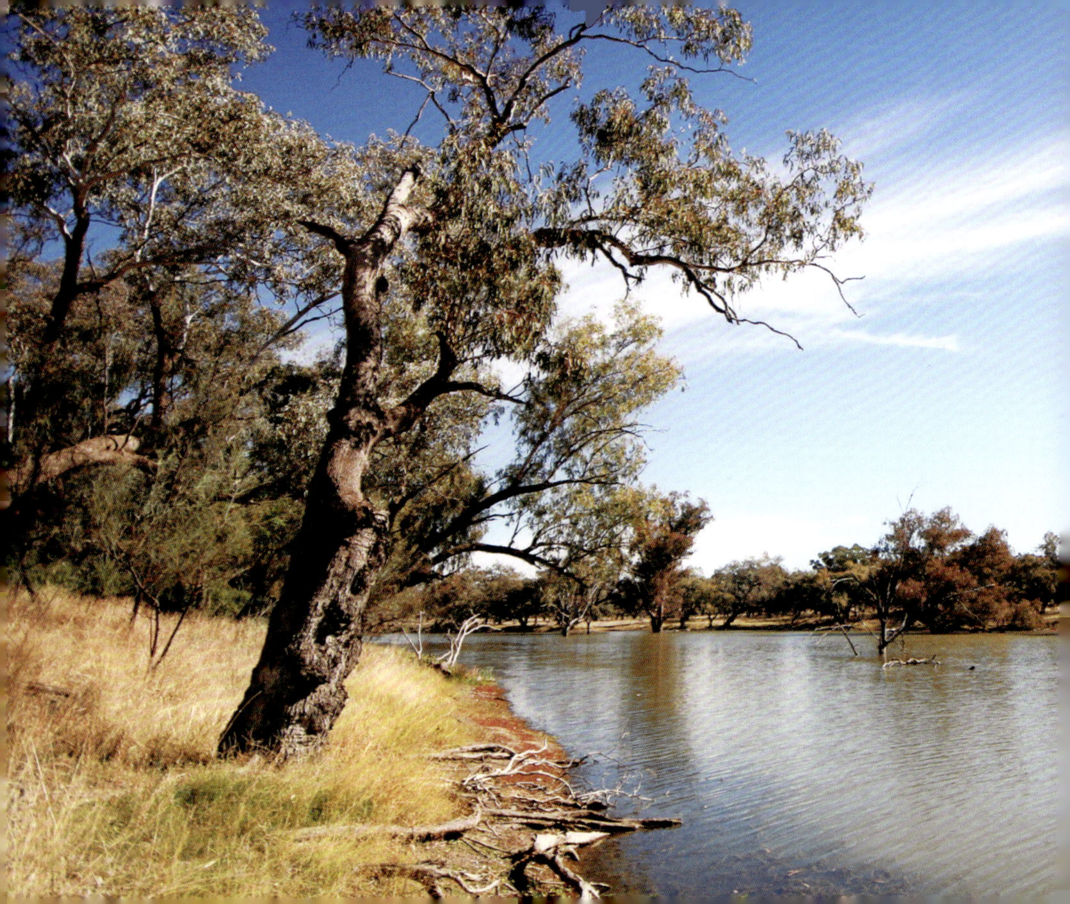

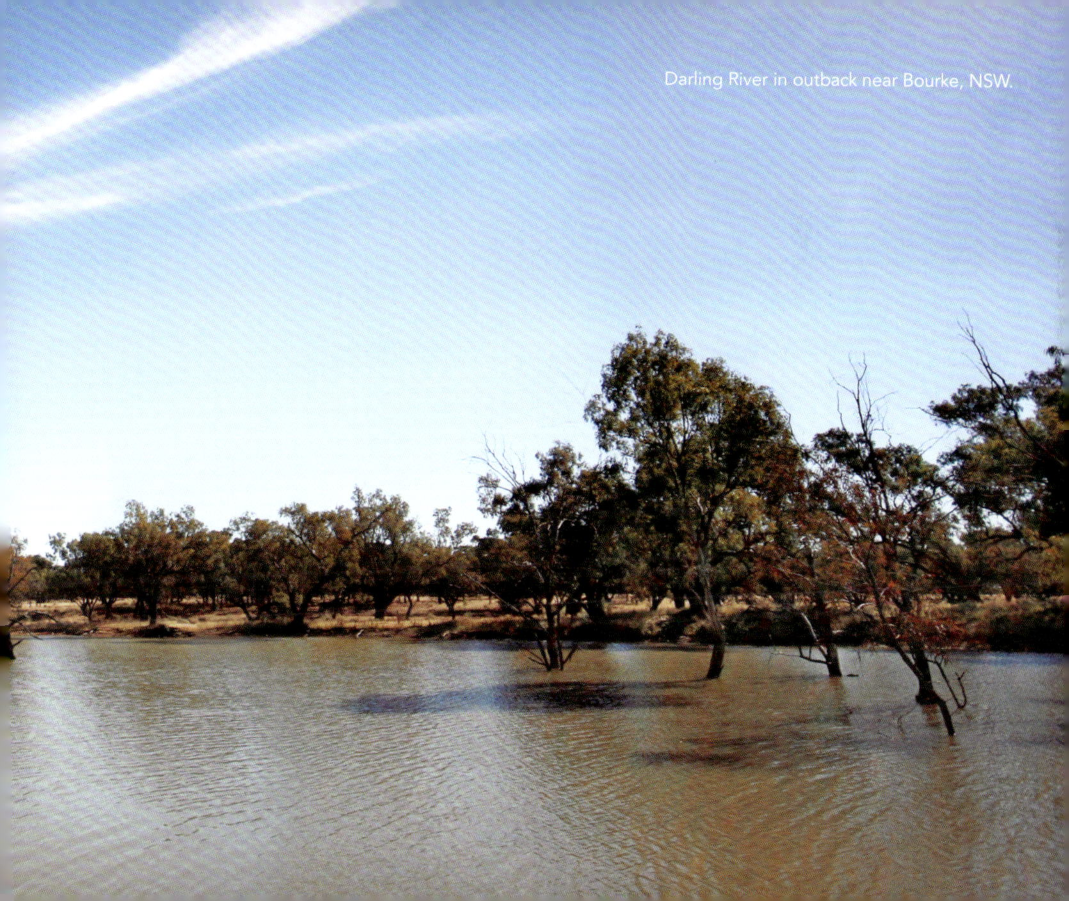

Darling River in outback near Bourke, NSW.

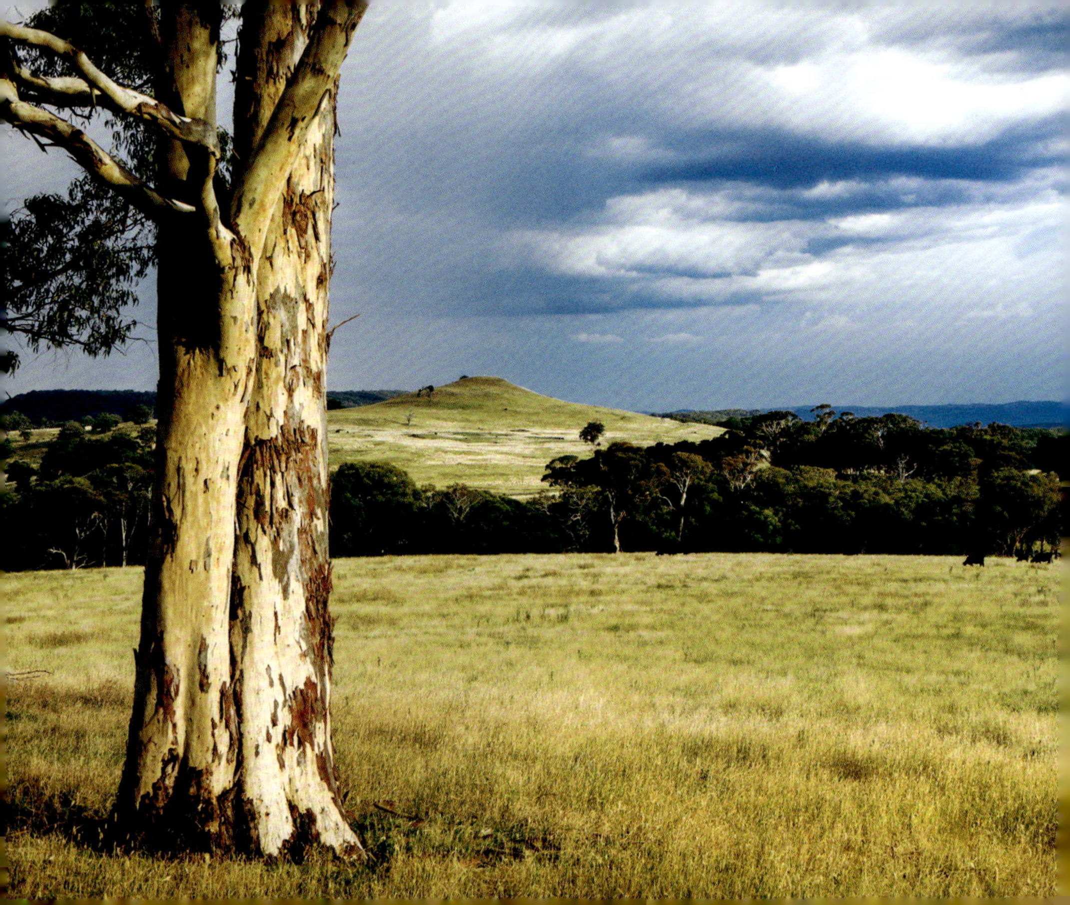

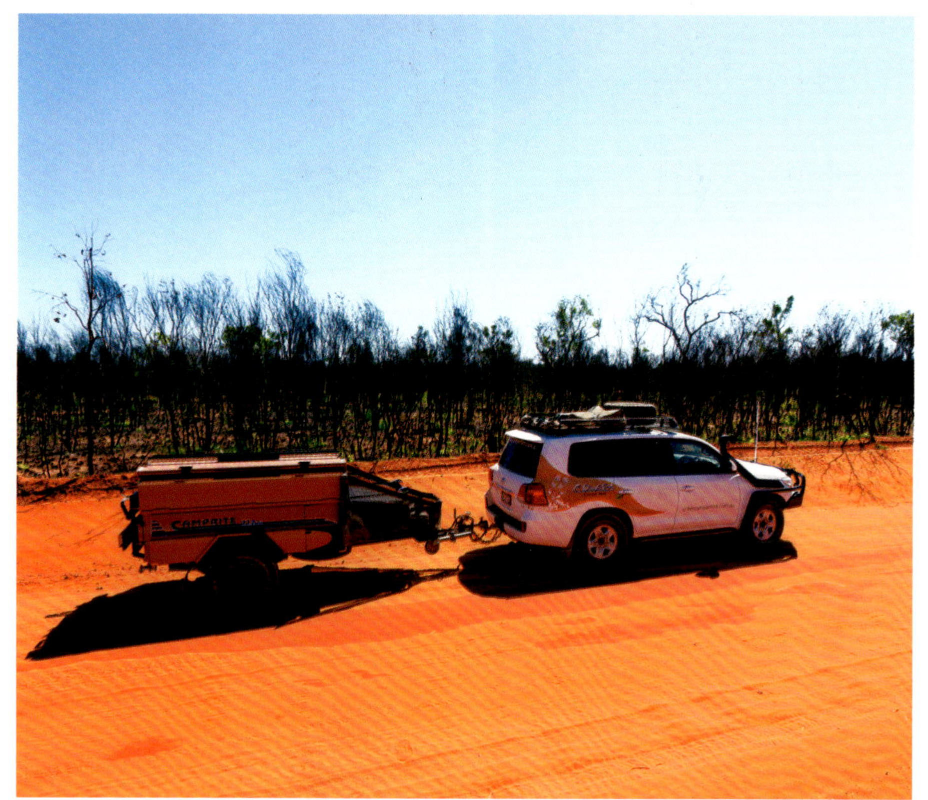
CAMPRITE

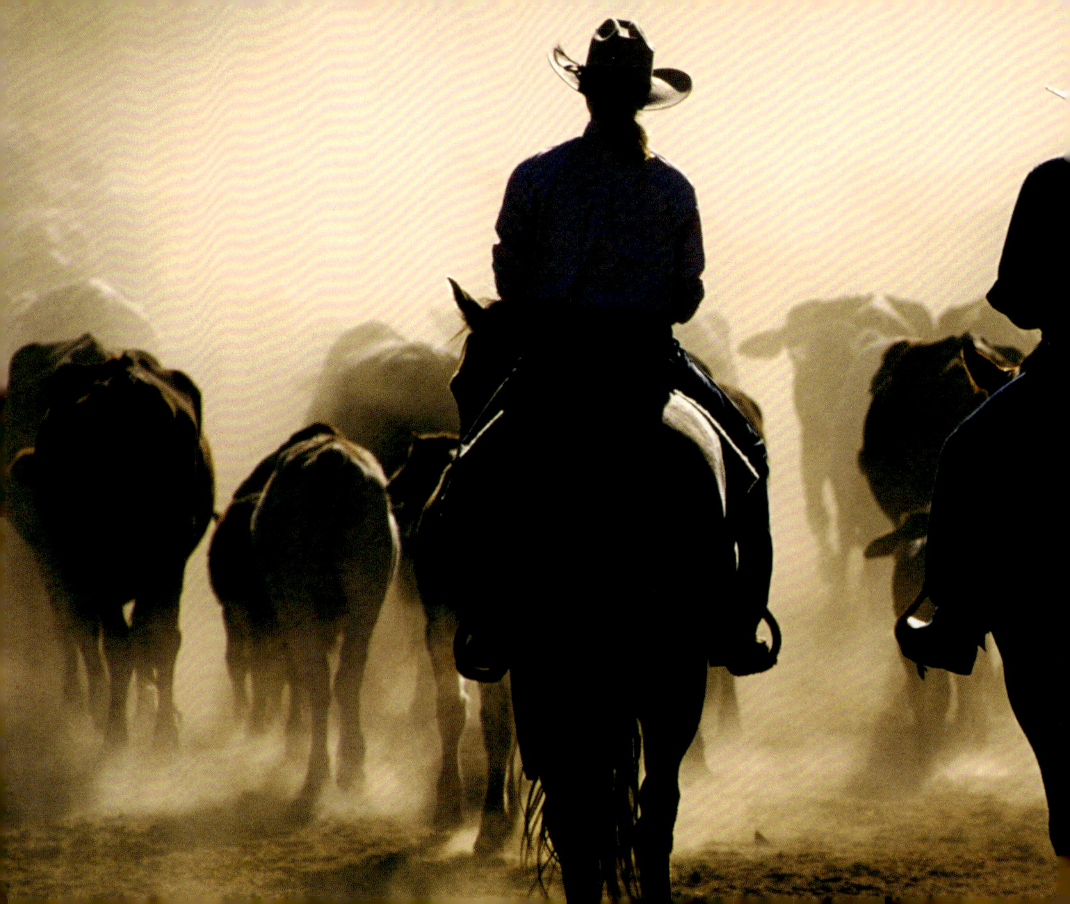

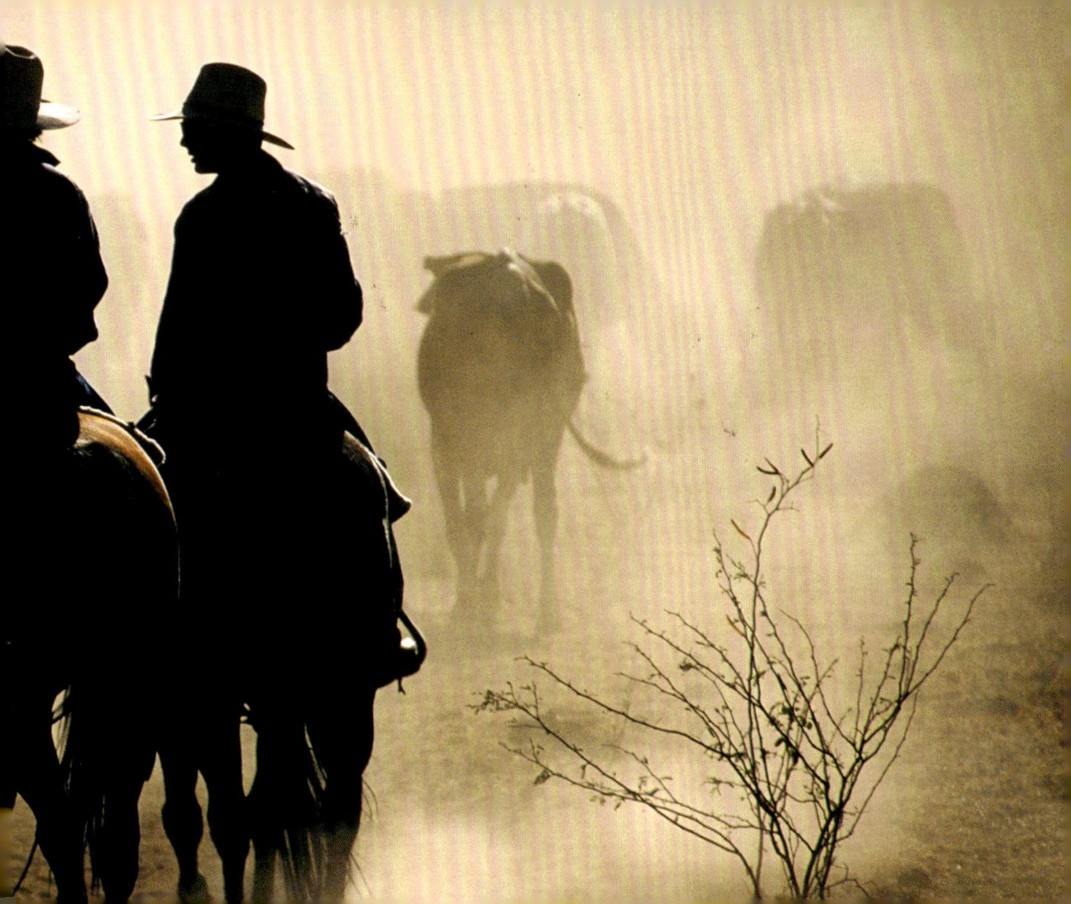

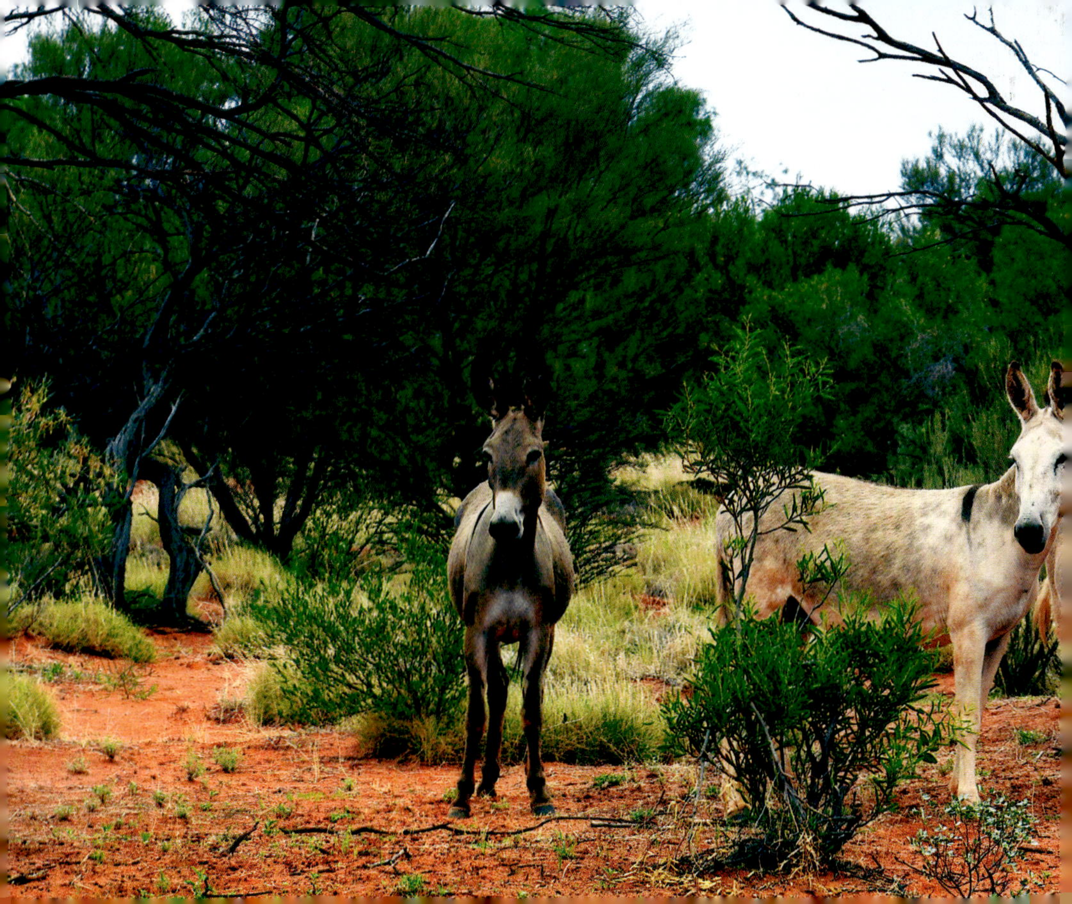

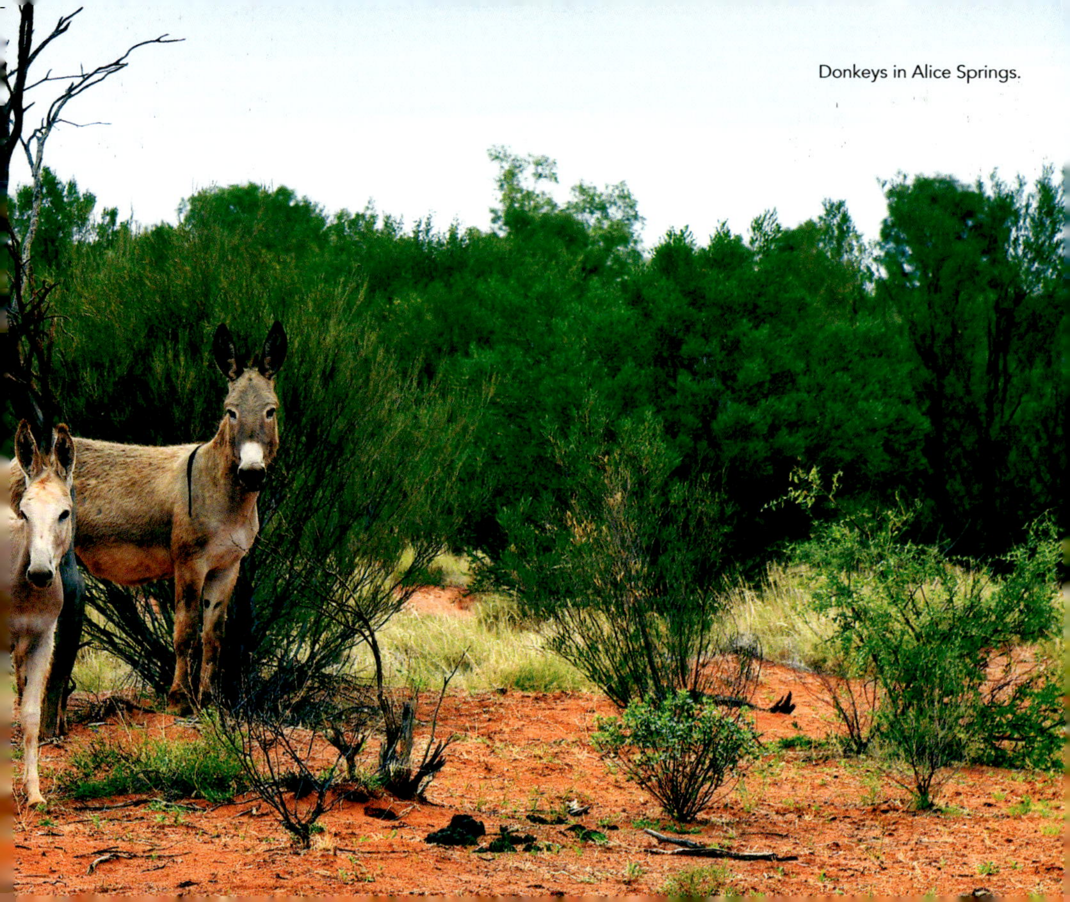

Donkeys in Alice Springs.

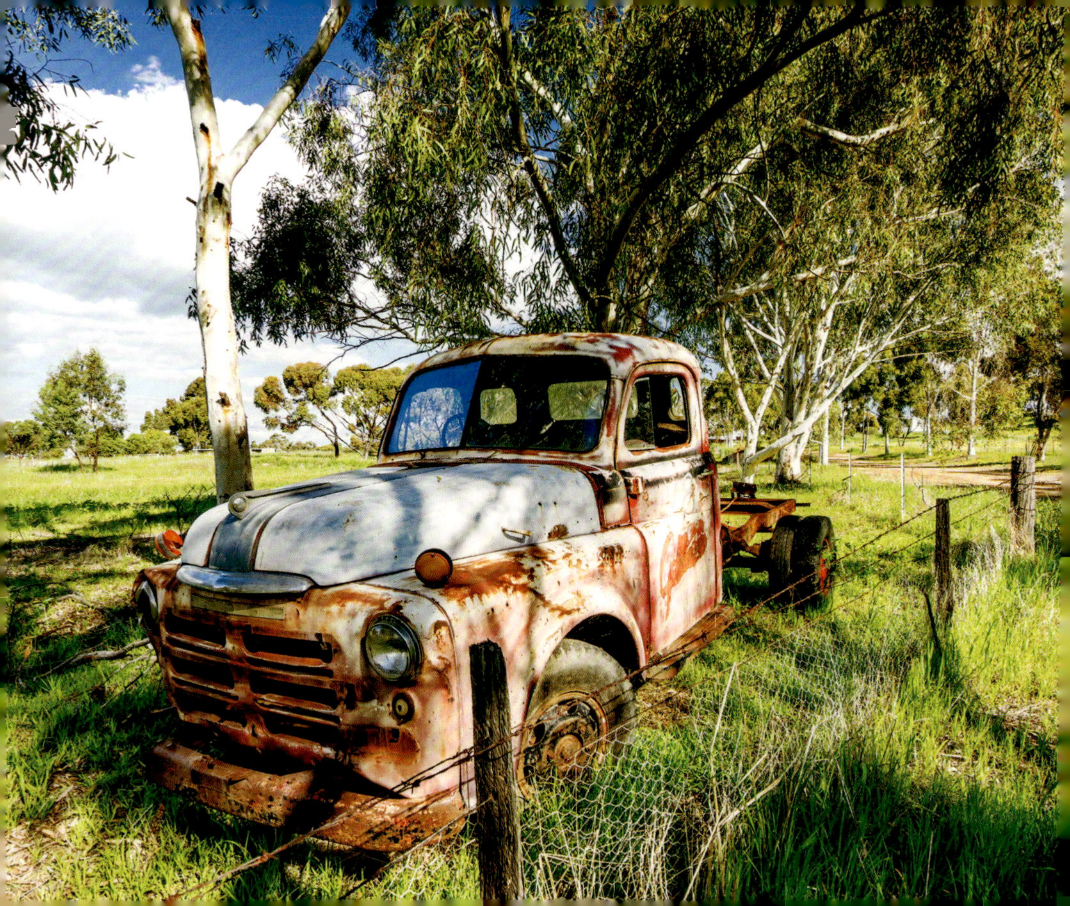

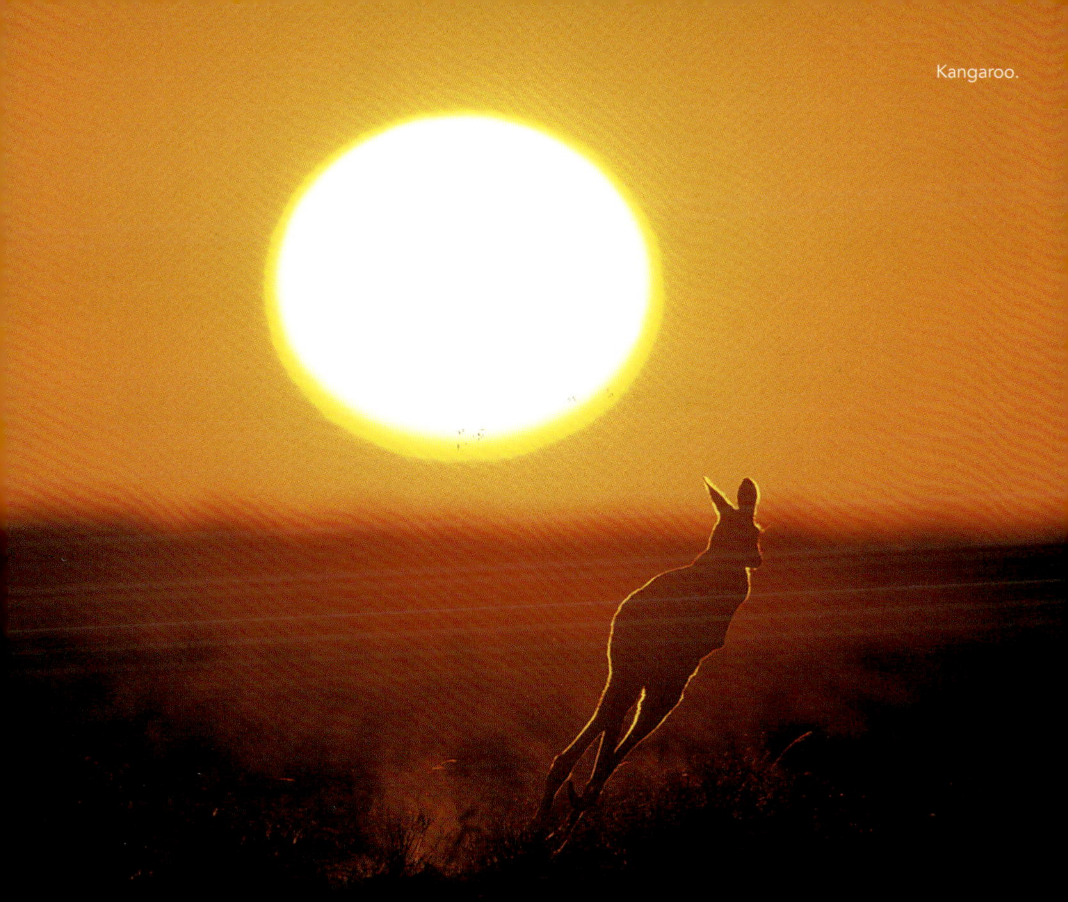

Kangaroo.

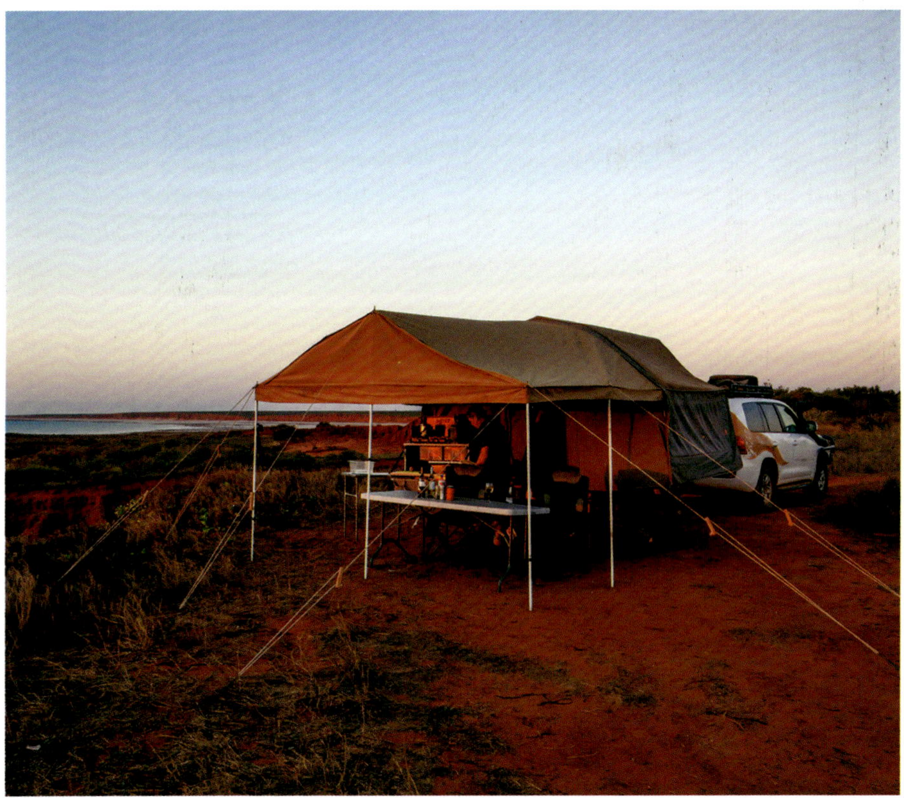

James Price Point, Kimberley Australia.

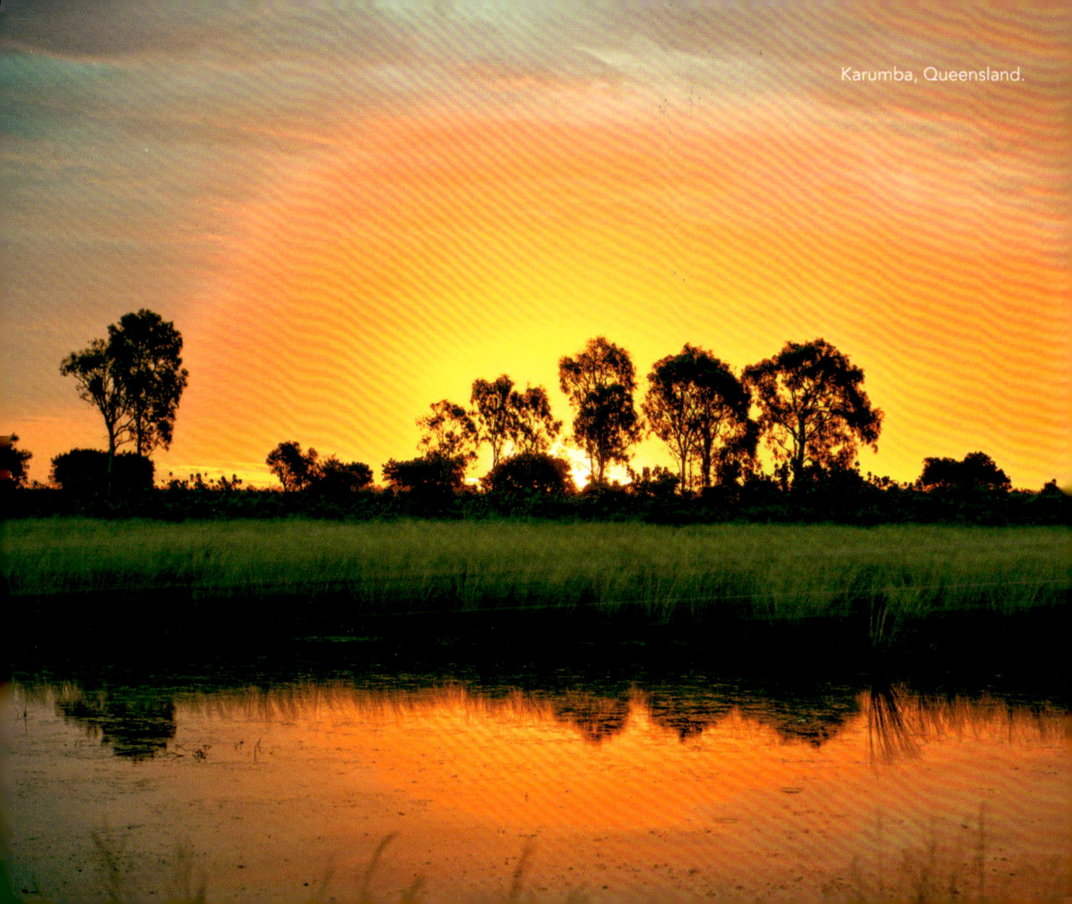
Karumba, Queensland.

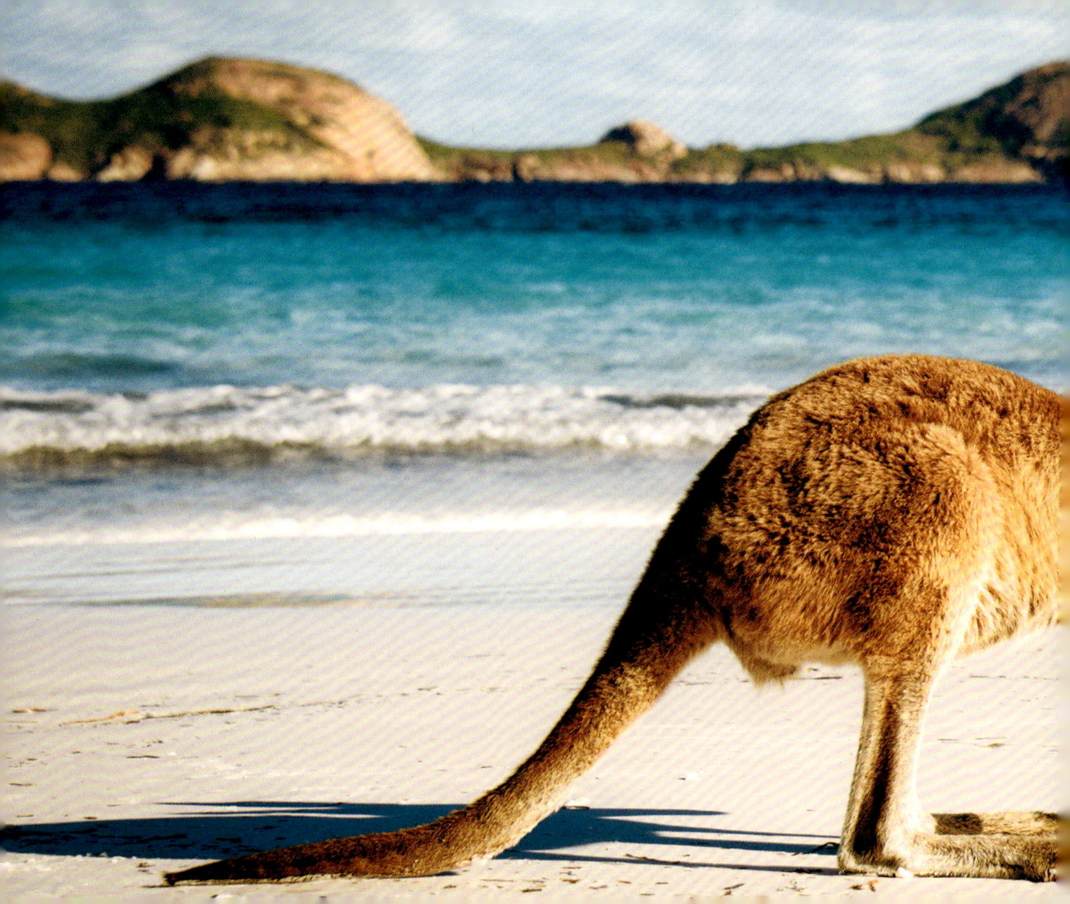

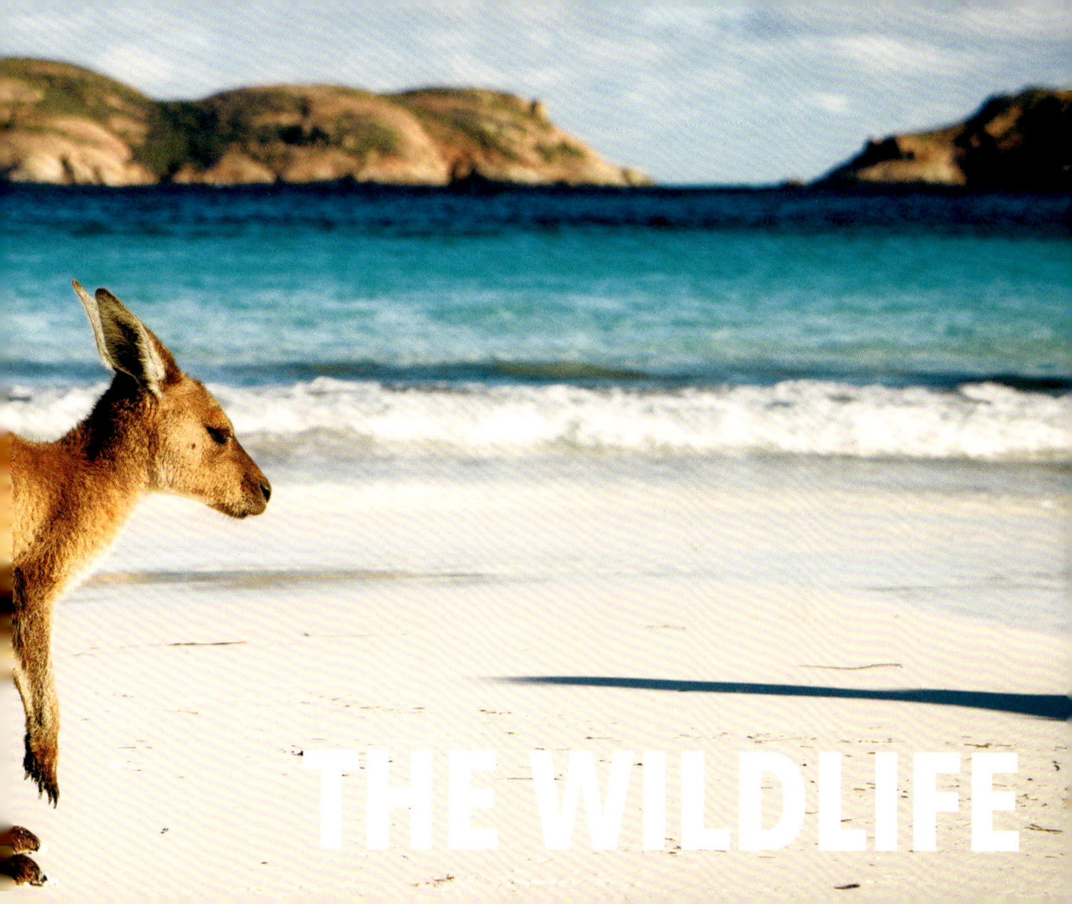
THE WILDLIFE

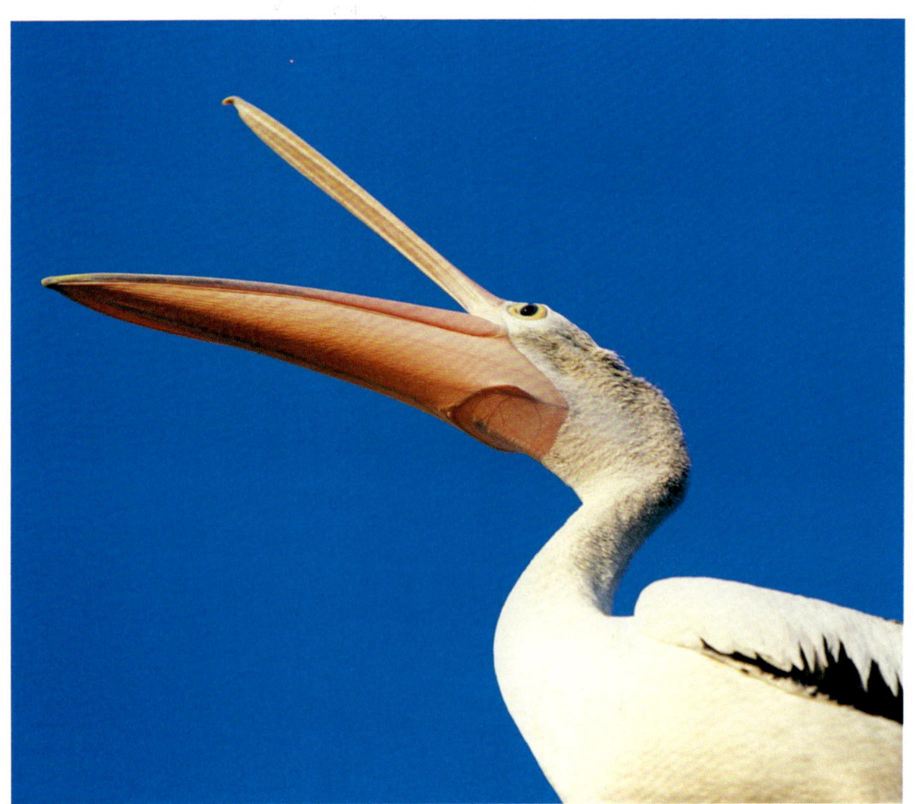

Pelican.

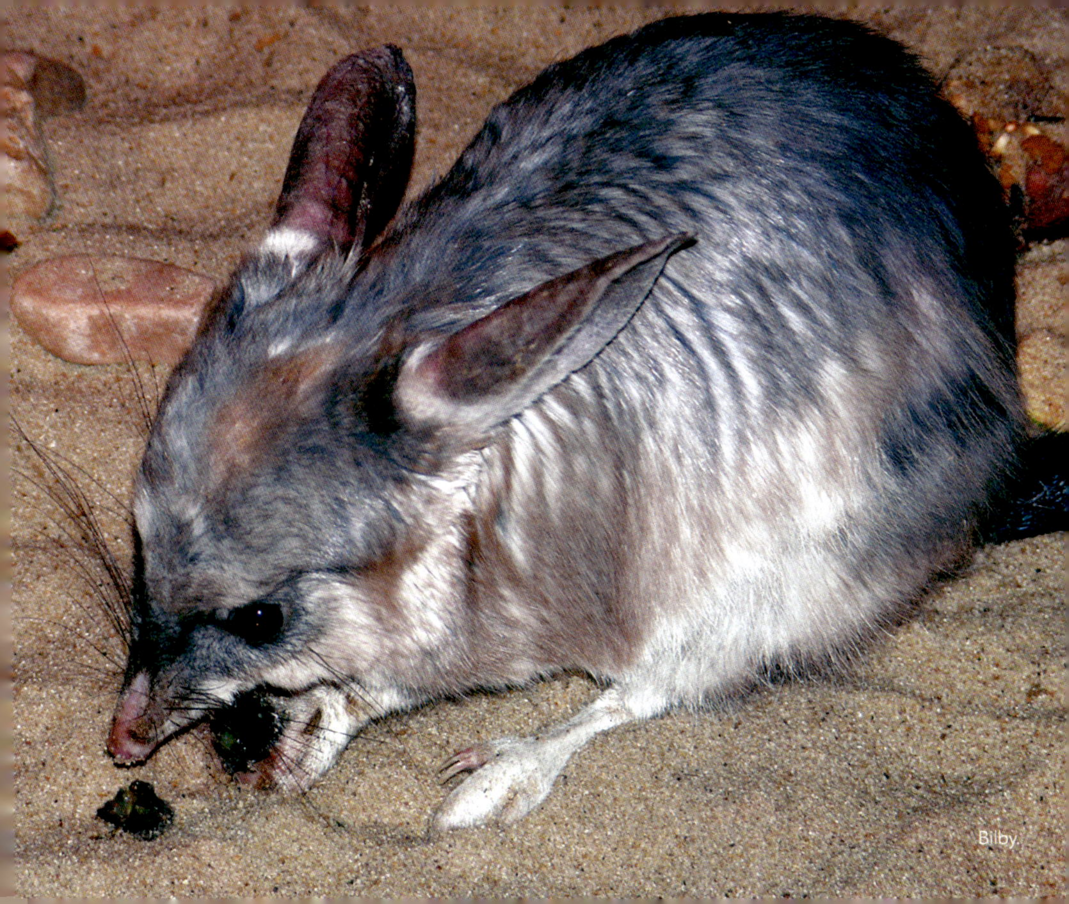

Bilby.

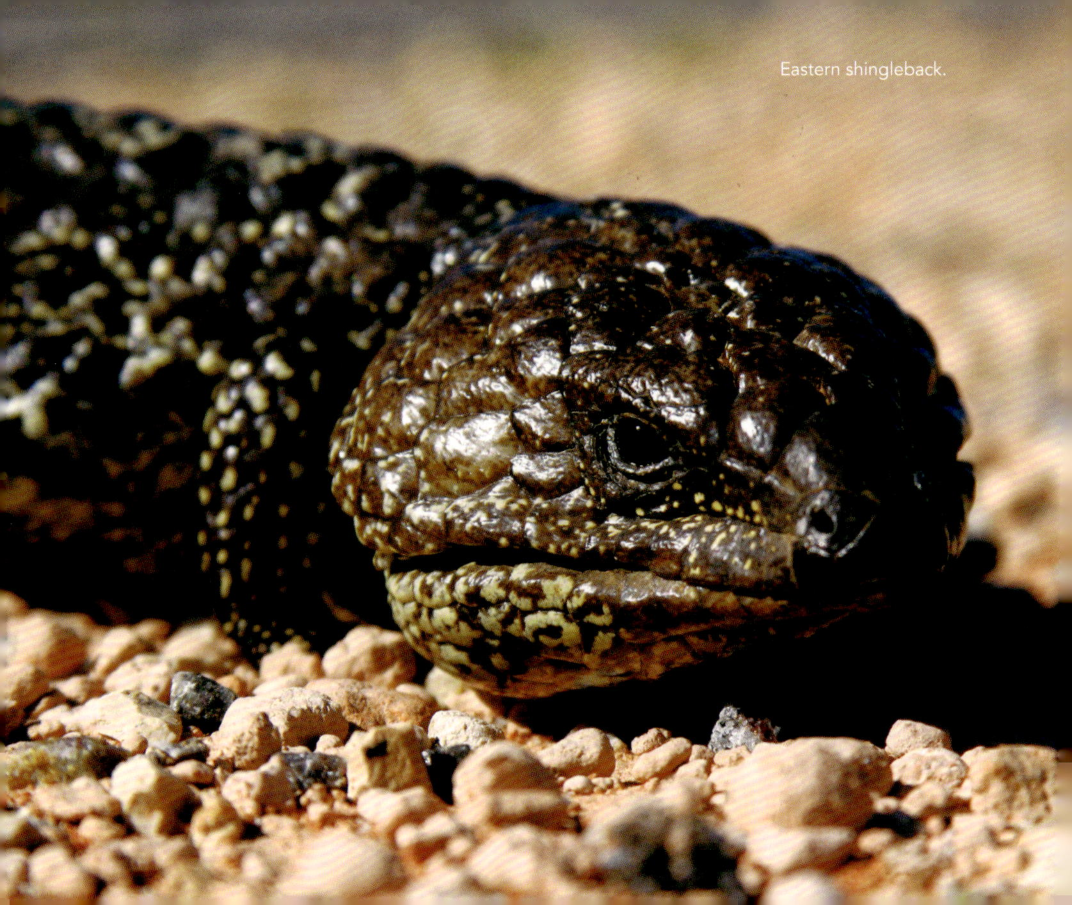

Eastern shingleback.

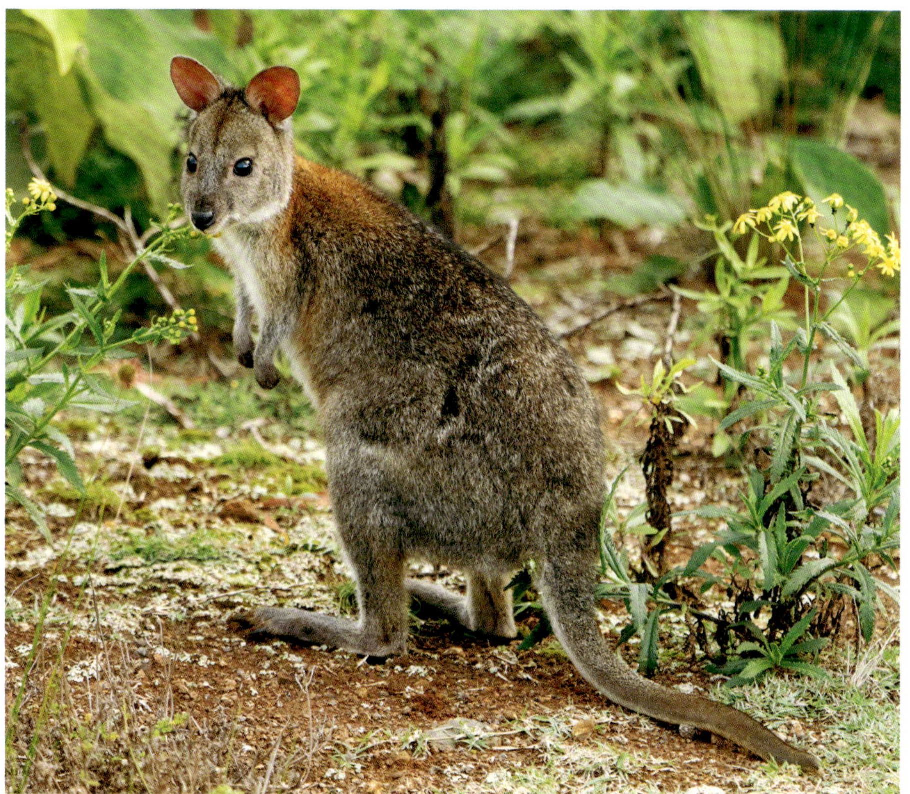

Red Necked Pademelon.

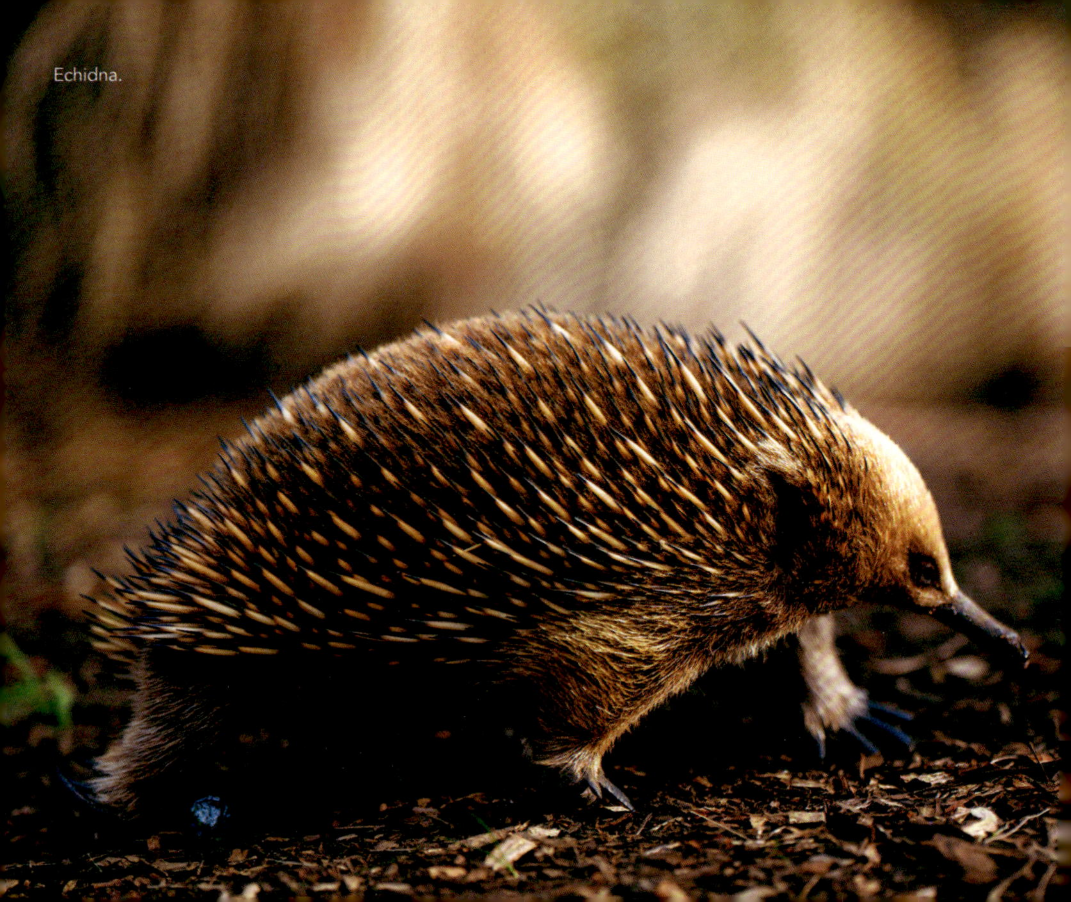
Echidna.

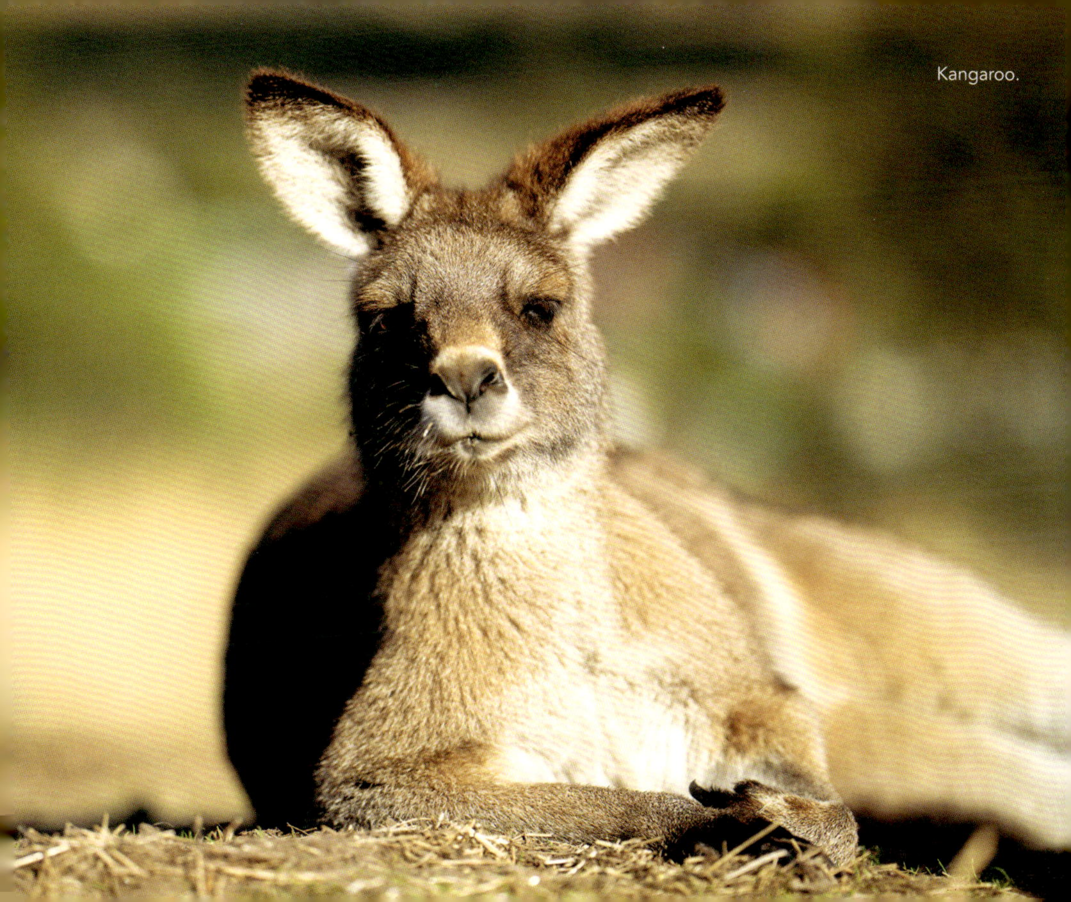

Kangaroo.

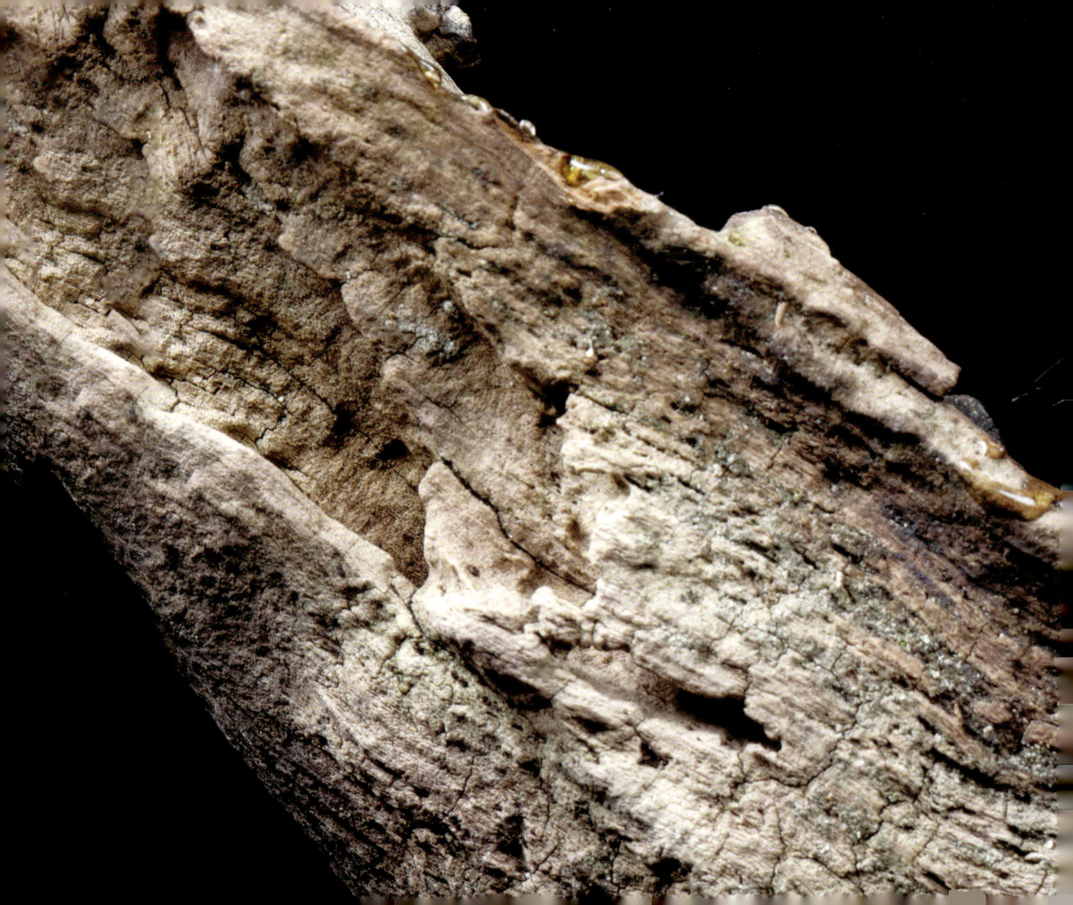

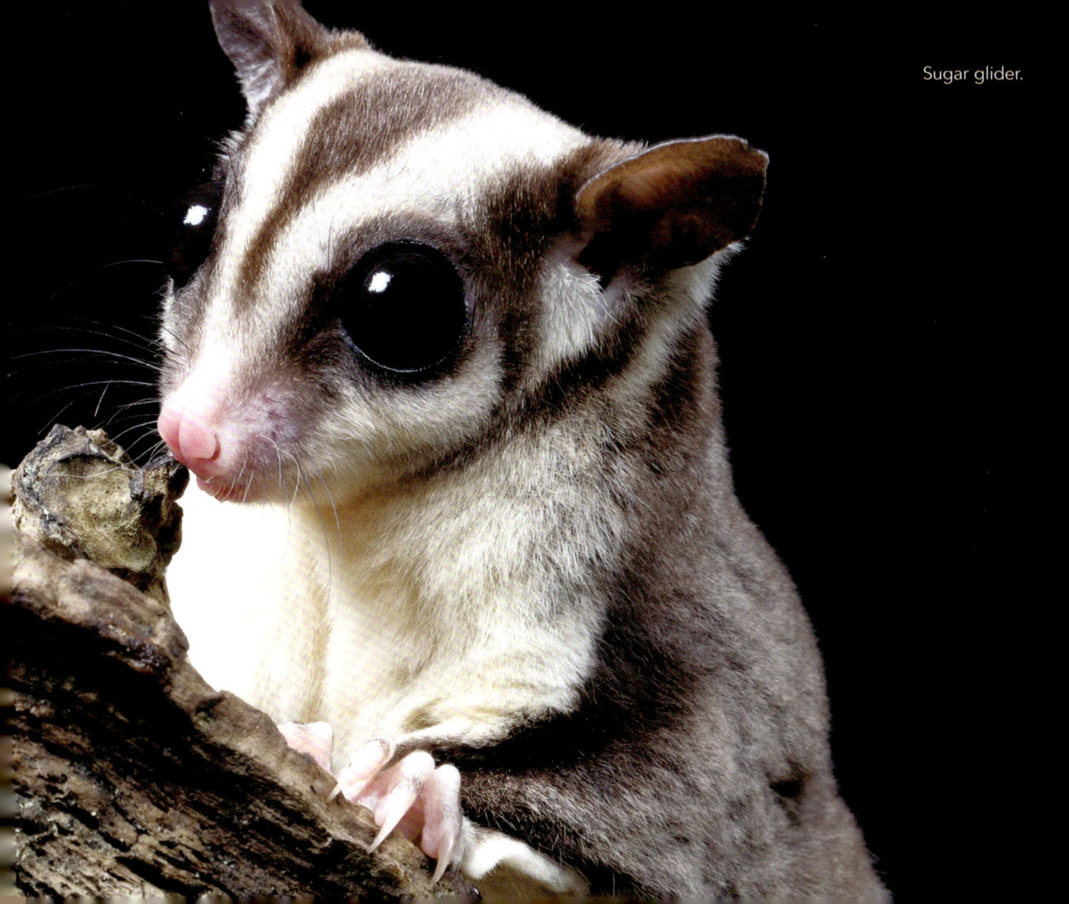

Sugar glider.

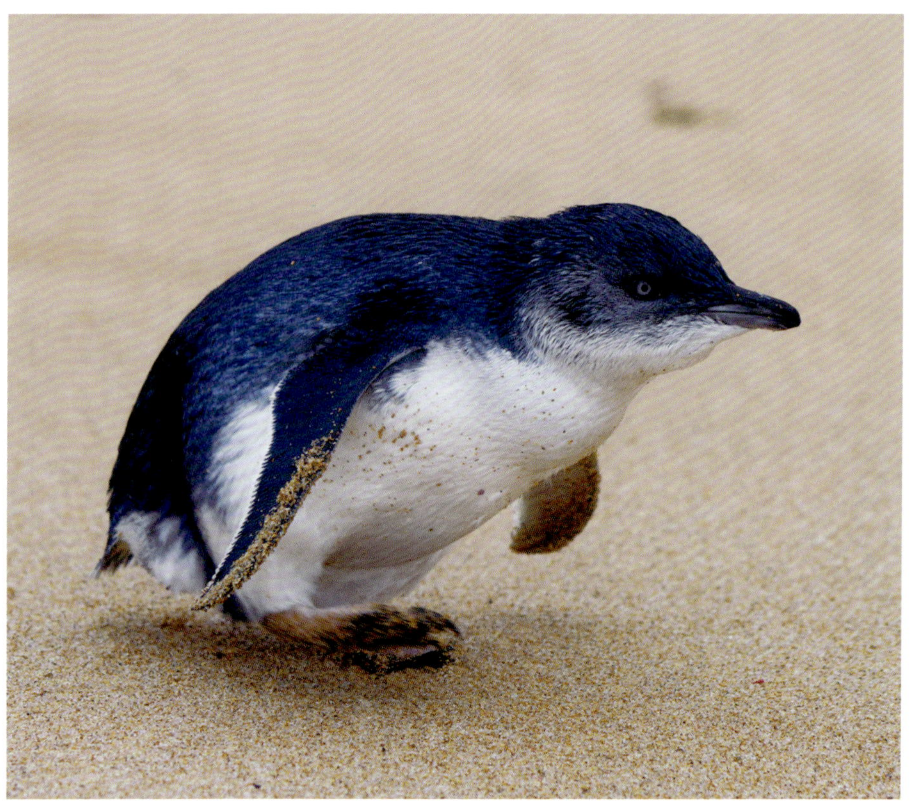

Fairy Penguin.

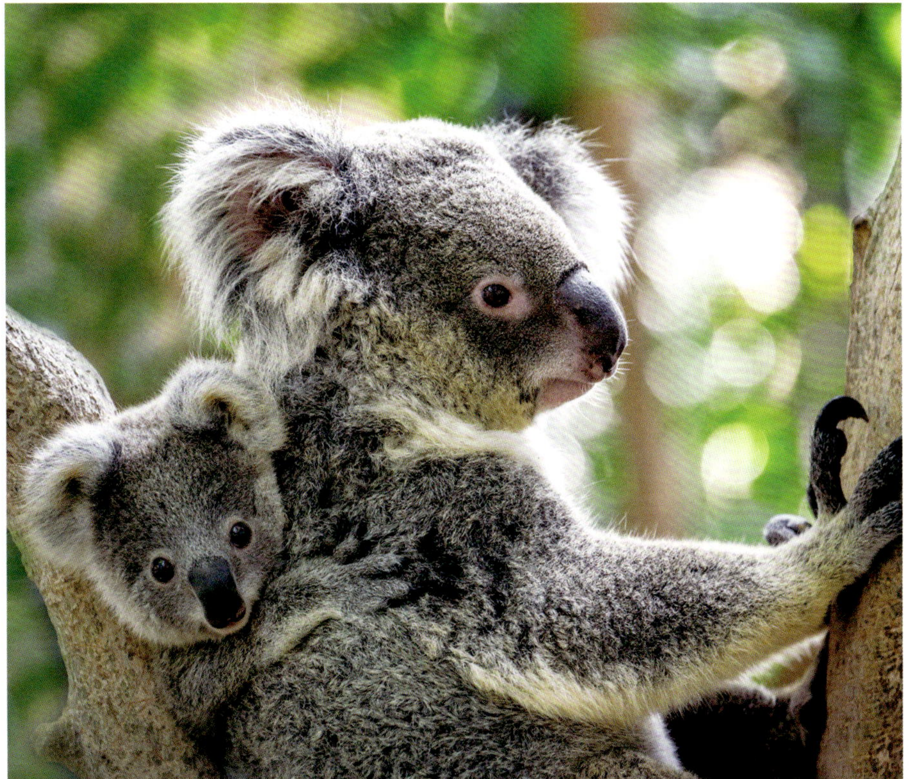

Koala and joey.

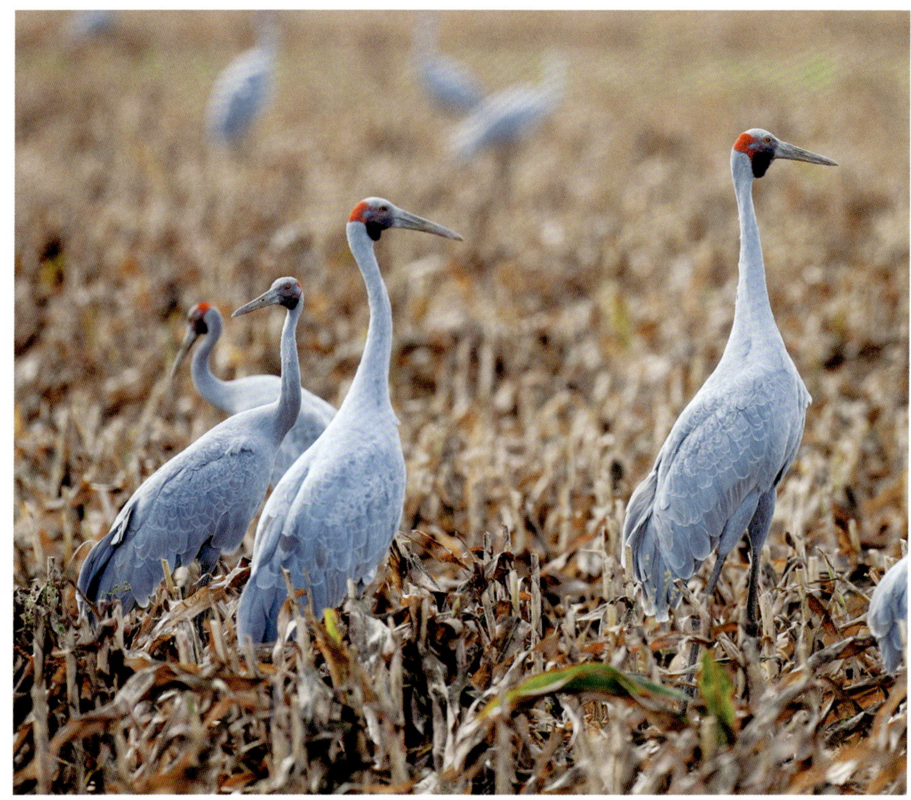
Brolga.

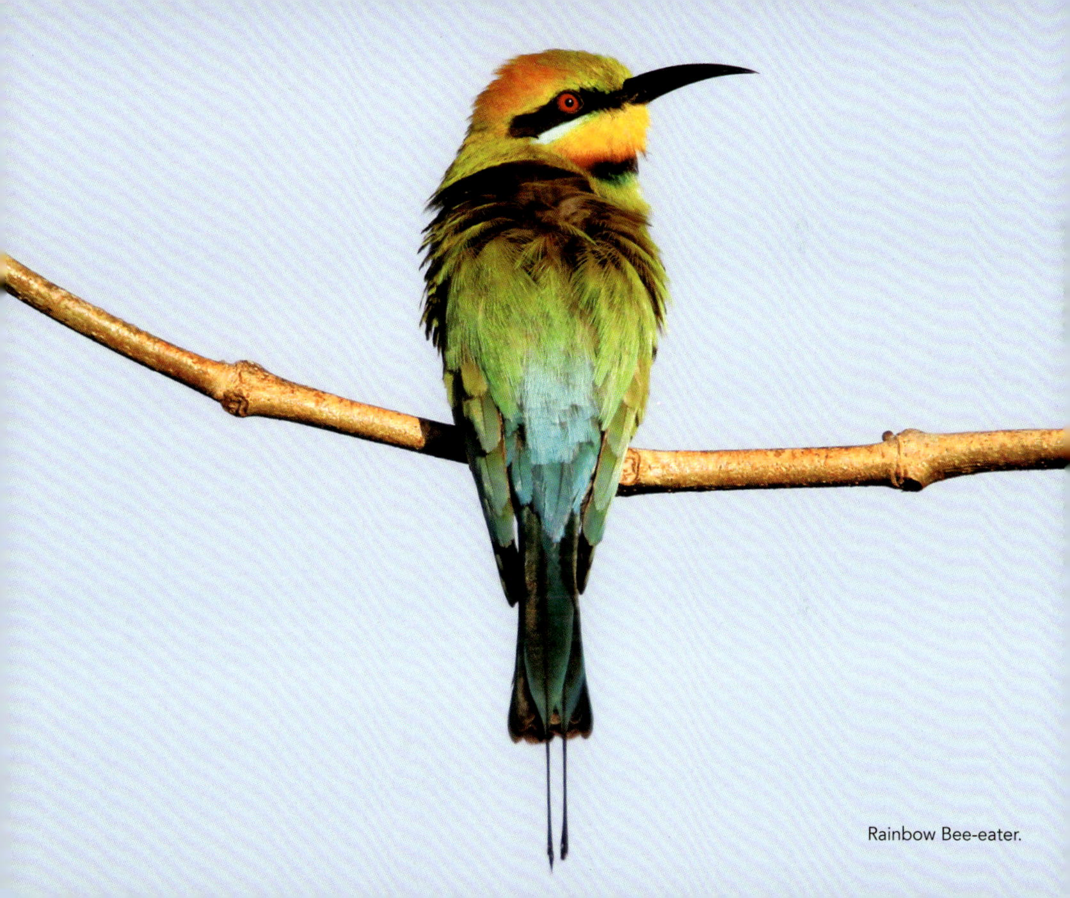
Rainbow Bee-eater.

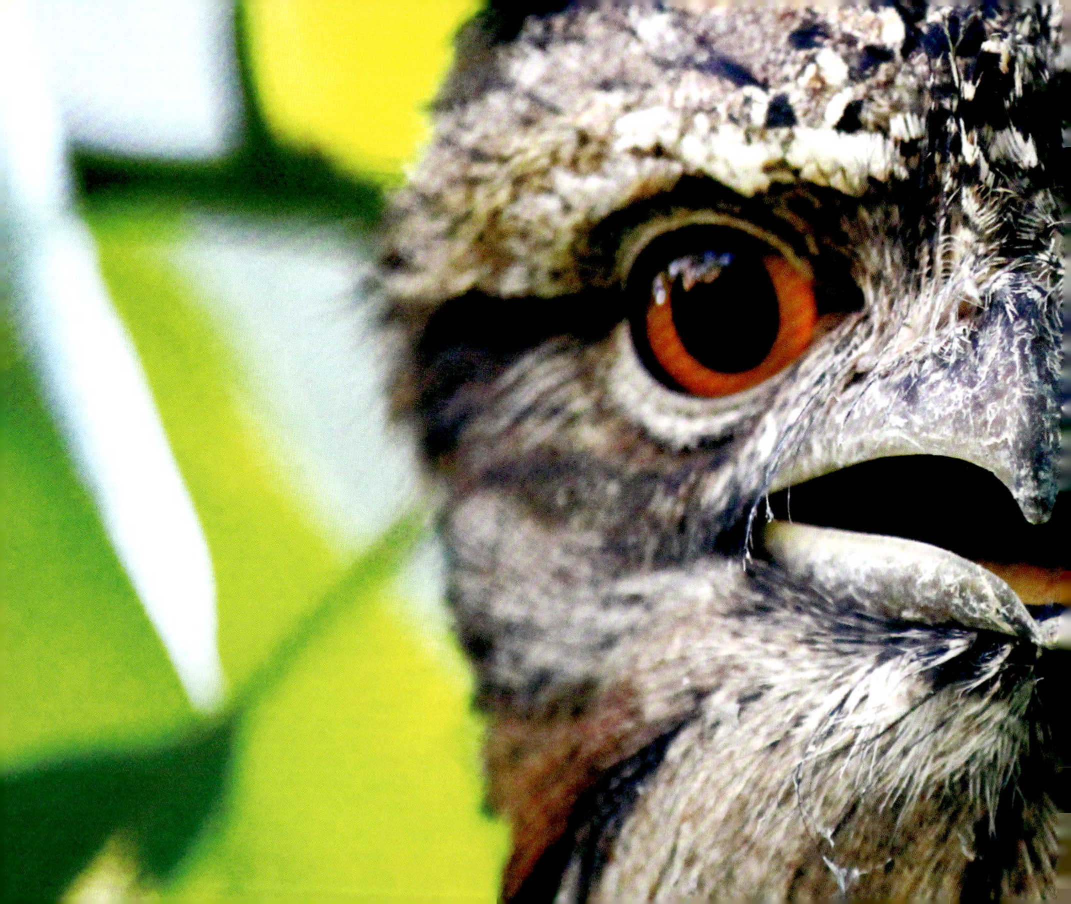

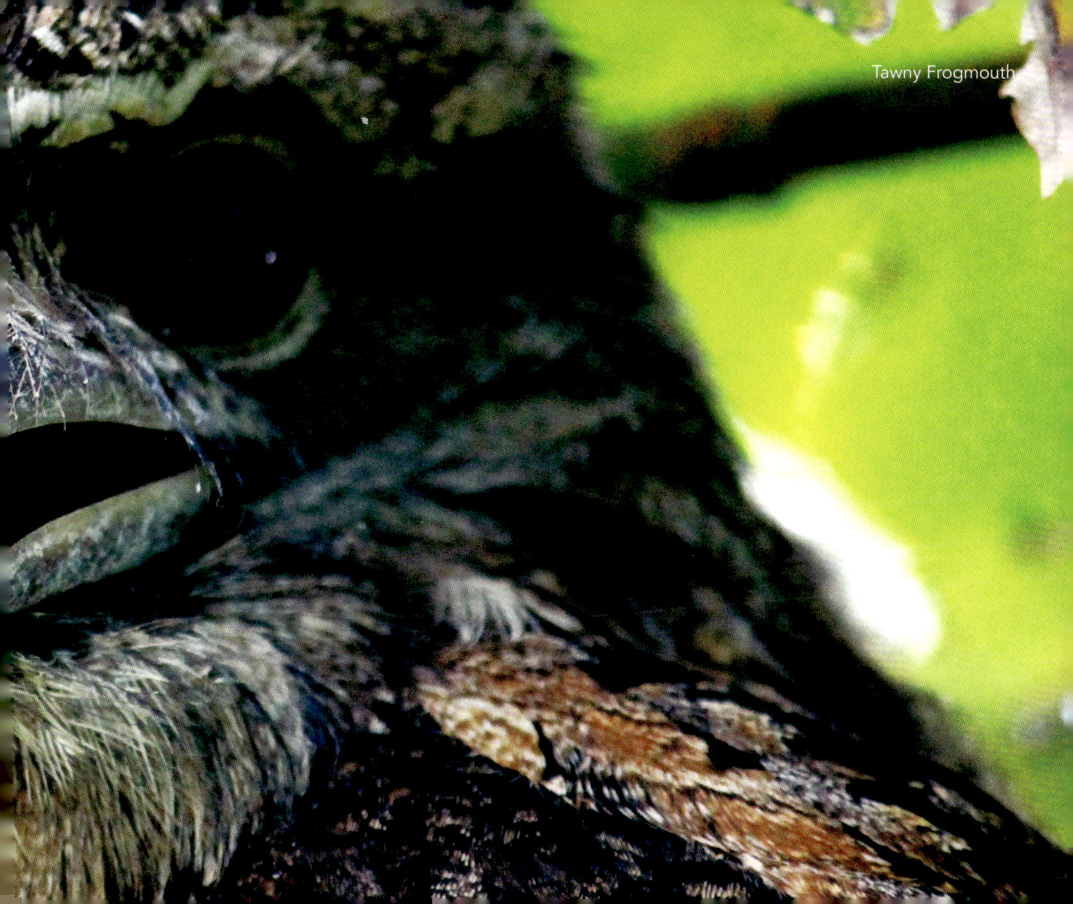

Tawny Frogmouth

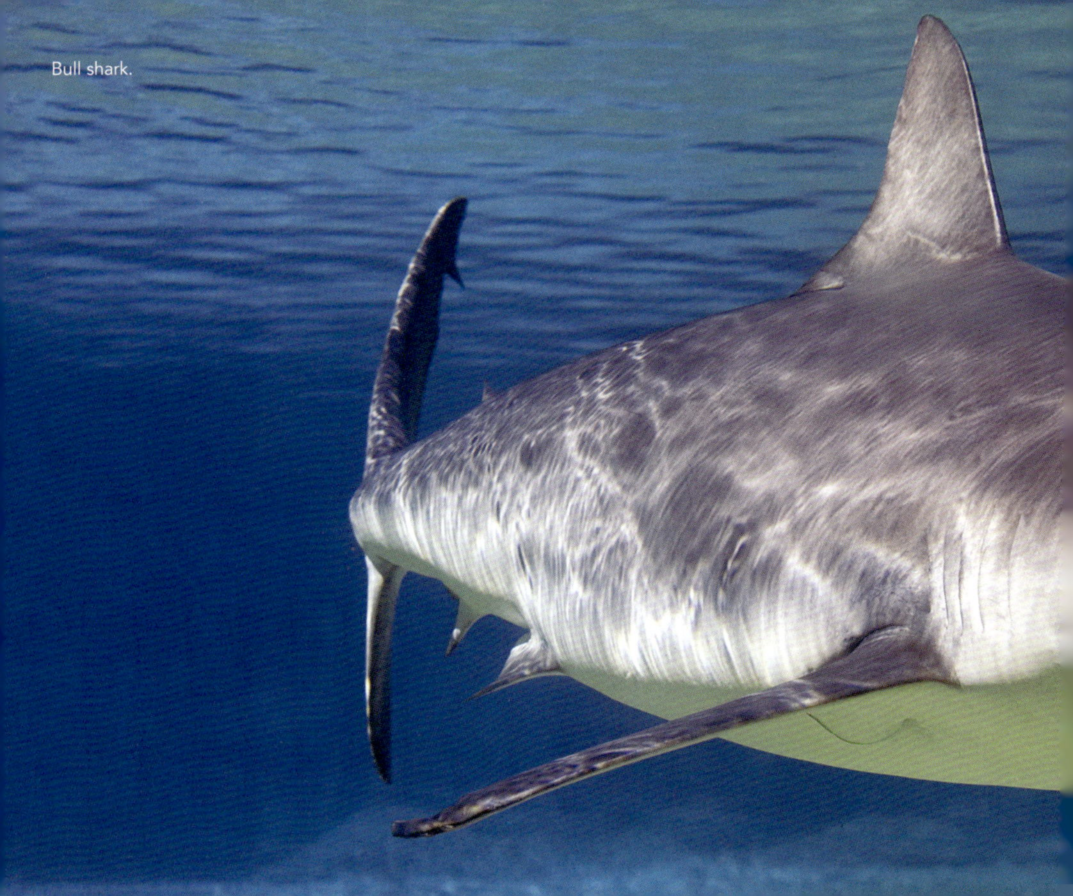
Bull shark.

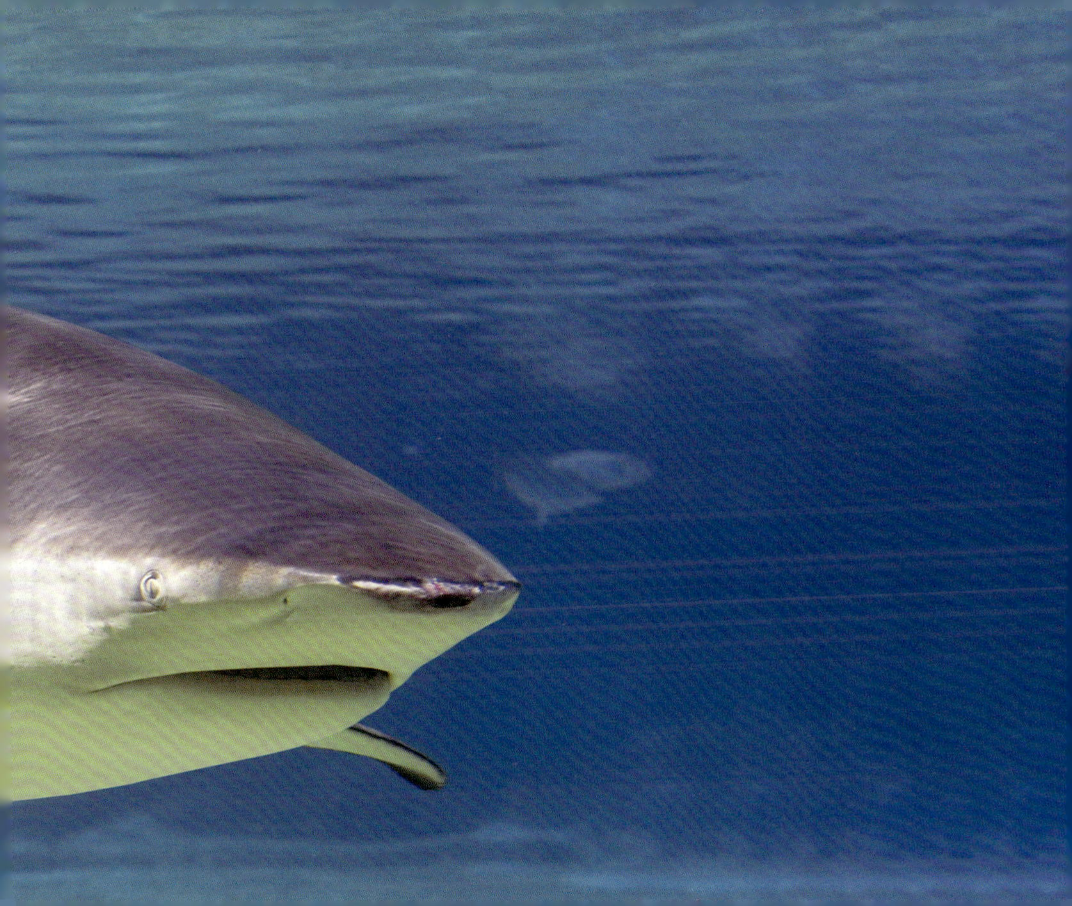

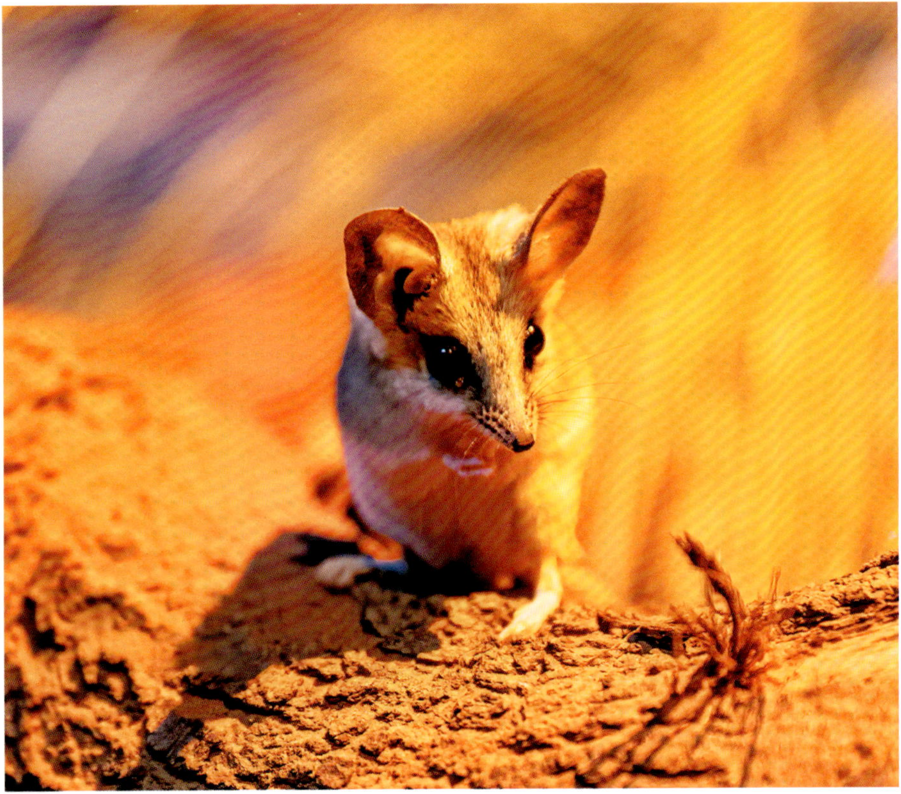

Fat-tailed Dunnart.

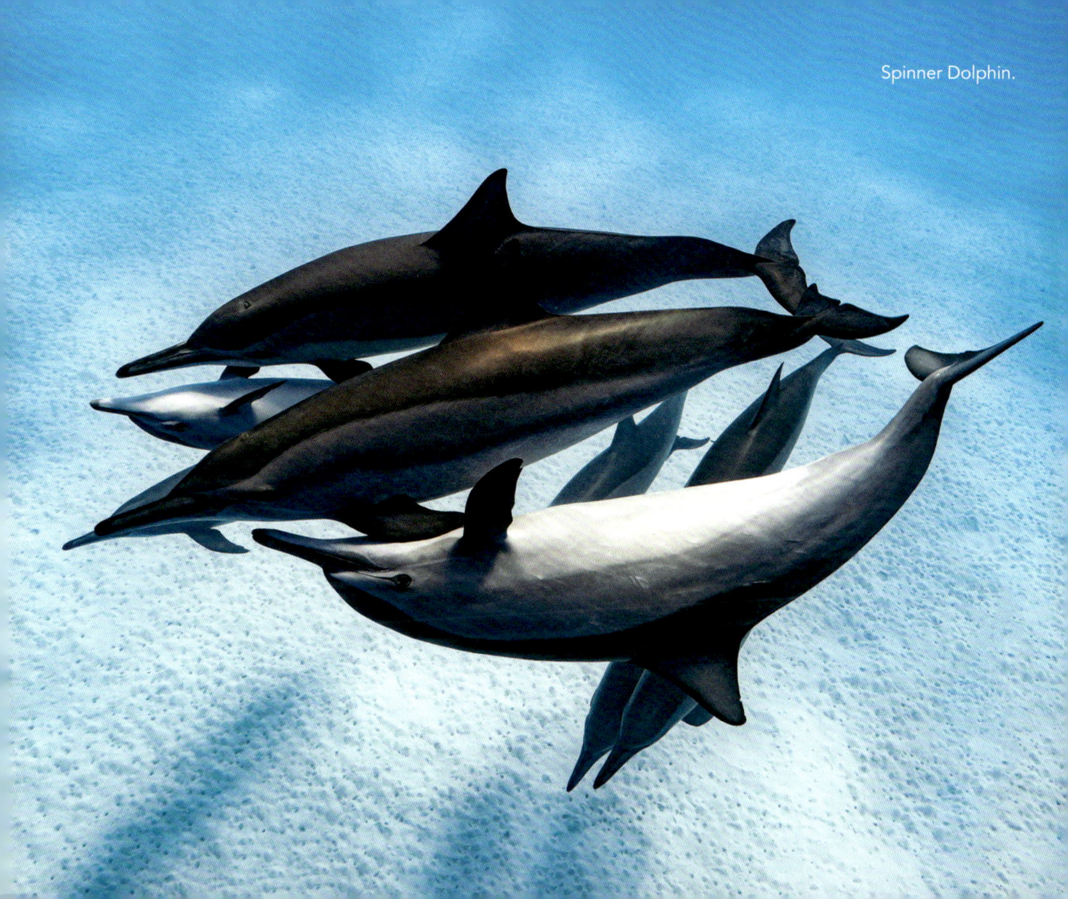

Spinner Dolphin.

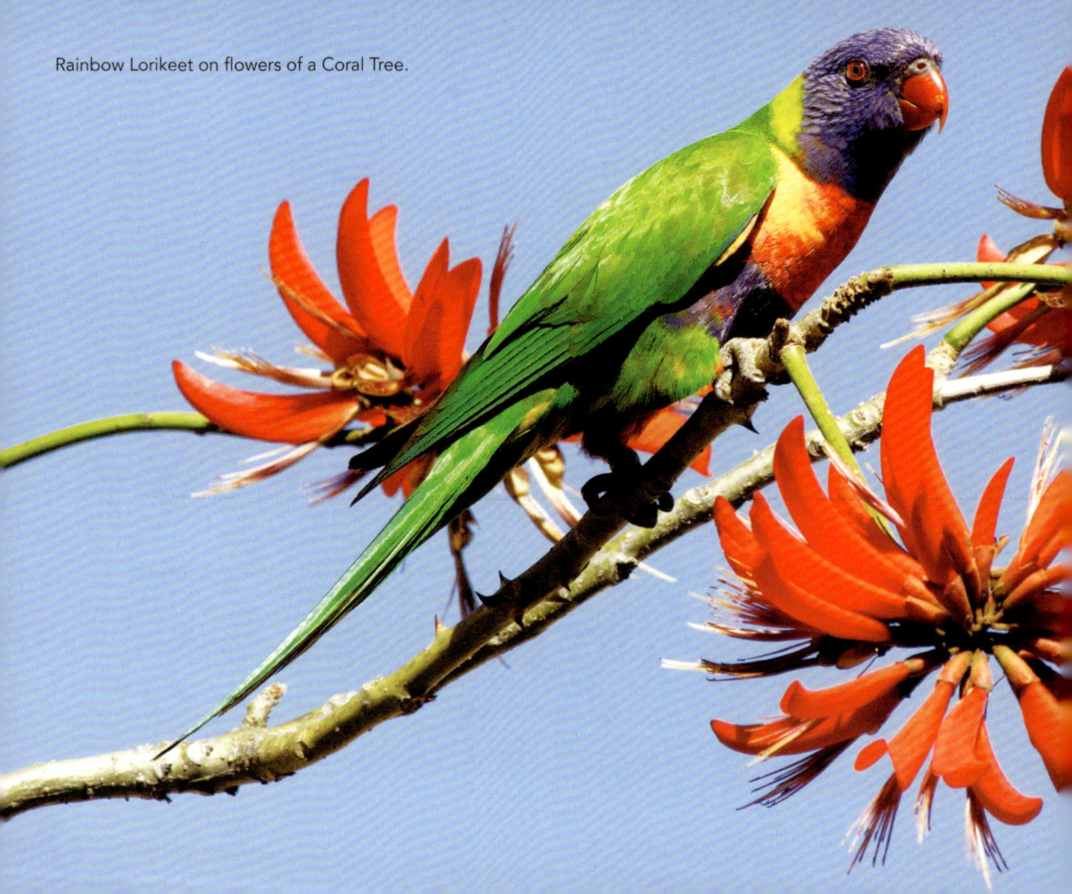
Rainbow Lorikeet on flowers of a Coral Tree.

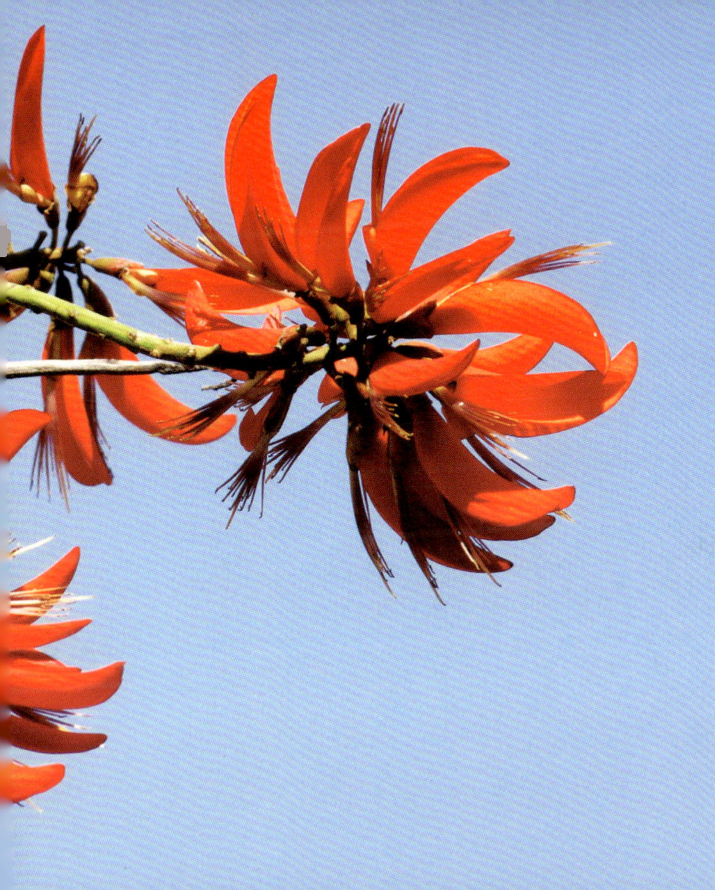

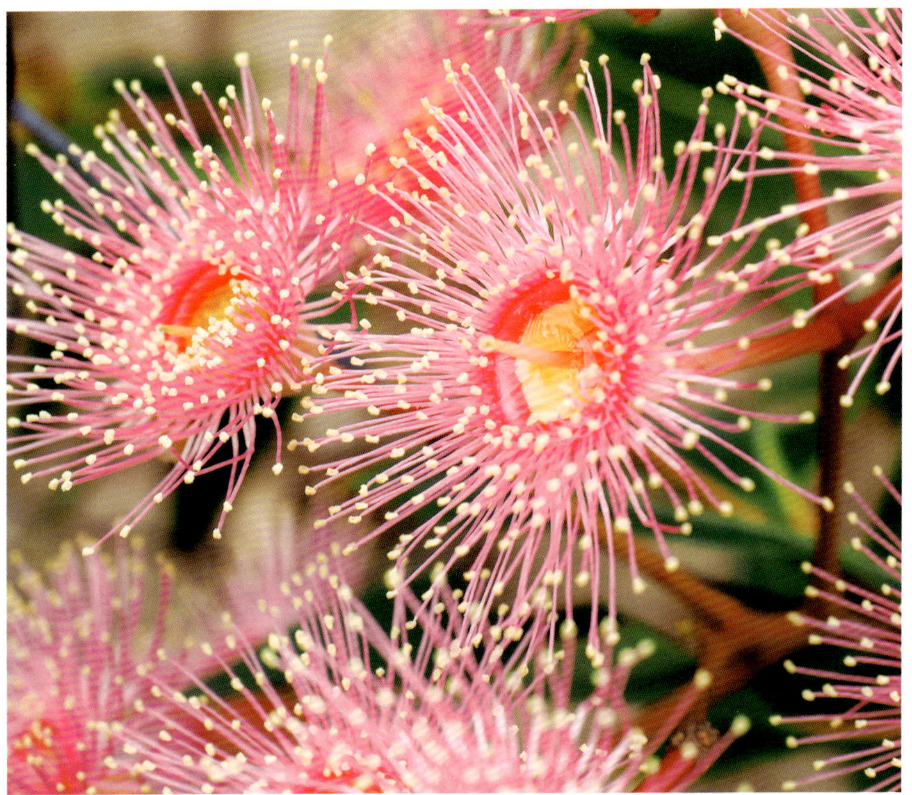

Corymbia ficifolia.

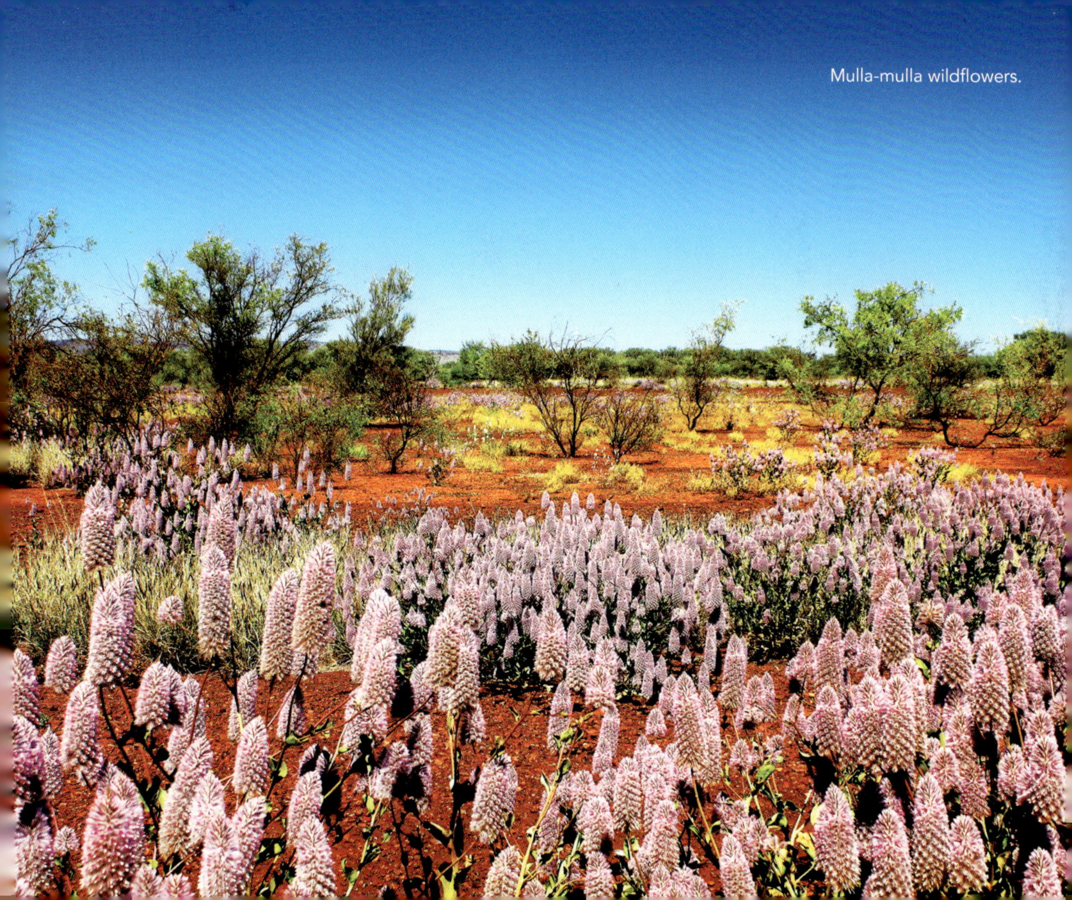

Mulla-mulla wildflowers.

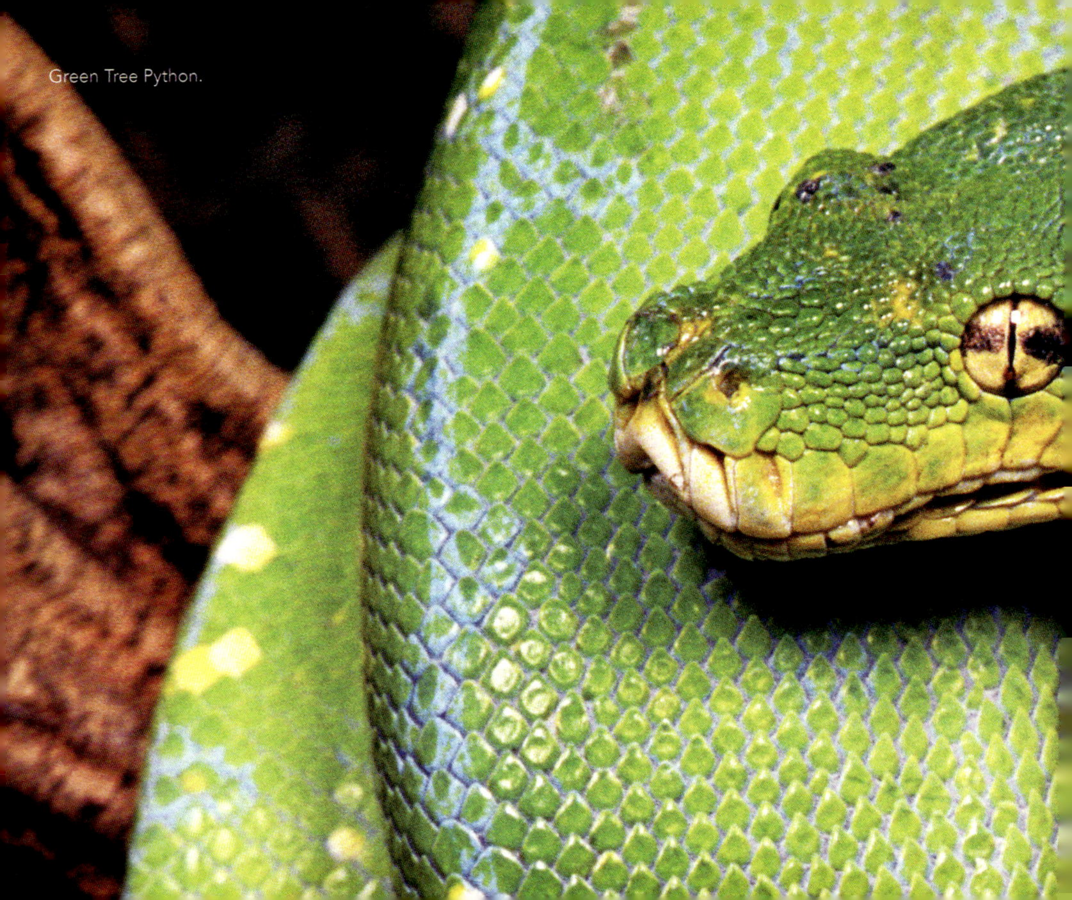

Green Tree Python.

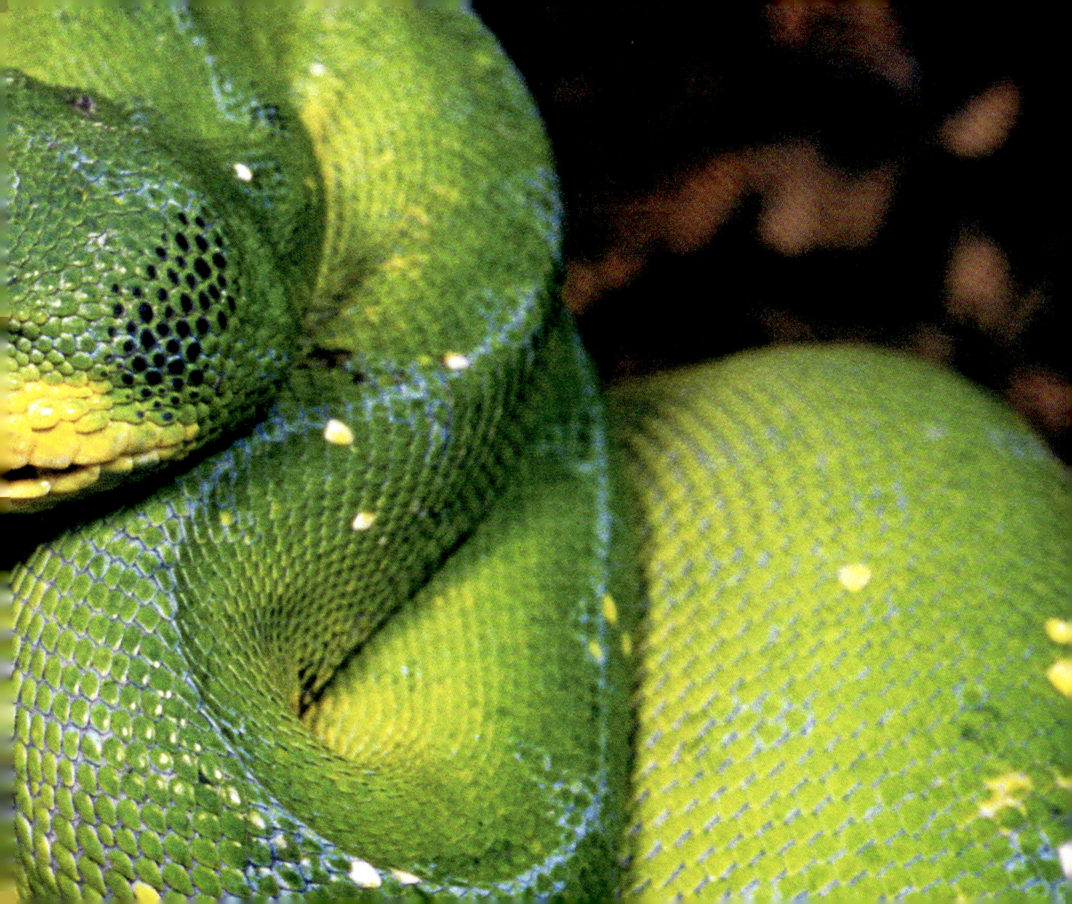

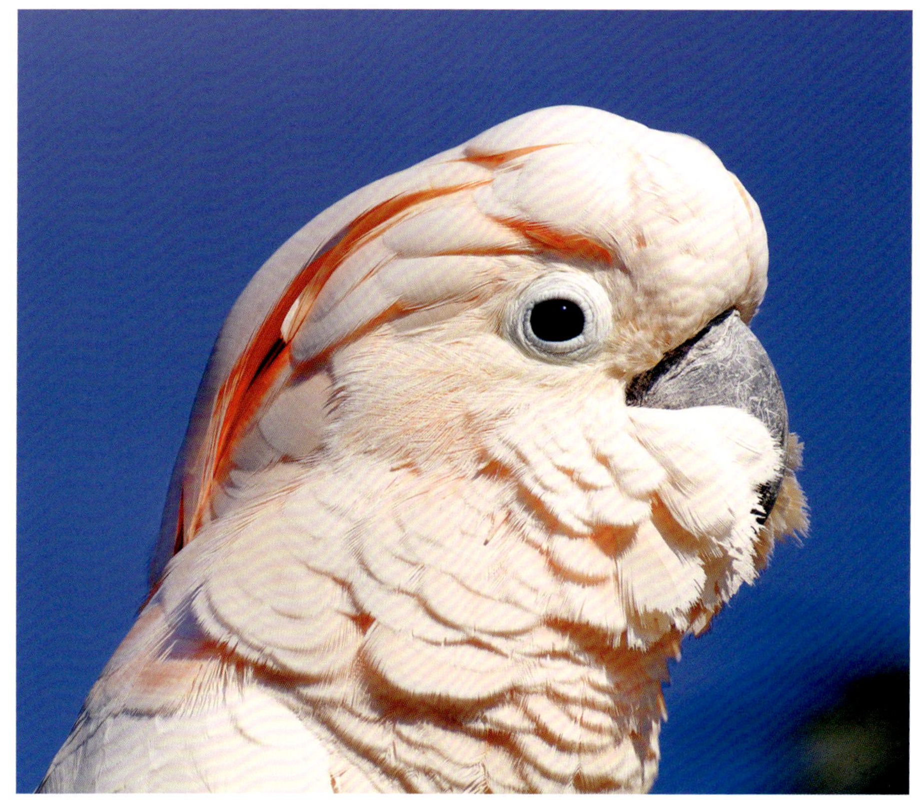

Major Mitchell's Cockatoo.

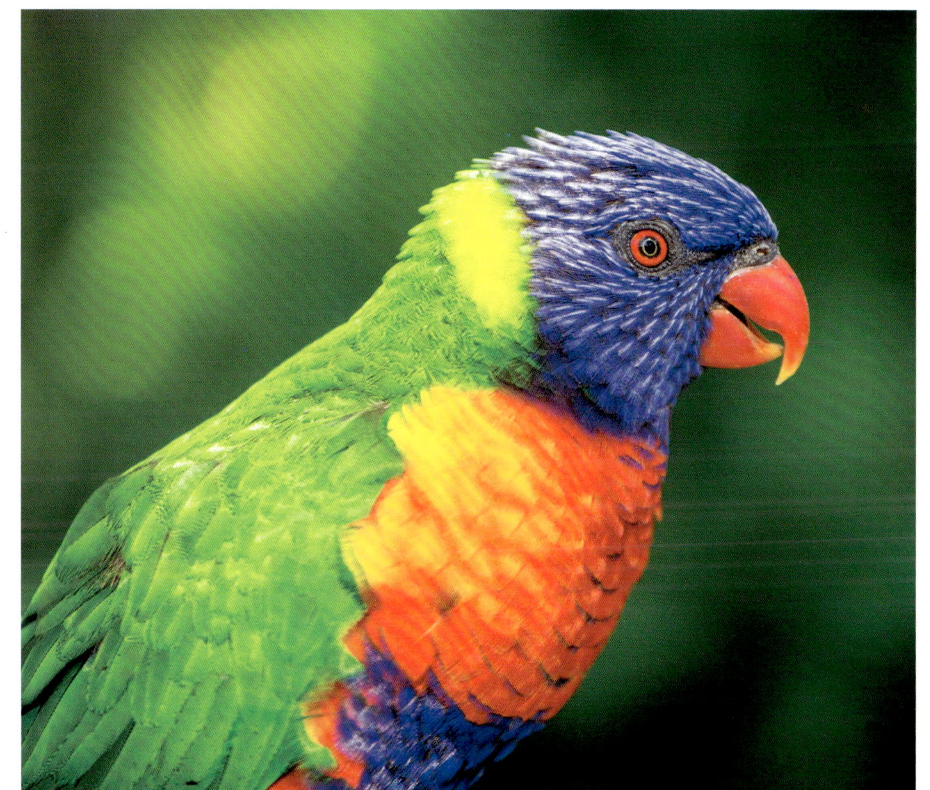

Rainbow Lorikeet.

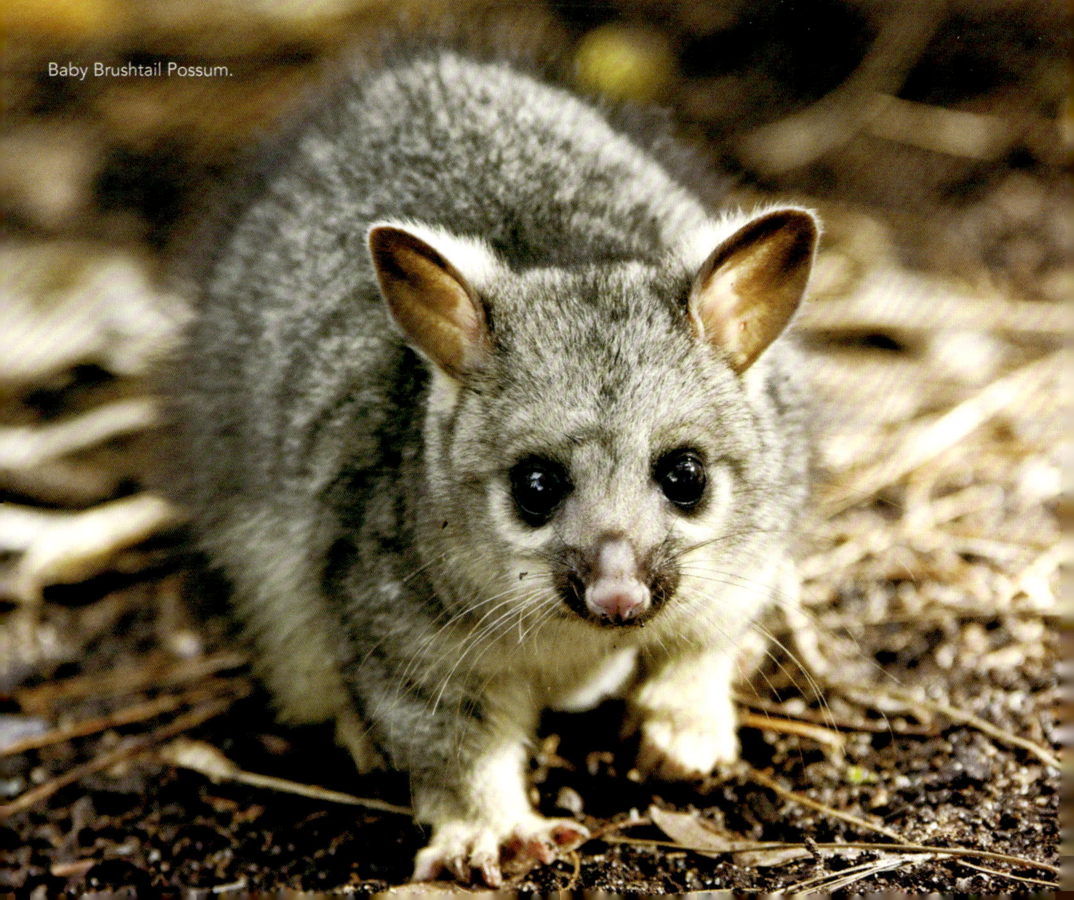

Baby Brushtail Possum.

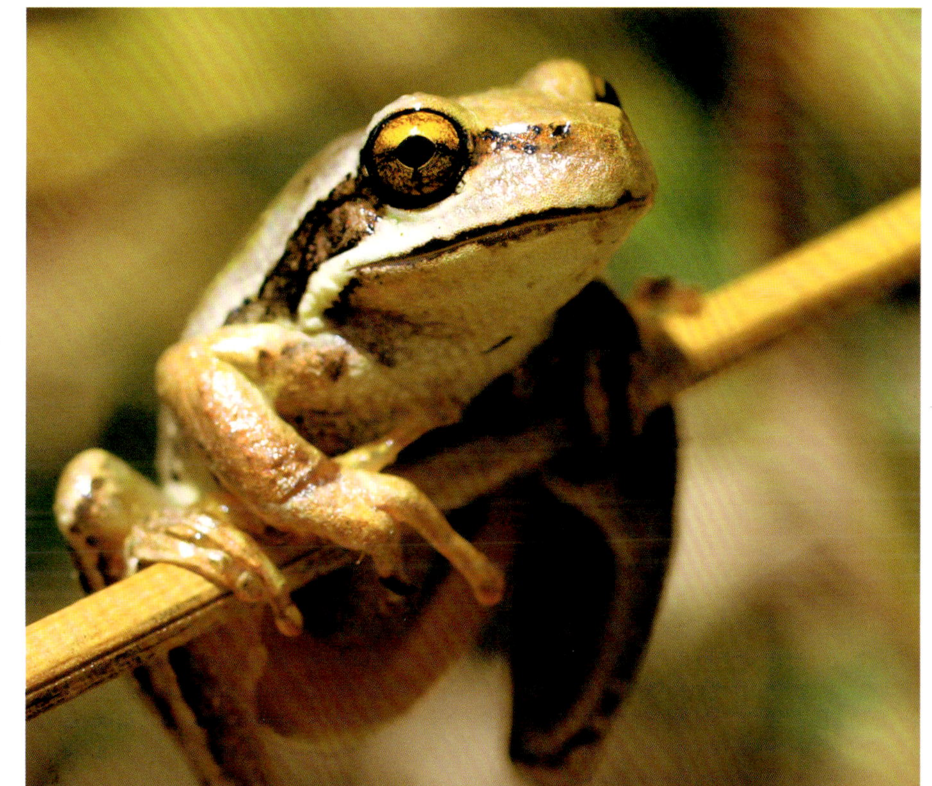

Brown Tree Frog.

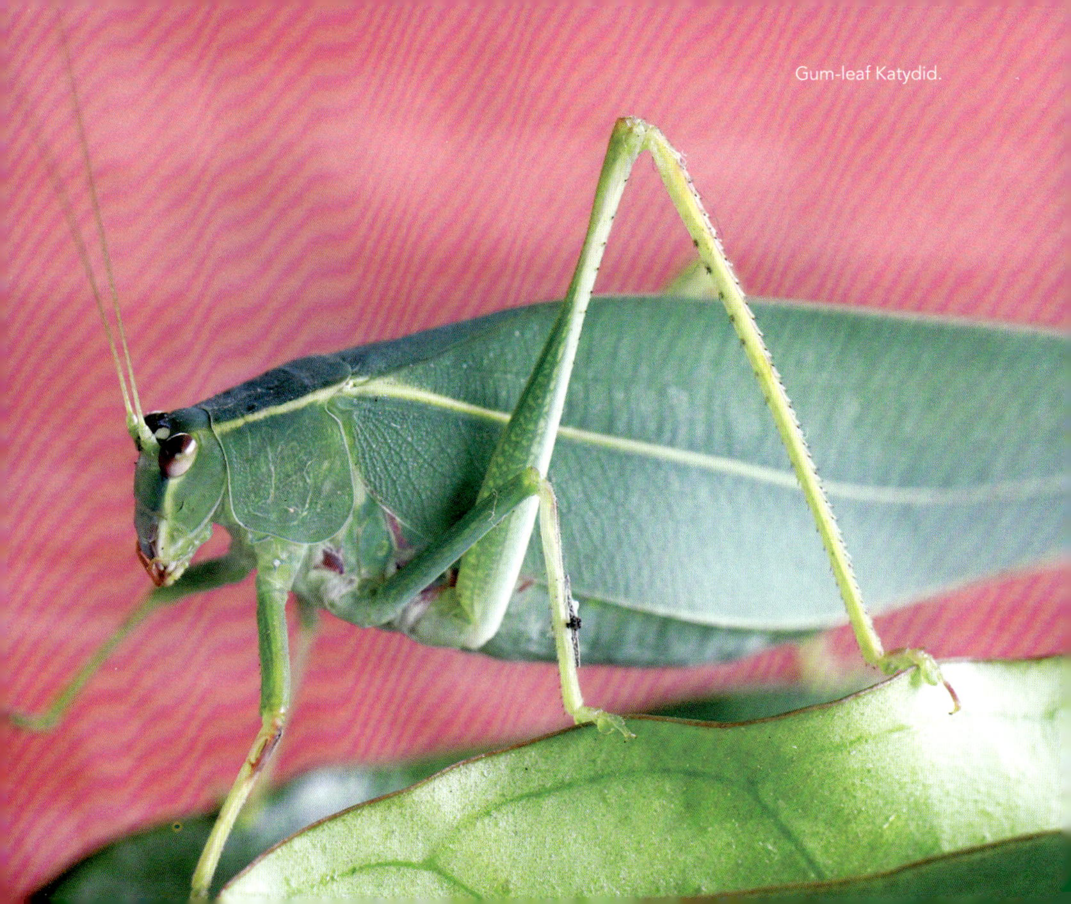

Gum-leaf Katydid.

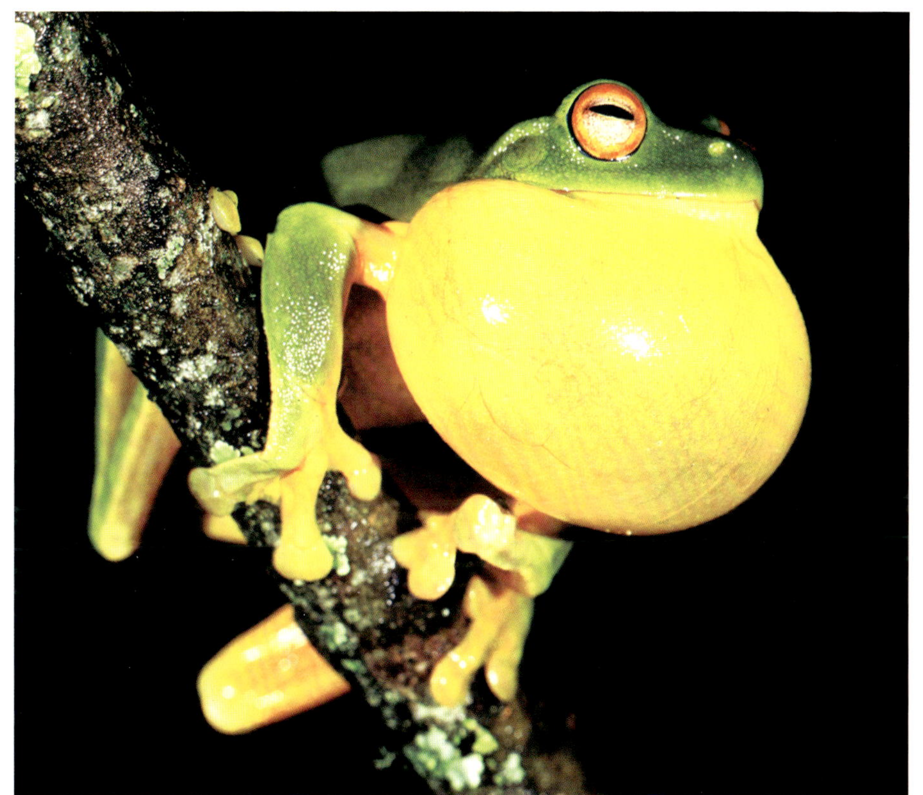

Red-eyed Tree Frog.

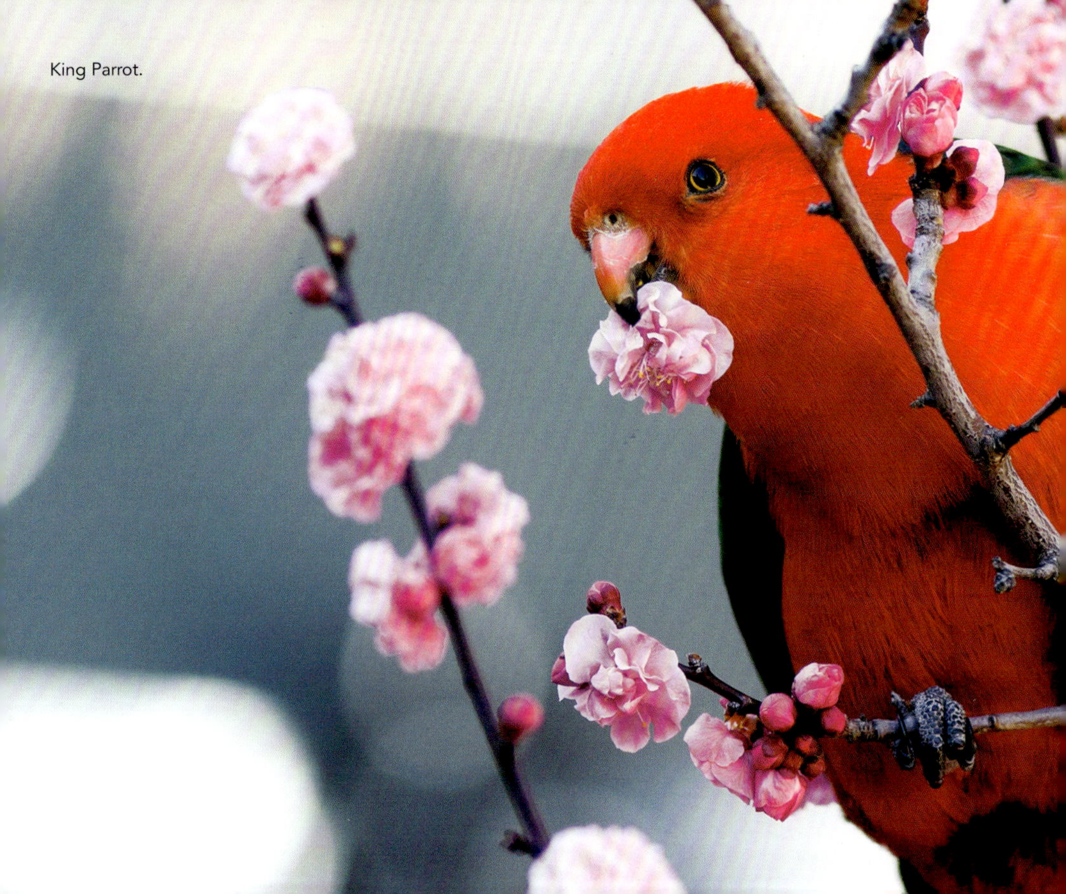

King Parrot.

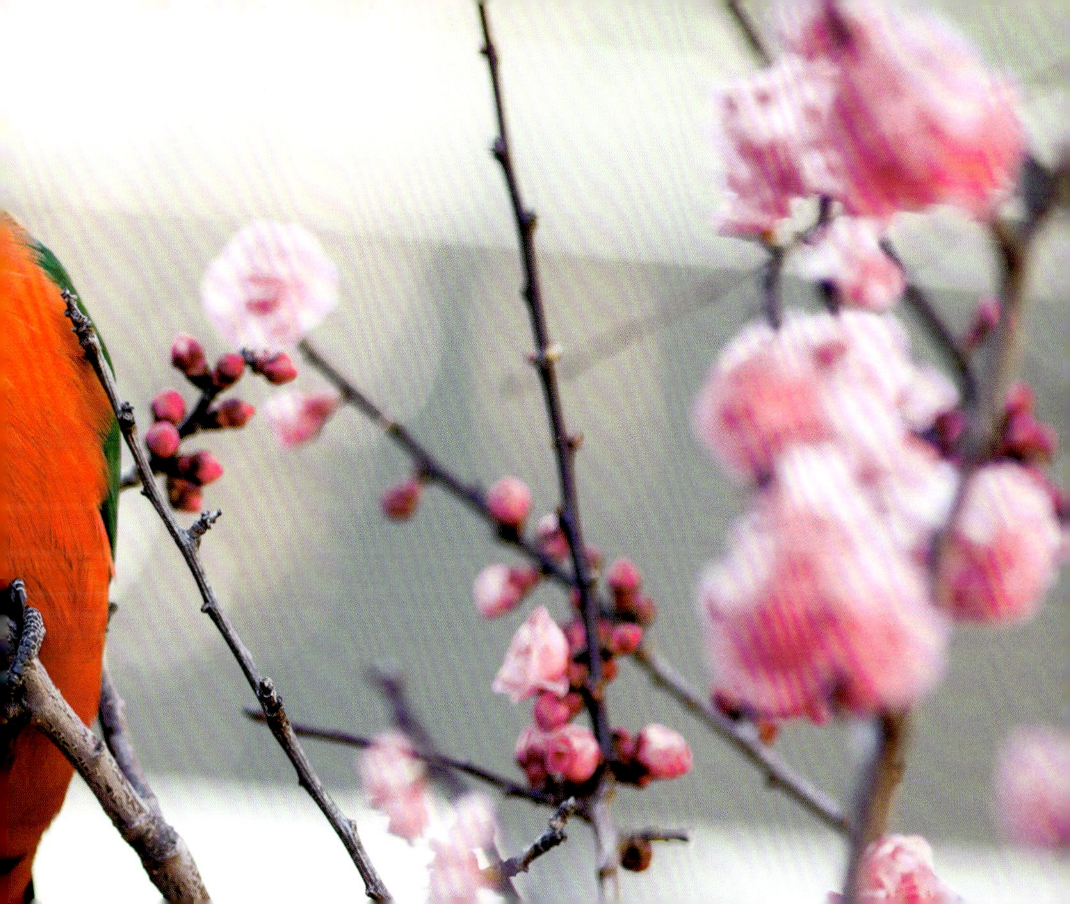

St Andrew's Cross Spider.

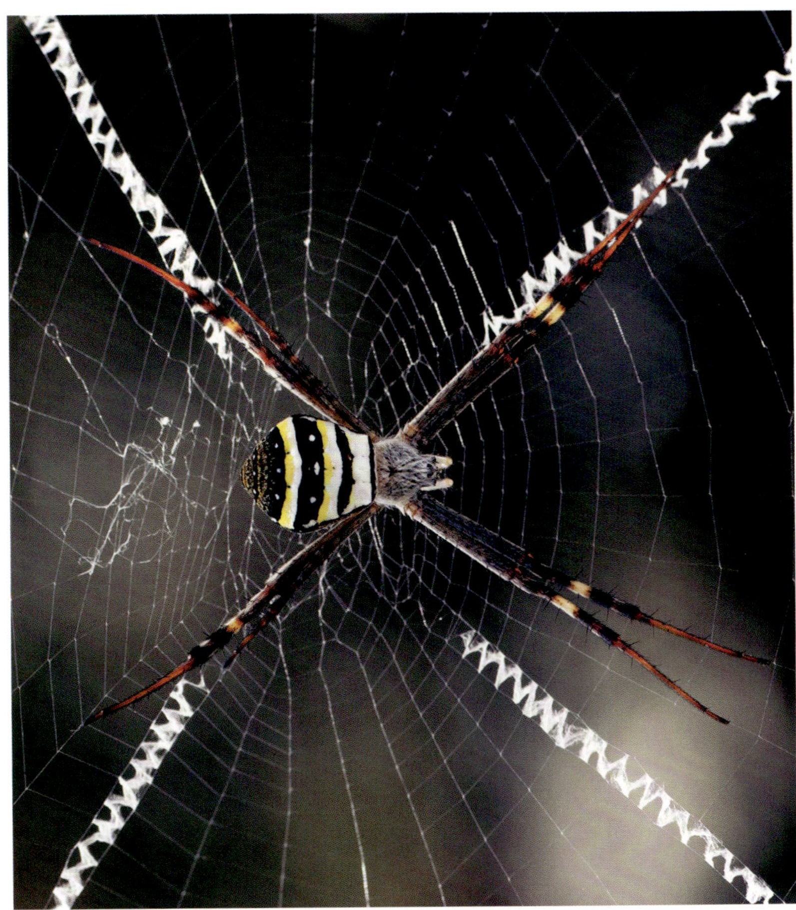

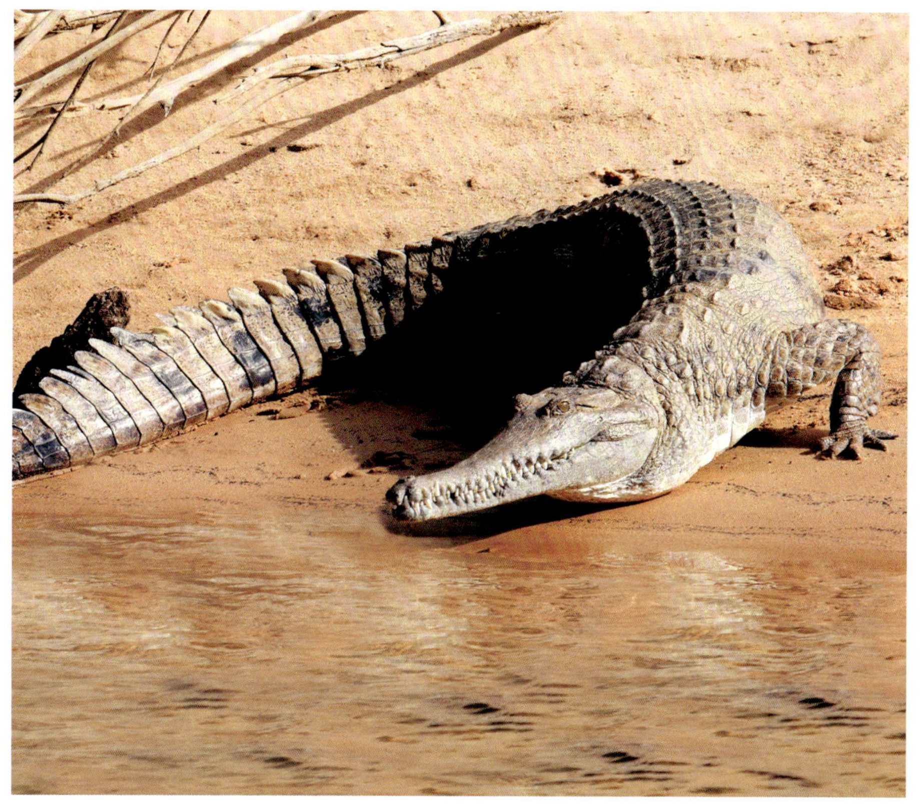

Freshwater Crocodile.

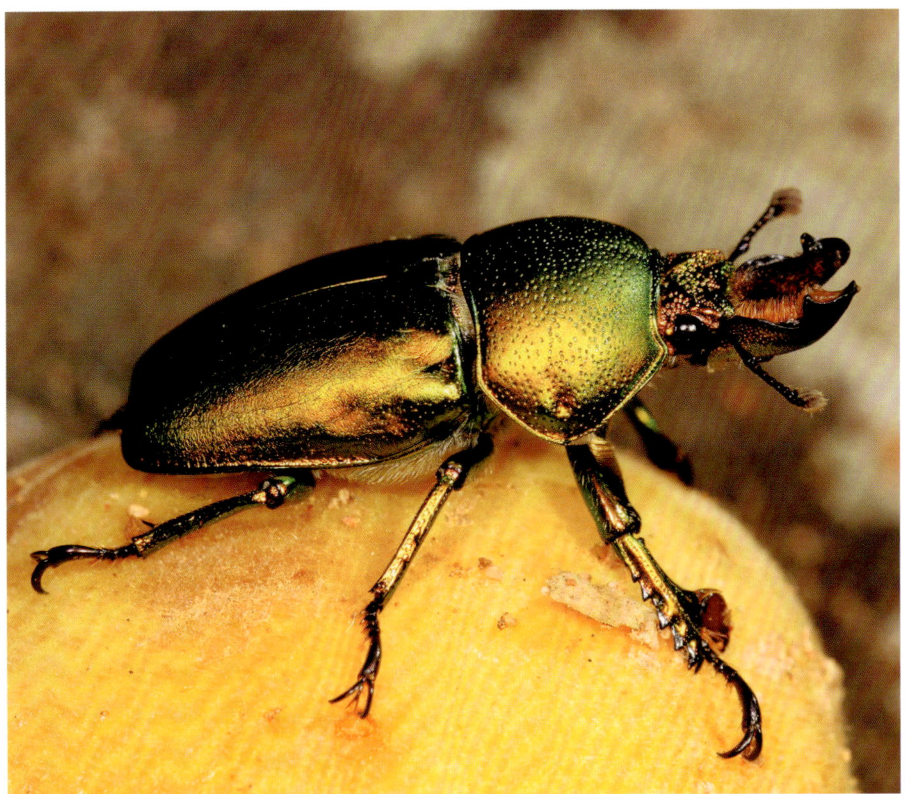

Golden Stag Beetle.

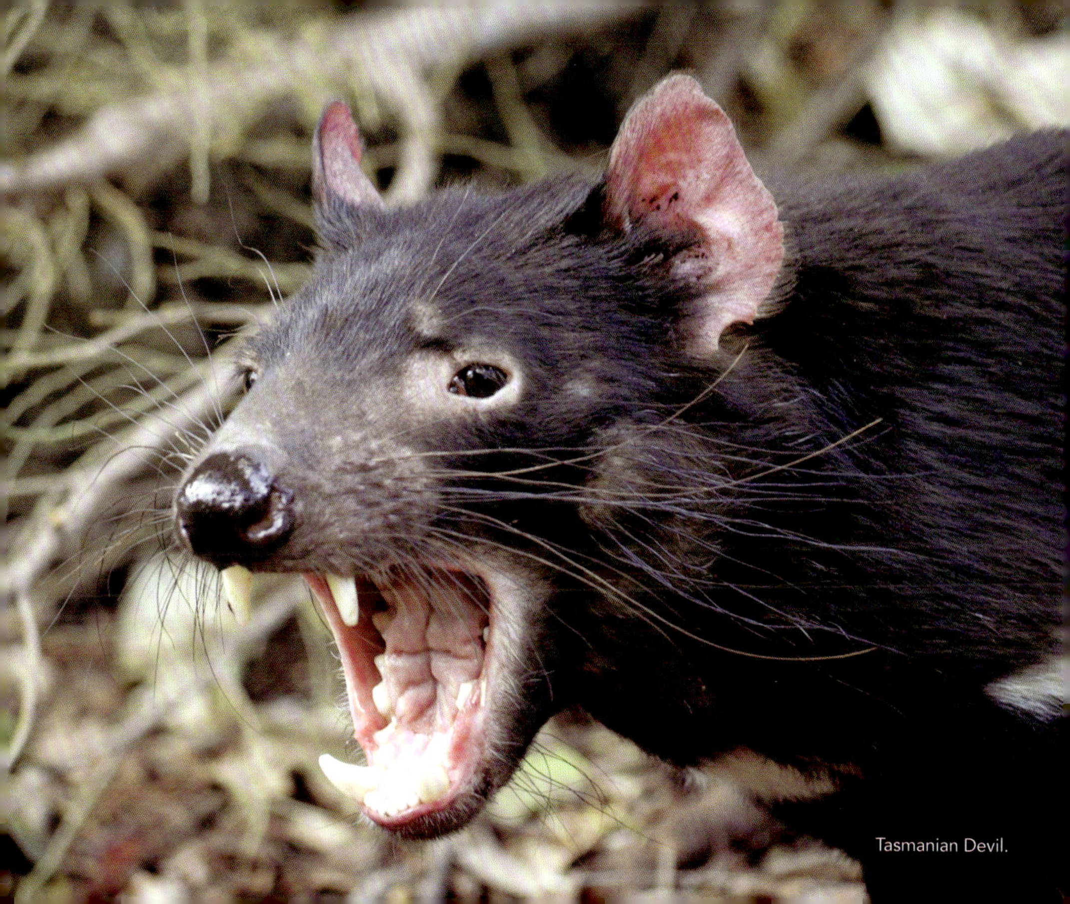
Tasmanian Devil.

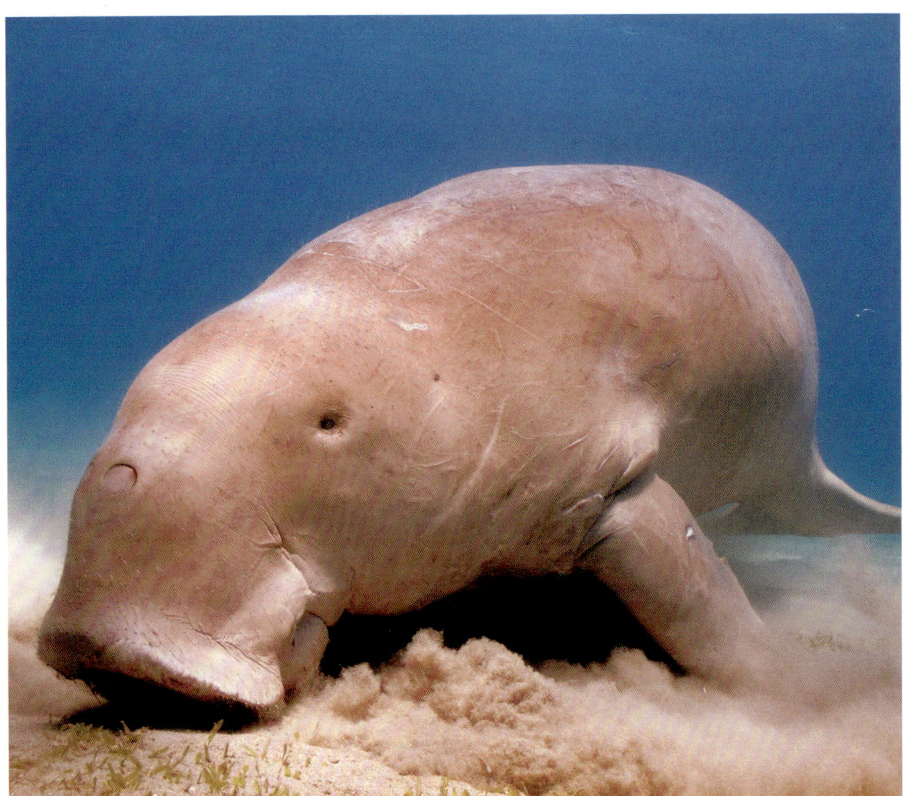

Dugong.

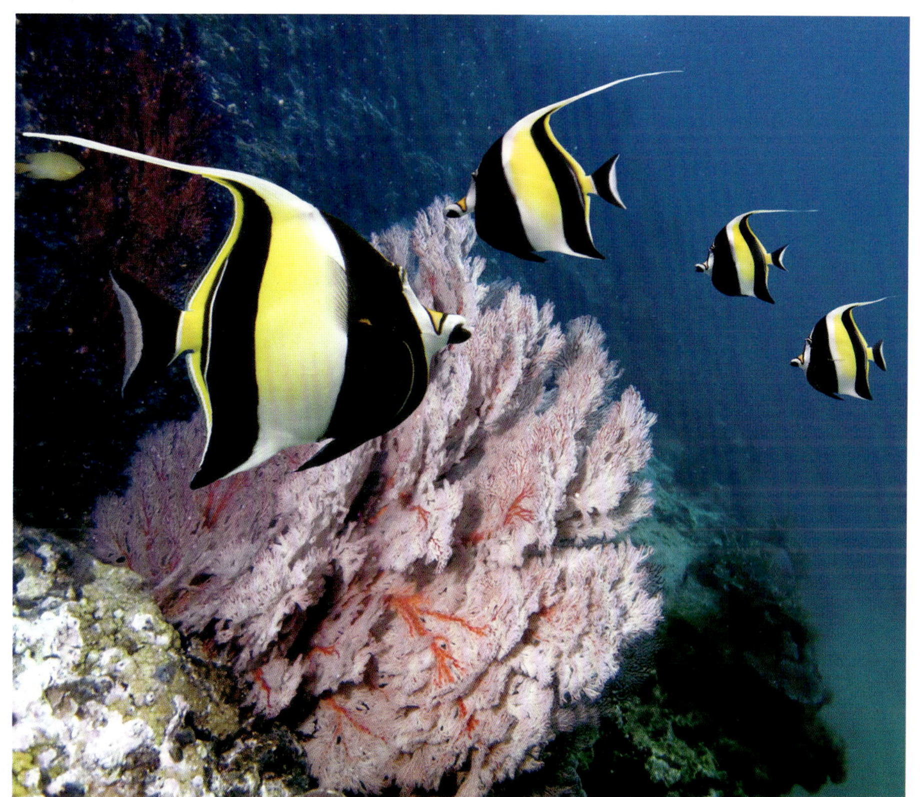

Moorish Idol.

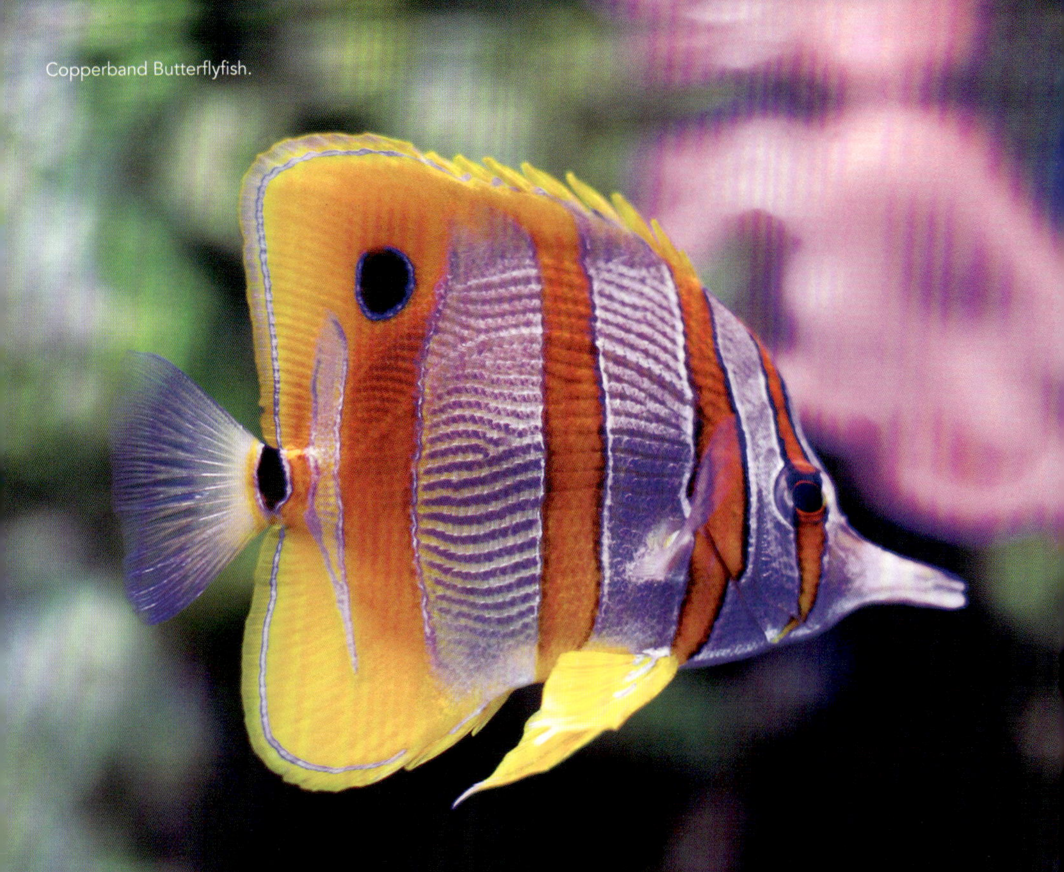
Copperband Butterflyfish.

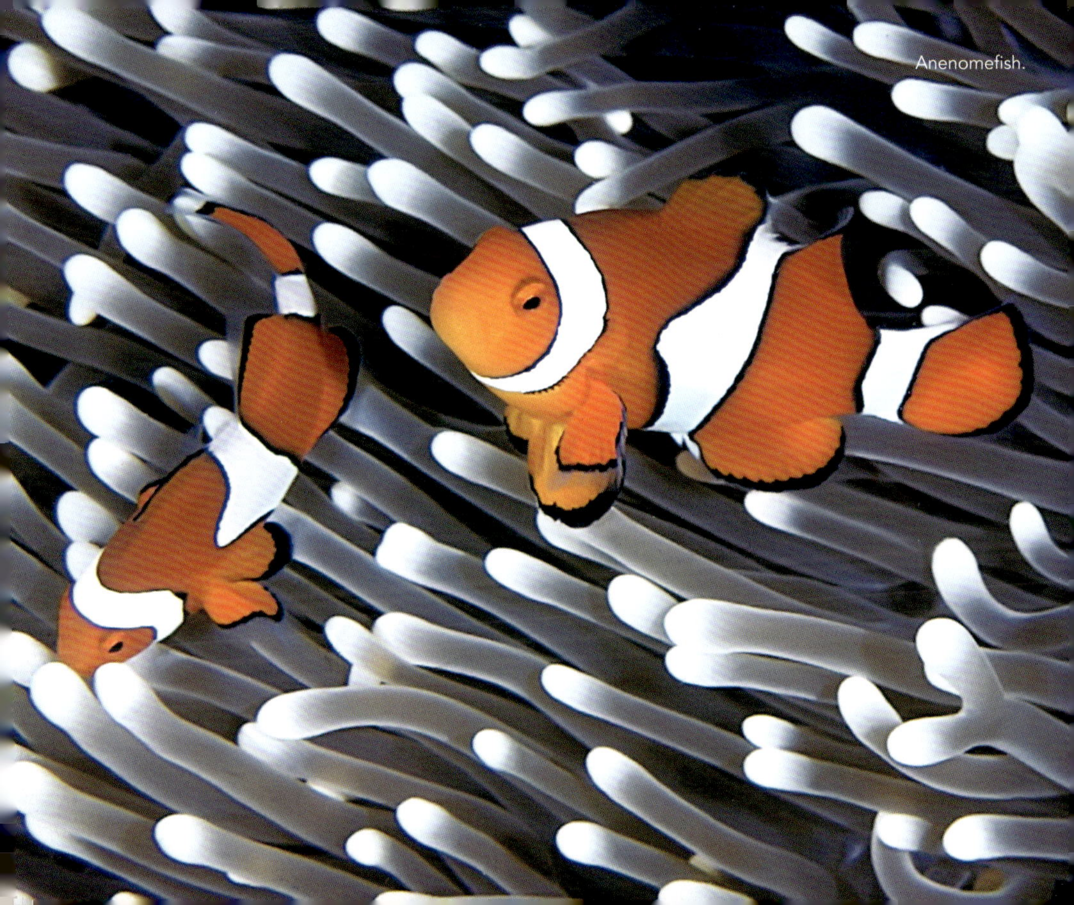

Anenomefish.

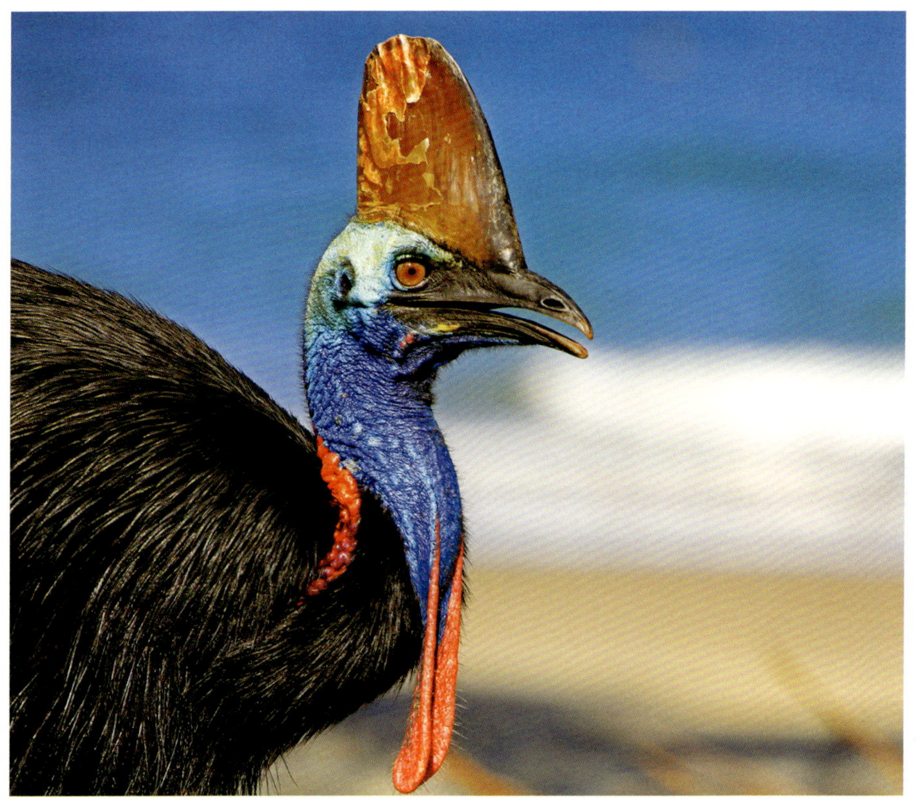

Cassowary.

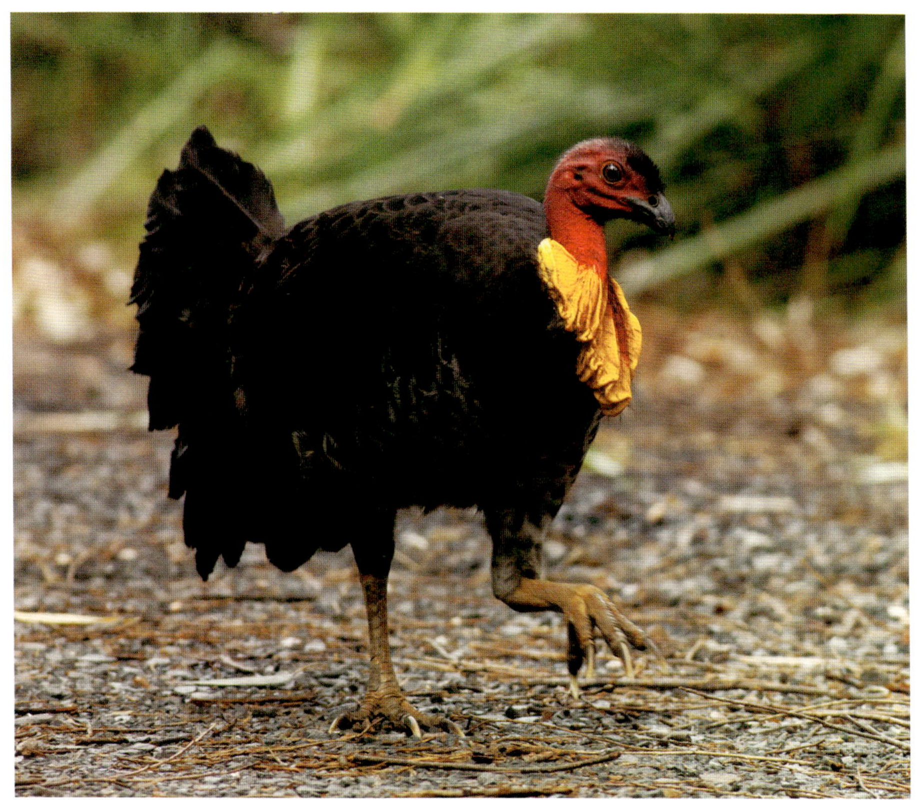

Brush Turkey.

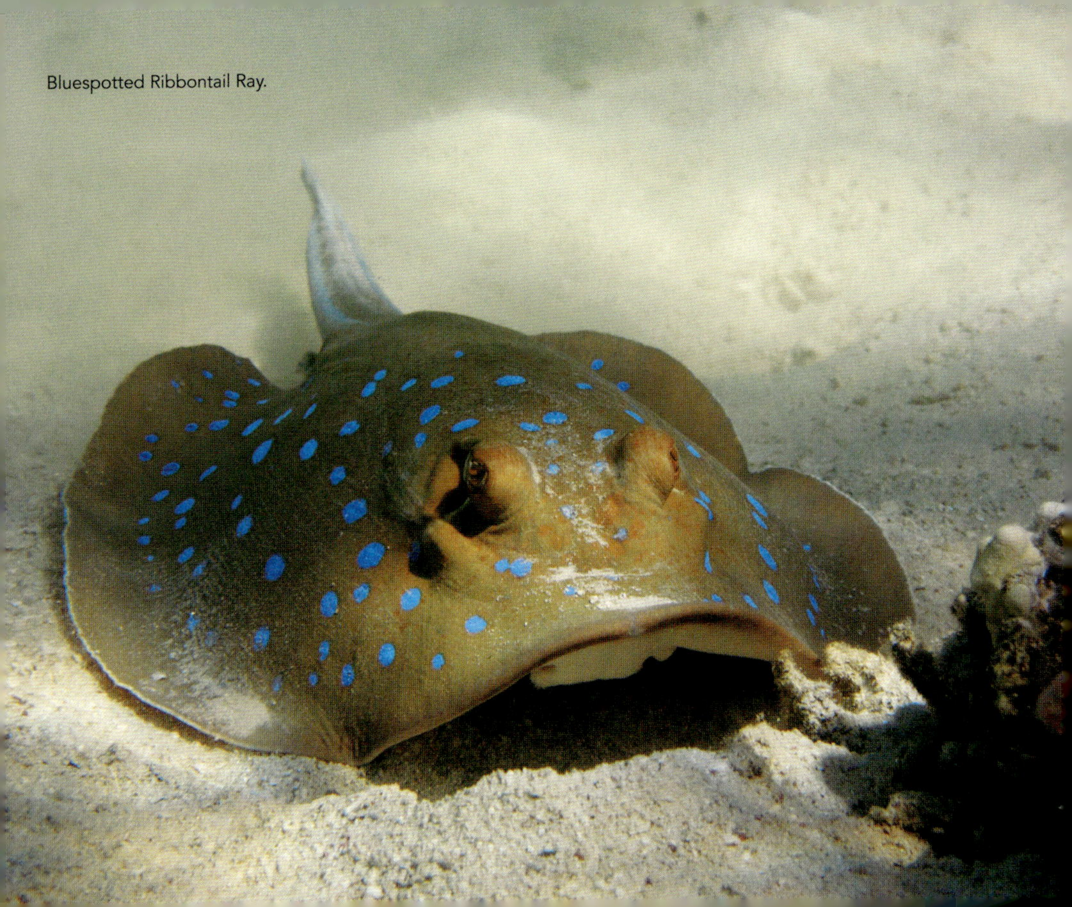

Bluespotted Ribbontail Ray.

Australian Pelican.

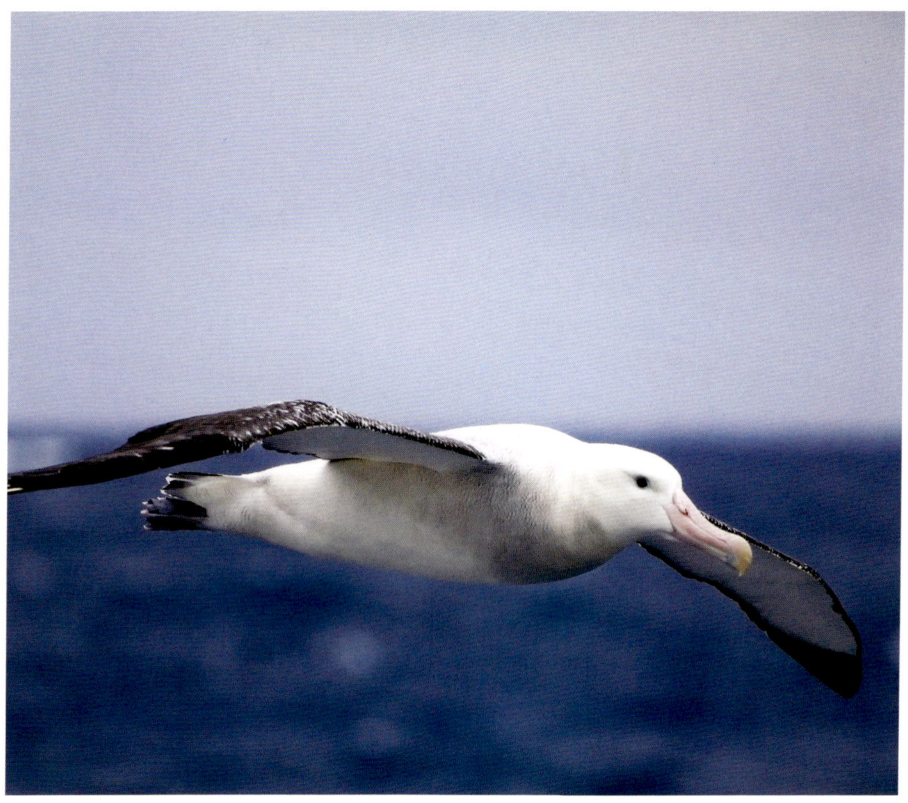

Wandering Albatross.

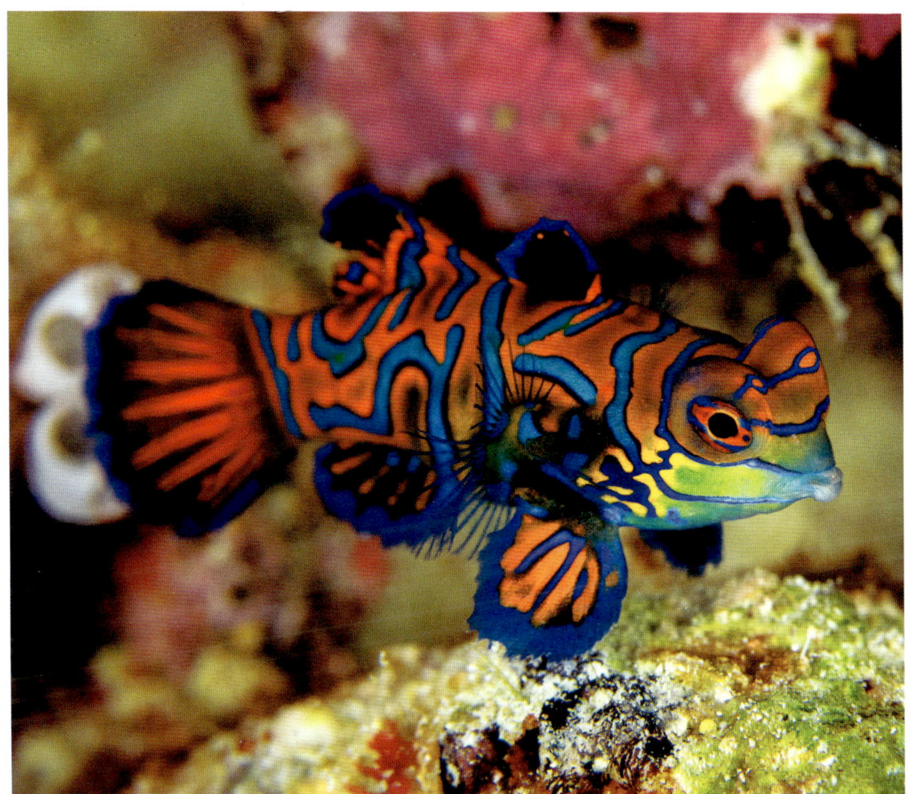

Mandarinfish.

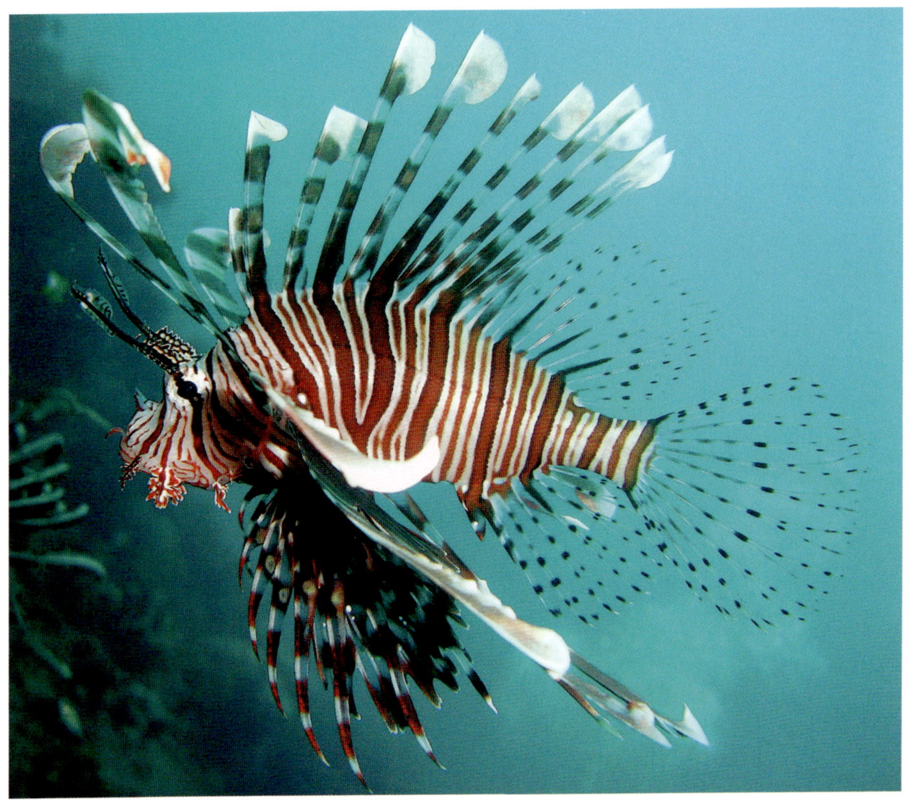

Lionfish.

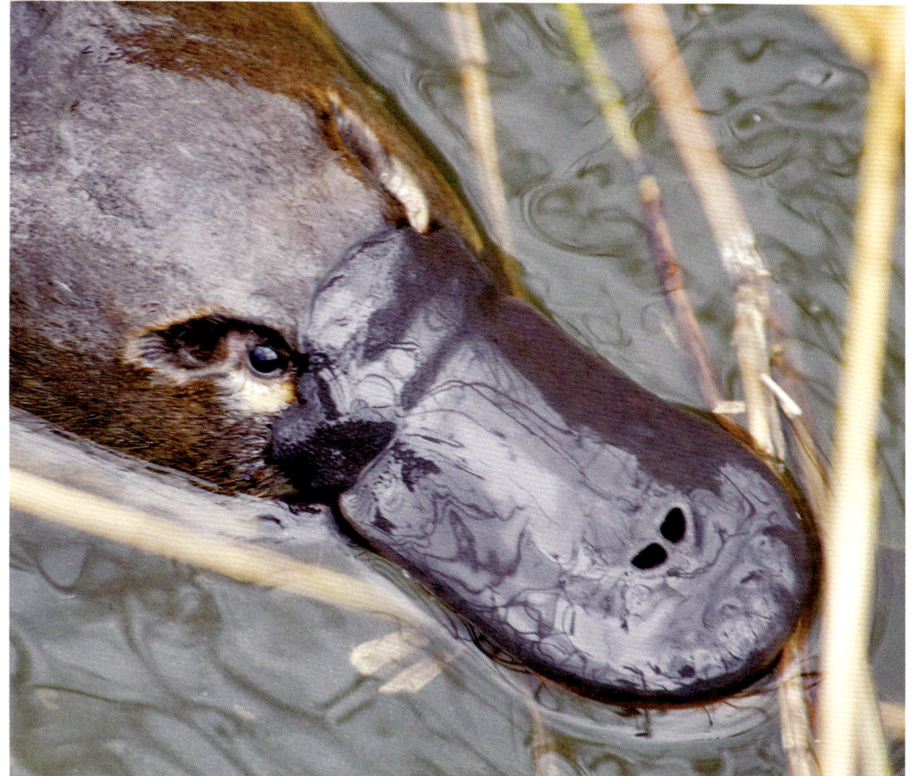

Platypus.

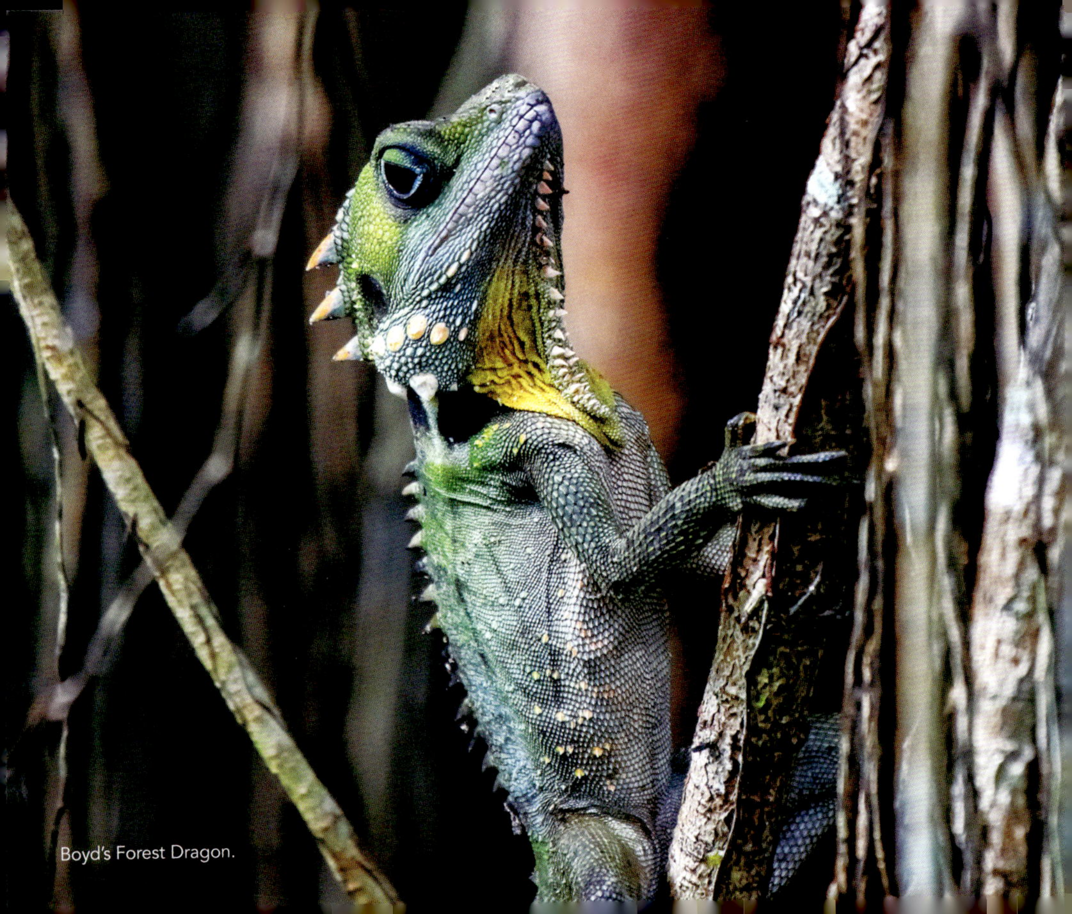

Boyd's Forest Dragon.

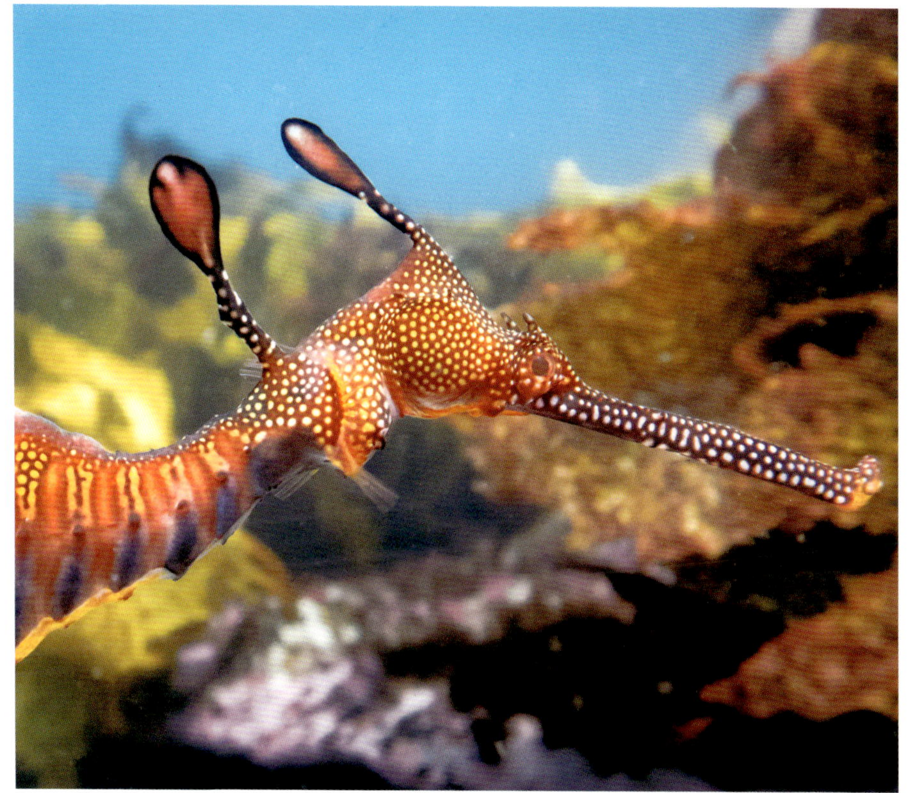

Weedy Seadragon.

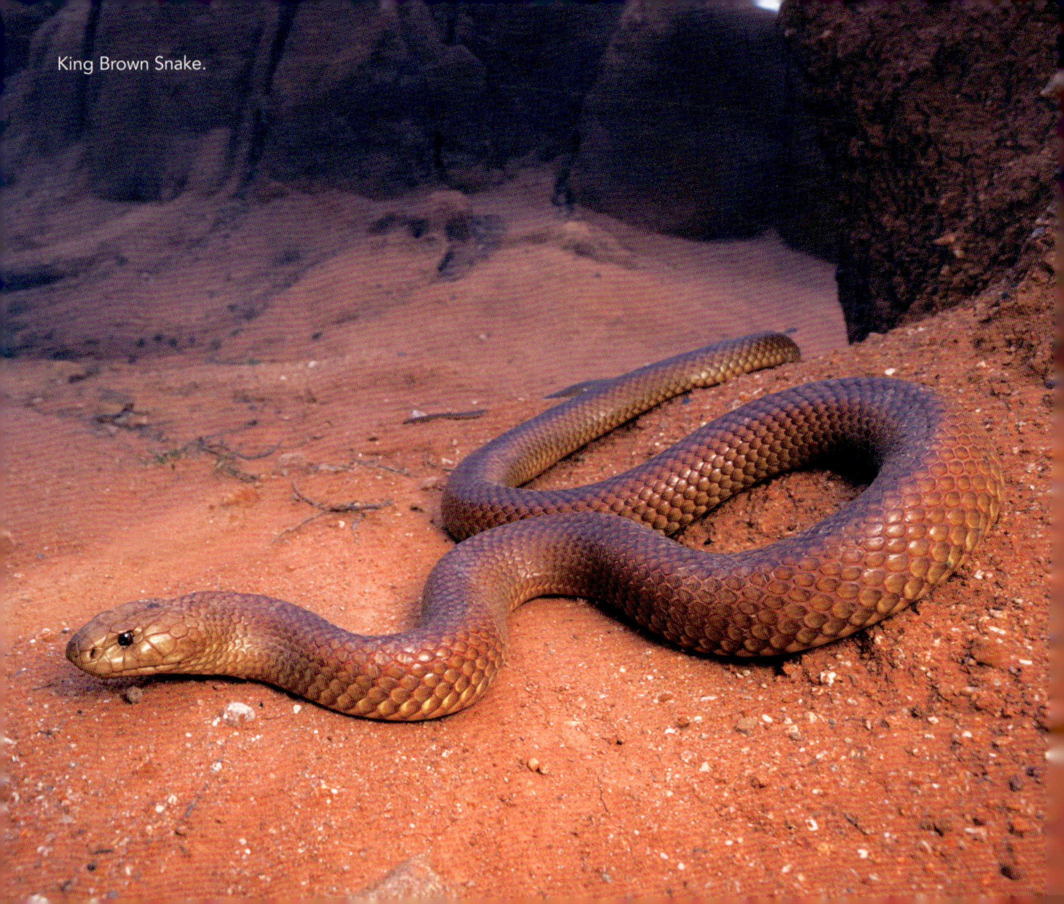

King Brown Snake.

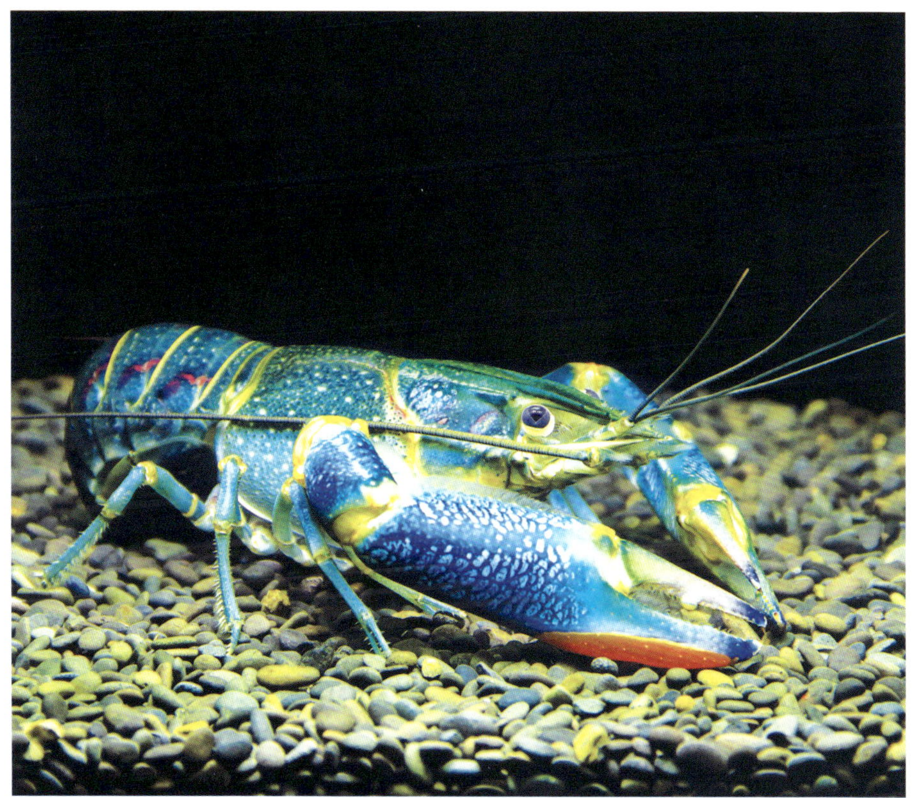

Rainbow Redclaw Crayfish Yabby.

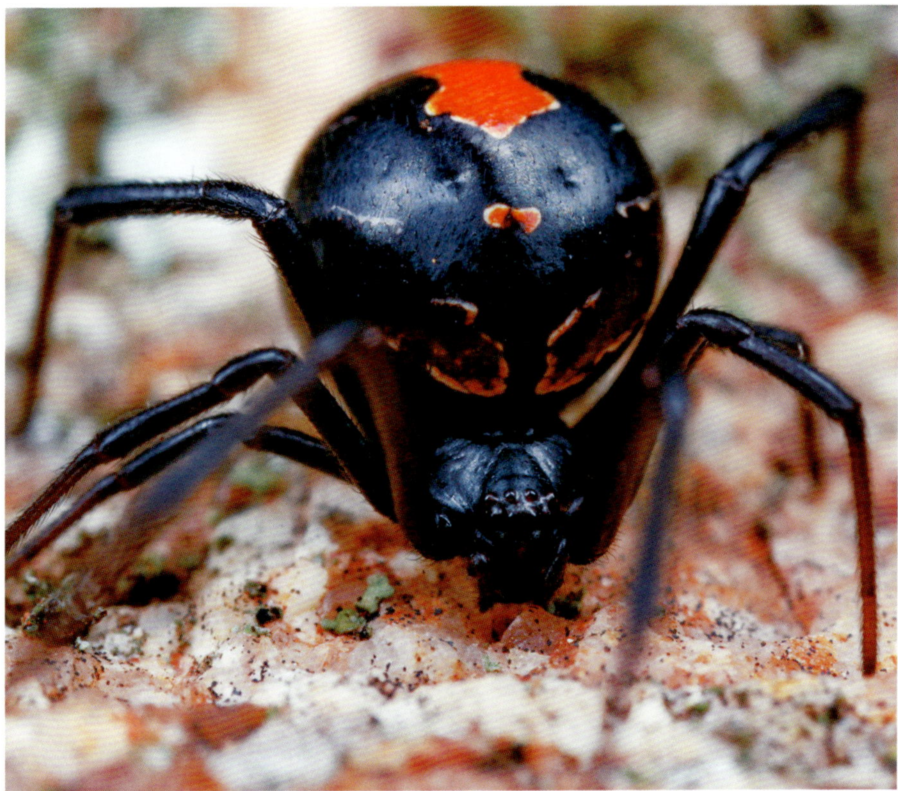

Redback Spider.

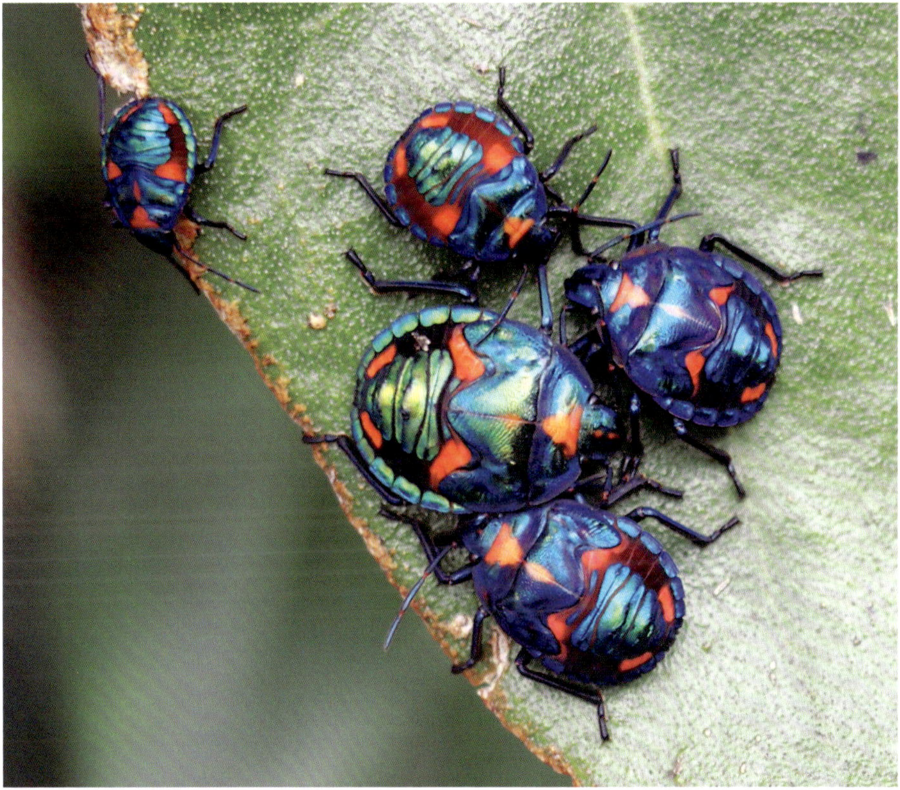

Hibiscus Harlequin Bug.

Blue-spotted Hawker Dragonfly.

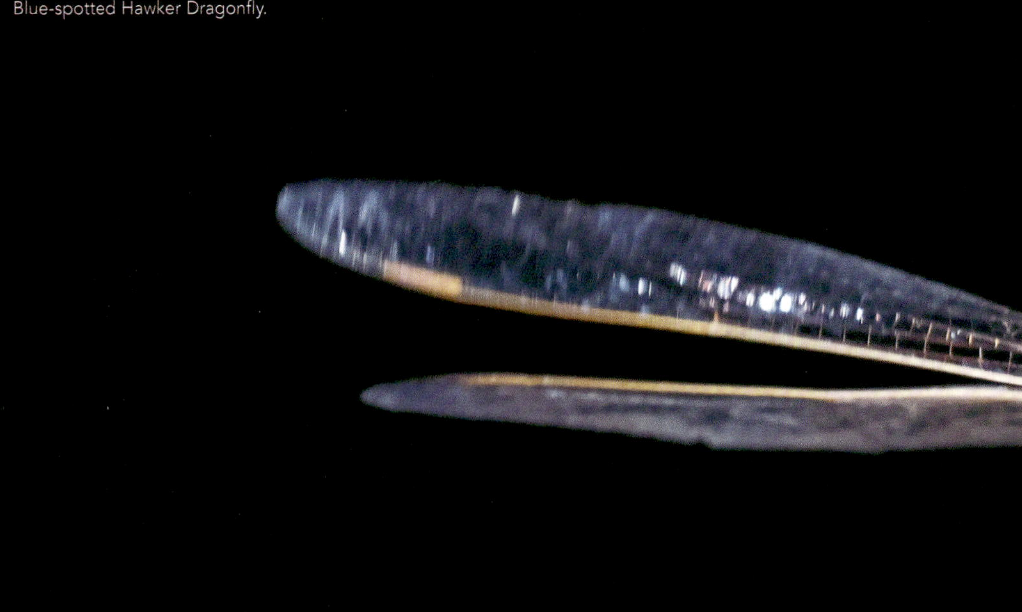

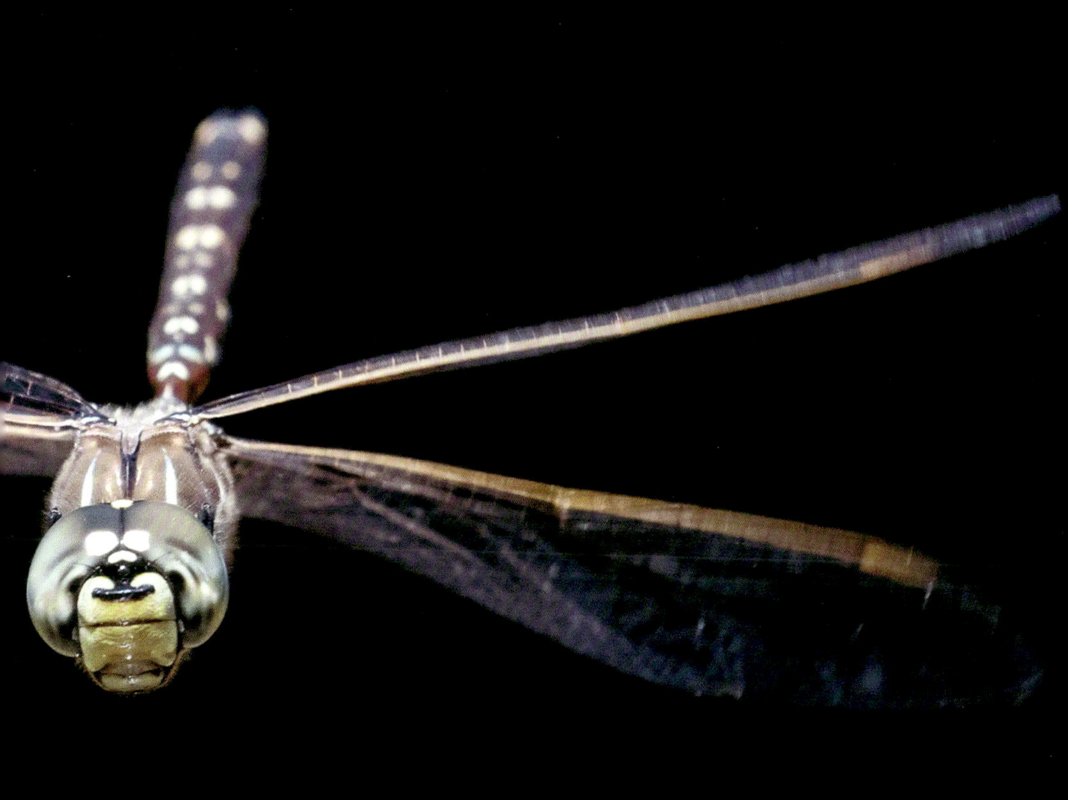

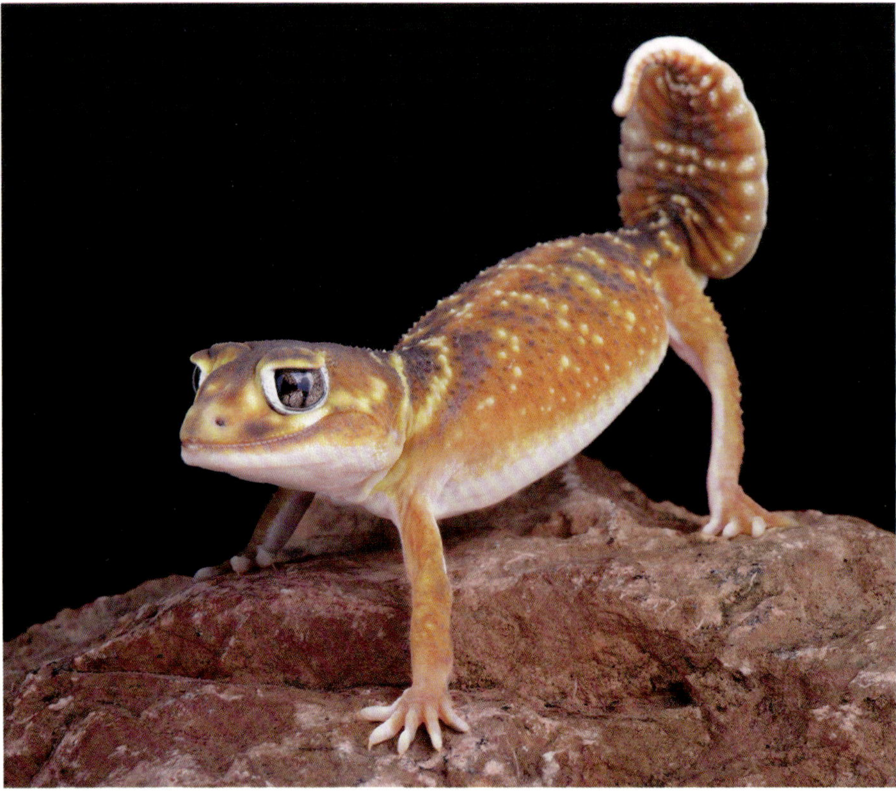

Smooth Knob-tailed Gecko.

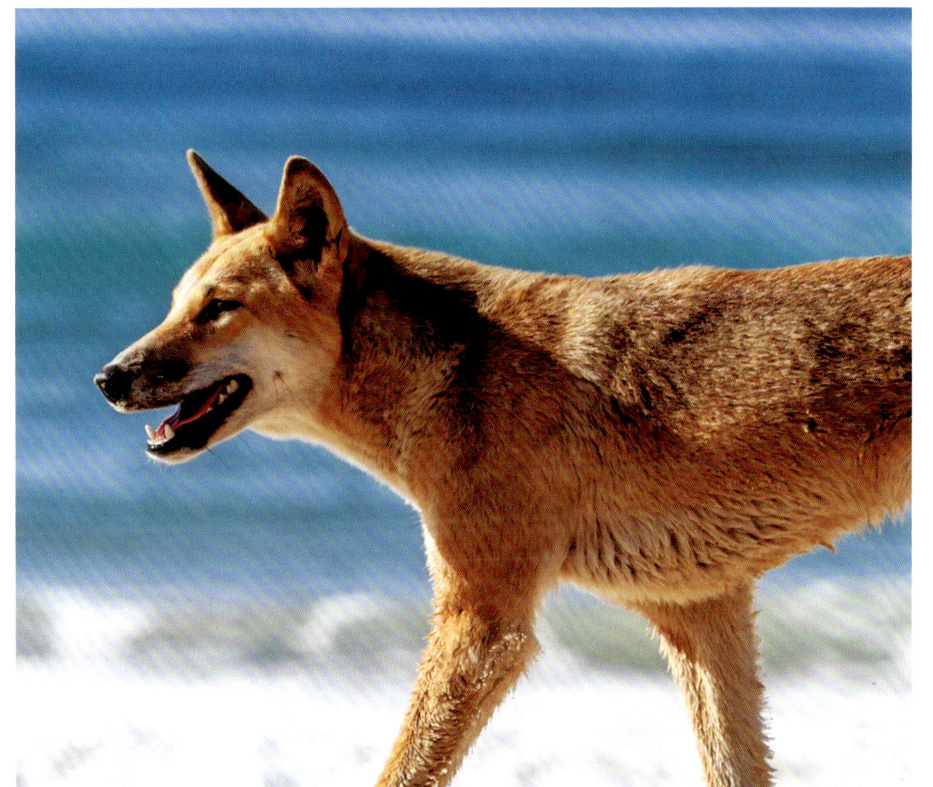

Dingo.

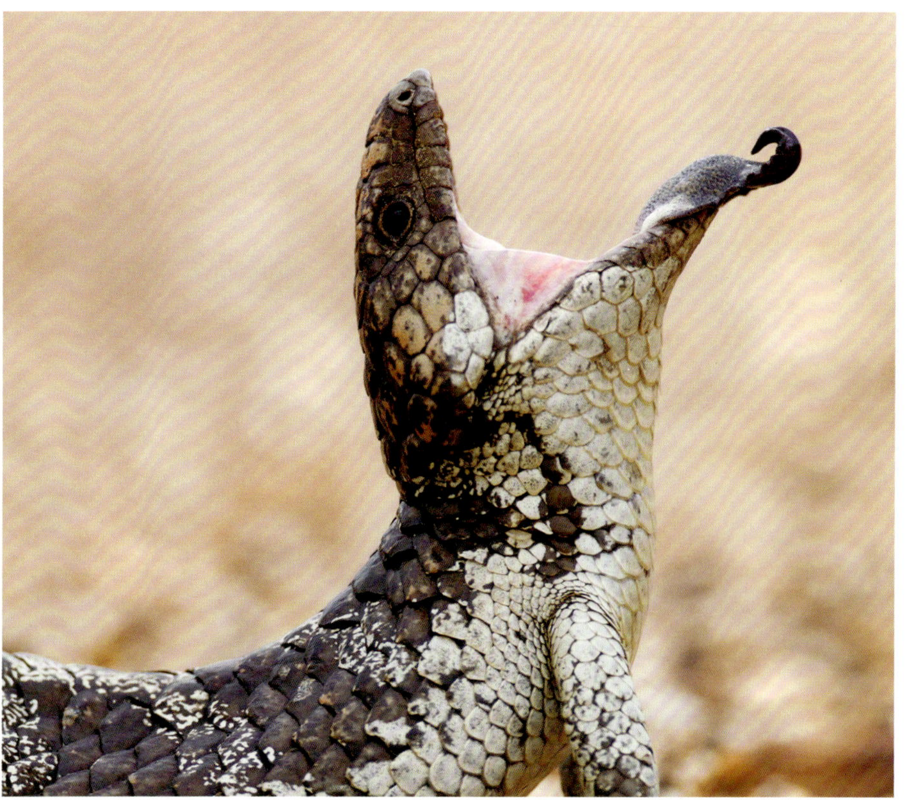
Shingleback Lizard.

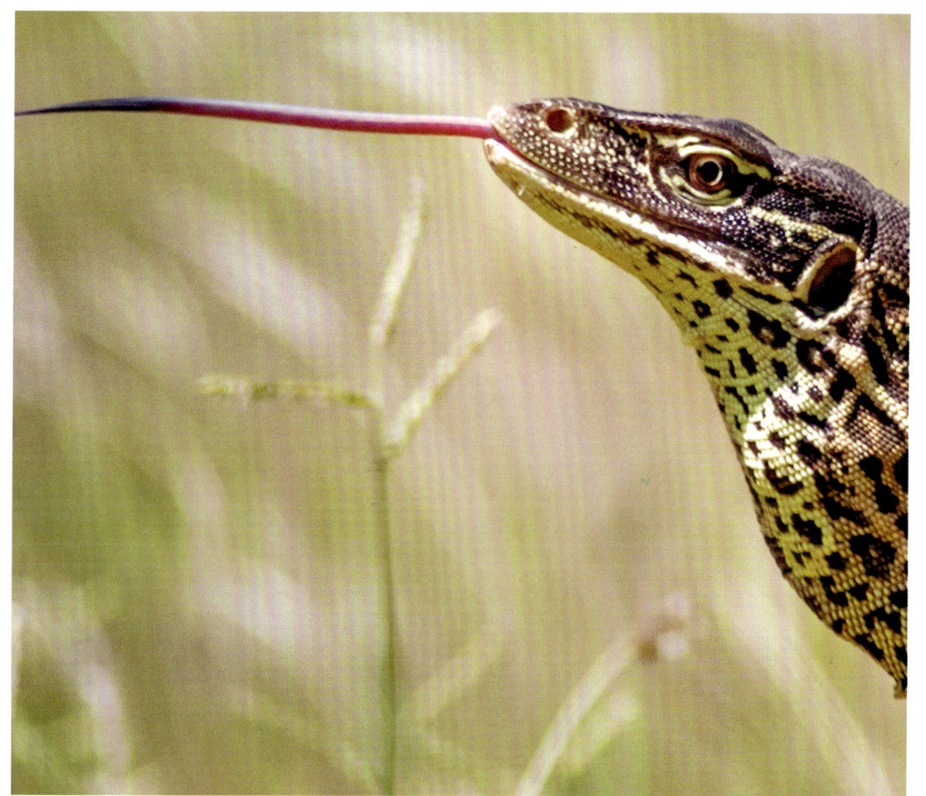

Goanna.

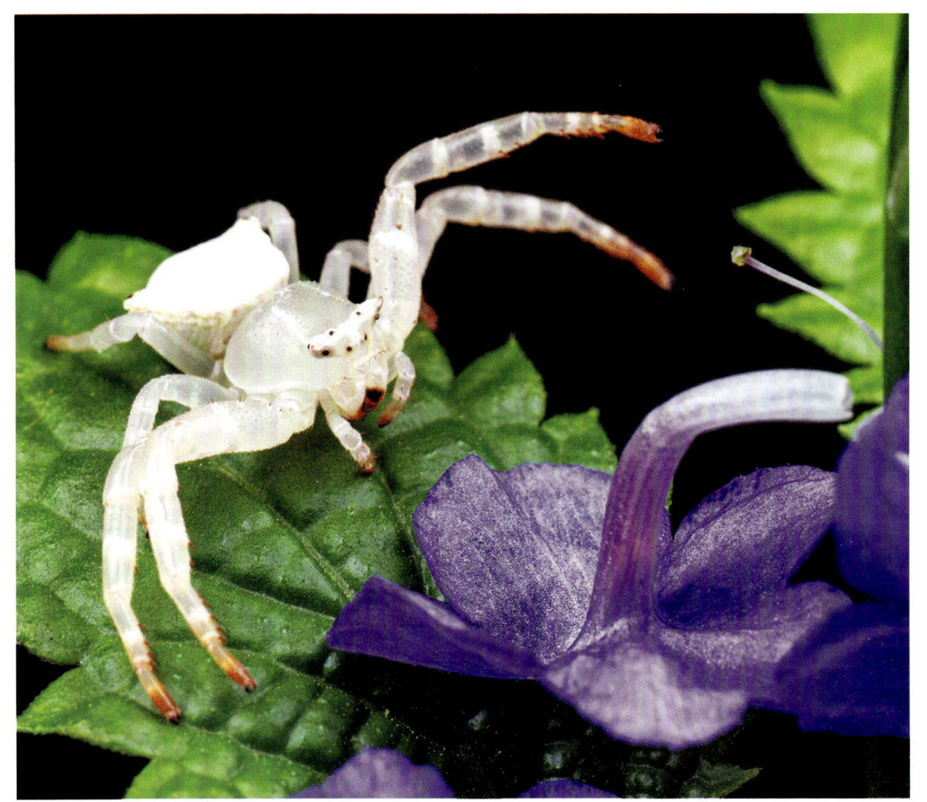

Crab Spider.

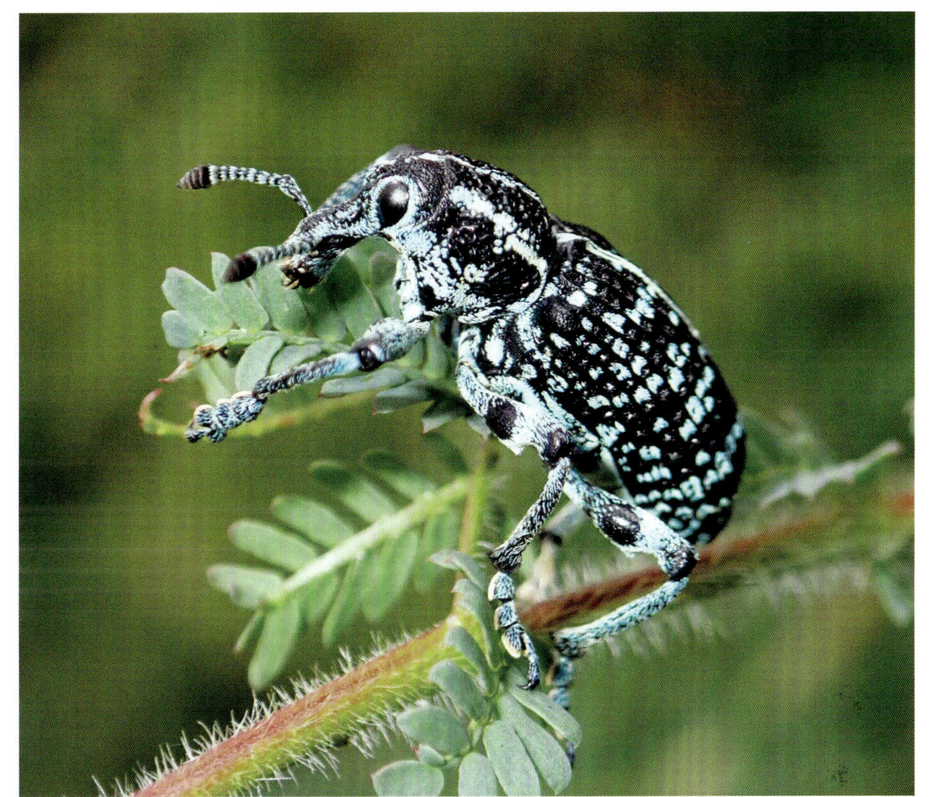

Botany Bay Weevil.

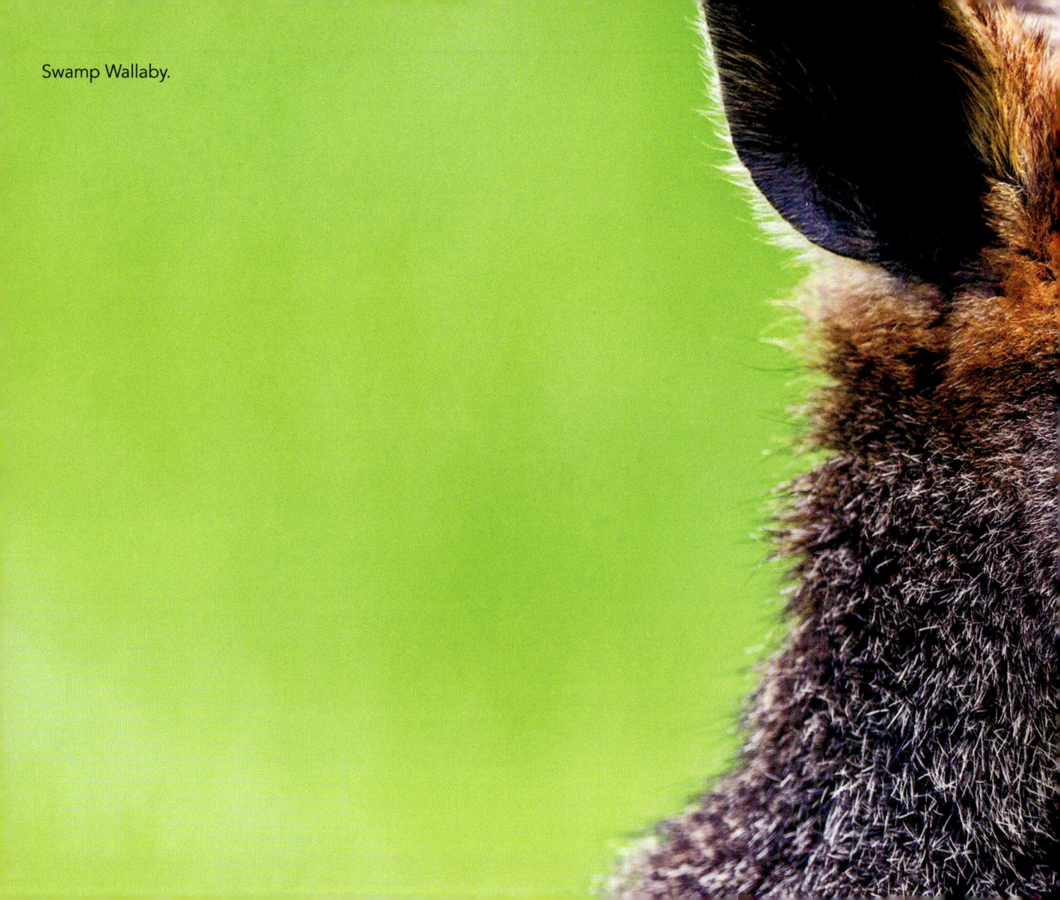

Swamp Wallaby.

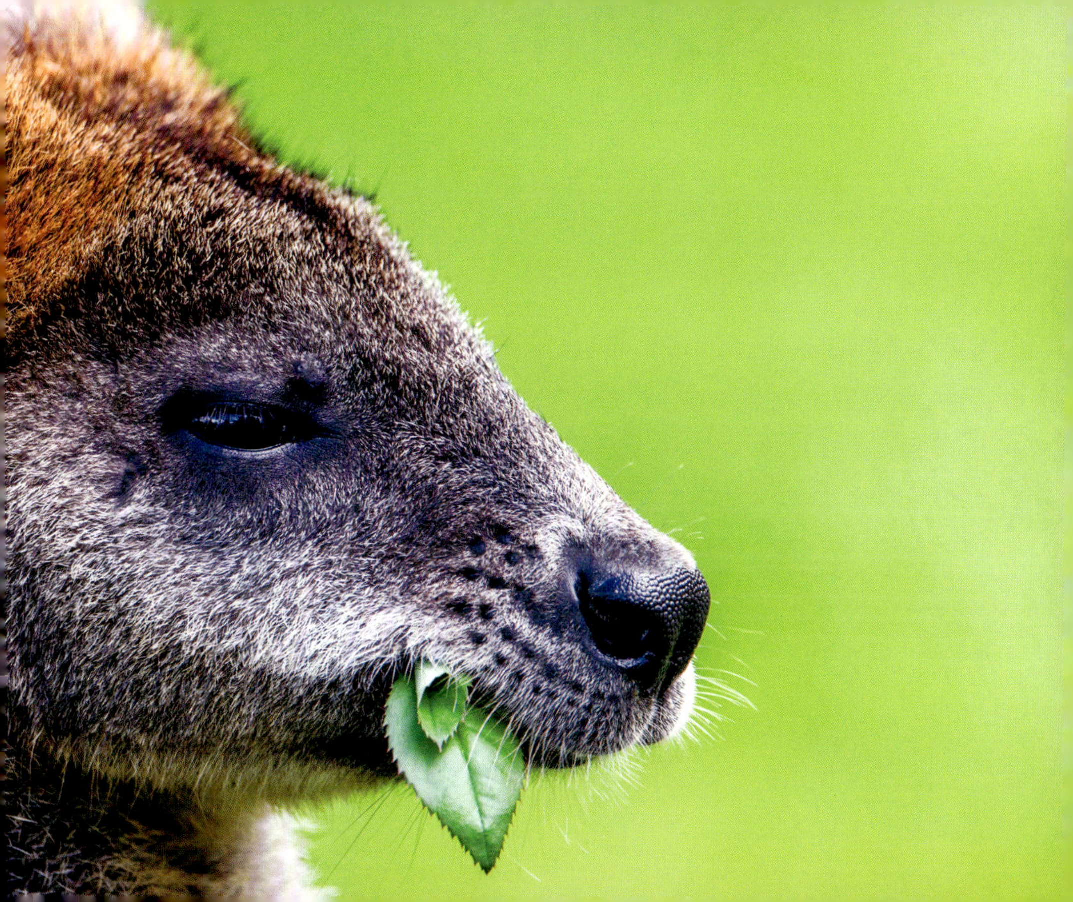

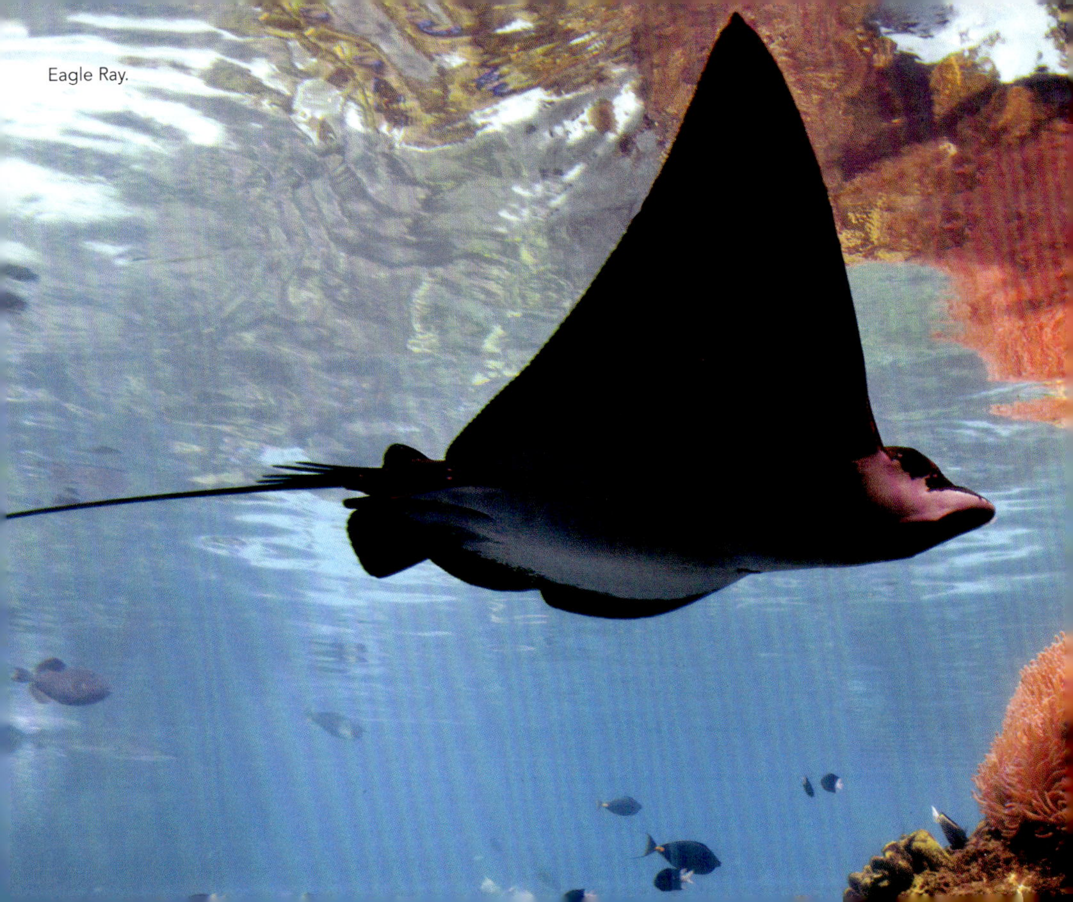
Eagle Ray.

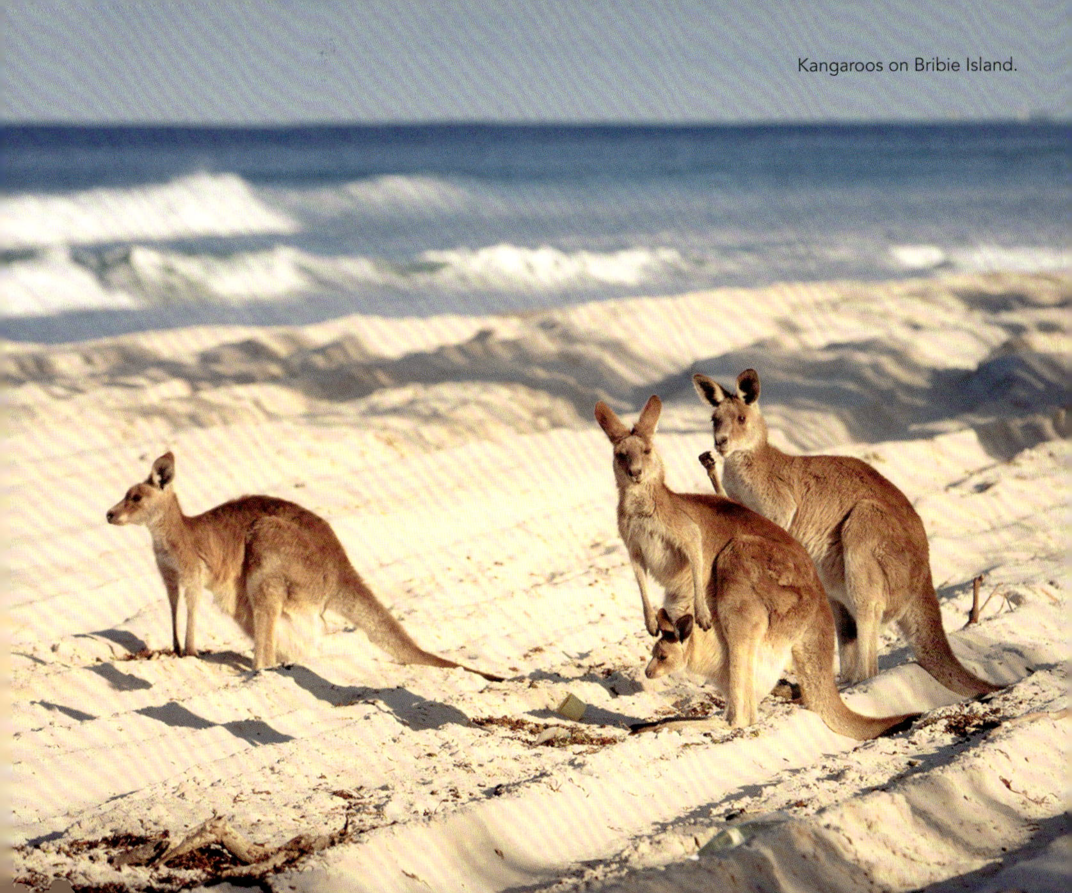

Kangaroos on Bribie Island.

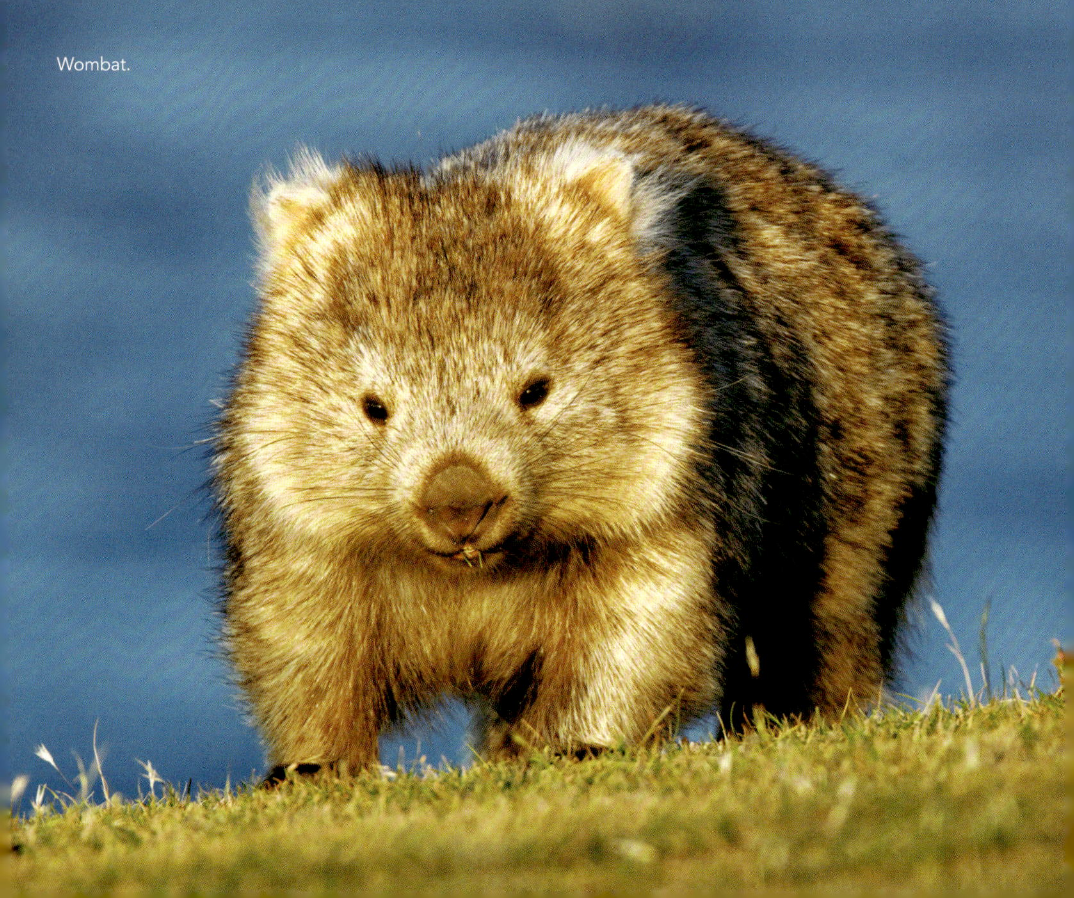

Wombat.

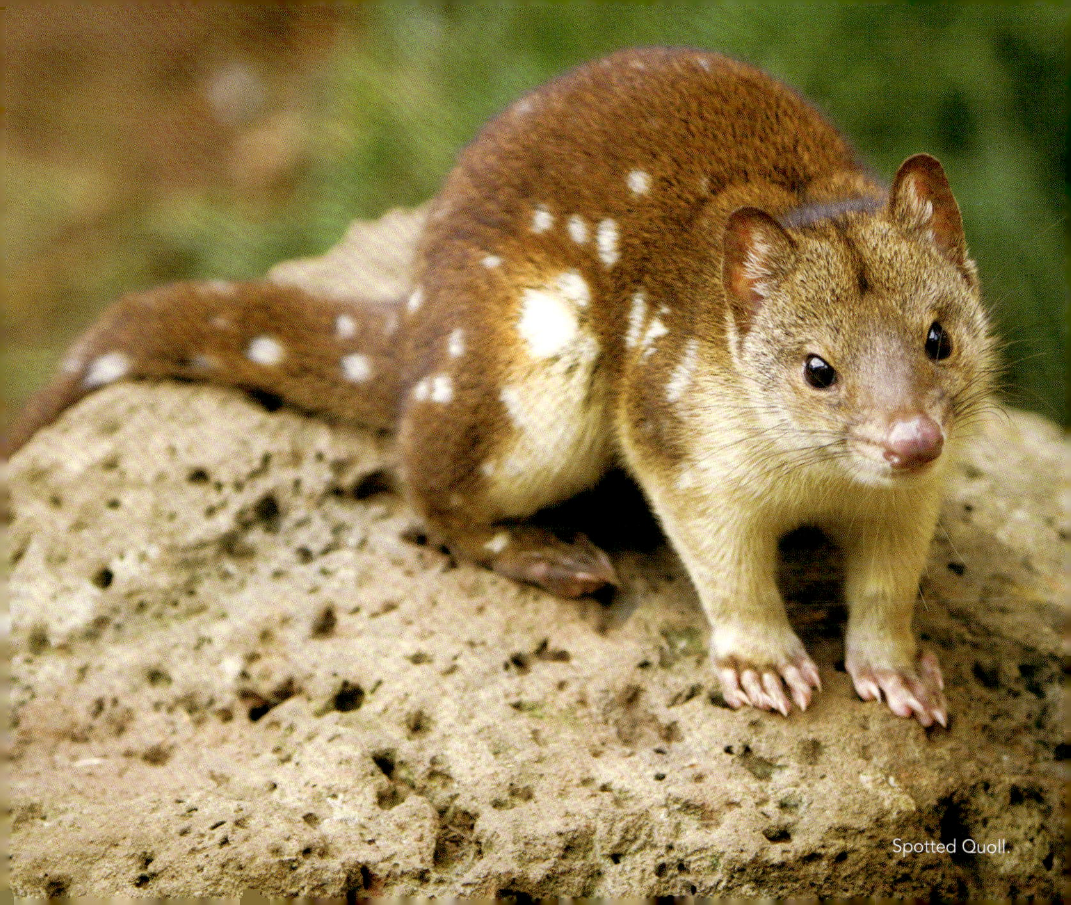

Spotted Quoll.

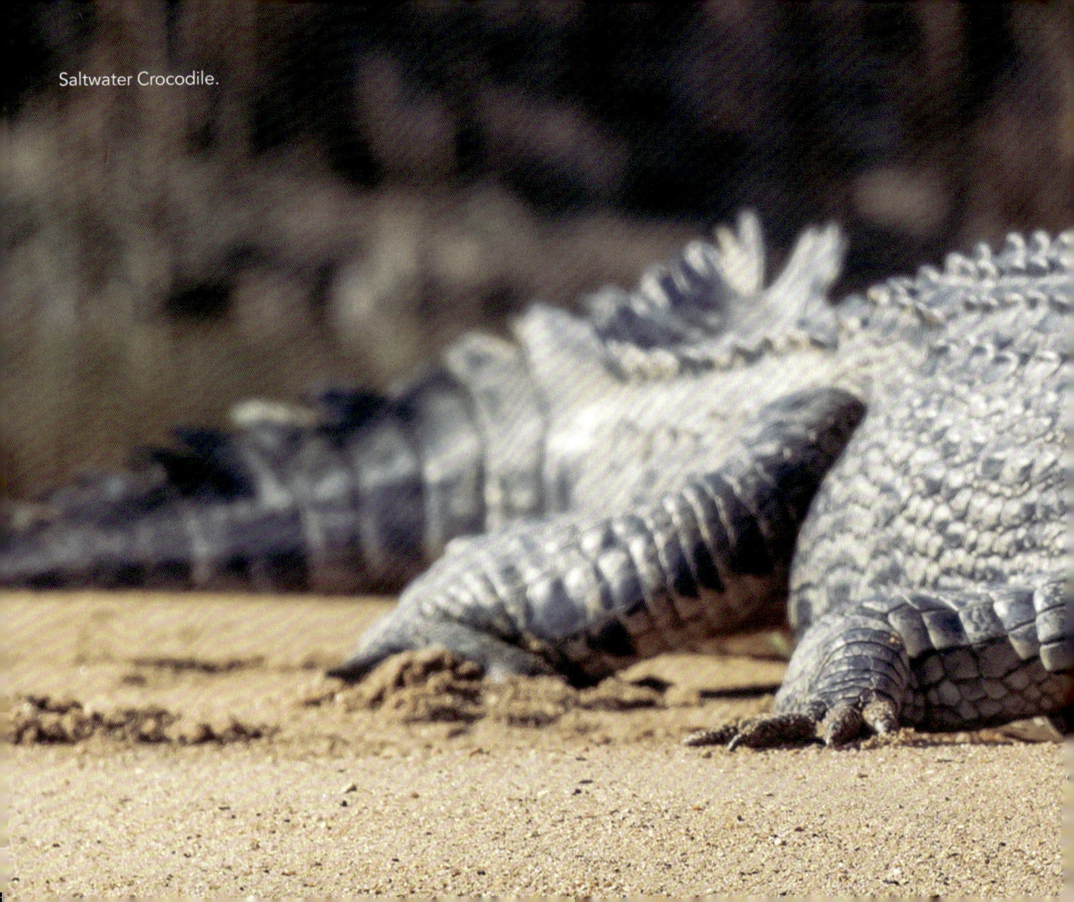
Saltwater Crocodile.

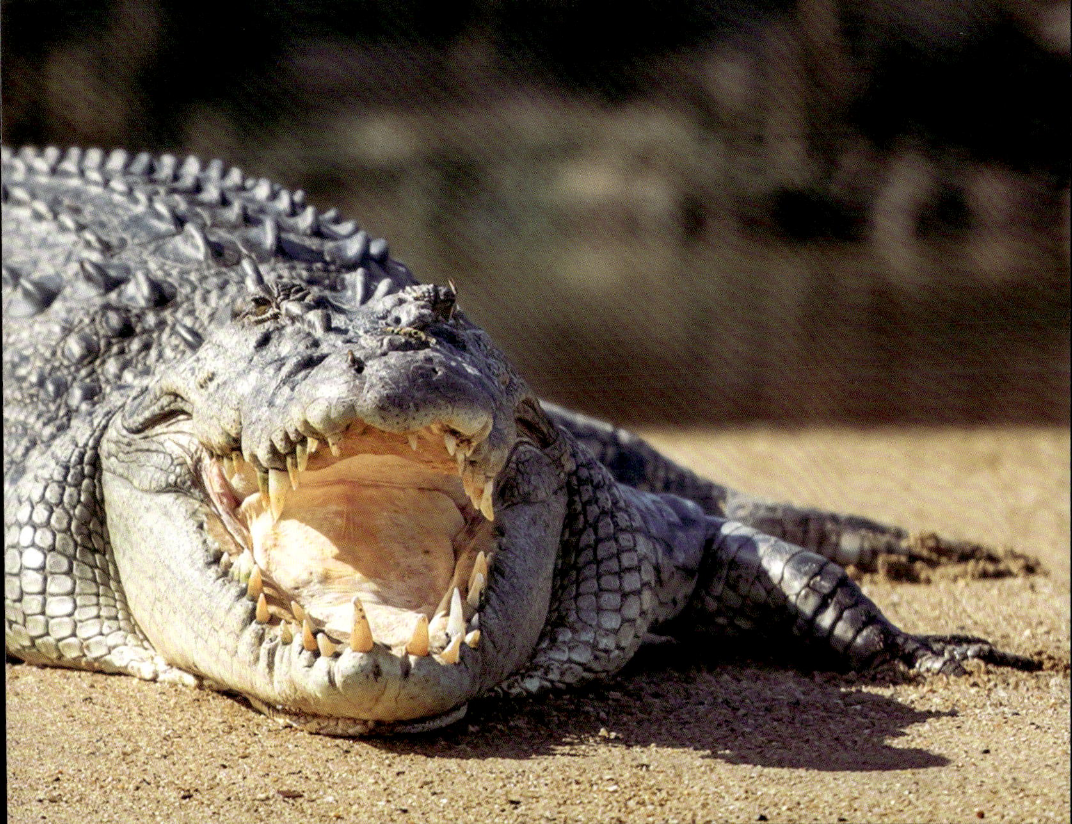

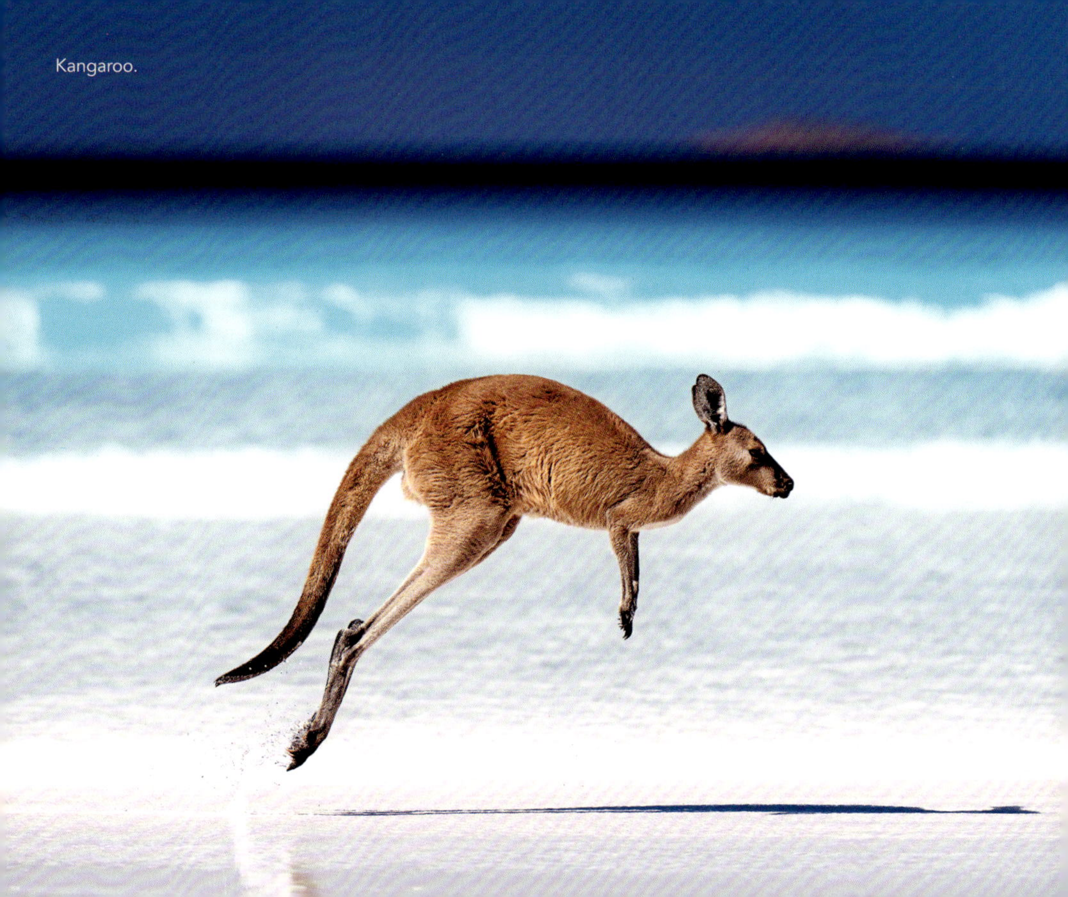

Kangaroo.

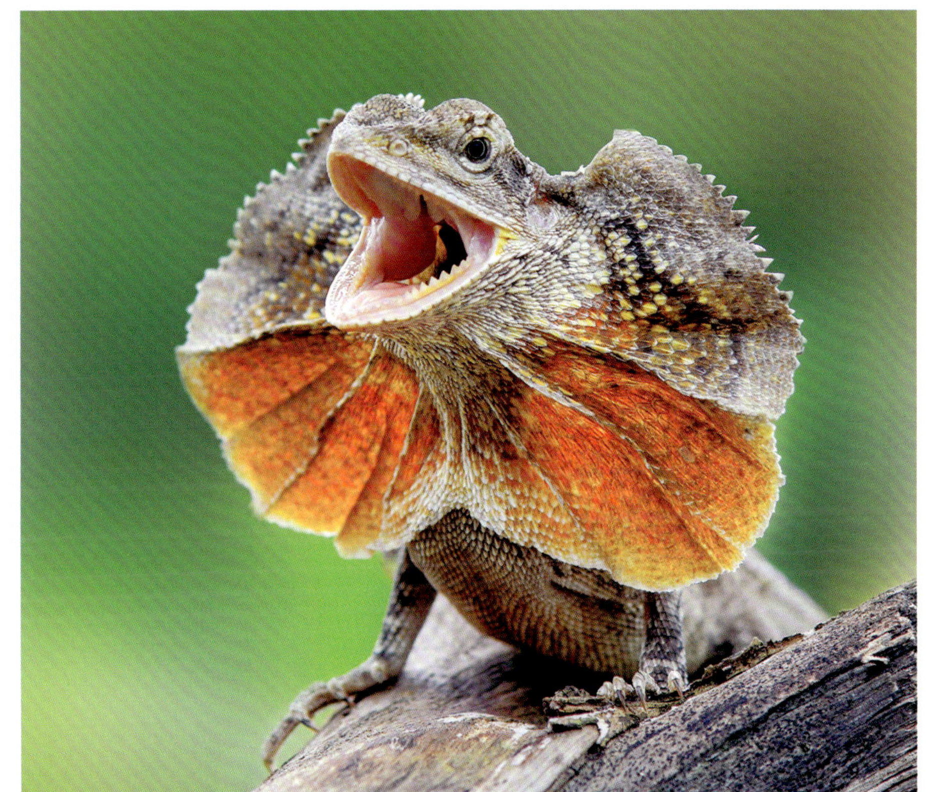

Frilled-neck Lizard.

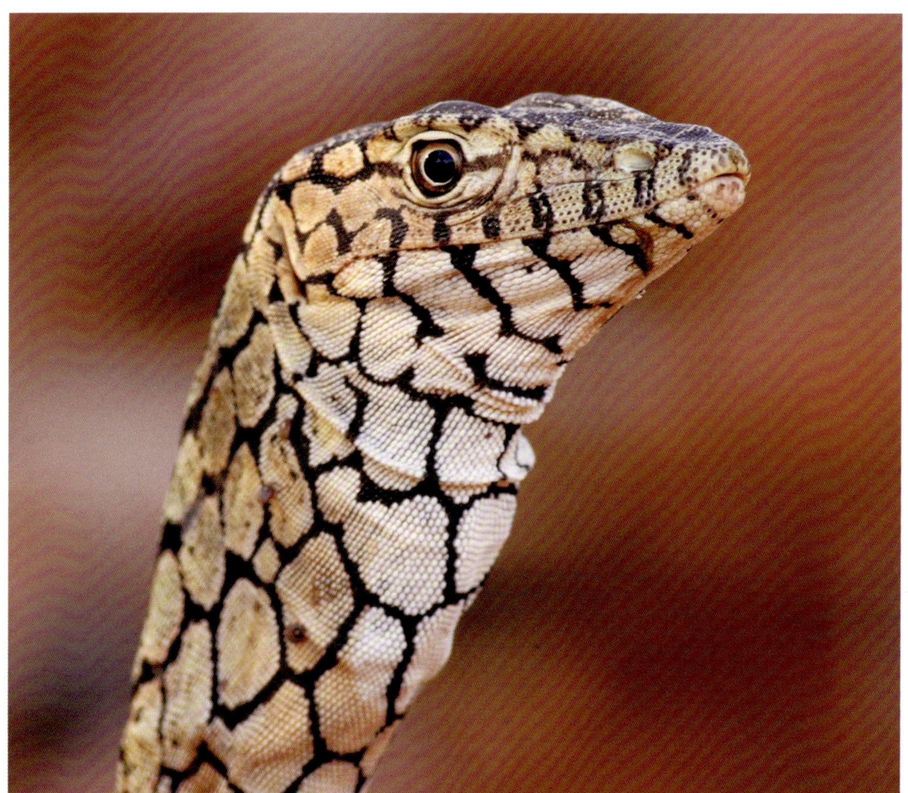

Perentie Monitor Lizard.

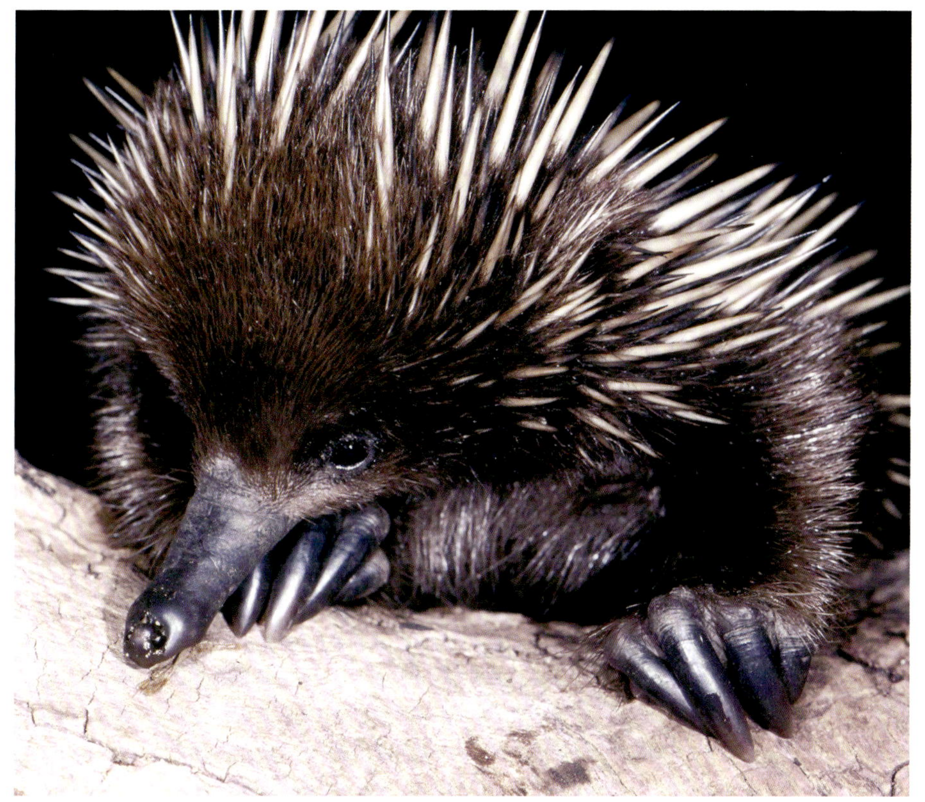

Echidna.

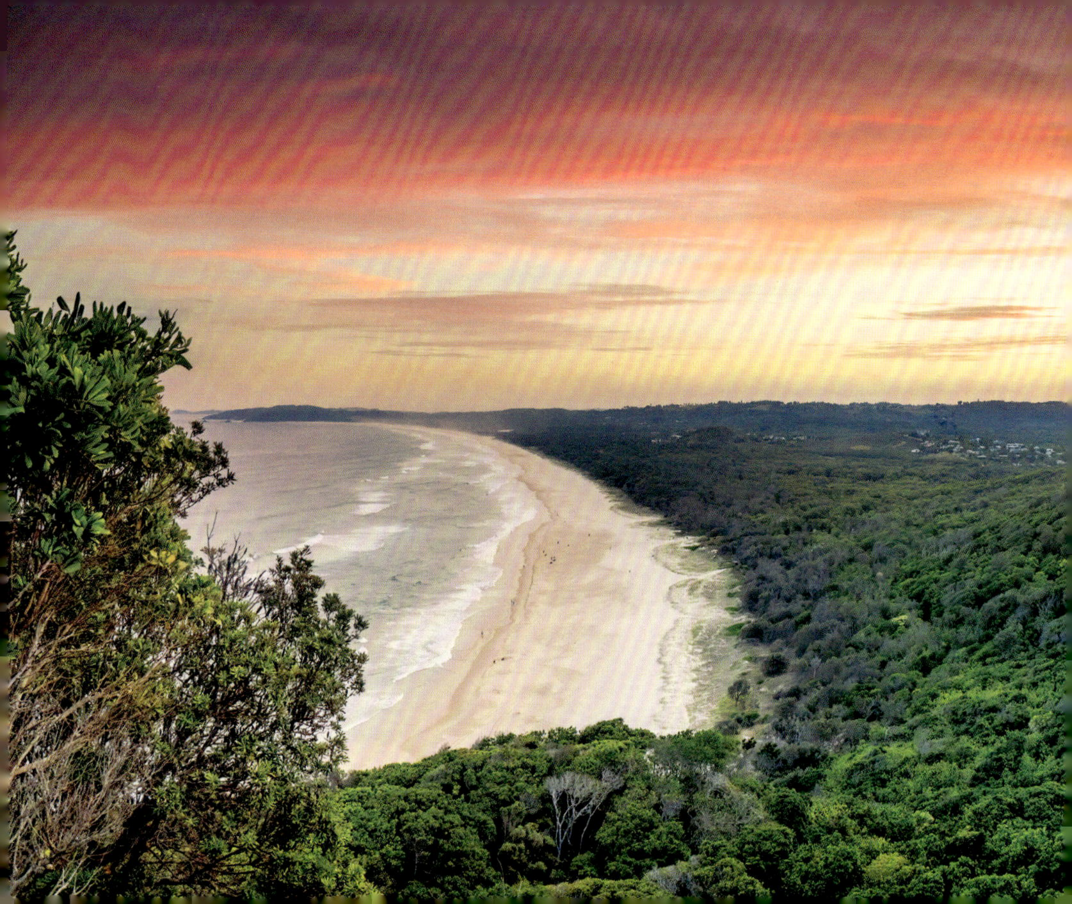

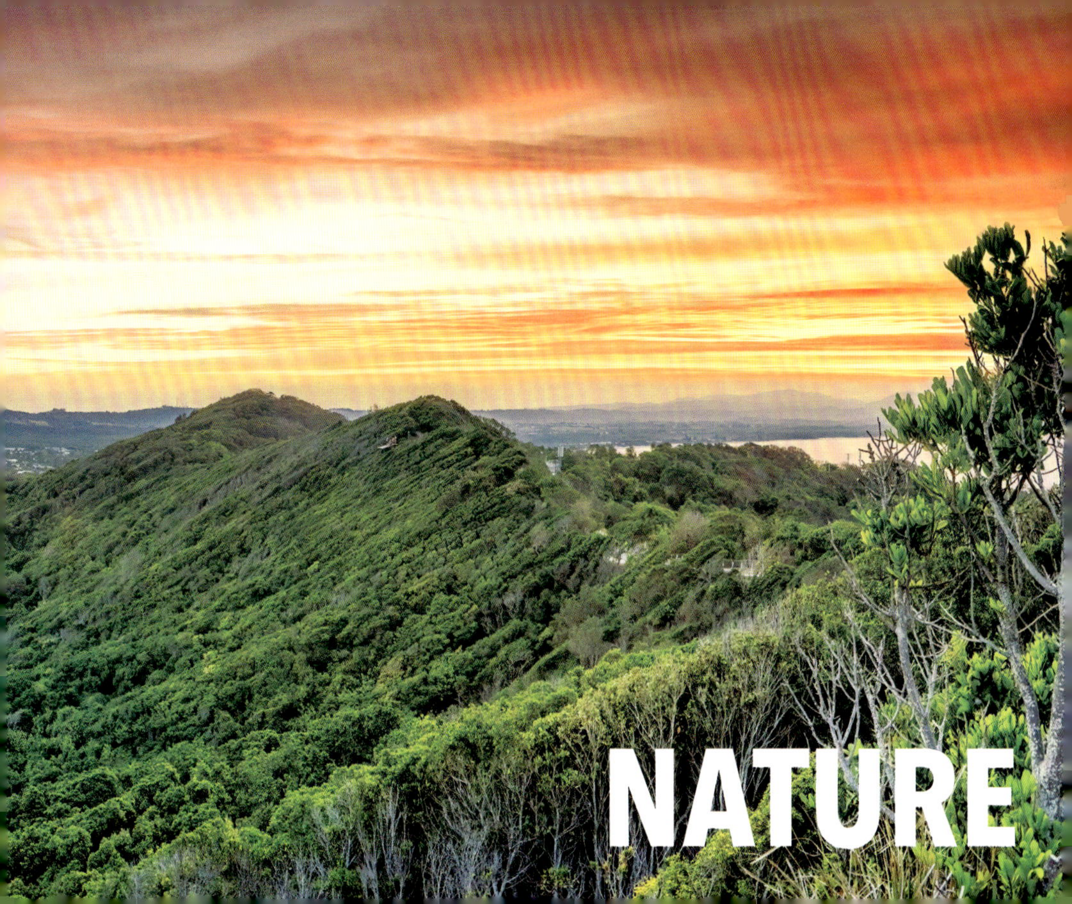
NATURE

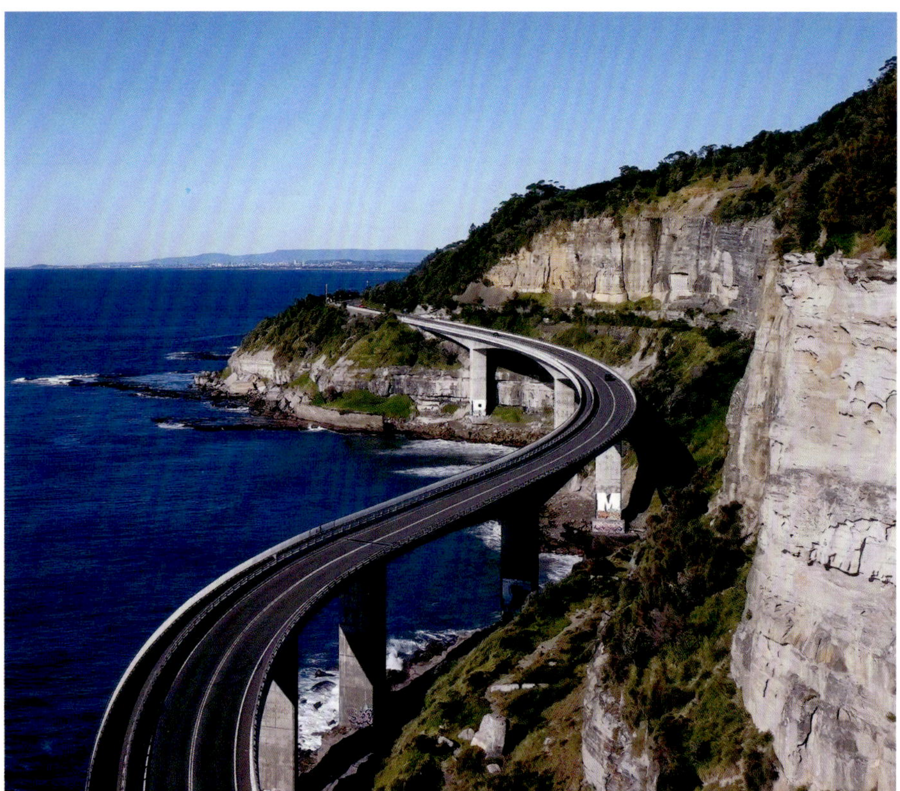

Sea Cliff Bridge, NSW.

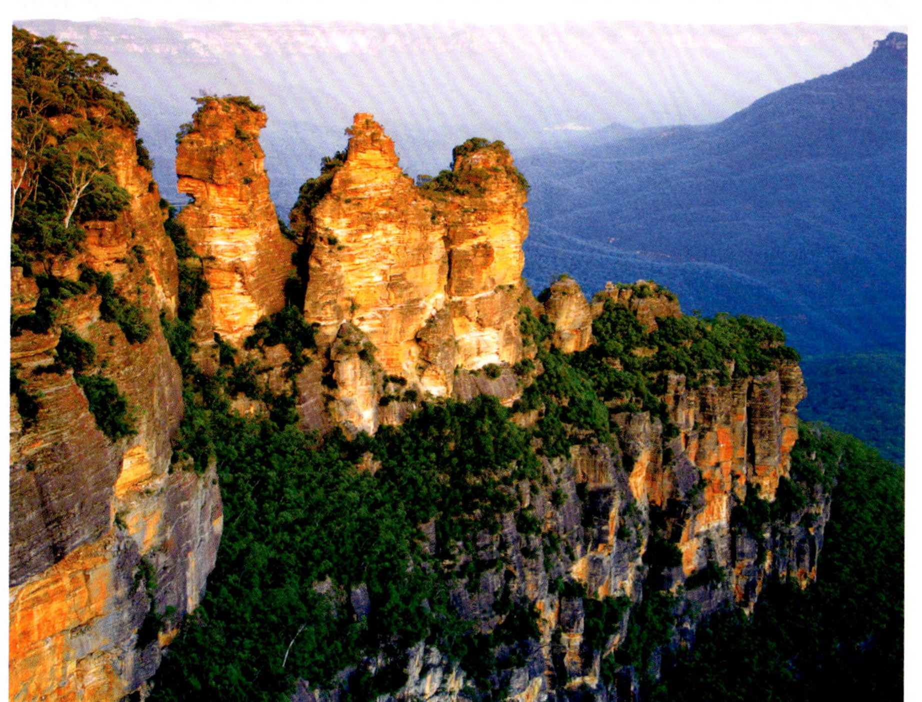

The Three Sisters, Blue Mountains, NSW.

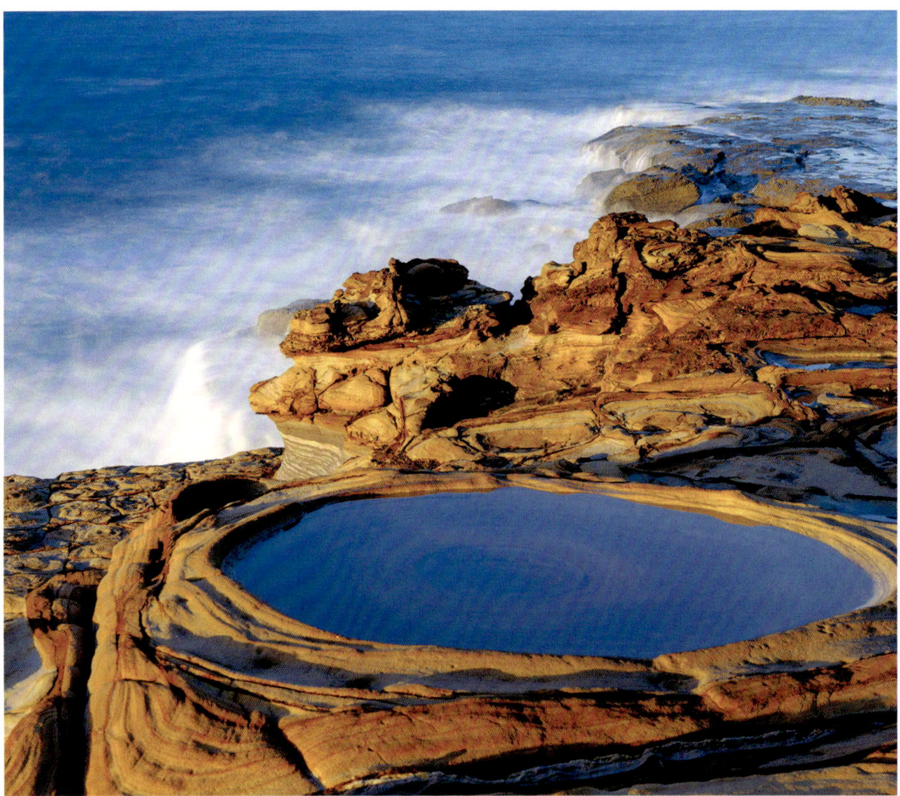

Putty Beach, Bouddi National Park, NSW,

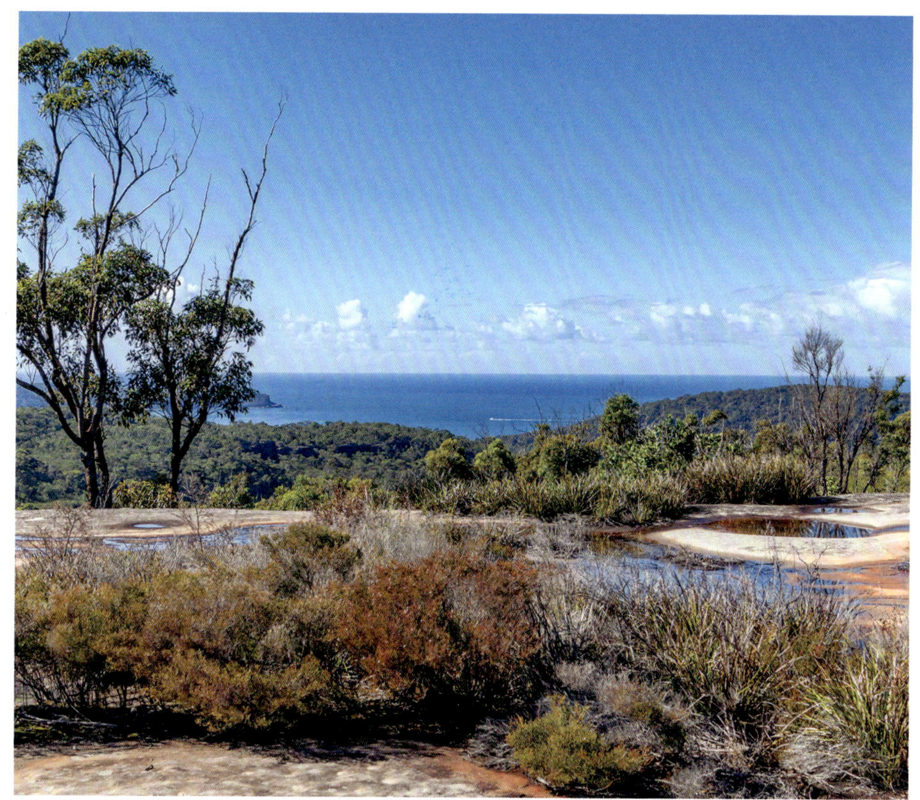

Bouddi National Park, NSW.

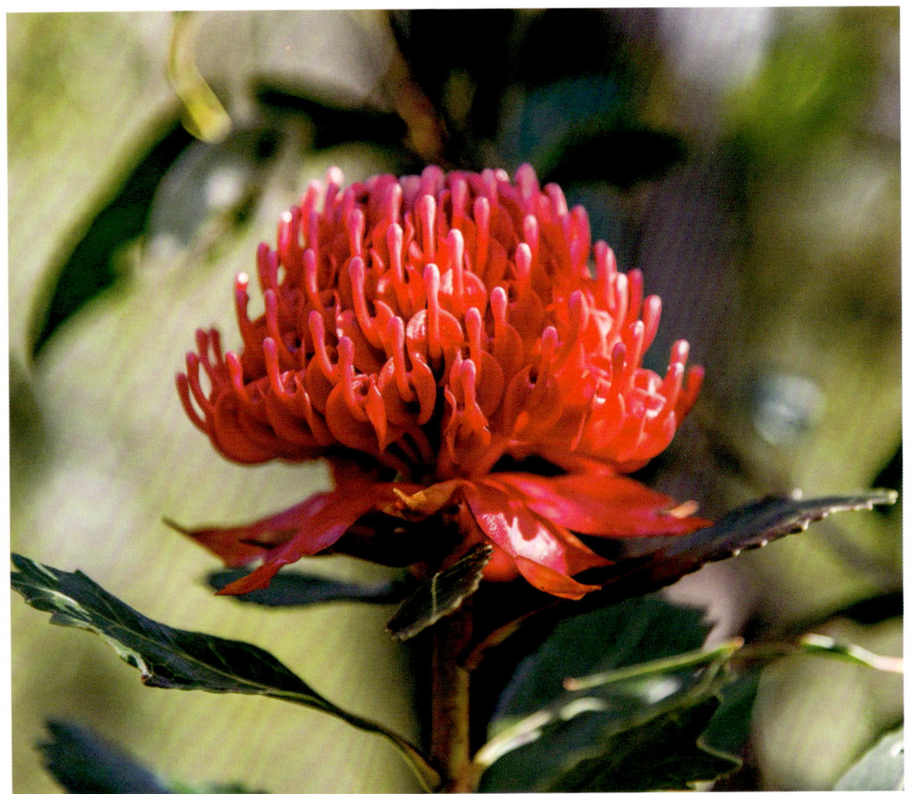

Waratah flower.

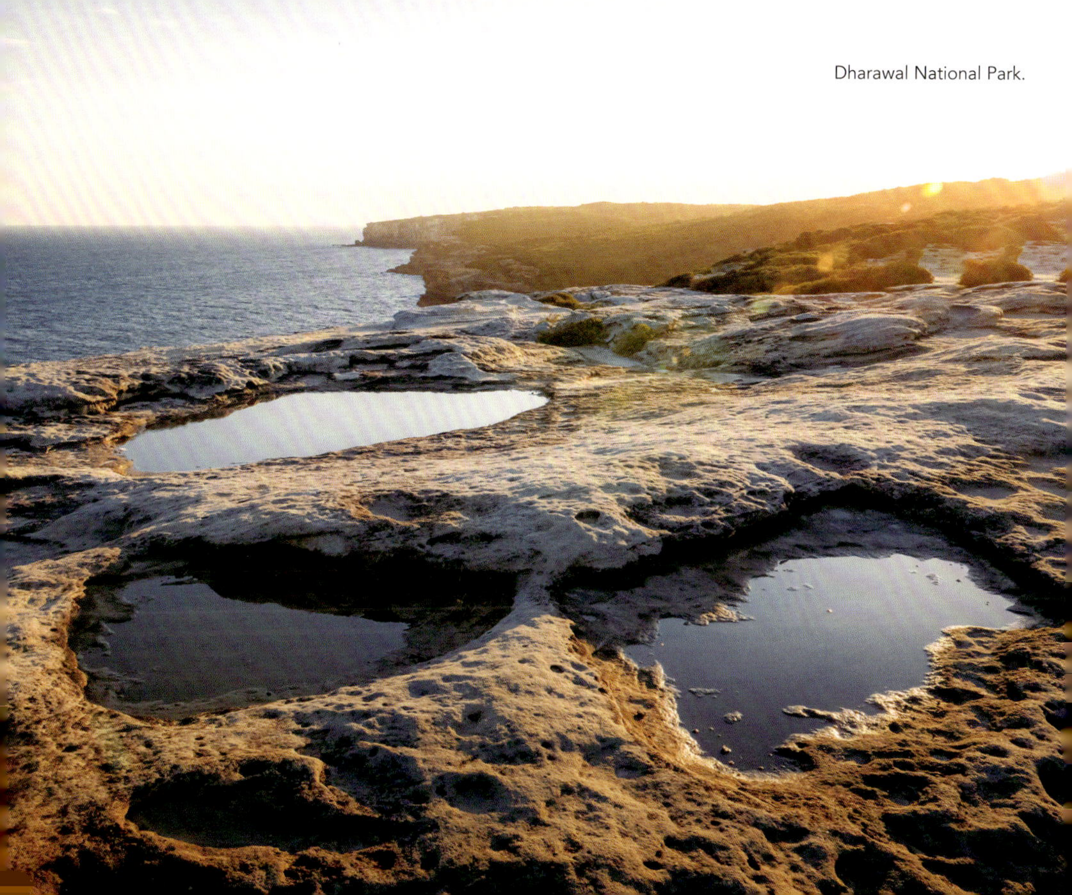

Dharawal National Park.

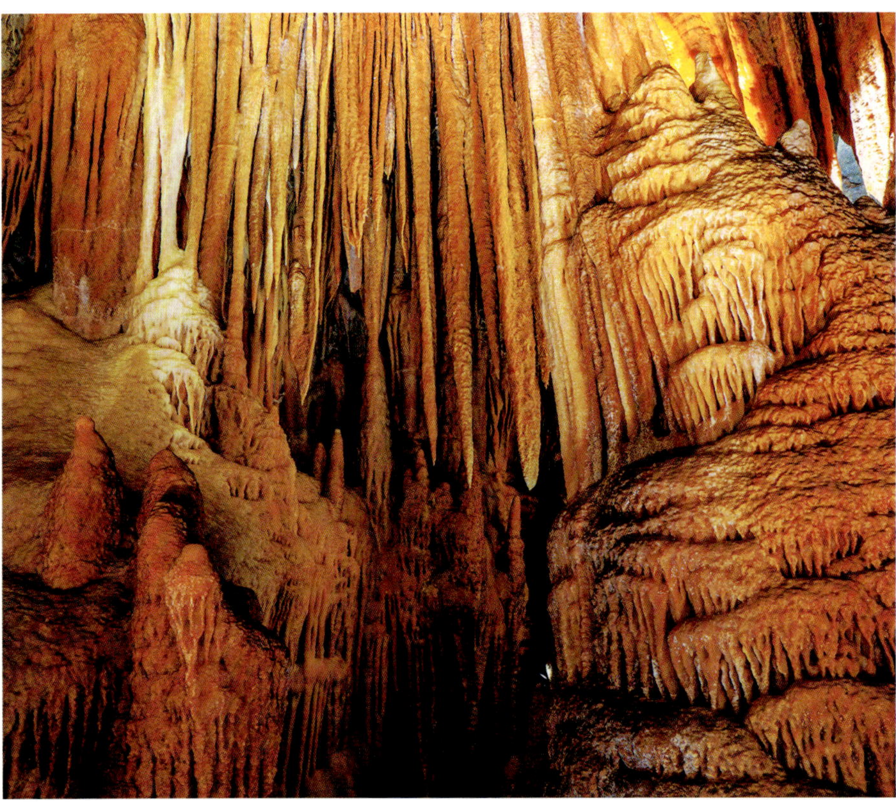

Jenolan Caves, NSW.

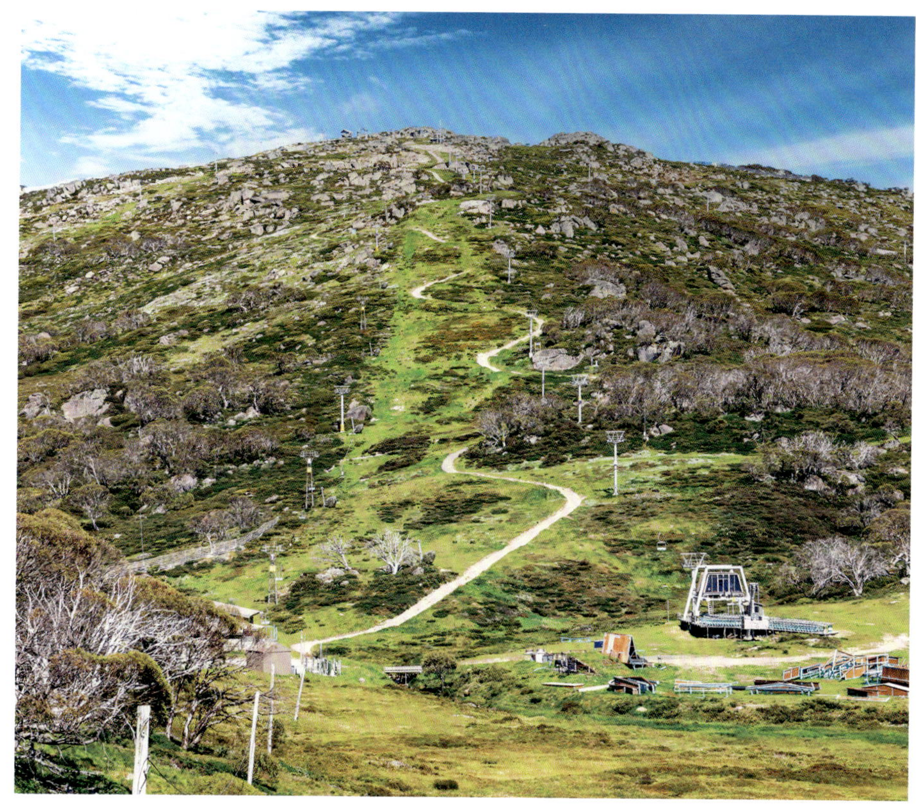

Perisher Valley, NSW.

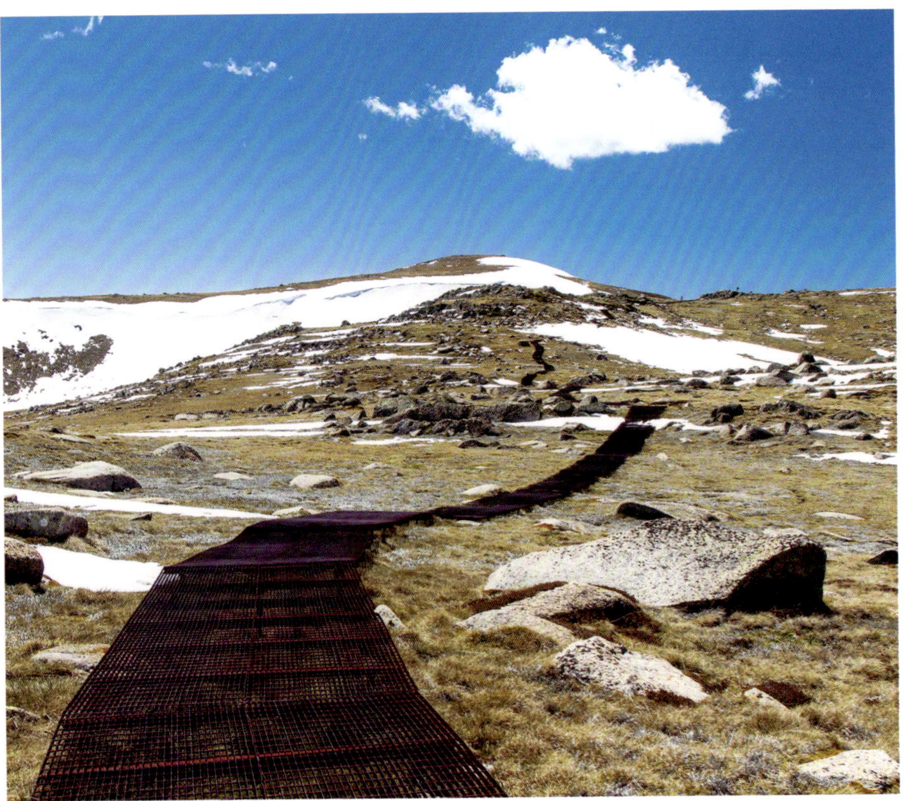

Mount Kosciuszko, NSW.

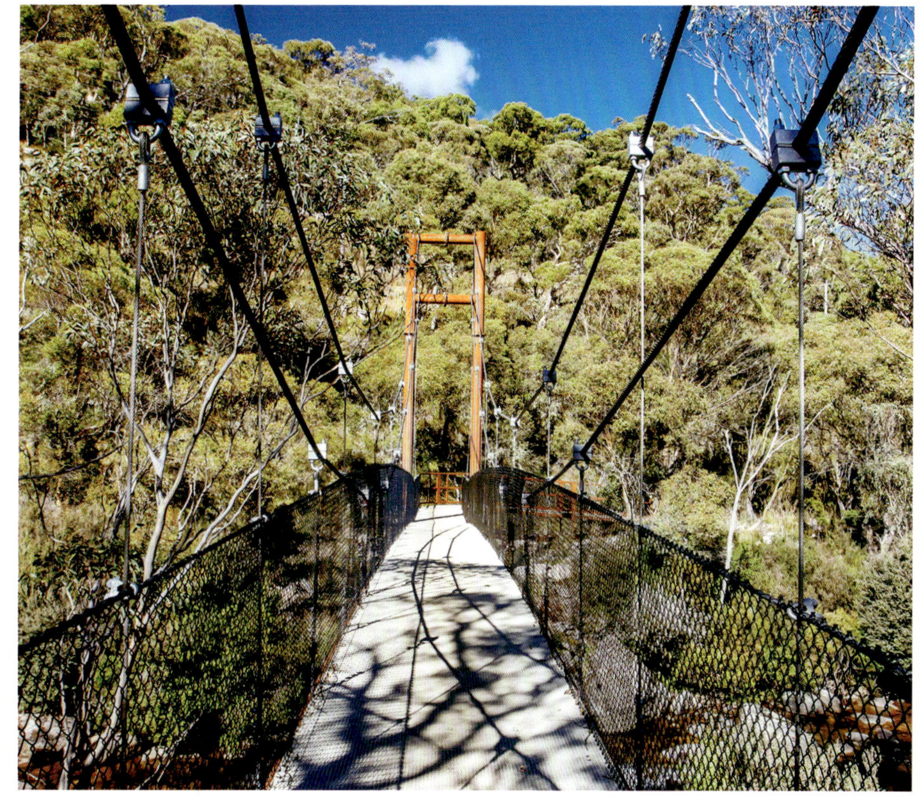

Threado Valley Track, NSW.

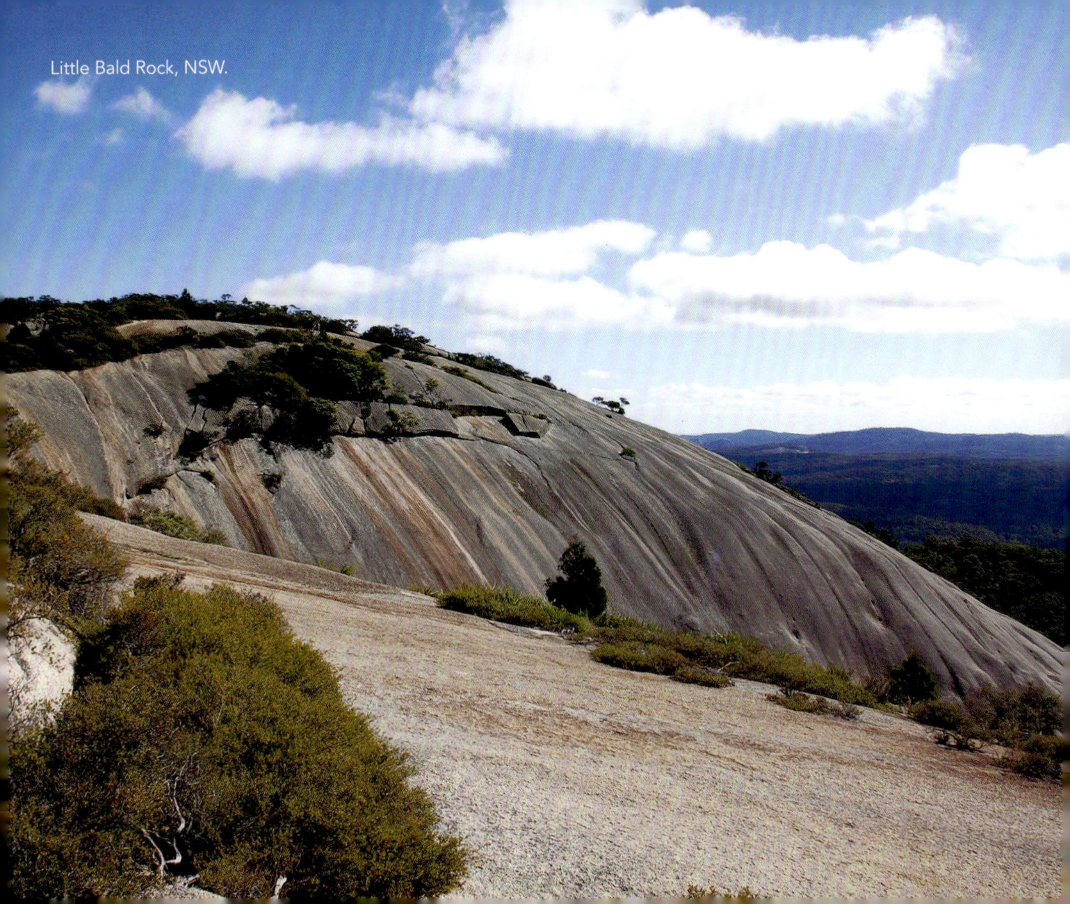

Little Bald Rock, NSW.

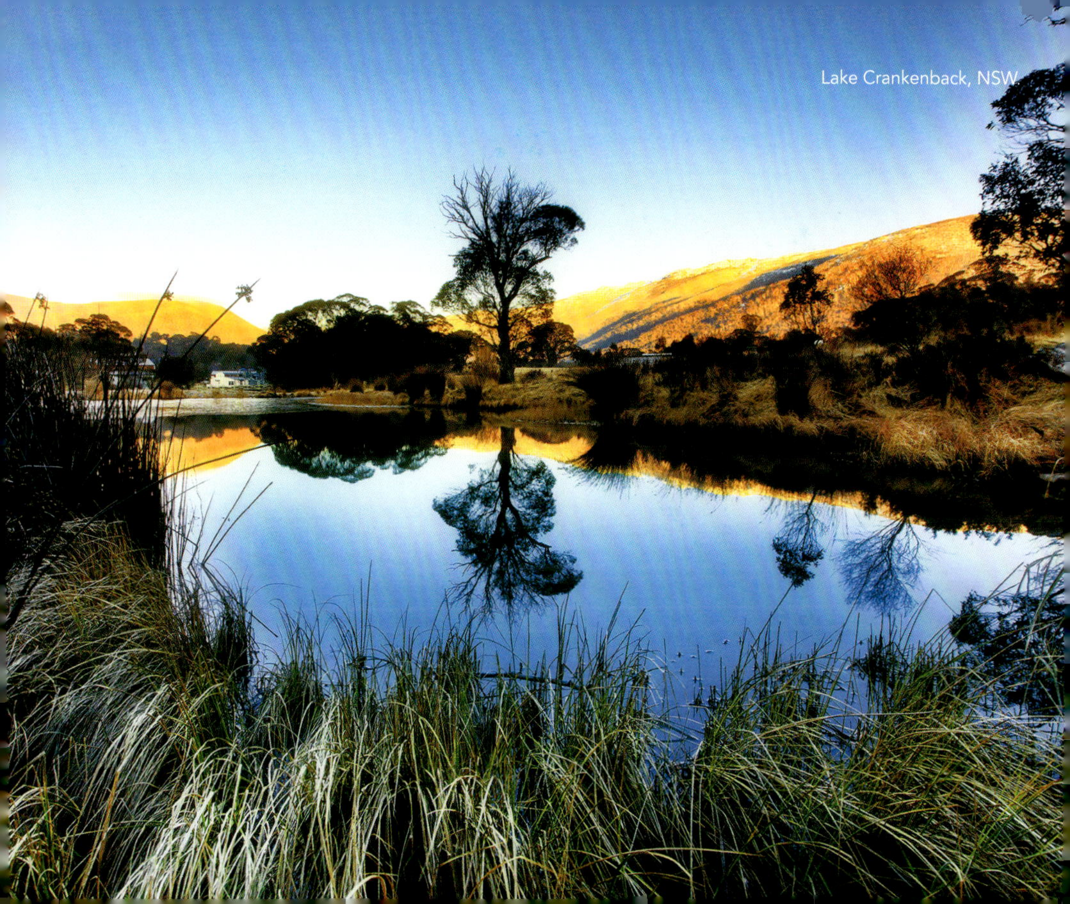

Lake Crankenback, NSW

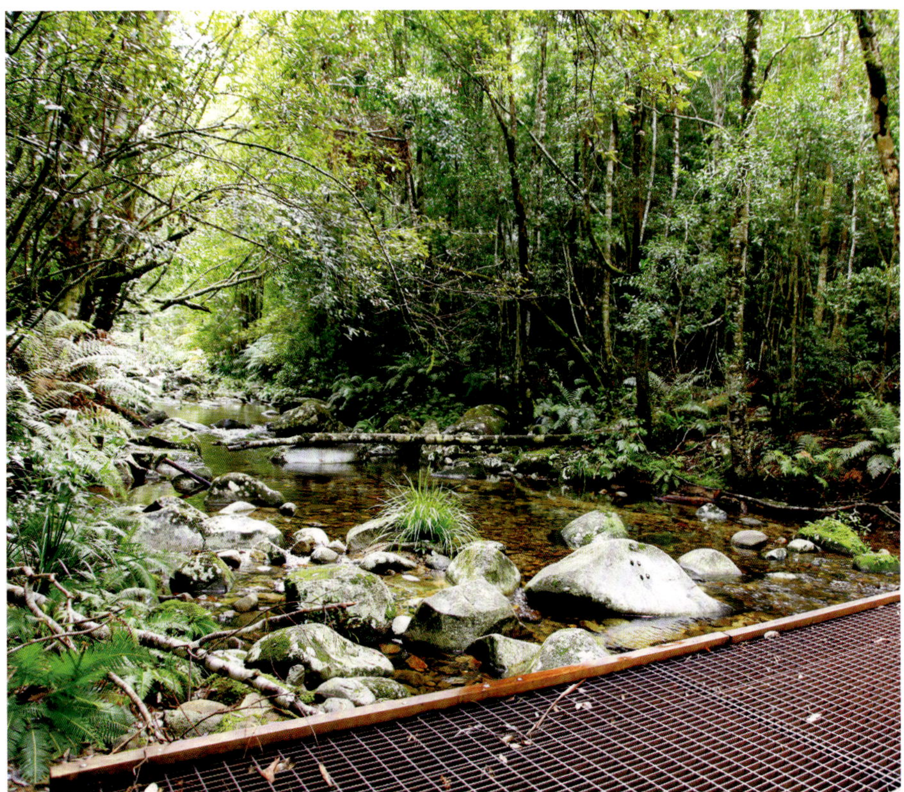

Washpool National Park, NSW.

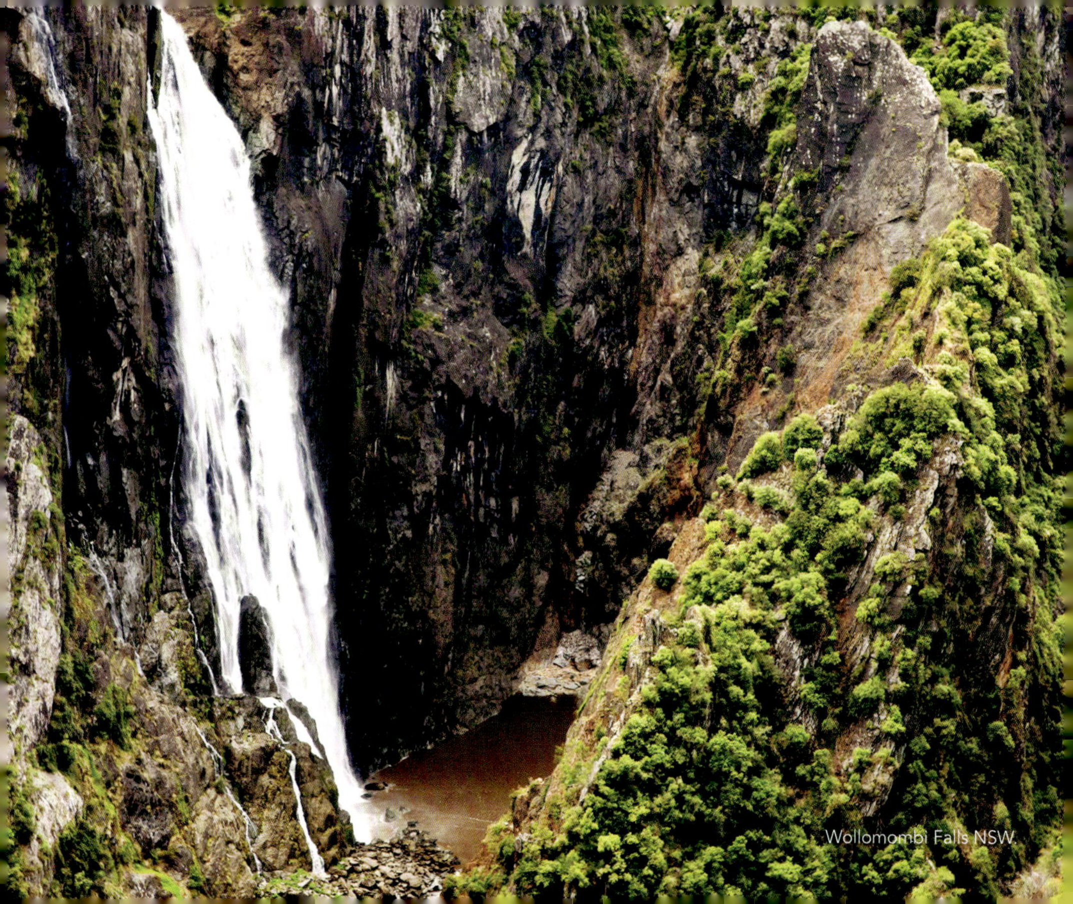

Wollomombi Falls NSW

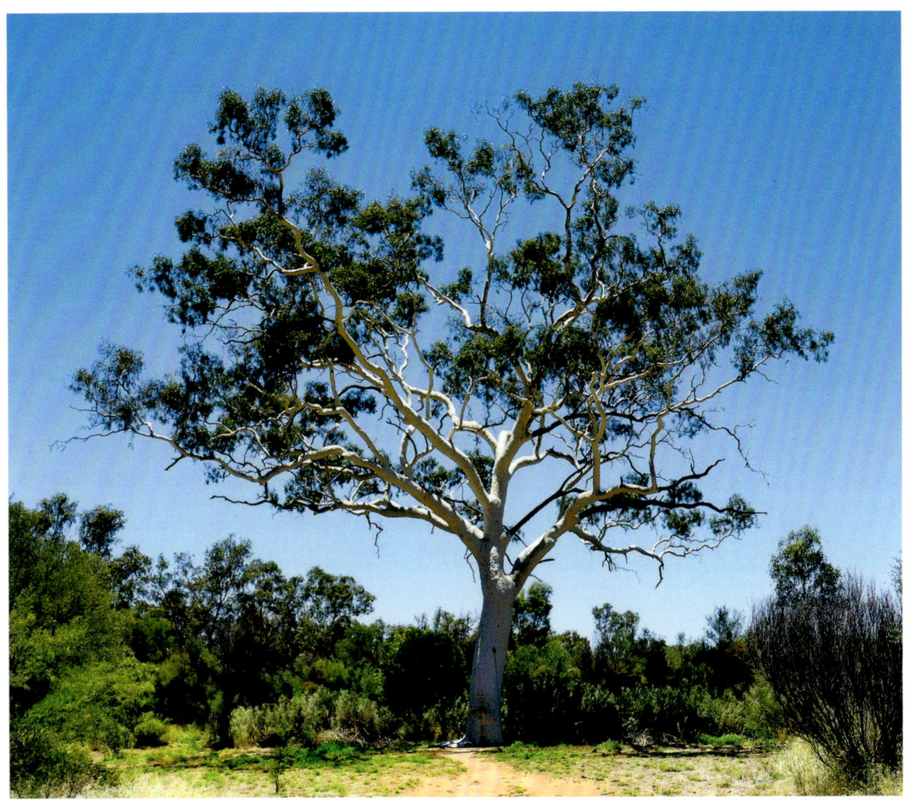

Ghost Gum Eucalyptus.

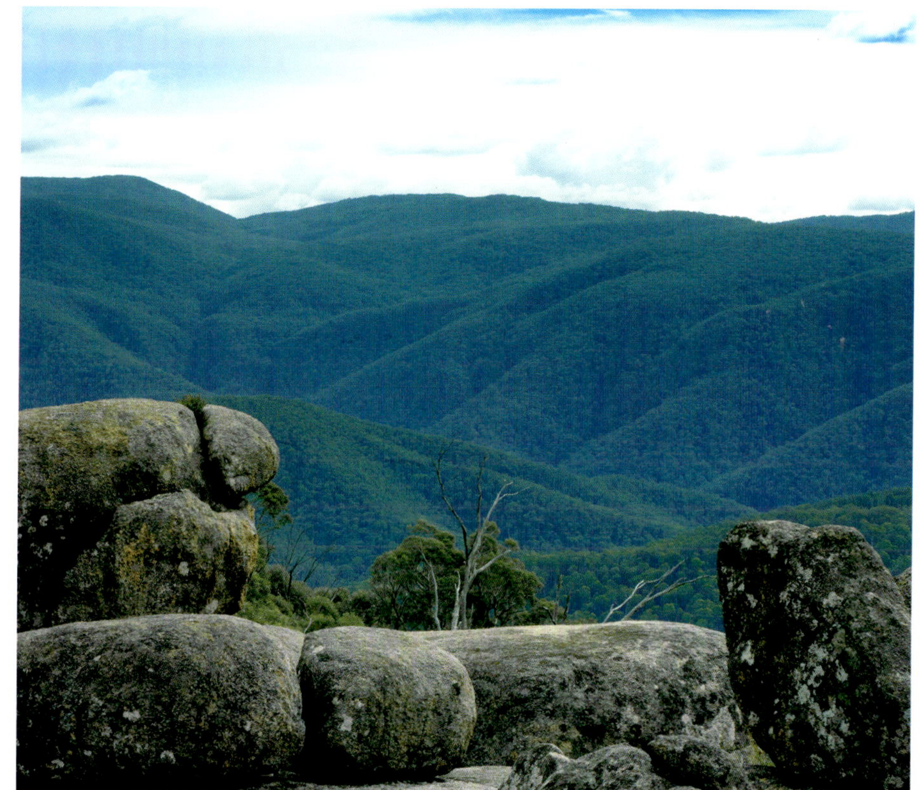

Namadgi National Park, Canberra.

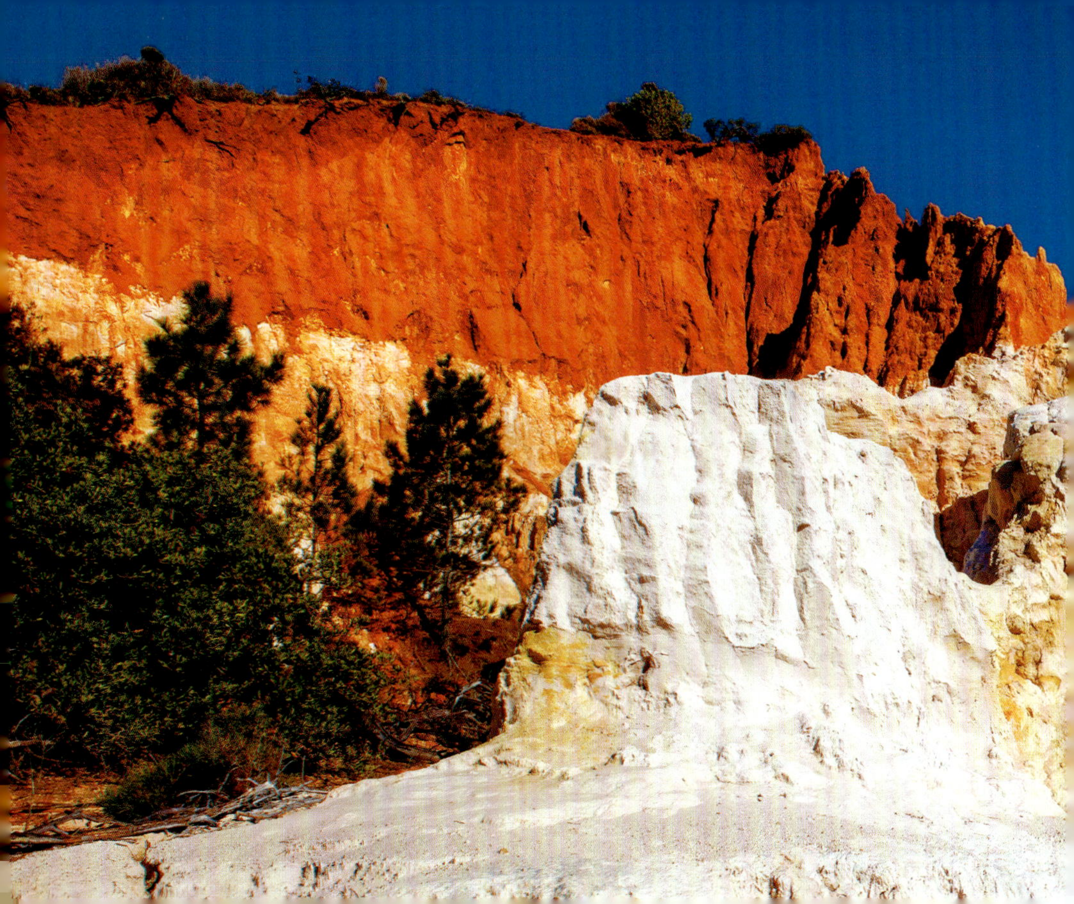

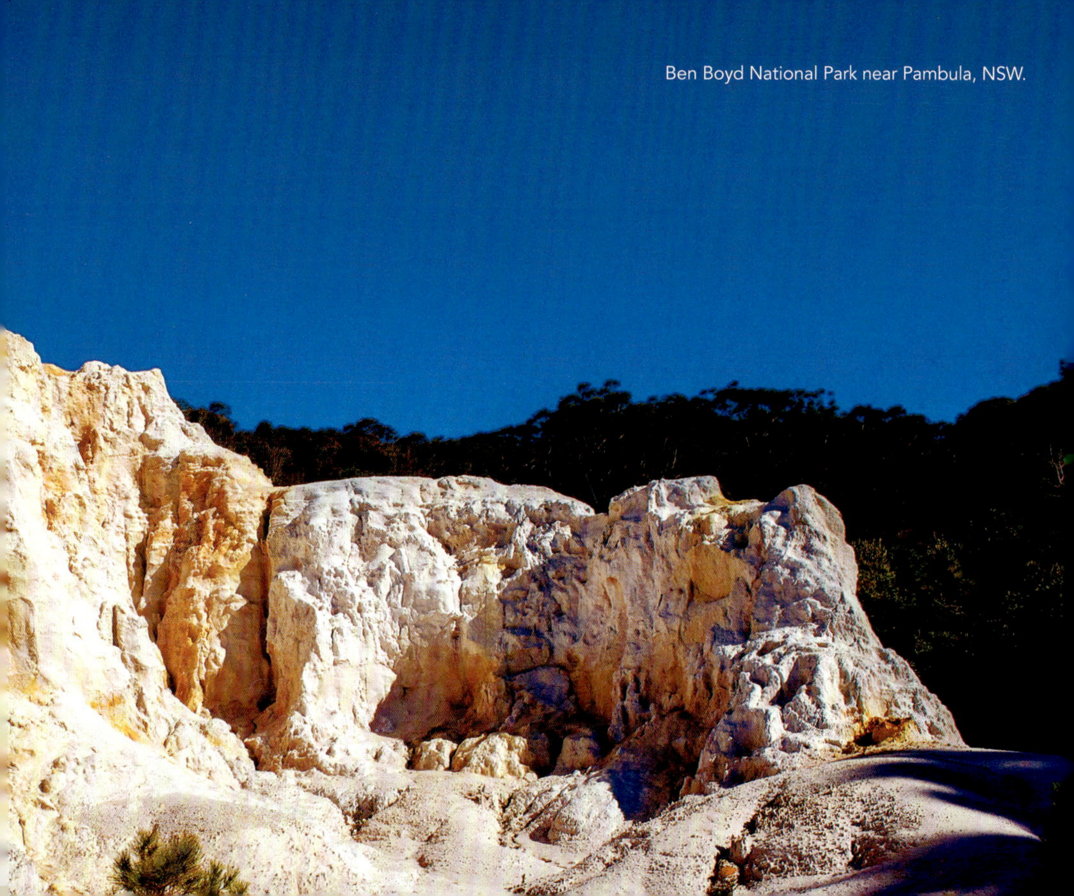
Ben Boyd National Park near Pambula, NSW.

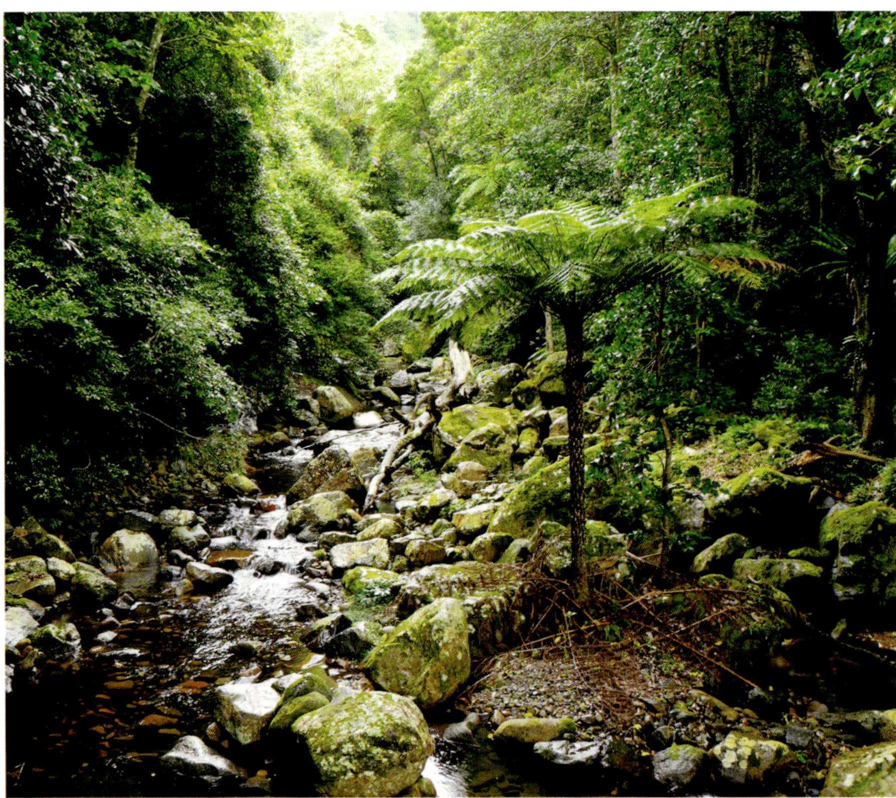

Minnamurra rainforest near Kiama, NSW.

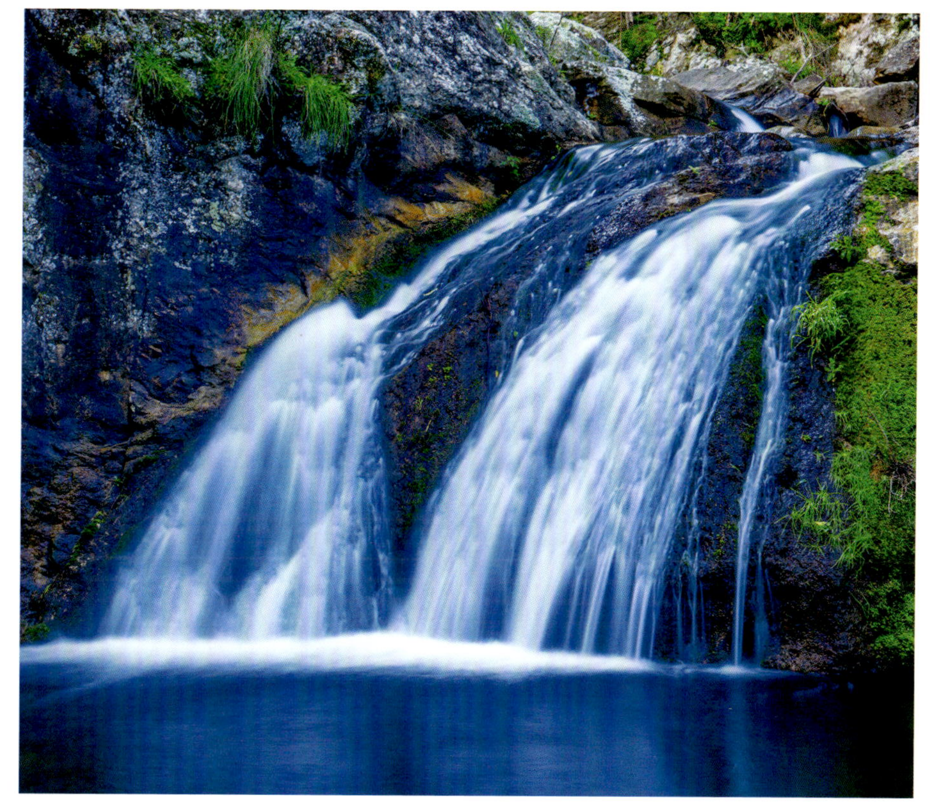

Jenolan Karst Conservation Reserve, NSW.

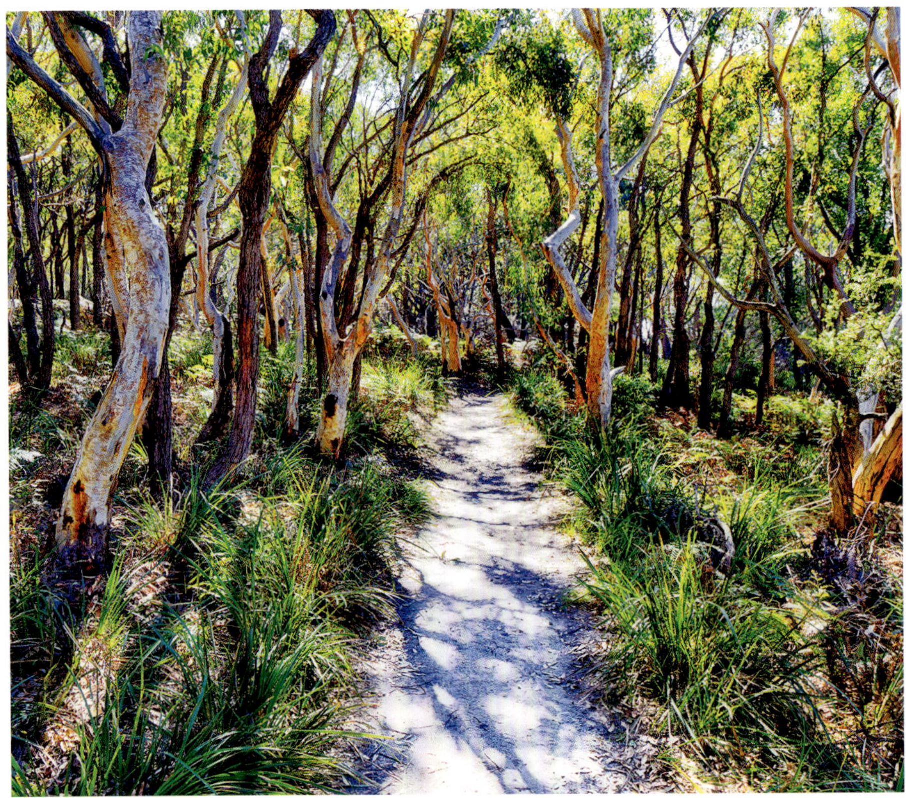

Booderee National Park, NSW.

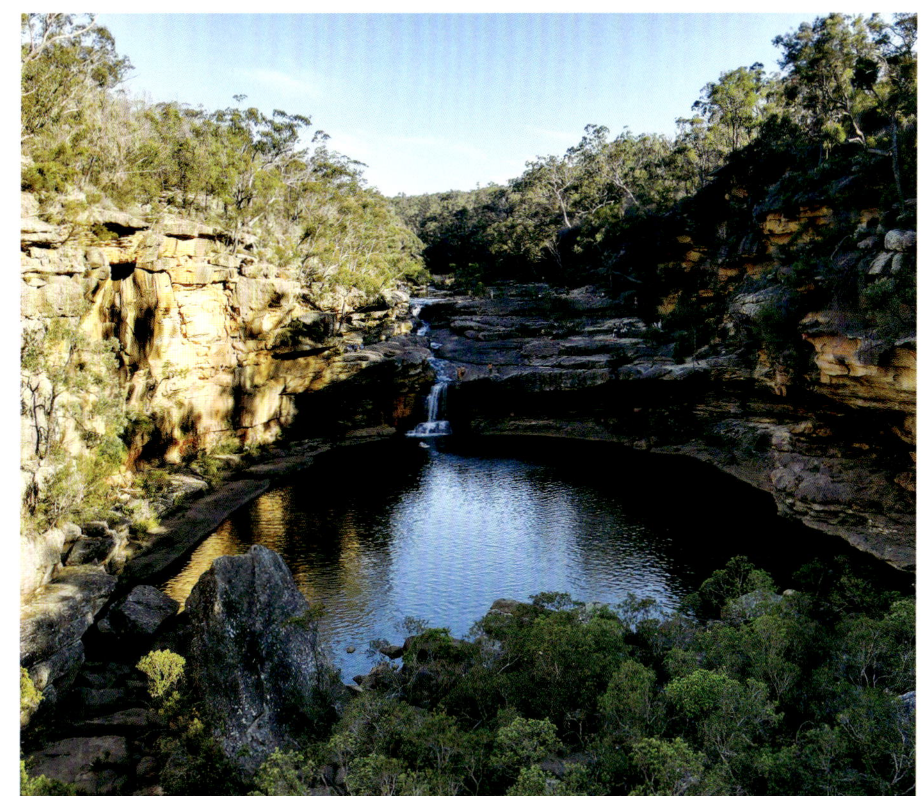

Mermaid Pools, NSW.

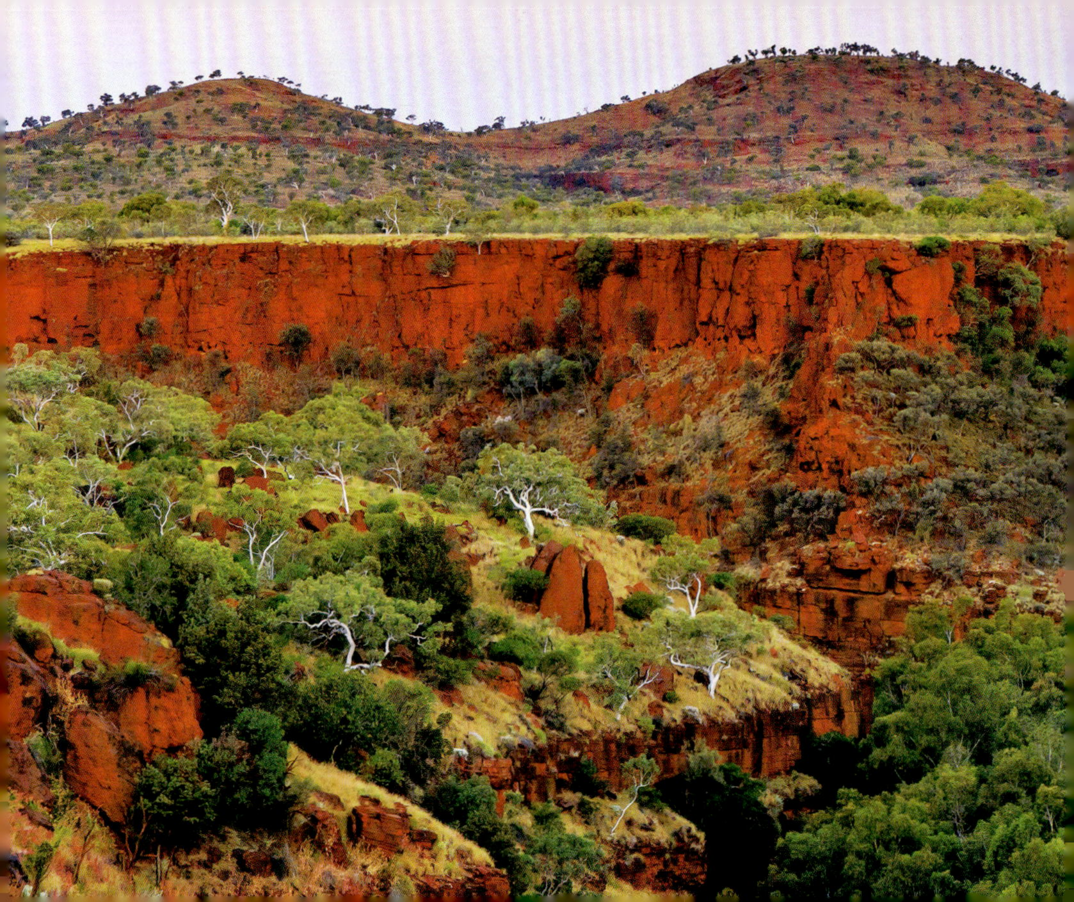

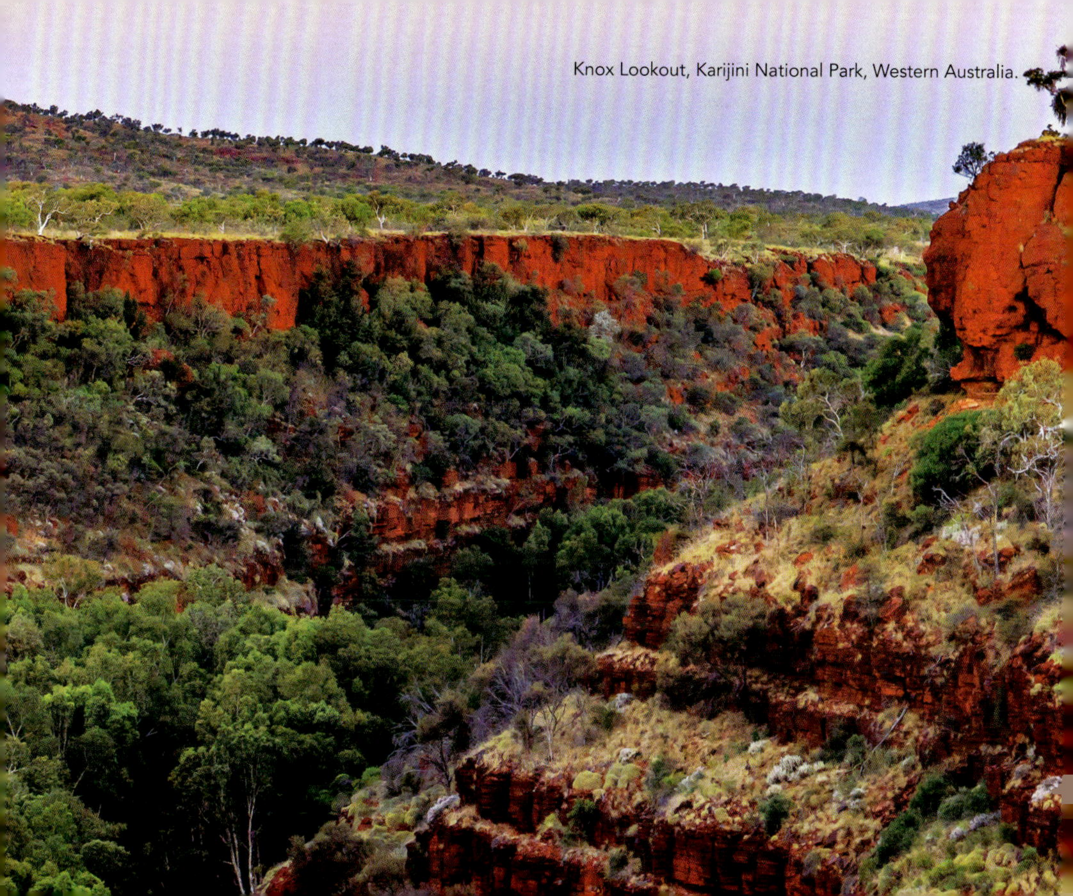

Knox Lookout, Karijini National Park, Western Australia.

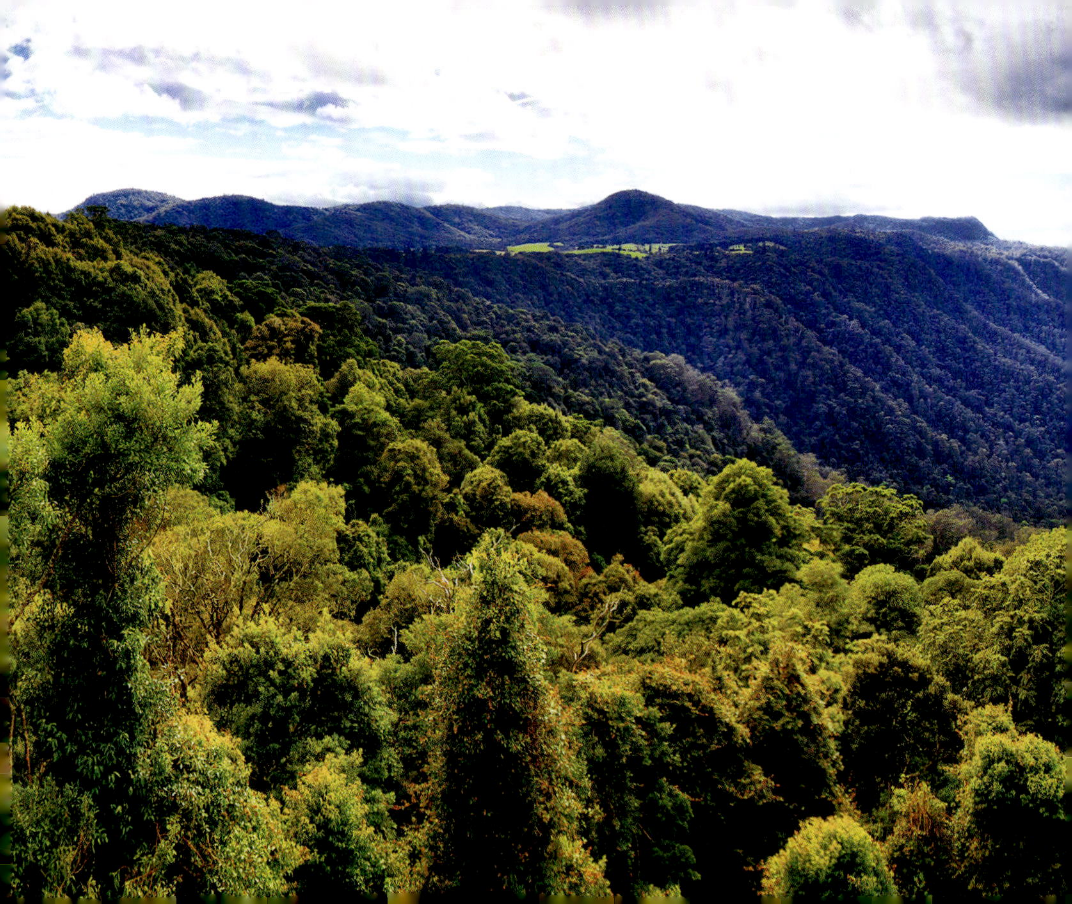

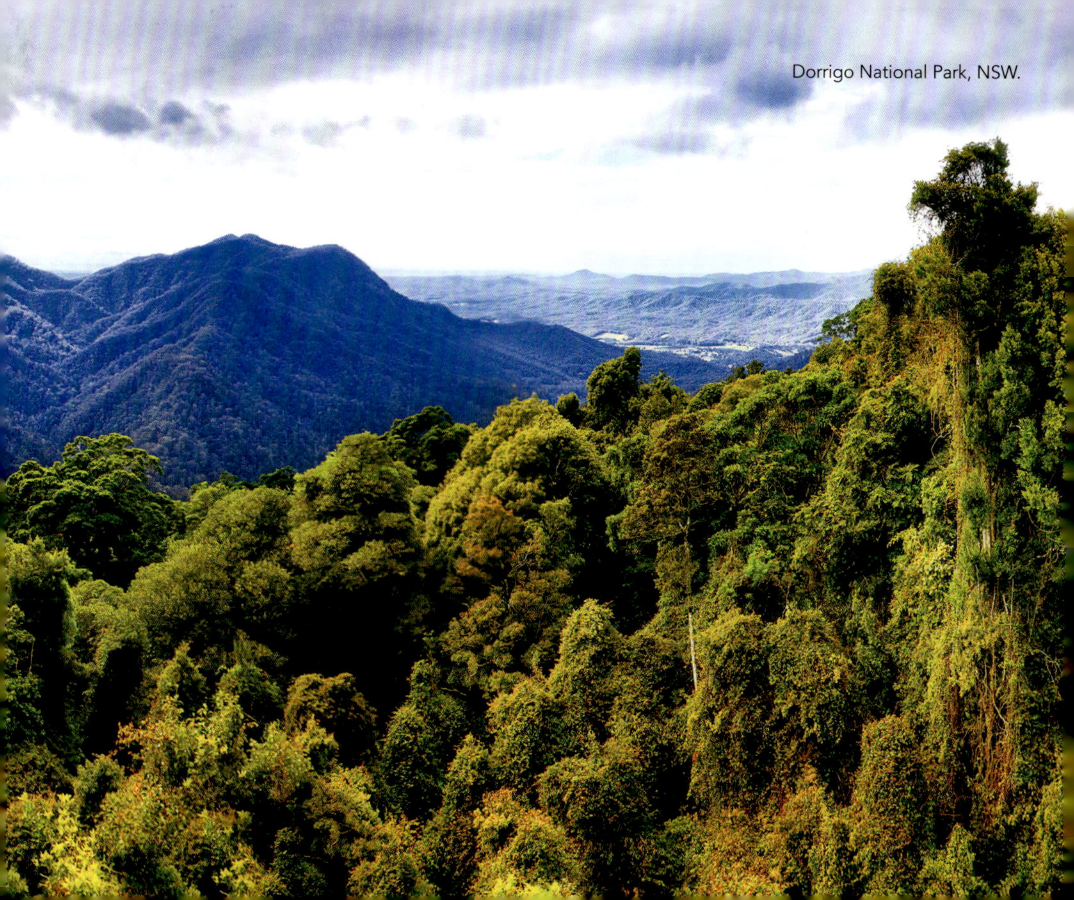

Dorrigo National Park, NSW.

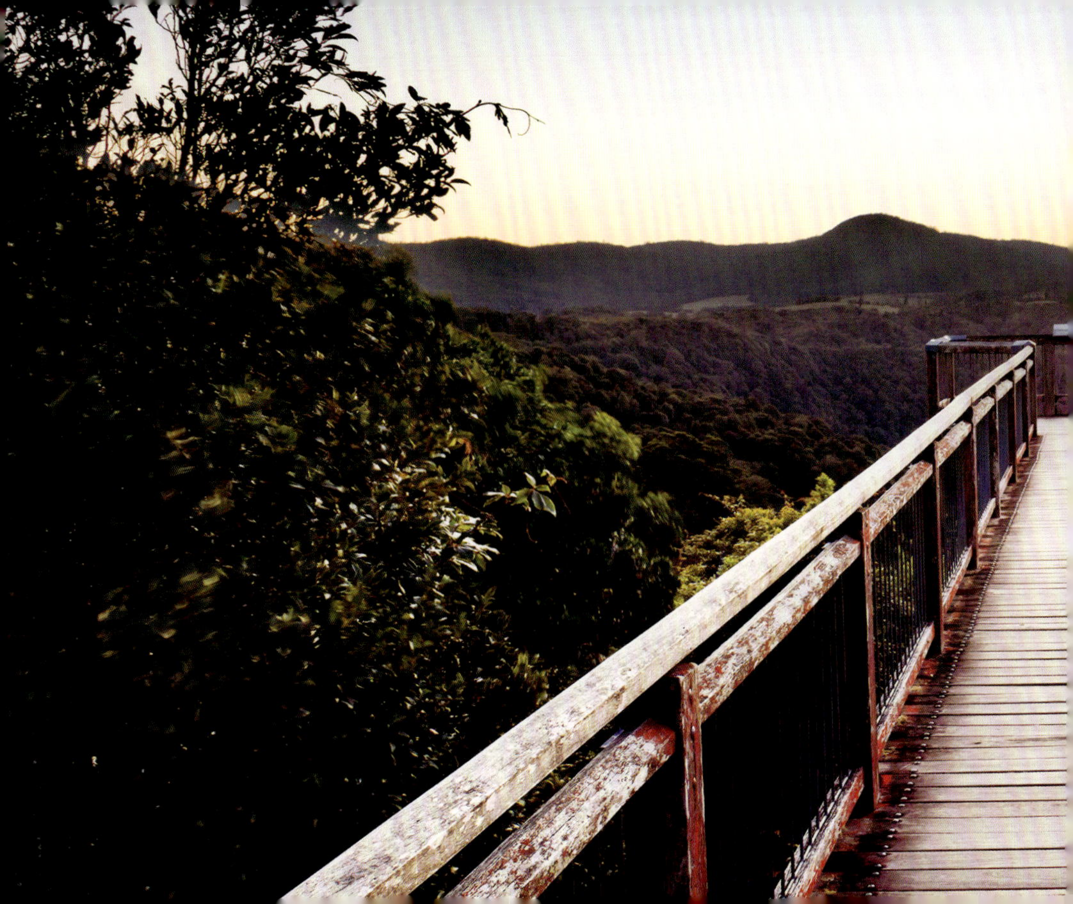

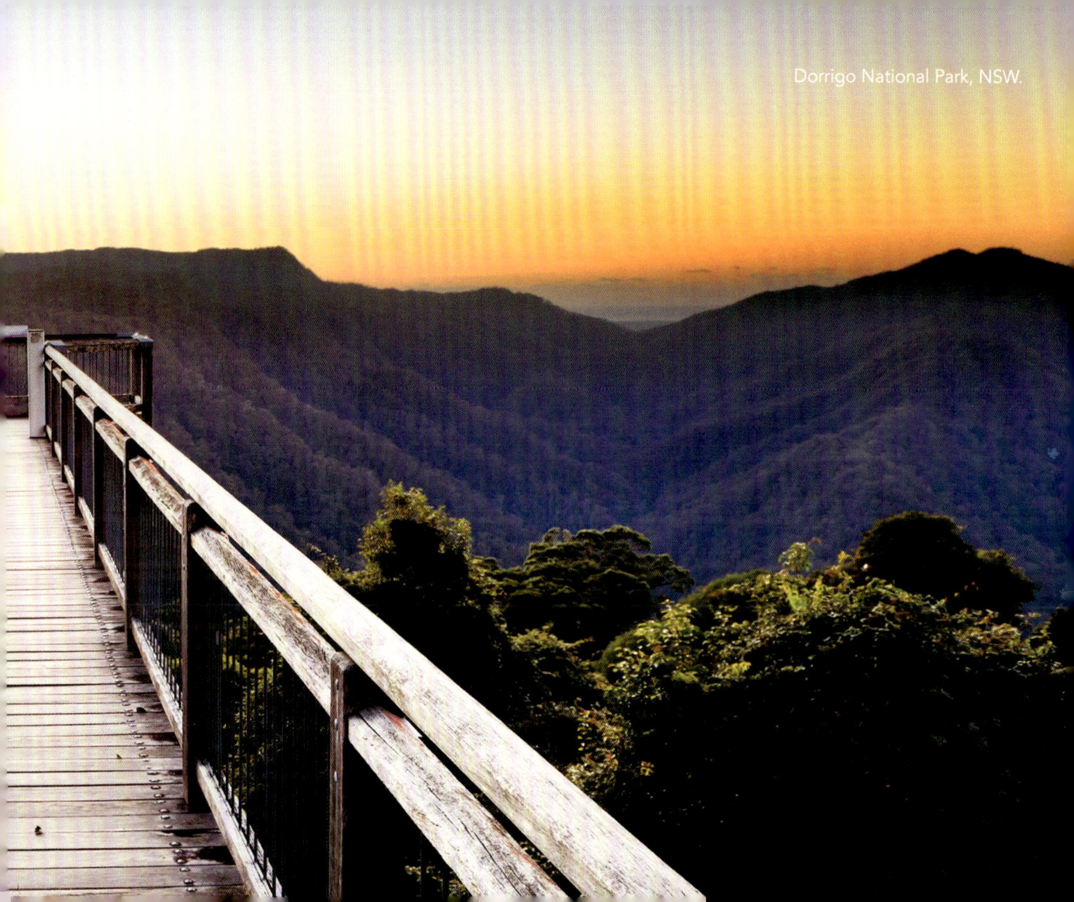
Dorrigo National Park, NSW.

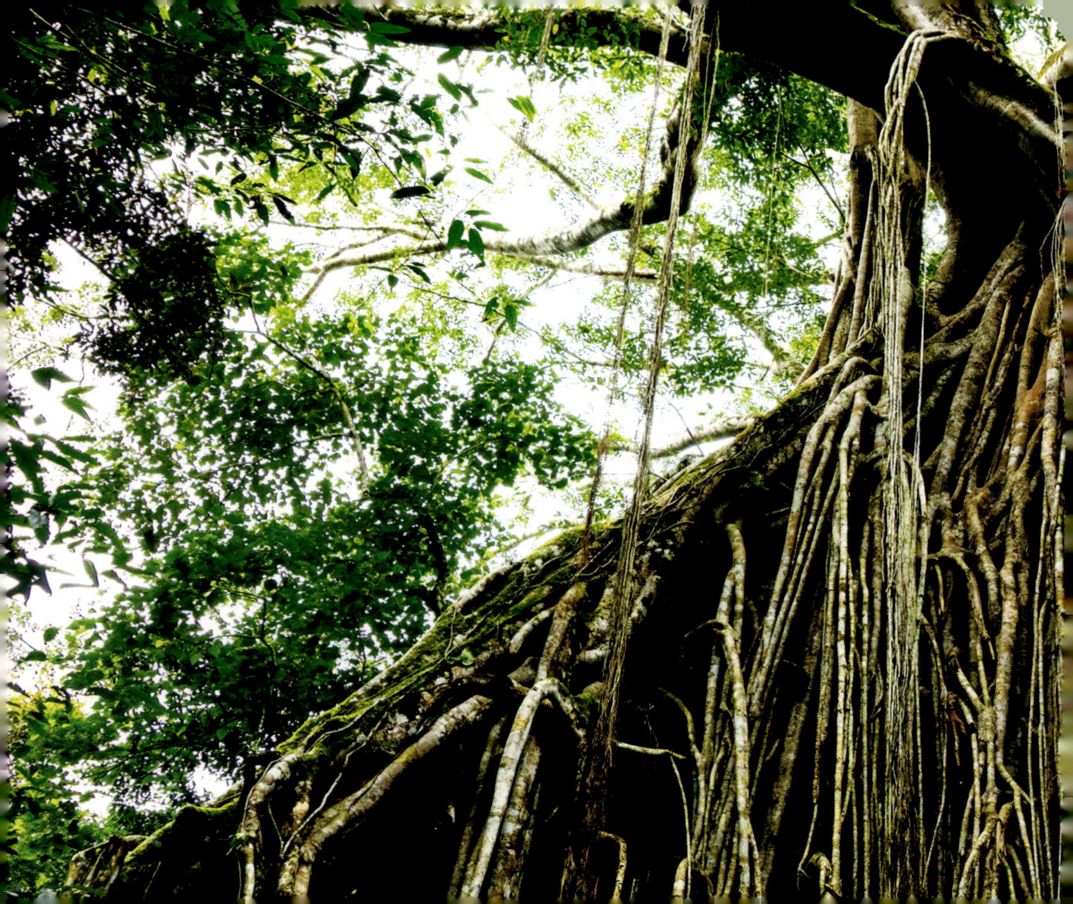

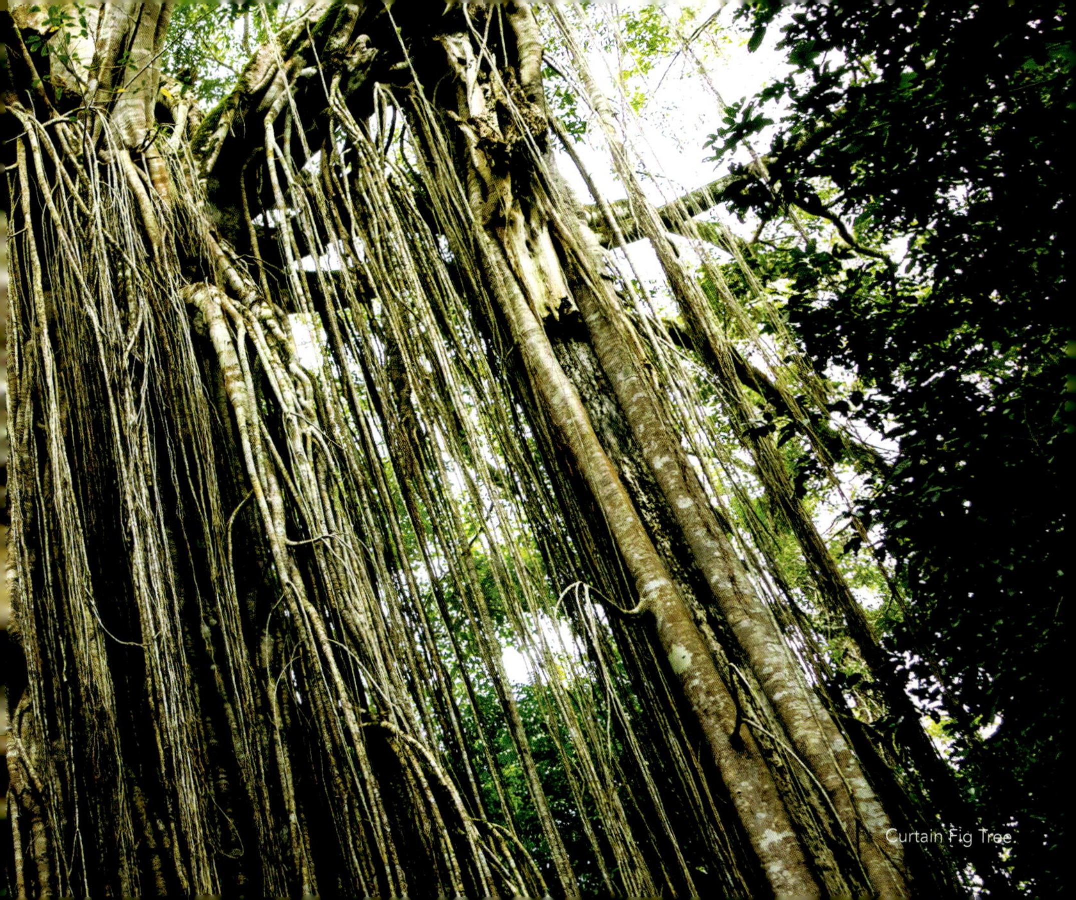
Curtain Fig Tree.

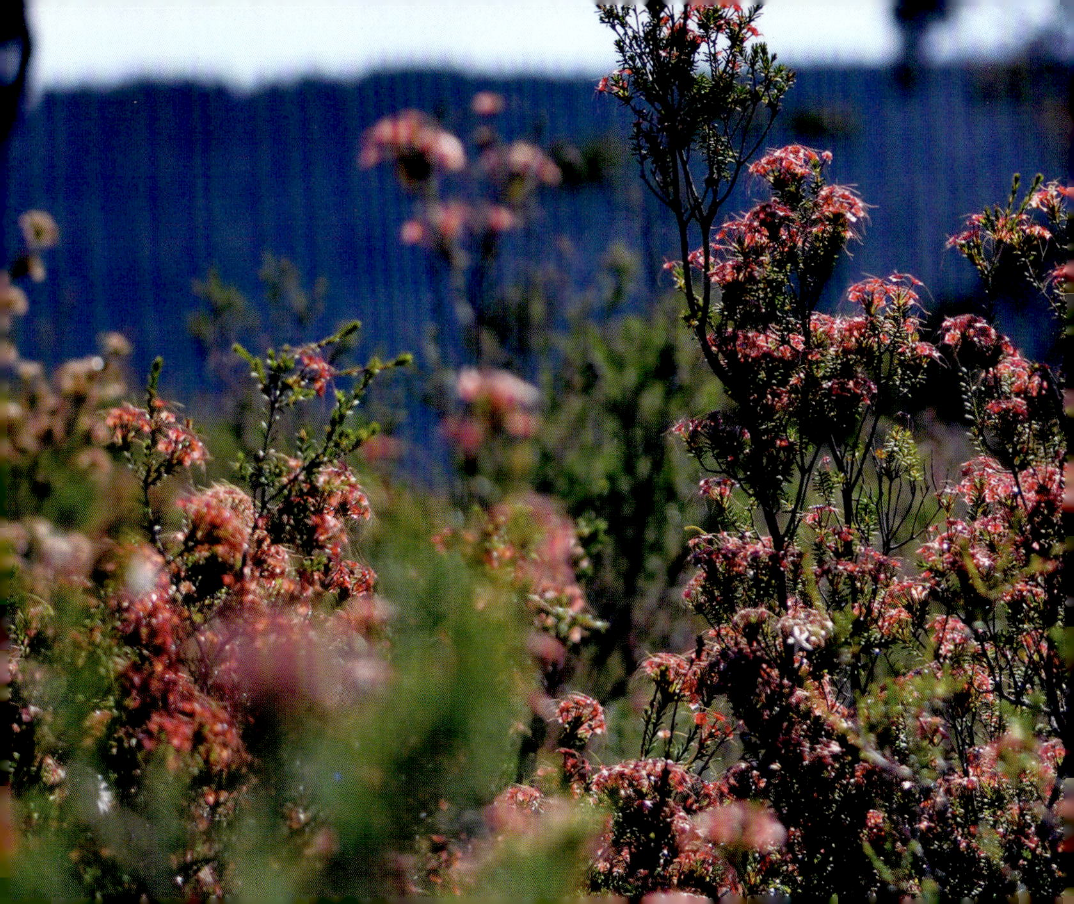

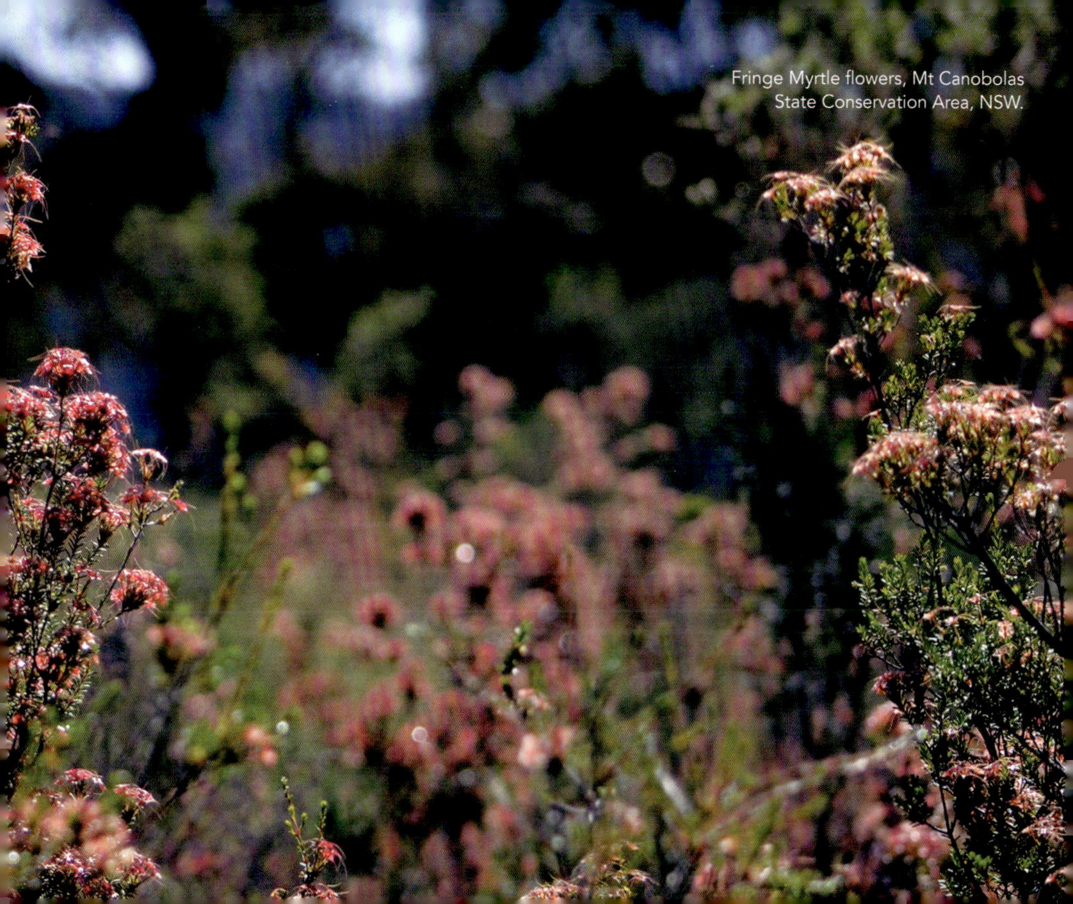

Fringe Myrtle flowers, Mt Canobolas State Conservation Area, NSW.

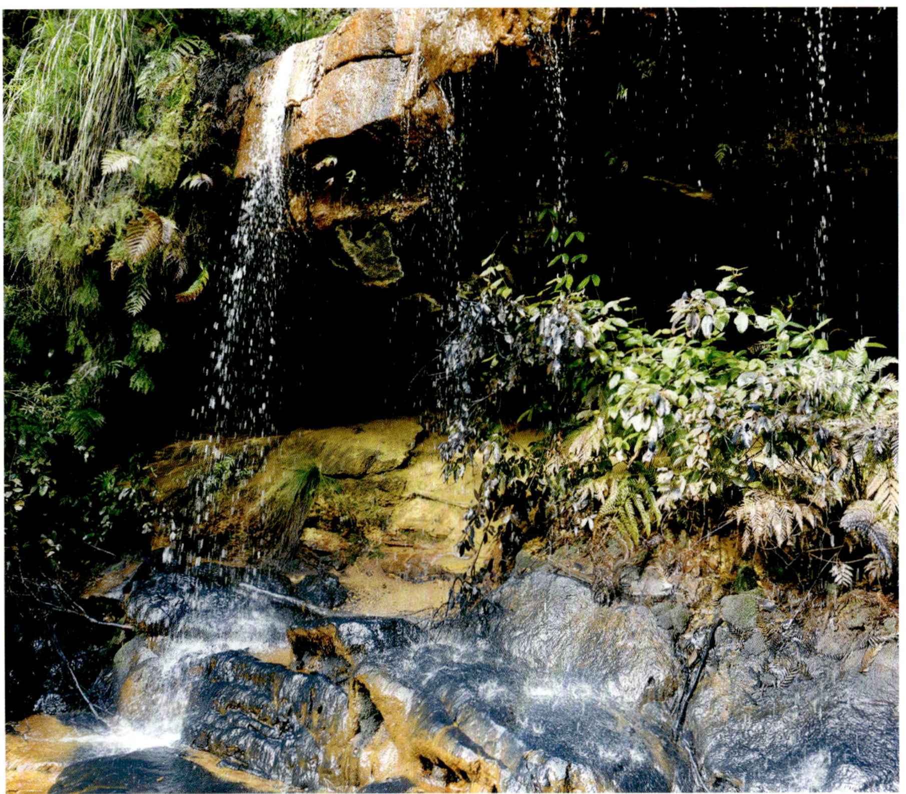

Fairy Falls, Blue Mountains, NSW.

Ovens Valley from the lookout on top of Mount Buffalo, Bright, Victoria.

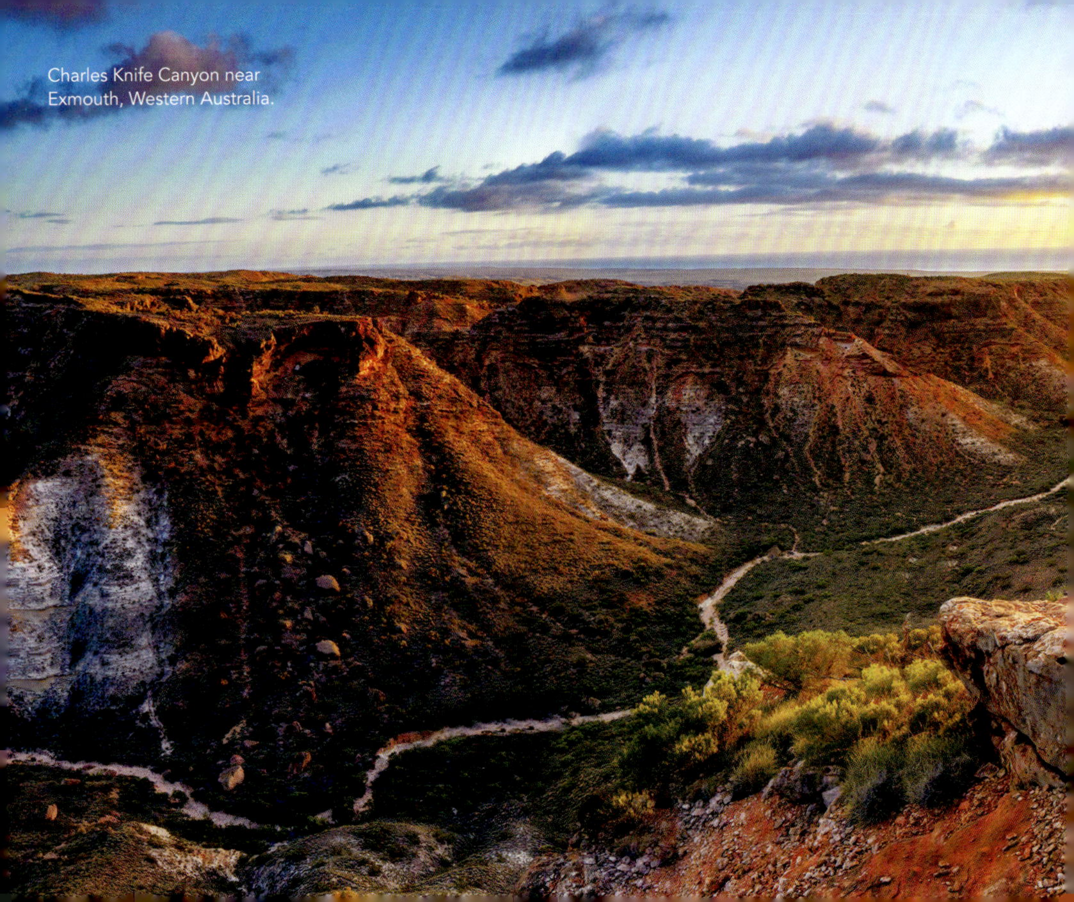

Charles Knife Canyon near Exmouth, Western Australia.

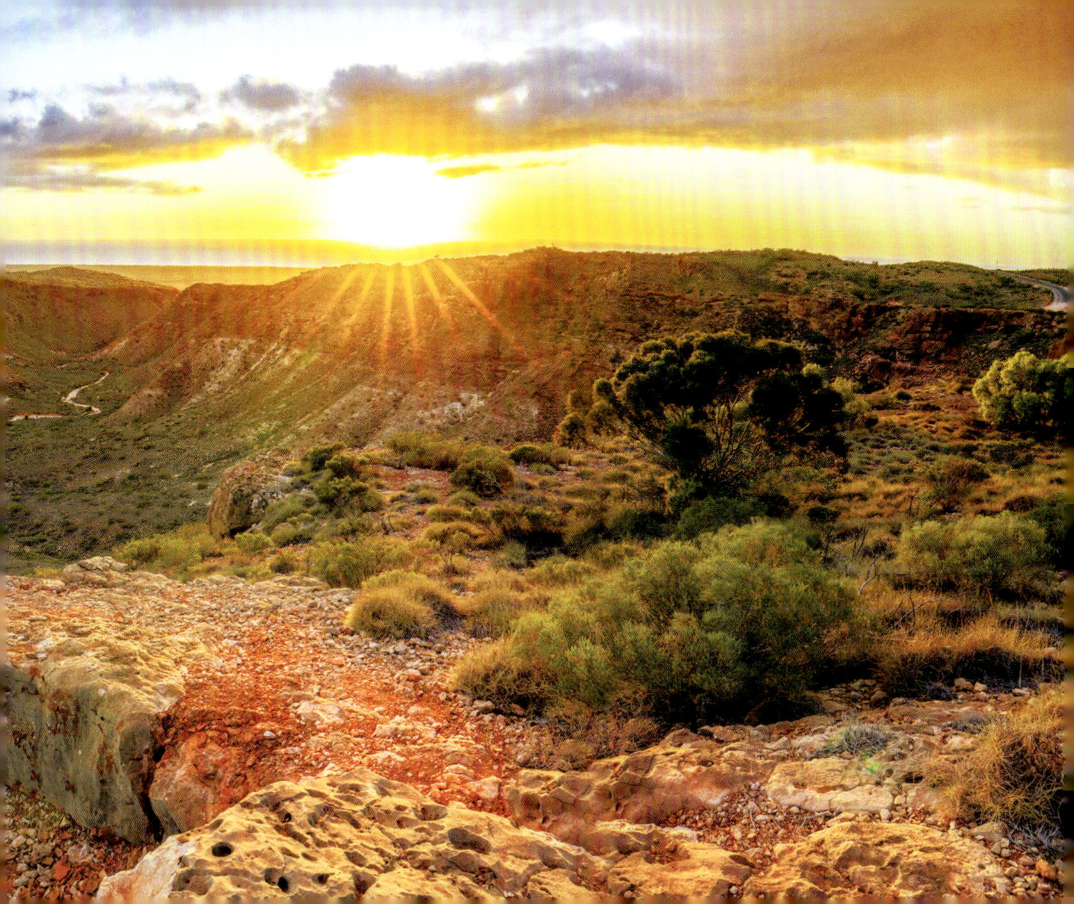

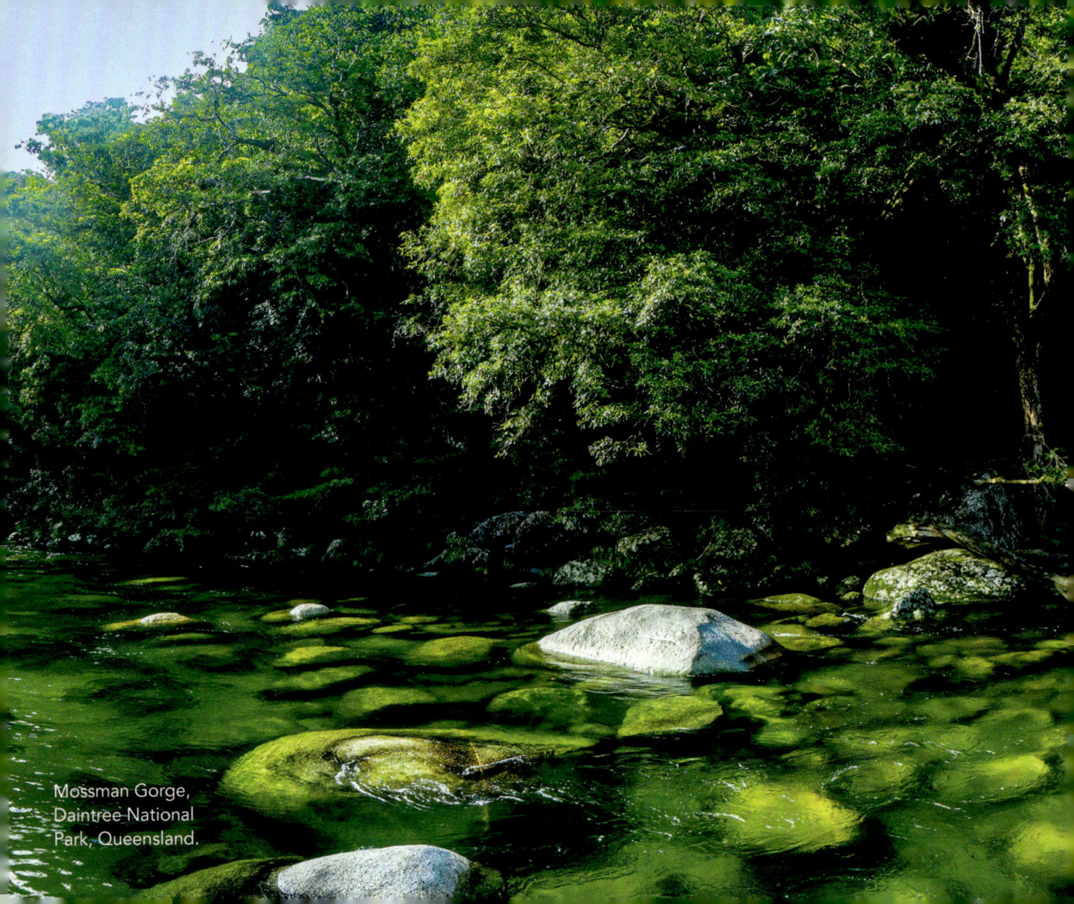

Mossman Gorge,
Daintree National
Park, Queensland.

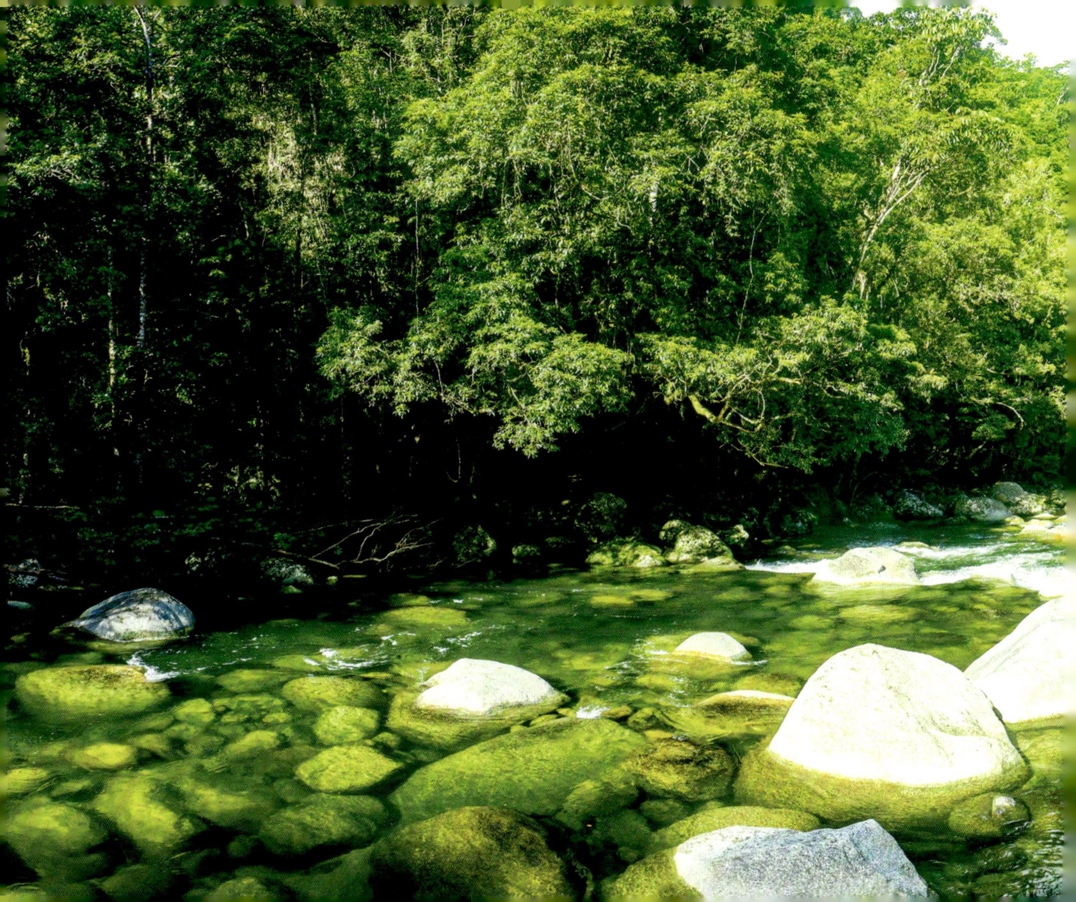

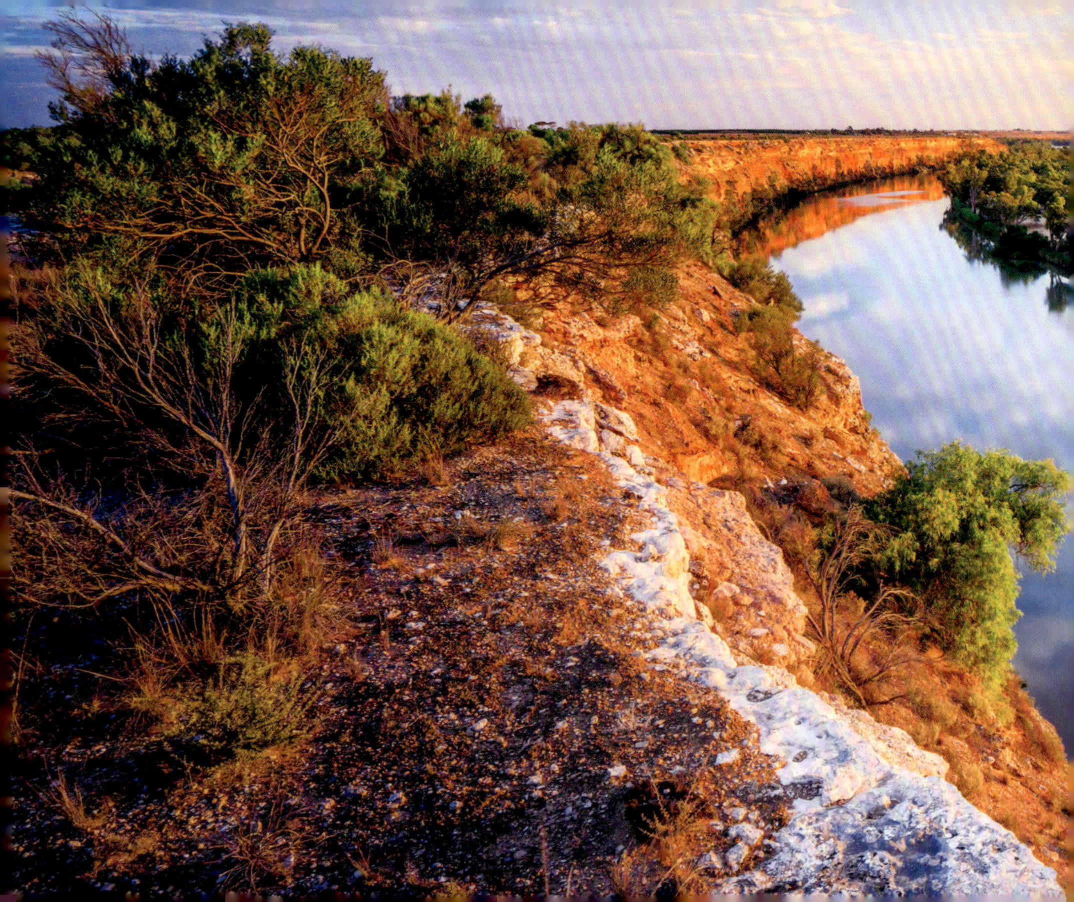

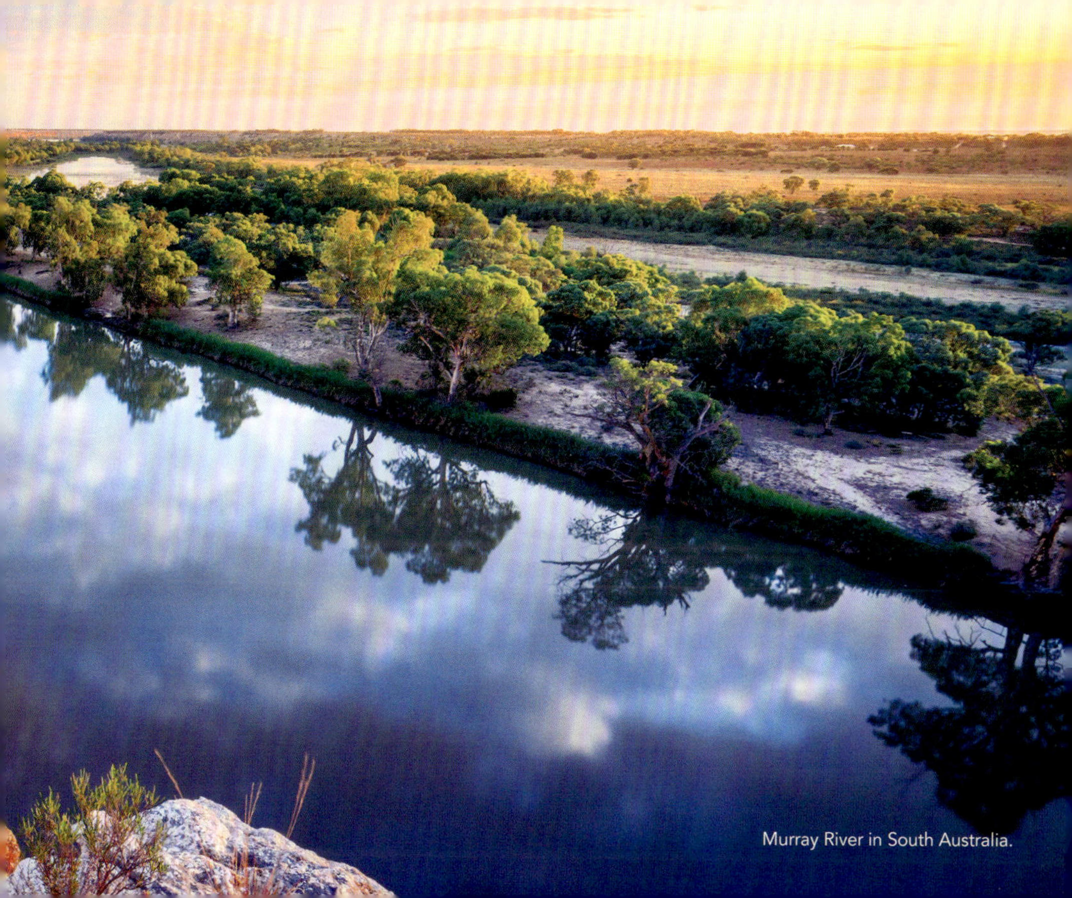

Murray River in South Australia.

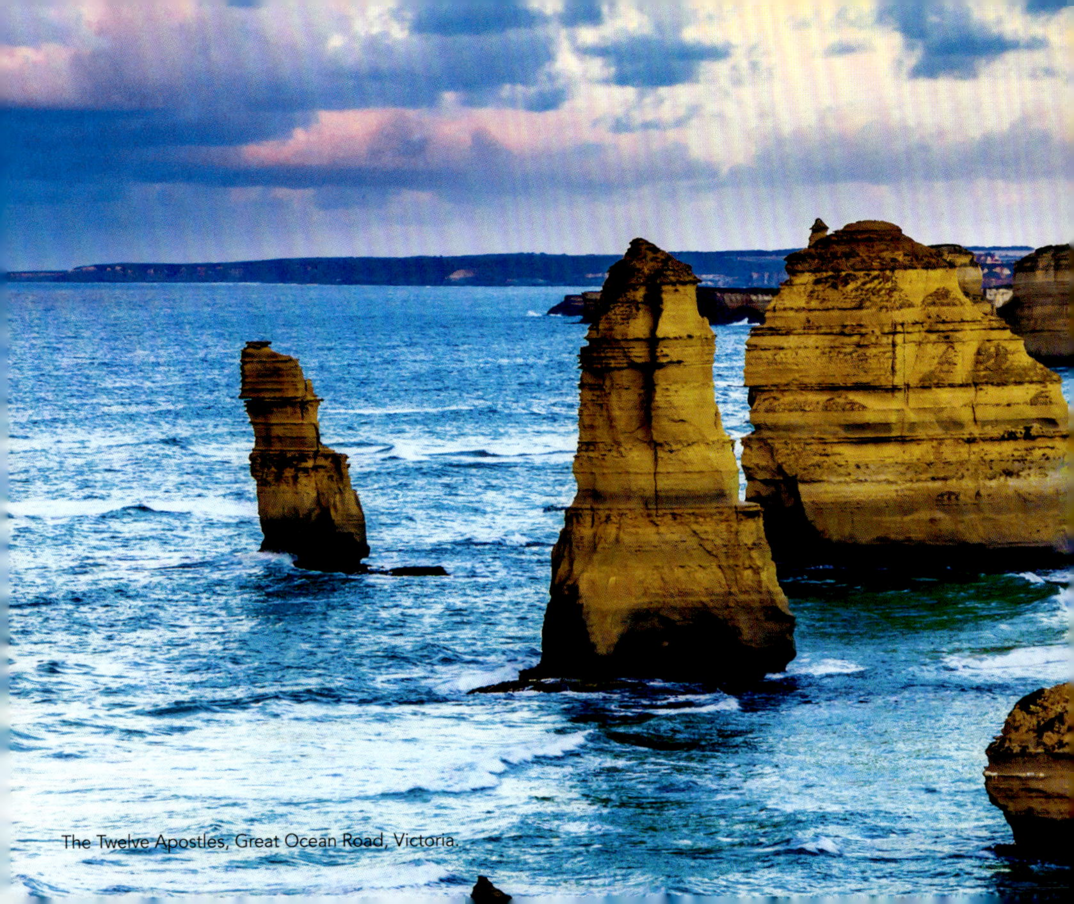
The Twelve Apostles, Great Ocean Road, Victoria.

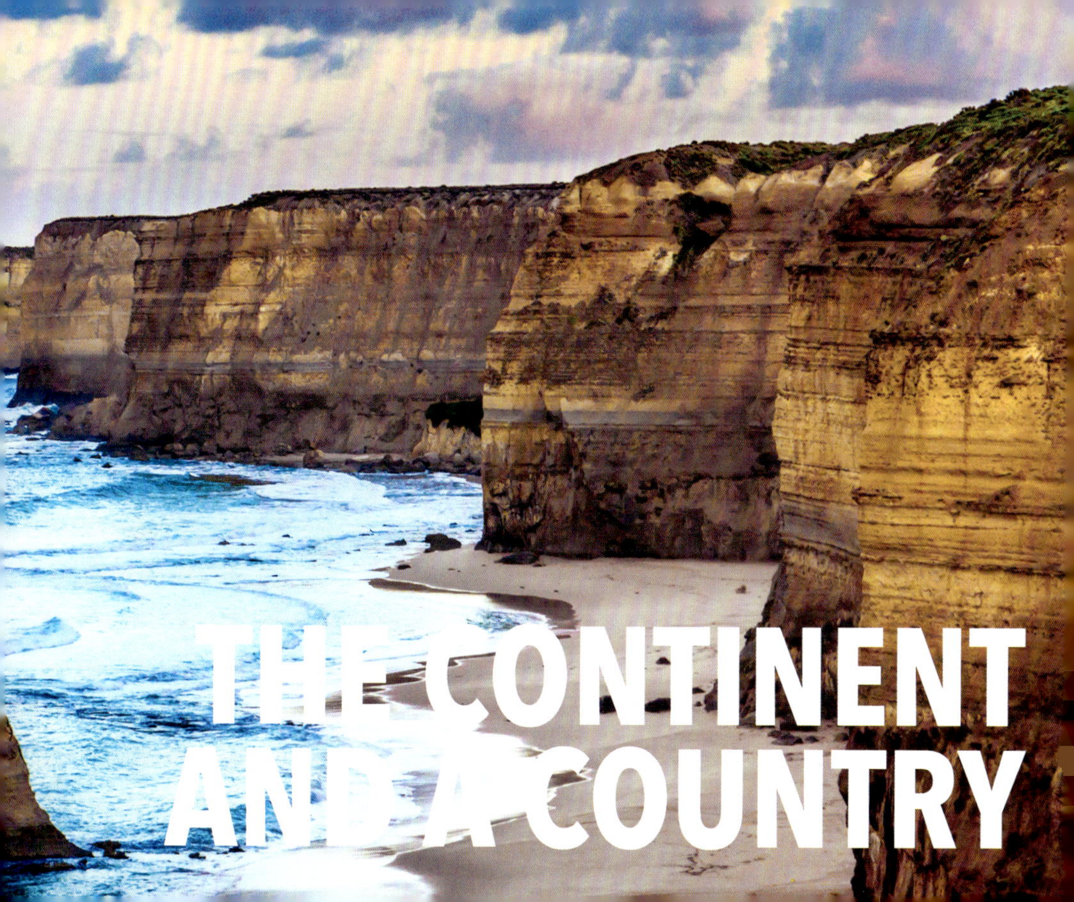

THE CONTINENT AND A COUNTRY

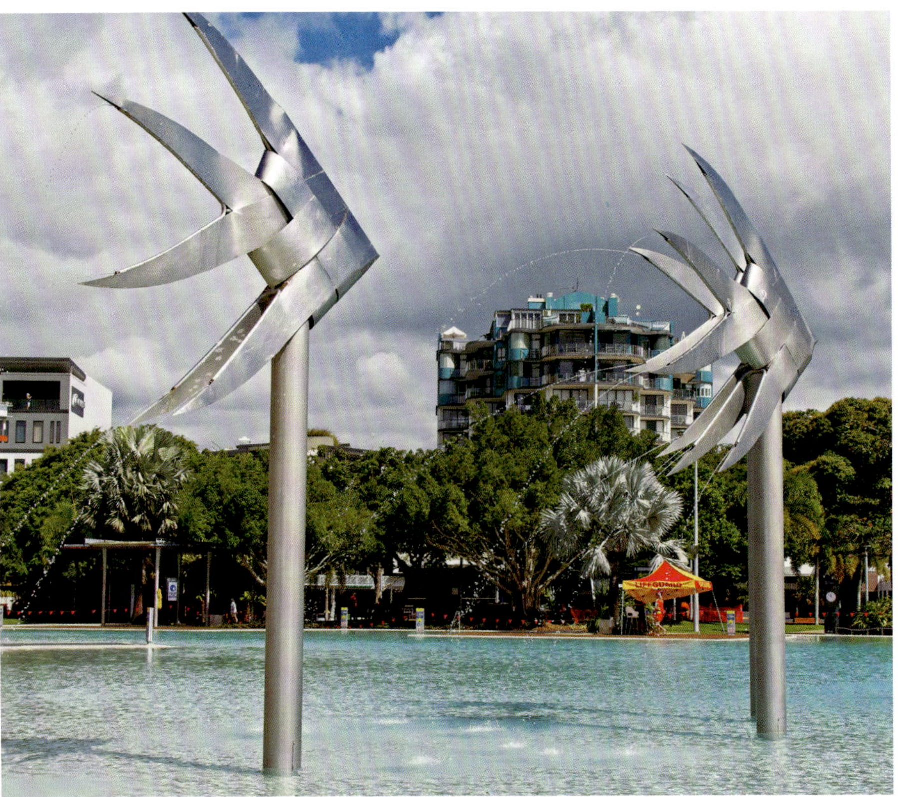

Cairns, Queensland.

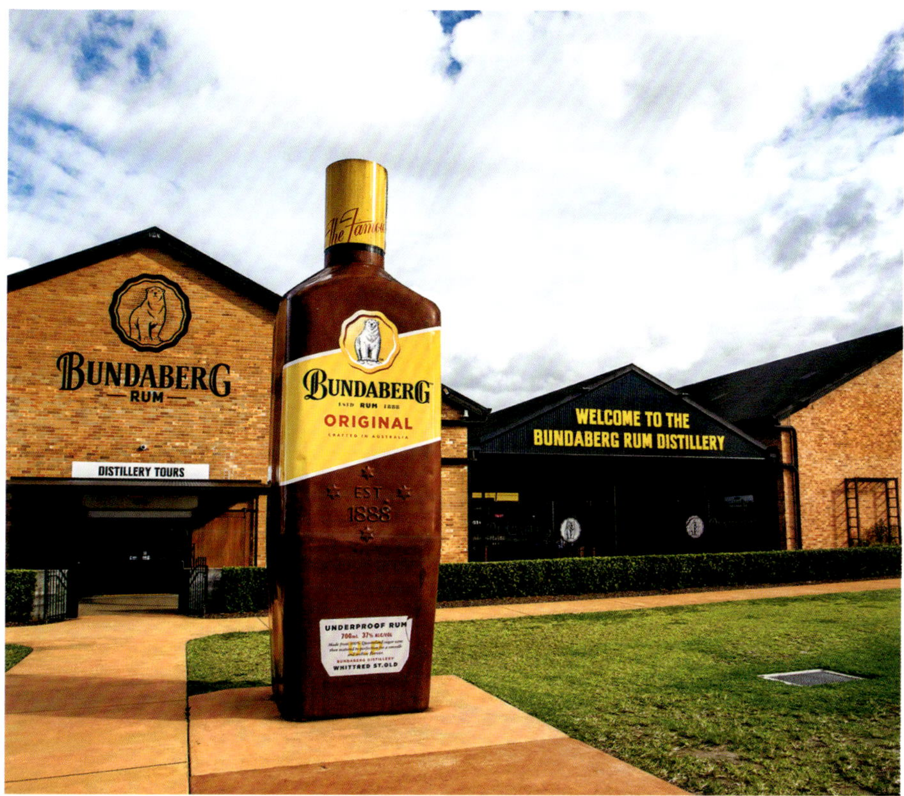

Bundaberg Rum Distillery, Bundaberg East, Queensland.

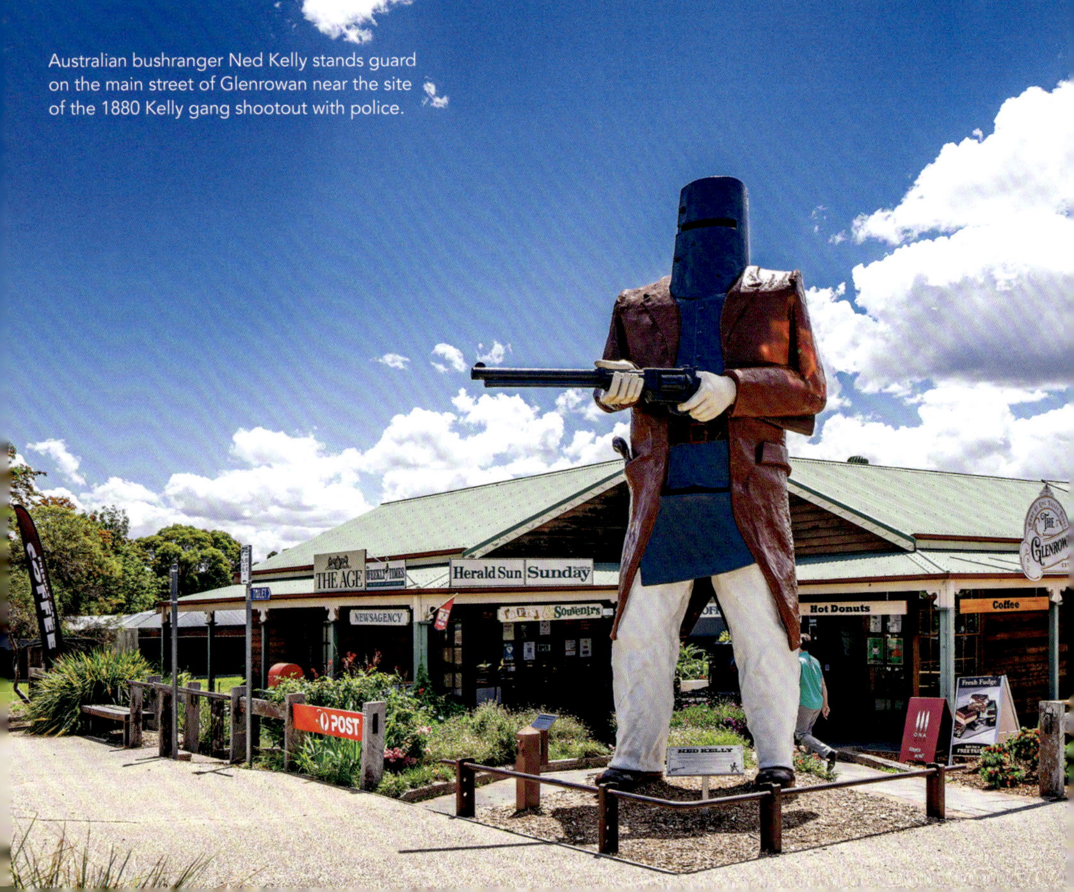

Australian bushranger Ned Kelly stands guard on the main street of Glenrowan near the site of the 1880 Kelly gang shootout with police.

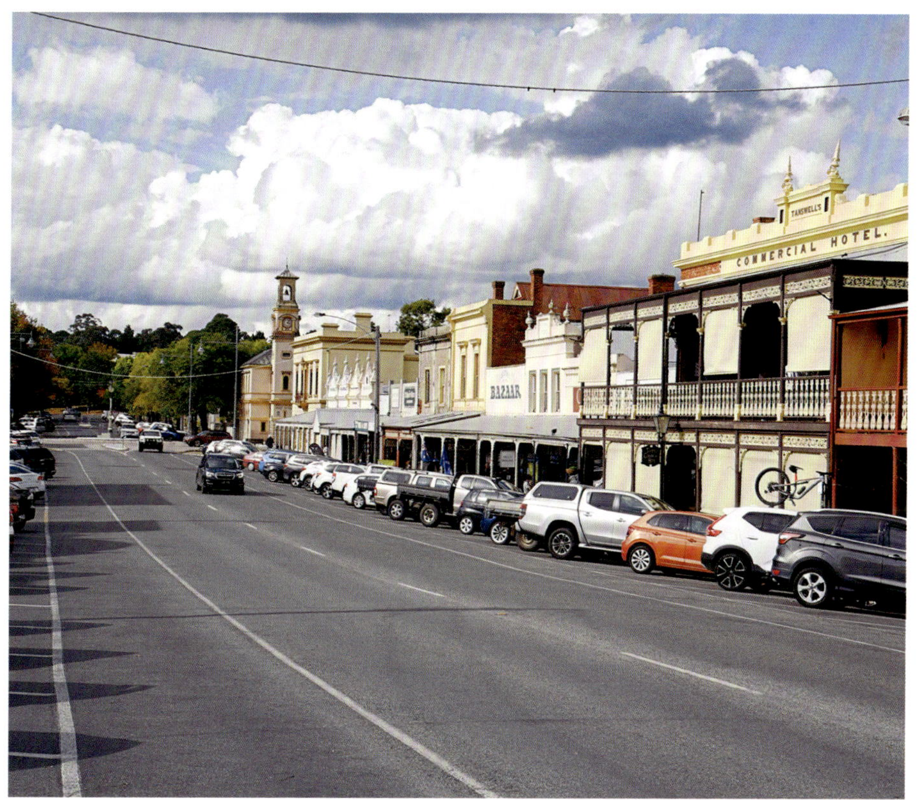

Beechworth, Victoria.

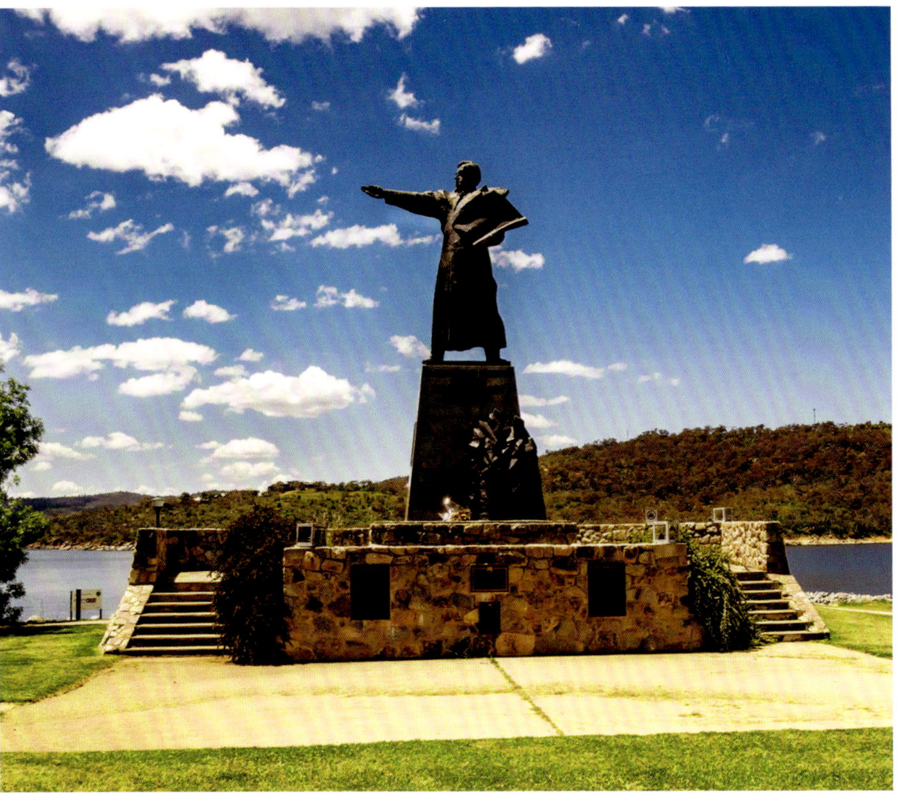

Bronze statue of Count Strzelecki, Jindabyne, NSW.

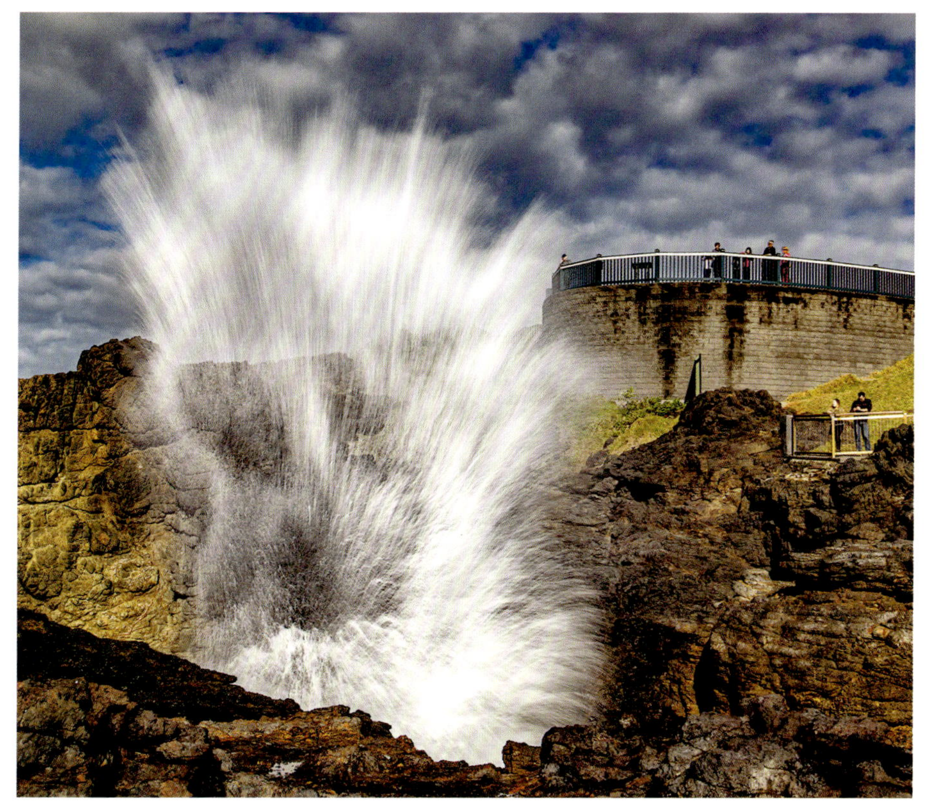

Kiama Blowhole, NSW.

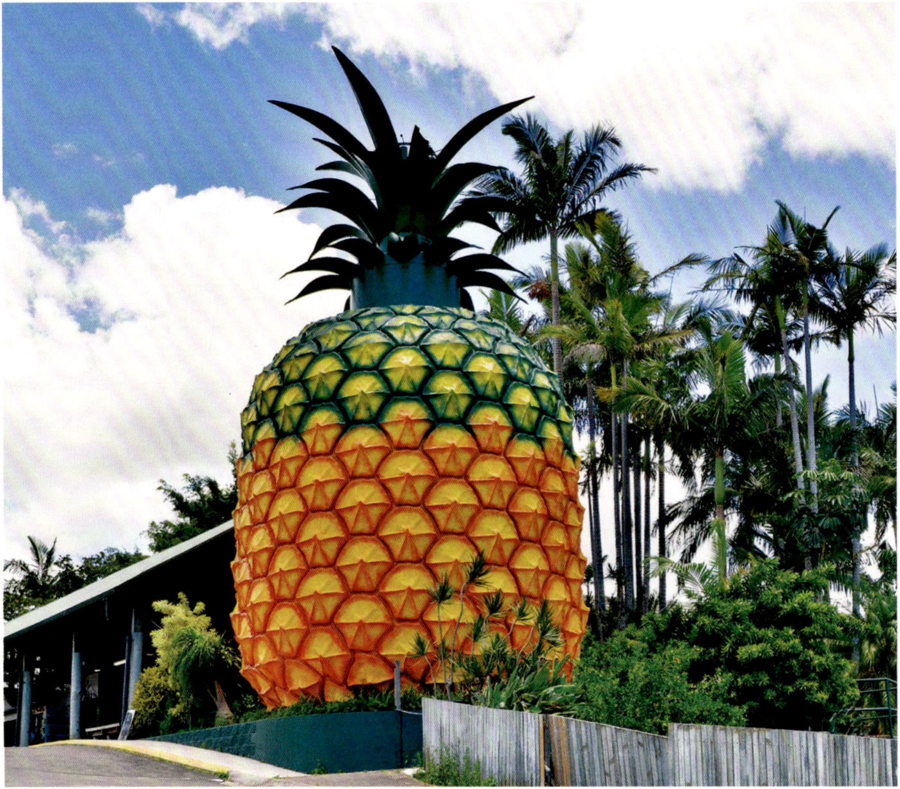

Big Pineapple in Woombye, Queensland.

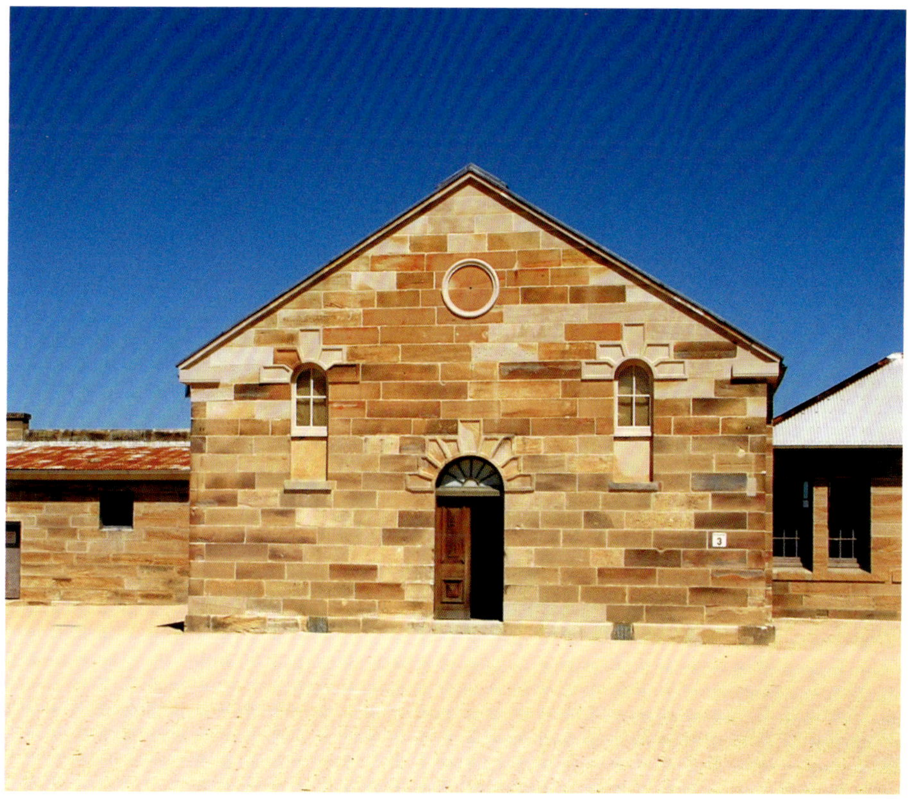

Cockatoo Island, Sydney.

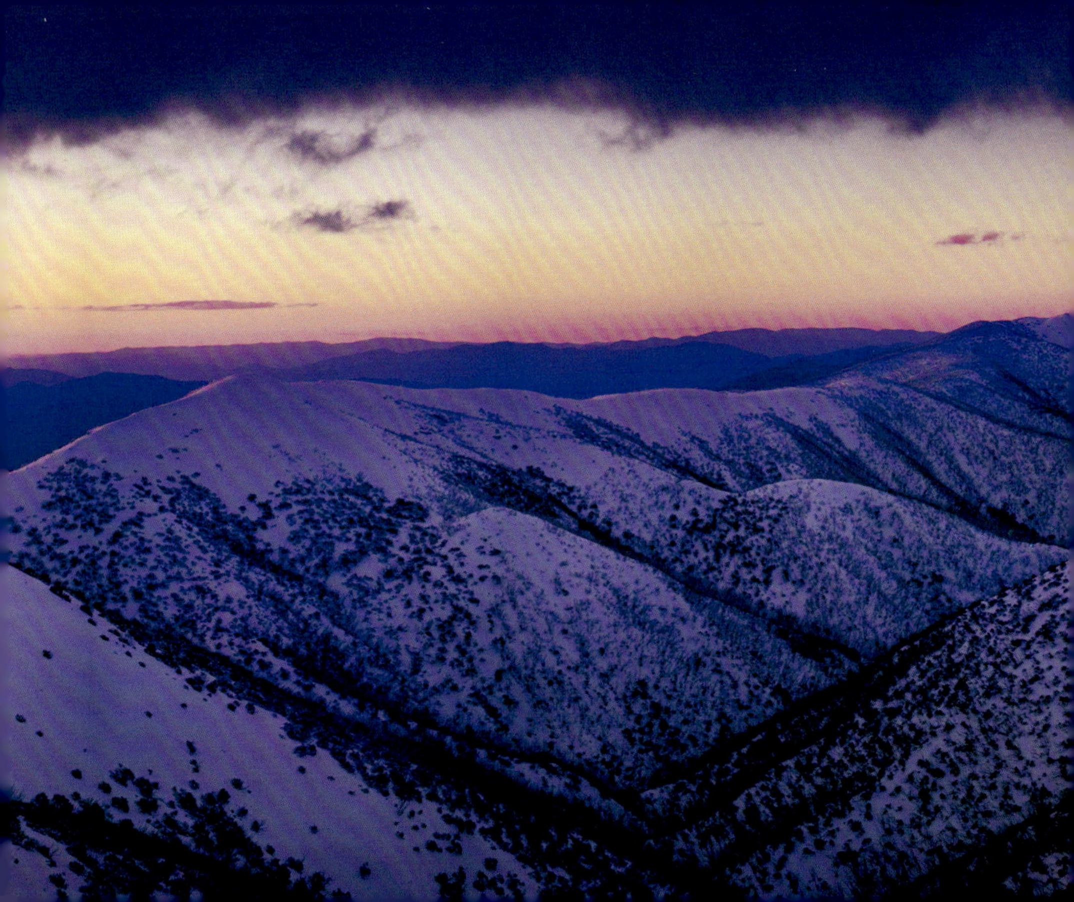

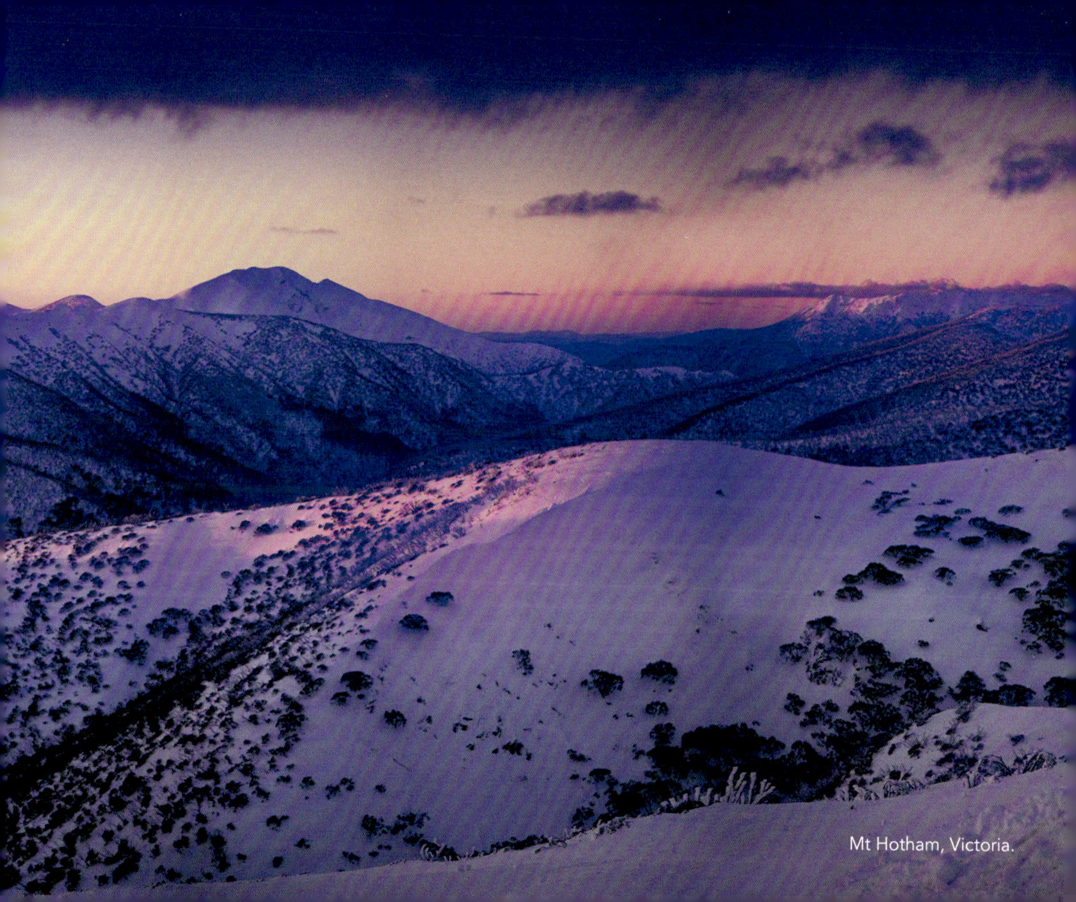

Mt Hotham, Victoria.

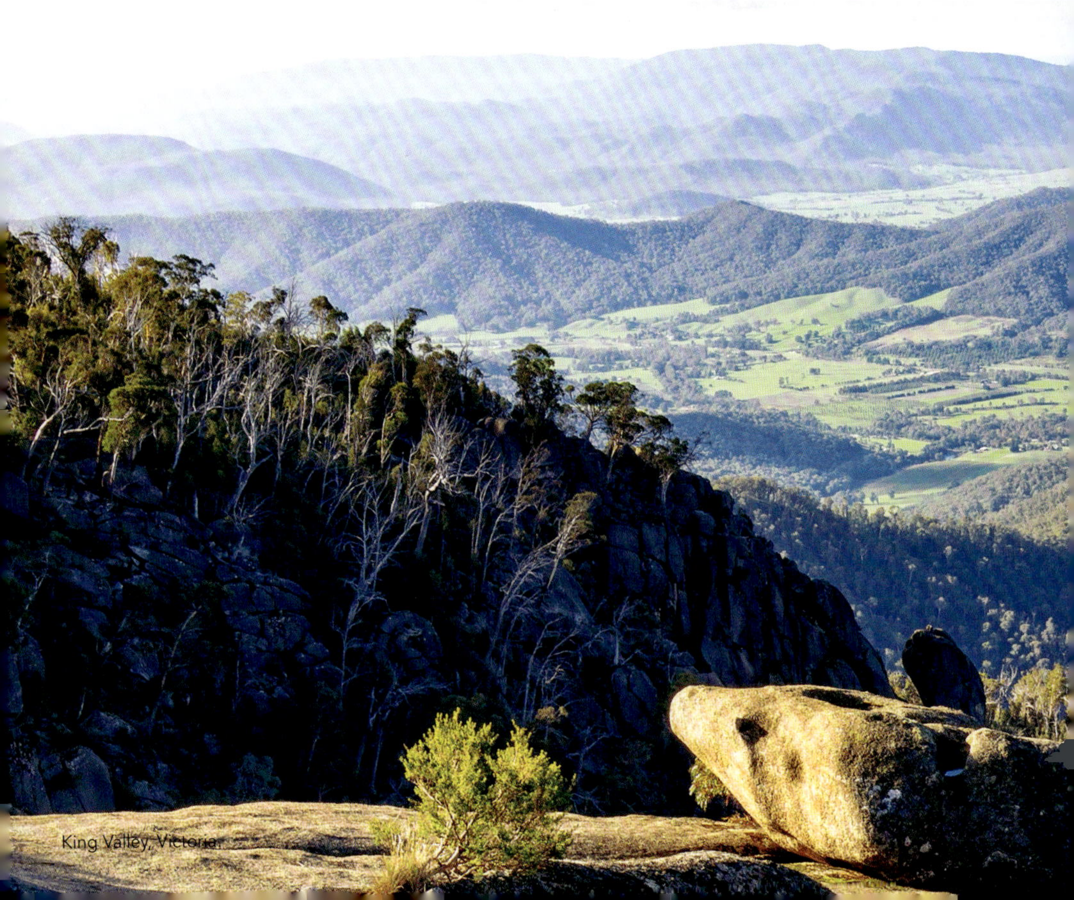
King Valley, Victoria

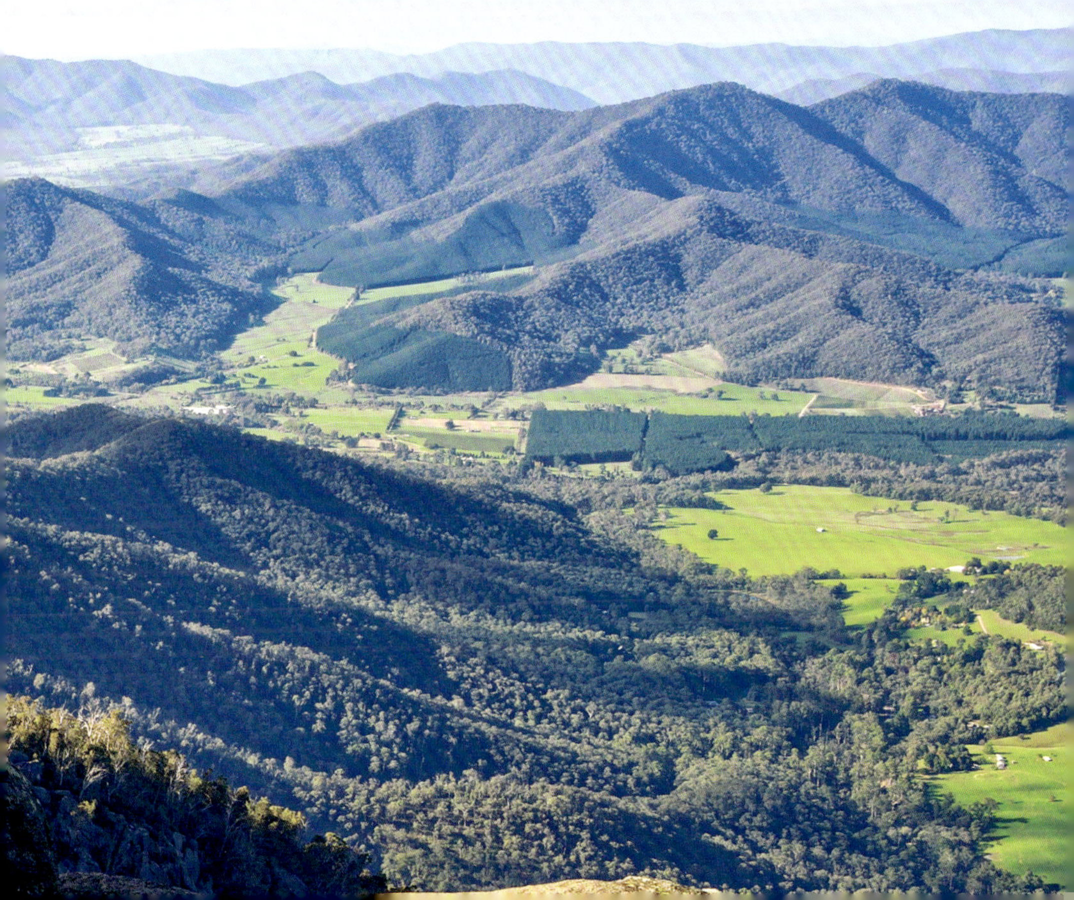

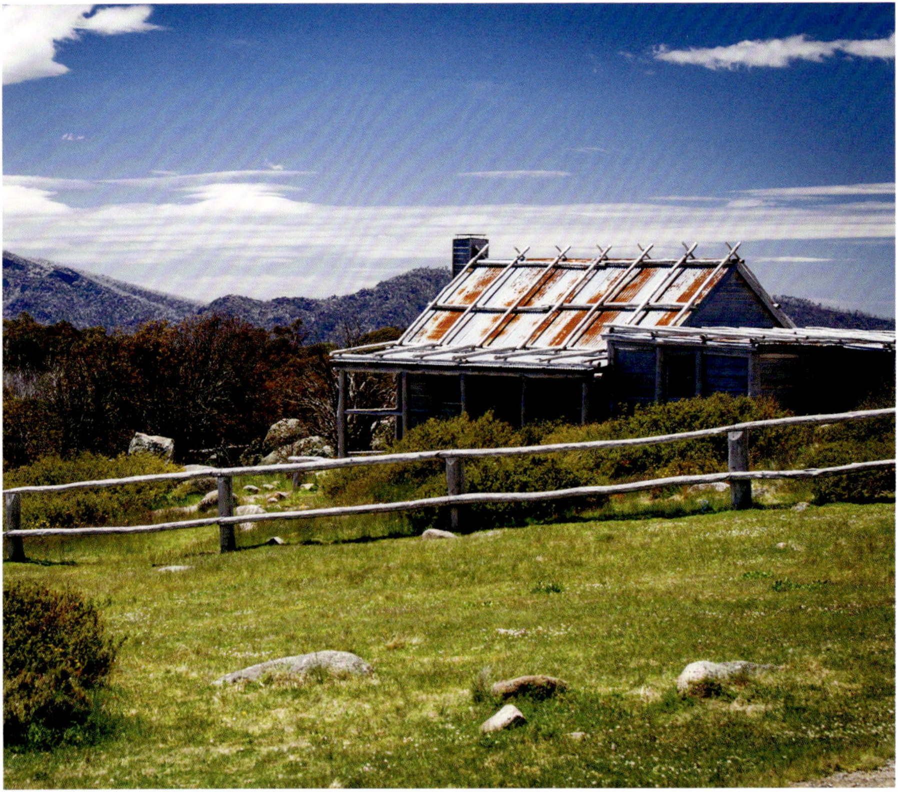

Craig's Hut (as seen in *The Man from Snowy River* movie) in the Victorian alps.

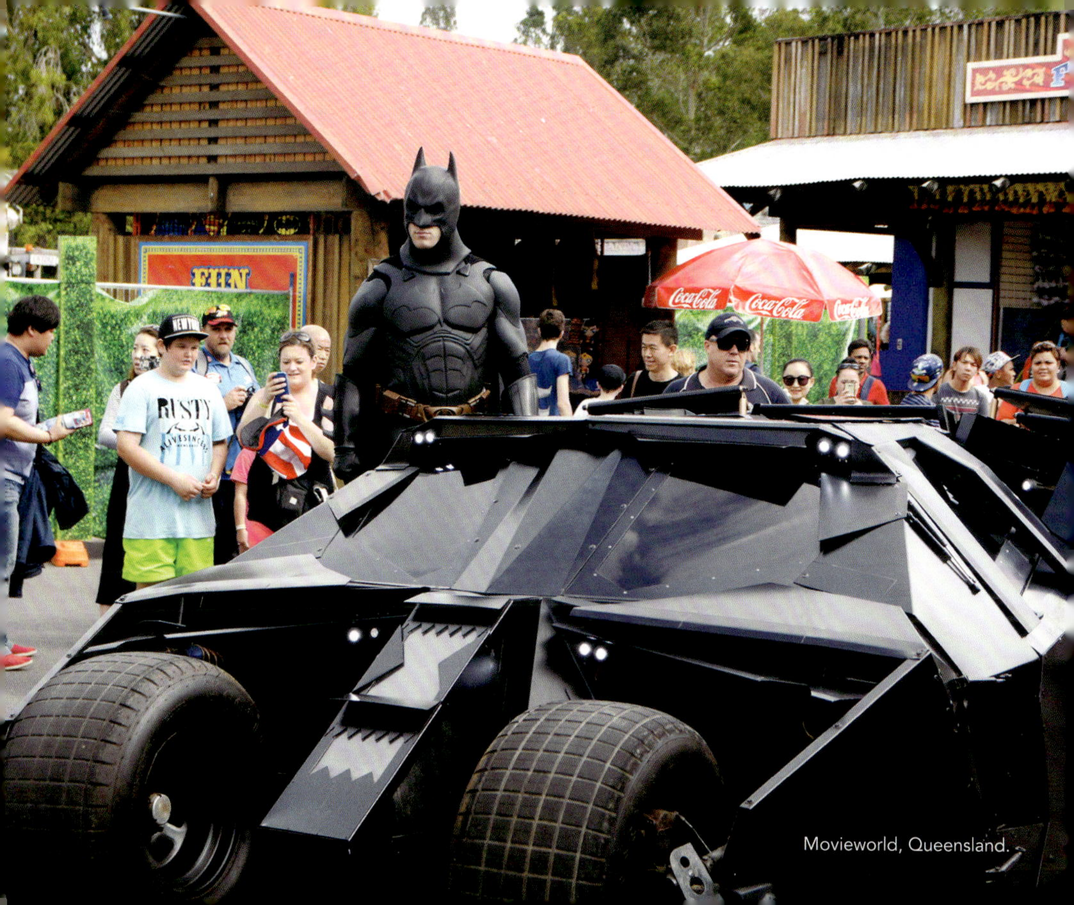

Movieworld, Queensland.

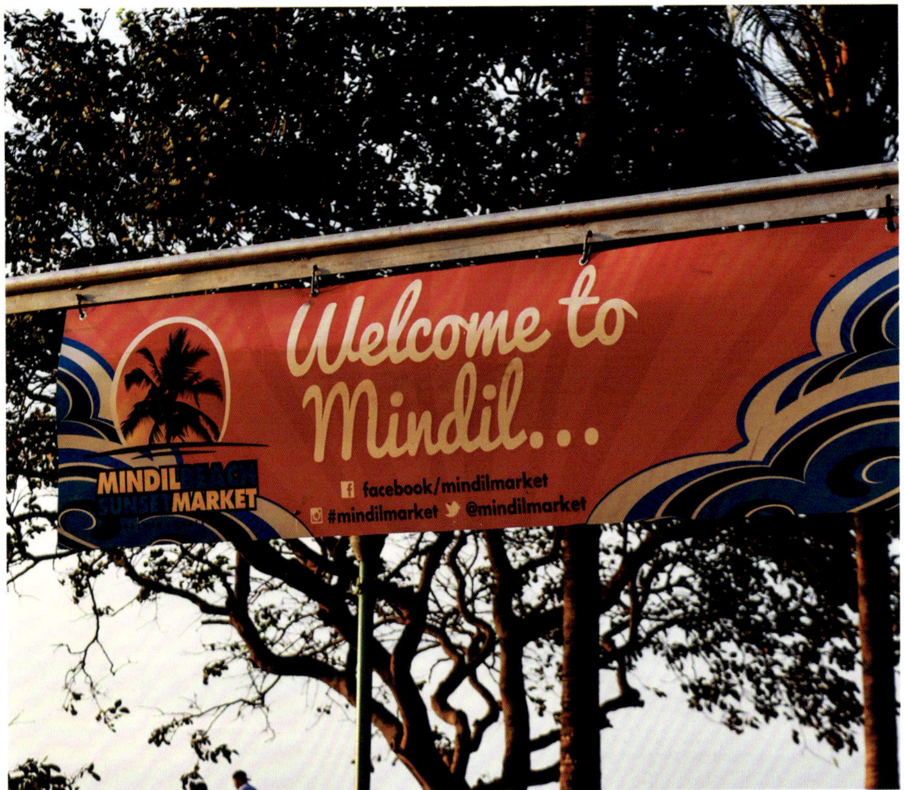

Darwin, Northern Territory.

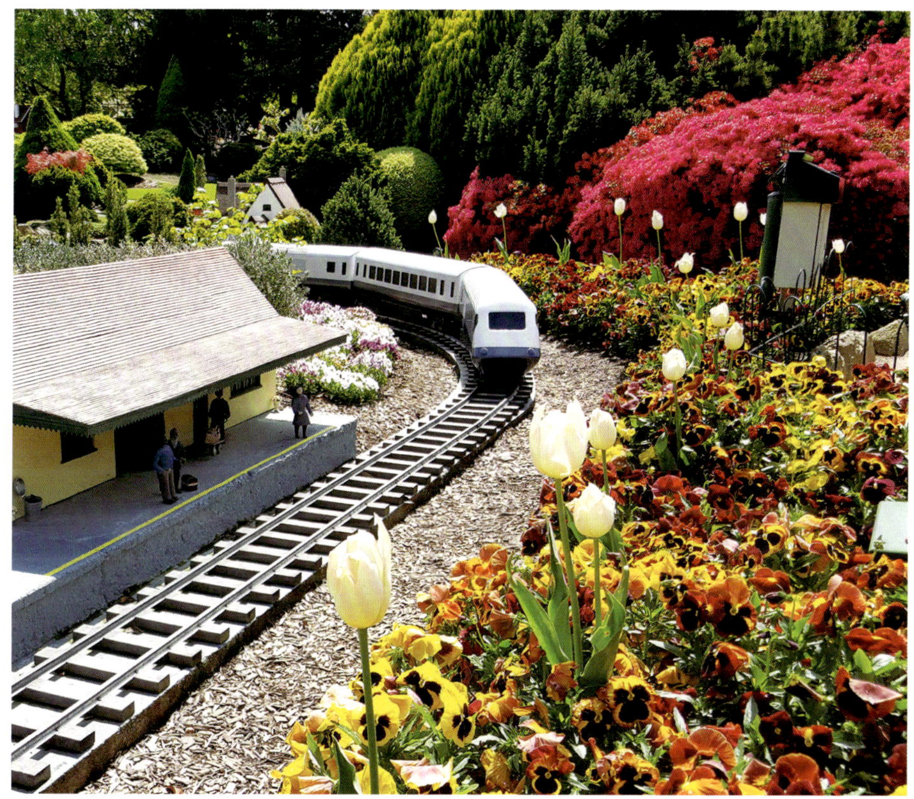

Cockington Green Gardens, ACT.

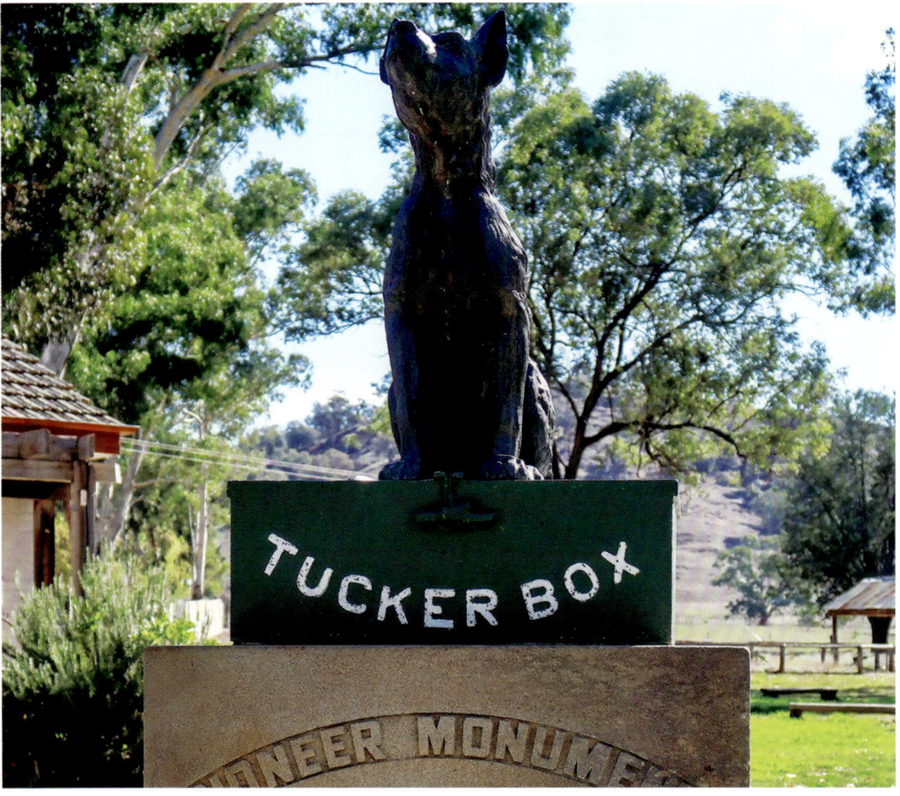

The Dog On The Tucker Box, NSW.

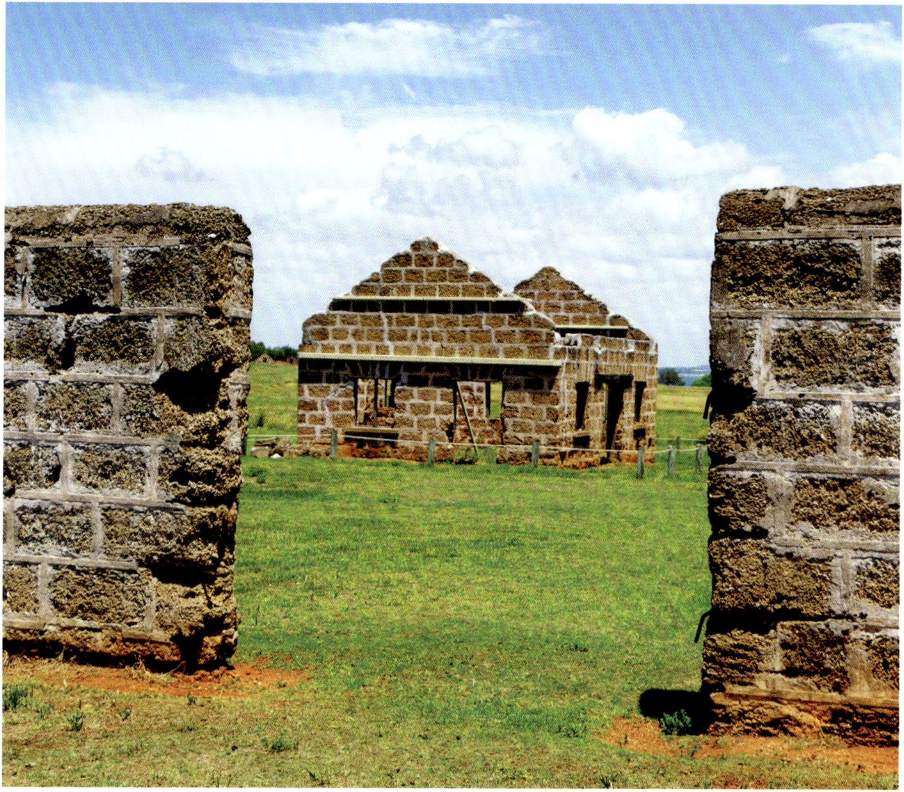

St Helena Island National Park, Brisbane, Queensland.

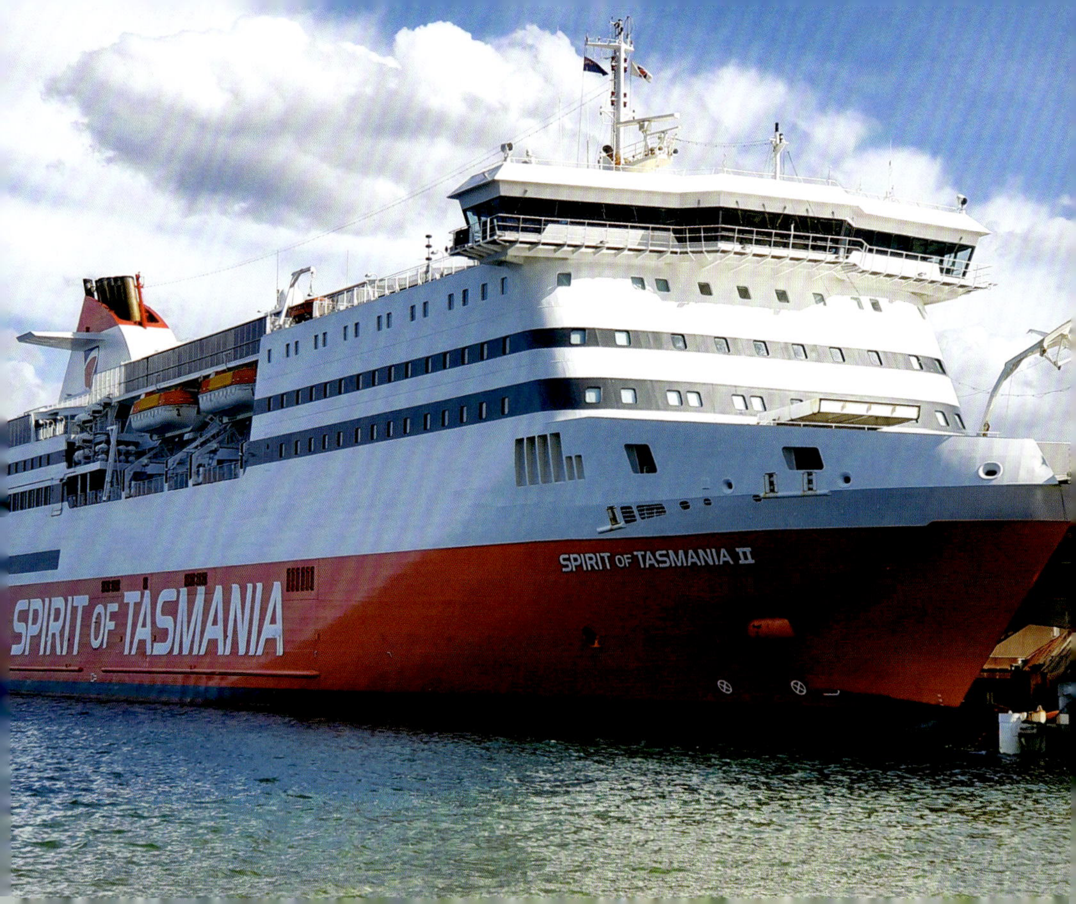
SPIRIT OF TASMANIA II
SPIRIT OF TASMANIA

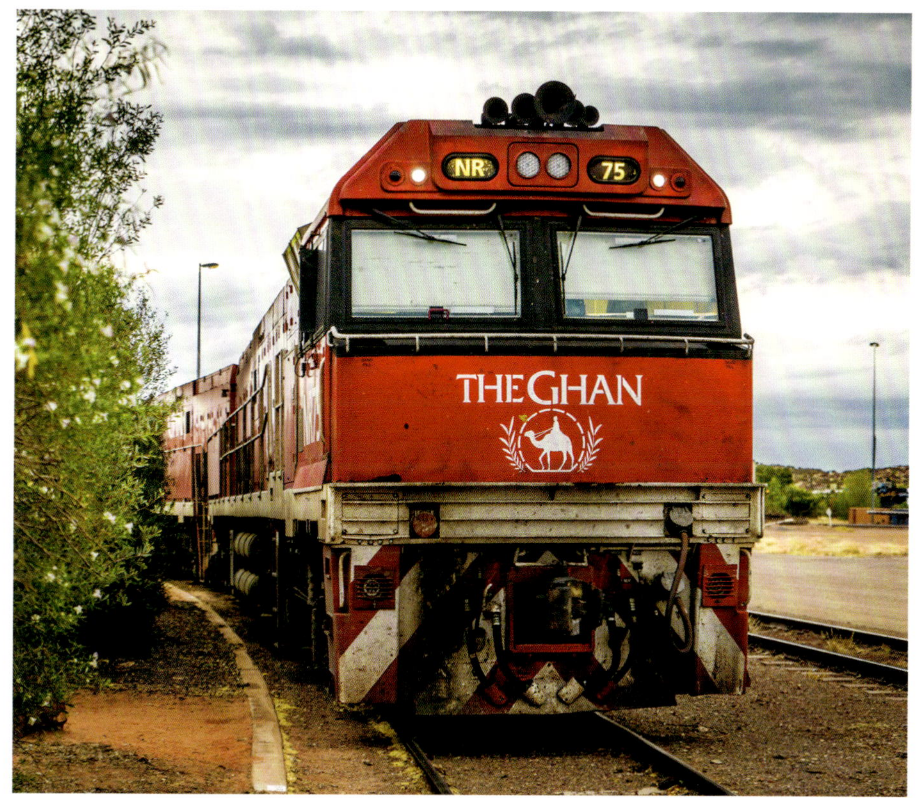

The Ghan.

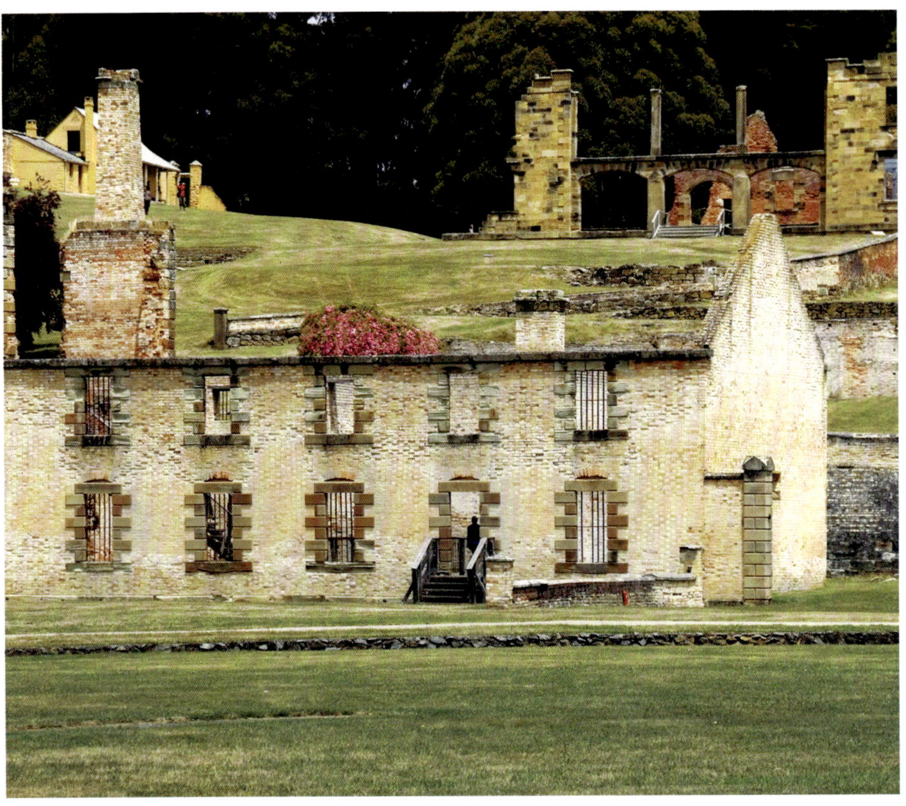

Port Arthur, Tasmania.

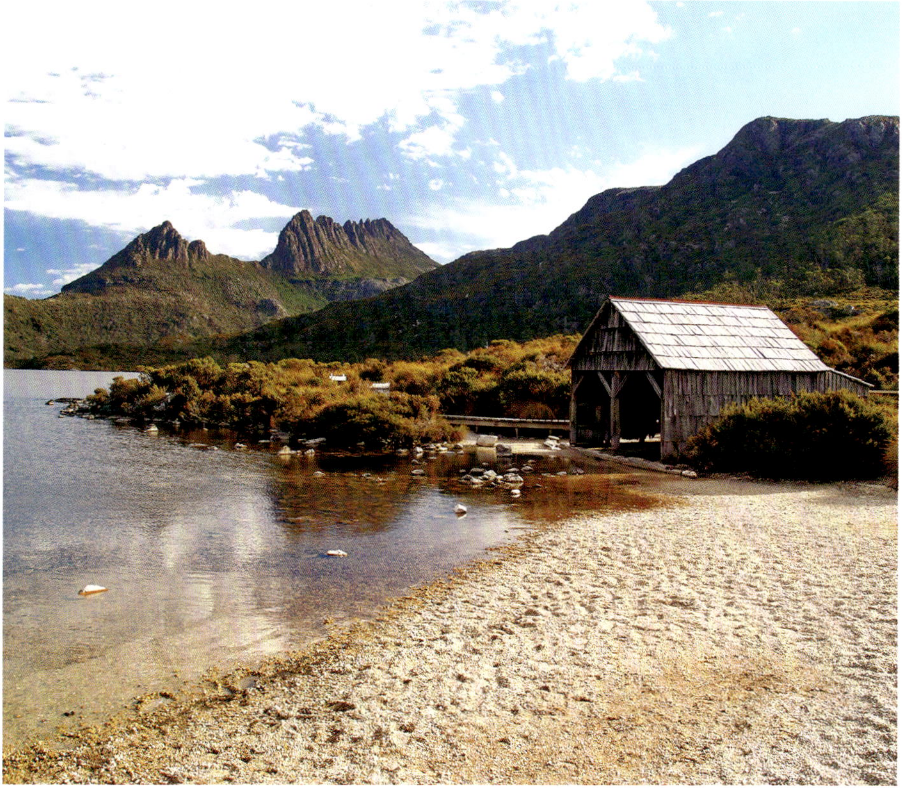

Cradle Mountain, Tasmania.

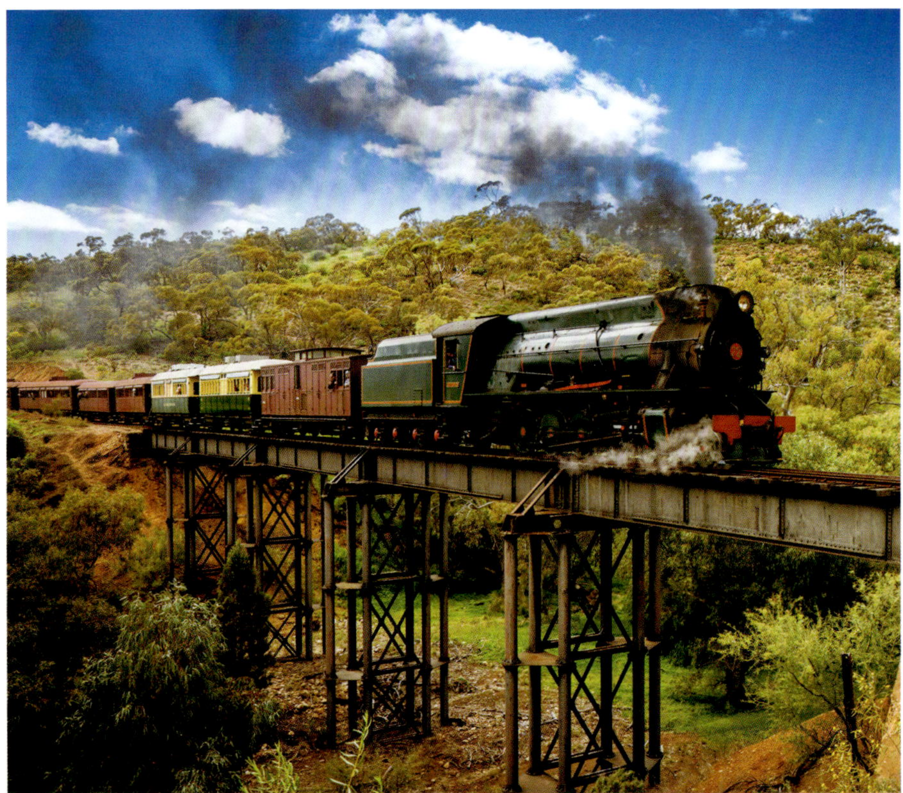

Pichi Richi Steam train ride in Flinders Ranges, South Australia.

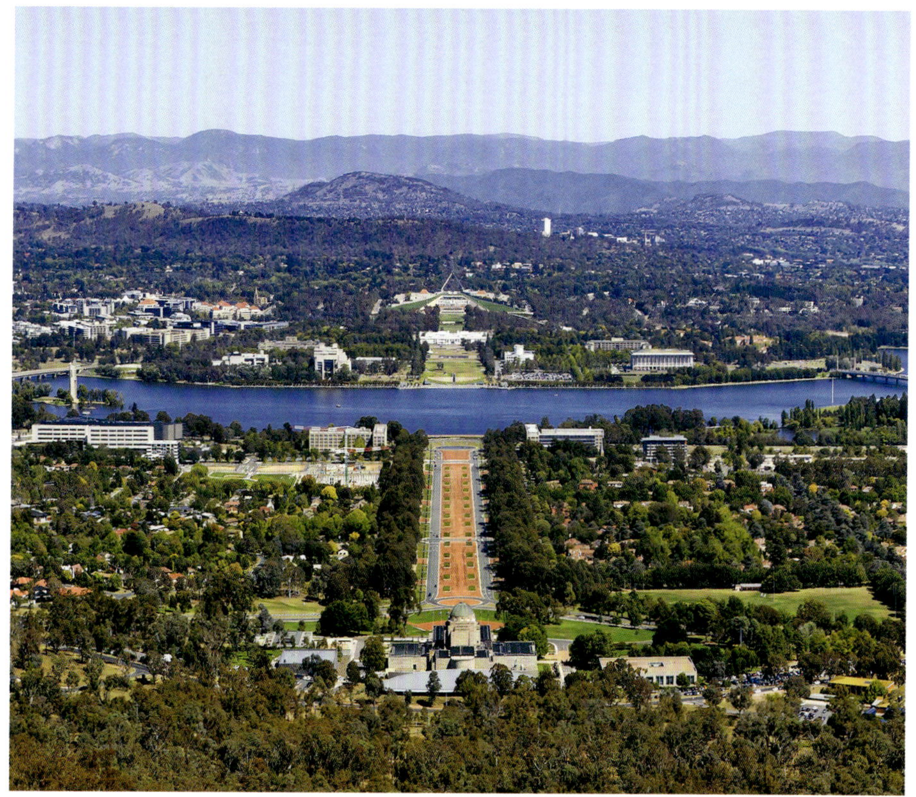

View fron Mt Ainslie, Canberra, ACT.

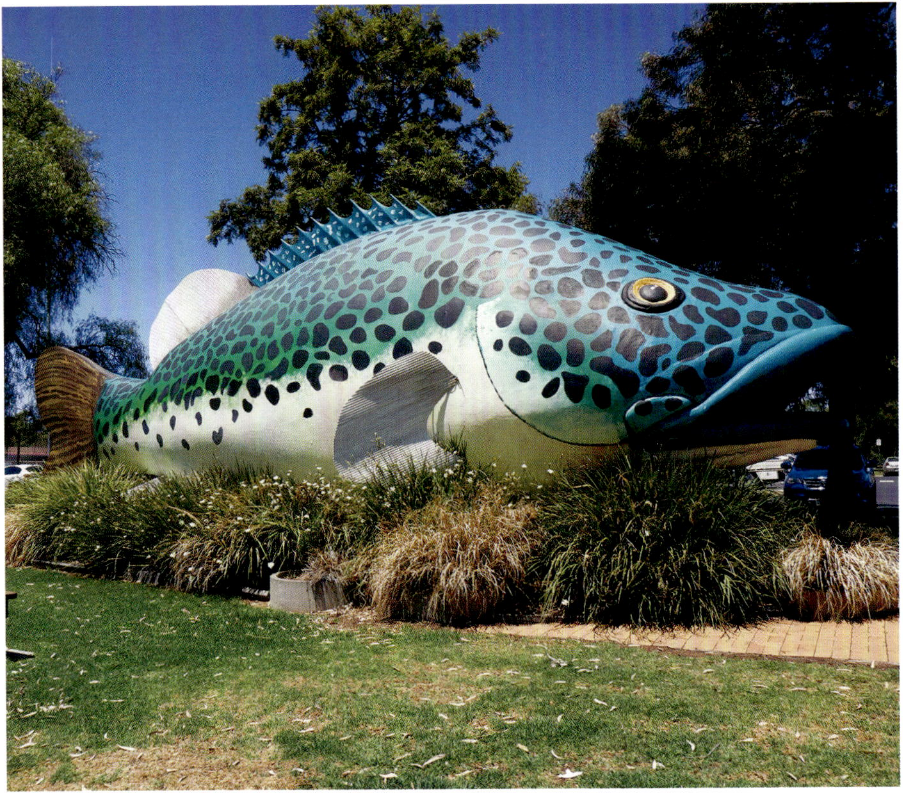

Model of the Giant Murray Cod nicknamed Arnold, Swan Hill, Victoria.

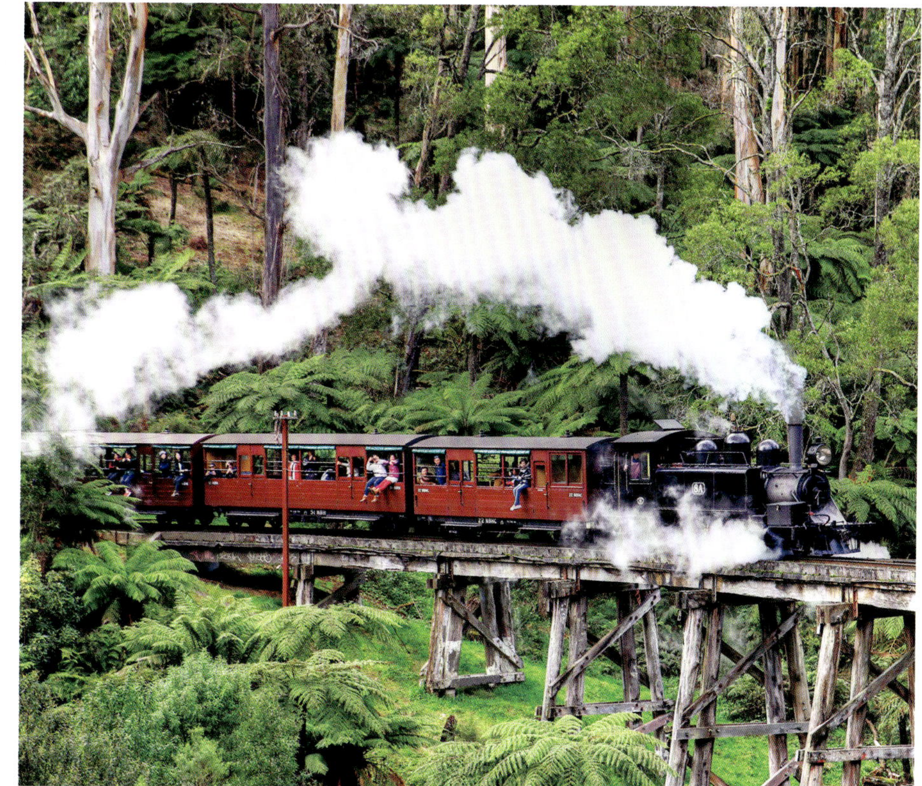

The Puffing Billy, the Dandenong Ranges, Victoria.

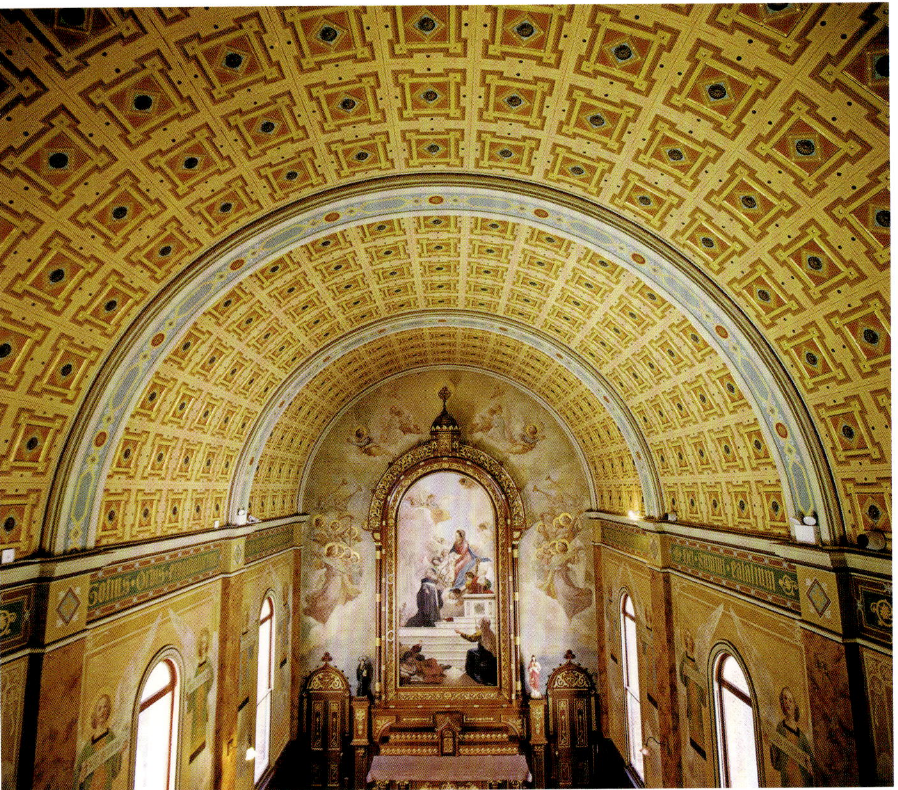

New Norcia, Western Australia.

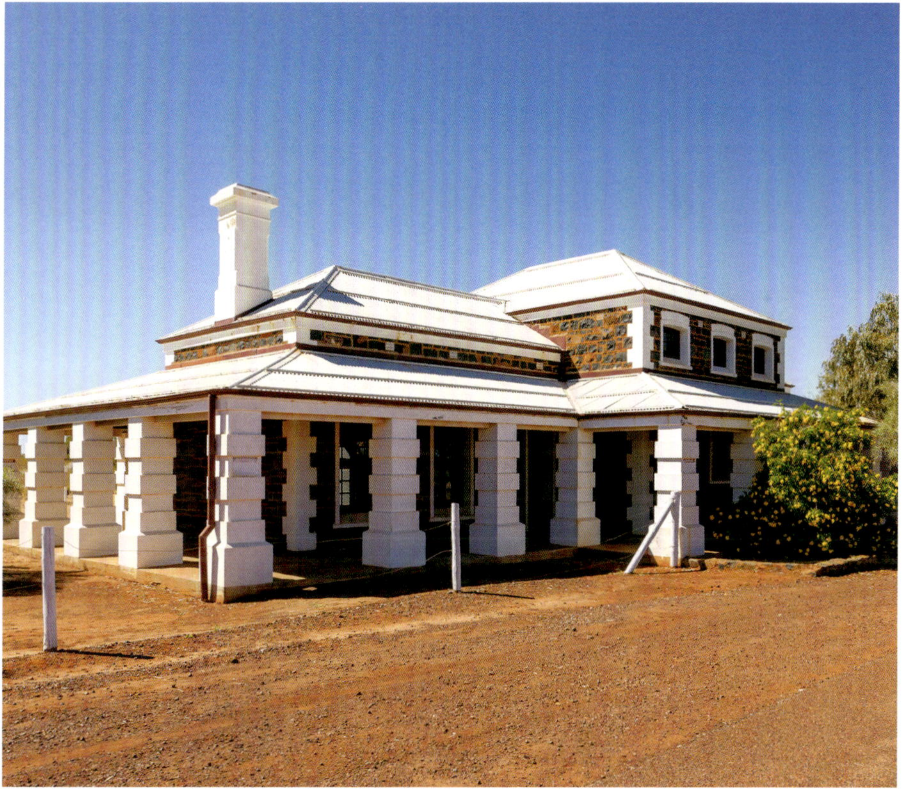

The restored Courthouse at Cossack in the Pilbara, Western Australia.

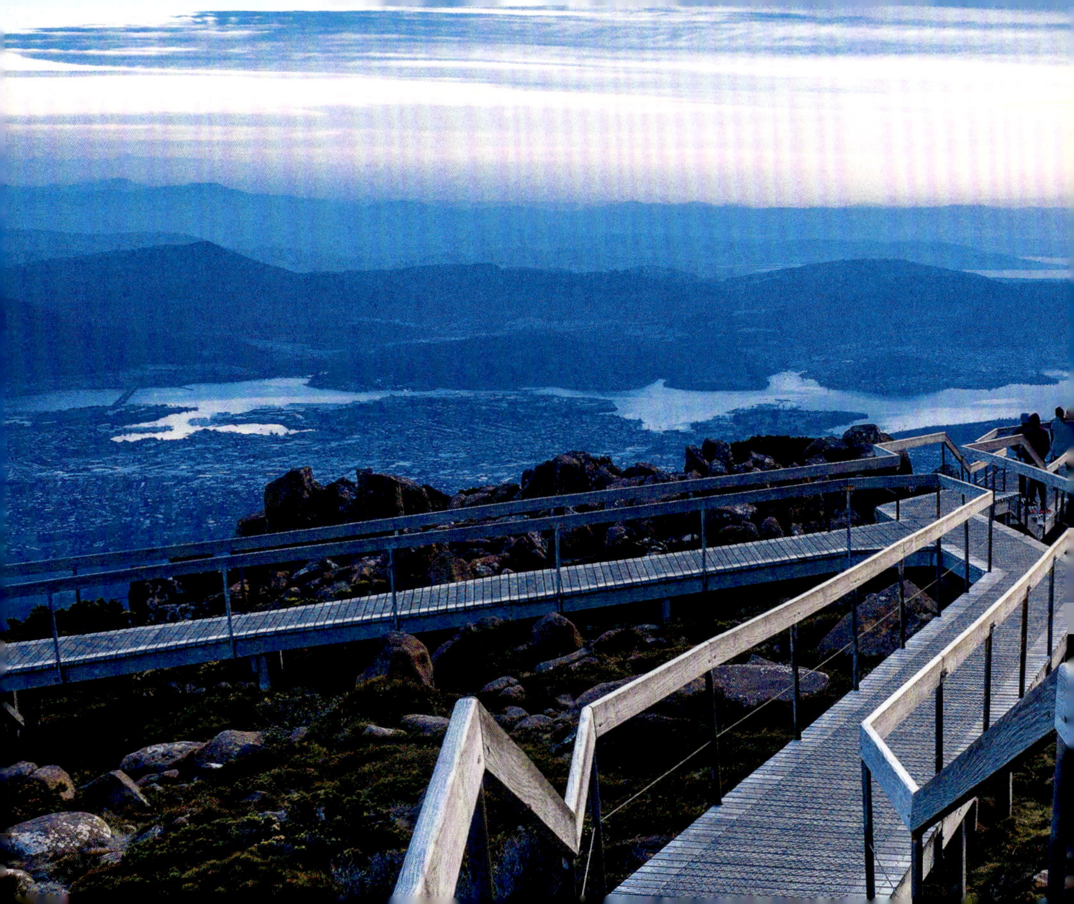

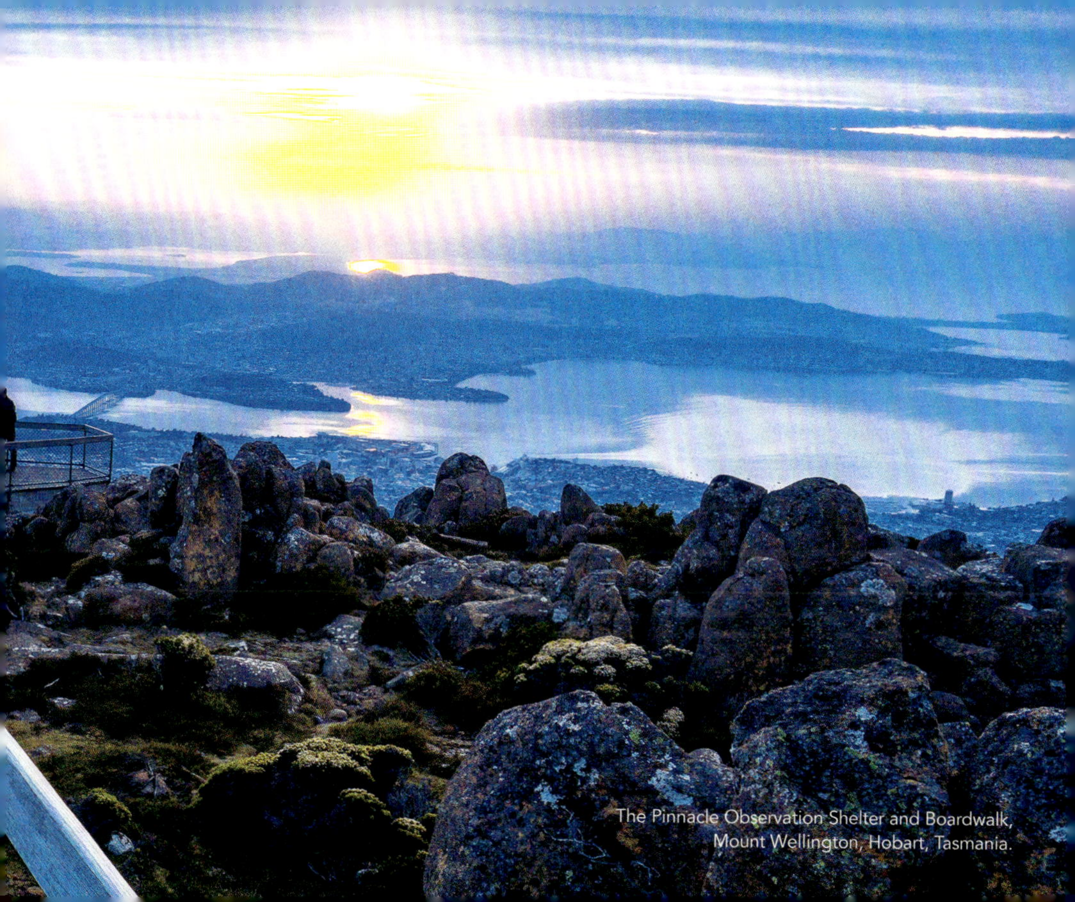

The Pinnacle Observation Shelter and Boardwalk,
Mount Wellington, Hobart, Tasmania.

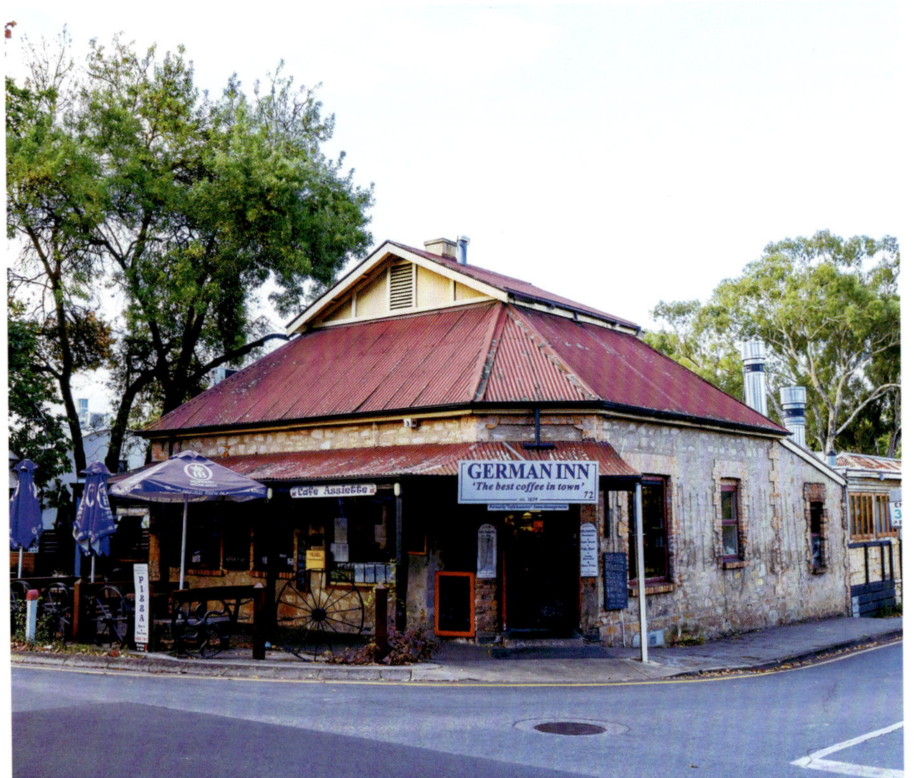

Iconic German town of Hahndorf, Adelaide Hills, South Australia.

Hahndorf, South Australia.

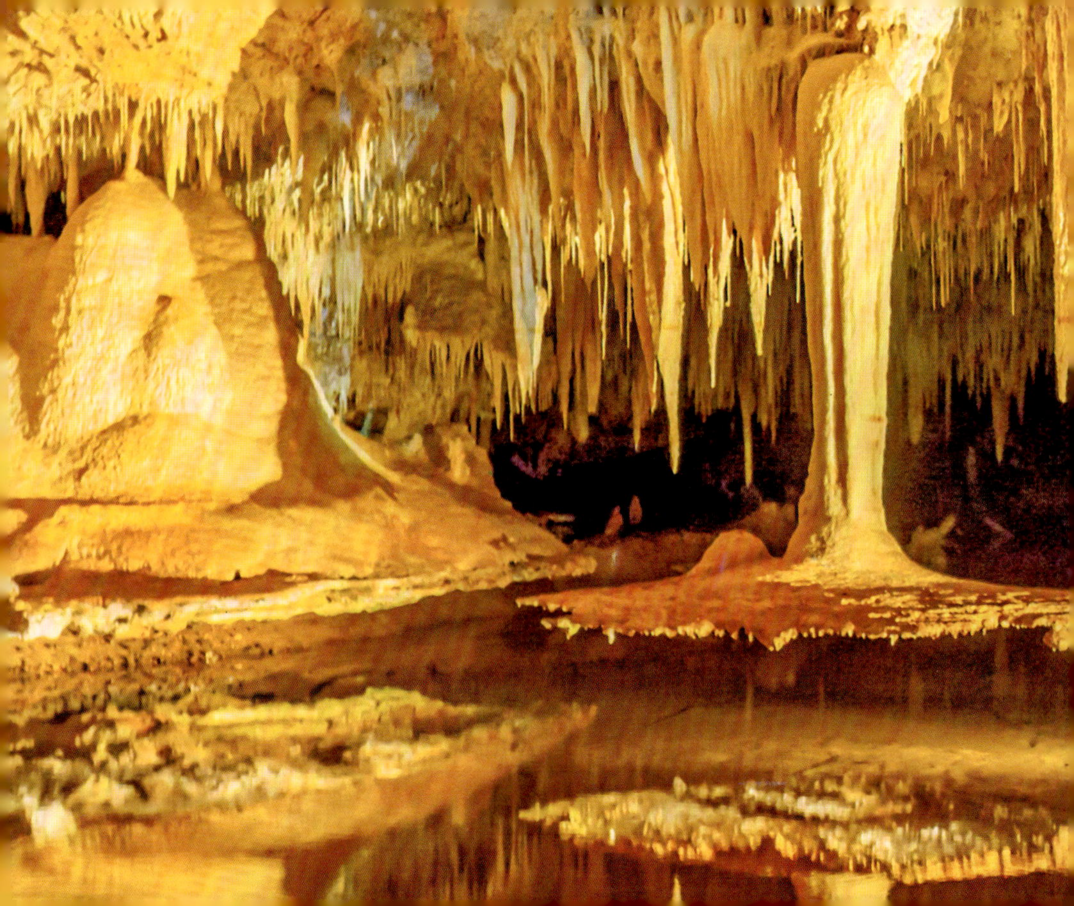

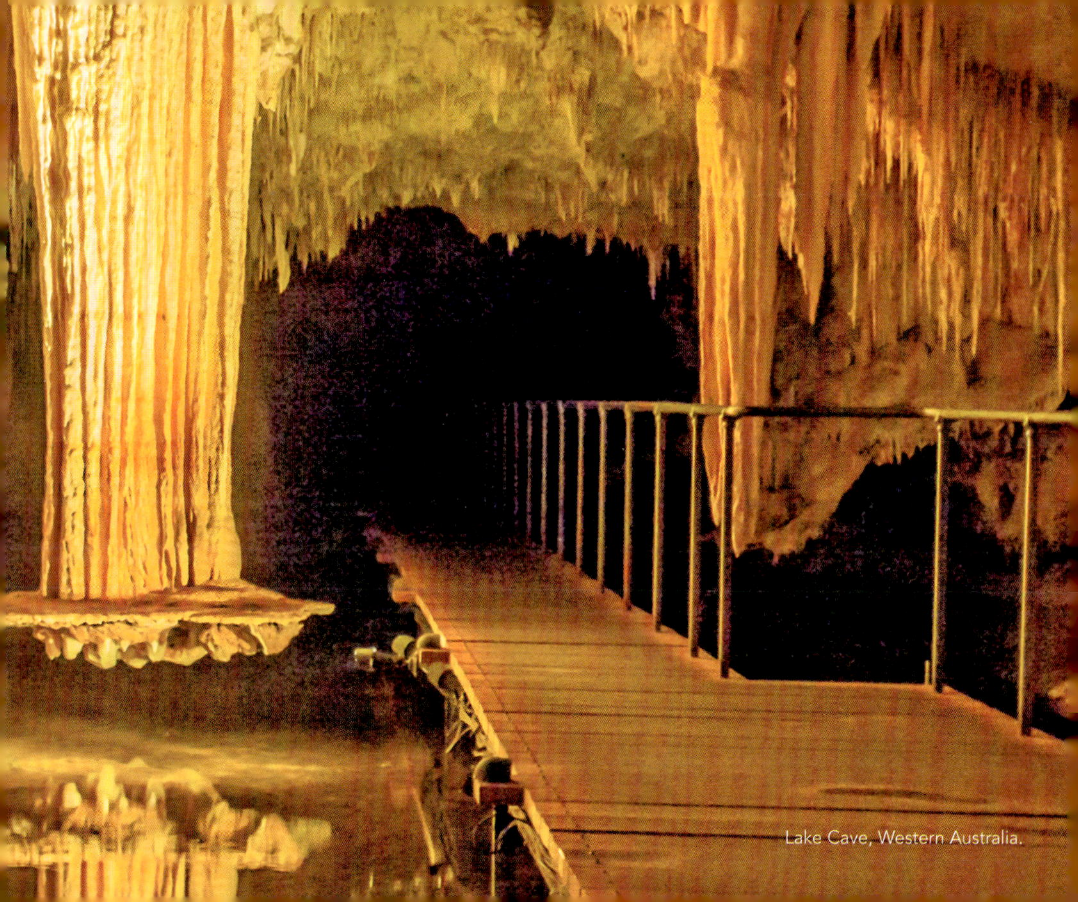

Lake Cave, Western Australia.

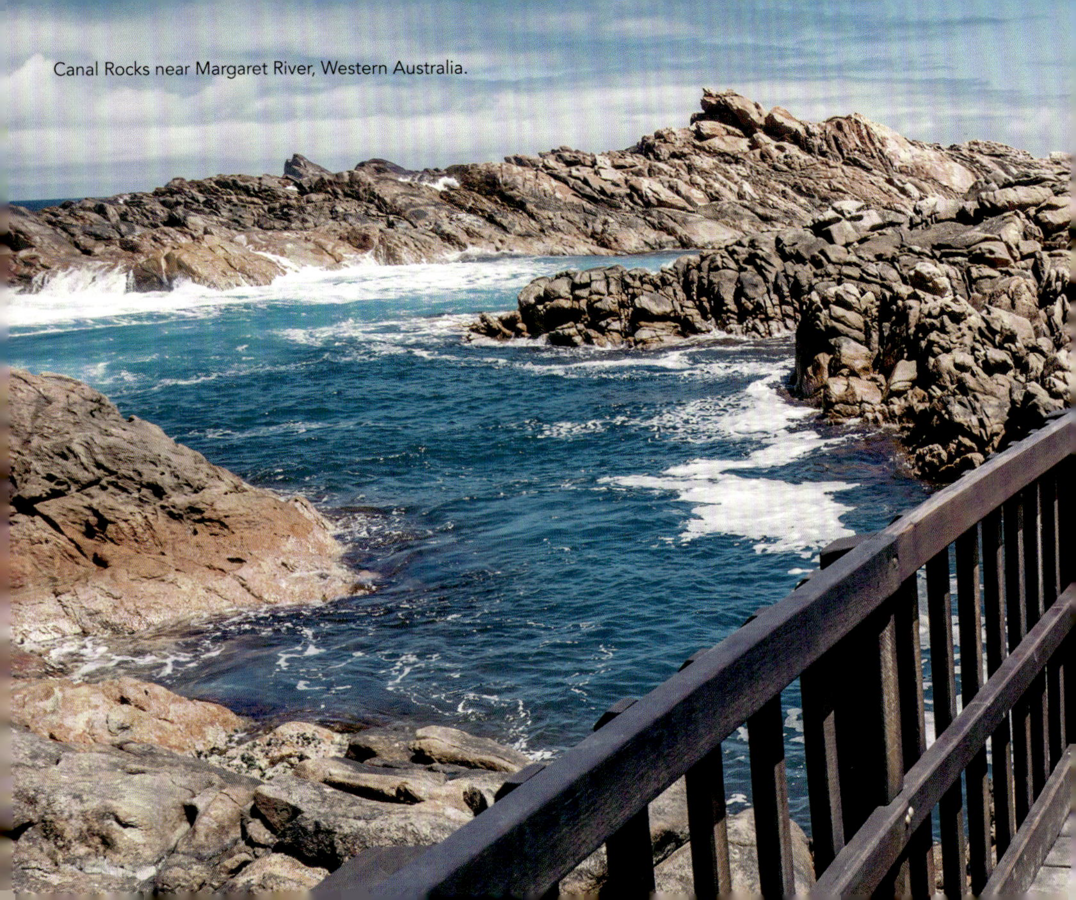
Canal Rocks near Margaret River, Western Australia.

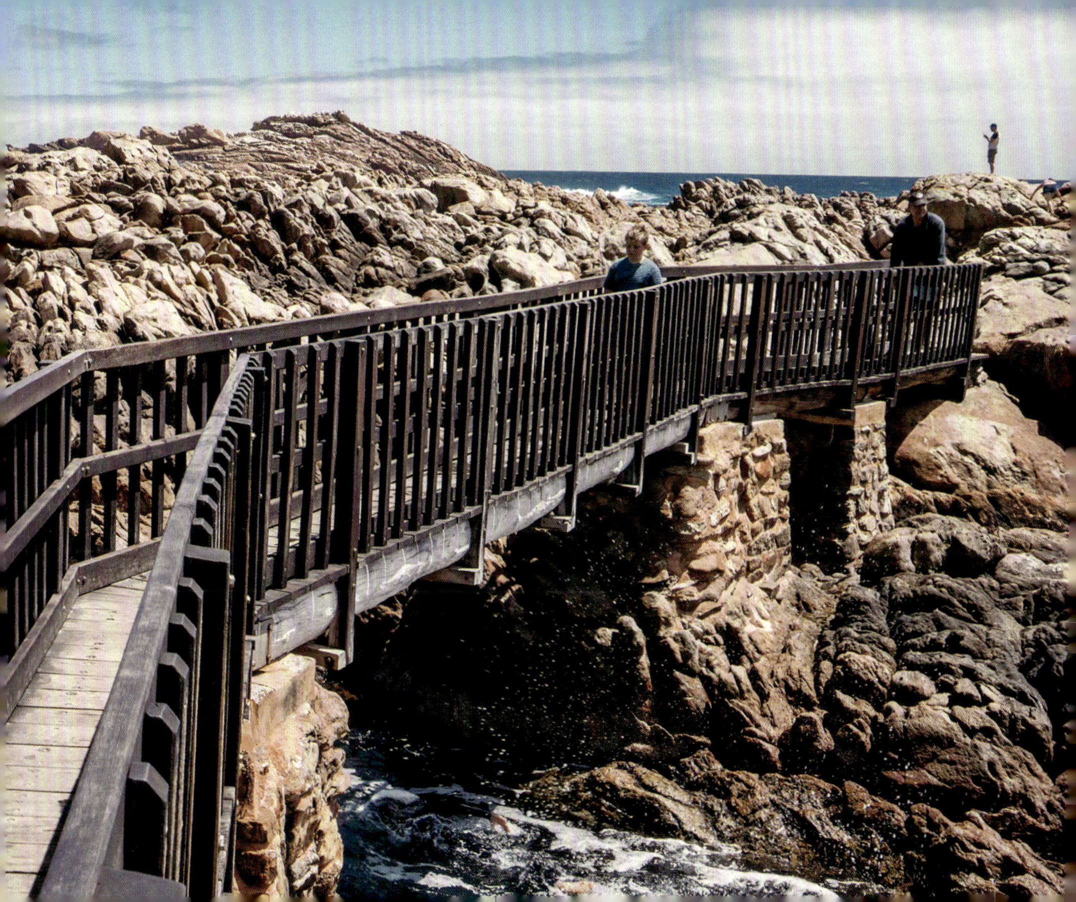

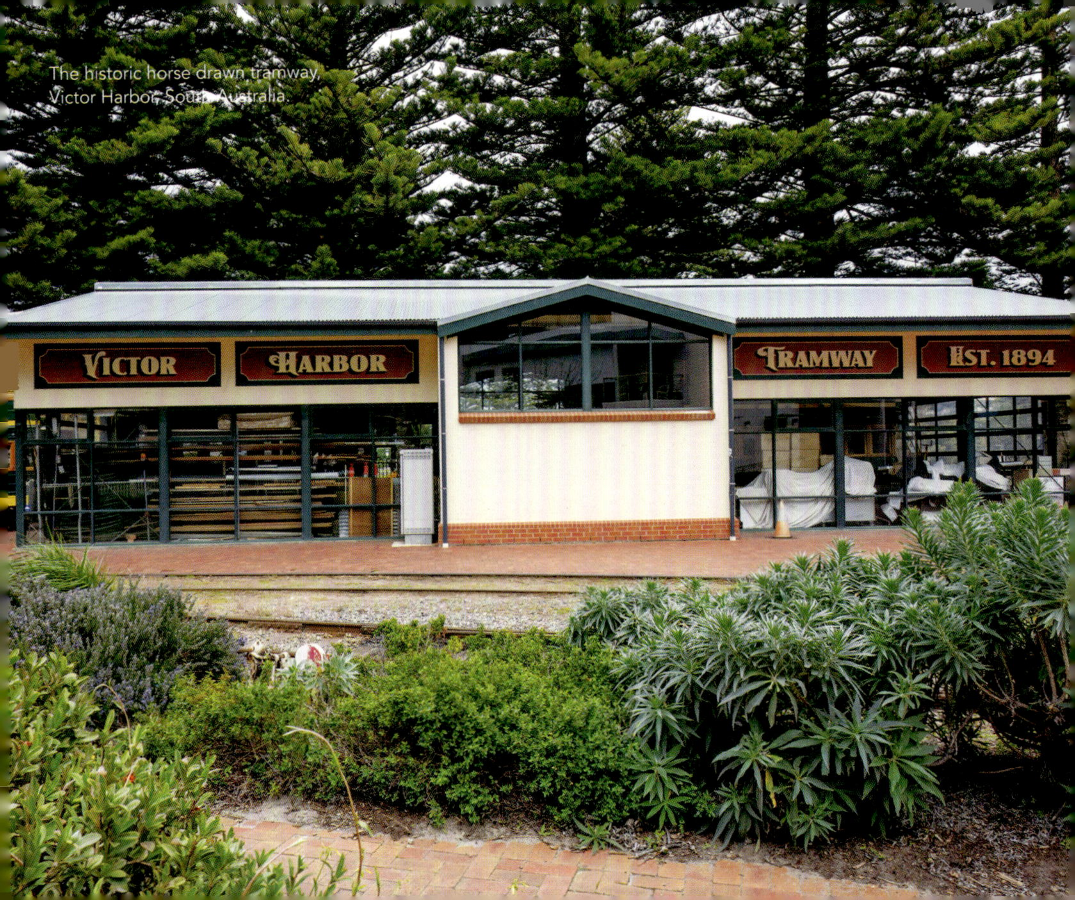

The historic horse drawn tramway, Victor Harbor, South Australia.

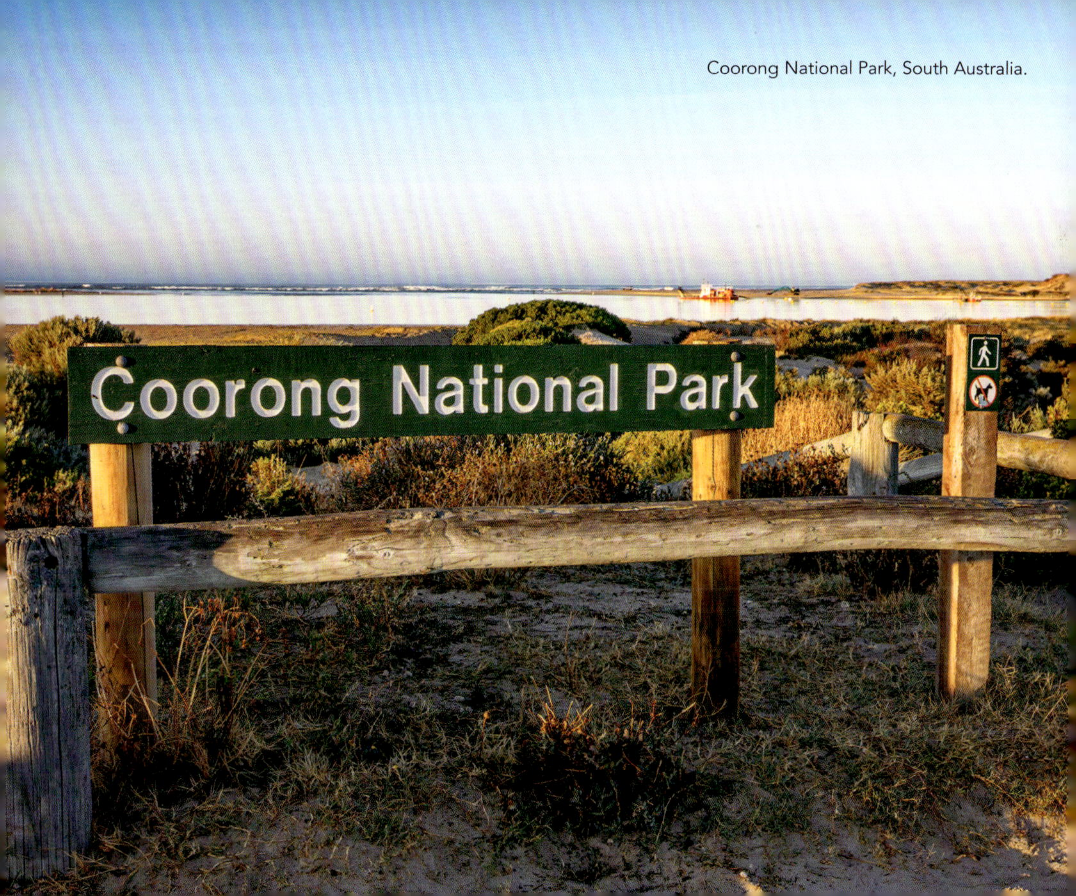

Coorong National Park, South Australia.

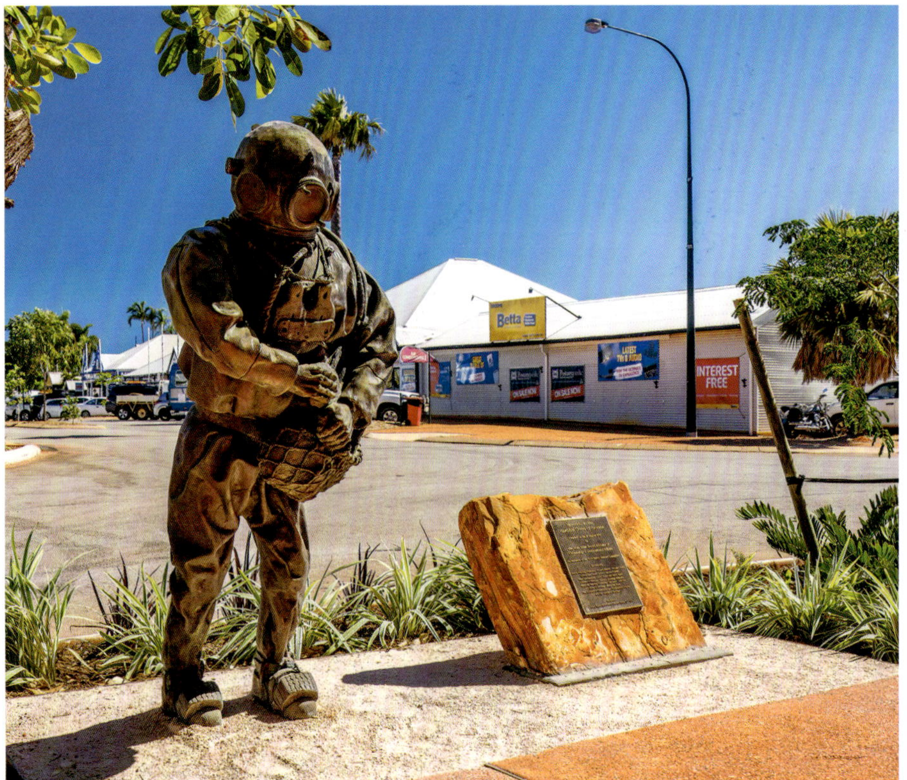

Memorial to the hard-hat divers of Broome, Western Australia.

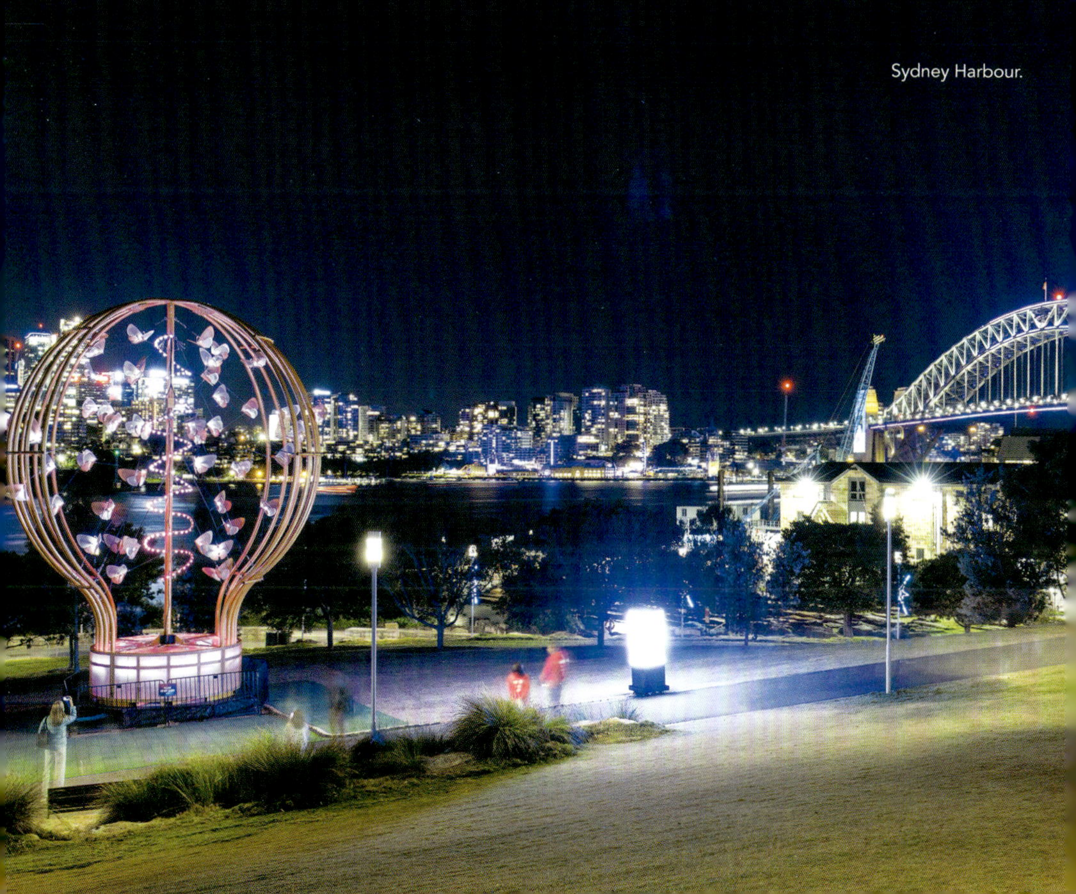

Sydney Harbour.

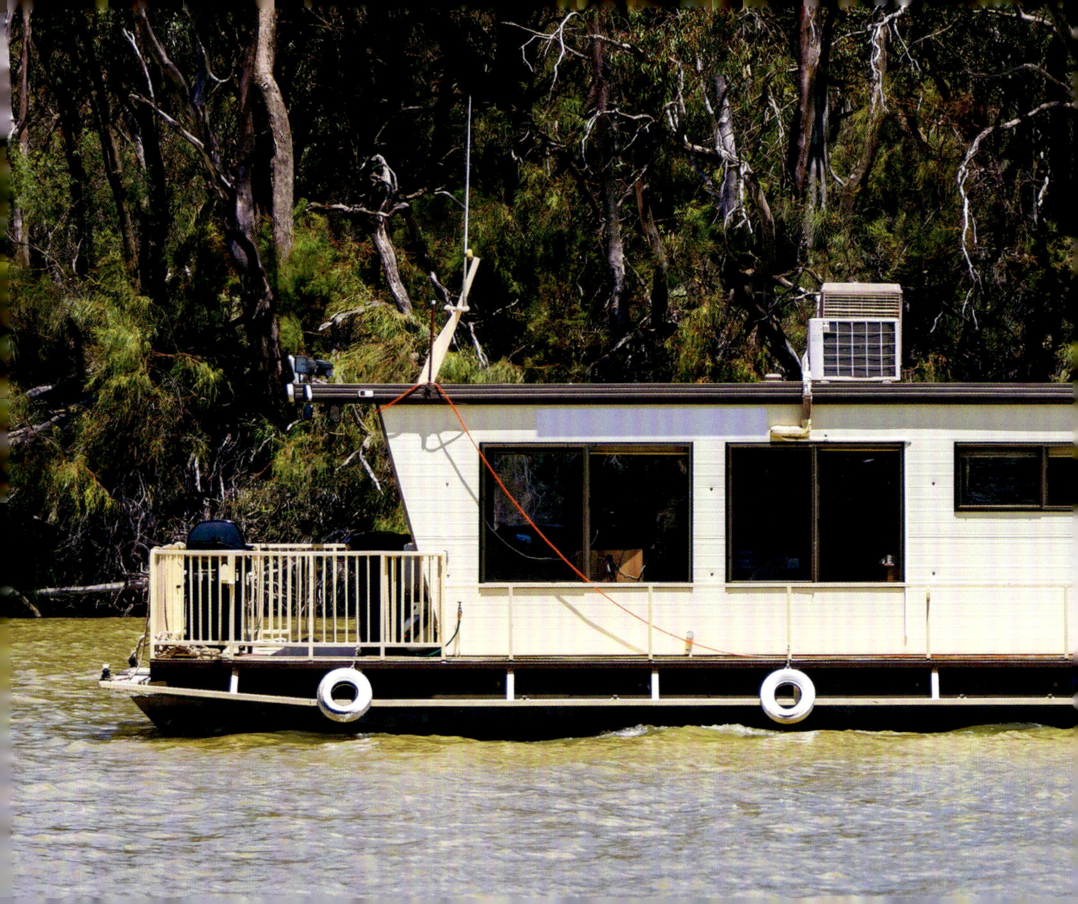

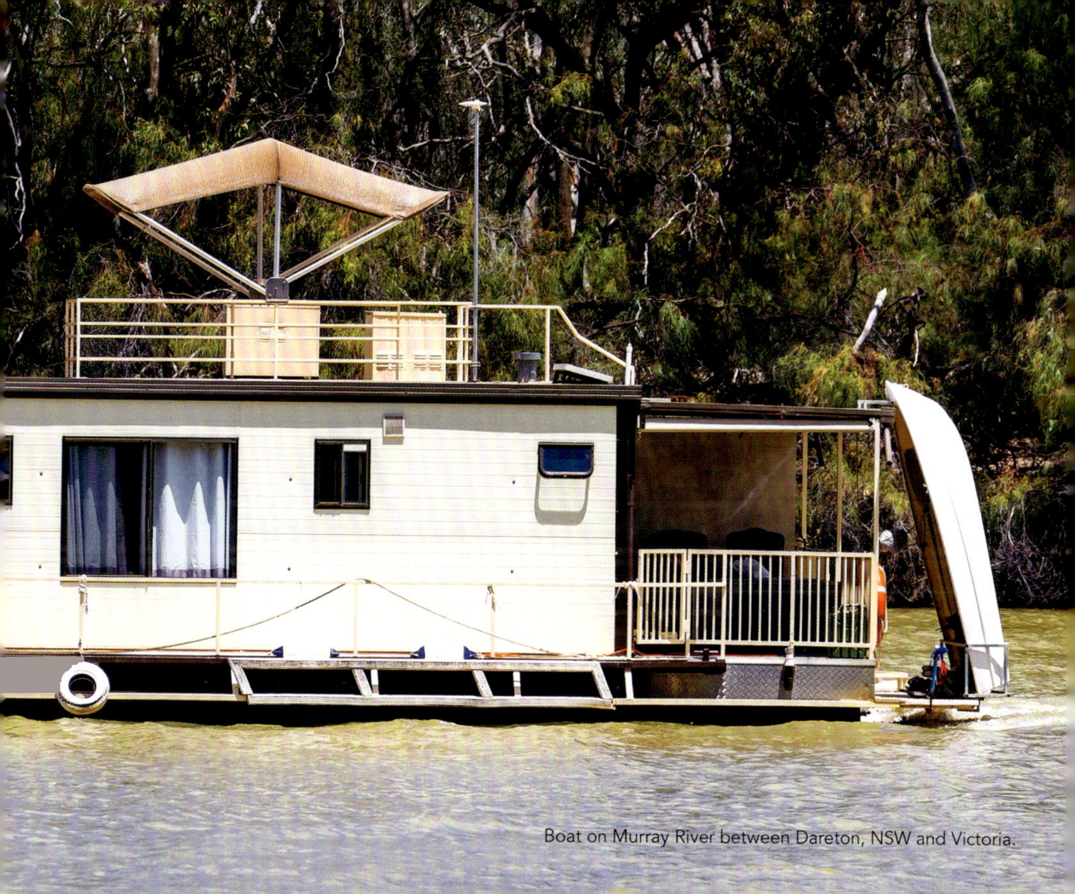

Boat on Murray River between Dareton, NSW and Victoria.

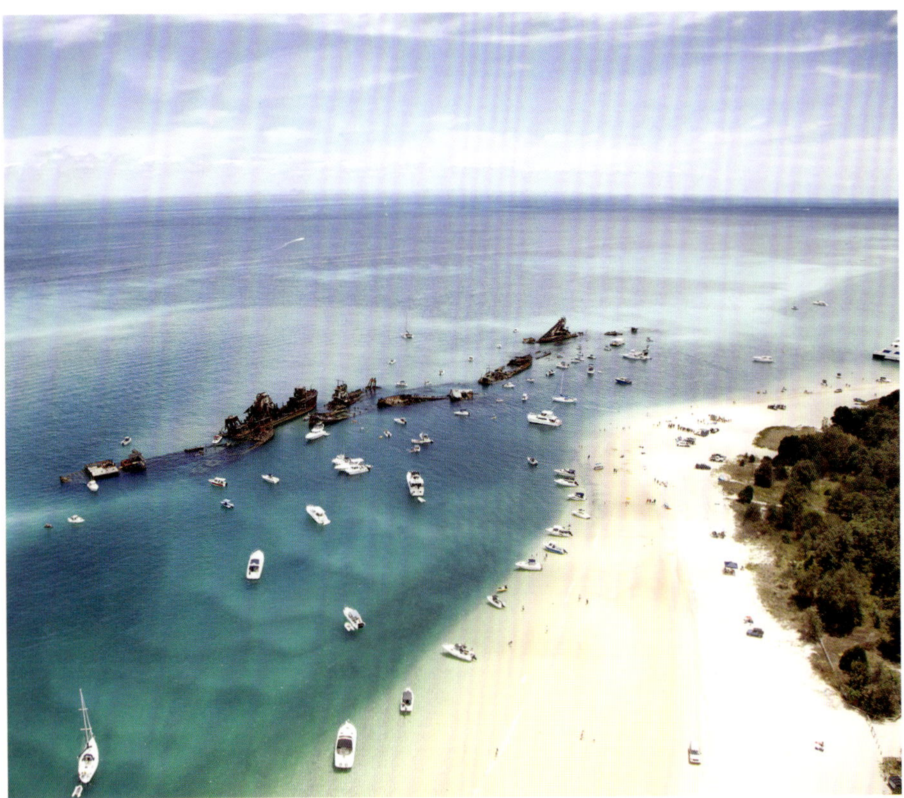

Moreton Island, Queensland.

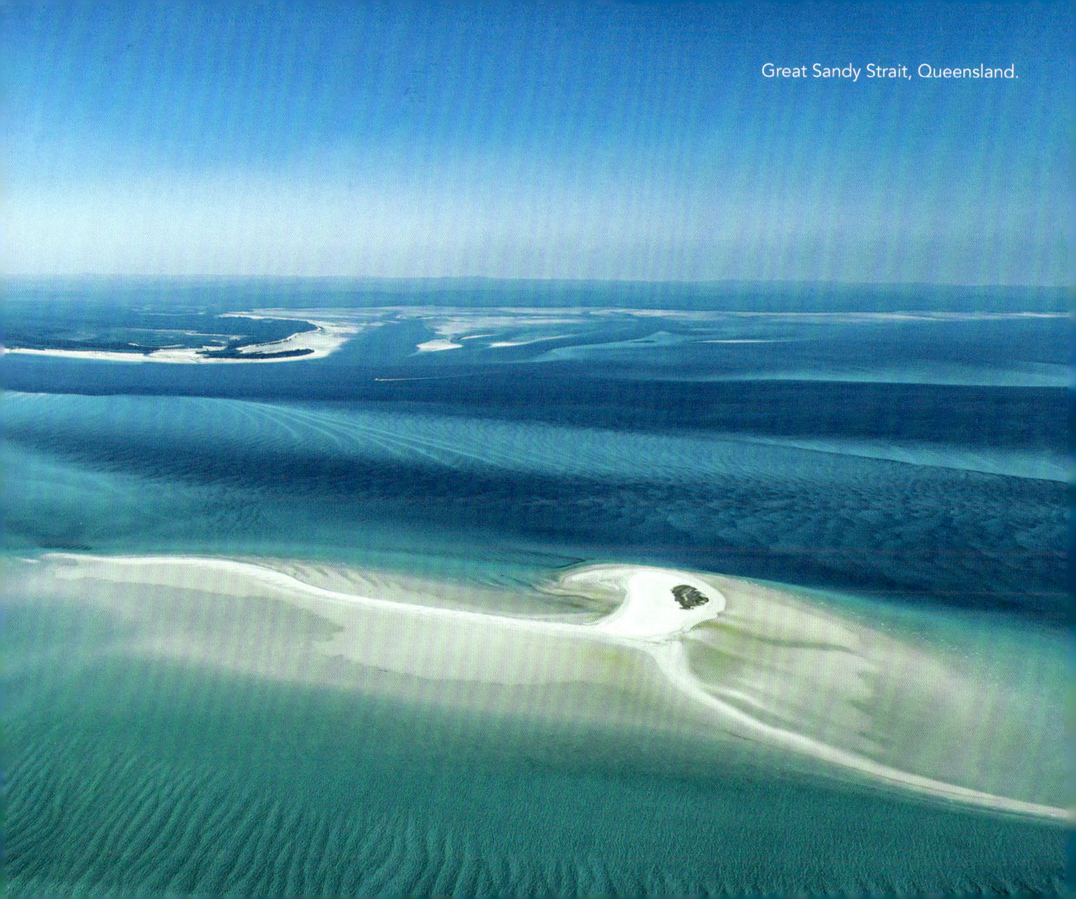
Great Sandy Strait, Queensland.

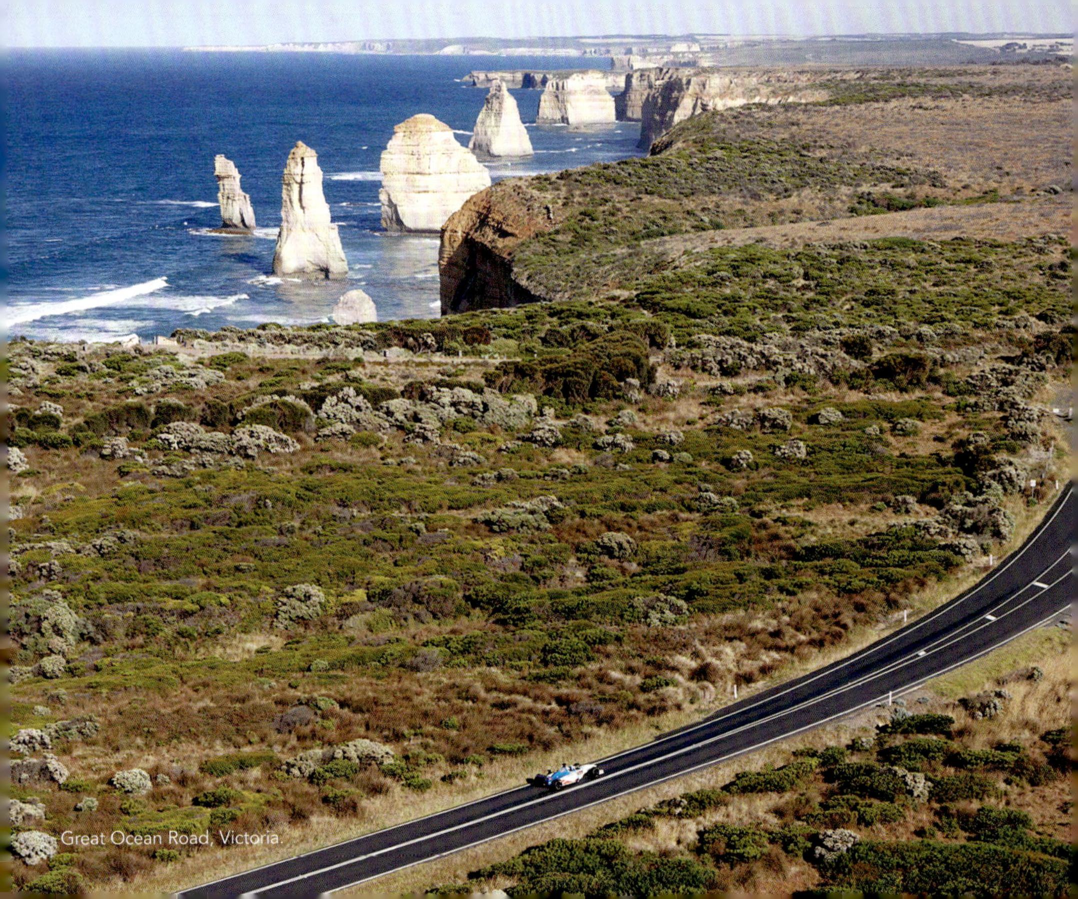

Great Ocean Road, Victoria.

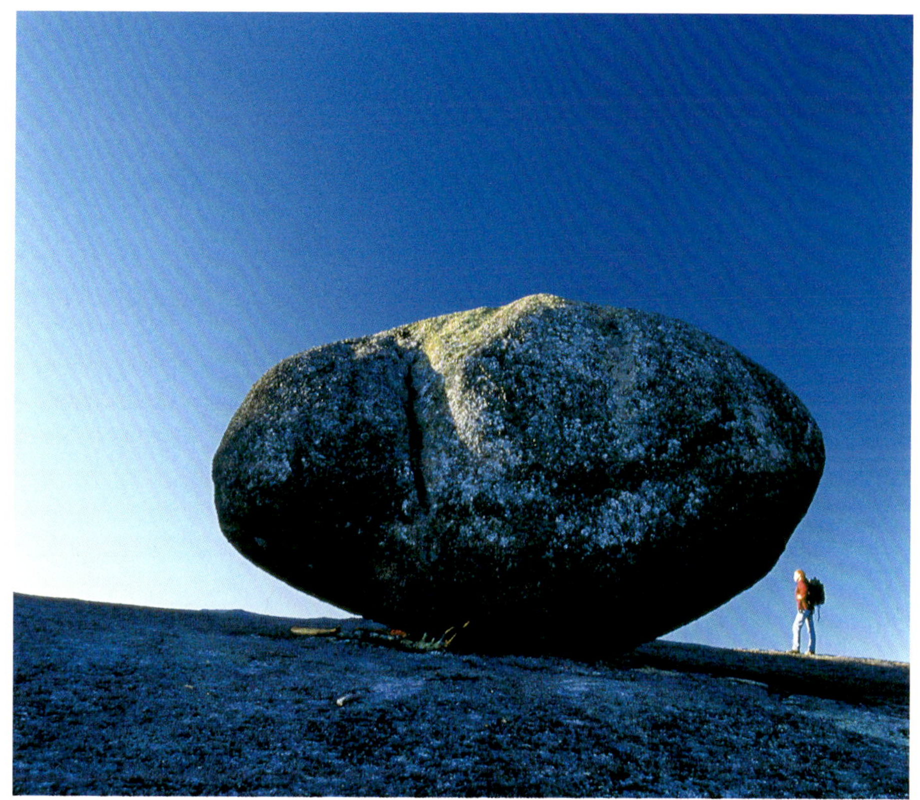

Southern Downs, Queensland.

First published in 2023 by New Holland Publishers
Sydney

Level 1, 178 Fox Valley Road, Wahroonga, NSW 2076, Australia

newhollandpublishers.com

A record of this book is held at the National Library of Australia.

ISBN 9781760796082

Managing Director: Fiona Schultz
Designer: Andrew Davies
Production Director: Arlene Gippert
Printed in China

10 9 8 7 6 5 4 3 2 1

Keep up with New Holland Publishers:

NewHollandPublishers

@newhollandpublishers

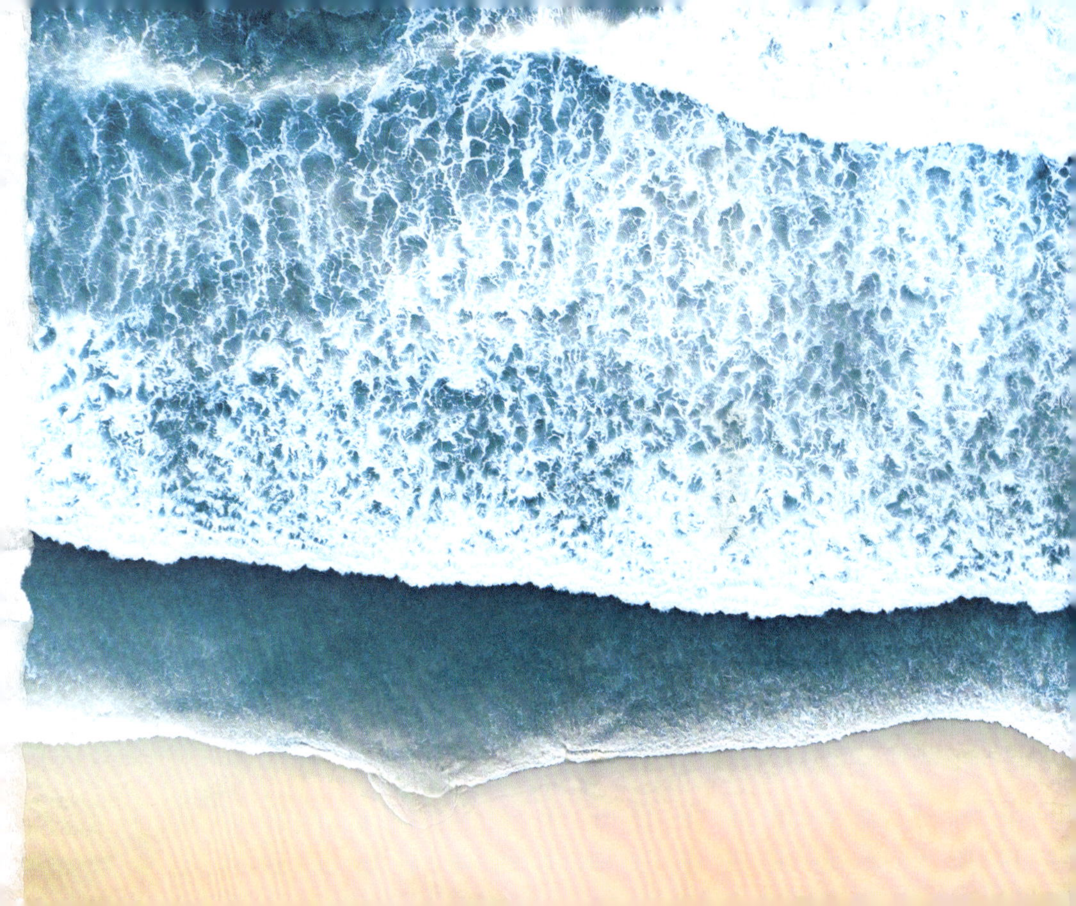

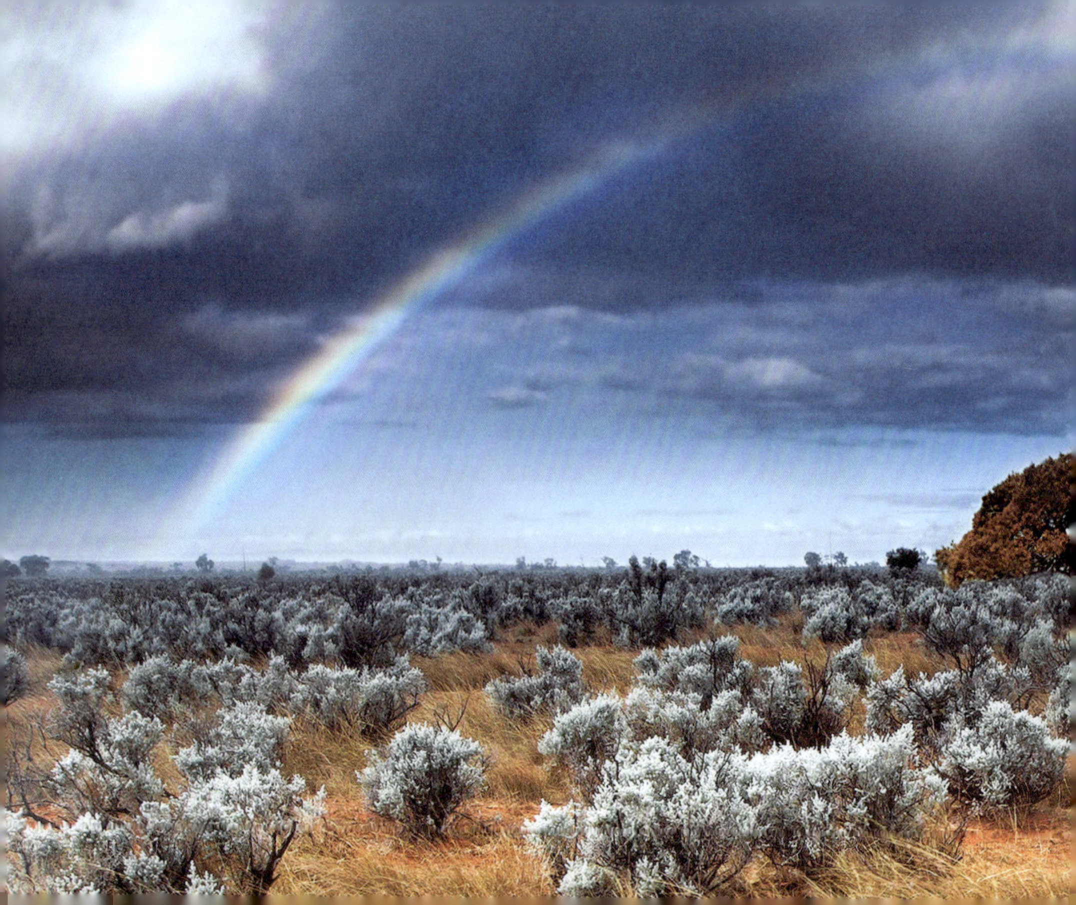